The

Holy Bible

———

NEW TESTAMENT
& PSALMS

American Standard Version

LOGOS♨LIGHT

ISBN (13) (Paperback): 978-1-68109-084-9
ISBN (10) (Paperback): 1-68109-084-8

ISBN (13) (ePub): 978-1-68109-085-6
ISBN (10) (ePub): 1-68109-085-6

Published by LOGOSLIGHT™
an imprint of TELLERBOOKS™

Visit us at TellerBooks.com/LogosLight
LogosLight@TellerBooks.com

t TellerBooks

Contents

I.   **WISDOM LITERATURE** **4**

    1.   PSALMS 4

II.   **THE GOSPELS AND THEIR PROCLAMATION** **102**

    2.   MATTHEW 102
    3.   MARK 148
    4.   LUKE 177
    5.   JOHN 226
    6.   ACTS 263

III.   **THE LETTERS OF THE APOSTLE PAUL** **311**

    7.   ROMANS 311
    8.   1 CORINTHIANS 329
    9.   2 CORINTHIANS 348
    10.   GALATIANS 360
    11.   EPHESIANS 366
    12.   PHILIPPIANS 373
    13.   COLOSSIANS 377
    14.   1 THESSALONIANS 381
    15.   2 THESSALONIANS 385
    16.   1 TIMOTHY 387
    17.   2 TIMOTHY 392
    18.   TITUS 395
    19.   PHILEMON 397

IV.   **LETTERS OF OTHER APOSTLES AND PROPHETS** **399**

    20.   HEBREWS 399
    21.   JAMES 413
    22.   1 PETER 417
    23.   2 PETER 422
    24.   1 JOHN 425
    25.   2 JOHN 430
    26.   3 JOHN 431
    27.   JUDE 431

V.   **REVELATION** **436**

    28.   REVELATION OF JESUS CHRIST 436

I. Wisdom Literature

1. Psalms

Chapter 1.

Psa 1:1 Blessed is the man that walketh not in the counsel of the wicked, Nor standeth in the way of sinners, Nor sitteth in the seat of scoffers:

Psa 1:2 But his delight is in the law of Jehovah; And on his law doth he meditate day and night.

Psa 1:3 And he shall be like a tree planted by the streams of water, That bringeth forth its fruit in its season, Whose leaf also doth not wither; And whatsoever he doeth shall prosper.

Psa 1:4 The wicked are not so, But are like the chaff which the wind driveth away.

Psa 1:5 Therefore the wicked shall not stand in the judgment, Nor sinners in the congregation of the righteous.

Psa 1:6 For Jehovah knoweth the way of the righteous; But the way of the wicked shall perish.

Chapter 2.

Psa 2:1 Why do the nations rage, And the peoples meditate a vain thing?

Psa 2:2 The kings of the earth set themselves, And the rulers take counsel together, Against Jehovah, and against his anointed, saying,

Psa 2:3 Let us break their bonds asunder, And cast away their cords from us.

Psa 2:4 He that sitteth in the heavens will laugh: The Lord will have them in derision.

Psa 2:5 Then will he speak unto them in his wrath, And vex them in his sore displeasure:

Psa 2:6 Yet I have set my king Upon my holy hill of Zion.

Psa 2:7 I will tell of the decree: Jehovah said unto me, Thou art my son; This day have I begotten thee.

Psa 2:8 Ask of me, and I will give thee the nations for thine inheritance, And the uttermost parts of the earth for thy possession.

Psa 2:9 Thou shalt break them with a rod of iron; Thou shalt dash them in pieces like a potter's vessel.

Psa 2:10 Now therefore be wise, O ye kings: Be instructed, ye judges of the earth.

Psa 2:11 Serve Jehovah with fear, And rejoice with trembling.

Psa 2:12 Kiss the son, lest he be angry, and ye perish in the way, For his wrath will soon be kindled. Blessed are all they that take refuge in him.

Chapter 3.

Psa 3:1 A Psalm of David, when he fled from Absalom his son. Jehovah, how are mine adversaries increased! Many are they that rise up against me.

Psa 3:2 Many there are that say of my soul, There is no help for him in God. Selah.

Psa 3:3 But thou, O Jehovah, art a shield about me; My glory and the lifter up of my head.

Psa 3:4 I cry unto Jehovah with my voice, And he answereth me out of his holy hill. Selah.

Psa 3:5 I laid me down and slept; I awaked; For Jehovah sustaineth me.

Psa 3:6 I will not be afraid of ten thousands of the people That have set themselves against me round about.

Psa 3:7 Arise, O Jehovah; save me, O my God: For thou hast smitten all mine enemies upon the cheek bone; Thou hast broken the teeth of the wicked.

Psa 3:8 Salvation belongeth unto Jehovah: Thy blessing be upon thy people. Selah.

Chapter 4.

Psa 4:1 For the Chief Musician; on stringed instruments. A Psalm of David. Answer me when I call, O God of my righteousness; Thou hast set me at large when I was in distress: Have mercy upon me, and hear my prayer.

Psa 4:2 O ye sons of men, how long shall my glory be turned into dishonor? How long will ye love vanity, and seek after falsehood? Selah.

Psa 4:3 But know that Jehovah hath set apart for himself him that is godly: Jehovah will hear when I call unto him.

Psa 4:4 Stand in awe, and sin not: Commune with your own heart upon your bed, and be still. Selah.

Psa 4:5 Offer the sacrifices of righteousness, And put your trust in Jehovah.

Psa 4:6 Many there are that say, Who will show us any good? Jehovah, lift thou up the light of thy countenance upon us.

Psa 4:7 Thou hast put gladness in my heart, More than they have when their grain and their new wine are increased.

Psa 4:8 In peace will I both lay me down and sleep; For thou, Jehovah, alone makest me dwell in safety.

Chapter 5.

Psa 5:1 For the Chief Musician; with the Nehiloth. A Psalm of David. Give ear to my words, O Jehovah, Consider my meditation.

Psa 5:2 Hearken unto the voice of my cry, my King, and my God; For unto thee do I pray.

Psa 5:3 O Jehovah, in the morning shalt thou hear my voice; In the morning will I order my prayer unto thee, and will keep watch.

Psa 5:4 For thou art not a God that hath pleasure in wickedness: Evil shall not sojourn with thee.

Psa 5:5 The arrogant shall not stand in thy sight: Thou hatest all workers of iniquity.

Psa 5:6 Thou wilt destroy them that speak lies: Jehovah abhorreth the blood-thirsty and deceitful man.

Psa 5:7 But as for me, in the abundance of thy lovingkindness will I come into thy house: In thy fear will I worship toward thy holy temple.

Psa 5:8 Lead me, O Jehovah, in thy righteousness because of mine enemies; Make thy way straight before my face.

Psa 5:9 For there is no faithfulness in their mouth; Their inward part is very wickedness; Their throat is an open sepulchre; They flatter with their tongue.

Psa 5:10 Hold them guilty, O God; Let them fall by their own counsels; Thrust them out in the multitude of their transgressions; For they have rebelled against thee.

Psa 5:11 But let all those that take refuge in thee rejoice, Let them ever shout for joy, because thou defendest them: Let them also that love thy name be joyful in thee.

Psa 5:12 For thou wilt bless the righteous; O Jehovah, thou wilt compass him with favor as with a shield.

Chapter 6.

Psa 6:1 For the Chief Musician; on stringed instruments, set to the Sheminith. A Psalm of David. O Jehovah, rebuke me not in thine anger, Neither chasten me in thy hot displeasure.

Psa 6:2 Have mercy upon me, O Jehovah; for I am withered away: O Jehovah, heal me; for my bones are troubled.

Psa 6:3 My soul also is sore troubled: And thou, O Jehovah, how long?

Psa 6:4 Return, O Jehovah, deliver my soul: Save me for thy lovingkindness' sake.

Psa 6:5 For in death there is no remembrance of thee: In Sheol who shall give thee thanks?

Psa 6:6 I am weary with my groaning; Every night make I my bed to swim; I water my couch with my tears.

Psa 6:7 Mine eye wasteth away because of grief; It waxeth old because of all mine adversaries.

Psa 6:8 Depart from me, all ye workers of iniquity; For Jehovah hath heard the voice of my weeping.

Psa 6:9 Jehovah hath heard my supplication; Jehovah will receive my prayer.

Psa 6:10 All mine enemies shall be put to shame and sore troubled: They shall turn back, they shall be put to shame suddenly.

Chapter 7.

Psa 7:1 Shiggaion of David, which he sang unto Jehovah, concerning the words of Cush a Benjamite. O Jehovah my God, in thee do I take refuge: Save me from all them that pursue me, and deliver me,

Psa 7:2 Lest they tear my soul like a lion, Rending it in pieces, while there is none to deliver.

Psa 7:3 O Jehovah my God, if I have done this; If there be iniquity in my hands;

Psa 7:4 If I have rewarded evil unto him that was at peace with me (Yea, I have delivered him that without cause was mine adversary);

Psa 7:5 Let the enemy pursue my soul, and overtake it; Yea, let him tread my life down to the earth, And lay my glory in the dust. Selah.

Psa 7:6 Arise, O Jehovah, in thine anger; Lift up thyself against the rage of mine adversaries, And awake for me; thou hast commanded judgment.

Psa 7:7 And let the congregation of the peoples compass thee about; And over them return thou on high.

Psa 7:8 Jehovah ministereth judgment to the peoples: Judge me, O Jehovah, according to my righteousness, and to mine integrity that is in me.

Psa 7:9 O let the wickedness of the wicked come to an end, but establish thou the righteous: For the righteous God trieth the minds and hearts.

Psa 7:10 My shield is with God, Who saveth the upright in heart.

Psa 7:11 God is a righteous judge, Yea, a God that hath indignation every day.

Psa 7:12 If a man turn not, he will whet his sword; He hath bent his bow, and made it ready.

Psa 7:13 He hath also prepared for him the instruments of death; He maketh his arrows fiery shafts.

Psa 7:14 Behold, he travaileth with iniquity; Yea, he hath conceived mischief, and brought forth falsehood.

Psa 7:15 He hath made a pit, and digged it, And is fallen into the ditch which he made.

Psa 7:16 His mischief shall return upon his own head, And his violence shall come down upon his own pate.

Psa 7:17 I will give thanks unto Jehovah according to his righteousness, And will sing praise to the name of Jehovah Most High.

Chapter 8.

Psa 8:1 For the Chief Musician; set to the Gittith. A Psalm of David. O Jehovah, our Lord, How excellent is thy name in all the earth, Who hast set thy glory upon the heavens!

Psa 8:2 Out of the mouth of babes and sucklings hast thou established strength, Because of thine adversaries, That thou mightest still the enemy and the avenger.

Psa 8:3 When I consider thy heavens, the work of thy fingers, The moon and the stars, which thou hast ordained;

Psa 8:4 What is man, that thou art mindful of him? And the son of man, that thou visitest him?

Psa 8:5 For thou hast made him but little lower than God, And crownest him with glory and honor.

Psa 8:6 Thou makest him to have dominion over the works of thy hands; Thou hast put all things under his feet:

Psa 8:7 All sheep and oxen, Yea, and the beasts of the field,

Psa 8:8 The birds of the heavens, and the fish of the sea, Whatsoever passeth through the paths of the seas.

Psa 8:9 O Jehovah, our Lord, How excellent is thy name in all the earth!

Chapter 9.

Psa 9:1 For the Chief Musician; set to Muth-labben. A Psalm of David. I will give thanks unto Jehovah with my whole heart; I will show forth all thy marvellous works.

Psa 9:2 I will be glad and exult in thee; I will sing praise to thy name, O thou Most High.

Psa 9:3 When mine enemies turn back, They stumble and perish at thy presence.

Psa 9:4 For thou hast maintained my right and my cause; Thou sittest in the throne judging righteously.

Psa 9:5 Thou hast rebuked the nations, thou hast destroyed the wicked; Thou hast blotted out their name for ever and ever.

Psa 9:6 The enemy are come to an end, they are desolate for ever; And the cities which thou hast overthrown, The very remembrance of them is perished.

Psa 9:7 But Jehovah sitteth as king for ever: He hath prepared his throne for judgment;

Psa 9:8 And he will judge the world in righteousness, He will minister judgment to the peoples in uprightness.

Psa 9:9 Jehovah also will be a high tower for the oppressed, A high tower in times of trouble;

Psa 9:10 And they that know thy name will put their trust in thee; For thou, Jehovah, hast not forsaken them that seek thee.

Psa 9:11 Sing praises to Jehovah, who dwelleth in Zion: Declare among the people his doings.

Psa 9:12 For he that maketh inquisition for blood remembereth them; He forgetteth not the cry of the poor.

Psa 9:13 Have mercy upon me, O Jehovah; Behold my affliction which I suffer of them that hate me, Thou that liftest me up from the gates of death;

Psa 9:14 That I may show forth all thy praise. In the gates of the daughter of Zion I will rejoice in thy salvation.

Psa 9:15 The nations are sunk down in the pit that they made: In the net which they hid is their own foot taken.

Psa 9:16 Jehovah hath made himself known, he hath executed judgment: The wicked is snared in the work of his own hands. Higgaion. Selah.

Psa 9:17 The wicked shall be turned back unto Sheol, Even all the nations that forget God.

Psa 9:18 For the needy shall not alway be forgotten, Nor the expectation of the poor perish for ever.

Psa 9:19 Arise, O Jehovah; let not man prevail: Let the nations be judged in thy sight.

Psa 9:20 Put them in fear, O Jehovah: Let the nations know themselves to be but men. Selah.

Chapter 10.

Psa 10:1 Why standest thou afar off, O Jehovah? Why hidest thou thyself in times of trouble?

Psa 10:2 In the pride of the wicked the poor is hotly pursued; Let them be taken in the devices that they have conceived.

Psa 10:3 For the wicked boasteth of his heart's desire, And the covetous renounceth, yea, contemneth Jehovah.

Psa 10:4 The wicked, in the pride of his countenance, saith, He will not require it. All his thoughts are, There is no God.

Psa 10:5 His ways are firm at all times; Thy judgments are far above out of his sight: As for all his adversaries, he puffeth at them.

Psa 10:6 He saith in his heart, I shall not be moved; To all generations I shall not be in adversity.

Psa 10:7 His mouth is full of cursing and deceit and oppression: Under his tongue is mischief and iniquity.

Psa 10:8 He sitteth in the lurking-places of the villages; In the secret places doth he murder the innocent; His eyes are privily set against the helpless.

Psa 10:9 He lurketh in secret as a lion in his covert; He lieth in wait to catch the poor: He doth catch the poor, when he draweth him in his net.

Psa 10:10 He croucheth, he boweth down, And the helpless fall by his strong ones.

Psa 10:11 He saith in his heart, God hath forgotten; He hideth his face; he will never see it.

Psa 10:12 Arise, O Jehovah; O God, lift up thy hand: Forget not the poor.

Psa 10:13 Wherefore doth the wicked contemn God, And say in his heart, Thou wilt not require it?

Psa 10:14 Thou hast seen it; for thou beholdest mischief and spite, to requite it with thy hand: The helpless committeth himself unto thee; Thou hast been the helper of the fatherless.

Psa 10:15 Break thou the arm of the wicked; And as for the evil man, seek out his wickedness till thou find none.

Psa 10:16 Jehovah is King for ever and ever: The nations are perished out of his land.

Psa 10:17 Jehovah, thou hast heard the desire of the meek: Thou wilt prepare their heart, thou wilt cause thine ear to hear;

Psa 10:18 To judge the fatherless and the oppressed, That man who is of the earth may be terrible no more.

Chapter 11.

Psa 11:1 For the Chief Musician. A Psalm of David. In Jehovah do I take refuge: How say ye to my soul, Flee as a bird to your mountain;

Psa 11:2 For, lo, the wicked bend the bow, They make ready their arrow upon the string, That they may shoot in darkness at the upright in heart;

Psa 11:3 If the foundations be destroyed, What can the righteous do?

Psa 11:4 Jehovah is in his holy temple; Jehovah, his throne is in heaven; His eyes behold, his eyelids try, the children of men.

Psa 11:5 Jehovah trieth the righteous; But the wicked and him that loveth violence his soul hateth.

Psa 11:6 Upon the wicked he will rain snares; Fire and brimstone and burning wind shall be the portion of their cup.

Psa 11:7 For Jehovah is righteous; He loveth righteousness: The upright shall behold his face.

Chapter 12.

Psa 12:1 For the Chief Musician; set to the Sheminith. A Psalm of David. Help, Jehovah; for the godly man ceaseth; For the faithful fail from among the children of men.

Psa 12:2 They speak falsehood every one with his neighbor: With flattering lip, and with a double heart, do they speak.

Psa 12:3 Jehovah will cut off all flattering lips, The tongue that speaketh great things;

Psa 12:4 Who have said, With our tongue will we prevail; Our lips are our own: who is lord over us?

Psa 12:5 Because of the oppression of the poor, because of the sighing of the needy, Now will I arise, saith Jehovah; I will set him in the safety he panteth for.

Psa 12:6 The words of Jehovah are pure words; As silver tried in a furnace on the earth, Purified seven times.

Psa 12:7 Thou wilt keep them, O Jehovah, Thou wilt preserve them from this generation for ever.

Psa 12:8 The wicked walk on every side, When vileness is exalted among the sons of men.

Chapter 13.

Psa 13:1 For the Chief Musician. A Psalm of David. How long, O Jehovah? wilt thou forget me for ever? How long wilt thou hide thy face from me?

Psa 13:2 How long shall I take counsel in my soul, Having sorrow in my heart all the day? How long shall mine enemy be exalted over me?

Psa 13:3 Consider and answer me, O Jehovah my God: Lighten mine eyes, lest I sleep the sleep of death;

Psa 13:4 Lest mine enemy say, I have prevailed against him; Lest mine adversaries rejoice when I am moved.

Psa 13:5 But I have trusted in thy lovingkindness; My heart shall rejoice in thy salvation.

Psa 13:6 I will sing unto Jehovah, Because he hath dealt bountifully with me.

Chapter 14.

Psa 14:1 For the Chief Musician. A Psalm of David. The fool hath said in his heart, There is no God. They are corrupt, they have done abominable works; There is none that doeth good.

Psa 14:2 Jehovah looked down from heaven upon the children of men, To see if there were any that did understand, That did seek after God.

Psa 14:3 They are all gone aside; they are together become filthy; There is none that doeth good, no, not one.

Psa 14:4 Have all the workers of iniquity no knowledge, Who eat up my people as they eat bread, And call not upon Jehovah?

Psa 14:5 There were they in great fear; For God is in the generation of the righteous.

Psa 14:6 Ye put to shame the counsel of the poor, Because Jehovah is his refuge.

Psa 14:7 Oh that the salvation of Israel were come out of Zion! When Jehovah bringeth back the captivity of his people, Then shall Jacob rejoice, and Israel shall be glad.

Chapter 15.

Psa 15:1 A Psalm of David. Jehovah, who shall sojourn in thy tabernacle? Who shall dwell in thy holy hill?

Psa 15:2 He that walketh uprightly, and worketh righteousness, And speaketh truth in his heart;

Psa 15:3 He that slandereth not with his tongue, Nor doeth evil to his friend, Nor taketh up a reproach against his neighbor;

Psa 15:4 In whose eyes a reprobate is despised, But who honoreth them that fear Jehovah; He that sweareth to his own hurt, and changeth not;

Psa 15:5 He that putteth not out his money to interest, Nor taketh reward against the innocent. He that doeth these things shall never be moved.

Chapter 16.

Psa 16:1 Michtam of David. Preserve me, O God; for in thee do I take refuge.

Psa 16:2 O my soul, thou hast said unto Jehovah, Thou art my Lord: I have no good beyond thee.

Psa 16:3 As for the saints that are in the earth, They are the excellent in whom is all my delight.

Psa 16:4 Their sorrows shall be multiplied that give gifts for another god: Their drink-offerings of blood will I not offer, Nor take their names upon my lips.

Psa 16:5 Jehovah is the portion of mine inheritance and of my cup: Thou maintainest my lot.

Psa 16:6 The lines are fallen unto me in pleasant places; Yea, I have a goodly heritage.

Psa 16:7 I will bless Jehovah, who hath given me counsel; Yea, my heart instructeth me in the night seasons.

Psa 16:8 I have set Jehovah always before me: Because he is at my right hand, I shall not be moved.

Psa 16:9 Therefore my heart is glad, and my glory rejoiceth; My flesh also shall dwell in safety.

Psa 16:10 For thou wilt not leave my soul to Sheol; Neither wilt thou suffer thy holy one to see corruption.

Psa 16:11 Thou wilt show me the path of life: In thy presence is fulness of joy; In thy right hand there are pleasures for evermore.

Chapter 17.

Psa 17:1 A Prayer of David. Hear the right, O Jehovah, attend unto my cry; Give ear unto my prayer, that goeth not out of feigned lips.

Psa 17:2 Let my sentence come forth from thy presence; Let thine eyes look upon equity.

Psa 17:3 Thou hast proved my heart; thou hast visited me in the night; Thou hast tried me, and findest nothing; I am purposed that my mouth shall not transgress.

Psa 17:4 As for the works of men, by the word of thy lips I have kept me from the ways of the violent.

Psa 17:5 My steps have held fast to thy paths, My feet have not slipped.

Psa 17:6 I have called upon thee, for thou wilt answer me, O God: Incline thine ear unto me, and hear my speech.

Psa 17:7 Show thy marvellous lovingkindness, O thou that savest by thy right hand them that take refuge in thee From those that rise up against them.

Psa 17:8 Keep me as the apple of the eye; Hide me under the shadow of thy wings,

Psa 17:9 From the wicked that oppress me, My deadly enemies, that compass me about.

Psa 17:10 They are inclosed in their own fat: With their mouth they speak proudly.

Psa 17:11 They have now compassed us in our steps; They set their eyes to cast us down to the earth.

Psa 17:12 He is like a lion that is greedy of his prey, And as it were a young lion lurking in secret places.

Psa 17:13 Arise, O Jehovah, Confront him, cast him down: Deliver my soul from the wicked by thy sword;

Psa 17:14 From men by thy hand, O Jehovah, From men of the world, whose portion is in this life, And whose belly thou fillest with thy treasure: They are satisfied with children, And leave the rest of their substance to their babes.

Psa 17:15 As for me, I shall behold thy face in righteousness; I shall be satisfied, when I awake, with beholding thy form.

Chapter 18.

Psa 18:1 For the Chief Musician. A Psalm of David the servant of Jehovah, who spake unto Jehovah the words of this song in the day that Jehovah delivered him from the hand of all his enemies, and from the hand of Saul: and he said, I love thee, O Jehovah, my strength.

Psa 18:2 Jehovah is my rock, and my fortress, and my deliverer; My God, my rock, in whom I will take refuge; My shield, and the horn of my salvation, my high tower.

Psa 18:3 I will call upon Jehovah, who is worthy to be praised: So shall I be saved from mine enemies.

Psa 18:4 The cords of death compassed me, And the floods of ungodliness made me afraid.

Psa 18:5 The cords of Sheol were round about me; The snares of death came upon me.

Psa 18:6 In my distress I called upon Jehovah, And cried unto my God: He heard my voice out of his temple, And my cry before him came into his ears.

Psa 18:7 Then the earth shook and trembled; The foundations also of the mountains quaked And were shaken, because he was wroth.

Psa 18:8 There went up a smoke out of his nostrils, And fire out of his mouth devoured: Coals were kindled by it.

Psa 18:9 He bowed the heavens also, and came down; And thick darkness was under his feet.

Psa 18:10 And he rode upon a cherub, and did fly; Yea, he soared upon the wings of the wind.

Psa 18:11 He made darkness his hiding-place, his pavilion round about him, Darkness of waters, thick clouds of the skies.

Psa 18:12 At the brightness before him his thick clouds passed, Hailstones and coals of fire.

Psa 18:13 Jehovah also thundered in the heavens, And the Most High uttered his voice, Hailstones and coals of fire.

Psa 18:14 And he sent out his arrows, and scattered them; Yea, lightnings manifold, and discomfited them.

Psa 18:15 Then the channels of waters appeared, And the foundations of the world were laid bare, At thy rebuke, O Jehovah, At the blast of the breath of thy nostrils.

Psa 18:16 He sent from on high, he took me; He drew me out of many waters.

Psa 18:17 He delivered me from my strong enemy, And from them that hated me; for they were too mighty for me.

Psa 18:18 They came upon me in the day of my calamity; But Jehovah was my stay.

Psa 18:19 He brought me forth also into a large place; He delivered me, because he delighted in me.

Psa 18:20 Jehovah hath rewarded me according to my righteousness; According to the cleanness of my hands hath he recompensed me.

Psa 18:21 For I have kept the ways of Jehovah, And have not wickedly departed from my God.

Psa 18:22 For all his ordinances were before me, And I put not away his statutes from me.

Psa 18:23 I was also perfect with him, And I kept myself from mine iniquity.

Psa 18:24 Therefore hath Jehovah recompensed me according to my righteousness, According to the cleanness of my hands in his eyesight.

Psa 18:25 With the merciful thou wilt show thyself merciful; With the perfect man thou wilt show thyself perfect;

Psa 18:26 With the pure thou wilt show thyself pure; And with the perverse thou wilt show thyself froward.

Psa 18:27 For thou wilt save the afflicted people; But the haughty eyes thou wilt bring down.

Psa 18:28 For thou wilt light my lamp: Jehovah my God will lighten my darkness.

Psa 18:29 For by thee I run upon a troop; And by my God do I leap over a wall.

Psa 18:30 As for God, his way is perfect: The word of Jehovah is tried; He is a shield unto all them that take refuge in him.

Psa 18:31 For who is God, save Jehovah? And who is a rock, besides our God,

Psa 18:32 The God that girdeth me with strength, And maketh my way perfect?

Psa 18:33 He maketh my feet like hinds' feet: And setteth me upon my high places.

Psa 18:34 He teacheth my hands to war; So that mine arms do bend a bow of brass.

Psa 18:35 Thou hast also given me the shield of thy salvation; And thy right hand hath holden me up, And thy gentleness hath made me great.

Psa 18:36 Thou hast enlarged my steps under me, And my feet have not slipped.

Psa 18:37 I will pursue mine enemies, and overtake them; Neither will I turn again till they are consumed.

Psa 18:38 I will smite them through, so that they shall not be able to rise: They shall fall under my feet.

Psa 18:39 For thou hast girded me with strength unto the battle: Thou hast subdued under me those that rose up against me.

Psa 18:40 Thou hast also made mine enemies turn their backs unto me, That I might cut off them that hate me.

Psa 18:41 They cried, but there was none to save; Even unto Jehovah, but he answered them not.

Psa 18:42 Then did I beat them small as the dust before the wind; I did cast them out as the mire of the streets.

Psa 18:43 Thou hast delivered me from the strivings of the people; Thou hast made me the head of the nations: A people whom I have not known shall serve me.

Psa 18:44 As soon as they hear of me they shall obey me; The foreigners shall submit themselves unto me.

Psa 18:45 The foreigners shall fade away, And shall come trembling out of their close places.

Psa 18:46 Jehovah liveth; and blessed be my rock; And exalted be the God of my salvation,

Psa 18:47 Even the God that executeth vengeance for me, And subdueth peoples under me.

Psa 18:48 He rescueth me from mine enemies; Yea, thou liftest me up above them that rise up against me; Thou deliverest me from the violent man.

Psa 18:49 Therefore I will give thanks unto thee, O Jehovah, among the nations, And will sing praises unto thy name.

Psa 18:50 Great deliverance giveth he to his king, And showeth lovingkindness to his anointed, To David and to his seed, for evermore.

Chapter 19.

Psa 19:1 For the Chief Musician. A Psalm of David. The heavens declare the glory of God; And the firmament showeth his handiwork.

Psa 19:2 Day unto day uttereth speech, And night unto night showeth knowledge.

Psa 19:3 There is no speech nor language; Their voice is not heard.

Psa 19:4 Their line is gone out through all the earth, And their words to the end of the world. In them hath he set a tabernacle for the sun,

Psa 19:5 Which is as a bridegroom coming out of his chamber, And rejoiceth as a strong man to run his course.

Psa 19:6 His going forth is from the end of the heavens, And his circuit unto the ends of it; And there is nothing hid from the heat thereof.

Psa 19:7 The law of Jehovah is perfect, restoring the soul: The testimony of Jehovah is sure, making wise the simple.

Psa 19:8 The precepts of Jehovah are right, rejoicing the heart: The commandment of Jehovah is pure, enlightening the eyes.

Psa 19:9 The fear of Jehovah is clean, enduring for ever: The ordinances of Jehovah are true, and righteous altogether.

Psa 19:10 More to be desired are they than gold, yea, than much fine gold; Sweeter also than honey and the droppings of the honeycomb.

Psa 19:11 Moreover by them is thy servant warned: In keeping them there is great reward.

Psa 19:12 Who can discern his errors? Clear thou me from hidden faults.

Psa 19:13 Keep back thy servant also from presumptuous sins; Let them not have dominion over me: Then shall I be upright, And I shall be clear from great transgression.

Psa 19:14 Let the words of my mouth and the meditation of my heart Be acceptable in thy sight, O Jehovah, my rock, and my redeemer.

Chapter 20.

Psa 20:1 For the Chief Musician. A Psalm of David. Jehovah answer thee in the day of trouble; The name of the God of Jacob set thee up on high;

Psa 20:2 Send thee help from the sanctuary, And strengthen thee out of Zion;

Psa 20:3 Remember all thy offerings, And accept thy burnt-sacrifice; Selah.

Psa 20:4 Grant thee thy heart's desire, And fulfil all thy counsel.

Psa 20:5 We will triumph in thy salvation, And in the name of our God we will set up our banners: Jehovah fulfil all thy petitions.

Psa 20:6 Now know I that Jehovah saveth his anointed; He will answer him from his holy heaven With the saving strength of his right hand.

Psa 20:7 Some trust in chariots, and some in horses; But we will make mention of the name of Jehovah our God.

Psa 20:8 They are bowed down and fallen; But we are risen, and stand upright.

Psa 20:9 Save, Jehovah: Let the King answer us when we call.

Chapter 21.

Psa 21:1 For the Chief Musician. A Psalm of David. The king shall joy in thy strength, O Jehovah; And in thy salvation how greatly shall he rejoice!

Psa 21:2 Thou hast given him his heart's desire, And hast not withholden the request of his lips. Selah.

Psa 21:3 For thou meetest him with the blessings of goodness: Thou settest a crown of fine gold on his head.

Psa 21:4 He asked life of thee, thou gavest it him, Even length of days for ever and ever.

Psa 21:5 His glory is great in thy salvation: Honor and majesty dost thou lay upon him.

Psa 21:6 For thou makest him most blessed for ever: Thou makest him glad with joy in thy presence.

Psa 21:7 For the king trusteth in Jehovah; And through the lovingkindness of the Most High he shall not be moved.

Psa 21:8 Thy hand will find out all thine enemies; Thy right hand will find out those that hate thee.

Psa 21:9 Thou wilt make them as a fiery furnace in the time of thine anger: Jehovah will swallow them up in his wrath, And the fire shall devour them.

Psa 21:10 Their fruit wilt thou destroy from the earth, And their seed from among the children of men.

Psa 21:11 For they intended evil against thee; They conceived a device which they are not able to perform.

Psa 21:12 For thou wilt make them turn their back; Thou wilt make ready with thy bowstrings against their face.

Psa 21:13 Be thou exalted, O Jehovah, in thy strength: So will we sing and praise thy power.

Chapter 22.

Psa 22:1 For the Chief Musician; set to Aijeleth hash-Shahar. A Psalm of David. My God, my God, why hast thou forsaken me? Why art thou so far from helping me, and from the words of my groaning?

Psa 22:2 O my God, I cry in the daytime, but thou answerest not; And in the night season, and am not silent.

Psa 22:3 But thou art holy, O thou that inhabitest the praises of Israel.

Psa 22:4 Our fathers trusted in thee: They trusted, and thou didst deliver them.

Psa 22:5 They cried unto thee, and were delivered: They trusted in thee, and were not put to shame.

Psa 22:6 But I am a worm, and no man; A reproach of men, and despised of the people.

Psa 22:7 All they that see me laugh me to scorn: They shoot out the lip, they shake the head, saying,

Psa 22:8 Commit thyself unto Jehovah; Let him deliver him: Let him rescue him, seeing he delighteth in him.

Psa 22:9 But thou art he that took me out of the womb; Thou didst make me trust when I was upon my mother's breasts.

Psa 22:10 I was cast upon thee from the womb; Thou art my God since my mother bare me.

Psa 22:11 Be not far from me; for trouble is near; For there is none to help.

Psa 22:12 Many bulls have compassed me; Strong bulls of Bashan have beset me round.

Psa 22:13 They gape upon me with their mouth, As a ravening and a roaring lion.

Psa 22:14 I am poured out like water, And all my bones are out of joint: My heart is like wax; It is melted within me.

Psa 22:15 My strength is dried up like a potsherd; And my tongue cleaveth to my jaws; And thou hast brought me into the dust of death.

Psa 22:16 For dogs have compassed me: A company of evil-doers have inclosed me; They pierced my hands and my feet.

Psa 22:17 I may count all my bones; They look and stare upon me.

Psa 22:18 They part my garments among them, And upon my vesture do they cast lots.

Psa 22:19 But be not thou far off, O Jehovah: O thou my succor, haste thee to help me.

Psa 22:20 Deliver my soul from the sword, My darling from the power of the dog.

Psa 22:21 Save me from the lion's mouth; Yea, from the horns of the wild-oxen thou hast answered me.

Psa 22:22 I will declare thy name unto my brethren: In the midst of the assembly will I praise thee.

Psa 22:23 Ye that fear Jehovah, praise him; All ye the seed of Jacob, glorify him; And stand in awe of him, all ye the seed of Israel.

Psa 22:24 For he hath not despised nor abhorred the affliction of the afflicted; Neither hath he hid his face from him; But when he cried unto him, he heard.

Psa 22:25 Of thee cometh my praise in the great assembly: I will pay my vows before them that fear him.

Psa 22:26 The meek shall eat and be satisfied; They shall praise Jehovah that seek after him: Let your heart live for ever.

Psa 22:27 All the ends of the earth shall remember and turn unto Jehovah; And all the kindreds of the nations shall worship before thee.

Psa 22:28 For the kingdom is Jehovah's; And he is the ruler over the nations.

Psa 22:29 All the fat ones of the earth shall eat and worship: All they that go down to the dust shall bow before him, Even he that cannot keep his soul alive.

Psa 22:30 A seed shall serve him; It shall be told of the Lord unto the next generation.

Psa 22:31 They shall come and shall declare his righteousness Unto a people that shall be born, that he hath done it.

Chapter 23.

Psa 23:1 A Psalm of David. Jehovah is my shepherd; I shall not want.

Psa 23:2 He maketh me to lie down in green pastures; He leadeth me beside still waters.

Psa 23:3 He restoreth my soul: He guideth me in the paths of righteousness for his name's sake.

Psa 23:4 Yea, thou I walk through the valley of the shadow of death, I will fear no evil; for thou art with me; Thy rod and thy staff, they comfort me.

Psa 23:5 Thou preparest a table before me in the presence of mine enemies: Thou hast anointed my head with oil; My cup runneth over.

Psa 23:6 Surely goodness and lovingkindness shall follow me all the days of my life; And I shall dwell in the house of Jehovah for ever.

Chapter 24.

Psa 24:1 A Psalm of David. The earth is Jehovah's, and the fulness thereof; The world, and they that dwell therein.

Psa 24:2 For he hath founded it upon the seas, And established it upon the floods.

Psa 24:3 Who shall ascend into the hill of Jehovah? And who shall stand in his holy place?

Psa 24:4 He that hath clean hands, and a pure heart; Who hath not lifted up his soul unto falsehood, And hath not sworn deceitfully.

Psa 24:5 He shall receive a blessing from Jehovah, And righteousness from the God of his salvation.

Psa 24:6 This is the generation of them that seek after him, That seek thy face, even Jacob. Selah.

Psa 24:7 Lift up your heads, O ye gates; And be ye lifted up, ye everlasting doors: And the King of glory will come in.

Psa 24:8 Who is the King of glory? Jehovah strong and mighty, Jehovah mighty in battle.

Psa 24:9 Lift up your heads, O ye gates; Yea, lift them up, ye everlasting doors: And the King of glory will come in.

Psa 24:10 Who is this King of glory? Jehovah of hosts, He is the King of glory. Selah.

Chapter 25.

Psa 25:1 A Psalm of David. Unto thee, O Jehovah, do I lift up my soul.

Psa 25:2 O my God, in thee have I trusted, Let me not be put to shame; Let not mine enemies triumph over me.

Psa 25:3 Yea, none that wait for thee shall be put to shame: They shall be put to shame that deal treacherously without cause.

Psa 25:4 Show me thy ways, O Jehovah; Teach me thy paths.

Psa 25:5 Guide me in thy truth, and teach me; For thou art the God of my salvation; For thee do I wait all the day.

Psa 25:6 Remember, O Jehovah, thy tender mercies and thy lovingkindness; For they have been ever of old.

Psa 25:7 Remember not the sins of my youth, nor my transgressions: According to thy lovingkindness remember thou me, For thy goodness' sake, O Jehovah.

Psa 25:8 Good and upright is Jehovah: Therefore will he instruct sinners in the way.

Psa 25:9 The meek will he guide in justice; And the meek will he teach his way.

Psa 25:10 All the paths of Jehovah are lovingkindness and truth Unto such as keep his covenant and his testimonies.

Psa 25:11 For thy name's sake, O Jehovah, Pardon mine iniquity, for it is great.

Psa 25:12 What man is he that feareth Jehovah? Him shall he instruct in the way that he shall choose.

Psa 25:13 His soul shall dwell at ease; And his seed shall inherit the land.

Psa 25:14 The friendship of Jehovah is with them that fear him; And he will show them his covenant.

Psa 25:15 Mine eyes are ever toward Jehovah; For he will pluck my feet out of the net.

Psa 25:16 Turn thee unto me, and have mercy upon me; For I am desolate and afflicted.

Psa 25:17 The troubles of my heart are enlarged: Oh bring thou me out of my distresses.

Psa 25:18 Consider mine affliction and my travail; And forgive all my sins.

Psa 25:19 Consider mine enemies, for they are many; And they hate me with cruel hatred.

Psa 25:20 Oh keep my soul, and deliver me: Let me not be put to shame, for I take refuge in thee.

Psa 25:21 Let integrity and uprightness preserve me, For I wait for thee.

Psa 25:22 Redeem Israel, O God, Out all of his troubles.

Chapter 26.

Psa 26:1 A Psalm of David. Judge me, O Jehovah, for I have walked in mine integrity: I have trusted also in Jehovah without wavering.

Psa 26:2 Examine me, O Jehovah, and prove me; Try my heart and my mind.

Psa 26:3 For thy lovingkindness is before mine eyes; And I have walked in thy truth.

Psa 26:4 I have not sat with men of falsehood; Neither will I go in with dissemblers.

Psa 26:5 I hate the assembly of evil-doers, And will not sit with the wicked.

Psa 26:6 I will wash my hands in innocency: So will I compass thine altar, O Jehovah;

Psa 26:7 That I may make the voice of thanksgiving to be heard, And tell of all thy wondrous works.

Psa 26:8 Jehovah, I love the habitation of thy house, And the place where thy glory dwelleth.

Psa 26:9 Gather not my soul with sinners, Nor my life with men of blood;

Psa 26:10 In whose hands is wickedness, And their right hand is full of bribes.

Psa 26:11 But as for me, I will walk in mine integrity: Redeem me, and be merciful unto me.

Psa 26:12 My foot standeth in an even place: In the congregations will I bless Jehovah.

Chapter 27.

Psa 27:1 A Psalm of David. Jehovah is my light and my salvation; Whom shall I fear? Jehovah is the strength of my life; Of whom shall I be afraid?

Psa 27:2 When evil-doers came upon me to eat up my flesh, Even mine adversaries and my foes, they stumbled and fell.

Psa 27:3 Though a host should encamp against me, My heart shall not fear: Though war should rise against me, Even then will I be confident.

Psa 27:4 One thing have I asked of Jehovah, that will I seek after; That I may dwell in the house of Jehovah all the days of my life, To behold the beauty of Jehovah, And to inquire in his temple.

Psa 27:5 For in the day of trouble he will keep me secretly in his pavilion: In the covert of his tabernacle will he hide me; He will lift me up upon a rock.

Psa 27:6 And now shall my head be lifted up above mine enemies round about me. And I will offer in his tabernacle sacrifices of joy; I will sing, yea, I will sing praises unto Jehovah.

Psa 27:7 Hear, O Jehovah, when I cry with my voice: Have mercy also upon me, and answer me.

Psa 27:8 When thou saidst, Seek ye my face; My heart said unto thee, Thy face, Jehovah, will I seek.

Psa 27:9 Hide not thy face from me; Put not thy servant away in anger: Thou hast been my help; Cast me not off, neither forsake me, O God of my salvation.

Psa 27:10 When my father and my mother forsake me, Then Jehovah will take me up.

Psa 27:11 Teach me thy way, O Jehovah; And lead me in a plain path, Because of mine enemies.

Psa 27:12 Deliver me not over unto the will of mine adversaries: For false witnesses are risen up against me, And such as breathe out cruelty.

Psa 27:13 I had fainted, unless I had believed to see the goodness of Jehovah In the land of the living.

Psa 27:14 Wait for Jehovah: Be strong, And let thy heart take courage; Yea, wait thou for Jehovah.

Chapter 28.

Psa 28:1 A Psalm of David. Unto thee, O Jehovah, will I call: My rock, be not thou deaf unto me; Lest, if thou be silent unto me, I become like them that go down into the pit.

Psa 28:2 Hear the voice of my supplications, when I cry unto thee, When I lift up my hands toward thy holy oracle.

Psa 28:3 Draw me not away with the wicked, And with the workers of iniquity; That speak peace with their neighbors, But mischief is in their hearts.

Psa 28:4 Give them according to their work, and according to the wickedness of their doings: Give them after the operation of their hands; Render to them their desert.

Psa 28:5 Because they regard not the works of Jehovah, Nor the operation of his hands, He will break them down and not build them up.

Psa 28:6 Blessed be Jehovah, Because he hath heard the voice of my supplications.

Psa 28:7 Jehovah is my strength and my shield; My heart hath trusted in him, and I am helped: Therefore my heart greatly rejoiceth; And with my song will I praise him.

Psa 28:8 Jehovah is their strength, And he is a stronghold of salvation to his anointed.

Psa 28:9 Save thy people, and bless thine inheritance: Be their shepherd also, and bear them up for ever.

Chapter 29.

Psa 29:1 A Psalm of David. Ascribe unto Jehovah, O ye sons of the mighty, Ascribe unto Jehovah glory and strength.

Psa 29:2 Ascribe unto Jehovah the glory due unto his name; Worship Jehovah in holy array.

Psa 29:3 The voice of Jehovah is upon the waters: The God of glory thundereth, Even Jehovah upon many waters.

Psa 29:4 The voice of Jehovah is powerful; The voice of Jehovah is full of majesty.

Psa 29:5 The voice of Jehovah breaketh the cedars; Yea, Jehovah breaketh in pieces the cedars of Lebanon.

Psa 29:6 He maketh them also to skip like a calf; Lebanon and Sirion like a young wild-ox.

Psa 29:7 The voice of Jehovah cleaveth the flames of fire.

Psa 29:8 The voice of Jehovah shaketh the wilderness; Jehovah shaketh the wilderness of Kadesh.

Psa 29:9 The voice of Jehovah maketh the hinds to calve, And strippeth the forests bare: And in his temple everything saith, Glory.

Psa 29:10 Jehovah sat as King at the Flood; Yea, Jehovah sitteth as King for ever.

Psa 29:11 Jehovah will give strength unto his people; Jehovah will bless his people with peace.

Chapter 30.

Psa 30:1 A Psalm; a song at the Dedication of the House. A Psalm of David. I will extol thee, O Jehovah; for thou hast raised me up, And hast not made my foes to rejoice over me.

Psa 30:2 O Jehovah my God, I cried unto thee, and thou hast healed me.

Psa 30:3 O Jehovah, thou hast brought up my soul from Sheol; Thou hast kept me alive, that I should not go down to the pit.

Psa 30:4 Sing praise unto Jehovah, O ye saints of his, And give thanks to his holy memorial name.

Psa 30:5 For his anger is but for a moment; His favor is for a life-time: Weeping may tarry for the night, But joy cometh in the morning.

Psa 30:6 As for me, I said in my prosperity, I shall never be moved.

Psa 30:7 Thou, Jehovah, of thy favor hadst made my mountain to stand strong: Thou didst hide thy face; I was troubled.

Psa 30:8 I cried to thee, O Jehovah; And unto Jehovah I made supplication:

Psa 30:9 What profit is there in my blood, when I go down to the pit? Shall the dust praise thee? shall it declare thy truth?

Psa 30:10 Hear, O Jehovah, and have mercy upon me: Jehovah, be thou my helper.

Psa 30:11 Thou hast turned for me my mourning into dancing; Thou hast loosed my sackcloth, and girded me with gladness;

Psa 30:12 To the end that my glory may sing praise to thee, and not be silent. O Jehovah my God, I will give thanks unto thee for ever.

Chapter 31.

Psa 31:1 For the Chief Musician. A Psalm of David. In thee, O Jehovah, do I take refuge; Let me never be put to shame: Deliver me in thy righteousness.

Psa 31:2 Bow down thine ear unto me; deliver me speedily: Be thou to me a strong rock, A house of defence to save me.

Psa 31:3 For thou art my rock and my fortress; Therefore for thy name's sake lead me and guide me.

Psa 31:4 Pluck me out of the net that they have laid privily for me; For thou art my stronghold.

Psa 31:5 Into thy hand I commend my spirit: Thou hast redeemed me, O Jehovah, thou God of truth.

Psa 31:6 I hate them that regard lying vanities; But I trust in Jehovah.

Psa 31:7 I will be glad and rejoice in thy lovingkindness; For thou hast seen my affliction: Thou hast known my soul in adversities;

Psa 31:8 And thou hast not shut me up into the hand of the enemy; Thou hast set my feet in a large place.

Psa 31:9 Have mercy upon me, O Jehovah, for I am in distress: Mine eye wasteth away with grief, yea, my soul and my body.

Psa 31:10 For my life is spent with sorrow, And my years with sighing: My strength faileth because of mine iniquity, And my bones are wasted away.

Psa 31:11 Because of all mine adversaries I am become a reproach, Yea, unto my neighbors exceedingly, And a fear to mine acquaintance: They that did see me without fled from me.

Psa 31:12 I am forgotten as a dead man out of mind: I am like a broken vessel.

Psa 31:13 For I have heard the defaming of many, Terror on every side: While they took counsel together against me, They devised to take away my life.

Psa 31:14 But I trusted in thee, O Jehovah: I said, Thou art my God.

Psa 31:15 My times are in thy hand: Deliver me from the hand of mine enemies, and from them that persecute me.

Psa 31:16 Make thy face to shine upon thy servant: Save me in thy lovingkindness.

Psa 31:17 Let me not be put to shame, O Jehovah; for I have called upon thee: Let the wicked be put to shame, let them be silent in Sheol.

Psa 31:18 Let the lying lips be dumb, Which speak against the righteous insolently, With pride and contempt.

Psa 31:19 Oh how great is thy goodness, Which thou hast laid up for them that fear thee, Which thou hast wrought for them that take refuge in thee, Before the sons of men!

Psa 31:20 In the covert of thy presence wilt thou hide them from the plottings of man: Thou wilt keep them secretly in a pavilion from the strife of tongues.

Psa 31:21 Blessed be Jehovah; For he hath showed me his marvellous lovingkindness in a strong city.

Psa 31:22 As for me, I said in my haste, I am cut off from before thine eyes: Nevertheless thou heardest the voice of my supplications When I cried unto thee.

Psa 31:23 Oh love Jehovah, all ye his saints: Jehovah preserveth the faithful, And plentifully rewardeth him that dealeth proudly.

Psa 31:24 Be strong, and let your heart take courage, All ye that hope in Jehovah.

Chapter 32.

Psa 32:1 A Psalm of David. Maschil. Blessed is he whose transgression is forgiven, Whose sin is covered.

Psa 32:2 Blessed is the man unto whom Jehovah imputeth not iniquity, And in whose spirit there is no guile.

Psa 32:3 When I kept silence, my bones wasted away Through my groaning all the day long.

Psa 32:4 For day and night thy hand was heavy upon me: My moisture was changed as with the drought of summer. Selah.

Psa 32:5 I acknowledged my sin unto thee, And mine iniquity did I not hide: I said, I will confess my transgressions unto Jehovah; And thou forgavest the iniquity of my sin. Selah.

Psa 32:6 For this let every one that is godly pray unto thee in a time when thou mayest be found: Surely when the great waters overflow they shall not reach unto him.

Psa 32:7 Thou art my hiding-place; thou wilt preserve me from trouble; Thou wilt compass me about with songs of deliverance. Selah.

Psa 32:8 I will instruct thee and teach thee in the way which thou shalt go: I will counsel thee with mine eye upon thee.

Psa 32:9 Be ye not as the horse, or as the mule, which have no understanding; Whose trappings must be bit and bridle to hold them in, Else they will not come near unto thee.

Psa 32:10 Many sorrows shall be to the wicked; But he that trusteth in Jehovah, lovingkindness shall compass him about.

Psa 32:11 Be glad in Jehovah, and rejoice, ye righteous; And shout for joy, all ye that are upright in heart.

Chapter 33.

Psa 33:1 Rejoice in Jehovah, O ye righteous: Praise is comely for the upright.

Psa 33:2 Give thanks unto Jehovah with the harp: Sing praises unto him with the psaltery of ten strings.

Psa 33:3 Sing unto him a new song; Play skilfully with a loud noise.

Psa 33:4 For the word of Jehovah is right; And all his work is done in faithfulness.

Psa 33:5 He loveth righteousness and justice: The earth is full of the lovingkindness of Jehovah.

Psa 33:6 By the word of Jehovah were the heavens made, And all the host of them by the breath of his mouth.

Psa 33:7 He gathereth the waters of the sea together as a heap: He layeth up the deeps in store-houses.

Psa 33:8 Let all the earth fear Jehovah: Let all the inhabitants of the world stand in awe of him.

Psa 33:9 For he spake, and it was done; He commanded, and it stood fast.

Psa 33:10 Jehovah bringeth the counsel of the nations to nought; He maketh the thoughts of the peoples to be of no effect.

Psa 33:11 The counsel of Jehovah standeth fast for ever, The thoughts of his heart to all generations.

Psa 33:12 Blessed is the nation whose God is Jehovah, The people whom he hath chosen for his own inheritance.

Psa 33:13 Jehovah looketh from heaven; He beholdeth all the sons of men;

Psa 33:14 From the place of his habitation he looketh forth Upon all the inhabitants of the earth,

Psa 33:15 He that fashioneth the hearts of them all, That considereth all their works.

Psa 33:16 There is no king saved by the multitude of a host: A mighty man is not delivered by great strength.

Psa 33:17 A horse is a vain thing for safety; Neither doth he deliver any by his great power.

Psa 33:18 Behold, the eye of Jehovah is upon them that fear him, Upon them that hope in his lovingkindness;

Psa 33:19 To deliver their soul from death, And to keep them alive in famine.

Psa 33:20 Our soul hath waited for Jehovah: He is our help and our shield.

Psa 33:21 For our heart shall rejoice in him, Because we have trusted in his holy name.

Psa 33:22 Let thy lovingkindness, O Jehovah, be upon us, According as we have hoped in thee.

Chapter 34.

Psa 34:1 A Psalm of David; when he changed his behavior before Abimelech, who drove him away, and he departed. I will bless Jehovah at all times: His praise shall continually be in my mouth.

Psa 34:2 My soul shall make her boast in Jehovah: The meek shall hear thereof, and be glad.

Psa 34:3 Oh magnify Jehovah with me, And let us exalt his name together.

Psa 34:4 I sought Jehovah, and he answered me, And delivered me from all my fears.

Psa 34:5 They looked unto him, and were radiant; And their faces shall never be confounded.

Psa 34:6 This poor man cried, and Jehovah heard him, And saved him out of all his troubles.

Psa 34:7 The angel of Jehovah encampeth round about them that fear him, And delivereth them.

Psa 34:8 Oh taste and see that Jehovah is good: Blessed is the man that taketh refuge in him.

Psa 34:9 Oh fear Jehovah, ye his saints; For there is no want to them that fear him.

Psa 34:10 The young lions do lack, and suffer hunger; But they that seek Jehovah shall not want any good thing.

Psa 34:11 Come, ye children, hearken unto me: I will teach you the fear of Jehovah.

Psa 34:12 What man is he that desireth life, And loveth many days, that he may see good?

Psa 34:13 Keep thy tongue from evil, And thy lips from speaking guile.

Psa 34:14 Depart from evil, and do good; Seek peace, and pursue it.

Psa 34:15 The eyes of Jehovah are toward the righteous, And his ears are open unto their cry.

Psa 34:16 The face of Jehovah is against them that do evil, To cut off the remembrance of them from the earth.

Psa 34:17 The righteous cried, and Jehovah heard, And delivered them out of all their troubles.

Psa 34:18 Jehovah is nigh unto them that are of a broken heart, And saveth such as are of a contrite spirit.

Psa 34:19 Many are the afflictions of the righteous; But Jehovah delivereth him out of them all.

Psa 34:20 He keepeth all his bones: Not one of them is broken.

Psa 34:21 Evil shall slay the wicked; And they that hate the righteous shall be condemned.

Psa 34:22 Jehovah redeemeth the soul of his servants; And none of them that take refuge in him shall be condemned.

Chapter 35.

Psa 35:1 A Psalm of David. Strive thou, O Jehovah, with them that strive with me: Fight thou against them that fight against me.

Psa 35:2 Take hold of shield and buckler, And stand up for my help.

Psa 35:3 Draw out also the spear, and stop the way against them that pursue me: Say unto my soul, I am thy salvation.

Psa 35:4 Let them be put to shame and brought to dishonor that seek after my soul: Let them be turned back and confounded that devise my hurt.

Psa 35:5 Let them be as chaff before the wind, And the angel of Jehovah driving them on.

Psa 35:6 Let their way be dark and slippery, And the angel of Jehovah pursuing them.

Psa 35:7 For without cause have they hid for me their net in a pit; Without cause have they digged a pit for my soul.

Psa 35:8 Let destruction come upon him unawares; And let his net that he hath hid catch himself: With destruction let him fall therein.

Psa 35:9 And my soul shall be joyful in Jehovah: It shall rejoice in his salvation.

Psa 35:10 All my bones shall say, Jehovah, who is like unto thee, Who deliverest the poor from him that is too strong for him, Yea, the poor and the needy from him that robbeth him?

Psa 35:11 Unrighteous witnesses rise up; They ask me of things that I know not.

Psa 35:12 They reward me evil for good, To the bereaving of my soul.

Psa 35:13 But as for me, when they were sick, my clothing was sackcloth: I afflicted my soul with fasting; And my prayer returned into mine own bosom.

Psa 35:14 I behaved myself as though it had been my friend or my brother: I bowed down mourning, as one that bewaileth his mother.

Psa 35:15 But in mine adversity they rejoiced, and gathered themselves together: The abjects gathered themselves together against me, and I knew it not; They did tear me, and ceased not:

Psa 35:16 Like the profane mockers in feasts, They gnashed upon me with their teeth.

Psa 35:17 Lord, how long wilt thou look on? Rescue my soul from their destructions, My darling from the lions.

Psa 35:18 I will give thee thanks in the great assembly: I will praise thee among much people.

Psa 35:19 Let not them that are mine enemies wrongfully rejoice over me; Neither let them wink with the eye that hate me without a cause.

Psa 35:20 For they speak not peace; But they devise deceitful words against them that are quiet in the land.

Psa 35:21 Yea, they opened their mouth wide against me; They said, Aha, aha, our eye hath seen it.

Psa 35:22 Thou hast seen it, O Jehovah; keep not silence: O Lord, be not far from me.

Psa 35:23 Stir up thyself, and awake to the justice due unto me, Even unto my cause, my God and my Lord.

Psa 35:24 Judge me, O Jehovah my God, according to thy righteousness; And let them not rejoice over me.

Psa 35:25 Let them not say in their heart, Aha, so would we have it: Let them not say, We have swallowed him up.

Psa 35:26 Let them be put to shame and confounded together that rejoice at my hurt: Let them be clothed with shame and dishonor that magnify themselves against me.

Psa 35:27 Let them shout for joy, and be glad, that favor my righteous cause: Yea, let them say continually, Jehovah be magnified, Who hath pleasure in the prosperity of his servant.

Psa 35:28 And my tongue shall talk of thy righteousness And of thy praise all the day long.

Chapter 36.

Psa 36:1 For the Chief Musician. A Psalm of David the servant of Jehovah. The transgression of the wicked saith within my heart, There is no fear of God before his eyes.

Psa 36:2 For he flattereth himself in his own eyes, That his iniquity will not be found out and be hated.

Psa 36:3 The words of his mouth are iniquity and deceit: He hath ceased to be wise and to do good.

Psa 36:4 He deviseth iniquity upon his bed; He setteth himself in a way that is not good; He abhorreth not evil.

Psa 36:5 Thy lovingkindness, O Jehovah, is in the heavens; Thy faithfulness reacheth unto the skies.

Psa 36:6 Thy righteousness is like the mountains of God; Thy judgments are a great deep: O Jehovah, thou preservest man and beast.

Psa 36:7 How precious is thy lovingkindness, O God! And the children of men take refuge under the shadow of thy wings.

Psa 36:8 They shall be abundantly satisfied with the fatness of thy house; And thou wilt make them drink of the river of thy pleasures.

Psa 36:9 For with thee is the fountain of life: In thy light shall we see light.

Psa 36:10 Oh continue thy lovingkindness unto them that know thee, And thy righteousness to the upright in heart.

Psa 36:11 Let not the foot of pride come against me, And let not the hand of the wicked drive me away.

Psa 36:12 There are the workers of iniquity fallen: They are thrust down, and shall not be able to rise.

Chapter 37.

Psa 37:1 A Psalm of David. Fret not thyself because of evil-doers, Neither be thou envious against them that work unrighteousness.

Psa 37:2 For they shall soon be cut down like the grass, And wither as the green herb.

Psa 37:3 Trust in Jehovah, and do good; Dwell in the land, and feed on his faithfulness.

Psa 37:4 Delight thyself also in Jehovah; And he will give thee the desires of thy heart.

Psa 37:5 Commit thy way unto Jehovah; Trust also in him, and he will bring it to pass.

Psa 37:6 And he will make thy righteousness to go forth as the light, And thy justice as the noon-day.

Psa 37:7 Rest in Jehovah, and wait patiently for him: Fret not thyself because of him who prospereth in his way, Because of the man who bringeth wicked devices to pass.

Psa 37:8 Cease from anger, and forsake wrath: Fret not thyself, it tendeth only to evil-doing.

Psa 37:9 For evil-doers shall be cut off; But those that wait for Jehovah, they shall inherit the land.

Psa 37:10 For yet a little while, and the wicked shall not be: Yea, thou shalt diligently consider his place, and he shall not be.

Psa 37:11 But the meek shall inherit the land, And shall delight themselves in the abundance of peace.

Psa 37:12 The wicked plotteth against the just, And gnasheth upon him with his teeth.

Psa 37:13 The Lord will laugh at him; For he seeth that his day is coming.

Psa 37:14 The wicked have drawn out the sword, and have bent their bow, To cast down the poor and needy, To slay such as are upright in the way.

Psa 37:15 Their sword shall enter into their own heart, And their bows shall be broken.

Psa 37:16 Better is a little that the righteous hath Than the abundance of many wicked.

Psa 37:17 For the arms of the wicked shall be broken; But Jehovah upholdeth the righteous.

Psa 37:18 Jehovah knoweth the days of the perfect; And their inheritance shall be for ever.

Psa 37:19 They shall not be put to shame in the time of evil; And in the days of famine they shall be satisfied.

Psa 37:20 But the wicked shall perish, And the enemies of Jehovah shall be as the fat of lambs: They shall consume; in smoke shall they consume away.

Psa 37:21 The wicked borroweth, and payeth not again; But the righteous dealeth graciously, and giveth.

Psa 37:22 For such as are blessed of him shall inherit the land; And they that are cursed of him shall be cut off.

Psa 37:23 A man's goings are established of Jehovah; And he delighteth in his way.

Psa 37:24 Though he fall, he shall not be utterly cast down; For Jehovah upholdeth him with his hand.

Psa 37:25 I have been young, and now am old; Yet have I not seen the righteous forsaken, Nor his seed begging bread.

Psa 37:26 All the day long he dealeth graciously, and lendeth; And his seed is blessed.

Psa 37:27 Depart from evil, and do good; And dwell for evermore.

Psa 37:28 For Jehovah loveth justice, And forsaketh not his saints; They are preserved for ever: But the seed of the wicked shall be cut off.

Psa 37:29 The righteous shall inherit the land, And dwell therein for ever.

Psa 37:30 The mouth of the righteous talketh of wisdom, And his tongue speaketh justice.

Psa 37:31 The law of his God is in his heart; None of his steps shall slide.

Psa 37:32 The wicked watcheth the righteous, And seeketh to slay him.

Psa 37:33 Jehovah will not leave him in his hand, Nor condemn him when he is judged.

Psa 37:34 Wait for Jehovah, and keep his way, And he will exalt thee to inherit the land: When the wicked are cut off, thou shalt see it.

Psa 37:35 I have seen the wicked in great power, And spreading himself like a green tree in its native soil.

Psa 37:36 But one passed by, and, lo, he was not: Yea, I sought him, but he could not be found.

Psa 37:37 Mark the perfect man, and behold the upright; For there is a happy end to the man of peace.

Psa 37:38 As for transgressors, they shall be destroyed together; The end of the wicked shall be cut off.

Psa 37:39 But the salvation of the righteous is of Jehovah; He is their stronghold in the time of trouble.

Psa 37:40 And Jehovah helpeth them, and rescueth them; He rescueth them from the wicked, and saveth them, Because they have taken refuge in him.

Chapter 38.

Psa 38:1 A Psalm of David, to bring remembrance. O Jehovah, rebuke me not in thy wrath; Neither chasten me in thy hot displeasure.

Psa 38:2 For thine arrows stick fast in me, And thy hand presseth me sore.

Psa 38:3 There is no soundness in my flesh because of thine indignation; Neither is there any health in my bones because of my sin.

Psa 38:4 For mine iniquities are gone over my head: As a heavy burden they are too heavy for me.

Psa 38:5 My wounds are loathsome and corrupt, Because of my foolishness.

Psa 38:6 I am pained and bowed down greatly; I go mourning all the day long.

Psa 38:7 For my loins are filled with burning; And there is no soundness in my flesh.

Psa 38:8 I am faint and sore bruised: I have groaned by reason of the disquietness of my heart.

Psa 38:9 Lord, all my desire is before thee; And my groaning is not hid from thee.

Psa 38:10 My heart throbbeth, my strength faileth me: As for the light of mine eyes, it also is gone from me.

Psa 38:11 My lovers and my friends stand aloof from my plague; And my kinsmen stand afar off.

Psa 38:12 They also that seek after my life lay snares for me; And they that seek my hurt speak mischievous things, And meditate deceits all the day long.

Psa 38:13 But I, as a deaf man, hear not; And I am as a dumb man that openeth not his mouth.

Psa 38:14 Yea, I am as a man that heareth not, And in whose mouth are no reproofs.

Psa 38:15 For in thee, O Jehovah, do I hope: Thou wilt answer, O Lord my God.

Psa 38:16 For I said, Lest they rejoice over me: When my foot slippeth, they magnify themselves against me.

Psa 38:17 For I am ready to fall, And my sorrow is continually before me.

Psa 38:18 For I will declare mine iniquity; I will be sorry for my sin.

Psa 38:19 But mine enemies are lively, and are strong; And they that hate me wrongfully are multiplied.

Psa 38:20 They also that render evil for good Are adversaries unto me, because I follow the thing that is good.

Psa 38:21 Forsake me not, O Jehovah: O my God, be not far from me.

Psa 38:22 Make haste to help me, O Lord, my salvation.

Chapter 39.

Psa 39:1 For the Chief Musician, for Jeduthun. A Psalm of David. I said, I will take heed to my ways, That I sin not with my tongue: I will keep my mouth with a bridle, While the wicked is before me.

Psa 39:2 I was dumb with silence, I held my peace, even from good; And my sorrow was stirred.

Psa 39:3 My heart was hot within me; While I was musing the fire burned: Then spake I with my tongue:

Psa 39:4 Jehovah, make me to know mine end, And the measure of my days, what it is; Let me know how frail I am.

Psa 39:5 Behold, thou hast made my days as handbreadths; And my life-time is as nothing before thee: Surely every man at his best estate is altogether vanity. Selah.

Psa 39:6 Surely every man walketh in a vain show; Surely they are disquieted in vain: He heapeth up riches, and knoweth not who shall gather them.

Psa 39:7 And now, Lord, what wait I for? My hope is in thee.

Psa 39:8 Deliver me from all my transgressions: Make me not the reproach of the foolish.

Psa 39:9 I was dumb, I opened not my mouth; Because thou didst it.

Psa 39:10 Remove thy stroke away from me: I am consumed by the blow of thy hand.

Psa 39:11 When thou with rebukes dost correct man for iniquity, Thou makest his beauty to consume away like a moth: Surely every man is vanity. Selah.

Psa 39:12 Hear my prayer, O Jehovah, and give ear unto my cry; Hold not thy peace at my tears: For I am a stranger with thee, A sojourner, as all my fathers were.

Psa 39:13 Oh spare me, that I may recover strength, Before I go hence, and be no more.

Chapter 40.

Psa 40:1 For the Chief Musician. A Psalm of David. I waited patiently for Jehovah; And he inclined unto me, and heard my cry.

Psa 40:2 He brought me up also out of a horrible pit, out of the miry clay; And he set my feet upon a rock, and established my goings.

Psa 40:3 And he hath put a new song in my mouth, even praise unto our God: Many shall see it, and fear, And shall trust in Jehovah.

Psa 40:4 Blessed is the man that maketh Jehovah his trust, And respecteth not the proud, nor such as turn aside to lies.

Psa 40:5 Many, O Jehovah my God, are the wonderful works which thou hast done, And thy thoughts which are to us-ward; They cannot be set in order unto thee; If I would declare and speak of them, They are more than can be numbered.

Psa 40:6 Sacrifice and offering thou hast no delight in; Mine ears hast thou opened: Burnt-offering and sin-offering hast thou not required.

Psa 40:7 Then said I, Lo, I am come; In the roll of the book it is written of me:

Psa 40:8 I delight to do thy will, O my God; Yea, thy law is within my heart.

Psa 40:9 I have proclaimed glad tidings of righteousness in the great assembly; Lo, I will not refrain my lips, O Jehovah, thou knowest.

Psa 40:10 I have not hid thy righteousness within my heart; I have declared thy faithfulness and thy salvation; I have not concealed thy lovingkindness and thy truth from the great assembly.

Psa 40:11 Withhold not thou thy tender mercies from me, O Jehovah; Let thy lovingkindness and thy truth continually preserve me.

Psa 40:12 For innumerable evils have compassed me about; Mine iniquities have overtaken me, so that I am not able to look up; They are more than the hairs of my head; And my heart hath failed me.

Psa 40:13 Be pleased, O Jehovah, to deliver me: Make haste to help me, O Jehovah.

Psa 40:14 Let them be put to shame and confounded together That seek after my soul to destroy it: Let them be turned backward and brought to dishonor That delight in my hurt.

Psa 40:15 Let them be desolate by reason of their shame That say unto me, Aha, aha.

Psa 40:16 Let all those that seek thee rejoice and be glad in thee: Let such as love thy salvation say continually, Jehovah be magnified.

Psa 40:17 But I am poor and needy; Yet the Lord thinketh upon me: Thou art my help and my deliverer; Make no tarrying, O my God.

Chapter 41.

Psa 41:1 For the Chief Musician. A Psalm of David. Blessed is he that considereth the poor: Jehovah will deliver him in the day of evil.

Psa 41:2 Jehovah will preserve him, and keep him alive, And he shall be blessed upon the earth; And deliver not thou him unto the will of his enemies.

Psa 41:3 Jehovah will support him upon the couch of languishing: Thou makest all his bed in his sickness.

Psa 41:4 I said, O Jehovah, have mercy upon me: Heal my soul; For I have sinned against thee.

Psa 41:5 Mine enemies speak evil against me, saying, When will he die, and his name perish?

Psa 41:6 And if he come to see me, he speaketh falsehood; His heart gathereth iniquity to itself: When he goeth abroad, he telleth it.

Psa 41:7 All that hate me whisper together against me; Against me do they devise my hurt.

Psa 41:8 An evil disease, say they, cleaveth fast unto him; And now that he lieth he shall rise up no more.

Psa 41:9 Yea, mine own familiar friend, in whom I trusted, Who did eat of my bread, Hath lifted up his heel against me.

Psa 41:10 But thou, O Jehovah, have mercy upon me, and raise me up, That I may requite them.

Psa 41:11 By this I know that thou delightest in me, Because mine enemy doth not triumph over me.

Psa 41:12 And as for me, thou upholdest me in mine integrity, And settest me before thy face for ever.

Psa 41:13 Blessed be Jehovah, the God of Israel, From everlasting and to everlasting. Amen, and Amen.

Chapter 42.

Psa 42:1 For the Chief Musician. Maschil of the sons of Korah. As the hart panteth after the water brooks, So panteth my soul after thee, O God.

Psa 42:2 My soul thirsteth for God, for the living God: When shall I come and appear before God?

Psa 42:3 My tears have been my food day and night, While they continually say unto me, Where is thy God?

Psa 42:4 These things I remember, and pour out my soul within me, How I went with the throng, and led them to the house of God, With the voice of joy and praise, a multitude keeping holyday.

Psa 42:5 Why art thou cast down, O my soul? And why art thou disquieted within me? Hope thou in God; for I shall yet praise him For the help of his countenance.

Psa 42:6 O my God, my soul is cast down within me: Therefore do I remember thee from the land of the Jordan, And the Hermons, from the hill Mizar.

Psa 42:7 Deep calleth unto deep at the noise of thy waterfalls: All thy waves and thy billows are gone over me.

Psa 42:8 Yet Jehovah will command his lovingkindness in the day-time; And in the night his song shall be with me, Even a prayer unto the God of my life.

Psa 42:9 I will say unto God my rock, Why hast thou forgotten me? Why go I mourning because of the oppression of the enemy?

Psa 42:10 As with a sword in my bones, mine adversaries reproach me, While they continually say unto me, Where is thy God?

Psa 42:11 Why art thou cast down, O my soul? And why art thou disquieted within me? Hope thou in God; For I shall yet praise him, Who is the help of my countenance, and my God.

Chapter 43.

Psa 43:1 Judge me, O God, and plead my cause against an ungodly nation: Oh deliver me from the deceitful and unjust man.

Psa 43:2 For thou art the God of my strength; why hast thou cast me off? Why go I mourning because of the oppression of the enemy?

Psa 43:3 Oh send out thy light and thy truth; let them lead me: Let them bring me unto thy holy hill, And to thy tabernacles.

Psa 43:4 Then will I go unto the altar of God, Unto God my exceeding joy; And upon the harp will I praise thee, O God, my God.

Psa 43:5 Why art thou cast down, O my soul? And why art thou disquieted within me? Hope thou in God; For I shall yet praise him, Who is the help of my countenance, and my God.

Chapter 44.

Psa 44:1 For the Chief Musician. A Psalm of the sons of Korah. Maschil. We have heard with our ears, O God, Our fathers have told us, What work thou didst in their days, In the days of old.

Psa 44:2 Thou didst drive out the nations with thy hand; But them thou didst plant: Thou didst afflict the peoples; But them thou didst spread abroad.

Psa 44:3 For they gat not the land in possession by their own sword, Neither did their own arm save them; But thy right hand, and thine arm, and the light of thy countenance, Because thou wast favorable unto them.

Psa 44:4 Thou art my King, O God: Command deliverance for Jacob.

Psa 44:5 Through thee will we push down our adversaries: Through thy name will we tread them under that rise up against us.

Psa 44:6 For I will not trust in my bow, Neither shall my sword save me.

Psa 44:7 But thou hast saved us from our adversaries, And hast put them to shame that hate us.

Psa 44:8 In God have we made our boast all the day long, And we will give thanks unto thy name for ever. Selah.

Psa 44:9 But now thou hast cast us off, and brought us to dishonor, And goest not forth with our hosts.

Psa 44:10 Thou makest us to turn back from the adversary; And they that hate us take spoil for themselves.

Psa 44:11 Thou hast made us like sheep appointed for food, And hast scattered us among the nations.

Psa 44:12 Thou sellest thy people for nought, And hast not increased thy wealth by their price.

Psa 44:13 Thou makest us a reproach to our neighbors, A scoffing and a derision to them that are round about us.

Psa 44:14 Thou makest us a byword among the nations, A shaking of the head among the peoples.

Psa 44:15 All the day long is my dishonor before me, And the shame of my face hath covered me,

Psa 44:16 For the voice of him that reproacheth and blasphemeth, By reason of the enemy and the avenger.

Psa 44:17 All this is come upon us; Yet have we not forgotten thee, Neither have we dealt falsely in thy covenant.

Psa 44:18 Our heart is not turned back, Neither have our steps declined from thy way,

Psa 44:19 That thou hast sore broken us in the place of jackals, And covered us with the shadow of death.

Psa 44:20 If we have forgotten the name of our God, Or spread forth our hands to a strange god;

Psa 44:21 Will not God search this out? For he knoweth the secrets of the heart.

Psa 44:22 Yea, for thy sake are we killed all the day long; We are accounted as sheep for the slaughter.

Psa 44:23 Awake, why sleepest thou, O Lord? Arise, cast us not off for ever.

Psa 44:24 Wherefore hidest thou thy face, And forgettest our affliction and our oppression?

Psa 44:25 For our soul is bowed down to the dust: Our body cleaveth unto the earth.

Psa 44:26 Rise up for our help, And redeem us for thy lovingkindness' sake.

Chapter 45.

Psa 45:1 For the Chief Musician; set to Shoshannim. A Psalm of the sons of Korah. Maschil. A Song of loves. My heart overfloweth with a goodly matter; I speak the things which I have made touching the king: My tongue is the pen of a ready writer.

Psa 45:2 Thou art fairer than the children of men; Grace is poured into thy lips: Therefore God hath blessed thee for ever.

Psa 45:3 Gird thy sword upon thy thigh, O mighty one, Thy glory and thy majesty.

Psa 45:4 And in thy majesty ride on prosperously, Because of truth and meekness and righteousness: And thy right hand shall teach thee terrible things.

Psa 45:5 Thine arrows are sharp; The peoples fall under thee; They are in the heart of the king's enemies.

Psa 45:6 Thy throne, O God, is for ever and ever: A sceptre of equity is the sceptre of thy kingdom.

Psa 45:7 Thou hast loved righteousness, and hated wickedness: Therefore God, thy God, hath anointed thee With the oil of gladness above thy fellows.

Psa 45:8 All thy garments smell of myrrh, and aloes, and cassia; Out of ivory palaces stringed instruments have made thee glad.

Psa 45:9 Kings' daughters are among thy honorable women: At thy right hand doth stand the queen in gold of Ophir.

Psa 45:10 Hearken, O daughter, and consider, and incline thine ear; Forget also thine own people, and thy father's house:

Psa 45:11 So will the king desire thy beauty; For he is thy lord; and reverence thou him.

Psa 45:12 And the daughter of Tyre shall be there with a gift; The rich among the people shall entreat thy favor.

Psa 45:13 The king's daughter within the palace is all glorious: Her clothing is inwrought with gold.

Psa 45:14 She shall be led unto the king in broidered work: The virgins her companions that follow her Shall be brought unto thee.

Psa 45:15 With gladness and rejoicing shall they be led: They shall enter into the king's palace.

Psa 45:16 Instead of thy fathers shall be thy children, Whom thou shalt make princes in all the earth.

Psa 45:17 I will make thy name to be remembered in all generations: Therefore shall the peoples give thee thanks for ever and ever.

Chapter 46.

Psa 46:1 For the Chief Musician. A Psalm of the sons of Korah; set to Alamoth. A Song. God is our refuge and strength, A very present help in trouble.

Psa 46:2 Therefore will we not fear, though the earth do change, And though the mountains be shaken into the heart of the seas;

Psa 46:3 Though the waters thereof roar and be troubled, Though the mountains tremble with the swelling thereof. Selah.

Psa 46:4 There is a river, the streams whereof make glad the city of God, The holy place of the tabernacles of the Most High.

Psa 46:5 God is in the midst of her; She shall not be moved: God will help her, and that right early.

Psa 46:6 The nations raged, the kingdoms were moved: He uttered his voice, the earth melted.

Psa 46:7 Jehovah of hosts is with us; The God of Jacob is our refuge. Selah.

Psa 46:8 Come, behold the works of Jehovah, What desolations he hath made in the earth.

Psa 46:9 He maketh wars to cease unto the end of the earth; He breaketh the bow, and cutteth the spear in sunder; He burneth the chariots in the fire.

Psa 46:10 Be still, and know that I am God: I will be exalted among the nations, I will be exalted in the earth.

Psa 46:11 Jehovah of hosts is with us; The God of Jacob is our refuge. Selah.

Chapter 47.

Psa 47:1 For the Chief Musician. A Psalm of the sons of Korah. Oh clap your hands, all ye peoples; Shout unto God with the voice of triumph.

Psa 47:2 For Jehovah Most High is terrible; He is a great King over all the earth.

Psa 47:3 He subdueth peoples under us, And nations under our feet.

Psa 47:4 He chooseth our inheritance for us, The glory of Jacob whom he loved. Selah.

Psa 47:5 God is gone up with a shout, Jehovah with the sound of a trumpet.

Psa 47:6 Sing praise to God, sing praises: Sing praises unto our King, sing praises.

Psa 47:7 For God is the King of all the earth: Sing ye praises with understanding.

Psa 47:8 God reigneth over the nations: God sitteth upon his holy throne.

Psa 47:9 The princes of the peoples are gathered together To be the people of the God of Abraham: For the shields of the earth belong unto God; He is greatly exalted.

Chapter 48.

Psa 48:1 A Song; a Psalm of the sons of Korah. Great is Jehovah, and greatly to be praised, In the city of our God, in his holy mountain.

Psa 48:2 Beautiful in elevation, the joy of the whole earth, Is mount Zion, on the sides of the north, The city of the great King.

Psa 48:3 God hath made himself known in her palaces for a refuge.

Psa 48:4 For, lo, the kings assembled themselves, They passed by together.

Psa 48:5 They saw it, then were they amazed; They were dismayed, they hasted away.

Psa 48:6 Trembling took hold of them there, Pain, as of a woman in travail.

Psa 48:7 With the east wind Thou breakest the ships of Tarshish.

Psa 48:8 As we have heard, so have we seen In the city of Jehovah of hosts, in the city of our God: God will establish it for ever. Selah.

Psa 48:9 We have thought on thy lovingkindness, O God, In the midst of thy temple.

Psa 48:10 As is thy name, O God, So is thy praise unto the ends of the earth: Thy right hand is full of righteousness.

Psa 48:11 Let mount Zion be glad, Let the daughters of Judah rejoice, Because of thy judgments.

Psa 48:12 Walk about Zion, and go round about her; Number the towers thereof;

Psa 48:13 Mark ye well her bulwarks; Consider her palaces: That ye may tell it to the generation following.

Psa 48:14 For this God is our God for ever and ever: He will be our guide even unto death.

Chapter 49.

Psa 49:1 For the Chief Musician. A Psalm of the sons of Korah. Hear this, all ye peoples; Give ear, all ye inhabitants of the world,

Psa 49:2 Both low and high, Rich and poor together.

Psa 49:3 My mouth shall speak wisdom; And the meditation of my heart shall be of understanding.

Psa 49:4 I will incline mine ear to a parable: I will open my dark saying upon the harp.

Psa 49:5 Wherefore should I fear in the days of evil, When iniquity at my heels compasseth me about?

Psa 49:6 They that trust in their wealth, And boast themselves in the multitude of their riches;

Psa 49:7 None of them can by any means redeem his brother, Nor give to God a ransom for him

Psa 49:8 (For the redemption of their life is costly, And it faileth for ever),

Psa 49:9 That he should still live alway, That he should not see corruption.

Psa 49:10 For he shall see it. Wise men die; The fool and the brutish alike perish, And leave their wealth to others.

Psa 49:11 Their inward thought is, that their houses shall continue for ever, And their dwelling-places to all generations; They call their lands after their own names.

Psa 49:12 But man being in honor abideth not: He is like the beasts that perish.

Psa 49:13 This their way is their folly: Yet after them men approve their sayings. Selah.

Psa 49:14 They are appointed as a flock for Sheol; Death shall be their shepherd; And the upright shall have dominion over them in the morning; And their beauty shall be for Sheol to consume, That there be no habitation for it.

Psa 49:15 But God will redeem my soul from the power of Sheol; For he will receive me. Selah.

Psa 49:16 Be not thou afraid when one is made rich, When the glory of his house is increased.

Psa 49:17 For when he dieth he shall carry nothing away; His glory shall not descend after him.

Psa 49:18 Though while he lived he blessed his soul (And men praise thee, when thou doest well to thyself),

Psa 49:19 He shall go to the generation of his fathers; They shall never see the light.

Psa 49:20 Man that is in honor, and understandeth not, Is like the beasts that perish.

Chapter 50.

Psa 50:1 A Psalm of Asaph. The Mighty One, God, Jehovah, hath spoken, And called the earth from the rising of the sun unto the going down thereof.

Psa 50:2 Out of Zion, the perfection of beauty, God hath shined forth.

Psa 50:3 Our God cometh, and doth not keep silence: A fire devoureth before him, And it is very tempestuous round about him.

Psa 50:4 He calleth to the heavens above, And to the earth, that he may judge his people:

Psa 50:5 Gather my saints together unto me, Those that have made a covenant with me by sacrifice.

Psa 50:6 And the heavens shall declare his righteousness; For God is judge himself. Selah.

Psa 50:7 Hear, O my people, and I will speak; O Israel, and I will testify unto thee: I am God, even thy God.

Psa 50:8 I will not reprove thee for thy sacrifices; And thy burnt-offerings are continually before me.

Psa 50:9 I will take no bullock out of thy house, Nor he-goats out of thy folds.

Psa 50:10 For every beast of the forest is mine, And the cattle upon a thousand hills.

Psa 50:11 I know all the birds of the mountains; And the wild beasts of the field are mine.

Psa 50:12 If I were hungry, I would not tell thee; For the world is mine, and the fulness thereof.

Psa 50:13 Will I eat the flesh of bulls, Or drink the blood of goats?

Psa 50:14 Offer unto God the sacrifice of thanksgiving; And pay thy vows unto the Most High:

Psa 50:15 And call upon me in the day of trouble; I will deliver thee, and thou shalt glorify me.

Psa 50:16 But unto the wicked God saith, What hast thou to do to declare my statutes, And that thou hast taken my covenant in thy mouth,

Psa 50:17 Seeing thou hatest instruction, And castest my words behind thee?

Psa 50:18 When thou sawest a thief, thou consentedst with him, And hast been partaker with adulterers.

Psa 50:19 Thou givest thy mouth to evil, And thy tongue frameth deceit.

Psa 50:20 Thou sittest and speakest against thy brother; Thou slanderest thine own mother's son.

Psa 50:21 These things hast thou done, and I kept silence; Thou thoughtest that I was altogether such a one as thyself: But I will reprove thee, and set them in order before thine eyes.

Psa 50:22 Now consider this, ye that forget God, Lest I tear you in pieces, and there be none to deliver:

Psa 50:23 Whoso offereth the sacrifice of thanksgiving glorifieth me; And to him that ordereth his way aright Will I show the salvation of God.

Chapter 51.

Psa 51:1 For the Chief Musician. A Psalm of David; when Nathan the prophet came unto him, after he had gone in to Bathsheba. Have mercy upon me, O God, according to thy lovingkindness: According to the multitude of thy tender mercies blot out my transgressions.

Psa 51:2 Wash me thoroughly from mine iniquity, And cleanse me from my sin.

Psa 51:3 For I know my transgressions; And my sin is ever before me.

Psa 51:4 Against thee, thee only, have I sinned, And done that which is evil in thy sight; That thou mayest be justified when thou speakest, And be clear when thou judgest.

Psa 51:5 Behold, I was brought forth in iniquity; And in sin did my mother conceive me.

Psa 51:6 Behold, thou desirest truth in the inward parts; And in the hidden part thou wilt make me to know wisdom.

Psa 51:7 Purify me with hyssop, and I shall be clean: Wash me, and I shall be whiter than snow.

Psa 51:8 Make me to hear joy and gladness, That the bones which thou hast broken may rejoice.

Psa 51:9 Hide thy face from my sins, And blot out all mine iniquities.

Psa 51:10 Create in me a clean heart, O God; And renew a right spirit within me.

Psa 51:11 Cast me not away from thy presence; And take not thy holy spirit from me.

Psa 51:12 Restore unto me the joy of thy salvation; And uphold me with a willing spirit.

Psa 51:13 Then will I teach transgressors thy ways; And sinners shall be converted unto thee.

Psa 51:14 Deliver me from bloodguiltiness, O God, thou God of my salvation; And my tongue shall sing aloud of thy righteousness.

Psa 51:15 O Lord, open thou my lips; And my mouth shall show forth thy praise.

Psa 51:16 For thou delightest not in sacrifice; Else would I give it: Thou hast no pleasure in burnt-offering.

Psa 51:17 The sacrifices of God are a broken spirit: A broken and contrite heart, O God, thou wilt not despise.

Psa 51:18 Do good in thy good pleasure unto Zion: Build thou the walls of Jerusalem.

Psa 51:19 Then will thou delight in the sacrifices of righteousness, In burnt-offering and in whole burnt-offering: Then will they offer bullocks upon thine altar.

Chapter 52.

Psa 52:1 For the Chief Musician. Maschil of David; when Doeg the Edomite came and told Saul, and said unto him, David is come to the house of Abimelech. Why boastest thou thyself in mischief, O mighty man? The lovingkindness of God endureth continually.

Psa 52:2 Thy tongue deviseth very wickedness, Like a sharp razor, working deceitfully.

Psa 52:3 Thou lovest evil more than good, And lying rather than to speak righteousness. Selah.

Psa 52:4 Thou lovest all devouring words, O thou deceitful tongue.

Psa 52:5 God will likewise destroy thee for ever; He will take thee up, and pluck thee out of thy tent, And root thee out of the land of the living. Selah.

Psa 52:6 The righteous also shall see it, and fear, And shall laugh at him, saying,

Psa 52:7 Lo, this is the man that made not God his strength, But trusted in the abundance of his riches, And strengthened himself in his wickedness.

Psa 52:8 But as for me, I am like a green olive-tree in the house of God: I trust in the lovingkindness of God for ever and ever.

Psa 52:9 I will give thee thanks for ever, because thou hast done it; And I will hope in thy name, for it is good, in the presence of thy saints.

Chapter 53.

Psa 53:1 For the Chief Musician; set to Mahakath. Maschil of David. The fool hath said in his heart, There is no God. Corrupt are they, and have done abominable iniquity; There is none that doeth good.

Psa 53:2 God looked down from heaven upon the children of men, To see if there were any that did understand, That did seek after God.

Psa 53:3 Every one of them is gone back; they are together become filthy; There is none that doeth good, no, not one.

Psa 53:4 Have the workers of iniquity no knowledge, Who eat up my people as they eat bread, And call not upon God?

Psa 53:5 There were they in great fear, where no fear was; For God hath scattered the bones of him that encampeth against thee: Thou hast put them to shame, because of God hath rejected them.

Psa 53:6 Oh that the salvation of Israel were come out of Zion! When God bringeth back the captivity of his people, Then shall Jacob rejoice, and Israel shall be glad.

Chapter 54.

Psa 54:1 For the Chief Musician; on stringed instruments. Maschil of David; when the Ziphites came and said to Saul Doth not David hide himself with us? Save me, O God, by thy name, And judge me in thy might.

Psa 54:2 Hear my prayer, O God; Give ear to the words of my mouth.

Psa 54:3 For strangers are risen up against me, And violent men have sought after my soul: They have not set God before them. Selah.

Psa 54:4 Behold, God is my helper: The Lord is of them that uphold my soul.

Psa 54:5 He will requite the evil unto mine enemies: Destroy thou them in thy truth.

Psa 54:6 With a freewill-offering will I sacrifice unto thee: I will give thanks unto thy name, O Jehovah, for it is good.

Psa 54:7 For he hath delivered me out of all trouble; And mine eye hath seen my desire upon mine enemies.

Chapter 55.

Psa 55:1 For the Chief Musician; on stringed instruments. Maschil of David. Give ear to my prayer, O God; And hide not thyself from my supplication.

Psa 55:2 Attend unto me, and answer me: I am restless in my complaint, and moan,

Psa 55:3 Because of the voice of the enemy, Because of the oppression of the wicked; For they cast iniquity upon me, And in anger they persecute me.

Psa 55:4 My heart is sore pained within me: And the terrors of death are fallen upon me.

Psa 55:5 Fearfulness and trembling are come upon me, And horror hath overwhelmed me.

Psa 55:6 And I said, Oh that I had wings like a dove! Then would I fly away, and be at rest.

Psa 55:7 Lo, then would I wander far off, I would lodge in the wilderness. Selah.

Psa 55:8 I would haste me to a shelter From the stormy wind and tempest.

Psa 55:9 Destroy, O Lord, and divide their tongue; For I have seen violence and strife in the city.

Psa 55:10 Day and night they go about it upon the walls thereof: Iniquity also and mischief are in the midst of it.

Psa 55:11 Wickedness is in the midst thereof: Oppression and guile depart not from its streets.

Psa 55:12 For it was not an enemy that reproached me; Then I could have borne it: Neither was it he that hated me that did magnify himself against me; Then I would have hid myself from him:

Psa 55:13 But it was thou, a man mine equal, My companion, and my familiar friend.

Psa 55:14 We took sweet counsel together; We walked in the house of God with the throng.

Psa 55:15 Let death come suddenly upon them, Let them go down alive into Sheol; For wickedness is in their dwelling, in the midst of them.

Psa 55:16 As for me, I will call upon God; And Jehovah will save me.

Psa 55:17 Evening, and morning, and at noonday, will I complain, and moan; And he will hear my voice.

Psa 55:18 He hath redeemed my soul in peace from the battle that was against me; For they were many that strove with me.

Psa 55:19 God will hear, and answer them, Even he that abideth of old, Selah. The men who have no changes, And who fear not God.

Psa 55:20 He hath put forth his hands against such as were at peace with him: He hath profaned his covenant.

Psa 55:21 His mouth was smooth as butter, But his heart was war: His words were softer than oil, Yet were they drawn swords.

Psa 55:22 Cast thy burden upon Jehovah, and he will sustain thee: He will never suffer the righteous to be moved.

Psa 55:23 But thou, O God, wilt bring them down into the pit of destruction: Bloodthirsty and deceitful men shall not live out half their days; But I will trust in thee.

Chapter 56.

Psa 56:1 For the Chief Musician; set to Jonath elem rehokim. A Psalm of David. Michtam; when the Philistines took him in Gath. Be merciful unto me, O God; for man would swallow me up: All the day long he fighting oppresseth me.

Psa 56:2 Mine enemies would swallow me up all the day long; For they are many that fight proudly against me.

Psa 56:3 What time I am afraid, I will put my trust in thee.

Psa 56:4 In God (I will praise his word), In God have I put my trust, I will not be afraid; What can flesh do unto me?

Psa 56:5 All the day long they wrest my words: All their thoughts are against me for evil.

Psa 56:6 They gather themselves together, they hide themselves, They mark my steps, Even as they have waited for my soul.

Psa 56:7 Shall they escape by iniquity? In anger cast down the peoples, O God.

Psa 56:8 Thou numberest my wanderings: Put thou my tears into thy bottle; Are they not in thy book?

Psa 56:9 Then shall mine enemies turn back in the day that I call: This I know, that God is for me.

Psa 56:10 In God (I will praise his word), In Jehovah (I will praise his word),

Psa 56:11 In God have I put my trust, I will not be afraid; What can man do unto me?

Psa 56:12 Thy vows are upon me, O God: I will render thank-offerings unto thee.

Psa 56:13 For thou hast delivered my soul from death: Hast thou not delivered my feet from falling, That I may walk before God In the light of the living?

Chapter 57.

Psa 57:1 For the Chief Musician; set to al-tashheth. A Psalm of David. A miktam. When he had fled from Saul into the cave. Be merciful unto me, O God, be merciful unto me; For my soul taketh refuge in thee: Yea, in the shadow of thy wings will I take refuge, Until these calamities be overpast.

Psa 57:2 I will cry unto God Most High, Unto God that performeth all things for me.

Psa 57:3 He will send from heaven, and save me, When he that would swallow me up reproacheth; Selah. God will send forth his lovingkindness and his truth.

Psa 57:4 My soul is among lions; I lie among them that are set on fire, Even the sons of men, whose teeth are spears and arrows, And their tongue a sharp sword.

Psa 57:5 Be thou exalted, O God, above the heavens; Let thy glory be above all the earth.

Psa 57:6 They have prepared a net for my steps; My soul is bowed down: They have digged a pit before me; They are fallen into the midst thereof themselves. Selah.

Psa 57:7 My heart is fixed, O God, my heart is fixed: I will sing, yea, I will sing praises.

Psa 57:8 Awake up, my glory; Awake, psaltery and harp: I myself will awake right early.

Psa 57:9 I will give thanks unto thee, O Lord, among the peoples: I will sing praises unto thee among the nations.

Psa 57:10 For thy lovingkindness is great unto the heavens, And thy truth unto the skies.

Psa 57:11 Be thou exalted, O God, above the heavens; Let thy glory be above all the earth.

Chapter 58.

Psa 58:1 For the Chief Musician; set to Al-tashheth. A Psalm of David. A miktam. Do ye indeed in silence speak righteousness? Do ye judge uprightly, O ye sons of men?

Psa 58:2 Nay, in heart ye work wickedness; Ye weigh out the violence of your hands in the earth.

Psa 58:3 The wicked are estranged from the womb: They go astray as soon as they are born, speaking lies.

Psa 58:4 Their poison is like the poison of a serpent: They are like the deaf adder that stoppeth her ear,

Psa 58:5 Which hearkeneth not to the voice of charmers, Charming never so wisely.

Psa 58:6 Break their teeth, O God, in their mouth: Break out the great teeth of the young lions, O Jehovah.

Psa 58:7 Let them melt away as water that runneth apace: When he aimeth his arrows, let them be as though they were cut off.

Psa 58:8 Let them be as a snail which melteth and passeth away, Like the untimely birth of a woman, that hath not seen the sun.

Psa 58:9 Before your pots can feel the thorns, He will take them away with a whirlwind, the green and the burning alike.

Psa 58:10 The righteous shall rejoice when he seeth the vengeance: He shall wash his feet in the blood of the wicked;

Psa 58:11 So that men shall say, Verily there is a reward for the righteous: Verily there is a God that judgeth in the earth.

Chapter 59.

Psa 59:1 For the Chief Musician; set to Al-tashheth. A Psalm of David. Michtam; when Saul sent, and they watched the house to kill him. Deliver me from mine enemies, O my God: Set me on high from them that rise up against me.

Psa 59:2 Deliver me from the workers of iniquity, And save me from the bloodthirsty men.

Psa 59:3 For, lo, they lie in wait for my soul; The mighty gather themselves together against me: Not for my transgression, nor for my sin, O Jehovah.

Psa 59:4 They run and prepare themselves without my fault: Awake thou to help me, and behold.

Psa 59:5 Even thou, O Jehovah God of hosts, the God of Israel, Arise to visit all the nations: Be not merciful to any wicked transgressors. Selah.

Psa 59:6 They return at evening, they howl like a dog, And go round about the city.

Psa 59:7 Behold, they belch out with their mouth; Swords are in their lips: For who, say they, doth hear?

Psa 59:8 But thou, O Jehovah, wilt laugh at them; Thou wilt have all the nations in derision.

Psa 59:9 Because of his strength I will give heed unto thee; For God is my high tower.

Psa 59:10 My God with his lovingkindness will meet me: God will let me see my desire upon mine enemies.

Psa 59:11 Slay them not, lest my people forget: Scatter them by thy power, and bring them down, O Lord our shield.

Psa 59:12 For the sin of their mouth, and the words of their lips, Let them even be taken in their pride, And for cursing and lying which they speak.

Psa 59:13 Consume them in wrath, consume them, so that they shall be no more: And let them know that God ruleth in Jacob, Unto the ends of the earth. Selah.

Psa 59:14 And at evening let them return, let them howl like a dog, And go round about the city.

Psa 59:15 They shall wander up and down for food, And tarry all night if they be not satisfied.

Psa 59:16 But I will sing of thy strength; Yea, I will sing aloud of thy lovingkindness in the morning: For thou hast been my high tower, And a refuge in the day of my distress.

Psa 59:17 Unto thee, O my strength, will I sing praises: For God is my high tower, the God of my mercy.

Chapter 60.

Psa 60:1 For the Chief Musician; set to Shushan Eduth. Michtam of David, to teach; when he strove with Aram-naharaim and with Aram-zobah, and Joab returned, and smote of Edom in the Valley of Salt twelve thousand. O God thou hast cast us off, thou hast broken us down; Thou hast been angry; oh restore us again.

Psa 60:2 Thou hast made the land to tremble; thou hast rent it: Heal the breaches thereof; for it shaketh.

Psa 60:3 Thou hast showed thy people hard things: Thou hast made us to drink the wine of staggering.

Psa 60:4 Thou hast given a banner to them that fear thee, That it may be displayed because of the truth. Selah.

Psa 60:5 That thy beloved may be delivered, Save with thy right hand, and answer us.

Psa 60:6 God hath spoken in his holiness: I will exult; I will divide Shechem, and mete out the valley of Succoth.

Psa 60:7 Gilead is mine, and Manasseh is mine; Ephraim also is the defence of my head; Judah is my sceptre.

Psa 60:8 Moab is my washpot; Upon Edom will I cast my shoe: Philistia, shout thou because of me.

Psa 60:9 Who will bring me into the strong city? Who hath led me unto Edom?

Psa 60:10 Hast not thou, O God, cast us off? And thou goest not forth, O God, with our hosts.

Psa 60:11 Give us help against the adversary; For vain is the help of man.

Psa 60:12 Through God we shall do valiantly; For he it is that will tread down our adversaries.

Chapter 61.

Psa 61:1 For the Chief Musician; on a stringed instrument. A Psalm of David. Hear my cry, O God; Attend unto my prayer.

Psa 61:2 From the end of the earth will I call unto thee, when my heart is overwhelmed: Lead me to the rock that is higher than I.

Psa 61:3 For thou hast been a refuge for me, A strong tower from the enemy.

Psa 61:4 I will dwell in thy tabernacle for ever: I will take refuge in the covert of thy wings. Selah.

Psa 61:5 For thou, O God, hast heard my vows: Thou hast given me the heritage of those that fear thy name.

Psa 61:6 Thou wilt prolong the king's life; His years shall be as many generations.

Psa 61:7 He shall abide before God for ever: Oh prepare lovingkindness and truth, that they may preserve him.

Psa 61:8 So will I sing praise unto thy name for ever, That I may daily perform my vows.

Chapter 62.

Psa 62:1 For the Chief Musician; after the manner of Jeduthun. A Psalm of David. My soul waiteth in silence for God only: From him cometh my salvation.

Psa 62:2 He only is my rock and my salvation: He is my high tower; I shall not be greatly moved.

Psa 62:3 How long will ye set upon a man, That ye may slay him, all of you, Like a leaning wall, like a tottering fence?

Psa 62:4 They only consult to thrust him down from his dignity; They delight in lies; They bless with their mouth, but they curse inwardly. Selah.

Psa 62:5 My soul, wait thou in silence for God only; For my expectation is from him.

Psa 62:6 He only is my rock and my salvation: He is my high tower; I shall not be moved.

Psa 62:7 With God is my salvation and my glory: The rock of my strength, and my refuge, is in God.

Psa 62:8 Trust in him at all times, ye people; Pour out your heart before him: God is a refuge for us. Selah.

Psa 62:9 Surely men of low degree are vanity, and men of high degree are a lie: In the balances they will go up; They are together lighter than vanity.

Psa 62:10 Trust not in oppression, And become not vain in robbery: If riches increase, set not your heart thereon.

Psa 62:11 God hath spoken once, Twice have I heard this, That power belongeth unto God.

Psa 62:12 Also unto thee, O Lord, belongeth lovingkindness; For thou renderest to every man according to his work.

Chapter 63.

Psa 63:1 A Psalm of David, when he was in the wilderness of Judah. O God, thou art my God; earnestly will I seek thee: My soul thirsteth for thee, my flesh longeth for thee, In a dry and weary land, where no water is.

Psa 63:2 So have I looked upon thee in the sanctuary, To see thy power and thy glory.

Psa 63:3 Because thy lovingkindness is better than life, My lips shall praise thee.

Psa 63:4 So will I bless thee while I live: I will lift up my hands in thy name.

Psa 63:5 My soul shall be satisfied as with marrow and fatness; And my mouth shall praise thee with joyful lips;

Psa 63:6 When I remember thee upon my bed, And meditate on thee in the night-watches.

Psa 63:7 For thou hast been my help, And in the shadow of thy wings will I rejoice.

Psa 63:8 My soul followeth hard after thee: Thy right hand upholdeth me.

Psa 63:9 But those that seek my soul, to destroy it, Shall go into the lower parts of the earth.

Psa 63:10 They shall be given over to the power of the sword: They shall be a portion for foxes.

Psa 63:11 But the king shall rejoice in God: Every one that sweareth by him shall glory; For the mouth of them that speak lies shall be stopped.

Chapter 64.

Psa 64:1 For the Chief Musician. A Psalm of David. Hear my voice, O God, in my complaint: Preserve my life from fear of the enemy.

Psa 64:2 Hide me from the secret counsel of evil-doers, From the tumult of the workers of iniquity;

Psa 64:3 Who have whet their tongue like a sword, And have aimed their arrows, even bitter words,

Psa 64:4 That they may shoot in secret places at the perfect: Suddenly do they shoot at him, and fear not.

Psa 64:5 They encourage themselves in an evil purpose; They commune of laying snares privily; They say, Who will see them?

Psa 64:6 They search out iniquities; We have accomplished, say they, a diligent search: And the inward thought and the heart of every one is deep.

Psa 64:7 But God will shoot at them; With an arrow suddenly shall they be wounded.

Psa 64:8 So they shall be made to stumble, their own tongue being against them: All that see them shall wag the head.

Psa 64:9 And all men shall fear; And they shall declare the work of God, And shall wisely consider of his doing.

Psa 64:10 The righteous shall be glad in Jehovah, and shall take refuge in him; And all the upright in heart shall glory.

Chapter 65.

Psa 65:1 For the Chief Musician. A Psalm. A song of David. Praise waiteth for thee, O God, in Zion; And unto thee shall the vow be performed.

Psa 65:2 O thou that hearest prayer, Unto thee shall all flesh come.

Psa 65:3 Iniquities prevail against me: As for our transgressions, thou wilt forgive them.

Psa 65:4 Blessed is the man whom thou choosest, and causest to approach unto thee, That he may dwell in thy courts: We shall be satisfied with the goodness of thy house, Thy holy temple.

Psa 65:5 By terrible things thou wilt answer us in righteousness, Oh God of our salvation, Thou that art the confidence of all the ends of the earth, And of them that are afar off upon the sea:

Psa 65:6 Who by his strength setteth fast the mountains, Being girded about with might;

Psa 65:7 Who stilleth the roaring of the seas, The roaring of their waves, And the tumult of the peoples.

Psa 65:8 They also that dwell in the uttermost parts are afraid at thy tokens: Thou makest the outgoings of the morning and evening to rejoice.

Psa 65:9 Thou visitest the earth, and waterest it, Thou greatly enrichest it; The river of God is full of water: Thou providest them grain, when thou hast so prepared the earth.

Psa 65:10 Thou waterest its furrows abundantly; Thou settlest the ridges thereof: Thou makest it soft with showers; Thou blessest the springing thereof.

Psa 65:11 Thou crownest the year with thy goodness; And thy paths drop fatness.

Psa 65:12 They drop upon the pastures of the wilderness; And the hills are girded with joy.

Psa 65:13 The pastures are clothed with flocks; The valleys also are covered over with grain; They shout for joy, they also sing.

Chapter 66.

Psa 66:1 For the Chief Musician. A Song, a Psalm. Make a joyful noise unto God, all the earth:

Psa 66:2 Sing forth the glory of his name: Make his praise glorious.

Psa 66:3 Say unto God, How terrible are thy works! Through the greatness of thy power shall thine enemies submit themselves unto thee.

Psa 66:4 All the earth shall worship thee, And shall sing unto thee; They shall sing to thy name. Selah.

Psa 66:5 Come, and see the works of God; He is terrible in his doing toward the children of men.

Psa 66:6 He turned the sea into dry land; They went through the river on foot: There did we rejoice in him.

Psa 66:7 He ruleth by his might for ever; His eyes observe the nations: Let not the rebellious exalt themselves. Selah.

Psa 66:8 Oh bless our God, ye peoples, And make the voice of his praise to be heard;

Psa 66:9 Who holdeth our soul in life, And suffereth not our feet to be moved.

Psa 66:10 For thou, O God, hast proved us: Thou hast tried us, as silver is tried.

Psa 66:11 Thou broughtest us into the net; Thou layedst a sore burden upon our loins.

Psa 66:12 Thou didst cause men to ride over our heads; We went through fire and through water; But thou broughtest us out into a wealthy place.

Psa 66:13 I will come into thy house with burnt-offerings; I will pay thee my vows,

Psa 66:14 Which my lips uttered, And my mouth spake, when I was in distress.

Psa 66:15 I will offer unto thee burnt-offerings of fatlings, With the incense of rams; I will offer bullocks with goats. Selah.

Psa 66:16 Come, and hear, all ye that fear God, And I will declare what he hath done for my soul.

Psa 66:17 I cried unto him with my mouth, And he was extolled with my tongue.

Psa 66:18 If I regard iniquity in my heart, The Lord will not hear:

Psa 66:19 But verily God hath heard; He hath attended to the voice of my prayer.

Psa 66:20 Blessed be God, Who hath not turned away my prayer, Nor his lovingkindness from me.

Chapter 67.

Psa 67:1 For the Chief Musician; on stringed instruments. A Psalm, a Song. God be merciful unto us, and bless us, And cause his face to shine upon us; Selah.

Psa 67:2 That thy way may be known upon earth, Thy salvation among all nations.

Psa 67:3 Let the peoples praise thee, O God; Let all the peoples praise thee.

Psa 67:4 Oh let the nations be glad and sing for joy; For thou wilt judge the peoples with equity, And govern the nations upon earth. Selah.

Psa 67:5 Let the peoples praise thee, O God; Let all the peoples praise thee.

Psa 67:6 The earth hath yielded its increase: God, even our own God, will bless us.

Psa 67:7 God will bless us; And all the ends of the earth shall fear him.

Chapter 68.

Psa 68:1 For the Chief Musician; A Psalm of David, a song. Let God arise, let his enemies be scattered; Let them also that hate him flee before him.

Psa 68:2 As smoke is driven away, so drive them away: As wax melteth before the fire, So let the wicked perish at the presence of God.

Psa 68:3 But let the righteous be glad; let them exult before God: Yea, let them rejoice with gladness.

Psa 68:4 Sing unto God, sing praises to his name: Cast up a highway for him that rideth through the deserts; His name is Jehovah; and exult ye before him.

Psa 68:5 A father of the fatherless, and a judge of the widows, Is God in his holy habitation.

Psa 68:6 God setteth the solitary in families: He bringeth out the prisoners into prosperity; But the rebellious dwell in a parched land.

Psa 68:7 O God, when thou wentest forth before thy people, When thou didst march through the wilderness; Selah.

Psa 68:8 The earth trembled, The heavens also dropped rain at the presence of God: Yon Sinai trembled at the presence of God, the God of Israel.

Psa 68:9 Thou, O God, didst send a plentiful rain, Thou didst confirm thine inheritance, when it was weary.

Psa 68:10 Thy congregation dwelt therein: Thou, O God, didst prepare of thy goodness for the poor.

Psa 68:11 The Lord giveth the word: The women that publish the tidings are a great host.

Psa 68:12 Kings of armies flee, they flee; And she that tarrieth at home divideth the spoil.

Psa 68:13 When ye lie among the sheepfolds, It is as the wings of a dove covered with silver, And her pinions with yellow gold.

Psa 68:14 When the Almighty scattered kings therein, It was as when it snoweth in Zalmon.

Psa 68:15 A mountain of God is the mountain of Bashan; A high mountain is the mountain of Bashan.

Psa 68:16 Why look ye askance, ye high mountains, At the mountain which God hath desired for his abode? Yea, Jehovah will dwell in it for ever.

Psa 68:17 The chariots of God are twenty thousand, even thousands upon thousands; The Lord is among them, as in Sinai, in the sanctuary.

Psa 68:18 Thou hast ascended on high, thou hast led away captives; Thou hast received gifts among men, Yea, among the rebellious also, that Jehovah God might dwell with them.

Psa 68:19 Blessed be the Lord, who daily beareth our burden, Even the God who is our salvation. Selah.

Psa 68:20 God is unto us a God of deliverances; And unto Jehovah the Lord belongeth escape from death.

Psa 68:21 But God will smite through the head of his enemies, The hairy scalp of such a one as goeth on still in his guiltiness.

Psa 68:22 The Lord said, I will bring again from Bashan, I will bring them again from the depths of the sea;

Psa 68:23 That thou mayest crush them, dipping thy foot in blood, That the tongue of thy dogs may have its portion from thine enemies.

Psa 68:24 They have seen thy goings, O God, Even the goings of my God, my King, into the sanctuary.

Psa 68:25 The singers went before, the minstrels followed after, In the midst of the damsels playing with timbrels.

Psa 68:26 Bless ye God in the congregations, Even the Lord, ye that are of the fountain of Israel.

Psa 68:27 There is little Benjamin their ruler, The princes of Judah and their council, The princes of Zebulun, the princes of Naphtali.

Psa 68:28 Thy God hath commanded thy strength: Strengthen, O God, that which thou hast wrought for us.

Psa 68:29 Because of thy temple at Jerusalem Kings shall bring presents unto thee.

Psa 68:30 Rebuke the wild beast of the reeds, The multitude of the bulls, with the calves of the peoples, Trampling under foot the pieces of silver: He hath scattered the peoples that delight in war.

Psa 68:31 Princes shall come out of Egypt; Ethiopia shall haste to stretch out her hands unto God.

Psa 68:32 Sing unto God, ye kingdoms of the earth; Oh sing praises unto the Lord; Selah.

Psa 68:33 To him that rideth upon the heaven of heavens, which are of old; Lo, he uttereth his voice, a mighty voice.

Psa 68:34 Ascribe ye strength unto God: His excellency is over Israel, And his strength is in the skies.

Psa 68:35 O God, thou art terrible out of thy holy places: The God of Israel, he giveth strength and power unto his people. Blessed be God.

Chapter 69.

Psa 69:1 For the Chief Musician; set to Shoshannim. A Psalm of David. Save me, O God; For the waters are come in unto my soul.

Psa 69:2 I sink in deep mire, where there is no standing: I am come into deep waters, where the floods overflow me.

Psa 69:3 I am weary with my crying; my throat is dried: Mine eyes fail while I wait for my God.

Psa 69:4 They that hate me without a cause are more than the hairs of my head: They that would cut me off, being mine enemies wrongfully, are mighty: That which I took not away I have to restore.

Psa 69:5 O God, thou knowest my foolishness; And my sins are not hid from thee.

Psa 69:6 Let not them that wait for thee be put to shame through me, O Lord Jehovah of hosts: Let not those that seek thee be brought to dishonor through me, O God of Israel.

Psa 69:7 Because for thy sake I have borne reproach; Shame hath covered my face.

Psa 69:8 I am become a stranger unto my brethren, And an alien unto my mother's children.

Psa 69:9 For the zeal of thy house hath eaten me up; And the reproaches of them that reproach thee are fallen upon me.

Psa 69:10 When I wept, and chastened my soul with fasting, That was to my reproach.

Psa 69:11 When I made sackcloth my clothing, I became a byword unto them.

Psa 69:12 They that sit in the gate talk of me; And I am the song of the drunkards.

Psa 69:13 But as for me, my prayer is unto thee, O Jehovah, in an acceptable time: O God, in the abundance of thy lovingkindness, Answer me in the truth of thy salvation.

Psa 69:14 Deliver me out of the mire, and let me not sink: Let me be delivered from them that hate me, and out of the deep waters.

Psa 69:15 Let not the waterflood overwhelm me, Neither let the deep shallow me up; And let not the pit shut its mouth upon me.

Psa 69:16 Answer me, O Jehovah; for thy lovingkindness is good: According to the multitude of thy tender mercies turn thou unto me.

Psa 69:17 And hide not thy face from thy servant; For I am in distress; answer me speedily.

Psa 69:18 Draw nigh unto my soul, and redeem it: Ransom me because of mine enemies.

Psa 69:19 Thou knowest my reproach, and my shame, and my dishonor: Mine adversaries are all before thee.

Psa 69:20 Reproach hath broken my heart; and I am full of heaviness: And I looked for some to take pity, but there was none; And for comforters, but I found none.

Psa 69:21 They gave me also gall for my food; And in my thirst they gave me vinegar to drink.

Psa 69:22 Let their table before them become a snare; And when they are in peace, let it become a trap.

Psa 69:23 Let their eyes be darkened, so that they cannot see; And make their loins continually to shake.

Psa 69:24 Pour out thine indignation upon them, And let the fierceness of thine anger overtake them.

Psa 69:25 Let their habitation be desolate; Let none dwell in their tents.

Psa 69:26 For they persecute him whom thou hast smitten; And they tell of the sorrow of those whom thou hast wounded.

Psa 69:27 Add iniquity unto their iniquity; And let them not come into thy righteousness.

Psa 69:28 Let them be blotted out of the book of life, And not be written with the righteous.

Psa 69:29 But I am poor and sorrowful: Let thy salvation, O God, set me up on high.

Psa 69:30 I will praise the name of God with a song, And will magnify him with thanksgiving.

Psa 69:31 And it will please Jehovah better than an ox, Or a bullock that hath horns and hoofs.

Psa 69:32 The meek have seen it, and are glad: Ye that seek after God, let your heart live.

Psa 69:33 For Jehovah heareth the needy, And despiseth not his prisoners.

Psa 69:34 Let heaven and earth praise him, The seas, and everything that moveth therein.

Psa 69:35 For God will save Zion, and build the cities of Judah; And they shall abide there, and have it in possession.

Psa 69:36 The seed also of his servants shall inherit it; And they that love his name shall dwell therein.

Chapter 70.

Psa 70:1 Make haste, O God, to deliver me; Make haste to help me, O Jehovah.

Psa 70:2 Let them be put to shame and confounded That seek after my soul: Let them be turned backward and brought to dishonor That delight in my hurt.

Psa 70:3 Let them be turned back by reason of their shame That say, Aha, aha.

Psa 70:4 Let all those that seek thee rejoice and be glad in thee; And let such as love thy salvation say continually, Let God be magnified.

Psa 70:5 But I am poor and needy; Make haste unto me, O God: Thou art my help and my deliverer; O Jehovah, make no tarrying.

Chapter 71.

Psa 71:1 In thee, O Jehovah, do I take refuge: Let me never be put to shame.

Psa 71:2 Deliver me in thy righteousness, and rescue me: Bow down thine ear unto me, and save me.

Psa 71:3 Be thou to me a rock of habitation, whereunto I may continually resort: Thou hast given commandment to save me; For thou art my rock and my fortress.

Psa 71:4 Rescue me, O my God, out of the hand of the wicked, Out of the hand of the unrighteous and cruel man.

Psa 71:5 For thou art my hope, O Lord Jehovah: Thou art my trust from my youth.

Psa 71:6 By thee have I been holden up from the womb; Thou art he that took me out of my mother's bowels: My praise shall be continually of thee.

Psa 71:7 I am as a wonder unto many; But thou art my strong refuge.

Psa 71:8 My mouth shall be filled with thy praise, And with thy honor all the day.

Psa 71:9 Cast me not off in the time of old age; Forsake me not when my strength faileth.

Psa 71:10 For mine enemies speak concerning me; And they that watch for my soul take counsel together,

Psa 71:11 Saying, God hath forsaken him: Pursue and take him; For there is none to deliver.

Psa 71:12 O God, be not far from me; O my God, make haste to help me.

Psa 71:13 Let them be put to shame and consumed that are adversaries to my soul; Let them be covered with reproach and dishonor that seek my hurt.

Psa 71:14 But I will hope continually, And will praise thee yet more and more.

Psa 71:15 My mouth shall tell of thy righteousness, And of thy salvation all the day; For I know not the numbers thereof.

Psa 71:16 I will come with the mighty acts of the Lord Jehovah: I will make mention of thy righteousness, even of thine only.

Psa 71:17 O God, thou hast taught me from my youth; And hitherto have I declared thy wondrous works.

Psa 71:18 Yea, even when I am old and grayheaded, O God, forsake me not, Until I have declared thy strength unto the next generation, Thy might to every one that is to come.

Psa 71:19 Thy righteousness also, O God, is very high; Thou who hast done great things, O God, who is like unto thee?

Psa 71:20 Thou, who hast showed us many and sore troubles, Wilt quicken us again, And wilt bring us up again from the depths of the earth.

Psa 71:21 Increase thou my greatness, And turn again and comfort me.

Psa 71:22 I will also praise thee with the psaltery, Even thy truth, O my God: Unto thee will I sing praises with the harp, O thou Holy One of Israel.

Psa 71:23 My lips shall shout for joy when I sing praises unto thee; And my soul, which thou hast redeemed.

Psa 71:24 My tongue also shall talk of thy righteousness all the day long; For they are put to shame, for they are confounded, that seek my hurt.

Chapter 72.

Psa 72:1 A Psalm of Solomon. Give the king thy judgments, O God, And thy righteousness unto the king's son.

Psa 72:2 He will judge thy people with righteousness, And thy poor with justice.

Psa 72:3 The mountains shall bring peace to the people, And the hills, in righteousness.

Psa 72:4 He will judge the poor of the people, He will save the children of the needy, And will break in pieces the oppressor.

Psa 72:5 They shall fear thee while the sun endureth, And so long as the moon, throughout all generations.

Psa 72:6 He will come down like rain upon the mown grass, As showers that water the earth.

Psa 72:7 In his days shall the righteous flourish, And abundance of peace, till the moon be no more.

Psa 72:8 He shall have dominion also from sea to sea, And from the River unto the ends of the earth.

Psa 72:9 They that dwell in the wilderness shall bow before him; And his enemies shall lick the dust.

Psa 72:10 The kings of Tarshish and of the isles shall render tribute: The kings of Sheba and Seba shall offer gifts.

Psa 72:11 Yea, all kings shall fall down before him; All nations shall serve him.

Psa 72:12 For he will deliver the needy when he crieth, And the poor, that hath no helper.

Psa 72:13 He will have pity on the poor and needy, And the souls of the needy he will save.

Psa 72:14 He will redeem their soul from oppression and violence; And precious will their blood be in his sight:

Psa 72:15 And they shall live; and to him shall be given of the gold of Sheba: And men shall pray for him continually; They shall bless him all the day long.

Psa 72:16 There shall be abundance of grain in the earth upon the top of the mountains; The fruit thereof shall shake like Lebanon: And they of the city shall flourish like grass of the earth.

Psa 72:17 His name shall endure for ever; His name shall be continued as long as the sun: And men shall be blessed in him; All nations shall call him happy.

Psa 72:18 Blessed be Jehovah God, the God of Israel, Who only doeth wondrous things:

Psa 72:19 And blessed be his glorious name for ever; And let the whole earth be filled with his glory. Amen, and Amen.

Psa 72:20 The prayers of David the son of Jesse are ended.

Chapter 73.

Psa 73:1 A Psalm of Asaph. Surely God is good to Israel, Even to such as are pure in heart.

Psa 73:2 But as for me, my feet were almost gone; My steps had well nigh slipped.

Psa 73:3 For I was envious at the arrogant, When I saw the prosperity of the wicked.

Psa 73:4 For there are no pangs in their death; But their strength is firm.

Psa 73:5 They are not in trouble as other men; Neither are they plagued like other men.

Psa 73:6 Therefore pride is as a chain about their neck; Violence covereth them as a garment.

Psa 73:7 Their eyes stand out with fatness: They have more than heart could wish.

Psa 73:8 They scoff, and in wickedness utter oppression: They speak loftily.

Psa 73:9 They have set their mouth in the heavens, And their tongue walketh through the earth.

Psa 73:10 Therefore his people return hither: And waters of a full cup are drained by them.

Psa 73:11 And they say, How doth God know? And is there knowledge in the Most High?

Psa 73:12 Behold, these are the wicked; And, being alway at ease, they increase in riches.

Psa 73:13 Surely in vain have I cleansed my heart, And washed my hands in innocency;

Psa 73:14 For all the day long have I been plagued, And chastened every morning.

Psa 73:15 If I had said, I will speak thus; Behold, I had dealt treacherously with the generation of thy children.

Psa 73:16 When I thought how I might know this, It was too painful for me;

Psa 73:17 Until I went into the sanctuary of God, And considered their latter end.

Psa 73:18 Surely thou settest them in slippery places: Thou castest them down to destruction.

Psa 73:19 How are they become a desolation in a moment! They are utterly consumed with terrors.

Psa 73:20 As a dream when one awaketh, So, O Lord, when thou awakest, thou wilt despise their image.

Psa 73:21 For my soul was grieved, And I was pricked in my heart:

Psa 73:22 So brutish was I, and ignorant; I was as a beast before thee.

Psa 73:23 Nevertheless I am continually with thee: Thou hast holden my right hand.

Psa 73:24 Thou wilt guide me with thy counsel, And afterward receive me to glory.

Psa 73:25 Whom have I in heaven but thee? And there is none upon earth that I desire besides thee.

Psa 73:26 My flesh and my heart faileth; But God is the strength of my heart and my portion for ever.

Psa 73:27 For, lo, they that are far from thee shall perish: Thou hast destroyed all them that play the harlot, departing from thee.

Psa 73:28 But it is good for me to draw near unto God: I have made the Lord Jehovah my refuge, That I may tell of all thy works.

Chapter 74.

Psa 74:1 Maschil of Asaph. O God, why hast thou cast us off for ever? Why doth thine anger smoke against the sheep of thy pasture?

Psa 74:2 Remember thy congregation, which thou hast gotten of old, Which thou hast redeemed to be the tribe of thine inheritance; And mount Zion, wherein thou hast dwelt.

Psa 74:3 Lift up thy feet unto the perpetual ruins, All the evil that the enemy hath done in the sanctuary.

Psa 74:4 Thine adversaries have roared in the midst of thine assembly; They have set up their ensigns for signs.

Psa 74:5 They seemed as men that lifted up Axes upon a thicket of trees.

Psa 74:6 And now all the carved work thereof They break down with hatchet and hammers.

Psa 74:7 They have set thy sanctuary on fire; They have profaned the dwelling-place of thy name by casting it to the ground.

Psa 74:8 They said in their heart, Let us make havoc of them altogether: They have burned up all the synagogues of God in the land.

Psa 74:9 We see not our signs: There is no more any prophet; Neither is there among us any that knoweth how long.

Psa 74:10 How long, O God, shall the adversary reproach? Shall the enemy blaspheme thy name for ever?

Psa 74:11 Why drawest thou back thy hand, even thy right hand? Pluck it out of thy bosom and consume them.

Psa 74:12 Yet God is my King of old, Working salvation in the midst of the earth.

Psa 74:13 Thou didst divide the sea by thy strength: Thou brakest the heads of the sea-monsters in the waters.

Psa 74:14 Thou brakest the heads of leviathan in pieces; Thou gavest him to be food to the people inhabiting the wilderness.

Psa 74:15 Thou didst cleave fountain and flood: Thou driedst up mighty rivers.

Psa 74:16 The day is thine, the night also is thine: Thou hast prepared the light and the sun.

Psa 74:17 Thou hast set all the borders of the earth: Thou hast made summer and winter.

Psa 74:18 Remember this, that the enemy hath reproached, O Jehovah, And that a foolish people hath blasphemed thy name.

Psa 74:19 Oh deliver not the soul of thy turtle-dove unto the wild beast: Forget not the life of thy poor for ever.

Psa 74:20 Have respect unto the covenant; For the dark places of the earth are full of the habitations of violence.

Psa 74:21 Oh let not the oppressed return ashamed: Let the poor and needy praise thy name.

Psa 74:22 Arise, O God, plead thine own cause: Remember how the foolish man reproacheth thee all the day.

Psa 74:23 Forget not the voice of thine adversaries: The tumult of those that rise up against thee ascendeth continually.

Chapter 75.

Psa 75:1 For the Chief Musician; set to Al-tashheth. A Psalm of Asaph, a song. We give thanks unto thee, O God; We give thanks, for thy name is near: Men tell of thy wondrous works.

Psa 75:2 When I shall find the set time, I will judge uprightly.

Psa 75:3 The earth and all the inhabitants thereof are dissolved: I have set up the pillars of it. Selah.

Psa 75:4 I said unto the arrogant, Deal not arrogantly; And to the wicked, Lift not up the horn:

Psa 75:5 Lift not up your horn on high; Speak not with a stiff neck.

Psa 75:6 For neither from the east, nor from the west, Nor yet from the south, cometh lifting up.

Psa 75:7 But God is the judge: He putteth down one, and lifteth up another.

Psa 75:8 For in the hand of Jehovah there is a cup, and the wine foameth; It is full of mixture, and he poureth out of the same: Surely the dregs thereof, all the wicked of the earth shall drain them, and drink them.

Psa 75:9 But I will declare for ever, I will sing praises to the God of Jacob.

Psa 75:10 All the horns of the wicked also will I cut off; But the horns of the righteous shall be lifted up.

Chapter 76.

Psa 76:1 For the Chief Musician; on stringed instruments. A Psalm of Asaph, a song. In Judah is God known: His name is great in Israel.

Psa 76:2 In Salem also is his tabernacle, And his dwelling-place in Zion.

Psa 76:3 There he brake the arrows of the bow; The shield, and the sword, and the battle. Selah.

Psa 76:4 Glorious art thou and excellent, From the mountains of prey.

Psa 76:5 The stouthearted are made a spoil, They have slept their sleep; And none of the men of might have found their hands.

Psa 76:6 At thy rebuke, O God of Jacob, Both chariot and horse are cast into a deep sleep.

Psa 76:7 Thou, even thou, art to be feared; And who may stand in thy sight when once thou art angry?

Psa 76:8 Thou didst cause sentence to be heard from heaven; The earth feared, and was still,

Psa 76:9 When God arose to judgment, To save all the meek of the earth. Selah.

Psa 76:10 Surely the wrath of man shall praise thee: The residue of wrath shalt thou gird upon thee.

Psa 76:11 Vow, and pay unto Jehovah your God: Let all that are round about him bring presents unto him that ought to be feared.

Psa 76:12 He will cut off the spirit of princes: He is terrible to the kings of the earth.

Chapter 77.

Psa 77:1 For the Chief Musician; after the manner of Jeduthun. A Psalm of Asaph. I will cry unto God with my voice, Even unto God with my voice; and he will give ear unto me.

Psa 77:2 In the day of my trouble I sought the Lord: My hand was stretched out in the night, and slacked not; My soul refused to be comforted.

Psa 77:3 I remember God, and am disquieted: I complain, and my spirit is overwhelmed. Selah.

Psa 77:4 Thou holdest mine eyes watching: I am so troubled that I cannot speak.

Psa 77:5 I have considered the days of old, The years of ancient times.

Psa 77:6 I call to remembrance my song in the night: I commune with mine own heart; And my spirit maketh diligent search.

Psa 77:7 Will the Lord cast off for ever? And will he be favorable no more?

Psa 77:8 Is his lovingkindness clean gone for ever? Doth his promise fail for evermore?

Psa 77:9 Hath God forgotten to be gracious? Hath he in anger shut up his tender mercies? Selah.

Psa 77:10 And I said, This is my infirmity; But I will remember the years of the right hand of the Most High.

Psa 77:11 I will make mention of the deeds of Jehovah; For I will remember thy wonders of old.

Psa 77:12 I will meditate also upon all thy work, And muse on thy doings.

Psa 77:13 Thy way, O God, is in the sanctuary: Who is a great god like unto God?

Psa 77:14 Thou art the God that doest wonders: Thou hast made known thy strength among the peoples.

Psa 77:15 Thou hast with thine arm redeemed thy people, The sons of Jacob and Joseph. Selah.

Psa 77:16 The waters saw thee, O God; The waters saw thee, they were afraid: The depths also trembled.

Psa 77:17 The clouds poured out water; The skies sent out a sound: Thine arrows also went abroad.

Psa 77:18 The voice of thy thunder was in the whirlwind; The lightnings lightened the world: The earth trembled and shook.

Psa 77:19 Thy way was in the sea, And thy paths in the great waters, And thy footsteps were not known.

Psa 77:20 Thou leddest thy people like a flock, By the hand of Moses and Aaron.

Chapter 78.

Psa 78:1 Maschil of Asaph. Give ear, O my people, to my law: Incline your ears to the words of my mouth.

Psa 78:2 I will open my mouth in a parable; I will utter dark sayings of old,

Psa 78:3 Which we have heard and known, And our fathers have told us.

Psa 78:4 We will not hide them from their children, Telling to the generation to come the praises of Jehovah, And his strength, and his wondrous works that he hath done.

Psa 78:5 For he established a testimony in Jacob, And appointed a law in Israel, Which he commanded our fathers, That they should make them known to their children;

Psa 78:6 That the generation to come might know them, even the children that should be born; Who should arise and tell them to their children,

Psa 78:7 That they might set their hope in God, And not forget the works of God, But keep his commandments,

Psa 78:8 And might not be as their fathers, A stubborn and rebellious generation, A generation that set not their heart aright, And whose spirit was not stedfast with God.

Psa 78:9 The children of Ephraim, being armed and carrying bows, Turned back in the day of battle.

Psa 78:10 They kept not the covenant of God, And refused to walk in his law;

Psa 78:11 And they forgat his doings, And his wondrous works that he had showed them.

Psa 78:12 Marvellous things did he in the sight of their fathers, In the land of Egypt, in the field of Zoan.

Psa 78:13 He clave the sea, and caused them to pass through; And he made the waters to stand as a heap.

Psa 78:14 In the day-time also he led them with a cloud, And all the night with a light of fire.

Psa 78:15 He clave rocks in the wilderness, And gave them drink abundantly as out of the depths.

Psa 78:16 He brought streams also out of the rock, And caused waters to run down like rivers.

Psa 78:17 Yet went they on still to sin against him, To rebel against the Most High in the desert.

Psa 78:18 And they tempted God in their heart By asking food according to their desire.

Psa 78:19 Yea, they spake against God; They said, Can God prepare a table in the wilderness?

Psa 78:20 Behold, he smote the rock, so that waters gushed out, And streams overflowed; Can he give bread also? Will he provide flesh for his people?

Psa 78:21 Therefore Jehovah heard, and was wroth; And a fire was kindled against Jacob, And anger also went up against Israel;

Psa 78:22 Because they believed not in God, And trusted not in his salvation.

Psa 78:23 Yet he commanded the skies above, And opened the doors of heaven;

Psa 78:24 And he rained down manna upon them to eat, And gave them food from heaven.

Psa 78:25 Man did eat the bread of the mighty: He sent them food to the full.

Psa 78:26 He caused the east wind to blow in the heavens; And by his power he guided the south wind.

Psa 78:27 He rained flesh also upon them as the dust, And winged birds as the sand of the seas:

Psa 78:28 And he let it fall in the midst of their camp, Round about their habitations.

Psa 78:29 So they did eat, and were well filled; And he gave them their own desire.

Psa 78:30 They were not estranged from that which they desired, Their food was yet in their mouths,

Psa 78:31 When the anger of God went up against them, And slew of the fattest of them, And smote down the young men of Israel.

Psa 78:32 For all this they sinned still, And believed not in his wondrous works.

Psa 78:33 Therefore their days did he consume in vanity, And their years in terror.

Psa 78:34 When he slew them, then they inquired after him; And they returned and sought God earnestly.

Psa 78:35 And they remembered that God was their rock, And the Most High God their redeemer.

Psa 78:36 But they flattered him with their mouth, And lied unto him with their tongue.

Psa 78:37 For their heart was not right with him, Neither were they faithful in his covenant.

Psa 78:38 But he, being merciful, forgave their iniquity, and destroyed them not: Yea, many a time turned he his anger away, And did not stir up all his wrath.

Psa 78:39 And he remembered that they were but flesh, A wind that passeth away, and cometh not again.

Psa 78:40 How oft did they rebel against him in the wilderness, And grieve him in the desert!

Psa 78:41 And they turned again and tempted God, And provoked the Holy One of Israel.

Psa 78:42 They remember not his hand, Nor the day when he redeemed them from the adversary;

Psa 78:43 How he set his signs in Egypt, And his wonders in the field of Zoan,

Psa 78:44 And turned their rivers into blood, And their streams, so that they could not drink.

Psa 78:45 He sent among them swarms of flies, which devoured them; And frogs, which destroyed them.

Psa 78:46 He gave also their increase unto the caterpillar, And their labor unto the locust.

Psa 78:47 He destroyed their vines with hail, And their sycomore-trees with frost.

Psa 78:48 He gave over their cattle also to the hail, And their flocks to hot thunderbolts.

Psa 78:49 He cast upon them the fierceness of his anger, Wrath, and indignation, and trouble, A band of angels of evil.

Psa 78:50 He made a path for his anger; He spared not their soul from death, But gave their life over to the pestilence,

Psa 78:51 And smote all the first-born in Egypt, The chief of their strength in the tents of Ham.

Psa 78:52 But he led forth his own people like sheep, And guided them in the wilderness like a flock.

Psa 78:53 And he led them safely, so that they feared not; But the sea overwhelmed their enemies.

Psa 78:54 And he brought them to the border of his sanctuary, To this mountain, which his right hand had gotten.

Psa 78:55 He drove out the nations also before them, And allotted them for an inheritance by line, And made the tribes of Israel to dwell in their tents.

Psa 78:56 Yet they tempted and rebelled against the Most High God, And kept not his testimonies;

Psa 78:57 But turned back, and dealt treacherously like their fathers: They were turned aside like a deceitful bow.

Psa 78:58 For they provoked him to anger with their high places, And moved him to jealousy with their graven images.

Psa 78:59 When God heard this, he was wroth, And greatly abhorred Israel;

Psa 78:60 So that he forsook the tabernacle of Shiloh, The tent which he placed among men;

Psa 78:61 And delivered his strength into captivity, And his glory into the adversary's hand.

Psa 78:62 He gave his people over also unto the sword, And was wroth with his inheritance.

Psa 78:63 Fire devoured their young men; And their virgins had no marriage-song.

Psa 78:64 Their priests fell by the sword; And their widows made no lamentation.

Psa 78:65 Then the Lord awaked as one out of sleep, Like a mighty man that shouteth by reason of wine.

Psa 78:66 And he smote his adversaries backward: He put them to a perpetual reproach.

Psa 78:67 Moreover he refused the tent of Joseph, And chose not the tribe of Ephraim,

Psa 78:68 But chose the tribe of Judah, The mount Zion which he loved.

Psa 78:69 And he built his sanctuary like the heights, Like the earth which he hath established for ever.

Psa 78:70 He chose David also his servant, And took him from the sheepfolds:

Psa 78:71 From following the ewes that have their young he brought him, To be the shepherd of Jacob his people, and Israel his inheritance.

Psa 78:72 So he was their shepherd according to the integrity of his heart, And guided them by the skilfulness of his hands.

Chapter 79.

Psa 79:1 A Psalm of Asaph. O God, the nations are come into thine inheritance; Thy holy temple have they defiled; They have laid Jerusalem in heaps.

Psa 79:2 The dead bodies of thy servants have they given to be food unto the birds of the heavens, The flesh of thy saints unto the beasts of the earth.

Psa 79:3 Their blood have they shed like water round about Jerusalem; And there was none to bury them.

Psa 79:4 We are become a reproach to our neighbors, A scoffing and derision to them that are round about us.

Psa 79:5 How long, O Jehovah? wilt thou be angry for ever? Shall thy jealousy burn like fire?

Psa 79:6 Pour out thy wrath upon the nations that know thee not, And upon the kingdoms that call not upon thy name.

Psa 79:7 For they have devoured Jacob, And laid waste his habitation.

Psa 79:8 Remember not against us the iniquities of our forefathers: Let thy tender mercies speedily meet us; For we are brought very low.

Psa 79:9 Help us, O God of our salvation, for the glory of thy name; And deliver us, and forgive our sins, for thy name's sake.

Psa 79:10 Wherefore should the nations say, Where is their God? Let the avenging of the blood of thy servants which is shed Be known among the nations in our sight.

Psa 79:11 Let the sighing of the prisoner come before thee: According to the greatness of thy power preserve thou those that are appointed to death;

Psa 79:12 And render unto our neighbors sevenfold into their bosom Their reproach, wherewith they have reproached thee, O Lord.

Psa 79:13 So we thy people and sheep of thy pasture Will give thee thanks for ever: We will show forth thy praise to all generations.

Chapter 80.

Psa 80:1 For the Chief Musician; set to Shoshannim Eduth. A Psalm of Asaph. Give ear, O Shepherd of Israel, Thou that leadest Joseph like a flock; Thou that sittest above the cherubim, shine forth.

Psa 80:2 Before Ephraim and Benjamin and Manasseh, stir up thy might, And come to save us.

Psa 80:3 Turn us again, O God; And cause thy face to shine, and we shall be saved.

Psa 80:4 O Jehovah God of hosts, How long wilt thou be angry against the prayer of thy people?

Psa 80:5 Thou hast fed them with the bread of tears, And given them tears to drink in large measure.

Psa 80:6 Thou makest us a strife unto our neighbors; And our enemies laugh among themselves.

Psa 80:7 Turn us again, O God of hosts; And cause thy face to shine, and we shall be saved.

Psa 80:8 Thou broughtest a vine out of Egypt: Thou didst drive out the nations, and plantedst it.

Psa 80:9 Thou preparedst room before it, And it took deep root, and filled the land.

Psa 80:10 The mountains were covered with the shadow of it, And the boughs thereof were like cedars of God.

Psa 80:11 It sent out its branches unto the sea, And its shoots unto the River.

Psa 80:12 Why hast thou broken down its walls, So that all they that pass by the way do pluck it?

Psa 80:13 The boar out of the wood doth ravage it, And the wild beasts of the field feed on it.

Psa 80:14 Turn again, we beseech thee, O God of hosts: Look down from heaven, and behold, and visit this vine,

Psa 80:15 And the stock which thy right hand planted, And the branch that thou madest strong for thyself.

Psa 80:16 It is burned with fire, it is cut down: They perish at the rebuke of thy countenance.

Psa 80:17 Let thy hand be upon the man of thy right hand, Upon the son of man whom thou madest strong for thyself.

Psa 80:18 So shall we not go back from thee: Quicken thou us, and we will call upon thy name.

Psa 80:19 Turn us again, O Jehovah God of hosts; Cause thy face to shine, and we shall be saved.

Chapter 81.

Psa 81:1 For the Chief Musician; set to the Gittith. A Psalm of Asaph. Sing aloud unto God our strength: Make a joyful noise unto the God of Jacob.

Psa 81:2 Raise a song, and bring hither the timbrel, The pleasant harp with the psaltery.

Psa 81:3 Blow the trumpet at the new moon, At the full moon, on our feast-day.

Psa 81:4 For it is a statute for Israel, An ordinance of the God of Jacob.

Psa 81:5 He appointed it in Joseph for a testimony, When he went out over the land of Egypt, Where I heard a language that I knew not.

Psa 81:6 I removed his shoulder from the burden: His hands were freed from the basket.

Psa 81:7 Thou calledst in trouble, and I delivered thee; I answered thee in the secret place of thunder; I proved thee at the waters of Meribah. Selah.

Psa 81:8 Hear, O my people, and I will testify unto thee: O Israel, if thou wouldest hearken unto me!

Psa 81:9 There shall no strange god be in thee; Neither shalt thou worship any foreign god.

Psa 81:10 I am Jehovah thy God, Who brought thee up out of the land of Egypt: Open thy mouth wide, and I will fill it.

Psa 81:11 But my people hearkened not to my voice; And Israel would none of me.

Psa 81:12 So I let them go after the stubbornness of their heart, That they might walk in their own counsels.

Psa 81:13 Oh that my people would hearken unto me, That Israel would walk in my ways!

Psa 81:14 I would soon subdue their enemies, And turn my hand against their adversaries.

Psa 81:15 The haters of Jehovah should submit themselves unto him: But their time should endure for ever.

Psa 81:16 He would feed them also with the finest of the wheat; And with honey out of the rock would I satisfy thee.

Chapter 82.

Psa 82:1 A Psalm of Asaph. God standeth in the congregation of God; He judgeth among the gods.

Psa 82:2 How long will ye judge unjustly, And respect the persons of the wicked? Selah.

Psa 82:3 Judge the poor and fatherless: Do justice to the afflicted and destitute.

Psa 82:4 Rescue the poor and needy: Deliver them out of the hand of the wicked.

Psa 82:5 They know not, neither do they understand; They walk to and fro in darkness: All the foundations of the earth are shaken.

Psa 82:6 I said, Ye are gods, And all of you sons of the Most High.

Psa 82:7 Nevertheless ye shall die like men, And fall like one of the princes.

Psa 82:8 Arise, O God, judge the earth; For thou shalt inherit all the nations.

Chapter 83.

Psa 83:1 A Song, a Psalm of Asaph. O God, keep not thou silence: Hold not thy peace, and be not still, O God.

Psa 83:2 For, lo, thine enemies make a tumult; And they that hate thee have lifted up the head.

Psa 83:3 Thy take crafty counsel against thy people, And consult together against thy hidden ones.

Psa 83:4 They have said, Come, and let us cut them off from being a nation; That the name of Israel may be no more in remembrance.

Psa 83:5 For they have consulted together with one consent; Against thee do they make a covenant:

Psa 83:6 The tents of Edom and the Ishmaelites; Moab, and the Hagarenes;

Psa 83:7 Gebal, and Ammon, and Amalek; Philistia with the inhabitants of Tyre:

Psa 83:8 Assyria also is joined with them; They have helped the children of Lot. Selah.

Psa 83:9 Do thou unto them as unto Midian, As to Sisera, as to Jabin, at the river Kishon;

Psa 83:10 Who perished at Endor, Who became as dung for the earth.

Psa 83:11 Make their nobles like Oreb and Zeeb; Yea, all their princes like Zebah and Zalmunna;

Psa 83:12 Who said, Let us take to ourselves in possession The habitations of God.

Psa 83:13 O my God, make them like the whirling dust; As stubble before the wind.

Psa 83:14 As the fire that burneth the forest, And as the flame that setteth the mountains on fire,

Psa 83:15 So pursue them with thy tempest, And terrify them with thy storm.

Psa 83:16 Fill their faces with confusion, That they may seek thy name, O Jehovah.

Psa 83:17 Let them be put to shame and dismayed for ever; Yea, let them be confounded and perish;

Psa 83:18 That they may know that thou alone, whose name is Jehovah, Art the Most High over all the earth.

Chapter 84.

Psa 84:1 For the Chief Musician; set to the Gittith. A Psalm of the Sons of Korah. How amiable are thy tabernacles, O Jehovah of hosts!

Psa 84:2 My soul longeth, yea, even fainteth for the courts of Jehovah; My heart and my flesh cry out unto the living God.

Psa 84:3 Yea, the sparrow hath found her a house, And the swallow a nest for herself, where she may lay her young, Even thine altars, O Jehovah of hosts, My King, and my God.

Psa 84:4 Blessed are they that dwell in thy house: They will be still praising thee. Selah.

Psa 84:5 Blessed is the man whose strength is in thee; In whose heart are the highways to Zion.

Psa 84:6 Passing through the valley of Weeping they make it a place of springs; Yea, the early rain covereth it with blessings.

Psa 84:7 They go from strength to strength; Every one of them appeareth before God in Zion.

Psa 84:8 O Jehovah God of hosts, hear my prayer; Give ear, O God of Jacob. Selah.

Psa 84:9 Behold, O God our shield, And look upon the face of thine anointed.

Psa 84:10 For a day in thy courts is better than a thousand. I had rather be a doorkeeper in the house of my God, Than to dwell in the tents of wickedness.

Psa 84:11 For Jehovah God is a sun and a shield: Jehovah will give grace and glory; No good thing will he withhold from them that walk uprightly.

Psa 84:12 O Jehovah of hosts, Blessed is the man that trusteth in thee.

Chapter 85.

Psa 85:1 For the Chief Musician. A Psalm of the Sons of Korah. Jehovah, thou hast been favorable unto thy land; Thou hast brought back the captivity of Jacob.

Psa 85:2 Thou hast forgiven the iniquity of thy people; Thou hast covered all their sin. Selah.

Psa 85:3 Thou hast taken away all thy wrath; Thou hast turned thyself from the fierceness of thine anger.

Psa 85:4 Turn us, O God of our salvation, And cause thine indignation toward us to cease.

Psa 85:5 Wilt thou be angry with us for ever? Wilt thou draw out thine anger to all generations?

Psa 85:6 Wilt thou not quicken us again, That thy people may rejoice in thee?

Psa 85:7 Show us thy lovingkindness, O Jehovah, And grant us thy salvation.

Psa 85:8 I will hear what God Jehovah will speak; For he will speak peace unto his people, and to his saints: But let them not turn again to folly.

Psa 85:9 Surely his salvation is nigh them that fear him, That glory may dwell in our land.

Psa 85:10 Mercy and truth are met together; Righteousness and peace have kissed each other.

Psa 85:11 Truth springeth out of the earth; And righteousness hath looked down from heaven.

Psa 85:12 Yea, Jehovah will give that which is good; And our land shall yield its increase.

Psa 85:13 Righteousness shall go before him, And shall make his footsteps a way to walk in.

Chapter 86.

Psa 86:1 A Prayer of David. Bow down thine ear, O Jehovah, and answer me; For I am poor and needy.

Psa 86:2 Preserve my soul; For I am godly: O thou my God, save thy servant that trusteth in thee.

Psa 86:3 Be merciful unto me, O Lord; For unto thee do I cry all the day long.

Psa 86:4 Rejoice the soul of thy servant; For unto thee, O Lord, do I lift up my soul.

Psa 86:5 For thou, Lord, art good, and ready to forgive, And abundant in lovingkindness unto all them that call upon thee.

Psa 86:6 Give ear, O Jehovah, unto my prayer; And hearken unto the voice of my supplications.

Psa 86:7 In the day of my trouble I will call upon thee; For thou wilt answer me.

Psa 86:8 There is none like unto thee among the gods, O Lord; Neither are there any works like unto thy works.

Psa 86:9 All nations whom thou hast made shall come and worship before thee, O Lord; And they shall glorify thy name.

Psa 86:10 For thou art great, and doest wondrous things: Thou art God alone.

Psa 86:11 Teach me thy way, O Jehovah; I will walk in thy truth: Unite my heart to fear thy name.

Psa 86:12 I will praise thee, O Lord my God, with my whole heart; And I will glorify thy name for evermore.

Psa 86:13 For great is thy lovingkindness toward me; And thou hast delivered my soul from the lowest Sheol.

Psa 86:14 O God, the proud are risen up against me, And a company of violent men have sought after my soul, And have not set thee before them.

Psa 86:15 But thou, O Lord, art a God merciful and gracious, Slow to anger, and abundant in lovingkindness and truth.

Psa 86:16 Oh turn unto me, and have mercy upon me; Give thy strength unto thy servant, And save the son of thy handmaid.

Psa 86:17 Show me a token for good, That they who hate me may see it, and be put to shame, Because thou, Jehovah, hast helped me, and comforted me.

Chapter 87.

Psa 87:1 A Psalm of the sons of Korah; a song. His foundation is in the holy mountains.

Psa 87:2 Jehovah loveth the gates of Zion More than all the dwellings of Jacob.

Psa 87:3 Glorious things are spoken of thee, O city of God. Selah.

Psa 87:4 I will make mention of Rahab and Babylon as among them that know me: Behold, Philistia, and Tyre, with Ethiopia: This one was born there.

Psa 87:5 Yea, of Zion it shall be said, This one and that one was born in her; And the Most High himself will establish her.

Psa 87:6 Jehovah will count, when he writeth up the peoples, This one was born there. Selah.

Psa 87:7 They that sing as well as they that dance shall say, All my fountains are in thee.

Chapter 88.

Psa 88:1 A Song, a Psalm of the sons of Korah; for the Chief Musician; set to Mahalath Leannoth. Maschil of Herman the Ezrahite. O Jehovah, the God of my salvation, I have cried day and night before thee.

Psa 88:2 Let my prayer enter into thy presence; Incline thine ear unto my cry.

Psa 88:3 For my soul is full of troubles, And my life draweth nigh unto Sheol.

Psa 88:4 I am reckoned with them that go down into the pit; I am as a man that hath no help,

Psa 88:5 Cast off among the dead, Like the slain that lie in the grave, Whom thou rememberest no more, And they are cut off from thy hand.

Psa 88:6 Thou hast laid me in the lowest pit, In dark places, in the deeps.

Psa 88:7 Thy wrath lieth hard upon me, And thou hast afflicted me with all thy waves. Selah.

Psa 88:8 Thou hast put mine acquaintance far from me; Thou hast made me an abomination unto them: I am shut up, and I cannot come forth.

Psa 88:9 Mine eye wasteth away by reason of affliction: I have called daily upon thee, O Jehovah; I have spread forth my hands unto thee.

Psa 88:10 Wilt thou show wonders to the dead? Shall they that are deceased arise and praise thee? Selah.

Psa 88:11 Shall thy lovingkindness be declared in the grave? Or thy faithfulness in Destruction?

Psa 88:12 Shall thy wonders be known in the dark? And thy righteousness in the land of forgetfulness?

Psa 88:13 But unto thee, O Jehovah, have I cried; And in the morning shall my prayer come before thee.

Psa 88:14 Jehovah, why castest thou off my soul? Why hidest thou thy face from me?

Psa 88:15 I am afflicted and ready to die from my youth up: While I suffer thy terrors I am distracted.

Psa 88:16 Thy fierce wrath is gone over me; Thy terrors have cut me off.

Psa 88:17 They came round about me like water all the day long; They compassed me about together.

Psa 88:18 Lover and friend hast thou put far from me, And mine acquaintance into darkness.

Chapter 89.

Psa 89:1 Maschil of Ethan the Ezrahite. I will sing of the lovingkindness of Jehovah for ever: With my mouth will I make known thy faithfulness to all generations.

Psa 89:2 For I have said, Mercy shall be built up for ever; Thy faithfulness wilt thou establish in the very heavens.

Psa 89:3 I have made a covenant with my chosen, I have sworn unto David my servant:

Psa 89:4 Thy seed will I establish for ever, And build up thy throne to all generations. Selah.

Psa 89:5 And the heavens shall praise thy wonders, O Jehovah; Thy faithfulness also in the assembly of the holy ones.

Psa 89:6 For who in the skies can be compared unto Jehovah? Who among the sons of the mighty is like unto Jehovah,

Psa 89:7 A God very terrible in the council of the holy ones, And to be feared above all them that are round about him?

Psa 89:8 O Jehovah God of hosts, Who is a mighty one, like unto thee, O Jehovah? And thy faithfulness is round about thee.

Psa 89:9 Thou rulest the pride of the sea: When the waves thereof arise, thou stillest them.

Psa 89:10 Thou hast broken Rahab in pieces, as one that is slain; Thou hast scattered thine enemies with the arm of thy strength.

Psa 89:11 The heavens are thine, the earth also is thine: The world and the fulness thereof, thou hast founded them.

Psa 89:12 The north and the south, thou hast created them: Tabor and Hermon rejoice in thy name.

Psa 89:13 Thou hast a mighty arm; Strong is thy hand, and high is thy right hand.

Psa 89:14 Righteousness and justice are the foundation of thy throne: Lovingkindness and truth go before thy face.

Psa 89:15 Blessed is the people that know the joyful sound: They walk, O Jehovah, in the light of thy countenance.

Psa 89:16 In thy name do they rejoice all the day; And in thy righteousness are they exalted.

Psa 89:17 For thou art the glory of their strength; And in thy favor our horn shall be exalted.

Psa 89:18 For our shield belongeth unto Jehovah; And our king to the Holy One of Israel.

Psa 89:19 Then thou spakest in vision to thy saints, And saidst, I have laid help upon one that is mighty; I have exalted one chosen out of the people.

Psa 89:20 I have found David my servant; With my holy oil have I anointed him:

Psa 89:21 With whom my hand shall be established; Mine arm also shall strengthen him.

Psa 89:22 The enemy shall not exact from him, Nor the son of wickedness afflict him.

Psa 89:23 And I will beat down his adversaries before him, And smite them that hate him.

Psa 89:24 But my faithfulness and my lovingkindness shall be with him; And in my name shall his horn be exalted.

Psa 89:25 I will set his hand also on the sea, And his right hand on the rivers.

Psa 89:26 He shall cry unto me, Thou art my Father, My God, and the rock of my salvation.

Psa 89:27 I also will make him my first-born, The highest of the kings of the earth.

Psa 89:28 My lovingkindness will I keep for him for evermore; And my covenant shall stand fast with him.

Psa 89:29 His seed also will I make to endure for ever, And his throne as the days of heaven.

Psa 89:30 If his children forsake my law, And walk not in mine ordinances;

Psa 89:31 If they break my statutes, And keep not my commandments;

Psa 89:32 Then will I visit their transgression with the rod, And their iniquity with stripes.

Psa 89:33 But my lovingkindness will I not utterly take from him, Nor suffer my faithfulness to fail.

Psa 89:34 My covenant will I not break, Nor alter the thing that is gone out of my lips.

Psa 89:35 Once have I sworn by my holiness: I will not lie unto David:

Psa 89:36 His seed shall endure for ever, And his throne as the sun before me.

Psa 89:37 It shall be established for ever as the moon, And as the faithful witness in the sky. Selah.

Psa 89:38 But thou hast cast off and rejected, Thou hast been wroth with thine anointed.

Psa 89:39 Thou hast abhorred the covenant of thy servant: Thou hast profaned his crown by casting it to the ground.

Psa 89:40 Thou hast broken down all his hedges; Thou hast brought his strongholds to ruin.

Psa 89:41 All that pass by the way rob him: He is become a reproach to his neighbors.

Psa 89:42 Thou hast exalted the right hand of his adversaries; Thou hast made all his enemies to rejoice.

Psa 89:43 Yea, thou turnest back the edge of his sword, And hast not made him to stand in the battle.

Psa 89:44 Thou hast made his brightness to cease, And cast his throne down to the ground.

Psa 89:45 The days of his youth hast thou shortened: Thou hast covered him with shame. Selah.

Psa 89:46 How long, O Jehovah? wilt thou hide thyself for ever? How long shall thy wrath burn like fire?

Psa 89:47 Oh remember how short my time is: For what vanity hast thou created all the children of men!

Psa 89:48 What man is he that shall live and not see death, That shall deliver his soul from the power of Sheol? Selah.

Psa 89:49 Lord, where are thy former lovingkindnesses, Which thou swarest unto David in thy faithfulness?

Psa 89:50 Remember, Lord, the reproach of thy servants; How I do bear in my bosom the reproach of all the mighty peoples,

Psa 89:51 Wherewith thine enemies have reproached, O Jehovah, Wherewith they have reproached the footsteps of thine anointed.

Psa 89:52 Blessed be Jehovah for evermore. Amen, and Amen.

Chapter 90.

Psa 90:1 A prayer of Moses the man of God. Lord, thou hast been our dwelling-place In all generations.

Psa 90:2 Before the mountains were brought forth, Or ever thou hadst formed the earth and the world, Even from everlasting to everlasting, thou art God.

Psa 90:3 Thou turnest man to destruction, And sayest, Return, ye children of men.

Psa 90:4 For a thousand years in thy sight Are but as yesterday when it is past, And as a watch in the night.

Psa 90:5 Thou carriest them away as with a flood; they are as a sleep: In the morning they are like grass which groweth up.

Psa 90:6 In the morning it flourisheth, and groweth up; In the evening it is cut down, and withereth.

Psa 90:7 For we are consumed in thine anger, And in thy wrath are we troubled.

Psa 90:8 Thou hast set our iniquities before thee, Our secret sins in the light of thy countenance.

Psa 90:9 For all our days are passed away in thy wrath: We bring our years to an end as a sigh.

Psa 90:10 The days of our years are threescore years and ten, Or even by reason of strength fourscore years; Yet is their pride but labor and sorrow; For it is soon gone, and we fly away.

Psa 90:11 Who knoweth the power of thine anger, And thy wrath according to the fear that is due unto thee?

Psa 90:12 So teach us to number our days, That we may get us a heart of wisdom.

Psa 90:13 Return, O Jehovah; How long? And let it repent thee concerning thy servants.

Psa 90:14 Oh satisfy us in the morning with thy lovingkindness, That we may rejoice and be glad all our days.

Psa 90:15 Make us glad according to the days wherein thou hast afflicted us, And the years wherein we have seen evil.

Psa 90:16 Let thy work appear unto thy servants, And thy glory upon their children.

Psa 90:17 And let the favor of the Lord our God be upon us; And establish thou the work of our hands upon us; Yea, the work of our hands establish thou it.

Chapter 91.

Psa 91:1 He that dwelleth in the secret place of the Most High Shall abide under the shadow of the Almighty.

Psa 91:2 I will say of Jehovah, He is my refuge and my fortress; My God, in whom I trust.

Psa 91:3 For he will deliver thee from the snare of the fowler, And from the deadly pestilence.

Psa 91:4 He will cover thee with his pinions, And under his wings shalt thou take refuge: His truth is a shield and a buckler.

Psa 91:5 Thou shalt not be afraid for the terror by night, Nor for the arrow that flieth by day;

Psa 91:6 For the pestilence that walketh in darkness, Nor for the destruction that wasteth at noonday.

Psa 91:7 A thousand shall fall at thy side, And ten thousand at thy right hand; But it shall not come nigh thee.

Psa 91:8 Only with thine eyes shalt thou behold, And see the reward of the wicked.

Psa 91:9 For thou, O Jehovah, art my refuge! Thou hast made the Most High thy habitation;

Psa 91:10 There shall no evil befall thee, Neither shall any plague come nigh thy tent.

Psa 91:11 For he will give his angels charge over thee, To keep thee in all thy ways.

Psa 91:12 They shall bear thee up in their hands, Lest thou dash thy foot against a stone.

Psa 91:13 Thou shalt tread upon the lion and adder: The young lion and the serpent shalt thou trample under foot.

Psa 91:14 Because he hath set his love upon me, therefore will I deliver him: I will set him on high, because he hath known my name.

Psa 91:15 He shall call upon me, and I will answer him; I will be with him in trouble: I will deliver him, and honor him.

Psa 91:16 With long life will I satisfy him, And show him my salvation.

Chapter 92.

Psa 92:1 A Psalm, a song for the sabbath day. It is a good thing to give thanks unto Jehovah, And to sing praises unto thy name, O Most High;

Psa 92:2 To show forth thy lovingkindness in the morning, And thy faithfulness every night,

Psa 92:3 With an instrument of ten strings, and with the psaltery; With a solemn sound upon the harp.

Psa 92:4 For thou, Jehovah, hast made me glad through thy work: I will triumph in the works of thy hands.

Psa 92:5 How great are thy works, O Jehovah! Thy thoughts are very deep.

Psa 92:6 A brutish man knoweth not; Neither doth a fool understand this:

Psa 92:7 When the wicked spring as the grass, And when all the workers of iniquity do flourish; It is that they shall be destroyed for ever.

Psa 92:8 But thou, O Jehovah, art on high for evermore.

Psa 92:9 For, lo, thine enemies, O Jehovah, For, lo, thine enemies shall perish; All the workers of iniquity shall be scattered.

Psa 92:10 But my horn hast thou exalted like the horn of the wild-ox: I am anointed with fresh oil.

Psa 92:11 Mine eye also hath seen my desire on mine enemies, Mine ears have heard my desire of the evil-doers that rise up against me.

Psa 92:12 The righteous shall flourish like the palm-tree: He shall grow like a cedar in Lebanon.

Psa 92:13 They are planted in the house of Jehovah; They shall flourish in the courts of our God.

Psa 92:14 They shall still bring forth fruit in old age; They shall be full of sap and green:

Psa 92:15 To show that Jehovah is upright; He is my rock, and there is no unrighteousness in him.

Chapter 93.

Psa 93:1 Jehovah reigneth; He is clothed with majesty; Jehovah is clothed with strength; he hath girded himself therewith: The world also is established, that it cannot be moved.

Psa 93:2 Thy throne is established of old: Thou art from everlasting.

Psa 93:3 The floods have lifted up, O Jehovah, The floods have lifted up their voice; The floods lift up their waves.

Psa 93:4 Above the voices of many waters, The mighty breakers of the sea, Jehovah on high is mighty.

Psa 93:5 Thy testimonies are very sure: Holiness becometh thy house, O Jehovah, for evermore.

Chapter 94.

Psa 94:1 O Jehovah, thou God to whom vengeance belongeth, Thou God to whom vengeance belongeth, shine forth.

Psa 94:2 Lift up thyself, thou judge of the earth: Render to the proud their desert.

Psa 94:3 Jehovah, how long shall the wicked, How long shall the wicked triumph?

Psa 94:4 They prate, they speak arrogantly: All the workers of iniquity boast themselves.

Psa 94:5 They break in pieces thy people, O Jehovah, And afflict thy heritage.

Psa 94:6 They slay the widow and the sojourner, And murder the fatherless.

Psa 94:7 And they say, Jehovah will not see, Neither will the God of Jacob consider.

Psa 94:8 Consider, ye brutish among the people; And ye fools, when will ye be wise?

Psa 94:9 He that planted the ear, shall he not hear? He that formed the eye, shall he not see?

Psa 94:10 He that chastiseth the nations, shall not he correct, Even he that teacheth man knowledge?

Psa 94:11 Jehovah knoweth the thoughts of man, That they are vanity.

Psa 94:12 Blessed is the man whom thou chastenest, O Jehovah, And teachest out of thy law;

Psa 94:13 That thou mayest give him rest from the days of adversity, Until the pit be digged for the wicked.

Psa 94:14 For Jehovah will not cast off his people, Neither will he forsake his inheritance.

Psa 94:15 For judgment shall return unto righteousness; And all the upright in heart shall follow it.

Psa 94:16 Who will rise up for me against the evil-doers? Who will stand up for me against the workers of iniquity?

Psa 94:17 Unless Jehovah had been my help, My soul had soon dwelt in silence.

Psa 94:18 When I said, My foot slippeth; Thy lovingkindness, O Jehovah, held me up.

Psa 94:19 In the multitude of my thoughts within me Thy comforts delight my soul.

Psa 94:20 Shall the throne of wickedness have fellowship with thee, Which frameth mischief by statute?

Psa 94:21 They gather themselves together against the soul of the righteous, And condemn the innocent blood.

Psa 94:22 But Jehovah hath been my high tower, And my God the rock of my refuge.

Psa 94:23 And he hath brought upon them their own iniquity, And will cut them off in their own wickedness; Jehovah our God will cut them off.

Chapter 95.

Psa 95:1 Oh come, let us sing unto Jehovah; Let us make a joyful noise to the rock of our salvation.

Psa 95:2 Let us come before his presence with thanksgiving; Let us make a joyful noise unto him with psalms.

Psa 95:3 For Jehovah is a great God, And a great King above all gods.

Psa 95:4 In his hand are the deep places of the earth; The heights of the mountains are his also.

Psa 95:5 The sea is his, and he made it; And his hands formed the dry land.

Psa 95:6 Oh come, let us worship and bow down; Let us kneel before Jehovah our Maker:

Psa 95:7 For he is our God, And we are the people of his pasture, and the sheep of his hand. To-day, oh that ye would hear his voice!

Psa 95:8 Harden not your heart, as at Meribah, As in the day of Massah in the wilderness;

Psa 95:9 When your fathers tempted me, Proved me, and saw my work.

Psa 95:10 Forty years long was I grieved with that generation, And said, It is a people that do err in their heart, And they have not known my ways:

Psa 95:11 Wherefore I sware in my wrath, That they should not enter into my rest.

Chapter 96.

Psa 96:1 Oh sing unto Jehovah a new song: Sing unto Jehovah, all the earth.

Psa 96:2 Sing unto Jehovah, bless his name; Show forth his salvation from day to day.

Psa 96:3 Declare his glory among the nations, His marvellous works among all the peoples.

Psa 96:4 For great is Jehovah, and greatly to be praised: He is to be feared above all gods.

Psa 96:5 For all the gods of the peoples are idols; But Jehovah made the heavens.

Psa 96:6 Honor and majesty are before him: Strength and beauty are in his sanctuary.

Psa 96:7 Ascribe unto Jehovah, ye kindreds of the peoples, Ascribe unto Jehovah glory and strength.

Psa 96:8 Ascribe unto Jehovah the glory due unto his name: Bring an offering, and come into his courts.

Psa 96:9 Oh worship Jehovah in holy array: Tremble before him, all the earth.

Psa 96:10 Say among the nations, Jehovah reigneth: The world also is established that it cannot be moved: He will judge the peoples with equity.

Psa 96:11 Let the heavens be glad, and let the earth rejoice; Let the sea roar, and the fulness thereof;

Psa 96:12 Let the field exult, and all that is therein; Then shall all the trees of the wood sing for joy

Psa 96:13 Before Jehovah; for he cometh, For he cometh to judge the earth: He will judge the world with righteousness, And the peoples with his truth.

Chapter 97.

Psa 97:1 Jehovah reigneth; let the earth rejoice; Let the multitude of isles be glad.

Psa 97:2 Clouds and darkness are round about him: Righteousness and justice are the foundation of his throne.

Psa 97:3 A fire goeth before him, And burneth up his adversaries round about.

Psa 97:4 His lightnings lightened the world: The earth saw, and trembled.

Psa 97:5 The mountains melted like wax at the presence of Jehovah, At the presence of the Lord of the whole earth.

Psa 97:6 The heavens declare his righteousness, And all the peoples have seen his glory.

Psa 97:7 Let all them be put to shame that serve graven images, That boast themselves of idols: Worship him, all ye gods.

Psa 97:8 Zion heard and was glad, And the daughters of Judah rejoiced, Because of thy judgments, O Jehovah.

Psa 97:9 For thou, Jehovah, art most high above all the earth: Thou art exalted far above all gods.

Psa 97:10 O ye that love Jehovah, hate evil: He preserveth the souls of his saints; He delivereth them out of the hand of the wicked.

Psa 97:11 Light is sown for the righteous, And gladness for the upright in heart.

Psa 97:12 Be glad in Jehovah, ye righteous; And give thanks to his holy memorial name.

Chapter 98.

Psa 98:1 A Psalm. Oh sing unto Jehovah a new song; For he hath done marvellous things: His right hand, and his holy arm, hath wrought salvation for him.

Psa 98:2 Jehovah hath made known his salvation: His righteousness hath he openly showed in the sight of the nations.

Psa 98:3 He hath remembered his lovingkindness and his faithfulness toward the house of Israel: All the ends of the earth have seen the salvation of our God.

Psa 98:4 Make a joyful noise unto Jehovah, all the earth: Break forth and sing for joy, yea, sing praises.

Psa 98:5 Sing praises unto Jehovah with the harp; With the harp and the voice of melody.

Psa 98:6 With trumpets and sound of cornet Make a joyful noise before the King, Jehovah.

Psa 98:7 Let the sea roar, and the fulness thereof; The world, and they that dwell therein;

Psa 98:8 Let the floods clap their hands; Let the hills sing for joy together

Psa 98:9 Before Jehovah; for he cometh to judge the earth: He will judge the world with righteousness, And the peoples with equity.

Chapter 99.

Psa 99:1 Jehovah reigneth; let the peoples tremble: He sitteth above the cherubim; let the earth be moved.

Psa 99:2 Jehovah is great in Zion; And he is high above all the peoples.

Psa 99:3 Let them praise thy great and terrible name: Holy is he.

Psa 99:4 The king's strength also loveth justice; Thou dost establish equity; Thou executest justice and righteousness in Jacob.

Psa 99:5 Exalt ye Jehovah our God, And worship at his footstool: Holy is he.

Psa 99:6 Moses and Aaron among his priests, And Samuel among them that call upon his name; They called upon Jehovah, and he answered them.

Psa 99:7 He spake unto them in the pillar of cloud: They kept his testimonies, And the statute that he gave them.

Psa 99:8 Thou answeredst them, O Jehovah our God: Thou wast a God that forgavest them, Though thou tookest vengeance of their doings.

Psa 99:9 Exalt ye Jehovah our God, And worship at his holy hill; For Jehovah our God is holy.

Chapter 100.

Psa 100:1 A Psalm of thanksgiving. Make a joyful noise unto Jehovah, all ye lands.

Psa 100:2 Serve Jehovah with gladness: Come before his presence with singing.

Psa 100:3 Know ye that Jehovah, he is God: It is he that hath made us, and we are his; We are his people, and the sheep of his pasture.

Psa 100:4 Enter into his gates with thanksgiving, And into his courts with praise: Give thanks unto him, and bless his name.

Psa 100:5 For Jehovah is good; his lovingkindness endureth for ever, And his faithfulness unto all generations.

Chapter 101.

Psa 101:1 A Psalm of David. I will sing of lovingkindness and justice: Unto thee, O Jehovah, will I sing praises.

Psa 101:2 I will behave myself wisely in a perfect way: Oh when wilt thou come unto me? I will walk within my house with a perfect heart.

Psa 101:3 I will set no base thing before mine eyes: I hate the work of them that turn aside; It shall not cleave unto me.

Psa 101:4 A perverse heart shall depart from me: I will know no evil thing.

Psa 101:5 Whoso privily slandereth his neighbor, him will I destroy: Him that hath a high look and a proud heart will I not suffer.

Psa 101:6 Mine eyes shall be upon the faithful of the land, that they may dwell with me: He that walketh in a perfect way, he shall minister unto me.

Psa 101:7 He that worketh deceit shall not dwell within my house: He that speaketh falsehood shall not be established before mine eyes.

Psa 101:8 Morning by morning will I destroy all the wicked of the land; To cut off all the workers of iniquity from the city of Jehovah.

Chapter 102.

Psa 102:1 A Prayer of the afflicted, when he is overwhelmed and poureth out his complaint before Jehovah. Hear my prayer, O Jehovah, And let my cry come unto thee.

Psa 102:2 Hide not thy face from me in the day of my distress: Incline thine ear unto me; In the day when I call answer me speedily.

Psa 102:3 For my days consume away like smoke, And my bones are burned as a firebrand.

Psa 102:4 My heart is smitten like grass, and withered; For I forget to eat my bread.

Psa 102:5 By reason of the voice of my groaning My bones cleave to my flesh.

Psa 102:6 I am like a pelican of the wilderness; I am become as an owl of the waste places.

Psa 102:7 I watch, and am become like a sparrow That is alone upon the house-top.

Psa 102:8 Mine enemies reproach me all the day; They that are mad against me do curse by me.

Psa 102:9 For I have eaten ashes like bread, And mingled my drink with weeping,

Psa 102:10 Because of thine indignation and thy wrath: For thou hast taken me up, and cast me away.

Psa 102:11 My days are like a shadow that declineth; And I am withered like grass.

Psa 102:12 But thou, O Jehovah, wilt abide for ever; And thy memorial name unto all generations.

Psa 102:13 Thou wilt arise, and have mercy upon Zion; For it is time to have pity upon her, Yea, the set time is come.

Psa 102:14 For thy servants take pleasure in her stones, And have pity upon her dust.

Psa 102:15 So the nations shall fear the name of Jehovah, And all the kings of the earth thy glory.

Psa 102:16 For Jehovah hath built up Zion; He hath appeared in his glory.

Psa 102:17 He hath regarded the prayer of the destitute, And hath not despised their prayer.

Psa 102:18 This shall be written for the generation to come; And a people which shall be created shall praise Jehovah.

Psa 102:19 For he hath looked down from the height of his sanctuary; From heaven did Jehovah behold the earth;

Psa 102:20 To hear the sighing of the prisoner; To loose those that are appointed to death;

Psa 102:21 That men may declare the name of Jehovah in Zion, And his praise in Jerusalem;

Psa 102:22 When the peoples are gathered together, And the kingdoms, to serve Jehovah.

Psa 102:23 He weakened my strength in the way; He shortened my days.

Psa 102:24 I said, O my God, take me not away in the midst of my days: Thy years are throughout all generations.

Psa 102:25 Of old didst thou lay the foundation of the earth; And the heavens are the work of thy hands.

Psa 102:26 They shall perish, but thou shalt endure; Yea, all of them shall wax old like a garment; As a vesture shalt thou change them, and they shall be changed:

Psa 102:27 But thou art the same, And thy years shall have no end.

Psa 102:28 The children of thy servants shall continue, And their seed shall be established before thee.

Chapter 103.

Psa 103:1 A Psalm of David. Bless Jehovah, O my soul; And all that is within me, bless his holy name.

Psa 103:2 Bless Jehovah, O my soul, And forget not all his benefits:

Psa 103:3 Who forgiveth all thine iniquities; Who healeth all thy diseases;

Psa 103:4 Who redeemeth thy life from destruction; Who crowneth thee with lovingkindness and tender mercies;

Psa 103:5 Who satisfieth thy desire with good things, So that thy youth is renewed like the eagle.

Psa 103:6 Jehovah executeth righteous acts, And judgments for all that are oppressed.

Psa 103:7 He made known his ways unto Moses, His doings unto the children of Israel.

Psa 103:8 Jehovah is merciful and gracious, Slow to anger, and abundant in lovingkindness.

Psa 103:9 He will not always chide; Neither will he keep his anger for ever.

Psa 103:10 He hath not dealt with us after our sins, Nor rewarded us after our iniquities.

Psa 103:11 For as the heavens are high above the earth, So great is his lovingkindness toward them that fear him.

Psa 103:12 As far as the east is from the west, So far hath he removed our transgressions from us.

Psa 103:13 Like as a father pitieth his children, So Jehovah pitieth them that fear him.

Psa 103:14 For he knoweth our frame; He remembereth that we are dust.

Psa 103:15 As for man, his days are as grass; As a flower of the field, so he flourisheth.

Psa 103:16 For the wind passeth over it, and it is gone; And the place thereof shall know it no more.

Psa 103:17 But the lovingkindness of Jehovah is from everlasting to everlasting upon them that fear him, And his righteousness unto children's children;

Psa 103:18 To such as keep his covenant, And to those that remember his precepts to do them.

Psa 103:19 Jehovah hath established his throne in the heavens; And his kingdom ruleth over all.

Psa 103:20 Bless Jehovah, ye his angels, That are mighty in strength, that fulfil his word, Hearkening unto the voice of his word.

Psa 103:21 Bless Jehovah, all ye his hosts, Ye ministers of his, that do his pleasure.

Psa 103:22 Bless Jehovah, all ye his works, In all places of his dominion: Bless Jehovah, O my soul.

Chapter 104.

Psa 104:1 Bless Jehovah, O my soul. O Jehovah my God, thou art very great; Thou art clothed with honor and majesty:

Psa 104:2 Who coverest thyself with light as with a garment; Who stretchest out the heavens like a curtain;

Psa 104:3 Who layeth the beams of his chambers in the waters; Who maketh the clouds his chariot; Who walketh upon the wings of the wind;

Psa 104:4 Who maketh winds his messengers; Flames of fire his ministers;

Psa 104:5 Who laid the foundations of the earth, That it should not be moved for ever.

Psa 104:6 Thou coveredst it with the deep as with a vesture; The waters stood above the mountains.

Psa 104:7 At thy rebuke they fled; At the voice of thy thunder they hasted away

Psa 104:8 (The mountains rose, the valleys sank down) Unto the place which thou hadst founded for them.

Psa 104:9 Thou hast set a bound that they may not pass over; That they turn not again to cover the earth.

Psa 104:10 He sendeth forth springs into the valleys; They run among the mountains;

Psa 104:11 They give drink to every beast of the field; The wild asses quench their thirst.

Psa 104:12 By them the birds of the heavens have their habitation; They sing among the branches.

Psa 104:13 He watereth the mountains from his chambers: The earth is filled with the fruit of thy works.

Psa 104:14 He causeth the grass to grow for the cattle, And herb for the service of man; That he may bring forth food out of the earth,

Psa 104:15 And wine that maketh glad the heart of man, And oil to make his face to shine, And bread that strengtheneth man's heart.

Psa 104:16 The trees of Jehovah are filled with moisture, The cedars of Lebanon, which he hath planted;

Psa 104:17 Where the birds make their nests: As for the stork, the fir-trees are her house.

Psa 104:18 The high mountains are for the wild goats; The rocks are a refuge for the conies.

Psa 104:19 He appointed the moon for seasons: The sun knoweth his going down.

Psa 104:20 Thou makest darkness, and it is night, Wherein all the beasts of the forest creep forth.

Psa 104:21 The young lions roar after their prey, And seek their food from God.

Psa 104:22 The sun ariseth, they get them away, And lay them down in their dens.

Psa 104:23 Man goeth forth unto his work And to his labor until the evening.

Psa 104:24 O Jehovah, how manifold are thy works! In wisdom hast thou made them all: The earth is full of thy riches.

Psa 104:25 Yonder is the sea, great and wide, Wherein are things creeping innumerable, Both small and great beasts.

Psa 104:26 There go the ships; There is leviathan, whom thou hast formed to play therein.

Psa 104:27 These wait all for thee, That thou mayest give them their food in due season.

Psa 104:28 Thou givest unto them, they gather; Thou openest thy hand, they are satisfied with good.

Psa 104:29 Thou hidest thy face, they are troubled; Thou takest away their breath, they die, And return to their dust.

Psa 104:30 Thou sendest forth thy Spirit, they are created; And thou renewest the face of the ground.

Psa 104:31 Let the glory of Jehovah endure for ever; Let Jehovah rejoice in his works:

Psa 104:32 Who looketh on the earth, and it trembleth; He toucheth the mountains, and they smoke.

Psa 104:33 I will sing unto Jehovah as long as I live: I will sing praise to my God while I have any being.

Psa 104:34 Let thy meditation be sweet unto him: I will rejoice in Jehovah.

Psa 104:35 Let sinners be consumed out of the earth. And let the wicked be no more. Bless Jehovah, O my soul. Praise ye Jehovah.

Chapter 105.

Psa 105:1 Oh give thanks unto Jehovah, call upon his name; Make known among the peoples his doings.

Psa 105:2 Sing unto him, sing praises unto him; Talk ye of all his marvelous works.

Psa 105:3 Glory ye in his holy name: Let the heart of them rejoice that seek Jehovah.

Psa 105:4 Seek ye Jehovah and his strength; Seek his face evermore.

Psa 105:5 Remember his marvellous works that he hath done, His wonders, and the judgments of his mouth,

Psa 105:6 O ye seed of Abraham his servant, Ye children of Jacob, his chosen ones.

Psa 105:7 He is Jehovah our God: His judgments are in all the earth.

Psa 105:8 He hath remembered his covenant for ever, The word which he commanded to a thousand generations,

Psa 105:9 The covenant which he made with Abraham, And his oath unto Isaac,

Psa 105:10 And confirmed the same unto Jacob for a statute, To Israel for an everlasting covenant,

Psa 105:11 Saying, Unto thee will I give the land of Canaan, The lot of your inheritance;

Psa 105:12 When they were but a few men in number, Yea, very few, and sojourners in it.

Psa 105:13 And they went about from nation to nation, From one kingdom to another people.

Psa 105:14 He suffered no man to do them wrong; Yea, he reproved kings for their sakes,

Psa 105:15 Saying, Touch not mine anointed ones, And do my prophets no harm.

Psa 105:16 And he called for a famine upon the land; He brake the whole staff of bread.

Psa 105:17 He sent a man before them; Joseph was sold for a servant:

Psa 105:18 His feet they hurt with fetters: He was laid in chains of iron,

Psa 105:19 Until the time that his word came to pass, The word of Jehovah tried him.

Psa 105:20 The king sent and loosed him; Even the ruler of peoples, and let him go free.

Psa 105:21 He made him lord of his house, And ruler of all his substance;

Psa 105:22 To bind his princes at his pleasure, And teach his elders wisdom.

Psa 105:23 Israel also came into Egypt; And Jacob sojourned in the land of Ham.

Psa 105:24 And he increased his people greatly, And made them stronger than their adversaries.

Psa 105:25 He turned their heart to hate his people, To deal subtly with his servants.

Psa 105:26 He sent Moses his servant, And Aaron whom he had chosen.

Psa 105:27 They set among them his signs, And wonders in the land of Ham.

Psa 105:28 He sent darkness, and made it dark; And they rebelled not against his words.

Psa 105:29 He turned their waters into blood, And slew their fish.

Psa 105:30 Their land swarmed with frogs In the chambers of their kings.

Psa 105:31 He spake, and there came swarms of flies, And lice in all their borders.

Psa 105:32 He gave them hail for rain, And flaming fire in their land.

Psa 105:33 He smote their vines also and their fig-trees, And brake the trees of their borders.

Psa 105:34 He spake, and the locust came, And the grasshopper, and that without number,

Psa 105:35 And did eat up every herb in their land, And did eat up the fruit of their ground.

Psa 105:36 He smote also all the first-born in their land, The chief of all their strength.

Psa 105:37 And he brought them forth with silver and gold; And there was not one feeble person among his tribes.

Psa 105:38 Egypt was glad when they departed; For the fear of them had fallen upon them.

Psa 105:39 He spread a cloud for a covering, And fire to give light in the night.

Psa 105:40 They asked, and he brought quails, And satisfied them with the bread of heaven.

Psa 105:41 He opened the rock, and waters gushed out; They ran in the dry places like a river.

Psa 105:42 For he remembered his holy word, And Abraham his servant.

Psa 105:43 And he brought forth his people with joy, And his chosen with singing.

Psa 105:44 And he gave them the lands of the nations; And they took the labor of the peoples in possession:

Psa 105:45 That they might keep his statutes, And observe his laws. Praise ye Jehovah.

Chapter 106.

Psa 106:1 Praise ye Jehovah. Oh give thanks unto Jehovah; for he is good; For his lovingkindness endureth forever.

Psa 106:2 Who can utter the mighty acts of Jehovah, Or show forth all his praise?

Psa 106:3 Blessed are they that keep justice, And he that doeth righteousness at all times.

Psa 106:4 Remember me, O Jehovah, with the favor that thou bearest unto thy people; Oh visit me with thy salvation,

Psa 106:5 That I may see the prosperity of thy chosen, That I may rejoice in the gladness of thy nation, That I may glory with thine inheritance.

Psa 106:6 We have sinned with our fathers, We have committed iniquity, we have done wickedly.

Psa 106:7 Our fathers understood not thy wonders in Egypt; They remembered not the multitude of thy lovingkindnesses, But were rebellious at the sea, even at the Red Sea.

Psa 106:8 Nevertheless he saved them for his name's sake, That he might make his mighty power to be known.

Psa 106:9 He rebuked the Red Sea also, and it was dried up: So he led them through the depths, as through a wilderness.

Psa 106:10 And he saved them from the hand of him that hated them, And redeemed them from the hand of the enemy.

Psa 106:11 And the waters covered their adversaries; There was not one of them left.

Psa 106:12 Then believed they his words; They sang his praise.

Psa 106:13 They soon forgat his works; They waited not for his counsel,

Psa 106:14 But lusted exceedingly in the wilderness, And tempted God in the desert.

Psa 106:15 And he gave them their request, But sent leanness into their soul.

Psa 106:16 They envied Moses also in the camp, And Aaron the saint of Jehovah.

Psa 106:17 The earth opened and swallowed up Dathan, And covered the company of Abiram.

Psa 106:18 And a fire was kindled in their company; The flame burned up the wicked.

Psa 106:19 They made a calf in Horeb, And worshipped a molten image.

Psa 106:20 Thus they changed their glory For the likeness of an ox that eateth grass.

Psa 106:21 They forgat God their Saviour, Who had done great things in Egypt,

Psa 106:22 Wondrous works in the land of Ham, And terrible things by the Red Sea.

Psa 106:23 Therefore he said that he would destroy them, Had not Moses his chosen stood before him in the breach, To turn away his wrath, lest he should destroy them.

Psa 106:24 Yea, they despised the pleasant land, They believed not his word,

Psa 106:25 But murmured in their tents, And hearkened not unto the voice of Jehovah.

Psa 106:26 Therefore he sware unto them, That he would overthrow them in the wilderness,

Psa 106:27 And that he would overthrow their seed among the nations, And scatter them in the lands.

Psa 106:28 They joined themselves also unto Baal-peor, And ate the sacrifices of the dead.

Psa 106:29 Thus they provoked him to anger with their doings; And the plague brake in upon them.

Psa 106:30 Then stood up Phinehas, and executed judgment; And so the plague was stayed.

Psa 106:31 And that was reckoned unto him for righteousness, Unto all generations for evermore.

Psa 106:32 They angered him also at the waters of Meribah, So that it went ill with Moses for their sakes;

Psa 106:33 Because they were rebellious against his spirit, And he spake unadvisedly with his lips.

Psa 106:34 They did not destroy the peoples, As Jehovah commanded them,

Psa 106:35 But mingled themselves with the nations, And learned their works,

Psa 106:36 And served their idols, Which became a snare unto them.

Psa 106:37 Yea, they sacrificed their sons and their daughters unto demons,

Psa 106:38 And shed innocent blood, Even the blood of their sons and of their daughters, Whom they sacrificed unto the idols of Canaan; And the land was polluted with blood.

Psa 106:39 Thus were they defiled with their works, And played the harlot in their doings.

Psa 106:40 Therefore was the wrath of Jehovah kindled against his people, And he abhorred his inheritance.

Psa 106:41 And he gave them into the hand of the nations; And they that hated them ruled over them.

Psa 106:42 Their enemies also oppressed them, And they were brought into subjection under their hand.

Psa 106:43 Many times did he deliver them; But they were rebellious in their counsel, And were brought low in their iniquity.

Psa 106:44 Nevertheless he regarded their distress, When he heard their cry:

Psa 106:45 And he remembered for them his covenant, And repented according to the multitude of his lovingkindnesses.

Psa 106:46 He made them also to be pitied Of all those that carried them captive.

Psa 106:47 Save us, O Jehovah our God, And gather us from among the nations, To give thanks unto thy holy name, And to triumph in thy praise.

Psa 106:48 Blessed be Jehovah, the God of Israel, From everlasting even to everlasting. And let all the people say, Amen. Praise ye Jehovah.

Chapter 107.

Psa 107:1 O give thanks unto Jehovah; For he is good; For his lovingkindness endureth for ever.

Psa 107:2 Let the redeemed of Jehovah say so, Whom he hath redeemed from the hand of the adversary,

Psa 107:3 And gathered out of the lands, From the east and from the west, From the north and from the south.

Psa 107:4 They wandered in the wilderness in a desert way; They found no city of habitation.

Psa 107:5 Hungry and thirsty, Their soul fainted in them.

Psa 107:6 Then they cried unto Jehovah in their trouble, And he delivered them out of their distresses,

Psa 107:7 He led them also by a straight way, That they might go to a city of habitation.

Psa 107:8 Oh that men would praise Jehovah for his lovingkindness, And for his wonderful works to the children of men!

Psa 107:9 For he satisfieth the longing soul, And the hungry soul he filleth with good.

Psa 107:10 Such as sat in darkness and in the shadow of death, Being bound in affliction and iron,

Psa 107:11 Because they rebelled against the words of God, And contemned the counsel of the Most High:

Psa 107:12 Therefore he brought down their heart with labor; They fell down, and there was none to help.

Psa 107:13 Then they cried unto Jehovah in their trouble, And he saved them out of their distresses.

Psa 107:14 He brought them out of darkness and the shadow of death, And brake their bonds in sunder.

Psa 107:15 Oh that men would praise Jehovah for his lovingkindness, And for his wonderful works to the children of men!

Psa 107:16 For he hath broken the gates of brass, And cut the bars of iron in sunder.

Psa 107:17 Fools because of their transgression, And because of their iniquities, are afflicted.

Psa 107:18 Their soul abhorreth all manner of food; And they draw near unto the gates of death.

Psa 107:19 Then they cry unto Jehovah in their trouble, And he saveth them out of their distresses.

Psa 107:20 He sendeth his word, and healeth them, And delivereth them from their destructions.

Psa 107:21 Oh that men would praise Jehovah for his lovingkindness, And for his wonderful works to the children of men!

Psa 107:22 And let them offer the sacrifices of thanksgiving, And declare his works with singing.

Psa 107:23 They that go down to the sea in ships, That do business in great waters;

Psa 107:24 These see the works of Jehovah, And his wonders in the deep.

Psa 107:25 For he commandeth, and raiseth the stormy wind, Which lifteth up the waves thereof.

Psa 107:26 They mount up to the heavens, they go down again to the depths: Their soul melteth away because of trouble.

Psa 107:27 They reel to and fro, and stagger like a drunken man, And are at their wits' end.

Psa 107:28 Then they cry unto Jehovah in their trouble, And he bringeth them out of their distresses.

Psa 107:29 He maketh the storm a calm, So that the waves thereof are still.

Psa 107:30 Then are they glad because they are quiet; So he bringeth them unto their desired haven.

Psa 107:31 Oh that men would praise Jehovah for his lovingkindness, And for his wonderful works to the children of men!

Psa 107:32 Let them exalt him also in the assembly of the people, And praise him in the seat of the elders.

Psa 107:33 He turneth rivers into a wilderness, And watersprings into a thirsty ground;

Psa 107:34 A fruitful land into a salt desert, For the wickedness of them that dwell therein.

Psa 107:35 He turneth a wilderness into a pool of water, And a dry land into watersprings.

Psa 107:36 And there he maketh the hungry to dwell, That they may prepare a city of habitation,

Psa 107:37 And sow fields, and plant vineyards, And get them fruits of increase.

Psa 107:38 He blesseth them also, so that they are multiplied greatly; And he suffereth not their cattle to decrease.

Psa 107:39 Again, they are diminished and bowed down Through oppression, trouble, and sorrow.

Psa 107:40 He poureth contempt upon princes, And causeth them to wander in the waste, where there is no way.

Psa 107:41 Yet setteth he the needy on high from affliction, And maketh him families like a flock.

Psa 107:42 The upright shall see it, and be glad; And all iniquity shall stop her mouth.

Psa 107:43 Whoso is wise will give heed to these things; And they will consider the lovingkindnesses of Jehovah.

Chapter 108.

Psa 108:1 A Song, a Psalm of David. My heart is fixed, O God; I will sing, yea, I will sing praises, even with my glory.

Psa 108:2 Awake, psaltery and harp: I myself will awake right early.

Psa 108:3 I will give thanks unto thee, O Jehovah, among the peoples; And I will sing praises unto thee among the nations.

Psa 108:4 For thy lovingkindness is great above the heavens; And thy truth reacheth unto the skies.

Psa 108:5 Be thou exalted, O God, above the heavens, And thy glory above all the earth.

Psa 108:6 That thy beloved may be delivered, Save with thy right hand, and answer us.

Psa 108:7 God hath spoken in his holiness: I will exult; I will divide Shechem, and mete out the valley of Succoth.

Psa 108:8 Gilead is mine; Manasseh is mine; Ephraim also is the defence of my head; Judah is my sceptre.

Psa 108:9 Moab is my washpot; Upon Edom will I cast my shoe; Over Philistia will I shout.

Psa 108:10 Who will bring me into the fortified city? Who hath led me unto Edom?

Psa 108:11 Hast not thou cast us off, O God? And thou goest not forth, O God, with our hosts.

Psa 108:12 Give us help against the adversary; For vain is the help of man.

Psa 108:13 Through God we shall do valiantly: For he it is that will tread down our adversaries.

Chapter 109.

Psa 109:1 For the Chief Musician. A Psalm of David. Hold not thy peace, O God of my praise;

Psa 109:2 For the mouth of the wicked and the mouth of deceit have they opened against me: They have spoken unto me with a lying tongue.

Psa 109:3 They have compassed me about also with words of hatred, And fought against me without a cause.

Psa 109:4 For my love they are my adversaries: But I give myself unto prayer.

Psa 109:5 And they have rewarded me evil for good, And hatred for my love.

Psa 109:6 Set thou a wicked man over him; And let an adversary stand at his right hand.

Psa 109:7 When he is judged, let him come forth guilty; And let his prayer be turned into sin.

Psa 109:8 Let his days be few; And let another take his office.

Psa 109:9 Let his children be fatherless, And his wife a widow.

Psa 109:10 Let his children be vagabonds, and beg; And let them seek their bread out of their desolate places.

Psa 109:11 Let the extortioner catch all that he hath; And let strangers make spoil of his labor.

Psa 109:12 Let there be none to extend kindness unto him; Neither let there be any to have pity on his fatherless children.

Psa 109:13 Let his posterity be cut off; In the generation following let their name be blotted out.

Psa 109:14 Let the iniquity of his fathers be remembered with Jehovah; And let not the sin of his mother be blotted out.

Psa 109:15 Let them be before Jehovah continually, That he may cut off the memory of them from the earth;

Psa 109:16 Because he remembered not to show kindness, But persecuted the poor and needy man, And the broken in heart, to slay them.

Psa 109:17 Yea, he loved cursing, and it came unto him; And he delighted not in blessing, and it was far from him.

Psa 109:18 He clothed himself also with cursing as with his garment, And it came into his inward parts like water, And like oil into his bones.

Psa 109:19 Let it be unto him as the raiment wherewith he covereth himself, And for the girdle wherewith he is girded continually.

Psa 109:20 This is the reward of mine adversaries from Jehovah, And of them that speak evil against my soul.

Psa 109:21 But deal thou with me, O Jehovah the Lord, for thy name's sake: Because thy lovingkindness is good, deliver thou me;

Psa 109:22 For I am poor and needy, And my heart is wounded within me.

Psa 109:23 I am gone like the shadow when it declineth: I am tossed up and down as the locust.

Psa 109:24 My knees are weak through fasting; And my flesh faileth of fatness.

Psa 109:25 I am become also a reproach unto them: When they see me, they shake their head.

Psa 109:26 Help me, O Jehovah my God; Oh save me according to thy lovingkindness:

Psa 109:27 That they may know that this is thy hand; That thou, Jehovah, hast done it.

Psa 109:28 Let them curse, but bless thou: When they arise, they shall be put to shame, But thy servant shall rejoice.

Psa 109:29 Let mine adversaries be clothed with dishonor, And let them cover themselves with their own shame as with a robe.

Psa 109:30 I will give great thanks unto Jehovah with my mouth; Yea, I will praise him among the multitude.

Psa 109:31 For he will stand at the right hand of the needy, To save him from them that judge his soul.

Chapter 110.

Psa 110:1 A Psalm of David. Jehovah saith unto my Lord, Sit thou at my right hand, Until I make thine enemies thy footstool.

Psa 110:2 Jehovah will send forth the rod of thy strength out of Zion: Rule thou in the midst of thine enemies.

Psa 110:3 Thy people offer themselves willingly In the day of thy power, in holy array: Out of the womb of the morning Thou hast the dew of thy youth.

Psa 110:4 Jehovah hath sworn, and will not repent: Thou art a priest for ever After the order of Melchizedek.

Psa 110:5 The Lord at thy right hand Will strike through kings in the day of his wrath.

Psa 110:6 He will judge among the nations, He will fill the places with dead bodies; He will strike through the head in many countries.

Psa 110:7 He will drink of the brook in the way: Therefore will he lift up the head.

Chapter 111.

Psa 111:1 Praise ye Jehovah. I will give thanks unto Jehovah with my whole heart, In the council of the upright, and in the congregation.

Psa 111:2 The works of Jehovah are great, Sought out of all them that have pleasure therein.

Psa 111:3 His work is honor and majesty; And his righteousness endureth for ever.

Psa 111:4 He hath made his wonderful works to be remembered: Jehovah is gracious and merciful.

Psa 111:5 He hath given food unto them that fear him: He will ever be mindful of his covenant.

Psa 111:6 He hath showed his people the power of his works, In giving them the heritage of the nations.

Psa 111:7 The works of his hands are truth and justice; All his precepts are sure.

Psa 111:8 They are established for ever and ever; They are done in truth and uprightness.

Psa 111:9 He hath sent redemption unto his people; He hath commanded his covenant for ever: Holy and reverend is his name.

Psa 111:10 The fear of Jehovah is the beginning of wisdom; A good understanding have all they that do his commandments: His praise endureth for ever.

Chapter 112.

Psa 112:1 Praise ye Jehovah. Blessed is the man that feareth Jehovah, That delighteth greatly in his commandments.

Psa 112:2 His seed shall be mighty upon earth: The generation of the upright shall be blessed.

Psa 112:3 Wealth and riches are in his house; And his righteousness endureth for ever.

Psa 112:4 Unto the upright there ariseth light in the darkness: He is gracious, and merciful, and righteous.

Psa 112:5 Well is it with the man that dealeth graciously and lendeth; He shall maintain his cause in judgment.

Psa 112:6 For he shall never be moved; The righteous shall be had in everlasting remembrance.

Psa 112:7 He shall not be afraid of evil tidings: His heart is fixed, trusting in Jehovah.

Psa 112:8 His heart is established, he shall not be afraid, Until he see his desire upon his adversaries.

Psa 112:9 He hath dispersed, he hath given to the needy; His righteousness endureth for ever: His horn shall be exalted with honor.

Psa 112:10 The wicked shall see it, and be grieved; He shall gnash with his teeth, and melt away: The desire of the wicked shall perish.

Chapter 113.

Psa 113:1 Praise ye Jehovah. Praise, O ye servants of Jehovah, Praise the name of Jehovah.

Psa 113:2 Blessed be the name of Jehovah From this time forth and for evermore.

Psa 113:3 From the rising of the sun unto the going down of the same Jehovah's name is to be praised.

Psa 113:4 Jehovah is high above all nations, And his glory above the heavens.

Psa 113:5 Who is like unto Jehovah our God, That hath his seat on high,

Psa 113:6 That humbleth himself to behold The things that are in heaven and in the earth?

Psa 113:7 He raiseth up the poor out of the dust, And lifteth up the needy from the dunghill;

Psa 113:8 That he may set him with princes, Even with the princes of his people.

Psa 113:9 He maketh the barren woman to keep house, And to be a joyful mother of children. Praise ye Jehovah.

Chapter 114.

Psa 114:1 When Israel went forth out of Egypt, The house of Jacob from a people of strange language;

Psa 114:2 Judah became his sanctuary, Israel his dominion.

Psa 114:3 The sea saw it, and fled; The Jordan was driven back.

Psa 114:4 The mountains skipped like rams, The little hills like lambs.

Psa 114:5 What aileth thee, O thou sea, that thou fleest? Thou Jordan, that thou turnest back?

Psa 114:6 Ye mountains, that ye skip like rams; Ye little hills, like lambs?

Psa 114:7 Tremble, thou earth, at the presence of the Lord, At the presence of the God of Jacob,

Psa 114:8 Who turned the rock into a pool of water, The flint into a fountain of waters.

Chapter 115.

Psa 115:1 Not unto us, O Jehovah, not unto us, But unto thy name give glory, For thy lovingkindness, and for thy truth's sake.

Psa 115:2 Wherefore should the nations say, Where is now their God?

Psa 115:3 But our God is in the heavens: He hath done whatsoever he pleased.

Psa 115:4 Their idols are silver and gold, The work of men's hands.

Psa 115:5 They have mouths, but they speak not; Eyes have they, but they see not;

Psa 115:6 They have ears, but they hear not; Noses have they, but they smell not;

Psa 115:7 They have hands, but they handle not; Feet have they, but they walk not; Neither speak they through their throat.

Psa 115:8 They that make them shall be like unto them; Yea, every one that trusteth in them.

Psa 115:9 O Israel, trust thou in Jehovah: He is their help and their shield.

Psa 115:10 O house of Aaron, trust ye in Jehovah: He is their help and their shield.

Psa 115:11 Ye that fear Jehovah, trust in Jehovah: He is their help and their shield.

Psa 115:12 Jehovah hath been mindful of us; he will bless us: He will bless the house of Israel; He will bless the house of Aaron.

Psa 115:13 He will bless them that fear Jehovah, Both small and great.

Psa 115:14 Jehovah increase you more and more, You and your children.

Psa 115:15 Blessed are ye of Jehovah, Who made heaven and earth.

Psa 115:16 The heavens are the heavens of Jehovah; But the earth hath he given to the children of men.

Psa 115:17 The dead praise not Jehovah, Neither any that go down into silence;

Psa 115:18 But we will bless Jehovah From this time forth and for evermore. Praise ye Jehovah.

Chapter 116.

Psa 116:1 I love Jehovah, because he heareth My voice and my supplications.

Psa 116:2 Because he hath inclined his ear unto me, Therefore will I call upon him as long as I live.

Psa 116:3 The cords of death compassed me, And the pains of Sheol gat hold upon me: I found trouble and sorrow.

Psa 116:4 Then called I upon the name of Jehovah: O Jehovah, I beseech thee, deliver my soul.

Psa 116:5 Gracious is Jehovah, and righteous; Yea, our God is merciful.

Psa 116:6 Jehovah preserveth the simple: I was brought low, and he saved me.

Psa 116:7 Return unto thy rest, O my soul; For Jehovah hath dealt bountifully with thee.

Psa 116:8 For thou hast delivered my soul from death, Mine eyes from tears, And my feet from falling.

Psa 116:9 I will walk before Jehovah In the land of the living.

Psa 116:10 I believe, for I will speak: I was greatly afflicted:

Psa 116:11 I said in my haste, All men are liars.

Psa 116:12 What shall I render unto Jehovah For all his benefits toward me?

Psa 116:13 I will take the cup of salvation, And call upon the name of Jehovah.

Psa 116:14 I will pay my vows unto Jehovah, Yea, in the presence of all his people.

Psa 116:15 Precious in the sight of Jehovah Is the death of his saints.

Psa 116:16 O Jehovah, truly I am thy servant: I am thy servant, the son of thy handmaid; Thou hast loosed my bonds.

Psa 116:17 I will offer to thee the sacrifice of thanksgiving, And will call upon the name of Jehovah.

Psa 116:18 I will pay my vows unto Jehovah, Yea, in the presence of all his people,

Psa 116:19 In the courts of Jehovah's house, In the midst of thee, O Jerusalem. Praise ye Jehovah.

Chapter 117.

Psa 117:1 O praise Jehovah, all ye nations; Laud him, all ye peoples.

Psa 117:2 For his lovingkindness is great toward us; And the truth of Jehovah endureth for ever. Praise ye Jehovah.

Chapter 118.

Psa 118:1 Oh give thanks unto Jehovah; for he is good; For his lovingkindness endureth for ever.

Psa 118:2 Let Israel now say, That his lovingkindness endureth for ever.

Psa 118:3 Let the house of Aaron now say, That his lovingkindness endureth for ever.

Psa 118:4 Let them now that fear Jehovah say, That his lovingkindness endureth for ever.

Psa 118:5 Out of my distress I called upon Jehovah: Jehovah answered me and set me in a large place.

Psa 118:6 Jehovah is on my side; I will not fear: What can man do unto me?

Psa 118:7 Jehovah is on my side among them that help me: Therefore shall I see my desire upon them that hate me.

Psa 118:8 It is better to take refuge in Jehovah Than to put confidence in man.

Psa 118:9 It is better to take refuge in Jehovah Than to put confidence in princes.

Psa 118:10 All nations compassed me about: In the name of Jehovah I will cut them off.

Psa 118:11 They compassed me about; yea, they compassed me about: In the name of Jehovah I will cut them off.

Psa 118:12 They compassed me about like bees; They are quenched as the fire of thorns: In the name of Jehovah I will cut them off.

Psa 118:13 Thou didst thrust sore at me that I might fall; But Jehovah helped me.

Psa 118:14 Jehovah is my strength and song; And he is become my salvation.

Psa 118:15 The voice of rejoicing and salvation is in the tents of the righteous: The right hand of Jehovah doeth valiantly.

Psa 118:16 The right hand of Jehovah is exalted: The right hand of Jehovah doeth valiantly.

Psa 118:17 I shall not die, but live, And declare the works of Jehovah.

Psa 118:18 Jehovah hath chastened me sore; But he hath not given me over unto death.

Psa 118:19 Open to me the gates of righteousness: I will enter into them, I will give thanks unto Jehovah.

Psa 118:20 This is the gate of Jehovah; The righteous shall enter into it.

Psa 118:21 I will give thanks unto thee; for thou hast answered me, And art become my salvation.

Psa 118:22 The stone which the builders rejected Is become the head of the corner.

Psa 118:23 This is Jehovah's doing; It is marvellous in our eyes.

Psa 118:24 This is the day which Jehovah hath made; We will rejoice and be glad in it.

Psa 118:25 Save now, we beseech thee, O Jehovah: O Jehovah, we beseech thee, send now prosperity.

Psa 118:26 Blessed be he that cometh in the name of Jehovah: We have blessed you out of the house of Jehovah.

Psa 118:27 Jehovah is God, and he hath given us light: Bind the sacrifice with cords, even unto the horns of the altar.

Psa 118:28 Thou art my God, and I will give thanks unto thee: Thou art my God, I will exalt thee.

Psa 118:29 Oh give thanks unto Jehovah; for he is good; For his lovingkindness endureth for ever.

Chapter 119.

Psa 119:1 Aleph. Blessed are they that are perfect in the way, Who walk in the law of Jehovah.

Psa 119:2 Blessed are they that keep his testimonies, That seek him with the whole heart.

Psa 119:3 Yea, they do no unrighteousness; They walk in his ways.

Psa 119:4 Thou hast commanded us thy precepts, That we should observe them diligently.

Psa 119:5 Oh that my ways were established To observe thy statutes!

Psa 119:6 Then shall I not be put to shame, When I have respect unto all thy commandments.

Psa 119:7 I will give thanks unto thee with uprightness of heart, When I learn thy righteous judgments.

Psa 119:8 I will observe thy statutes: Oh forsake me not utterly.

Psa 119:9 Beth. Wherewith shall a young man cleanse his way? By taking heed thereto according to thy word.

Psa 119:10 With my whole heart have I sought thee: Oh let me not wander from thy commandments.

Psa 119:11 Thy word have I laid up in my heart, That I might not sin against thee.

Psa 119:12 Blessed art thou, O Jehovah: Teach me thy statutes.

Psa 119:13 With my lips have I declared All the ordinances of thy mouth.

Psa 119:14 I have rejoiced in the way of thy testimonies, As much as in all riches.

Psa 119:15 I will meditate on thy precepts, And have respect unto thy ways.

Psa 119:16 I will delight myself in thy statutes: I will not forget thy word.

Psa 119:17 Gimel. Deal bountifully with thy servant, that I may live; So will I observe thy word.

Psa 119:18 Open thou mine eyes, that I may behold Wondrous things out of thy law.

Psa 119:19 I am a sojourner in the earth: Hide not thy commandments from me.

Psa 119:20 My soul breaketh for the longing That it hath unto thine ordinances at all times.

Psa 119:21 Thou hast rebuked the proud that are cursed, That do wander from thy commandments.

Psa 119:22 Take away from me reproach and contempt; For I have kept thy testimonies.

Psa 119:23 Princes also sat and talked against me; But thy servant did meditate on thy statutes.

Psa 119:24 Thy testimonies also are my delight And my counsellors.

Psa 119:25 Daleth. My soul cleaveth unto the dust: Quicken thou me according to thy word.

Psa 119:26 I declared my ways, and thou answeredst me: Teach me thy statutes.

Psa 119:27 Make me to understand the way of thy precepts: So shall I meditate on thy wondrous works.

Psa 119:28 My soul melteth for heaviness: Strengthen thou me according unto thy word.

Psa 119:29 Remove from me the way of falsehood; And grant me thy law graciously.

Psa 119:30 I have chosen the way of faithfulness: Thine ordinances have I set before me.

Psa 119:31 I cleave unto thy testimonies: O Jehovah, put me not to shame.

Psa 119:32 I will run the way of thy commandments, When thou shalt enlarge my heart.

Psa 119:33 He. Teach me, O Jehovah, the way of thy statutes; And I shall keep it unto the end.

Psa 119:34 Give me understanding, and I shall keep thy law; Yea, I shall observe it with my whole heart.

Psa 119:35 Make me to go in the path of thy commandments; For therein do I delight.

Psa 119:36 Incline my heart unto thy testimonies, And not to covetousness.

Psa 119:37 Turn away mine eyes from beholding vanity, And quicken me in thy ways.

Psa 119:38 Confirm unto thy servant thy word, Which is in order unto the fear of thee.

Psa 119:39 Turn away my reproach whereof I am afraid; For thine ordinances are good.

Psa 119:40 Behold, I have longed after thy precepts: Quicken me in thy righteousness.

Psa 119:41 Vav. Let thy lovingkindnesses also come unto me, O Jehovah, Even thy salvation, according to thy word.

Psa 119:42 So shall I have an answer for him that reproacheth me; For I trust in thy word.

Psa 119:43 And take not the word of truth utterly out of my mouth; For I have hoped in thine ordinances.

Psa 119:44 So shall I observe thy law continually For ever and ever.

Psa 119:45 And I shall walk at liberty; For I have sought thy precepts.

Psa 119:46 I will also speak of thy testimonies before kings, And shall not be put to shame.

Psa 119:47 And I will delight myself in thy commandments, Which I have loved.

Psa 119:48 I will lift up my hands also unto thy commandments, which I have loved; And I will meditate on thy statutes.

Psa 119:49 Zayin. Remember the word unto thy servant, Because thou hast made me to hope.

Psa 119:50 This is my comfort in my affliction; For thy word hath quickened me.

Psa 119:51 The proud have had me greatly in derision: Yet have I not swerved from thy law.

Psa 119:52 I have remembered thine ordinances of old, O Jehovah, And have comforted myself.

Psa 119:53 Hot indignation hath taken hold upon me, Because of the wicked that forsake thy law.

Psa 119:54 Thy statutes have been my songs In the house of my pilgrimage.

Psa 119:55 I have remembered thy name, O Jehovah, in the night, And have observed thy law.

Psa 119:56 This I have had, Because I have kept thy precepts.

Psa 119:57 Heth. Jehovah is my portion: I have said that I would observe thy words.

Psa 119:58 I entreated thy favor with my whole heart: Be merciful unto me according to thy word.

Psa 119:59 I thought on my ways, And turned my feet unto thy testimonies.

Psa 119:60 I made haste, and delayed not, To observe thy commandments.

Psa 119:61 The cords of the wicked have wrapped me round; But I have not forgotten thy law.

Psa 119:62 At midnight I will rise to give thanks unto thee Because of thy righteous ordinances.

Psa 119:63 I am a companion of all them that fear thee, And of them that observe thy precepts.

Psa 119:64 The earth, O Jehovah, is full of thy lovingkindness: Teach me thy statutes.

Psa 119:65 Teth. Thou hast dealt well with thy servant, O Jehovah, according unto thy word.

Psa 119:66 Teach me good judgment and knowledge; For I have believed in thy commandments.

Psa 119:67 Before I was afflicted I went astray; But now I observe thy word.

Psa 119:68 Thou art good, and doest good; Teach me thy statutes.

Psa 119:69 The proud have forged a lie against me: With my whole heart will I keep thy precepts.

Psa 119:70 Their heart is as fat as grease; But I delight in thy law.

Psa 119:71 It is good for me that I have been afflicted; That I may learn thy statutes.

Psa 119:72 The law of thy mouth is better unto me Than thousands of gold and silver.

Psa 119:73 Yodh. Thy hands have made me and fashioned me: Give me understanding, that I may learn thy commandments.

Psa 119:74 They that fear thee shall see me and be glad, Because I have hoped in thy word.

Psa 119:75 I know, O Jehovah, that thy judgments are righteous, And that in faithfulness thou hast afflicted me.

Psa 119:76 Let, I pray thee, thy lovingkindness be for my comfort, According to thy word unto thy servant.

Psa 119:77 Let thy tender mercies come unto me, that I may live; For thy law is my delight.

Psa 119:78 Let the proud be put to shame; for they have overthrown me wrongfully: But I will meditate on thy precepts.

Psa 119:79 Let those that fear thee turn unto me; And they shall know thy testimonies.

Psa 119:80 Let my heart be perfect in thy statutes, That I be not put to shame.

Psa 119:81 Kaph. My soul fainteth for thy salvation; But I hope in thy word.

Psa 119:82 Mine eyes fail for thy word, While I say, When wilt thou comfort me?

Psa 119:83 For I am become like a wine-skin in the smoke; Yet do I not forget thy statutes.

Psa 119:84 How many are the days of thy servant? When wilt thou execute judgment on them that persecute me?

Psa 119:85 The proud have digged pits for me, Who are not according to thy law.

Psa 119:86 All thy commandments are faithful: They persecute me wrongfully; Help thou me.

Psa 119:87 They had almost consumed me upon earth; But I forsook not thy precepts.

Psa 119:88 Quicken me after thy lovingkindness; So shall I observe the testimony of thy mouth.

Psa 119:89 Lamedh. For ever, O Jehovah, Thy word is settled in heaven.

Psa 119:90 Thy faithfulness is unto all generations: Thou hast established the earth, and it abideth.

Psa 119:91 They abide this day according to thine ordinances; For all things are thy servants.

Psa 119:92 Unless thy law had been my delight, I should then have perished in mine affliction.

Psa 119:93 I will never forget thy precepts; For with them thou hast quickened me.

Psa 119:94 I am thine, save me; For I have sought thy precepts.

Psa 119:95 The wicked have waited for me, to destroy me; But I will consider thy testimonies.

Psa 119:96 I have seen an end of all perfection; But thy commandment is exceeding broad.

Psa 119:97 Mem. Oh how love I thy law! It is my meditation all the day.

Psa 119:98 Thy commandments make me wiser than mine enemies; For they are ever with me.

Psa 119:99 I have more understanding than all my teachers; For thy testimonies are my meditation.

Psa 119:100 I understand more than the aged, Because I have kept thy precepts.

Psa 119:101 I have refrained my feet from every evil way, That I might observe thy word.

Psa 119:102 I have not turned aside from thine ordinances; For thou hast taught me.

Psa 119:103 How sweet are thy words unto my taste! Yea, sweeter than honey to my mouth!

Psa 119:104 Through thy precepts I get understanding: Therefore I hate every false way.

Psa 119:105 Nun. Thy word is a lamp unto my feet, And light unto my path.

Psa 119:106 I have sworn, and have confirmed it, That I will observe thy righteous ordinances.

Psa 119:107 I am afflicted very much: Quicken me, O Jehovah, according unto thy word.

Psa 119:108 Accept, I beseech thee, the freewill-offerings of my mouth, O Jehovah, And teach me thine ordinances.

Psa 119:109 My soul is continually in my hand; Yet do I not forget thy law.

Psa 119:110 The wicked have laid a snare for me; Yet have I not gone astray from thy precepts.

Psa 119:111 Thy testimonies have I taken as a heritage for ever; For they are the rejoicing of my heart.

Psa 119:112 I have inclined my heart to perform thy statutes For ever, even unto the end.

Psa 119:113 Samekh. I hate them that are of a double mind; But thy law do I love.

Psa 119:114 Thou art my hiding-place and my shield: I hope in thy word.

Psa 119:115 Depart from me, ye evil-doers, That I may keep the commandments of my God.

Psa 119:116 Uphold me according unto thy word, that I may live; And let me not be ashamed of my hope.

Psa 119:117 Hold thou me up, and I shall be safe, And shall have respect unto thy statutes continually.

Psa 119:118 Thou hast set at nought all them that err from thy statutes; For their deceit is falsehood.

Psa 119:119 Thou puttest away all the wicked of the earth like dross: Therefore I love thy testimonies.

Psa 119:120 My flesh trembleth for fear of thee; And I am afraid of thy judgments.

Psa 119:121 Ayin. I have done justice and righteousness: Leave me not to mine oppressors.

Psa 119:122 Be surety for thy servant for good: Let not the proud oppress me.

Psa 119:123 Mine eyes fail for thy salvation, And for thy righteous word.

Psa 119:124 Deal with thy servant according unto thy lovingkindness, And teach me thy statutes.

Psa 119:125 I am thy servant; Give me understanding, That I may know thy testimonies.

Psa 119:126 It is time for Jehovah to work; For they have made void thy law.

Psa 119:127 Therefore I love thy commandments Above gold, yea, above fine gold.

Psa 119:128 Therefore I esteem all thy precepts concerning all things to be right; And I hate every false way.

Psa 119:129 Pe. Thy testimonies are wonderful; Therefore doth my soul keep them.

Psa 119:130 The opening of thy words giveth light; It giveth understanding unto the simple.

Psa 119:131 I opened wide my mouth, and panted; For I longed for thy commandments.

Psa 119:132 Turn thee unto me, and have mercy upon me, As thou usest to do unto those that love thy name.

Psa 119:133 Establish my footsteps in thy word; And let not any iniquity have dominion over me.

Psa 119:134 Redeem me from the oppression of man: So will I observe thy precepts.

Psa 119:135 Make thy face to shine upon thy servant; And teach me thy statutes.

Psa 119:136 Streams of water run down mine eyes, Because they observe not thy law.

Psa 119:137 Tsadhe. Righteous art thou, O Jehovah, And upright are thy judgments.

Psa 119:138 Thou hast commanded thy testimonies in righteousness And very faithfulness.

Psa 119:139 My zeal hath consumed me, Because mine adversaries have forgotten thy words.

Psa 119:140 Thy word is very pure; Therefore thy servant loveth it.

Psa 119:141 I am small and despised; Yet do I not forget thy precepts.

Psa 119:142 Thy righteousness is an everlasting righteousness, And thy law is truth.

Psa 119:143 Trouble and anguish have taken hold on me; Yet thy commandments are my delight.

Psa 119:144 Thy testimonies are righteous for ever: Give me understanding, and I shall live.

Psa 119:145 Qoph. I have called with my whole heart; answer me, O Jehovah: I will keep thy statutes.

Psa 119:146 I have called unto thee; Save me, And I shall observe thy testimonies.

Psa 119:147 I anticipated the dawning of the morning, and cried: I hoped in thy words.

Psa 119:148 Mine eyes anticipated the night-watches, That I might meditate on thy word.

Psa 119:149 Hear my voice according unto thy lovingkindness: Quicken me, O Jehovah, according to thine ordinances.

Psa 119:150 They draw nigh that follow after wickedness; They are far from thy law.

Psa 119:151 Thou art nigh, O Jehovah; And all thy commandments are truth.

Psa 119:152 Of old have I known from thy testimonies, That thou hast founded them for ever.

Psa 119:153 Resh. Consider mine affliction, and deliver me; For I do not forget thy law.

Psa 119:154 Plead thou my cause, and redeem me: Quicken me according to thy word.

Psa 119:155 Salvation is far from the wicked; For they seek not thy statutes.

Psa 119:156 Great are thy tender mercies, O Jehovah: Quicken me according to thine ordinances.

Psa 119:157 Many are my persecutors and mine adversaries; Yet have I not swerved from thy testimonies.

Psa 119:158 I beheld the treacherous, and was grieved, Because they observe not thy word.

Psa 119:159 Consider how I love thy precepts: Quicken me, O Jehovah, according to thy lovingkindness.

Psa 119:160 The sum of thy word is truth; And every one of thy righteous ordinances endureth for ever.

Psa 119:161 Shin. Princes have persecuted me without a cause; But my heart standeth in awe of thy words.

Psa 119:162 I rejoice at thy word, As one that findeth great spoil.

Psa 119:163 I hate and abhor falsehood; But thy law do I love.

Psa 119:164 Seven times a day do I praise thee, Because of thy righteous ordinances.

Psa 119:165 Great peace have they that love thy law; And they have no occasion of stumbling.

Psa 119:166 I have hoped for thy salvation, O Jehovah, And have done thy commandments.

Psa 119:167 My soul hath observed thy testimonies; And I love them exceedingly.

Psa 119:168 I have observed thy precepts and thy testimonies; For all my ways are before thee.

Psa 119:169 Tav. Let my cry come near before thee, O Jehovah: Give me understanding according to thy word.

Psa 119:170 Let my supplication come before thee: Deliver me according to thy word.

Psa 119:171 Let my lips utter praise; For thou teachest me thy statutes.

Psa 119:172 Let my tongue sing of thy word; For all thy commandments are righteousness.

Psa 119:173 Let thy hand be ready to help me; For I have chosen thy precepts.

Psa 119:174 I have longed for thy salvation, O Jehovah; And thy law is my delight.

Psa 119:175 Let my soul live, and it shall praise thee; And let thine ordinances help me.

Psa 119:176 I have gone astray like a lost sheep; seek thy servant; For I do not forget thy commandments.

Chapter 120.

Psa 120:1 A Song of Ascents. In my distress I cried unto Jehovah, And he answered me.

Psa 120:2 Deliver my soul, O Jehovah, from lying lips, And from a deceitful tongue.

Psa 120:3 What shall be given unto thee, and what shall be done more unto thee, Thou deceitful tongue?

Psa 120:4 Sharp arrows of the mighty, With coals of juniper.

Psa 120:5 Woe is me, that I sojourn in Meshech, That I dwell among the tents of Kedar!

Psa 120:6 My soul hath long had her dwelling With him that hateth peace.

Psa 120:7 I am for peace: But when I speak, they are for war.

Chapter 121.

Psa 121:1 A Song of Ascents. I will lift up mine eyes unto the mountains: From whence shall my help come?

Psa 121:2 My help cometh from Jehovah, Who made heaven and earth.

Psa 121:3 He will not suffer thy foot to be moved: He that keepeth thee will not slumber.

Psa 121:4 Behold, he that keepeth Israel Will neither slumber nor sleep.

Psa 121:5 Jehovah is thy keeper: Jehovah is thy shade upon thy right hand.

Psa 121:6 The sun shall not smite thee by day, Nor the moon by night.

Psa 121:7 Jehovah will keep thee from all evil; He will keep thy soul.

Psa 121:8 Jehovah will keep thy going out and thy coming in From this time forth and for evermore.

Chapter 122.

Psa 122:1 A Song of Ascents; of David. I was glad when they said unto me, Let us go unto the house of Jehovah.

Psa 122:2 Our feet are standing Within thy gates, O Jerusalem,

Psa 122:3 Jerusalem, that art builded As a city that is compact together;

Psa 122:4 Whither the tribes go up, even the tribes of Jehovah, For an ordinance for Israel, To give thanks unto the name of Jehovah.

Psa 122:5 For there are set thrones for judgment, The thrones of the house of David.

Psa 122:6 Pray for the peace of Jerusalem: They shall prosper that love thee.

Psa 122:7 Peace be within thy walls, And prosperity within thy palaces.

Psa 122:8 For my brethren and companions' sakes, I will now say, Peace be within thee.

Psa 122:9 For the sake of the house of Jehovah our God I will seek thy good.

Chapter 123.

Psa 123:1 A Song of Ascents. Unto thee do I lift up mine eyes, O thou that sittest in the heavens.

Psa 123:2 Behold, as the eyes of servants look unto the hand of their master, As the eyes of a maid unto the hand of her mistress; So our eyes look unto Jehovah our God, Until he have mercy upon us.

Psa 123:3 Have mercy upon us, O Jehovah, have mercy upon us; For we are exceedingly filled with contempt.

Psa 123:4 Our soul is exceedingly filled With the scoffing of those that are at ease, And with the contempt of the proud.

Chapter 124.

Psa 124:1 A Song of Ascents; of David. If it had not been Jehovah who was on our side, Let Israel now say,

Psa 124:2 If it had not been Jehovah who was on our side, When men rose up against us;

Psa 124:3 Then they had swallowed us up alive, When their wrath was kindled against us;

Psa 124:4 Then the waters had overwhelmed us, The stream had gone over our soul;

Psa 124:5 Then the proud waters had gone over our soul.

Psa 124:6 Blessed be Jehovah, Who hath not given us as a prey to their teeth.

Psa 124:7 Our soul is escaped as a bird out of the snare of the fowlers: The snare is broken, and we are escaped.

Psa 124:8 Our help is in the name of Jehovah, Who made heaven and earth.

Chapter 125.

Psa 125:1 A Song of Ascents. They that trust in Jehovah Are as mount Zion, which cannot be moved, but abideth for ever.

Psa 125:2 As the mountains are round about Jerusalem, So Jehovah is round about his people From this time forth and for evermore.

Psa 125:3 For the sceptre of wickedness shall not rest upon the lot of the righteous; That the righteous put not forth their hands unto iniquity.

Psa 125:4 Do good, O Jehovah, unto those that are good, And to them that are upright in their hearts.

Psa 125:5 But as for such as turn aside unto their crooked ways, Jehovah will lead them forth with the workers of iniquity. Peace be upon Israel.

Chapter 126.

Psa 126:1 A Song of Ascents. When Jehovah brought back those that returned to Zion, We were like unto them that dream.

Psa 126:2 Then was our mouth filled with laughter, And our tongue with singing: Then said they among the nations, Jehovah hath done great things for them.

Psa 126:3 Jehovah hath done great things for us, Whereof we are glad.

Psa 126:4 Turn again our captivity, O Jehovah, As the streams in the South.

Psa 126:5 They that sow in tears shall reap in joy.

Psa 126:6 He that goeth forth and weepeth, bearing seed for sowing, Shall doubtless come again with joy, bringing his sheaves with him.

Chapter 127.

Psa 127:1 A Song of Ascents; of Solomon. Except Jehovah build the house, They labor in vain that build it: Except Jehovah keep the city, The watchman waketh but in vain.

Psa 127:2 It is vain for you to rise up early, To take rest late, To eat the bread of toil; For so he giveth unto his beloved sleep.

Psa 127:3 Lo, children are a heritage of Jehovah; And the fruit of the womb is his reward.

Psa 127:4 As arrows in the hand of a mighty man, So are the children of youth.

Psa 127:5 Happy is the man that hath his quiver full of them: They shall not be put to shame, When they speak with their enemies in the gate.

Chapter 128.

Psa 128:1 A Song of Ascents. Blessed is every one that feareth Jehovah, That walketh in his ways.

Psa 128:2 For thou shalt eat the labor of thy hands: Happy shalt thou be, and it shall be well with thee.

Psa 128:3 Thy wife shall be as a fruitful vine, In the innermost parts of thy house; Thy children like olive plants, Round about thy table.

Psa 128:4 Behold, thus shall the man be blessed That feareth Jehovah.

Psa 128:5 Jehovah bless thee out of Zion: And see thou the good of Jerusalem all the days of thy life.

Psa 128:6 Yea, see thou thy children's children. Peace be upon Israel.

Chapter 129.

Psa 129:1 Many a time have they afflicted me from my youth up, Let Israel now say,

Psa 129:2 Many a time have they afflicted me from my youth up: Yet they have not prevailed against me.

Psa 129:3 The plowers plowed upon my back; They made long their furrows.

Psa 129:4 Jehovah is righteous: He hath cut asunder the cords of the wicked.

Psa 129:5 Let them be put to shame and turned backward, All they that hate Zion.

Psa 129:6 Let them be as the grass upon the housetops, Which withereth before it groweth up;

Psa 129:7 Wherewith the reaper filleth not his hand, Nor he that bindeth sheaves his bosom.

Psa 129:8 Neither do they that go by say, The blessing of Jehovah be upon you; We bless you in the name of Jehovah.

Chapter 130.

Psa 130:1 A Song of Ascents. Out of the depths have I cried unto thee, O Jehovah.

Psa 130:2 Lord, hear my voice: Let thine ears be attentive To the voice of my supplications.

Psa 130:3 If thou, Jehovah, shouldest mark iniquities, O Lord, who could stand?

Psa 130:4 But there is forgiveness with thee, That thou mayest be feared.

Psa 130:5 I wait for Jehovah, my soul doth wait, And in his word do I hope.

Psa 130:6 My soul waiteth for the Lord More than watchmen wait for the morning; Yea, more than watchmen for the morning.

Psa 130:7 O Israel, hope in Jehovah; For with Jehovah there is lovingkindness, And with him is plenteous redemption.

Psa 130:8 And he will redeem Israel From all his iniquities.

Chapter 131.

Psa 131:1 A Song of Ascents; of David. Jehovah, my heart is not haughty, nor mine eyes lofty; Neither do I exercise myself in great matters, Or in things too wonderful for me.

Psa 131:2 Surely I have stilled and quieted my soul; Like a weaned child with his mother, Like a weaned child is my soul within me.

Psa 131:3 O Israel, hope in Jehovah From this time forth and for evermore.

Chapter 132.

Psa 132:1 A Song of Ascents. Jehovah, remember for David All his affliction;

Psa 132:2 How he sware unto Jehovah, And vowed unto the Mighty One of Jacob:

Psa 132:3 Surely I will not come into the tabernacle of my house, Nor go up into my bed;

Psa 132:4 I will not give sleep to mine eyes, Or slumber to mine eyelids;

Psa 132:5 Until I find out a place for Jehovah, A tabernacle for the Mighty One of Jacob.

Psa 132:6 Lo, we heard of it in Ephrathah: We found it in the field of the wood.

Psa 132:7 We will go into his tabernacles; We will worship at his footstool.

Psa 132:8 Arise, O Jehovah, into thy resting-place; Thou, and the ark of thy strength.

Psa 132:9 Let thy priest be clothed with righteousness; And let thy saints shout for joy.

Psa 132:10 For thy servant David's sake Turn not away the face of thine anointed.

Psa 132:11 Jehovah hath sworn unto David in truth; He will not turn from it: Of the fruit of thy body will I set upon thy throne.

Psa 132:12 If thy children will keep my covenant And my testimony that I shall teach them, Their children also shall sit upon thy throne for evermore.

Psa 132:13 For Jehovah hath chosen Zion; He hath desired it for his habitation.

Psa 132:14 This is my resting-place for ever: Here will I dwell; For I have desired it.

Psa 132:15 I will abundantly bless her provision: I will satisfy her poor with bread.

Psa 132:16 Her priests also will I clothe with salvation; And her saints shall shout aloud for joy.

Psa 132:17 There will I make the horn of David to bud: I have ordained a lamp for mine anointed.

Psa 132:18 His enemies will I clothe with shame; But upon himself shall his crown flourish.

Chapter 133.

Psa 133:1 A Song of Ascents; of David. Behold, how good and how pleasant it is For brethren to dwell together in unity!

Psa 133:2 It is like the precious oil upon the head, That ran down upon the beard, Even Aaron's beard; That came down upon the skirt of his garments;

Psa 133:3 Like the dew of Hermon, That cometh down upon the mountains of Zion: For there Jehovah commanded the blessing, Even life for evermore.

Chapter 134.

Psa 134:1 A Song of Ascents. Behold, bless ye Jehovah, all ye servants of Jehovah, That by night stand in the house of Jehovah.

Psa 134:2 Lift up your hands to the sanctuary, And bless ye Jehovah.

Psa 134:3 Jehovah bless thee out of Zion; Even he that made heaven and earth.

Chapter 135.

Psa 135:1 Praise ye Jehovah. Praise ye the name of Jehovah; Praise him, O ye servants of Jehovah,

Psa 135:2 Ye that stand in the house of Jehovah, In the courts of the house of our God.

Psa 135:3 Praise ye Jehovah; for Jehovah is good: Sing praises unto his name; for it is pleasant.

Psa 135:4 For Jehovah hath chosen Jacob unto himself, And Israel for his own possession.

Psa 135:5 For I know that Jehovah is great, And that our Lord is above all gods.

Psa 135:6 Whatsoever Jehovah pleased, that hath he done, In heaven and in earth, in the seas and in all deeps;

Psa 135:7 Who causeth the vapors to ascend from the ends of the earth; Who maketh lightnings for the rain; Who bringeth forth the wind out of his treasuries;

Psa 135:8 Who smote the first-born of Egypt, Both of man and beast;

Psa 135:9 Who sent signs and wonders into the midst of thee, O Egypt, Upon Pharaoh, and upon all his servants;

Psa 135:10 Who smote many nations, And slew mighty kings,

Psa 135:11 Sihon king of the Amorites, And Og king of Bashan, And all the kingdoms of Canaan,

Psa 135:12 And gave their land for a heritage, A heritage unto Israel his people.

Psa 135:13 Thy name, O Jehovah, endureth for ever; Thy memorial name, O Jehovah, throughout all generations.

Psa 135:14 For Jehovah will judge his people, And repent himself concerning his servants.

Psa 135:15 The idols of the nations are silver and gold, The work of men's hands.

Psa 135:16 They have mouths, but they speak not; Eyes have they, but they see not;

Psa 135:17 They have ears, but they hear not; Neither is there any breath in their mouths.

Psa 135:18 They that make them shall be like unto them; Yea, every one that trusteth in them.

Psa 135:19 O house of Israel, bless ye Jehovah: O house of Aaron, bless ye Jehovah:

Psa 135:20 O house of Levi, bless ye Jehovah: Ye that fear Jehovah, bless ye Jehovah.

Psa 135:21 Blessed be Jehovah out of Zion, Who dwelleth at Jerusalem. Praise ye Jehovah.

Chapter 136.

Psa 136:1 Oh give thanks unto Jehovah; for he is good; For his lovingkindness endureth for ever.

Psa 136:2 Oh give thanks unto the God of gods; For his lovingkindness endureth for ever.

Psa 136:3 Oh give thanks unto the Lord of lords; For his lovingkindness endureth for ever:

Psa 136:4 To him who alone doeth great wonders; For his lovingkindness endureth for ever:

Psa 136:5 To him that by understanding made the heavens; For his lovingkindness endureth for ever:

Psa 136:6 To him that spread forth the earth above the waters; For his lovingkindness endureth for ever:

Psa 136:7 To him that made great lights; For his lovingkindness endureth for ever:

Psa 136:8 The sun to rule by day; For his lovingkindness endureth for ever;

Psa 136:9 The moon and stars to rule by night; For his lovingkindness endureth for ever:

Psa 136:10 To him that smote Egypt in their first-born; For his lovingkindness endureth for ever;

Psa 136:11 And brought out Israel from among them; For his lovingkindness endureth for ever;

Psa 136:12 With a strong hand, and with an outstretched arm; For his lovingkindness endureth for ever:

Psa 136:13 To him that divided the Red Sea in sunder; For his lovingkindness endureth for ever;

Psa 136:14 And made Israel to pass through the midst of it; For his lovingkindness endureth for ever;

Psa 136:15 But overthrew Pharaoh and his host in the Red Sea; For his lovingkindness endureth for ever:

Psa 136:16 To him that led his people through the wilderness; For his lovingkindness endureth for ever:

Psa 136:17 To him that smote great kings; For his lovingkindness endureth for ever;

Psa 136:18 And slew famous kings; For his lovingkindness endureth for ever:

Psa 136:19 Sihon king of the Amorites; For his lovingkindness endureth forever;

Psa 136:20 And Og king of Bashan; For his lovingkindness endureth for ever;

Psa 136:21 And gave their land for a heritage; For his lovingkindness endureth for ever;

Psa 136:22 Even a heritage unto Israel his servant; For his lovingkindness endureth for ever:

Psa 136:23 Who remembered us in our low estate; For his lovingkindness endureth for ever;

Psa 136:24 And hath delivered us from our adversaries; For his lovingkindness endureth for ever:

Psa 136:25 Who giveth food to all flesh; For his lovingkindness endureth for ever.

Psa 136:26 Oh give thanks unto the God of heaven; For his lovingkindness endureth for ever.

Chapter 137.

Psa 137:1 By the rivers of Babylon, There we sat down, yea, we wept, When we remembered Zion.

Psa 137:2 Upon the willows in the midst thereof We hanged up our harps.

Psa 137:3 For there they that led us captive required of us songs, And they that wasted us required of us mirth, saying, Sing us one of the songs of Zion.

Psa 137:4 How shall we sing Jehovah's song In a foreign land?

Psa 137:5 If I forget thee, O Jerusalem, Let my right hand forget her skill.

Psa 137:6 Let my tongue cleave to the roof of my mouth, If I remember thee not; If I prefer not Jerusalem Above my chief joy.

Psa 137:7 Remember, O Jehovah, against the children of Edom The day of Jerusalem; Who said, Rase it, rase it, Even to the foundation thereof.

Psa 137:8 O daughter of Babylon, that art to be destroyed, Happy shall he be, that rewardeth thee As thou hast served us.

Psa 137:9 Happy shall he be, that taketh and dasheth thy little ones Against the rock.

Chapter 138.

Psa 138:1 A Psalm of David. I will give thee thanks with my whole heart: Before the gods will I sing praises unto thee.

Psa 138:2 I will worship toward thy holy temple, And give thanks unto thy name for thy lovingkindness and for thy truth: For thou hast magnified thy word above all thy name.

Psa 138:3 In the day that I called thou answeredst me, Thou didst encourage me with strength in my soul.

Psa 138:4 All the kings of the earth shall give thee thanks, O Jehovah, For they have heard the words of thy mouth.

Psa 138:5 Yea, they shall sing of the ways of Jehovah; For great is the glory of Jehovah.

Psa 138:6 For though Jehovah is high, yet hath he respect unto the lowly; But the haughty he knoweth from afar.

Psa 138:7 Though I walk in the midst of trouble, thou wilt revive me; Thou wilt stretch forth thy hand against the wrath of mine enemies, And thy right hand will save me.

Psa 138:8 Jehovah will perfect that which concerneth me: Thy lovingkindness, O Jehovah, endureth for ever; Forsake not the works of thine own hands.

Chapter 139.

Psa 139:1 For the Chief Musician. A Psalm of David. O Jehovah, thou hast searched me, and known me.

Psa 139:2 Thou knowest my downsitting and mine uprising; Thou understandest my thought afar off.

Psa 139:3 Thou searchest out my path and my lying down, And art acquainted with all my ways.

Psa 139:4 For there is not a word in my tongue, But, lo, O Jehovah, thou knowest it altogether.

Psa 139:5 Thou hast beset me behind and before, And laid thy hand upon me.

Psa 139:6 Such knowledge is too wonderful for me; It is high, I cannot attain unto it.

Psa 139:7 Whither shall I go from thy Spirit? Or whither shall I flee from thy presence?

Psa 139:8 If I ascend up into heaven, thou art there: If I make my bed in Sheol, behold, thou art there.

Psa 139:9 If I take the wings of the morning, And dwell in the uttermost parts of the sea;

Psa 139:10 Even there shall thy hand lead me, And thy right hand shall hold me.

Psa 139:11 If I say, Surely the darkness shall overwhelm me, And the light about me shall be night;

Psa 139:12 Even the darkness hideth not from thee, But the night shineth as the day: The darkness and the light are both alike to thee.

Psa 139:13 For thou didst form my inward parts: Thou didst cover me in my mother's womb.

Psa 139:14 I will give thanks unto thee; for I am fearfully and wonderfully made: Wonderful are thy works; And that my soul knoweth right well.

Psa 139:15 My frame was not hidden from thee, When I was made in secret, And curiously wrought in the lowest parts of the earth.

Psa 139:16 Thine eyes did see mine unformed substance; And in thy book they were all written, Even the days that were ordained for me, When as yet there was none of them.

Psa 139:17 How precious also are thy thoughts unto me, O God! How great is the sum of them!

Psa 139:18 If I should count them, they are more in number than the sand: When I awake, I am still with thee.

Psa 139:19 Surely thou wilt slay the wicked, O God: Depart from me therefore, ye bloodthirsty men.

Psa 139:20 For they speak against thee wickedly, And thine enemies take thy name in vain.

Psa 139:21 Do not I hate them, O Jehovah, that hate thee? And am not I grieved with those that rise up against thee?

Psa 139:22 I hate them with perfect hatred: They are become mine enemies.

Psa 139:23 Search me, O God, and know my heart: Try me, and know my thoughts;

Psa 139:24 And see if there be any wicked way in me, And lead me in the way everlasting.

Chapter 140.

Psa 140:1 For the Chief Musician. A Psalm of David. Deliver me, O Jehovah, from the evil man; Preserve me from the violent man:

Psa 140:2 Who devise mischiefs in their heart; Continually do they gather themselves together for war.

Psa 140:3 They have sharpened their tongue like a serpent; Adders' poison is under their lips. Selah.

Psa 140:4 Keep me, O Jehovah, from the hands of the wicked; Preserve me from the violent man: Who have purposed to thrust aside my steps.

Psa 140:5 The proud have hid a snare for me, and cords; They have spread a net by the wayside; They have set gins for me. Selah.

Psa 140:6 I said unto Jehovah, Thou art my God: Give ear unto the voice of my supplications, O Jehovah.

Psa 140:7 O Jehovah the Lord, the strength of my salvation, Thou hast covered my head in the day of battle.

Psa 140:8 Grant not, O Jehovah, the desires of the wicked; Further not his evil device, lest they exalt themselves. Selah.

Psa 140:9 As for the head of those that compass me about, Let the mischief of their own lips cover them.

Psa 140:10 Let burning coals fall upon them: Let them be cast into the fire, Into deep pits, whence they shall not rise.

Psa 140:11 An evil speaker shall not be established in the earth: Evil shall hunt the violent man to overthrow him.

Psa 140:12 I know that Jehovah will maintain the cause of the afflicted, And justice for the needy.

Psa 140:13 Surely the righteous shall give thanks unto thy name: The upright shall dwell in thy presence.

Chapter 141.

Psa 141:1 A Psalm of David. Jehovah, I have called upon thee; make haste unto me: Give ear unto my voice, when I call unto thee.

Psa 141:2 Let my prayer be set forth as incense before thee; The lifting up of my hands as the evening sacrifice.

Psa 141:3 Set a watch, O Jehovah, before my mouth; Keep the door of my lips.

Psa 141:4 Incline not my heart to any evil thing, To practise deeds of wickedness With men that work iniquity: And let me not eat of their dainties.

Psa 141:5 Let the righteous smite me, it shall be a kindness; And let him reprove me, it shall be as oil upon the head; Let not my head refuse it: For even in their wickedness shall my prayer continue.

Psa 141:6 Their judges are thrown down by the sides of the rock; And they shall hear my words; For they are sweet.

Psa 141:7 As when one ploweth and cleaveth the earth, Our bones are scattered at the mouth of Sheol.

Psa 141:8 For mine eyes are unto thee, O Jehovah the Lord: In thee do I take refuge; leave not my soul destitute.

Psa 141:9 Keep me from the snare which they have laid for me, And from the gins of the workers of iniquity.

Psa 141:10 Let the wicked fall into their own nets, Whilst that I withal escape.

Chapter 142.

Psa 142:1 Maschil of David, when he was in the cave; a Prayer. I cry with my voice unto Jehovah; With my voice unto Jehovah do I make supplication.

Psa 142:2 I pour out my complaint before him; I show before him my trouble.

Psa 142:3 When my spirit was overwhelmed within me, Thou knewest my path. In the way wherein I walk Have they hidden a snare for me.

Psa 142:4 Look on my right hand, and see; For there is no man that knoweth me: Refuge hath failed me; No man careth for my soul.

Psa 142:5 I cried unto thee, O Jehovah; I said, Thou art my refuge, My portion in the land of the living.

Psa 142:6 Attend unto my cry; For I am brought very low: Deliver me from my persecutors; For they are stronger than I.

Psa 142:7 Bring my soul out of prison, That I may give thanks unto thy name: The righteous shall compass me about; For thou wilt deal bountifully with me.

Chapter 143.

Psa 143:1 A Psalm of David. Hear my prayer, O Jehovah; give ear to my supplications: In thy faithfulness answer me, and in thy righteousness.

Psa 143:2 And enter not into judgment with thy servant; For in thy sight no man living is righteous.

Psa 143:3 For the enemy hath persecuted my soul; He hath smitten my life down to the ground: He hath made me to dwell in dark places, as those that have been long dead.

Psa 143:4 Therefore is my spirit overwhelmed within me; My heart within me is desolate.

Psa 143:5 I remember the days of old; I meditate on all thy doings; I muse on the work of thy hands.

Psa 143:6 I spread forth my hands unto thee: My soul thirsteth after thee, as a weary land. Selah.

Psa 143:7 Make haste to answer me, O Jehovah; my spirit faileth: Hide not thy face from me, Lest I become like them that go down into the pit.

Psa 143:8 Cause me to hear thy lovingkindness in the morning; For in thee do I trust: Cause me to know the way wherein I should walk; For I lift up my soul unto thee.

Psa 143:9 Deliver me, O Jehovah, from mine enemies: I flee unto thee to hide me.

Psa 143:10 Teach me to do thy will; For thou art my God: Thy Spirit is good; Lead me in the land of uprightness.

Psa 143:11 Quicken me, O Jehovah, for thy name's sake: In thy righteousness bring my soul out of trouble.

Psa 143:12 And in thy lovingkindness cut off mine enemies, And destroy all them that afflict my soul; For I am thy servant.

Chapter 144.

Psa 144:1 A Psalm of David. Blessed be Jehovah my rock, Who teacheth my hands to war, And my fingers to fight:

Psa 144:2 My lovingkindness, and my fortress, My high tower, and my deliverer; My shield, and he in whom I take refuge; Who subdueth my people under me.

Psa 144:3 Jehovah, what is man, that thou takest knowledge of him? Or the son of man, that thou makest account of him?

Psa 144:4 Man is like to vanity: His days are as a shadow that passeth away.

Psa 144:5 Bow thy heavens, O Jehovah, and come down: Touch the mountains, and they shall smoke.

Psa 144:6 Cast forth lightning, and scatter them; Send out thine arrows, and discomfit them.

Psa 144:7 Stretch forth thy hand from above; Rescue me, and deliver me out of great waters, Out of the hand of aliens;

Psa 144:8 Whose mouth speaketh deceit, And whose right hand is a right hand of falsehood.

Psa 144:9 I will sing a new song unto thee, O God: Upon a psaltery of ten strings will I sing praises unto thee.

Psa 144:10 Thou art he that giveth salvation unto kings; Who rescueth David his servant from the hurtful sword.

Psa 144:11 Rescue me, and deliver me out of the hand of aliens, Whose mouth speaketh deceit, And whose right hand is a right hand of falsehood.

Psa 144:12 When our sons shall be as plants grown up in their youth, And our daughters as corner-stones hewn after the fashion of a palace;

Psa 144:13 When our garners are full, affording all manner of store, And our sheep bring forth thousands and ten thousands in our fields;

Psa 144:14 When our oxen are well laden; When there is no breaking in, and no going forth, And no outcry in our streets:

Psa 144:15 Happy is the people that is in such a case; Yea, happy is the people whose God is Jehovah.

Chapter 145.

Psa 145:1 A Psalm of praise; of David. I will extol thee, my God, O King; And I will bless thy name for ever and ever.

Psa 145:2 Every day will I bless thee; And I will praise thy name for ever and ever.

Psa 145:3 Great is Jehovah, and greatly to be praised; And his greatness is unsearchable.

Psa 145:4 One generation shall laud thy works to another, And shall declare thy mighty acts.

Psa 145:5 Of the glorious majesty of thine honor, And of thy wondrous works, will I meditate.

Psa 145:6 And men shall speak of the might of thy terrible acts; And I will declare thy greatness.

Psa 145:7 They shall utter the memory of thy great goodness, And shall sing of thy righteousness.

Psa 145:8 Jehovah is gracious, and merciful; Slow to anger, and of great lovingkindness.

Psa 145:9 Jehovah is good to all; And his tender mercies are over all his works.

Psa 145:10 All thy works shall give thanks unto thee, O Jehovah; And thy saints shall bless thee.

Psa 145:11 They shall speak of the glory of thy kingdom, And talk of thy power;

Psa 145:12 To make known to the sons of men his mighty acts, And the glory of the majesty of his kingdom.

Psa 145:13   Thy kingdom is an everlasting kingdom, And thy dominion endureth throughout all generations.

Psa 145:14   Jehovah upholdeth all that fall, And raiseth up all those that are bowed down.

Psa 145:15   The eyes of all wait for thee; And thou givest them their food in due season.

Psa 145:16   Thou openest thy hand, And satisfiest the desire of every living thing.

Psa 145:17   Jehovah is righteous in all his ways, And gracious in all his works.

Psa 145:18   Jehovah is nigh unto all them that call upon him, To all that call upon him in truth.

Psa 145:19   He will fulfil the desire of them that fear him; He also will hear their cry and will save them.

Psa 145:20   Jehovah preserveth all them that love him; But all the wicked will he destroy.

Psa 145:21   My mouth shall speak the praise of Jehovah; And let all flesh bless his holy name for ever and ever.

Chapter 146.

Psa 146:1   Praise ye Jehovah. Praise Jehovah, O my soul.

Psa 146:2   While I live will I praise Jehovah: I will sing praises unto my God while I have any being.

Psa 146:3   Put not your trust in princes, Nor in the son of man, in whom there is no help.

Psa 146:4   His breath goeth forth, he returneth to his earth; In that very day his thoughts perish.

Psa 146:5   Happy is he that hath the God of Jacob for his help, Whose hope is in Jehovah his God:

Psa 146:6   Who made heaven and earth, The sea, and all that in them is; Who keepeth truth for ever;

Psa 146:7   Who executeth justice for the oppressed; Who giveth food to the hungry. Jehovah looseth the prisoners;

Psa 146:8   Jehovah openeth the eyes of the blind; Jehovah raiseth up them that are bowed down; Jehovah loveth the righteous;

Psa 146:9   Jehovah preserveth the sojourners; He upholdeth the fatherless and widow; But the way of the wicked he turneth upside down.

Psa 146:10   Jehovah will reign for ever, Thy God, O Zion, unto all generations. Praise ye Jehovah.

Chapter 147.

Psa 147:1   Praise ye Jehovah; For it is good to sing praises unto our God; For it is pleasant, and praise is comely.

Psa 147:2   Jehovah doth build up Jerusalem; He gathereth together the outcasts of Israel.

Psa 147:3   He healeth the broken in heart, And bindeth up their wounds.

Psa 147:4   He counteth the number of the stars; He calleth them all by their names.

Psa 147:5   Great is our Lord, and mighty in power; His understanding is infinite.

Psa 147:6   Jehovah upholdeth the meek: He bringeth the wicked down to the ground.

Psa 147:7 Sing unto Jehovah with thanksgiving; Sing praises upon the harp unto our God,

Psa 147:8 Who covereth the heavens with clouds, Who prepareth rain for the earth, Who maketh grass to grow upon the mountains.

Psa 147:9 He giveth to the beast his food, And to the young ravens which cry.

Psa 147:10 He delighteth not in the strength of the horse: He taketh no pleasure in the legs of a man.

Psa 147:11 Jehovah taketh pleasure in them that fear him, In those that hope in his lovingkindness.

Psa 147:12 Praise Jehovah, O Jerusalem; Praise thy God, O Zion.

Psa 147:13 For he hath strengthened the bars of thy gates; He hath blessed thy children within thee.

Psa 147:14 He maketh peace in thy borders; He filleth thee with the finest of the wheat.

Psa 147:15 He sendeth out his commandment upon earth; His word runneth very swiftly.

Psa 147:16 He giveth snow like wool; He scattereth the hoar-frost like ashes.

Psa 147:17 He casteth forth his ice like morsels: Who can stand before his cold?

Psa 147:18 He sendeth out his word, and melteth them: He causeth his wind to blow, and the waters flow.

Psa 147:19 He showeth his word unto Jacob, His statutes and his ordinances unto Israel.

Psa 147:20 He hath not dealt so with any nation; And as for his ordinances, they have not known them. Praise ye Jehovah.

Chapter 148.

Psa 148:1 Praise ye Jehovah. Praise ye Jehovah from the heavens: Praise him in the heights.

Psa 148:2 Praise ye him, all his angels: Praise ye him, all his host.

Psa 148:3 Praise ye him, sun and moon: Praise him, all ye stars of light.

Psa 148:4 Praise him, ye heavens of heavens, And ye waters that are above the heavens.

Psa 148:5 Let them praise the name of Jehovah; For he commanded, and they were created.

Psa 148:6 He hath also established them for ever and ever: He hath made a decree which shall not pass away.

Psa 148:7 Praise Jehovah from the earth, Ye sea-monsters, and all deeps.

Psa 148:8 Fire and hail, snow and vapor; Stormy wind, fulfilling his word;

Psa 148:9 Mountains and all hills; Fruitful trees and all cedars;

Psa 148:10 Beasts and all cattle; Creeping things and flying birds;

Psa 148:11 Kings of the earth and all peoples; Princes and all judges of the earth;

Psa 148:12 Both young men and virgins; Old men and children:

Psa 148:13 Let them praise the name of Jehovah; For his name alone is exalted; His glory is above the earth and the heavens.

Psa 148:14 And he hath lifted up the horn of his people, The praise of all his saints; Even of the children of Israel, a people near unto him. Praise ye Jehovah.

Chapter 149.

Psa 149:1 Praise ye Jehovah. Sing unto Jehovah a new song, And his praise in the assembly of the saints.

Psa 149:2 Let Israel rejoice in him that made him: Let the children of Zion be joyful in their King.

Psa 149:3 Let them praise his name in the dance: Let them sing praises unto him with timbrel and harp.

Psa 149:4 For Jehovah taketh pleasure in his people: He will beautify the meek with salvation.

Psa 149:5 Let the saints exult in glory: Let them sing for joy upon their beds.

Psa 149:6 Let the high praises of God be in their mouth, And a two-edged sword in their hand;

Psa 149:7 To execute vengeance upon the nations, And punishments upon the peoples;

Psa 149:8 To bind their kings with chains, And their nobles with fetters of iron;

Psa 149:9 To execute upon them the judgment written: This honor have all his saints. Praise ye Jehovah.

Chapter 150.

Psa 150:1 Praise ye Jehovah. Praise God in his sanctuary: Praise him in the firmament of his power.

Psa 150:2 Praise him for his mighty acts: Praise him according to his excellent greatness.

Psa 150:3 Praise him with trumpet sound: Praise him with psaltery and harp.

Psa 150:4 Praise him with timbrel and dance: Praise him with stringed instruments and pipe.

Psa 150:5 Praise him with loud cymbals: Praise him with high sounding cymbals.

Psa 150:6 Let everything that hath breath praise Jehovah. Praise ye Jehovah.

II. The Gospels and Their Proclamation

2. Matthew

Chapter 1.

Mat 1:1 The book of the generation of Jesus Christ, the son of David, the son of Abraham.

Mat 1:2 Abraham begat Isaac; and Isaac begat Jacob; and Jacob begat Judah and his brethren;

Mat 1:3 and Judah begat Perez and Zerah of Tamar; and Perez begat Hezron; and Hezron begat Ram;

Mat 1:4 and Ram begat Amminadab; and Amminadab begat Nahshon; and Nahshon begat Salmon;

Mat 1:5 and Salmon begat Boaz of Rahab; and Boaz begat Obed of Ruth; and Obed begat Jesse;

Mat 1:6 and Jesse begat David the king. And David begat Solomon of her that had been the wife of Uriah;

Mat 1:7 and Solomon begat Rehoboam; and Rehoboam begat Abijah; and Abijah begat Asa;

Mat 1:8 and Asa begat Jehoshaphat; and Jehoshaphat begat Joram; and Joram begat Uzziah;

Mat 1:9 and Uzziah begat Jotham; and Jotham begat Ahaz; and Ahaz begat Hezekiah;

Mat 1:10 and Hezekiah begat Manasseh; and Manasseh begat Amon; and Amon begat Josiah;

Mat 1:11 and Josiah begat Jechoniah and his brethren, at the time of the carrying away to Babylon.

Mat 1:12 And after the carrying away to Babylon, Jechoniah begat Shealtiel; and Shealtiel begat Zerubbabel;

Mat 1:13 and Zerubbabel begat Abiud; and Abiud begat Eliakim; and Eliakim begat Azor;

Mat 1:14 and Azor begat Sadoc; and Sadoc begat Achim; and Achim begat Eliud;

Mat 1:15 and Eliud begat Eleazar; and Eleazar begat Matthan; and Matthan begat Jacob;

Mat 1:16 and Jacob begat Joseph the husband of Mary, of whom was born Jesus, who is called Christ.

Mat 1:17 So all the generations from Abraham unto David are fourteen generations; and from David unto the carrying away to Babylon fourteen generations; and from the carrying away to Babylon unto the Christ fourteen generations.

Mat 1:18 Now the birth of Jesus Christ was on this wise: When his mother Mary had been betrothed to Joseph, before they came together she was found with child of the Holy Spirit.

Mat 1:19 And Joseph her husband, being a righteous man, and not willing to make her a public example, was minded to put her away privily.

Mat 1:20 But when he thought on these things, behold, an angel of the Lord appeared unto him in a dream, saying, Joseph, thou son of David, fear not to take unto thee Mary thy wife: for that which is conceived in her is of the Holy Spirit.

Mat 1:21 And she shall bring forth a son; and thou shalt call his name JESUS; for it is he that shall save his people from their sins.

Mat 1:22 Now all this is come to pass, that it might be fulfilled which was spoken by the Lord through the prophet, saying,

Mat 1:23 Behold, the virgin shall be with child, and shall bring forth a son, And they shall call his name Immanuel; which is, being interpreted, God with us.

Mat 1:24 And Joseph arose from his sleep, and did as the angel of the Lord commanded him, and took unto him his wife;

Mat 1:25 and knew her not till she had brought forth a son: and he called his name JESUS.

Chapter 2.

Mat 2:1 Now when Jesus was born in Bethlehem of Judaea in the days of Herod the king, behold, Wise-men from the east came to Jerusalem, saying,

Mat 2:2 Where is he that is born King of the Jews? for we saw his star in the east, and are come to worship him.

Mat 2:3 And when Herod the king heard it, he was troubled, and all Jerusalem with him.

Mat 2:4 And gathering together all the chief priests and scribes of the people, he inquired of them where the Christ should be born.

Mat 2:5 And they said unto him, In Bethlehem of Judaea: for thus it is written through the prophet,

Mat 2:6 And thou Bethlehem, land of Judah, Art in no wise least among the princes of Judah: For out of thee shall come forth a governor, Who shall be shepherd of my people Israel.

Mat 2:7 Then Herod privily called the Wise-men, and learned of them exactly what time the star appeared.

Mat 2:8 And he sent them to Bethlehem, and said, Go and search out exactly concerning the young child; and when ye have found him, bring me word, that I also may come and worship him.

Mat 2:9 And they, having heard the king, went their way; and lo, the star, which they saw in the east, went before them, till it came and stood over where the young child was.

Mat 2:10 And when they saw the star, they rejoiced with exceeding great joy.

Mat 2:11 And they came into the house and saw the young child with Mary his mother; and they fell down and worshipped him; and opening their treasures they offered unto him gifts, gold and frankincense and myrrh.

Mat 2:12 And being warned of God in a dream that they should not return to Herod, they departed into their own country another way.

Mat 2:13 Now when they were departed, behold, an angel of the Lord appeareth to Joseph in a dream, saying, Arise and take the young child and his mother, and flee into Egypt, and be thou there until I tell thee: for Herod will seek the young child to destroy him.

Mat 2:14 And he arose and took the young child and his mother by night, and departed into Egypt;

Mat 2:15 and was there until the death of Herod: that it might be fulfilled which was spoken by the Lord through the prophet, saying, Out of Egypt did I call my son.

Mat 2:16 Then Herod, when he saw that he was mocked of the Wise-men, was exceeding wroth, and sent forth, and slew all the male children that were in

Bethlehem, and in all the borders thereof, from two years old and under, according to the time which he had exactly learned of the Wise-men.

Mat 2:17 Then was fulfilled that which was spoken through Jeremiah the prophet, saying,

Mat 2:18 A voice was heard in Ramah, Weeping and great mourning, Rachel weeping for her children; And she would not be comforted, because they are not.

Mat 2:19 But when Herod was dead, behold, an angel of the Lord appeareth in a dream to Joseph in Egypt, saying,

Mat 2:20 Arise and take the young child and his mother, and go into the land of Israel: for they are dead that sought the young child's life.

Mat 2:21 And he arose and took the young child and his mother, and came into the land of Israel.

Mat 2:22 But when he heard that Archelaus was reigning over Judaea in the room of his father Herod, he was afraid to go thither; and being warned of God in a dream, he withdrew into the parts of Galilee,

Mat 2:23 and came and dwelt in a city called Nazareth; that it might be fulfilled which was spoken through the prophets, that he should be called a Nazarene.

Chapter 3.

Mat 3:1 And in those days cometh John the Baptist, preaching in the wilderness of Judaea, saying,

Mat 3:2 Repent ye; for the kingdom of heaven is at hand.

Mat 3:3 For this is he that was spoken of through Isaiah the prophet, saying, The voice of one crying in the wilderness, Make ye ready the way of the Lord, Make his paths straight.

Mat 3:4 Now John himself had his raiment of camel's hair, and a leathern girdle about his loins; and his food was locusts and wild honey.

Mat 3:5 Then went out unto him Jerusalem, and all Judaea, and all the region round about the Jordan;

Mat 3:6 and they were baptized of him in the river Jordan, confessing their sins.

Mat 3:7 But when he saw many of the Pharisees and Sadducees coming to his baptism, he said unto them, Ye offspring of vipers, who warned you to flee from the wrath to come?

Mat 3:8 Bring forth therefore fruit worthy of repentance:

Mat 3:9 and think not to say within yourselves, We have Abraham to our father: for I say unto you, that God is able of these stones to raise up children unto Abraham.

Mat 3:10 And even now the axe lieth at the root of the trees: every tree therefore that bringeth not forth good fruit is hewn down, and cast into the fire.

Mat 3:11 I indeed baptize you in water unto repentance: but he that cometh after me is mightier than I, whose shoes I am not worthy to bear: he shall baptize you in the Holy Spirit and in fire:

Mat 3:12 whose fan is in his hand, and he will thoroughly cleanse his threshing-floor; and he will gather his wheat into the garner, but the chaff he will burn up with unquenchable fire.

Mat 3:13 Then cometh Jesus from Galilee to the Jordan unto John, to be baptized of him.

Mat 3:14 But John would have hindered him, saying, I have need to be baptized of thee, and comest thou to me?

Mat 3:15 But Jesus answering said unto him, Suffer it now: for thus it becometh us to fulfil all righteousness. Then he suffereth him.

Mat 3:16 And Jesus when he was baptized, went up straightway from the water: and lo, the heavens were opened unto him, and he saw the Spirit of God descending as a dove, and coming upon him;

Mat 3:17 and lo, a voice out of the heavens, saying, This is my beloved Son, in whom I am well pleased.

Chapter 4.

Mat 4:1 Then was Jesus led up of the Spirit into the wilderness to be tempted of the devil.

Mat 4:2 And when he had fasted forty days and forty nights, he afterward hungered.

Mat 4:3 And the tempter came and said unto him, If thou art the Son of God, command that these stones become bread.

Mat 4:4 But he answered and said, It is written, Man shall not live by bread alone, but by every word that proceedeth out of the mouth of God.

Mat 4:5 Then the devil taketh him into the holy city; and he set him on the pinnacle of the temple,

Mat 4:6 and saith unto him, If thou art the Son of God, cast thyself down: for it is written, He shall give his angels charge concerning thee: and, On their hands they shall bear thee up, Lest haply thou dash thy foot against a stone.

Mat 4:7 Jesus said unto him, Again it is written, Thou shalt not make trial of the Lord thy God.

Mat 4:8 Again, the devil taketh him unto an exceeding high mountain, and showeth him all the kingdoms of the world, and the glory of them;

Mat 4:9 and he said unto him, All these things will I give thee, if thou wilt fall down and worship me.

Mat 4:10 Then saith Jesus unto him, Get thee hence, Satan: for it is written, Thou shalt worship the Lord thy God, and him only shalt thou serve.

Mat 4:11 Then the devil leaveth him; and behold, angels came and ministered unto him.

Mat 4:12 Now when he heard that John was delivered up, he withdrew into Galilee;

Mat 4:13 and leaving Nazareth, he came and dwelt in Capernaum, which is by the sea, in the borders of Zebulun and Naphtali:

Mat 4:14 that it might be fulfilled which was spoken through Isaiah the prophet, saying,

Mat 4:15 The land of Zebulun and the land of Naphtali, Toward the sea, beyond the Jordan, Galilee of the Gentiles,

Mat 4:16 The people that sat in darkness Saw a great light, And to them that sat in the region and shadow of death, To them did light spring up.

Mat 4:17 From that time began Jesus to preach, and to say, Repent ye; for the kingdom of heaven is at hand.

Mat 4:18 And walking by the sea of Galilee, he saw two brethren, Simon who is called Peter, and Andrew his brother, casting a net into the sea; for they were fishers.

Mat 4:19 And he saith unto them, Come ye after me, and I will make you fishers of men.

Mat 4:20 And they straightway left the nets, and followed him.

Mat 4:21 And going on from thence he saw two other brethren, James the son of Zebedee, and John his brother, in the boat with Zebedee their father, mending their nets; and he called them.

Mat 4:22 And they straightway left the boat and their father, and followed him.

Mat 4:23 And Jesus went about in all Galilee, teaching in their synagogues, and preaching the gospel of the kingdom, and healing all manner of disease and all manner of sickness among the people.

Mat 4:24 And the report of him went forth into all Syria: and they brought unto him all that were sick, holden with divers diseases and torments, possessed with demons, and epileptic, and palsied; and he healed them.

Mat 4:25 And there followed him great multitudes from Galilee and Decapolis and Jerusalem and Judaea and from beyond the Jordan.

Chapter 5.

Mat 5:1 And seeing the multitudes, he went up into the mountain: and when he had sat down, his disciples came unto him:

Mat 5:2 and he opened his mouth and taught them, saying,

Mat 5:3 Blessed are the poor in spirit: for theirs is the kingdom of heaven.

Mat 5:4 Blessed are they that mourn: for they shall be comforted.

Mat 5:5 Blessed are the meek: for they shall inherit the earth.

Mat 5:6 Blessed are they that hunger and thirst after righteousness: for they shall be filled.

Mat 5:7 Blessed are the merciful: for they shall obtain mercy.

Mat 5:8 Blessed are the pure in heart: for they shall see God.

Mat 5:9 Blessed are the peacemakers: for they shall be called sons of God.

Mat 5:10 Blessed are they that have been persecuted for righteousness' sake: for theirs is the kingdom of heaven.

Mat 5:11 Blessed are ye when men shall reproach you, and persecute you, and say all manner of evil against you falsely, for my sake.

Mat 5:12 Rejoice, and be exceeding glad: for great is your reward in heaven: for so persecuted they the prophets that were before you.

Mat 5:13 Ye are the salt of the earth: but if the salt have lost its savor, wherewith shall it be salted? it is thenceforth good for nothing, but to be cast out and trodden under foot of men.

Mat 5:14 Ye are the light of the world. A city set on a hill cannot be hid.

Mat 5:15 Neither do men light a lamp, and put it under the bushel, but on the stand; and it shineth unto all that are in the house.

Mat 5:16 Even so let your light shine before men; that they may see your good works, and glorify your Father who is in heaven.

Mat 5:17 Think not that I came to destroy the law or the prophets: I came not to destroy, but to fulfil.

Mat 5:18 For verily I say unto you, Till heaven and earth pass away, one jot or one tittle shall in no wise pass away from the law, till all things be accomplished.

Mat 5:19 Whosoever therefore shall break one of these least commandments, and shall teach men so, shall be called least in the kingdom of heaven: but whosoever shall do and teach them, he shall be called great in the kingdom of heaven.

Mat 5:20   For I say unto you, that except your righteousness shall exceed the righteousness of the scribes and Pharisees, ye shall in no wise enter into the kingdom of heaven.

Mat 5:21 Ye have heard that it was said to them of old time, Thou shalt not kill; and whosoever shall kill shall be in danger of the judgment:

Mat 5:22 but I say unto you, that every one who is angry with his brother shall be in danger of the judgment; and whosoever shall say to his brother, Raca, shall be in danger of the council; and whosoever shall say, Thou fool, shall be in danger of the hell of fire.

Mat 5:23 If therefore thou art offering thy gift at the altar, and there rememberest that thy brother hath aught against thee,

Mat 5:24 leave there thy gift before the altar, and go thy way, first be reconciled to thy brother, and then come and offer thy gift.

Mat 5:25 Agree with thine adversary quickly, while thou art with him in the way; lest haply the adversary deliver thee to the judge, and the judge deliver thee to the officer, and thou be cast into prison.

Mat 5:26 Verily I say unto thee, thou shalt by no means come out thence, till thou have paid the last farthing.

Mat 5:27 Ye have heard that it was said, Thou shalt not commit adultery:

Mat 5:28 but I say unto you, that every one that looketh on a woman to lust after her hath committed adultery with her already in his heart.

Mat 5:29 And if thy right eye causeth thee to stumble, pluck it out, and cast it from thee: for it is profitable for thee that one of thy members should perish, and not thy whole body be cast into hell.

Mat 5:30 And if thy right hand causeth thee to stumble, cut it off, and cast it from thee: for it is profitable for thee that one of thy members should perish, and not thy whole body go into hell.

Mat 5:31   It was said also, Whosoever shall put away his wife, let him give her a writing of divorcement:

Mat 5:32 but I say unto you, that every one that putteth away his wife, saving for the cause of fornication, maketh her an adulteress: and whosoever shall marry her when she is put away committeth adultery.

Mat 5:33   Again, ye have heard that it was said to them of old time, Thou shalt not forswear thyself, but shalt perform unto the Lord thine oaths:

Mat 5:34 but I say unto you, swear not at all; neither by the heaven, for it is the throne of God;

Mat 5:35 nor by the earth, for it is the footstool of his feet; nor by Jerusalem, for it is the city of the great King.

Mat 5:36 Neither shalt thou swear by thy head, for thou canst not make one hair white or black.

Mat 5:37 But let your speech be, Yea, yea; Nay, nay: and whatsoever is more than these is of the evil one.

Mat 5:38 Ye have heard that it was said, An eye for an eye, and a tooth for a tooth:

Mat 5:39 but I say unto you, resist not him that is evil: but whosoever smiteth thee on thy right cheek, turn to him the other also.

Mat 5:40 And if any man would go to law with thee, and take away thy coat, let him have thy cloak also.

Mat 5:41 And whosoever shall compel thee to go one mile, go with him two.

Mat 5:42 Give to him that asketh thee, and from him that would borrow of thee turn not thou away.

Mat 5:43 Ye have heard that it was said, Thou shalt love thy neighbor, and hate thine enemy:

Mat 5:44 but I say unto you, love your enemies, and pray for them that persecute you;

Mat 5:45 that ye may be sons of your Father who is in heaven: for he maketh his sun to rise on the evil and the good, and sendeth rain on the just and the unjust.

Mat 5:46 For if ye love them that love you, what reward have ye? do not even the publicans the same?

Mat 5:47 And if ye salute your brethren only, what do ye more than others? do not even the Gentiles the same?

Mat 5:48 Ye therefore shall be perfect, as your heavenly Father is perfect.

Chapter 6.

Mat 6:1 Take heed that ye do not your righteousness before men, to be seen of them: else ye have no reward with your Father who is in heaven.

Mat 6:2 When therefore thou doest alms, sound not a trumpet before thee, as the hypocrites do in the synagogues and in the streets, that they may have glory of men. Verily I say unto you, They have received their reward.

Mat 6:3 But when thou doest alms, let not thy left hand know what thy right hand doeth:

Mat 6:4 that thine alms may be in secret: and thy Father who seeth in secret shall recompense thee.

Mat 6:5 And when ye pray, ye shall not be as the hypocrites: for they love to stand and pray in the synagogues and in the corners of the streets, that they may be seen of men. Verily I say unto you, They have received their reward.

Mat 6:6 But thou, when thou prayest, enter into thine inner chamber, and having shut thy door, pray to thy Father who is in secret, and thy Father who seeth in secret shall recompense thee.

Mat 6:7 And in praying use not vain repetitions, as the Gentiles do: for they think that they shall be heard for their much speaking.

Mat 6:8 Be not therefore like unto them: for your Father knoweth what things ye have need of, before ye ask him.

Mat 6:9 After this manner therefore pray ye. Our Father who art in heaven, Hallowed be thy name.

Mat 6:10 Thy kingdom come. Thy will be done, as in heaven, so on earth.

Mat 6:11 Give us this day our daily bread.

Mat 6:12 And forgive us our debts, as we also have forgiven our debtors.

Mat 6:13 And bring us not into temptation, but deliver us from the evil one.

Mat 6:14 For if ye forgive men their trespasses, your heavenly Father will also forgive you.

Mat 6:15 But if ye forgive not men their trespasses, neither will your Father forgive your trespasses.

Mat 6:16 Moreover when ye fast, be not, as the hypocrites, of a sad countenance: for they disfigure their faces, that they may be seen of men to fast. Verily I say unto you, They have received their reward.

Mat 6:17 But thou, when thou fastest, anoint thy head, and wash thy face;

Mat 6:18 that thou be not seen of men to fast, but of thy Father who is in secret: and thy Father, who seeth in secret, shall recompense thee.

Mat 6:19 Lay not up for yourselves treasures upon the earth, where moth and rust consume, and where thieves break through and steal:

Mat 6:20 but lay up for yourselves treasures in heaven, where neither moth nor rust doth consume, and where thieves do not break through nor steal:

Mat 6:21 for where thy treasure is, there will thy heart be also.

Mat 6:22 The lamp of the body is the eye: if therefore thine eye be single, thy whole body shall be full of light.

Mat 6:23 But if thine eye be evil, thy whole body shall be full of darkness. If therefore the light that is in thee be darkness, how great is the darkness!

Mat 6:24 No man can serve two masters; for either he will hate the one, and love the other; or else he will hold to one, and despise the other. Ye cannot serve God and mammon.

Mat 6:25 Therefore I say unto you, be not anxious for your life, what ye shall eat, or what ye shall drink; nor yet for your body, what ye shall put on. Is not the life more than the food, and the body than the raiment?

Mat 6:26 Behold the birds of the heaven, that they sow not, neither do they reap, nor gather into barns; and your heavenly Father feedeth them. Are not ye of much more value then they?

Mat 6:27 And which of you by being anxious can add one cubit unto the measure of his life?

Mat 6:28 And why are ye anxious concerning raiment? Consider the lilies of the field, how they grow; they toil not, neither do they spin:

Mat 6:29 yet I say unto you, that even Solomon in all his glory was not arrayed like one of these.

Mat 6:30 But if God doth so clothe the grass of the field, which to-day is, and to-morrow is cast into the oven, shall he not much more clothe you, O ye of little faith?

Mat 6:31 Be not therefore anxious, saying, What shall we eat? or, What shall we drink? or, Wherewithal shall we be clothed?

Mat 6:32 For after all these things do the Gentiles seek; for your heavenly Father knoweth that ye have need of all these things.

Mat 6:33 But seek ye first his kingdom, and his righteousness; and all these things shall be added unto you.

Mat 6:34 Be not therefore anxious for the morrow: for the morrow will be anxious for itself. Sufficient unto the day is the evil thereof.

Chapter 7.

Mat 7:1 Judge not, that ye be not judged.

Mat 7:2 For with what judgment ye judge, ye shall be judged: and with what measure ye mete, it shall be measured unto you.

Mat 7:3 And why beholdest thou the mote that is in thy brother's eye, but considerest not the beam that is in thine own eye?

Mat 7:4 Or how wilt thou say to thy brother, Let me cast out the mote out of thine eye; and lo, the beam is in thine own eye?

Mat 7:5 Thou hypocrite, cast out first the beam out of thine own eye; and then shalt thou see clearly to cast out the mote out of thy brother's eye.

Mat 7:6 Give not that which is holy unto the dogs, neither cast your pearls before the swine, lest haply they trample them under their feet, and turn and rend you.

Mat 7:7 Ask, and it shall be given you; seek, and ye shall find; knock, and it shall be opened unto you:

Mat 7:8 for every one that asketh receiveth; and he that seeketh findeth; and to him that knocketh it shall be opened.

Mat 7:9 Or what man is there of you, who, if his son shall ask him for a loaf, will give him a stone;

Mat 7:10 or if he shall ask for a fish, will give him a serpent?

Mat 7:11 If ye then, being evil, know how to give good gifts unto your children, how much more shall your Father who is in heaven give good things to them that ask him?

Mat 7:12 All things therefore whatsoever ye would that men should do unto you, even so do ye also unto them: for this is the law and the prophets.

Mat 7:13 Enter ye in by the narrow gate: for wide is the gate, and broad is the way, that leadeth to destruction, and many are they that enter in thereby.

Mat 7:14 For narrow is the gate, and straitened the way, that leadeth unto life, and few are they that find it.

Mat 7:15 Beware of false prophets, who come to you in sheep's clothing, but inwardly are ravening wolves.

Mat 7:16 By their fruits ye shall know them. Do men gather grapes of thorns, or figs of thistles?

Mat 7:17 Even so every good tree bringeth forth good fruit; but the corrupt tree bringeth forth evil fruit.

Mat 7:18 A good tree cannot bring forth evil fruit, neither can a corrupt tree bring forth good fruit.

Mat 7:19 Every tree that bringeth not forth good fruit is hewn down, and cast into the fire.

Mat 7:20 Therefore by their fruits ye shall know them.

Mat 7:21 Not every one that saith unto me, Lord, Lord, shall enter into the kingdom of heaven; but he that doeth the will of my Father who is in heaven.

Mat 7:22 Many will say to me in that day, Lord, Lord, did we not prophesy by thy name, and by thy name cast out demons, and by thy name do many mighty works?

Mat 7:23 And then will I profess unto them, I never knew you: depart from me, ye that work iniquity.

Mat 7:24 Every one therefore that heareth these words of mine, and doeth them, shall be likened unto a wise man, who built his house upon the rock:

Mat 7:25 and the rain descended, and the floods came, and the winds blew, and beat upon that house; and if fell not: for it was founded upon the rock.

Mat 7:26 And every one that heareth these words of mine, and doeth them not, shall be likened unto a foolish man, who built his house upon the sand:

Mat 7:27 and the rain descended, and the floods came, and the winds blew, and smote upon that house; and it fell: and great was the fall thereof.

Mat 7:28 And it came to pass, when Jesus had finished these words, the multitudes were astonished at his teaching:

Mat 7:29 for he taught them as one having authority, and not as their scribes.

Chapter 8.

Mat 8:1 And when he was come down from the mountain, great multitudes followed him.

Mat 8:2 And behold, there came to him a leper and worshipped him, saying, Lord, if thou wilt, thou canst make me clean.

Mat 8:3 And he stretched forth his hand, and touched him, saying, I will; be thou made clean. And straightway his leprosy was cleansed.

Mat 8:4 And Jesus saith unto him, See thou tell no man; but go, show thyself to the priest, and offer the gift that Moses commanded, for a testimony unto them.

Mat 8:5 And when he was entered into Capernaum, there came unto him a centurion, beseeching him,

Mat 8:6 and saying, Lord, my servant lieth in the house sick of the palsy, grievously tormented.

Mat 8:7 And he saith unto him, I will come and heal him.

Mat 8:8 And the centurion answered and said, Lord, I am not worthy that thou shouldest come under my roof; but only say the word, and my servant shall be healed.

Mat 8:9 For I also am a man under authority, having under myself soldiers: and I say to this one, Go, and he goeth; and to another, Come, and he cometh; and to my servant, Do this, and he doeth it.

Mat 8:10 And when Jesus heard it, he marvelled, and said to them that followed, Verily I say unto you, I have not found so great faith, no, not in Israel.

Mat 8:11 And I say unto you, that many shall come from the east and the west, and shall sit down with Abraham, and Isaac, and Jacob, in the kingdom of heaven:

Mat 8:12 but the sons of the kingdom shall be cast forth into the outer darkness: there shall be the weeping and the gnashing of teeth.

Mat 8:13 And Jesus said unto the centurion, Go thy way; as thou hast believed, so be it done unto thee. And the servant was healed in that hour.

Mat 8:14 And when Jesus was come into Peter's house, he saw his wife's mother lying sick of a fever.

Mat 8:15 And he touched her hand, and the fever left her; and she arose, and ministered unto him.

Mat 8:16 And when even was come, they brought unto him many possessed with demons: and he cast out the spirits with a word, and healed all that were sick:

Mat 8:17 that it might be fulfilled which was spoken through Isaiah the prophet, saying: Himself took our infirmities, and bare our diseases.

Mat 8:18 Now when Jesus saw great multitudes about him, he gave commandment to depart unto the other side.

Mat 8:19 And there came a scribe, and said unto him, Teacher, I will follow thee whithersoever thou goest.

Mat 8:20 And Jesus saith unto him, The foxes have holes, and the birds of the heaven have nests; but the Son of man hath not where to lay his head.

Mat 8:21 And another of the disciples said unto him, Lord, suffer me first to go and bury my father.

Mat 8:22 But Jesus saith unto him, Follow me; and leave the dead to bury their own dead.

Mat 8:23 And when he was entered into a boat, his disciples followed him.

Mat 8:24 And behold, there arose a great tempest in the sea, insomuch that the boat was covered with the waves: but he was asleep.

Mat 8:25 And they came to him, and awoke him, saying, Save, Lord; we perish.

Mat 8:26 And he saith unto them, Why are ye fearful, O ye of little faith? Then he arose, and rebuked the winds and the sea; and there was a great calm.

Mat 8:27 And the men marvelled, saying, What manner of man is this, that even the winds and the sea obey him?

Mat 8:28 And when he was come to the other side into the country of the Gadarenes, there met him two possessed with demons, coming forth out of the tombs, exceeding fierce, so that no man could pass by that way.

Mat 8:29 And behold, they cried out, saying, What have we to do with thee, thou Son of God? art thou come hither to torment us before the time?

Mat 8:30 Now there was afar off from them a herd of many swine feeding.

Mat 8:31 And the demons besought him, saying, If thou cast us out, send us away into the herd of swine.

Mat 8:32 And he said unto them, Go. And they came out, and went into the swine: and behold, the whole herd rushed down the steep into the sea, and perished in the waters.

Mat 8:33 And they that fed them fled, and went away into the city, and told everything, and what was befallen to them that were possessed with demons.

Mat 8:34 And behold, all the city came out to meet Jesus: and when they saw him, they besought him that he would depart from their borders.

Chapter 9.

Mat 9:1 And he entered into a boat, and crossed over, and came into his own city.

Mat 9:2 And behold, they brought to him a man sick of the palsy, lying on a bed: and Jesus seeing their faith said unto the sick of the palsy, Son, be of good cheer; thy sins are forgiven.

Mat 9:3 And behold, certain of the scribes said within themselves, This man blasphemeth.

Mat 9:4 And Jesus knowing their thoughts said, Wherefore think ye evil in your hearts?

Mat 9:5 For which is easier, to say, Thy sins are forgiven; or to say, Arise, and walk?

Mat 9:6 But that ye may know that the Son of man hath authority on earth to forgive sins (then saith he to the sick of the palsy), Arise, and take up thy bed, and go up unto thy house.

Mat 9:7 And he arose, and departed to his house.

Mat 9:8 But when the multitudes saw it, they were afraid, and glorified God, who had given such authority unto men.

Mat 9:9 And as Jesus passed by from thence, he saw a man, called Matthew, sitting at the place of toll: and he saith unto him, Follow me. And he arose, and followed him.

Mat 9:10 And it came to pass, as he sat at meat in the house, behold, many publicans and sinners came and sat down with Jesus and his disciples.

Mat 9:11 And when the Pharisees saw it, they said unto his disciples, Why eateth your Teacher with the publicans and sinners?

Mat 9:12 But when he heard it, he said, They that are whole have no need of a physician, but they that are sick.

Mat 9:13 But go ye and learn what this meaneth, I desire mercy, and not sacrifice, for I came not to call the righteous, but sinners.

Mat 9:14 Then come to him the disciples of John, saying, Why do we and the Pharisees fast oft, but thy disciples fast not?

Mat 9:15 And Jesus said unto them, Can the sons of the bridechamber mourn, as long as the bridegroom is with them? but the days will come, when the bridegroom shall be taken away from them, and then will they fast.

Mat 9:16 And no man putteth a piece of undressed cloth upon an old garment; for that which should fill it up taketh from the garment, and a worse rent is made.

Mat 9:17 Neither do men put new wine into old wine-skins: else the skins burst, and the wine is spilled, and the skins perish: but they put new wine into fresh wine-skins, and both are preserved.

Mat 9:18 While he spake these things unto them, behold, there came a ruler, and worshipped him, saying, My daughter is even now dead: but come and lay thy hand upon her, and she shall live.

Mat 9:19 And Jesus arose, and followed him, and so did his disciples.

Mat 9:20 And behold, a woman, who had an issue of blood twelve years, came behind him, and touched the border of his garment:

Mat 9:21 for she said within herself, If I do but touch his garment, I shall be made whole.

Mat 9:22 But Jesus turning and seeing her said, Daughter, be of good cheer; thy faith hath made thee whole. And the woman was made whole from that hour.

Mat 9:23 And when Jesus came into the ruler's house, and saw the flute-players, and the crowd making a tumult,

Mat 9:24 he said, Give place: for the damsel is not dead, but sleepeth. And they laughed him to scorn.

Mat 9:25 But when the crowd was put forth, he entered in, and took her by the hand; and the damsel arose.

Mat 9:26 And the fame hereof went forth into all that land.

Mat 9:27 And as Jesus passed by from thence, two blind men followed him, crying out, and saying, Have mercy on us, thou son of David.

Mat 9:28 And when he was come into the house, the blind men came to him: and Jesus saith unto them, Believe ye that I am able to do this? They say unto him, Yea, Lord.

Mat 9:29 Then touched he their eyes, saying, According to your faith be it done unto you.

Mat 9:30 And their eyes were opened. And Jesus strictly charged them, saying, See that no man know it.

Mat 9:31 But they went forth, and spread abroad his fame in all that land.

Mat 9:32 And as they went forth, behold, there was brought to him a dumb man possessed with a demon.

Mat 9:33 And when the demon was cast out, the dumb man spake: and the multitudes marvelled, saying, It was never so seen in Israel.

Mat 9:34 But the Pharisees said, By the prince of the demons casteth he out demons.

Mat 9:35 And Jesus went about all the cities and the villages, teaching in their synagogues, and preaching the gospel of the kingdom, and healing all manner of disease and all manner of sickness.

Mat 9:36 But when he saw the multitudes, he was moved with compassion for them, because they were distressed and scattered, as sheep not having a shepherd.

Mat 9:37 Then saith he unto his disciples, The harvest indeed is plenteous, but the laborers are few.

Mat 9:38 Pray ye therefore the Lord of the harvest, that he send forth laborers into his harvest.

Chapter 10.

Mat 10:1 And he called unto him his twelve disciples, and gave them authority over unclean spirits, to cast them out, and to heal all manner of disease and all manner of sickness.

Mat 10:2 Now the names of the twelve apostles are these: The first, Simon, who is called Peter, and Andrew his brother; James the son of Zebedee, and John his brother;

Mat 10:3 Philip, and Bartholomew; Thomas, and Matthew the publican; James the son of Alphaeus, and Thaddaeus;

Mat 10:4 Simon the Cananaean, and Judas Iscariot, who also betrayed him.

Mat 10:5 These twelve Jesus sent forth, and charged them, saying, Go not into any way of the Gentiles, and enter not into any city of the Samaritans:

Mat 10:6 but go rather to the lost sheep of the house of Israel.

Mat 10:7 And as ye go, preach, saying, The kingdom of heaven is at hand.

Mat 10:8 Heal the sick, raise the dead, cleanse the lepers, cast out demons: freely ye received, freely give.

Mat 10:9 Get you no gold, nor silver, nor brass in your purses;

Mat 10:10 no wallet for your journey, neither two coats, nor shoes, nor staff: for the laborer is worthy of his food.

Mat 10:11 And into whatsoever city or village ye shall enter, search out who in it is worthy; and there abide till ye go forth.

Mat 10:12 And as ye enter into the house, salute it.

Mat 10:13 And if the house be worthy, let your peace come upon it: but if it be not worthy, let your peace return to you.

Mat 10:14 And whosoever shall not receive you, nor hear your words, as ye go forth out of that house or that city, shake off the dust of your feet.

Mat 10:15 Verily I say unto you, It shall be more tolerable for the land of Sodom and Gomorrah in the day of judgment, than for that city.

Mat 10:16 Behold, I send you forth as sheep in the midst of wolves: be ye therefore wise as serpents, and harmless as doves.

Mat 10:17 But beware of men: for they will deliver you up to councils, and in their synagogues they will scourge you;

Mat 10:18 yea and before governors and kings shall ye be brought for my sake, for a testimony to them and to the Gentiles.

Mat 10:19 But when they deliver you up, be not anxious how or what ye shall speak: for it shall be given you in that hour what ye shall speak.

Mat 10:20 For it is not ye that speak, but the Spirit of your Father that speaketh in you.

Mat 10:21 And brother shall deliver up brother to death, and the father his child: and children shall rise up against parents, and cause them to be put to death.

Mat 10:22 And ye shall be hated of all men for my name's sake: but he that endureth to the end, the same shall be saved.

Mat 10:23 But when they persecute you in this city, flee into the next: for verily I say unto you, Ye shall not have gone through the cities of Israel, till the Son of man be come.

Mat 10:24 A disciple is not above his teacher, nor a servant above his lord.

Mat 10:25 It is enough for the disciple that he be as his teacher, and the servant as his lord. If they have called the master of the house Beelzebub, how much more them of his household!

Mat 10:26 Fear them not therefore: for there is nothing covered, that shall not be revealed; and hid, that shall not be known.

Mat 10:27 What I tell you in the darkness, speak ye in the light; and what ye hear in the ear, proclaim upon the house-tops.

Mat 10:28 And be not afraid of them that kill the body, but are not able to kill the soul: but rather fear him who is able to destroy both soul and body in hell.

Mat 10:29 Are not two sparrows sold for a penny? and not one of them shall fall on the ground without your Father:

Mat 10:30 but the very hairs of your head are all numbered.

Mat 10:31 Fear not therefore: ye are of more value than many sparrows.

Mat 10:32 Every one therefore who shall confess me before men, him will I also confess before my Father who is in heaven.

Mat 10:33 But whosoever shall deny me before men, him will I also deny before my Father who is in heaven.

Mat 10:34 Think not that I came to send peace on the earth: I came not to send peace, but a sword.

Mat 10:35 For I came to set a man at variance against his father, and the daughter against her mother, and the daughter in law against her mother in law:

Mat 10:36 and a man's foes shall be they of his own household.

Mat 10:37 He that loveth father or mother more than me is not worthy of me; and he that loveth son or daughter more than me is not worthy of me.

Mat 10:38 And he that doth not take his cross and follow after me, is not worthy of me.

Mat 10:39 He that findeth his life shall lose it; and he that loseth his life for my sake shall find it.

Mat 10:40 He that receiveth you receiveth me, and he that receiveth me receiveth him that sent me.

Mat 10:41 He that receiveth a prophet in the name of a prophet shall receive a prophet's reward: and he that receiveth a righteous man in the name of a righteous man shall receive a righteous man's reward.

Mat 10:42 And whosoever shall give to drink unto one of these little ones a cup of cold water only, in the name of a disciple, verily I say unto you he shall in no wise lose his reward.

Chapter 11.

Mat 11:1 And it came to pass when Jesus had finished commanding his twelve disciples, he departed thence to teach and preach in their cities.

Mat 11:2 Now when John heard in the prison the works of the Christ, he sent by his disciples

Mat 11:3 and said unto him, Art thou he that cometh, or look we for another?

Mat 11:4 And Jesus answered and said unto them, Go and tell John the things which ye hear and see:

Mat 11:5 the blind receive their sight, and the lame walk, the lepers are cleansed, and the deaf hear, and the dead are raised up, and the poor have good tidings preached to them.

Mat 11:6 And blessed is he, whosoever shall find no occasion of stumbling in me.

Mat 11:7 And as these went their way, Jesus began to say unto the multitudes concerning John, What went ye out into the wilderness to behold? a reed shaken with the wind?

Mat 11:8 But what went ye out to see? a man clothed in soft raiment? Behold, they that wear soft raiment are in king's houses.

Mat 11:9 But wherefore went ye out? to see a prophet? Yea, I say unto you, and much more than a prophet.

Mat 11:10 This is he, of whom it is written, Behold, I send my messenger before thy face, Who shall prepare thy way before thee.

Mat 11:11 Verily I say unto you, Among them that are born of women there hath not arisen a greater than John the Baptist: yet he that is but little in the kingdom of heaven is greater than he.

Mat 11:12 And from the days of John the Baptist until now the kingdom of heaven suffereth violence, and men of violence take it by force.

Mat 11:13 For all the prophets and the law prophesied until John.

Mat 11:14 And if ye are willing to receive it, this is Elijah, that is to come.

Mat 11:15 He that hath ears to hear, let him hear.

Mat 11:16 But whereunto shall I liken this generation? It is like unto children sitting in the marketplaces, who call unto their fellows

Mat 11:17 and say, We piped unto you, and ye did not dance; we wailed, and ye did not mourn.

Mat 11:18 For John came neither eating nor drinking, and they say, He hath a demon.

Mat 11:19 The Son of man came eating and drinking, and they say, Behold, a gluttonous man and a winebibber, a friend of publicans and sinners! And wisdom is justified by her works.

Mat 11:20 Then began he to upbraid the cities wherein most of his mighty works were done, because they repented not.

Mat 11:21 Woe unto thee, Chorazin! woe unto thee, Bethsaida! for if the mighty works had been done in Tyre and Sidon which were done in you, they would have repented long ago in sackcloth and ashes.

Mat 11:22 But I say unto you, it shall be more tolerable for Tyre and Sidon in the day of judgment than for you.

Mat 11:23 And thou, Capernaum, shalt thou be exalted unto heaven? thou shalt go down unto Hades: for if the mighty works had been done in Sodom which were done in thee, it would have remained until this day.

Mat 11:24 But I say unto you that it shall be more tolerable for the land of Sodom in the day of judgment, than for thee.

Mat 11:25 At that season Jesus answered and said, I thank thee, O Father, Lord of heaven and earth, that thou didst hide these things from the wise and understanding, and didst reveal them unto babes:

Mat 11:26 yea, Father, for so it was well-pleasing in thy sight.

Mat 11:27 All things have been delivered unto me of my Father: and no one knoweth the Son, save the Father; neither doth any know the Father, save the Son, and he to whomsoever the Son willeth to reveal him.

Mat 11:28 Come unto me, all ye that labor and are heavy laden, and I will give you rest.

Mat 11:29 Take my yoke upon you, and learn of me; for I am meek and lowly in heart: and ye shall find rest unto your souls.

Mat 11:30 For my yoke is easy, and my burden is light.

Chapter 12.

Mat 12:1 At that season Jesus went on the sabbath day through the grainfields; and his disciples were hungry and began to pluck ears and to eat.

Mat 12:2 But the Pharisees, when they saw it, said unto him, Behold, thy disciples do that which it is not lawful to do upon the sabbath.

Mat 12:3 But he said unto them, Have ye not read what David did, when he was hungry, and they that were with him;

Mat 12:4 how he entered into the house of God, and ate the showbread, which it was not lawful for him to eat, neither for them that were with him, but only for the priests?

Mat 12:5 Or have ye not read in the law, that on the sabbath day the priests in the temple profane the sabbath, and are guiltless?

Mat 12:6 But I say unto you, that one greater than the temple is here.

Mat 12:7 But if ye had known what this meaneth, I desire mercy, and not sacrifice, ye would not have condemned the guiltless.

Mat 12:8 For the Son of man is lord of the sabbath.

Mat 12:9 And he departed thence, and went into their synagogue:

Mat 12:10 and behold, a man having a withered hand. And they asked him, saying, Is it lawful to heal on the sabbath day? that they might accuse him.

Mat 12:11 And he said unto them, What man shall there be of you, that shall have one sheep, and if this fall into a pit on the sabbath day, will he not lay hold on it, and lift it out?

Mat 12:12 How much then is a man of more value than a sheep! Wherefore it is lawful to do good on the sabbath day.

Mat 12:13 Then saith he to the man, Stretch forth thy hand. And he stretched it forth; and it was restored whole, as the other.

Mat 12:14 But the Pharisees went out, and took counsel against him, how they might destroy him.

Mat 12:15 And Jesus perceiving it withdrew from thence: and many followed him; and he healed them all,

Mat 12:16 and charged them that they should not make him known:

Mat 12:17 that it might be fulfilled which was spoken through Isaiah the prophet, saying,

Mat 12:18 Behold, my servant whom I have chosen; My beloved in whom my soul is well pleased: I will put my Spirit upon him, And he shall declare judgment to the Gentiles.

Mat 12:19 He shall not strive, nor cry aloud; Neither shall any one hear his voice in the streets.

Mat 12:20 A bruised reed shall he not break, And smoking flax shall he not quench, Till he send forth judgment unto victory.

Mat 12:21 And in his name shall the Gentiles hope.

Mat 12:22 Then was brought unto him one possessed with a demon, blind and dumb: and he healed him, insomuch that the dumb man spake and saw.

Mat 12:23 And all the multitudes were amazed, and said, Can this be the son of David?

Mat 12:24 But when the Pharisees heard it, they said, This man doth not cast out demons, but by Beelzebub the prince of the demons.

Mat 12:25 And knowing their thoughts he said unto them, Every kingdom divided against itself is brought to desolation; and every city or house divided against itself shall not stand:

Mat 12:26 and if Satan casteth out Satan, he is divided against himself; how then shall his kingdom stand?

Mat 12:27 And if I by Beelzebub cast out demons, by whom do your sons cast them out? therefore shall they be your judges.

Mat 12:28 But if I by the Spirit of God cast out demons, then is the kingdom of God come upon you.

Mat 12:29 Or how can one enter into the house of the strong man, and spoil his goods, except he first bind the strong man? and then he will spoil his house.

Mat 12:30 He that is not with me is against me, and he that gathereth not with me scattereth.

Mat 12:31 Therefore I say unto you, Every sin and blasphemy shall be forgiven unto men; but the blasphemy against the Spirit shall not be forgiven.

Mat 12:32 And whosoever shall speak a word against the Son of man, it shall be forgiven him; but whosoever shall speak against the Holy Spirit, it shall not be forgiven him, neither in this world, nor in that which is to come.

Mat 12:33 Either make the tree good, and its fruit good; or make the tree corrupt, and its fruit corrupt: for the tree is known by its fruit.

Mat 12:34 Ye offspring of vipers, how can ye, being evil, speak good things? for out of the abundance of the heart the mouth speaketh.

Mat 12:35 The good man out of his good treasure bringeth forth good things: and the evil man out of his evil treasure bringeth forth evil things.

Mat 12:36 And I say unto you, that every idle word that men shall speak, they shall give account thereof in the day of judgment.

Mat 12:37 For by thy words thou shalt be justified, and by thy words thou shalt be condemned.

Mat 12:38 Then certain of the scribes and Pharisees answered him, saying, Teacher, we would see a sign from thee.

Mat 12:39 But he answered and said unto them, An evil and adulterous generation seeketh after a sign; and there shall no sign be given it but the sign of Jonah the prophet:

Mat 12:40 for as Jonah was three days and three nights in the belly of the whale; so shall the Son of man be three days and three nights in the heart of the earth.

Mat 12:41 The men of Nineveh shall stand up in the judgment with this generation, and shall condemn it: for they repented at the preaching of Jonah; and behold, a greater than Jonah is here.

Mat 12:42 The queen of the south shall rise up in the judgment with this generation, and shall condemn it: for she came from the ends of the earth to hear the wisdom of Solomon; and behold, a greater than Solomon is here.

Mat 12:43 But the unclean spirit, when he is gone out of the man, passeth through waterless places, seeking rest, and findeth it not.

Mat 12:44 Then he saith, I will return into my house whence I came out; and when he is come, he findeth it empty, swept, and garnished.

Mat 12:45 Then goeth he, and taketh with himself seven other spirits more evil than himself, and they enter in and dwell there: and the last state of that man becometh worse than the first. Even so shall it be also unto this evil generation.

Mat 12:46 While he was yet speaking to the multitudes, behold, his mother and his brethren stood without, seeking to speak to him.

Mat 12:47 And one said unto him, Behold, thy mother and thy brethren stand without, seeking to speak to thee.

Mat 12:48 But he answered and said unto him that told him, Who is my mother? and who are my brethren?

Mat 12:49 And he stretched forth his hand towards his disciples, and said, Behold, my mother and my brethren!

Mat 12:50 For whosoever shall do the will of my Father who is in heaven, he is my brother, and sister, and mother.

Chapter 13.

Mat 13:1 On that day went Jesus out of the house, and sat by the sea side.

Mat 13:2 And there were gathered unto him great multitudes, so that he entered into a boat, and sat; and all the multitude stood on the beach.

Mat 13:3 And he spake to them many things in parables, saying, Behold, the sower went forth to sow;

Mat 13:4 and as he sowed, some seeds fell by the way side, and the birds came and devoured them:

Mat 13:5 and others fell upon the rocky places, where they had not much earth: and straightway they sprang up, because they had no deepness of earth:

Mat 13:6 and when the sun was risen, they were scorched; and because they had no root, they withered away.

Mat 13:7 And others fell upon the thorns; and the thorns grew up and choked them:

Mat 13:8 and others fell upon the good ground, and yielded fruit, some a hundredfold, some sixty, some thirty.

Mat 13:9 He that hath ears, let him hear.

Mat 13:10 And the disciples came, and said unto him, Why speakest thou unto them in parables?

Mat 13:11 And he answered and said unto them, Unto you it is given to know the mysteries of the kingdom of heaven, but to them it is not given.

Mat 13:12 For whosoever hath, to him shall be given, and he shall have abundance: but whosoever hath not, from him shall be taken away even that which he hath.

Mat 13:13 Therefore speak I to them in parables; because seeing they see not, and hearing they hear not, neither do they understand.

Mat 13:14 And unto them is fulfilled the prophecy of Isaiah, which saith, By hearing ye shall hear, and shall in no wise understand; And seeing ye shall see, and shall in no wise perceive:

Mat 13:15 For this people's heart is waxed gross, And their ears are dull of hearing, And their eyes they have closed; Lest haply they should perceive with their eyes, And hear with their ears, And understand with their heart, And should turn again, And I should heal them.

Mat 13:16 But blessed are your eyes, for they see; and your ears, for they hear.

Mat 13:17 For verily I say unto you, that many prophets and righteous men desired to see the things which ye see, and saw them not; and to hear the things which ye hear, and heard them not.

Mat 13:18 Hear then ye the parable of the sower.

Mat 13:19 When any one heareth the word of the kingdom, and understandeth it not, then cometh the evil one, and snatcheth away that which hath been sown in his heart. This is he that was sown by the way side.

Mat 13:20 And he that was sown upon the rocky places, this is he that heareth the word, and straightway with joy receiveth it;

Mat 13:21   yet hath he not root in himself, but endureth for a while; and when tribulation or persecution ariseth because of the word, straightway he stumbleth.

Mat 13:22 And he that was sown among the thorns, this is he that heareth the word; and the care of the world, and the deceitfulness of riches, choke the word, and he becometh unfruitful.

Mat 13:23 And he that was sown upon the good ground, this is he that heareth the word, and understandeth it; who verily beareth fruit, and bringeth forth, some a hundredfold, some sixty, some thirty.

Mat 13:24 Another parable set he before them, saying, The kingdom of heaven is likened unto a man that sowed good seed in his field:

Mat 13:25   but while men slept, his enemy came and sowed tares also among the wheat, and went away.

Mat 13:26 But when the blade sprang up and brought forth fruit, then appeared the tares also.

Mat 13:27 And the servants of the householder came and said unto him, Sir, didst thou not sow good seed in thy field? whence then hath it tares?

Mat 13:28 And he said unto them, An enemy hath done this. And the servants say unto him, Wilt thou then that we go and gather them up?

Mat 13:29 But he saith, Nay; lest haply while ye gather up the tares, ye root up the wheat with them.

Mat 13:30 Let both grow together until the harvest: and in the time of the harvest I will say to the reapers, Gather up first the tares, and bind them in bundles to burn them; but gather the wheat into my barn.

Mat 13:31 Another parable set he before them, saying, The kingdom of heaven is like unto a grain of mustard seed, which a man took, and sowed in his field:

Mat 13:32 which indeed is less than all seeds; but when it is grown, it is greater than the herbs, and becometh a tree, so that the birds of the heaven come and lodge in the branches thereof.

Mat 13:33 Another parable spake he unto them; The kingdom of heaven is like unto leaven, which a woman took, and hid in three measures of meal, till it was all leavened.

Mat 13:34 All these things spake Jesus in parables unto the multitudes; and without a parable spake he nothing unto them:

Mat 13:35 that it might be fulfilled which was spoken through the prophet, saying, I will open my mouth in parables; I will utter things hidden from the foundation of the world.

Mat 13:36 Then he left the multitudes, and went into the house: and his disciples came unto him, saying, Explain unto us the parable of the tares of the field.

Mat 13:37 And he answered and said, He that soweth the good seed is the Son of man;

Mat 13:38 and the field is the world; and the good seed, these are the sons of the kingdom; and the tares are the sons of the evil one;

Mat 13:39 and the enemy that sowed them is the devil: and the harvest is the end of the world; and the reapers are angels.

Mat 13:40 As therefore the tares are gathered up and burned with fire; so shall it be in the end of the world.

Mat 13:41 The Son of man shall send forth his angels, and they shall gather out of his kingdom all things that cause stumbling, and them that do iniquity,

Mat 13:42 and shall cast them into the furnace of fire: there shall be the weeping and the gnashing of teeth.

Mat 13:43 Then shall the righteous shine forth as the sun in the kingdom of their Father. He that hath ears, let him hear.

Mat 13:44 The kingdom of heaven is like unto a treasure hidden in the field; which a man found, and hid; and in his joy he goeth and selleth all that he hath, and buyeth that field.

Mat 13:45 Again, the kingdom of heaven is like unto a man that is a merchant seeking goodly pearls:

Mat 13:46 and having found one pearl of great price, he went and sold all that he had, and bought it.

Mat 13:47 Again, the kingdom of heaven is like unto a net, that was cast into the sea, and gathered of every kind:

Mat 13:48 which, when it was filled, they drew up on the beach; and they sat down, and gathered the good into vessels, but the bad they cast away.

Mat 13:49 So shall it be in the end of the world: the angels shall come forth, and sever the wicked from among the righteous,

Mat 13:50 and shall cast them into the furnace of fire: there shall be the weeping and the gnashing of teeth.

Mat 13:51 Have ye understood all these things? They say unto him, Yea.

Mat 13:52 And he said unto them, Therefore every scribe who hath been made a disciple to the kingdom of heaven is like unto a man that is a householder, who bringeth forth out of his treasure things new and old.

Mat 13:53 And it came to pass, when Jesus had finished these parables, he departed thence.

Mat 13:54 And coming into his own country he taught them in their synagogue, insomuch that they were astonished, and said, Whence hath this man this wisdom, and these mighty works?

Mat 13:55 Is not this the carpenter's son? is not his mother called Mary? and his brethren, James, and Joseph, and Simon, and Judas?

Mat 13:56 And his sisters, are they not all with us? Whence then hath this man all these things?

Mat 13:57 And they were offended in him. But Jesus said unto them, A prophet is not without honor, save in his own country, and in his own house.

Mat 13:58 And he did not many mighty works there because of their unbelief.

Chapter 14.

Mat 14:1 At that season Herod the tetrarch heard the report concerning Jesus,

Mat 14:2 and said unto his servants, This is John the Baptist; he is risen from the dead; and therefore do these powers work in him.

Mat 14:3 For Herod had laid hold on John, and bound him, and put him in prison for the sake of Herodias, his brother Philip's wife.

Mat 14:4 For John said unto him, It is not lawful for thee to have her.

Mat 14:5 And when he would have put him to death, he feared the multitude, because they counted him as a prophet.

Mat 14:6 But when Herod's birthday came, the daughter of Herodias danced in the midst, and pleased Herod.

Mat 14:7 Whereupon he promised with an oath to give her whatsoever she should ask.

Mat 14:8 And she, being put forward by her mother, saith, Give me here on a platter the head of John the Baptist.

Mat 14:9 And the king was grieved; but for the sake of his oaths, and of them that sat at meat with him, he commanded it to be given;

Mat 14:10 and he sent and beheaded John in the prison.

Mat 14:11 And his head was brought on a platter, and given to the damsel: and she brought it to her mother.

Mat 14:12 And his disciples came, and took up the corpse, and buried him; and they went and told Jesus.

Mat 14:13 Now when Jesus heard it, he withdrew from thence in a boat, to a desert place apart: and when the multitudes heard thereof, they followed him on foot from the cities.

Mat 14:14 And he came forth, and saw a great multitude, and he had compassion on them, and healed their sick.

Mat 14:15 And when even was come, the disciples came to him, saying, The place is desert, and the time is already past; send the multitudes away, that they may go into the villages, and buy themselves food.

Mat 14:16 But Jesus said unto them, They have no need to go away; give ye them to eat.

Mat 14:17 And they say unto him, We have here but five loaves, and two fishes.

Mat 14:18 And he said, Bring them hither to me.

Mat 14:19 And he commanded the multitudes to sit down on the grass; and he took the five loaves, and the two fishes, and looking up to heaven, he blessed, and brake and gave the loaves to the disciples, and the disciples to the multitudes.

Mat 14:20 And they all ate, and were filled: and they took up that which remained over of the broken pieces, twelve baskets full.

Mat 14:21 And they that did eat were about five thousand men, besides women and children.

Mat 14:22 And straightway he constrained the disciples to enter into the boat, and to go before him unto the other side, till he should send the multitudes away.

Mat 14:23 And after he had sent the multitudes away, he went up into the mountain apart to pray: and when even was come, he was there alone.

Mat 14:24 But the boat was now in the midst of the sea, distressed by the waves; for the wind was contrary.

Mat 14:25 And in the fourth watch of the night he came unto them, walking upon the sea.

Mat 14:26 And when the disciples saw him walking on the sea, they were troubled, saying, It is a ghost; and they cried out for fear.

Mat 14:27 But straightway Jesus spake unto them, saying Be of good cheer; it is I; be not afraid.

Mat 14:28 And Peter answered him and said, Lord, if it be thou, bid me come unto thee upon the waters.

Mat 14:29 And he said, Come. And Peter went down from the boat, and walked upon the waters to come to Jesus.

Mat 14:30 But when he saw the wind, he was afraid; and beginning to sink, he cried out, saying, Lord, save me.

Mat 14:31 And immediately Jesus stretched forth his hand, and took hold of him, and saith unto him, O thou of little faith, wherefore didst thou doubt?

Mat 14:32 And when they were gone up into the boat, the wind ceased.

Mat 14:33 And they that were in the boat worshipped him, saying, Of a truth thou art the Son of God.

Mat 14:34 And when they had crossed over, they came to the land, unto Gennesaret.

Mat 14:35 And when the men of that place knew him, they sent into all that region round about, and brought unto him all that were sick,

Mat 14:36 and they besought him that they might only touch the border of his garment: and as many as touched were made whole.

Chapter 15.

Mat 15:1 Then there come to Jesus from Jerusalem Pharisees and scribes, saying,

Mat 15:2 Why do thy disciples transgress the tradition of the elders? for they wash not their hands when they eat bread.

Mat 15:3 And he answered and said unto them, Why do ye also transgress the commandment of God because of your tradition?

Mat 15:4 For God said, Honor thy father and thy mother: and, He that speaketh evil of father or mother, let him die the death.

Mat 15:5 But ye say, whosoever shall say to his father or his mother, That wherewith thou mightest have been profited by me is given to God;

Mat 15:6 he shall not honor his father. And ye have made void the word of God because of your tradition.

Mat 15:7 Ye hypocrites, well did Isaiah prophesy of you, saying,

Mat 15:8 This people honoreth me with their lips; But their heart is far from me.

Mat 15:9 But in vain do they worship me, Teaching as their doctrines the precepts of men.

Mat 15:10 And he called to him the multitude, and said unto them, Hear, and understand:

Mat 15:11 not that which entereth into the mouth defileth the man; but that which proceedeth out of the mouth, this defileth the man.

Mat 15:12 Then came the disciples, and said unto him, Knowest thou that the Pharisees were offended, when they heard this saying?

Mat 15:13 But he answered and said, Every plant which my heavenly Father planted not, shall be rooted up.

Mat 15:14 Let them alone: they are blind guides. And if the blind guide the blind, both shall fall into a pit.

Mat 15:15 And Peter answered and said unto him, Declare unto us the parable.

Mat 15:16 And he said, Are ye also even yet without understanding?

Mat 15:17 Perceive ye not, that whatsoever goeth into the mouth passeth into the belly, and is cast out into the draught?

Mat 15:18 But the things which proceed out of the mouth come forth out of the heart; and they defile the man.

Mat 15:19 For out of the heart come forth evil thoughts, murders, adulteries, fornications, thefts, false witness, railings:

Mat 15:20 these are the things which defile the man; but to eat with unwashen hands defileth not the man.

Mat 15:21 And Jesus went out thence, and withdrew into the parts of Tyre and Sidon.

Mat 15:22 And behold, a Canaanitish woman came out from those borders, and cried, saying, Have mercy on me, O Lord, thou son of David; my daughter is grievously vexed with a demon.

Mat 15:23 But he answered her not a word. And his disciples came and besought him, saying, Send her away; for she crieth after us.

Mat 15:24 But he answered and said, I was not sent but unto the lost sheep of the house of Israel.

Mat 15:25 But she came and worshipped him, saying, Lord, help me.

Mat 15:26 And he answered and said, It is not meet to take the children's bread and cast it to the dogs.

Mat 15:27 But she said, Yea, Lord: for even the dogs eat of the crumbs which fall from their masters' table.

Mat 15:28 Then Jesus answered and said unto her, O woman, great is thy faith: be it done unto thee even as thou wilt. And her daughter was healed from that hour.

Mat 15:29 And Jesus departed thence, and came nigh unto the sea of Galilee; and he went up into the mountain, and sat there.

Mat 15:30 And there came unto him great multitudes, having with them the lame, blind, dumb, maimed, and many others, and they cast them down at this feet; and he healed them:

Mat 15:31 insomuch that the multitude wondered, when they saw the dumb speaking, the maimed whole, and lame walking, and the blind seeing: and they glorified the God of Israel.

Mat 15:32 And Jesus called unto him his disciples, and said, I have compassion on the multitude, because they continue with me now three days and have nothing to eat: and I would not send them away fasting, lest haply they faint on the way.

Mat 15:33 And the disciples say unto him, Whence should we have so many loaves in a desert place as to fill so great a multitude?

Mat 15:34 And Jesus said unto them, How many loaves have ye? And they said, Seven, and a few small fishes.

Mat 15:35 And he commanded the multitude to sit down on the ground;

Mat 15:36 and he took the seven loaves and the fishes; and he gave thanks and brake, and gave to the disciples, and the disciples to the multitudes.

Mat 15:37 And they all ate, and were filled: and they took up that which remained over of the broken pieces, seven baskets full.

Mat 15:38 And they that did eat were four thousand men, besides women and children.

Mat 15:39 And he sent away the multitudes, and entered into the boat, and came into the borders of Magadan.

Chapter 16.

Mat 16:1 And the Pharisees and Sadducees came, and trying him asked him to show them a sign from heaven.

Mat 16:2 But he answered and said unto them, When it is evening, ye say, It will be fair weather: for the heaven is red.

Mat 16:3 And in the morning, It will be foul weather to-day: for the heaven is red and lowering. Ye know how to discern the face of the heaven; but ye cannot discern the signs of the times.

Mat 16:4 An evil and adulterous generation seeketh after a sign; and there shall no sign be given unto it, but the sign of Jonah. And he left them, and departed.

Mat 16:5 And the disciples came to the other side and forgot to take bread.

Mat 16:6 And Jesus said unto them, Take heed and beware of the leaven of the Pharisees and Sadducees.

Mat 16:7 And they reasoned among themselves, saying, We took no bread.

Mat 16:8 And Jesus perceiving it said, O ye of little faith, why reason ye among yourselves, because ye have no bread?

Mat 16:9 Do ye not yet perceive, neither remember the five loaves of the five thousand, and how many baskets ye took up?

Mat 16:10 Neither the seven loaves of the four thousand, and how many baskets ye took up?

Mat 16:11 How is it that ye do not perceive that I spake not to you concerning bread? But beware of the leaven of the Pharisees and Sadducees.

Mat 16:12 Then understood they that he bade them not beware of the leaven of bread, but of the teaching of the Pharisees and Sadducees.

Mat 16:13 Now when Jesus came into the parts of Caesarea Philippi, he asked his disciples, saying, Who do men say that the Son of man is?

Mat 16:14 And they said, Some say John the Baptist; some, Elijah; and others, Jeremiah, or one of the prophets.

Mat 16:15 He saith unto them, But who say ye that I am?

Mat 16:16 And Simon Peter answered and said, Thou art the Christ, the Son of the living God.

Mat 16:17 And Jesus answered and said unto him, Blessed art thou, Simon Bar-Jonah: for flesh and blood hath not revealed it unto thee, but my Father who is in heaven.

Mat 16:18 And I also say unto thee, that thou art Peter, and upon this rock I will build my church; and the gates of Hades shall not prevail against it.

Mat 16:19 I will give unto thee the keys of the kingdom of heaven: and whatsoever thou shalt bind on earth shall be bound in heaven; and whatsoever thou shalt loose on earth shall be loosed in heaven.

Mat 16:20 Then charged he the disciples that they should tell no man that he was the Christ.

Mat 16:21 From that time began Jesus to show unto his disciples, that he must go unto Jerusalem, and suffer many things of the elders and chief priests and scribes, and be killed, and the third day be raised up.

Mat 16:22 And Peter took him, and began to rebuke him, saying, Be it far from thee, Lord: this shall never be unto thee.

Mat 16:23 But he turned, and said unto Peter, Get thee behind me, Satan: thou art a stumbling-block unto me: for thou mindest not the things of God, but the things of men.

Mat 16:24 Then said Jesus unto his disciples, If any man would come after me, let him deny himself, and take up his cross, and follow me.

Mat 16:25 For whosoever would save his life shall lose it: and whosoever shall lose his life for my sake shall find it.

Mat 16:26 For what shall a man be profited, if he shall gain the whole world, and forfeit his life? or what shall a man give in exchange for his life?

Mat 16:27 For the Son of man shall come in the glory of his Father with his angels; and then shall he render unto every man according to his deeds.

Mat 16:28 Verily I say unto you, there are some of them that stand here, who shall in no wise taste of death, till they see the Son of man coming in his kingdom.

Chapter 17.

Mat 17:1 And after six days Jesus taketh with him Peter, and James, and John his brother, and bringeth them up into a high mountain apart:

Mat 17:2 and he was transfigured before them; and his face did shine as the sun, and his garments became white as the light.

Mat 17:3 And behold, there appeared unto them Moses and Elijah talking with him.

Mat 17:4 And Peter answered, and said unto Jesus, Lord, it is good for us to be here: if thou wilt, I will make here three tabernacles; one for thee, and one for Moses, and one for Elijah.

Mat 17:5 While he was yet speaking, behold, a bright cloud overshadowed them: and behold, a voice out of the cloud, saying, This is my beloved Son, in whom I am well pleased; hear ye him.

Mat 17:6 And when the disciples heard it, they fell on their face, and were sore afraid.

Mat 17:7 And Jesus came and touched them and said, Arise, and be not afraid.

Mat 17:8 And lifting up their eyes, they saw no one, save Jesus only.

Mat 17:9 And as they were coming down from the mountain, Jesus commanded them, saying, Tell the vision to no man, until the Son of man be risen from the dead.

Mat 17:10 And his disciples asked him, saying, Why then say the scribes that Elijah must first come?

Mat 17:11 And he answered and said, Elijah indeed cometh, and shall restore all things:

Mat 17:12 but I say into you, that Elijah is come already, and they knew him not, but did unto him whatsoever they would. Even so shall the Son of man also suffer of them.

Mat 17:13 Then understood the disciples that he spake unto them of John the Baptist.

Mat 17:14 And when they were come to the multitude, there came to him a man, kneeling to him, saying,

Mat 17:15 Lord, have mercy on my son: for he is epileptic, and suffereth grievously; for oft-times he falleth into the fire, and off-times into the water.

Mat 17:16 And I brought him to thy disciples, and they could not cure him.

Mat 17:17 And Jesus answered and said, O faithless and perverse generation, how long shall I be with you? how long shall I bear with you? bring him hither to me.

Mat 17:18 And Jesus rebuked him; and the demon went out of him: and the boy was cured from that hour.

Mat 17:19 Then came the disciples to Jesus apart, and said, Why could not we cast it out?

Mat 17:20 And he saith unto them, Because of your little faith: for verily I say unto you, If ye have faith as a grain of mustard seed, ye shall say unto this mountain, Remove hence to yonder place; and it shall remove; and nothing shall be impossible unto you.

Mat 17:21 But this kind goeth not out save by prayer and fasting.

Mat 17:22 And while they abode in Galilee, Jesus said unto them, The Son of man shall be delivered up into the hands of men;

Mat 17:23 and they shall kill him, and the third day he shall be raised up. And they were exceeding sorry.

Mat 17:24 And when they were come to Capernaum, they that received the half-shekel came to Peter, and said, Doth not your teacher pay the half-shekel?

Mat 17:25 He saith, Yea. And when he came into the house, Jesus spake first to him, saying, What thinkest thou, Simon? the kings of the earth, from whom do they receive toll or tribute? from their sons, or from strangers?

Mat 17:26 And when he said, From strangers, Jesus said unto him, Therefore the sons are free.

Mat 17:27 But, lest we cause them to stumble, go thou to the sea, and cast a hook, and take up the fish that first cometh up; and when thou hast opened his mouth, thou shalt find a shekel: that take, and give unto them for me and thee.

Chapter 18.

Mat 18:1 In that hour came the disciples unto Jesus, saying, Who then is greatest in the kingdom of heaven?

Mat 18:2 And he called to him a little child, and set him in the midst of them,

Mat 18:3 and said, Verily I say unto you, Except ye turn, and become as little children, ye shall in no wise enter into the kingdom of heaven.

Mat 18:4 Whosoever therefore shall humble himself as this little child, the same is the greatest in the kingdom of heaven.

Mat 18:5 And whoso shall receive one such little child in my name receiveth me:

Mat 18:6 But whoso shall cause one of these little ones that believe on me to stumble, it is profitable for him that a great millstone should be hanged about his neck, and that he should be sunk in the depth of the sea.

Mat 18:7 Woe unto the world because of occasions of stumbling! for it must needs be that the occasions come; but woe to that man through whom the occasion cometh!

Mat 18:8 And if thy hand or thy foot causeth thee to stumble, cut it off, and cast it from thee: it is good for thee to enter into life maimed or halt, rather than having two hands or two feet to be cast into the eternal fire.

Mat 18:9 And if thine eye causeth thee to stumble, pluck it out, and cast it from thee: it is good for thee to enter into life with one eye, rather than having two eyes to be cast into the hell of fire.

Mat 18:10 See that ye despise not one of these little ones; for I say unto you, that in heaven their angels do always behold the face of my Father who is in heaven.

Mat 18:11 For the Son of man came to save that which was lost.

Mat 18:12 How think ye? if any man have a hundred sheep, and one of them be gone astray, doth he not leave the ninety and nine, and go unto the mountains, and seek that which goeth astray?

Mat 18:13 And if so be that he find it, verily I say unto you, he rejoiceth over it more than over the ninety and nine which have not gone astray.

Mat 18:14 Even so it is not the will of your Father who is in heaven, that one of these little ones should perish.

Mat 18:15 And if thy brother sin against thee, go, show him his fault between thee and him alone: if he hear thee, thou hast gained thy brother.

Mat 18:16 But if he hear thee not, take with thee one or two more, that at the mouth of two witnesses or three every word may be established.

Mat 18:17 And if he refuse to hear them, tell it unto the church: and if he refuse to hear the church also, let him be unto thee as the Gentile and the publican.

Mat 18:18 Verily I say unto you, what things soever ye shall bind on earth shall be bound in heaven; and what things soever ye shall loose on earth shall be loosed in heaven.

Mat 18:19 Again I say unto you, that if two of you shall agree on earth as touching anything that they shall ask, it shall be done for them of my Father who is in heaven.

Mat 18:20 For where two or three are gathered together in my name, there am I in the midst of them.

Mat 18:21 Then came Peter and said to him, Lord, how oft shall my brother sin against me, and I forgive him? until seven times?

Mat 18:22 Jesus saith unto him, I say not unto thee, Until seven times; but, Until seventy times seven.

Mat 18:23 Therefore is the kingdom of heaven likened unto a certain king, who would make a reckoning with his servants.

Mat 18:24 And when he had begun to reckon, one was brought unto him, that owed him ten thousand talents.

Mat 18:25 But forasmuch as he had not wherewith to pay, his lord commanded him to be sold, and his wife, and children, and all that he had, and payment to be made.

Mat 18:26 The servant therefore fell down and worshipped him, saying, Lord, have patience with me, and I will pay thee all.

Mat 18:27 And the lord of that servant, being moved with compassion, released him, and forgave him the debt.

Mat 18:28 But that servant went out, and found one of his fellow-servants, who owed him a hundred shillings: and he laid hold on him, and took him by the throat, saying, Pay what thou owest.

Mat 18:29 So his fellow-servant fell down and besought him, saying, Have patience with me, and I will pay thee.

Mat 18:30 And he would not: but went and cast him into prison, till he should pay that which was due.

Mat 18:31 So when his fellow-servants saw what was done, they were exceeding sorry, and came and told unto their lord all that was done.

Mat 18:32 Then his lord called him unto him, and saith to him, Thou wicked servant, I forgave thee all that debt, because thou besoughtest me:

Mat 18:33 shouldest not thou also have had mercy on thy fellow-servant, even as I had mercy on thee?

Mat 18:34 And his lord was wroth, and delivered him to the tormentors, till he should pay all that was due.

Mat 18:35 So shall also my heavenly Father do unto you, if ye forgive not every one his brother from your hearts.

Chapter 19.

Mat 19:1 And it came to pass when Jesus had finished these words, he departed from Galilee, and came into the borders of Judaea beyond the Jordan;

Mat 19:2 and great multitudes followed him; and he healed them there.

Mat 19:3 And there came unto him Pharisees, trying him, and saying, Is it lawful for a man to put away his wife for every cause?

Mat 19:4 And he answered and said, Have ye not read, that he who made them from the beginning made them male and female,

Mat 19:5 and said, For this cause shall a man leave his father and mother, and shall cleave to his wife; and the two shall become one flesh?

Mat 19:6 So that they are no more two, but one flesh. What therefore God hath joined together, let not man put asunder.

Mat 19:7 They say unto him, Why then did Moses command to give a bill of divorcement, and to put her away?

Mat 19:8 He saith unto them, Moses for your hardness of heart suffered you to put away your wives: but from the beginning it hath not been so.

Mat 19:9 And I say unto you, Whosoever shall put away his wife, except for fornication, and shall marry another, committeth adultery: and he that marrieth her when she is put away committeth adultery.

Mat 19:10 The disciples say unto him, If the case of the man is so with his wife, it is not expedient to marry.

Mat 19:11 But he said unto them, Not all men can receive this saying, but they to whom it is given.

Mat 19:12 For there are eunuchs, that were so born from their mother's womb: and there are eunuchs, that were made eunuchs by men: and there are eunuchs, that made themselves eunuchs for the kingdom of heaven's sake. He that is able to receive it, let him receive it.

Mat 19:13 Then were there brought unto him little children, that he should lay his hands on them, and pray: and the disciples rebuked them.

Mat 19:14 But Jesus said, Suffer the little children, and forbid them not, to come unto me: for to such belongeth the kingdom of heaven.

Mat 19:15 And he laid his hands on them, and departed thence.

Mat 19:16 And behold, one came to him and said, Teacher, what good thing shall I do, that I may have eternal life?

Mat 19:17 And he said unto him, Why askest thou me concerning that which is good? One there is who is good: but if thou wouldest enter into life, keep the commandments.

Mat 19:18 He saith unto him, Which? And Jesus said, Thou shalt not kill, Thou shalt not commit adultery, Thou shalt not steal, Thou shalt not bear false witness,

Mat 19:19 Honor thy father and mother; and, Thou shalt love thy neighbor as thyself.

Mat 19:20 The young man saith unto him, All these things have I observed: what lack I yet?

Mat 19:21 Jesus said unto him, If thou wouldest be perfect, go, sell that which thou hast, and give to the poor, and thou shalt have treasure in heaven: and come, follow me.

Mat 19:22 But when the young man heard the saying, he went away sorrowful; for he was one that had great possessions.

Mat 19:23 And Jesus said unto his disciples, Verily I say unto you, It is hard for a rich man to enter into the kingdom of heaven.

Mat 19:24 And again I say unto you, It is easier for a camel to go through a needle's eye, than for a rich man to enter into the kingdom of God.

Mat 19:25 And when the disciples heard it, they were astonished exceedingly, saying, Who then can be saved?

Mat 19:26 And Jesus looking upon them said to them, With men this is impossible; but with God all things are possible.

Mat 19:27 Then answered Peter and said unto him, Lo, we have left all, and followed thee; what then shall we have?

Mat 19:28 And Jesus said unto them, Verily I say unto you, that ye who have followed me, in the regeneration when the Son of man shall sit on the throne of his glory, ye also shall sit upon twelve thrones, judging the twelve tribes of Israel.

Mat 19:29 And every one that hath left houses, or brethren, or sisters, or father, or mother, or children, or lands, for my name's sake, shall receive a hundredfold, and shall inherit eternal life.

Mat 19:30 But many shall be last that are first; and first that are last.

Chapter 20.

Mat 20:1 For the kingdom of heaven is like unto a man that was a householder, who went out early in the morning to hire laborers into his vineyard.

Mat 20:2 And when he had agreed with the laborers for a shilling a day, he sent them into his vineyard.

Mat 20:3 And he went out about the third hour, and saw others standing in the marketplace idle;

Mat 20:4 and to them he said, Go ye also into the vineyard, and whatsoever is right I will give you. And they went their way.

Mat 20:5 Again he went out about the sixth and the ninth hour, and did likewise.

Mat 20:6 And about the eleventh hour he went out, and found others standing; and he saith unto them, Why stand ye here all the day idle?

Mat 20:7 They say unto him, Because no man hath hired us. He saith unto them, Go ye also into the vineyard.

Mat 20:8 And when even was come, the lord of the vineyard saith unto his steward, Call the laborers, and pay them their hire, beginning from the last unto the first.

Mat 20:9 And when they came that were hired about the eleventh hour, they received every man a shilling.

Mat 20:10 And when the first came, they supposed that they would receive more; and they likewise received every man a shilling.

Mat 20:11 And when they received it, they murmured against the householder,

Mat 20:12 saying, These last have spent but one hour, and thou hast made them equal unto us, who have borne the burden of the day and the scorching heat.

Mat 20:13 But he answered and said to one of them, Friend, I do thee no wrong: didst not thou agree with me for a shilling?

Mat 20:14 Take up that which is thine, and go thy way; it is my will to give unto this last, even as unto thee.

Mat 20:15 Is it not lawful for me to do what I will with mine own? or is thine eye evil, because I am good?

Mat 20:16 So the last shall be first, and the first last.

Mat 20:17 And as Jesus was going up to Jerusalem, he took the twelve disciples apart, and on the way he said unto them,

Mat 20:18 Behold, we go up to Jerusalem; and the Son of man shall be delivered unto the chief priests and scribes; and they shall condemn him to death,

Mat 20:19 and shall deliver him unto the Gentiles to mock, and to scourge, and to crucify: and the third day he shall be raised up.

Mat 20:20 Then came to him the mother of the sons of Zebedee with her sons, worshipping him, and asking a certain thing of him.

Mat 20:21 And he said unto her, What wouldest thou? She saith unto him, Command that these my two sons may sit, one on thy right hand, and one on thy left hand, in thy kingdom.

Mat 20:22 But Jesus answered and said, Ye know not what ye ask. Are ye able to drink the cup that I am about to drink? They say unto him, We are able.

Mat 20:23 He saith unto them, My cup indeed ye shall drink: but to sit on my right hand, and on my left hand, is not mine to give; but it is for them for whom it hath been prepared of my Father.

Mat 20:24 And when the ten heard it, they were moved with indignation concerning the two brethren.

Mat 20:25 But Jesus called them unto him, and said, Ye know that the rulers of the Gentiles lord it over them, and their great ones exercise authority over them.

Mat 20:26 Not so shall it be among you: but whosoever would become great among you shall be your minister;

Mat 20:27 and whosoever would be first among you shall be your servant:

Mat 20:28 even as the Son of man came not to be ministered unto, but to minister, and to give his life a ransom for many.

Mat 20:29 And as they went out from Jericho, a great multitude followed him.

Mat 20:30 And behold, two blind men sitting by the way side, when they heard that Jesus was passing by, cried out, saying, Lord, have mercy on us, thou son of David.

Mat 20:31 And the multitude rebuked them, that they should hold their peace: but they cried out the more, saying, Lord, have mercy on us, thou son of David.

Mat 20:32 And Jesus stood still, and called them, and said, What will ye that I should do unto you?

Mat 20:33 They say unto him, Lord, that our eyes may be opened.

Mat 20:34 And Jesus, being moved with compassion, touched their eyes; and straightway they received their sight, and followed him.

Chapter 21.

Mat 21:1 And when they drew nigh unto Jerusalem, and came unto Bethphage, unto the mount of Olives, then Jesus sent two disciples,

Mat 21:2 saying unto them, Go into the village that is over against you, and straightway ye shall find an ass tied, and a colt with her: loose them, and bring them unto me.

Mat 21:3 And if any one say aught unto you, ye shall say, The Lord hath need of them; and straightway he will send them.

Mat 21:4 Now this is come to pass, that it might be fulfilled which was spoken through the prophet, saying,

Mat 21:5 Tell ye the daughter of Zion, Behold, thy King cometh unto thee, Meek, and riding upon an ass, And upon a colt the foal of an ass.

Mat 21:6 And the disciples went, and did even as Jesus appointed them,

Mat 21:7 and brought the ass, and the colt, and put on them their garments; and he sat thereon.

Mat 21:8 And the most part of the multitude spread their garments in the way; and others cut branches from the trees, and spread them in the way.

Mat 21:9 And the multitudes that went before him, and that followed, cried, saying, Hosanna to the son of David: Blessed is he that cometh in the name of the Lord; Hosanna in the highest.

Mat 21:10 And when he was come into Jerusalem, all the city was stirred, saying, Who is this?

Mat 21:11 And the multitudes said, This is the prophet, Jesus, from Nazareth of Galilee.

Mat 21:12 And Jesus entered into the temple of God, and cast out all them that sold and bought in the temple, and overthrew the tables of he money-changers, and the seats of them that sold the doves;

Mat 21:13 and he saith unto them, It is written, My house shall be called a house of prayer: but ye make it a den of robbers.

Mat 21:14 And the blind and the lame came to him in the temple; and he healed them.

Mat 21:15 But when the chief priests and the scribes saw the wonderful things that he did, and the children that were crying in the temple and saying, Hosanna to the son of David; they were moved with indignation,

Mat 21:16 and said unto him, Hearest thou what these are saying? And Jesus saith unto them, Yea: did ye never read, Out of the mouth of babes and sucklings thou has perfected praise?

Mat 21:17 And he left them, and went forth out of the city to Bethany, and lodged there.

Mat 21:18 Now in the morning as he returned to the city, he hungered.

Mat 21:19 And seeing a fig tree by the way side, he came to it, and found nothing thereon, but leaves only; and he saith unto it, Let there be no fruit from thee henceforward for ever. And immediately the fig tree withered away.

Mat 21:20 And when the disciples saw it, they marvelled, saying, How did the fig tree immediately wither away?

Mat 21:21 And Jesus answered and said unto them, Verily I say unto you, If ye have faith, and doubt not, ye shall not only do what is done to the fig tree, but even if ye shall say unto this mountain, Be thou taken up and cast into the sea, it shall be done.

Mat 21:22 And all things, whatsoever ye shall ask in prayer, believing, ye shall receive.

Mat 21:23 And when he was come into the temple, the chief priests and the elders of the people came unto him as he was teaching, and said, By what authority doest thou these things? and who gave thee this authority?

Mat 21:24 And Jesus answered and said unto them, I also will ask you one question, which if ye tell me, I likewise will tell you by what authority I do these things.

Mat 21:25 The baptism of John, whence was it? from heaven or from men? And they reasoned with themselves, saying, If we shall say, From heaven; he will say unto us, Why then did ye not believe him?

Mat 21:26 But if we shall say, From men; we fear the multitude; for all hold John as a prophet.

Mat 21:27 And they answered Jesus, and said, We know not. He also said unto them, Neither tell I you by what authority I do these things.

Mat 21:28 But what think ye? A man had two sons; and he came to the first, and said, Son, go work to-day in the vineyard.

Mat 21:29 And he answered and said, I will not: but afterward he repented himself, and went.

Mat 21:30 And he came to the second, and said likewise. And he answered and said, I go, sir: and went not.

Mat 21:31 Which of the two did the will of his father? They say, The first. Jesus saith unto them, Verily I say unto you, that the publicans and the harlots go into the kingdom of God before you.

Mat 21:32 For John came unto you in the way of righteousness, and ye believed him not; but the publicans and the harlots believed him: and ye, when ye saw it, did not even repent yourselves afterward, that ye might believe him.

Mat 21:33 Hear another parable: There was a man that was a householder, who planted a vineyard, and set a hedge about it, and digged a winepress in it, and built a tower, and let it out to husbandmen, and went into another country.

Mat 21:34 And when the season of the fruits drew near, he sent his servants to the husbandmen, to receive his fruits.

Mat 21:35 And the husbandmen took his servants, and beat one, and killed another, and stoned another.

Mat 21:36 Again, he sent other servants more than the first: and they did unto them in like manner.

Mat 21:37 But afterward he sent unto them his son, saying, They will reverence my son.

Mat 21:38 But the husbandmen, when they saw the son, said among themselves, This is the heir; come, let us kill him, and take his inheritance.

Mat 21:39 And they took him, and cast him forth out of the vineyard, and killed him.

Mat 21:40 When therefore the lord of the vineyard shall come, what will he do unto those husbandmen?

Mat 21:41 They say unto him, He will miserably destroy those miserable men, and will let out the vineyard unto other husbandmen, who shall render him the fruits in their seasons.

Mat 21:42 Jesus saith unto them, Did ye never read in the scriptures, The stone which the builders rejected, The same was made the head of the corner; This was from the Lord, And it is marvelous in our eyes?

Mat 21:43 Therefore say I unto you, The kingdom of God shall be taken away from you, and shall be given to a nation bringing forth the fruits thereof.

Mat 21:44 And he that falleth on this stone shall be broken to pieces: but on whomsoever it shall fall, it will scatter him as dust.

Mat 21:45 And when the chief priests and the Pharisees heard his parables, they perceived that he spake of them.

Mat 21:46 And when they sought to lay hold on him, they feared the multitudes, because they took him for a prophet.

Chapter 22.

Mat 22:1 And Jesus answered and spake again in parables unto them, saying,

Mat 22:2 The kingdom of heaven is likened unto a certain king, who made a marriage feast for his son,

Mat 22:3 and sent forth his servants to call them that were bidden to the marriage feast: and they would not come.

Mat 22:4 Again he sent forth other servants, saying, Tell them that are bidden, Behold, I have made ready my dinner; my oxen and my fatlings are killed, and all things are ready: come to the marriage feast.

Mat 22:5 But they made light of it, and went their ways, one to his own farm, another to his merchandise;

Mat 22:6 and the rest laid hold on his servants, and treated them shamefully, and killed them.

Mat 22:7 But the king was wroth; and he sent his armies, and destroyed those murderers, and burned their city.

Mat 22:8 Then saith he to his servants, The wedding is ready, but they that were bidden were not worthy.

Mat 22:9 Go ye therefore unto the partings of the highways, and as many as ye shall find, bid to the marriage feast.

Mat 22:10 And those servants went out into the highways, and gathered together all as many as they found, both bad and good: and the wedding was filled with guests.

Mat 22:11 But when the king came in to behold the guests, he saw there a man who had not on a wedding-garment:

Mat 22:12 and he saith unto him, Friend, how camest thou in hither not having a wedding-garment? And he was speechless.

Mat 22:13 Then the king said to the servants, Bind him hand and foot, and cast him out into the outer darkness; there shall be the weeping and the gnashing of teeth.

Mat 22:14 For many are called, but few chosen.

Mat 22:15 Then went the Pharisees, and took counsel how they might ensnare him in his talk.

Mat 22:16 And they send to him their disciples, with the Herodians, saying, Teacher, we know that thou art true, and teachest the way of God in truth, and carest not for any one: for thou regardest not the person of men.

Mat 22:17 Tell us therefore, What thinkest thou? Is it lawful to give tribute unto Caesar, or not?

Mat 22:18 But Jesus perceived their wickedness, and said, Why make ye trial of me, ye hypocrites?

Mat 22:19 Show me the tribute money. And they brought unto him a denarius.

Mat 22:20 And he saith unto them, Whose is this image and superscription?

Mat 22:21 They say unto him, Caesar's. Then saith he unto them, Render therefore unto Caesar the things that are Caesar's; and unto God the things that are God's.

Mat 22:22 And when they heard it, they marvelled, and left him, and went away.

Mat 22:23 On that day there came to him Sadducees, they that say that there is no resurrection: and they asked him,

Mat 22:24 saying, Teacher, Moses said, If a man die, having no children, his brother shall marry his wife, and raise up seed unto his brother.

Mat 22:25 Now there were with us seven brethren: and the first married and deceased, and having no seed left his wife unto his brother;

Mat 22:26 in like manner the second also, and the third, unto the seventh.

Mat 22:27 And after them all, the woman died.

Mat 22:28 In the resurrection therefore whose wife shall she be of the seven? for they all had her.

Mat 22:29 But Jesus answered and said unto them, Ye do err, not knowing the scriptures, nor the power of God.

Mat 22:30 For in the resurrection they neither marry, nor are given in marriage, but are as angels in heaven.

Mat 22:31 But as touching the resurrection of the dead, have ye not read that which was spoken unto you by God, saying,

Mat 22:32 I am the God of Abraham, and the God of Isaac, and the God of Jacob? God is not the God of the dead, but of the living.

Mat 22:33 And when the multitudes heard it, they were astonished at his teaching.

Mat 22:34 But the Pharisees, when they heard that he had put the Sadducees to silence, gathered themselves together.

Mat 22:35 And one of them, a lawyer, asked him a question, trying him:

Mat 22:36 Teacher, which is the great commandment in the law?

Mat 22:37 And he said unto him, Thou shalt love the Lord thy God with all thy heart, and with all thy soul, and with all thy mind.

Mat 22:38 This is the great and first commandment.

Mat 22:39 And a second like unto it is this, Thou shalt love thy neighbor as thyself.

Mat 22:40 On these two commandments the whole law hangeth, and the prophets.

Mat 22:41 Now while the Pharisees were gathered together, Jesus asked them a question,

Mat 22:42 saying, What think ye of the Christ? whose son is he? They say unto him, The son of David.

Mat 22:43 He saith unto them, How then doth David in the Spirit call him Lord, saying,

Mat 22:44 The Lord said unto my Lord, Sit thou on my right hand, Till I put thine enemies underneath thy feet?

Mat 22:45 If David then calleth him Lord, how is he his son?

Mat 22:46 And no one was able to answer him a word, neither durst any man from that day forth ask him any more questions.

Chapter 23.

Mat 23:1 Then spake Jesus to the multitudes and to his disciples,

Mat 23:2 saying, The scribes and the Pharisees sit on Moses seat:

Mat 23:3 all things therefore whatsoever they bid you, these do and observe: but do not ye after their works; for they say, and do not.

Mat 23:4 Yea, they bind heavy burdens and grievous to be borne, and lay them on men's shoulders; but they themselves will not move them with their finger.

Mat 23:5 But all their works they do to be seen of men: for they make broad their phylacteries, and enlarge the borders of their garments,

Mat 23:6 and love the chief place at feasts, and the chief seats in the synagogues,

Mat 23:7 and the salutations in the marketplaces, and to be called of men, Rabbi.

Mat 23:8 But be not ye called Rabbi: for one is your teacher, and all ye are brethren.

Mat 23:9 And call no man your father on the earth: for one is your Father, even he who is in heaven.

Mat 23:10 Neither be ye called masters: for one is your master, even the Christ.

Mat 23:11 But he that is greatest among you shall be your servant.

Mat 23:12 And whosoever shall exalt himself shall be humbled; and whosoever shall humble himself shall be exalted.

Mat 23:13 But woe unto you, scribes and Pharisees, hypocrites! because ye shut the kingdom of heaven against men: for ye enter not in yourselves, neither suffer ye them that are entering in to enter.

Mat 23:14 Woe unto you, scribes and Pharisees, hypocrites! for ye devour widows' houses, even while for a pretence ye make long prayers: therefore ye shall receive greater condemnation.

Mat 23:15 Woe unto you, scribes and Pharisees, hypocrites! for ye compass sea and land to make one proselyte; and when he is become so, ye make him twofold more a son of hell than yourselves.

Mat 23:16 Woe unto you, ye blind guides, that say, Whosoever shall swear by the temple, it is nothing; but whosoever shall swear by the gold of the temple, he is a debtor.

Mat 23:17 Ye fools and blind: for which is greater, the gold, or the temple that hath sanctified the gold?

Mat 23:18 And, Whosoever shall swear by the altar, it is nothing; but whosoever shall swear by the gift that is upon it, he is a debtor.

Mat 23:19 Ye blind: for which is greater, the gift, or the altar that sanctifieth the gift?

Mat 23:20 He therefore that sweareth by the altar, sweareth by it, and by all things thereon.

Mat 23:21 And he that sweareth by the temple, sweareth by it, and by him that dwelleth therein.

Mat 23:22 And he that sweareth by the heaven, sweareth by the throne of God, and by him that sitteth thereon.

Mat 23:23 Woe unto you, scribes and Pharisees, hypocrites! for ye tithe mint and anise and cummin, and have left undone the weightier matters of the law, justice, and mercy, and faith: but these ye ought to have done, and not to have left the other undone.

Mat 23:24 Ye blind guides, that strain out the gnat, and swallow the camel!

Mat 23:25 Woe unto you, scribes and Pharisees, hypocrites! for ye cleanse the outside of the cup and of the platter, but within they are full from extortion and excess.

Mat 23:26 Thou blind Pharisee, cleanse first the inside of the cup and of the platter, that the outside thereof may become clean also.

Mat 23:27 Woe unto you, scribes and Pharisees, hypocrites! for ye are like unto whited sepulchres, which outwardly appear beautiful, but inwardly are full of dead men's bones, and of all uncleanness.

Mat 23:28 Even so ye also outwardly appear righteous unto men, but inwardly ye are full of hypocrisy and iniquity.

Mat 23:29   Woe unto you, scribes and Pharisees, hypocrites! for ye build the sepulchres of the prophets, and garnish the tombs of the righteous,

Mat 23:30 and say, If we had been in the days of our fathers, we should not have been partakers with them in the blood of the prophets.

Mat 23:31 Wherefore ye witness to yourselves, that ye are sons of them that slew the prophets.

Mat 23:32 Fill ye up then the measure of your fathers.

Mat 23:33   Ye serpents, ye offspring of vipers, how shall ye escape the judgment of hell?

Mat 23:34   Therefore, behold, I send unto you prophets, and wise men, and scribes: some of them shall ye kill and crucify; and some of them shall ye scourge in your synagogues, and persecute from city to city:

Mat 23:35 that upon you may come all the righteous blood shed on the earth, from the blood of Abel the righteous unto the blood of Zachariah son of Barachiah, whom ye slew between the sanctuary and the altar.

Mat 23:36 Verily I say unto you, All these things shall come upon this generation.

Mat 23:37 O Jerusalem, Jerusalem, that killeth the prophets, and stoneth them that are sent unto her! how often would I have gathered thy children together, even as a hen gathereth her chickens under her wings, and ye would not!

Mat 23:38 Behold, your house is left unto you desolate.

Mat 23:39   For I say unto you, Ye shall not see me henceforth, till ye shall say, Blessed is he that cometh in the name of the Lord.

Chapter 24.

Mat 24:1   And Jesus went out from the temple, and was going on his way; and his disciples came to him to show him the buildings of the temple.

Mat 24:2 But he answered and said unto them, See ye not all these things? verily I say unto you, There shall not be left here one stone upon another, that shall not be thrown down.

Mat 24:3 And as he sat on the mount of Olives, the disciples came unto him privately, saying, Tell us, when shall these things be? and what shall be the sign of thy coming, and of the end of the world?

Mat 24:4 And Jesus answered and said unto them, Take heed that no man lead you astray.

Mat 24:5   For many shall come in my name, saying, I am the Christ; and shall lead many astray.

Mat 24:6 And ye shall hear of wars and rumors of wars; see that ye be not troubled: for these things must needs come to pass; but the end is not yet.

Mat 24:7 For nation shall rise against nation, and kingdom against kingdom; and there shall be famines and earthquakes in divers places.

Mat 24:8 But all these things are the beginning of travail.

Mat 24:9 Then shall they deliver you up unto tribulation, and shall kill you: and ye shall be hated of all the nations for my name's sake.

Mat 24:10 And then shall many stumble, and shall deliver up one another, and shall hate one another.

Mat 24:11 And many false prophets shall arise, and shall lead many astray.

Mat 24:12 And because iniquity shall be multiplied, the love of the many shall wax cold.

Mat 24:13 But he that endureth to the end, the same shall be saved.

Mat 24:14 And this gospel of the kingdom shall be preached in the whole world for a testimony unto all the nations; and then shall the end come.

Mat 24:15 When therefore ye see the abomination of desolation, which was spoken of through Daniel the prophet, standing in the holy place (let him that readeth understand),

Mat 24:16 then let them that are in Judaea flee unto the mountains:

Mat 24:17 let him that is on the housetop not go down to take out things that are in his house:

Mat 24:18 and let him that is in the field not return back to take his cloak.

Mat 24:19 But woe unto them that are with child and to them that give suck in those days!

Mat 24:20 And pray ye that your flight be not in the winter, neither on a sabbath:

Mat 24:21 for then shall be great tribulation, such as hath not been from the beginning of the world until now, no, nor ever shall be.

Mat 24:22 And except those days had been shortened, no flesh would have been saved: but for the elect's sake those days shall be shortened.

Mat 24:23 Then if any man shall say unto you, Lo, here is the Christ, or, Here; believe it not.

Mat 24:24 For there shall arise false Christs, and false prophets, and shall show great signs and wonders; so as to lead astray, if possible, even the elect.

Mat 24:25 Behold, I have told you beforehand.

Mat 24:26 If therefore they shall say unto you, Behold, he is in the wilderness; go not forth: Behold, he is in the inner chambers; believe it not.

Mat 24:27 For as the lightning cometh forth from the east, and is seen even unto the west; so shall be the coming of the Son of man.

Mat 24:28 Wheresoever the carcase is, there will the eagles be gathered together.

Mat 24:29 But immediately after the tribulation of those days the sun shall be darkened, and the moon shall not give her light, and the stars shall fall from heaven, and the powers of the heavens shall be shaken:

Mat 24:30 and then shall appear the sign of the Son of man in heaven: and then shall all the tribes of the earth mourn, and they shall see the Son of man coming on the clouds of heaven with power and great glory.

Mat 24:31 And he shall send forth his angels with a great sound of a trumpet, and they shall gather together his elect from the four winds, from one end of heaven to the other.

Mat 24:32 Now from the fig tree learn her parable: when her branch is now become tender, and putteth forth its leaves, ye know that the summer is nigh;

Mat 24:33 even so ye also, when ye see all these things, know ye that he is nigh, even at the doors.

Mat 24:34 Verily I say unto you, This generation shall not pass away, till all these things be accomplished.

Mat 24:35 Heaven and earth shall pass away, but my words shall not pass away.

Mat 24:36 But of that day and hour knoweth no one, not even the angels of heaven, neither the Son, but the Father only.

Mat 24:37 And as were the days of Noah, so shall be the coming of the Son of man.

Mat 24:38 For as in those days which were before the flood they were eating and drinking, marrying and giving in marriage, until the day that Noah entered into the ark,

Mat 24:39 and they knew not until the flood came, and took them all away; so shall be the coming of the Son of man.

Mat 24:40 Then shall two men be in the field; one is taken, and one is left:

Mat 24:41 two women shall be grinding at the mill; one is taken, and one is left.

Mat 24:42 Watch therefore: for ye know not on what day your Lord cometh.

Mat 24:43 But know this, that if the master of the house had known in what watch the thief was coming, he would have watched, and would not have suffered his house to be broken through.

Mat 24:44 Therefore be ye also ready; for in an hour that ye think not the Son of man cometh.

Mat 24:45 Who then is the faithful and wise servant, whom his lord hath set over his household, to give them their food in due season?

Mat 24:46 Blessed is that servant, whom his lord when he cometh shall find so doing.

Mat 24:47 Verily I say unto you, that he will set him over all that he hath.

Mat 24:48 But if that evil servant shall say in his heart, My lord tarrieth;

Mat 24:49 and shall begin to beat his fellow-servants, and shall eat and drink with the drunken;

Mat 24:50 the lord of that servant shall come in a day when he expecteth not, and in an hour when he knoweth not,

Mat 24:51 and shall cut him asunder, and appoint his portion with the hypocrites: there shall be the weeping and the gnashing of teeth.

Chapter 25.

Mat 25:1 Then shall the kingdom of heaven be likened unto ten virgins, who took their lamps, and went forth to meet the bridegroom.

Mat 25:2 And five of them were foolish, and five were wise.

Mat 25:3 For the foolish, when they took their lamps, took no oil with them:

Mat 25:4 but the wise took oil in their vessels with their lamps.

Mat 25:5 Now while the bridegroom tarried, they all slumbered and slept.

Mat 25:6 But at midnight there is a cry, Behold, the bridegroom! Come ye forth to meet him.

Mat 25:7 Then all those virgins arose, and trimmed their lamps.

Mat 25:8 And the foolish said unto the wise, Give us of your oil; for our lamps are going out.

Mat 25:9 But the wise answered, saying, Peradventure there will not be enough for us and you: go ye rather to them that sell, and buy for yourselves.

Mat 25:10 And while they went away to buy, the bridegroom came; and they that were ready went in with him to the marriage feast: and the door was shut.

Mat 25:11 Afterward came also the other virgins, saying, Lord, Lord, open to us.

Mat 25:12 But he answered and said, Verily I say unto you, I know you not.

Mat 25:13 Watch therefore, for ye know not the day nor the hour.

Mat 25:14 For it is as when a man, going into another country, called his own servants, and delivered unto them his goods.

Mat 25:15 And unto one he gave five talents, to another two, to another one; to each according to his several ability; and he went on his journey.

Mat 25:16 Straightway he that received the five talents went and traded with them, and made other five talents.

Mat 25:17 In like manner he also that received the two gained other two.

Mat 25:18 But he that received the one went away and digged in the earth, and hid his lord's money.

Mat 25:19 Now after a long time the lord of those servants cometh, and maketh a reckoning with them.

Mat 25:20 And he that received the five talents came and brought other five talents, saying, Lord, thou deliveredst unto me five talents: lo, I have gained other five talents.

Mat 25:21 His lord said unto him, Well done, good and faithful servant: thou hast been faithful over a few things, I will set thee over many things; enter thou into the joy of thy lord.

Mat 25:22 And he also that received the two talents came and said, Lord, thou deliveredst unto me two talents: lo, I have gained other two talents.

Mat 25:23 His lord said unto him, Well done, good and faithful servant: thou hast been faithful over a few things, I will set thee over many things; enter thou into the joy of thy lord.

Mat 25:24 And he also that had received the one talent came and said, Lord, I knew thee that thou art a hard man, reaping where thou didst not sow, and gathering where thou didst not scatter;

Mat 25:25 and I was afraid, and went away and hid thy talent in the earth: lo, thou hast thine own.

Mat 25:26 But his lord answered and said unto him, Thou wicked and slothful servant, thou knewest that I reap where I sowed not, and gather where I did not scatter;

Mat 25:27 thou oughtest therefore to have put my money to the bankers, and at my coming I should have received back mine own with interest.

Mat 25:28 Take ye away therefore the talent from him, and give it unto him that hath the ten talents.

Mat 25:29 For unto every one that hath shall be given, and he shall have abundance: but from him that hath not, even that which he hath shall be taken away.

Mat 25:30 And cast ye out the unprofitable servant into the outer darkness: there shall be the weeping and the gnashing of teeth.

Mat 25:31 But when the Son of man shall come in his glory, and all the angels with him, then shall he sit on the throne of his glory:

Mat 25:32 and before him shall be gathered all the nations: and he shall separate them one from another, as the shepherd separateth the sheep from the goats;

Mat 25:33 and he shall set the sheep on his right hand, but the goats on the left.

Mat 25:34 Then shall the King say unto them on his right hand, Come, ye blessed of my Father, inherit the kingdom prepared for you from the foundation of the world:

Mat 25:35 for I was hungry, and ye gave me to eat; I was thirsty, and ye gave me drink; I was a stranger, and ye took me in;

Mat 25:36 naked, and ye clothed me; I was sick, and ye visited me; I was in prison, and ye came unto me.

Mat 25:37 Then shall the righteous answer him, saying, Lord, when saw we thee hungry, and fed thee? or athirst, and gave thee drink?

Mat 25:38 And when saw we thee a stranger, and took thee in? or naked, and clothed thee?

Mat 25:39 And when saw we thee sick, or in prison, and came unto thee?

Mat 25:40 And the King shall answer and say unto them, Verily I say unto you, Inasmuch as ye did it unto one of these my brethren, even these least, ye did it unto me.

Mat 25:41 Then shall he say also unto them on the left hand, Depart from me, ye cursed, into the eternal fire which is prepared for the devil and his angels:

Mat 25:42 for I was hungry, and ye did not give me to eat; I was thirsty, and ye gave me no drink;

Mat 25:43 I was a stranger, and ye took me not in; naked, and ye clothed me not; sick, and in prison, and ye visited me not.

Mat 25:44 Then shall they also answer, saying, Lord, when saw we thee hungry, or athirst, or a stranger, or naked, or sick, or in prison, and did not minister unto thee?

Mat 25:45 Then shall he answer them, saying, Verily I say unto you, Inasmuch as ye did it not unto one of these least, ye did it not unto me.

Mat 25:46 And these shall go away into eternal punishment: but the righteous into eternal life.

Chapter 26.

Mat 26:1 And it came to pass, when Jesus had finished all these words, he said unto his disciples,

Mat 26:2 Ye know that after two days the passover cometh, and the Son of man is delivered up to be crucified.

Mat 26:3 Then were gathered together the chief priests, and the elders of the people, unto the court of the high priest, who was called Caiaphas;

Mat 26:4 and they took counsel together that they might take Jesus by subtlety, and kill him.

Mat 26:5 But they said, Not during the feast, lest a tumult arise among people.

Mat 26:6 Now when Jesus was in Bethany, in the house of Simon the leper,

Mat 26:7 there came unto him a woman having an alabaster cruse of exceeding precious ointment, and she poured it upon his head, as he sat at meat.

Mat 26:8 But when the disciples saw it, they had indignation, saying, To what purpose is this waste?

Mat 26:9 For this ointment might have been sold for much, and given to the poor.

Mat 26:10 But Jesus perceiving it said unto them, Why trouble ye the woman? for she hath wrought a good work upon me.

Mat 26:11 For ye have the poor always with you; but me ye have not always.

Mat 26:12 For in that she poured this ointment upon my body, she did it to prepare me for burial.

Mat 26:13 Verily I say unto you, Wheresoever this gospel shall be preached in the whole world, that also which this woman hath done shall be spoken of for a memorial of her.

Mat 26:14 Then one of the twelve, who was called Judas Iscariot, went unto the chief priests,

Mat 26:15 and said, What are ye willing to give me, and I will deliver him unto you? And they weighed unto him thirty pieces of silver.

Mat 26:16 And from that time he sought opportunity to deliver him unto them.

Mat 26:17 Now on the first day of unleavened bread the disciples came to Jesus, saying, Where wilt thou that we make ready for thee to eat the passover?

Mat 26:18 And he said, Go into the city to such a man, and say unto him, The Teacher saith, My time is at hand; I keep the passover at thy house with my disciples.

Mat 26:19 And the disciples did as Jesus appointed them; and they made ready the passover.

Mat 26:20 Now when even was come, he was sitting at meat with the twelve disciples;

Mat 26:21 and as they were eating, he said, Verily I say unto you, that one of you shall betray me.

Mat 26:22 And they were exceeding sorrowful, and began to say unto him every one, Is it I, Lord?

Mat 26:23 And he answered and said, He that dipped his hand with me in the dish, the same shall betray me.

Mat 26:24 The Son of man goeth, even as it is written of him: but woe unto that man through whom the Son of man is betrayed! good were it for that man if he had not been born.

Mat 26:25 And Judas, who betrayed him, answered and said, Is it I, Rabbi? He saith unto him, Thou hast said.

Mat 26:26 And as they were eating, Jesus took bread, and blessed, and brake it; and he gave to the disciples, and said, Take, eat; this is my body.

Mat 26:27 And he took a cup, and gave thanks, and gave to them, saying, Drink ye all of it;

Mat 26:28 for this is my blood of the covenant, which is poured out for many unto remission of sins.

Mat 26:29 But I say unto you, I shall not drink henceforth of this fruit of the vine, until that day when I drink it new with you in my Father's kingdom.

Mat 26:30 And when they had sung a hymn, they went out unto the mount of Olives.

Mat 26:31 Then saith Jesus unto them, All ye shall be offended in me this night: for it is written, I will smite the shepherd, and the sheep of the flock shall be scattered abroad.

Mat 26:32 But after I am raised up, I will go before you into Galilee.

Mat 26:33 But Peter answered and said unto him, If all shall be offended in thee, I will never be offended.

Mat 26:34 Jesus said unto him, Verily I say unto thee, that this night, before the cock crow, thou shalt deny me thrice.

Mat 26:35 Peter saith unto him, Even if I must die with thee, yet will I not deny thee. Likewise also said all the disciples.

Mat 26:36 Then cometh Jesus with them unto a place called Gethsemane, and saith unto his disciples, Sit ye here, while I go yonder and pray.

Mat 26:37 And he took with him Peter and the two sons of Zebedee, and began to be sorrowful and sore troubled.

Mat 26:38 Then saith he unto them, My soul is exceeding sorrowful, even unto death: abide ye here, and watch with me.

Mat 26:39 And he went forward a little, and fell on his face, and prayed, saying, My Father, if it be possible, let this cup pass away from me: nevertheless, not as I will, but as thou wilt.

Mat 26:40 And he cometh unto the disciples, and findeth them sleeping, and saith unto Peter, What, could ye not watch with me one hour?

Mat 26:41 Watch and pray, that ye enter not into temptation: the spirit indeed is willing, but the flesh is weak.

Mat 26:42 Again a second time he went away, and prayed, saying, My Father, if this cannot pass away, except I drink it, thy will be done.

Mat 26:43 And he came again and found them sleeping, for their eyes were heavy.

Mat 26:44 And he left them again, and went away, and prayed a third time, saying again the same words.

Mat 26:45 Then cometh he to the disciples, and saith unto them, Sleep on now, and take your rest: behold, the hour is at hand, and the Son of man is betrayed into the hands of sinners.

Mat 26:46 Arise, let us be going: behold, he is at hand that betrayeth me.

Mat 26:47 And while he yet spake, lo, Judas, one of the twelve, came, and with him a great multitude with swords and staves, from the chief priest and elders of the people.

Mat 26:48 Now he that betrayed him gave them a sign, saying, Whomsoever I shall kiss, that is he: take him.

Mat 26:49 And straightway he came to Jesus, and said, Hail, Rabbi; and kissed him.

Mat 26:50 And Jesus said unto him, Friend, do that for which thou art come. Then they came and laid hands on Jesus, and took him.

Mat 26:51 And behold, one of them that were with Jesus stretched out his hand, and drew his sword, and smote the servant of the high priest, and struck off his ear.

Mat 26:52 Then saith Jesus unto him, Put up again thy sword into its place: for all they that take the sword shall perish with the sword.

Mat 26:53 Or thinkest thou that I cannot beseech my Father, and he shall even now send me more than twelve legions of angels?

Mat 26:54 How then should the scriptures be fulfilled that thus it must be?

Mat 26:55 In that hour said Jesus to the multitudes, Are ye come out as against a robber with swords and staves to seize me? I sat daily in the temple teaching, and ye took me not.

Mat 26:56 But all this is come to pass, that the scriptures of the prophets might be fulfilled. Then all the disciples left him, and fled.

Mat 26:57 And they that had taken Jesus led him away to the house of Caiaphas the high priest, where the scribes and the elders were gathered together.

Mat 26:58 But Peter followed him afar off, unto the court of the high priest, and entered in, and sat with the officers, to see the end.

Mat 26:59 Now the chief priests and the whole council sought false witness against Jesus, that they might put him to death;

Mat 26:60 and they found it not, though many false witnesses came. But afterward came two,

Mat 26:61 and said, This man said, I am able to destroy the temple of God, and to build it in three days.

Mat 26:62 And the high priest stood up, and said unto him, Answerest thou nothing? what is it which these witness against thee?

Mat 26:63 But Jesus held his peace. And the high priest said unto him, I adjure thee by the living God, that thou tell us whether thou art the Christ, the Son of God.

Mat 26:64 Jesus said unto him, Thou hast said: nevertheless I say unto you, Henceforth ye shall see the Son of man sitting at the right hand of Power, and coming on the clouds of heaven.

Mat 26:65 Then the high priest rent his garments, saying, He hath spoken blasphemy: what further need have we of witnesses? behold, now ye have heard the blasphemy:

Mat 26:66 what think ye? They answered and said, He is worthy of death.

Mat 26:67 Then did they spit in his face and buffet him: and some smote him with the palms of their hands,

Mat 26:68 saying, Prophesy unto us, thou Christ: who is he that struck thee?

Mat 26:69 Now Peter was sitting without in the court: and a maid came unto him, saying, Thou also wast with Jesus the Galilaean.

Mat 26:70 But he denied before them all, saying, I know not what thou sayest.

Mat 26:71 And when he was gone out into the porch, another maid saw him, and saith unto them that were there, This man also was with Jesus of Nazareth.

Mat 26:72 And again he denied with an oath, I know not the man.

Mat 26:73 And after a little while they that stood by came and said to Peter, Of a truth thou also art one of them; for thy speech maketh thee known.

Mat 26:74 Then began he to curse and to swear, I know not the man. And straightway the cock crew.

Mat 26:75 And Peter remembered the word which Jesus had said, Before the cock crow, thou shalt deny me thrice. And he went out, and wept bitterly.

Chapter 27.

Mat 27:1 Now when morning was come, all the chief priests and the elders of the people took counsel against Jesus to put him to death:

Mat 27:2 and they bound him, and led him away, and delivered him up to Pilate the governor.

Mat 27:3 Then Judas, who betrayed him, when he saw that he was condemned, repented himself, and brought back the thirty pieces of silver to the chief priests and elders,

Mat 27:4 saying, I have sinned in that I betrayed innocent blood. But they said, What is that to us? see thou to it.

Mat 27:5 And he cast down the pieces of silver into the sanctuary, and departed; and he went away and hanged himself.

Mat 27:6 And the chief priests took the pieces of silver, and said, It is not lawful to put them into the treasury, since it is the price of blood.

Mat 27:7 And they took counsel, and bought with them the potter's field, to bury strangers in.

Mat 27:8 Wherefore that field was called, the field of blood, unto this day.

Mat 27:9 Then was fulfilled that which was spoken through Jeremiah the prophet, saying, And they took the thirty pieces of silver, the price of him that was priced, whom certain of the children of Israel did price;

Mat 27:10 and they gave them for the potter's field, as the Lord appointed me.

Mat 27:11 Now Jesus stood before the governor: and the governor asked him, saying, Art thou the King of the Jews? And Jesus said unto him, Thou sayest.

Mat 27:12 And when he was accused by the chief priests and elders, he answered nothing.

Mat 27:13 Then saith Pilate unto him, Hearest thou not how many things they witness against thee?

Mat 27:14 And he gave him no answer, not even to one word: insomuch that the governor marvelled greatly.

Mat 27:15 Now at the feast the governor was wont to release unto the multitude one prisoner, whom they would.

Mat 27:16 And they had then a notable prisoner, called Barabbas.

Mat 27:17 When therefore they were gathered together, Pilate said unto them, Whom will ye that I release unto you? Barabbas, or Jesus who is called Christ?

Mat 27:18 For he knew that for envy they had delivered him up.

Mat 27:19 And while he was sitting on the judgment-seat, his wife sent unto him, saying, Have thou nothing to do with that righteous man; for I have suffered many things this day in a dream because of him.

Mat 27:20 Now the chief priests and the elders persuaded the multitudes that they should ask for Barabbas, and destroy Jesus.

Mat 27:21 But the governor answered and said unto them, Which of the two will ye that I release unto you? And they said, Barabbas.

Mat 27:22 Pilate saith unto them, What then shall I do unto Jesus who is called Christ? They all say, Let him be crucified.

Mat 27:23 And he said, Why, what evil hath he done? But they cried out exceedingly, saying, Let him be crucified.

Mat 27:24 So when Pilate saw that he prevailed nothing, but rather that a tumult was arising, he took water, and washed his hands before the multitude, saying, I am innocent of the blood of this righteous man; see ye to it.

Mat 27:25 And all the people answered and said, His blood be on us, and on our children.

Mat 27:26 Then released he unto them Barabbas; but Jesus he scourged and delivered to be crucified.

Mat 27:27 Then the soldiers of the governor took Jesus into the Praetorium, and gathered unto him the whole band.

Mat 27:28 And they stripped him, and put on him a scarlet robe.

Mat 27:29 And they platted a crown of thorns and put it upon his head, and a reed in his right hand; and they kneeled down before him, and mocked him, saying, Hail, King of the Jews!

Mat 27:30 And they spat upon him, and took the reed and smote him on the head.

Mat 27:31 And when they had mocked him, they took off from him the robe, and put on him his garments, and led him away to crucify him.

Mat 27:32 And as they came out, they found a man of Cyrene, Simon by name: him they compelled to go with them, that he might bear his cross.

Mat 27:33 And they were come unto a place called Golgotha, that is to say, The place of a skull,

Mat 27:34 they gave him wine to drink mingled with gall: and when he had tasted it, he would not drink.

Mat 27:35 And when they had crucified him, they parted his garments among them, casting lots;

Mat 27:36 and they sat and watched him there.

Mat 27:37 And they set up over his head his accusation written, THIS IS JESUS THE KING OF THE JEWS.

Mat 27:38 Then are there crucified with him two robbers, one on the right hand and one on the left.

Mat 27:39 And they that passed by railed on him, wagging their heads,

Mat 27:40 and saying, Thou that destroyest the temple, and buildest it in three days, save thyself: if thou art the Son of God, come down from the cross.

Mat 27:41 In like manner also the chief priests mocking him, with the scribes and elders, said,

Mat 27:42 He saved others; himself he cannot save. He is the King of Israel; let him now come down from the cross, and we will believe on him.

Mat 27:43 He trusteth on God; let him deliver him now, if he desireth him: for he said, I am the Son of God.

Mat 27:44 And the robbers also that were crucified with him cast upon him the same reproach.

Mat 27:45 Now from the sixth hour there was darkness over all the land until the ninth hour.

Mat 27:46 And about the ninth hour Jesus cried with a loud voice, saying, Eli, Eli, lama sabachthani? that is, My God, my God, why hast thou forsaken me?

Mat 27:47 And some of them stood there, when they heard it, said, This man calleth Elijah.

Mat 27:48 And straightway one of them ran, and took a sponge, and filled it with vinegar, and put it on a reed, and gave him to drink.

Mat 27:49 And the rest said, Let be; let us see whether Elijah cometh to save him.

Mat 27:50 And Jesus cried again with a loud voice, and yielded up his spirit.

Mat 27:51 And behold, the veil of the temple was rent in two from the top to the bottom; and the earth did quake; and the rocks were rent;

Mat 27:52 and the tombs were opened; and many bodies of the saints that had fallen asleep were raised;

Mat 27:53 and coming forth out of the tombs after his resurrection they entered into the holy city and appeared unto many.

Mat 27:54 Now the centurion, and they that were with him watching Jesus, when they saw the earthquake, and the things that were done, feared exceedingly, saying, Truly this was the Son of God.

Mat 27:55 And many women were there beholding from afar, who had followed Jesus from Galilee, ministering unto him:

Mat 27:56 among whom was Mary Magdalene, and Mary the mother of James and Joses, and the mother of the sons of Zebedee.

Mat 27:57 And when even was come, there came a rich man from Arimathaea, named Joseph, who also himself was Jesus' disciple:

Mat 27:58 this man went to Pilate, and asked for the body of Jesus. Then Pilate commanded it to be given up.

Mat 27:59 And Joseph took the body, and wrapped it in a clean linen cloth,

Mat 27:60 and laid it in his own new tomb, which he had hewn out in the rock: and he rolled a great stone to the door of the tomb, and departed.

Mat 27:61 And Mary Magdalene was there, and the other Mary, sitting over against the sepulchre.

Mat 27:62 Now on the morrow, which is the day after the Preparation, the chief priests and the Pharisees were gathered together unto Pilate,

Mat 27:63 saying, Sir, we remember that that deceiver said while he was yet alive, After three days I rise again.

Mat 27:64 Command therefore that the sepulchre be made sure until the third day, lest haply his disciples come and steal him away, and say unto the people, He is risen from the dead: and the last error will be worse than the first.

Mat 27:65 Pilate said unto them, Ye have a guard: go, make it as sure as ye can.

Mat 27:66 So they went, and made the sepulchre sure, sealing the stone, the guard being with them.

Chapter 28.

Mat 28:1 Now late on the sabbath day, as it began to dawn toward the first day of the week, came Mary Magdalene and the other Mary to see the sepulchre.

Mat 28:2 And behold, there was a great earthquake; for an angel of the Lord descended from heaven, and came and rolled away the stone, and sat upon it.

Mat 28:3 His appearance was as lightning, and his raiment white as snow:

Mat 28:4 and for fear of him the watchers did quake, and became as dead men.

Mat 28:5 And the angel answered and said unto the women, Fear not ye; for I know that ye seek Jesus, who hath been crucified.

Mat 28:6 He is not here; for he is risen, even as he said. Come, see the place where the Lord lay.

Mat 28:7 And go quickly, and tell his disciples, He is risen from the dead; and lo, he goeth before you into Galilee; there shall ye see him: lo, I have told you.

Mat 28:8 And they departed quickly from the tomb with fear and great joy, and ran to bring his disciples word.

Mat 28:9 And behold, Jesus met them, saying, All hail. And they came and took hold of his feet, and worshipped him.

Mat 28:10 Then saith Jesus unto them, Fear not: go tell my brethren that they depart into Galilee, and there shall they see me.

Mat 28:11 Now while they were going, behold, some of the guard came into the city, and told unto the chief priests all the things that were come to pass.

Mat 28:12 And when they were assembled with the elders, and had taken counsel, they gave much money unto the soldiers,

Mat 28:13 saying, Say ye, His disciples came by night, and stole him away while we slept.

Mat 28:14 And if this come to the governor's ears, we will persuade him, and rid you of care.

Mat 28:15 So they took the money, and did as they were taught: and this saying was spread abroad among the Jews, and continueth until this day.

Mat 28:16 But the eleven disciples went into Galilee, unto the mountain where Jesus had appointed them.

Mat 28:17 And when they saw him, they worshipped him; but some doubted.

Mat 28:18 And Jesus came to them and spake unto them, saying, All authority hath been given unto me in heaven and on earth.

Mat 28:19 Go ye therefore, and make disciples of all the nations, baptizing them into the name of the Father and of the Son and of the Holy Spirit:

Mat 28:20 teaching them to observe all things whatsoever I commanded you: and lo, I am with you always, even unto the end of the world.

3. Mark

Chapter 1.

Mar 1:1 The beginning of the gospel of Jesus Christ, the Son of God.

Mar 1:2 Even as it is written in Isaiah the prophet, Behold, I send my messenger before thy face, Who shall prepare thy way.

Mar 1:3 The voice of one crying in the wilderness, Make ye ready the way of the Lord, Make his paths straight;

Mar 1:4 John came, who baptized in the wilderness and preached the baptism of repentance unto remission of sins.

Mar 1:5 And there went out unto him all the country of Judaea, and all they of Jerusalem; And they were baptized of him in the river Jordan, confessing their sins.

Mar 1:6 And John was clothed with camel's hair, and had a leathern girdle about his loins, and did eat locusts and wild honey.

Mar 1:7 And he preached, saying, There cometh after me he that is mightier than I, the latchet of whose shoes I am not worthy to stoop down and unloose.

Mar 1:8 I baptized you in water; But he shall baptize you in the Holy Spirit.

Mar 1:9 And it came to pass in those days, that Jesus came from Nazareth of Galilee, and was baptized of John in the Jordan.

Mar 1:10 And straightway coming up out of the water, he saw the heavens rent asunder, and the Spirit as a dove descending upon him:

Mar 1:11 and a voice came out of the heavens, Thou art my beloved Son, in thee I am well pleased.

Mar 1:12 And straightway the Spirit driveth him forth into the wilderness.

Mar 1:13 And he was in the wilderness forty days tempted of Satan; and he was with the wild beasts; and the angels ministered unto him.

Mar 1:14 Now after John was delivered up, Jesus came into Galilee, preaching the gospel of God,

Mar 1:15 and saying, The time is fulfilled, and the kingdom of God is at hand: repent ye, and believe in the gospel.

Mar 1:16 And passing along by the sea of Galilee, he saw Simon and Andrew the brother of Simon casting a net in the sea; for they were fishers.

Mar 1:17 And Jesus said unto them, Come ye after me, and I will make you to become fishers of men.

Mar 1:18 And straightway they left the nets, and followed him.

Mar 1:19 And going on a little further, he saw James the son of Zebedee, and John his brother, who also were in the boat mending the nets.

Mar 1:20 And straightway he called them: and they left their father Zebedee in the boat with the hired servants, and went after him.

Mar 1:21 And they go into Capernaum; and straightway on the sabbath day he entered into the synagogue and taught.

Mar 1:22 And they were astonished at his teaching: for he taught them as having authority, and not as the scribes.

Mar 1:23 And straightway there was in their synagogue a man with an unclean spirit; and he cried out,

Mar 1:24 saying, What have we to do with thee, Jesus thou Nazarene? art thou come to destroy us? I know thee who thou art, the Holy One of God.

Mar 1:25 And Jesus rebuked him, saying, Hold thy peace, and come out of him.

Mar 1:26 And the unclean spirit, tearing him and crying with a loud voice, came out of him.

Mar 1:27 And they were all amazed, insomuch that they questioned among themselves, saying, What is this? a new teaching! with authority he commandeth even the unclean spirits, and they obey him.

Mar 1:28 And the report of him went out straightway everywhere into all the region of Galilee round about.

Mar 1:29 And straightway, when they were come out of the synagogue, they came into the house of Simon and Andrew, with James and John.

Mar 1:30 Now Simon's wife's mother lay sick of a fever; and straightway they tell him of her:

Mar 1:31 and he came and took her by the hand, and raised her up; and the fever left her, and she ministered unto them.

Mar 1:32 And at even, when the sun did set, they brought unto him all that were sick, and them that were possessed with demons.

Mar 1:33 And all the city was gathered together at the door.

Mar 1:34 And he healed many that were sick with divers diseases, and cast out many demons; and he suffered not the demons to speak, because they knew him.

Mar 1:35 And in the morning, a great while before day, he rose up and went out, and departed into a desert place, and there prayed.

Mar 1:36 And Simon and they that were with him followed after him;

Mar 1:37 and they found him, and say unto him, All are seeking thee.

Mar 1:38 And he saith unto them, Let us go elsewhere into the next towns, that I may preach there also; for to this end came I forth.

Mar 1:39 And he went into their synagogues throughout all Galilee, preaching and casting out demons.

Mar 1:40 And there cometh to him a leper, beseeching him, and kneeling down to him, and saying unto him, If thou wilt, thou canst make me clean.

Mar 1:41 And being moved with compassion, he stretched forth his hand, and touched him, and saith unto him, I will; be thou made clean.

Mar 1:42 And straightway the leprosy departed from him, and he was made clean.

Mar 1:43 And he strictly charged him, and straightway sent him out,

Mar 1:44 and saith unto him, See thou say nothing to any man: but go show thyself to the priest, and offer for thy cleansing the things which Moses commanded, for a testimony unto them.

Mar 1:45 But he went out, and began to publish it much, and to spread abroad the matter, insomuch that Jesus could no more openly enter into a city, but was without in desert places: and they came to him from every quarter.

Chapter 2.

Mar 2:1 And when he entered again into Capernaum after some days, it was noised that he was in the house.

Mar 2:2 And many were gathered together, so that there was no longer room for them, no, not even about the door: and he spake the word unto them.

Mar 2:3 And they come, bringing unto him a man sick of the palsy, borne of four.

Mar 2:4 And when they could not come nigh unto him for the crowd, they uncovered the roof where he was: and when they had broken it up, they let down the bed whereon the sick of the palsy lay.

Mar 2:5 And Jesus seeing their faith saith unto the sick of the palsy, Son, thy sins are forgiven.

Mar 2:6 But there were certain of the scribes sitting there, and reasoning in their hearts,

Mar 2:7 Why doth this man thus speak? he blasphemeth: who can forgive sins but one, even God?

Mar 2:8 And straightway Jesus, perceiving in his spirit that they so reasoned within themselves, saith unto them, Why reason ye these things in your hearts?

Mar 2:9 Which is easier, to say to the sick of the palsy, Thy sins are forgiven; or to say, Arise, and take up thy bed, and walk?

Mar 2:10 But that ye may know that the Son of man hath authority on earth to forgive sins (he saith to the sick of the palsy),

Mar 2:11 I say unto thee, Arise, take up thy bed, and go unto thy house.

Mar 2:12 And he arose, and straightway took up the bed, and went forth before them all; insomuch that they were all amazed, and glorified God, saying, We never saw it on this fashion.

Mar 2:13 And he went forth again by the sea side; and all the multitude resorted unto him, and he taught them.

Mar 2:14 And as he passed by, he saw Levi the son of Alphaeus sitting at the place of toll, and he saith unto him, Follow me. And he arose and followed him.

Mar 2:15 And it came to pass, that he was sitting at meat in his house, and many publicans and sinners sat down with Jesus and his disciples: for there were many, and they followed him.

Mar 2:16 And the scribes of the Pharisees, when they saw that he was eating with the sinners and publicans, said unto his disciples, How is it that he eateth and drinketh with publicans and sinners?

Mar 2:17 And when Jesus heard it, he saith unto them, They that are whole have no need of a physician, but they that are sick: I came not to call the righteous, but sinners.

Mar 2:18 And John's disciples and the Pharisees were fasting: and they come and say unto him, Why do John's disciples and the disciples of the Pharisees fast, but thy disciples fast not?

Mar 2:19 And Jesus said unto them, Can the sons of the bridechamber fast, while the bridegroom is with them? as long as they have the bridegroom with them, they cannot fast.

Mar 2:20 But the days will come, when the bridegroom shall be taken away from them, and then will they fast in that day.

Mar 2:21 No man seweth a piece of undressed cloth on an old garment: else that which should fill it up taketh from it, the new from the old, and a worse rent is made.

Mar 2:22 And no man putteth new wine into old wineskins; else the wine will burst the skins, and the wine perisheth, and the skins: but they put new wine into fresh wine-skins.

Mar 2:23 And it came to pass, that he was going on the sabbath day through the grainfields; and his disciples began, as they went, to pluck the ears.

Mar 2:24 And the Pharisees said unto him, Behold, why do they on the sabbath day that which is not lawful?

Mar 2:25 And he said unto them, Did ye never read what David did, when he had need, and was hungry, he, and they that were with him?

Mar 2:26 How he entered into the house of God when Abiathar was high priest, and ate the showbread, which it is not lawful to eat save for the priests, and gave also to them that were with him?

Mar 2:27 And he said unto them, The sabbath was made for man, and not man for the sabbath:

Mar 2:28 so that the Son of man is lord even of the sabbath.

Chapter 3.

Mar 3:1 And he entered again into the synagogue; and there was a man there who had his hand withered.

Mar 3:2 And they watched him, whether he would heal him on the sabbath day; that they might accuse him.

Mar 3:3 And he saith unto the man that had his hand withered, Stand forth.

Mar 3:4 And he saith unto them, Is it lawful on the sabbath day to do good, or to do harm? to save a life, or to kill? But they held their peace.

Mar 3:5 And when he had looked round about on them with anger, being grieved at the hardening of their heart, he saith unto the man, Stretch forth thy hand. And he stretched it forth; and his hand was restored.

Mar 3:6 And the Pharisees went out, and straightway with the Herodians took counsel against him, how they might destroy him.

Mar 3:7 And Jesus with his disciples withdrew to the sea: and a great multitude from Galilee followed; and from Judaea,

Mar 3:8 and from Jerusalem, and from Idumaea, and beyond the Jordan, and about Tyre and Sidon, a great multitude, hearing what great things he did, came unto him.

Mar 3:9 And he spake to his disciples, that a little boat should wait on him because of the crowd, lest they should throng him:

Mar 3:10 for he had healed many; insomuch that as many as had plagues pressed upon him that they might touch him.

Mar 3:11 And the unclean spirits, whensoever they beheld him, fell down before him, and cried, saying, Thou art the Son of God.

Mar 3:12 And he charged them much that they should not make him known.

Mar 3:13 And he goeth up into the mountain, and calleth unto him whom he himself would; and they went unto him.

Mar 3:14 And he appointed twelve, that they might be with him, and that he might send them forth to preach,

Mar 3:15 and to have authority to cast out demons:

Mar 3:16 and Simon he surnamed Peter;

Mar 3:17 and James the son of Zebedee, and John the brother of James; and them he surnamed Boanerges, which is, Sons of thunder:

Mar 3:18 and Andrew, and Philip, and Bartholomew, and Matthew, and Thomas, and James the son of Alphaeus, and Thaddaeus, and Simon the Cananaean,

Mar 3:19 and Judas Iscariot, who also betrayed him. And he cometh into a house.

Mar 3:20 And the multitude cometh together again, so that they could not so much as eat bread.

Mar 3:21 And when his friends heard it, they went out to lay hold on him: for they said, He is beside himself.

Mar 3:22 And the scribes that came down from Jerusalem said, He hath Beelzebub, and, By the prince of the demons casteth he out the demons.

Mar 3:23 And he called them unto him, and said unto them in parables, How can Satan cast out Satan?

Mar 3:24 And if a kingdom be divided against itself, that kingdom cannot stand.

Mar 3:25 And if a house be divided against itself, that house will not be able to stand.

Mar 3:26 And if Satan hath rise up against himself, and is divided, he cannot stand, but hath an end.

Mar 3:27 But no one can enter into the house of the strong man, and spoil his goods, except he first bind the strong man; and then he will spoil his house.

Mar 3:28 Verily I say unto you, All their sins shall be forgiven unto the sons of men, and their blasphemies wherewith soever they shall blaspheme:

Mar 3:29 but whosoever shall blaspheme against the Holy Spirit hath never forgiveness, but is guilty of an eternal sin:

Mar 3:30 because they said, He hath an unclean spirit.

Mar 3:31 And there come his mother and his brethren; and, standing without, they sent unto him, calling him.

Mar 3:32 And a multitude was sitting about him; and they say unto him, Behold, thy mother and thy brethren without seek for thee.

Mar 3:33 And he answereth them, and saith, Who is my mother and my brethren?

Mar 3:34 And looking round on them that sat round about him, he saith, Behold, my mother and my brethren!

Mar 3:35 For whosoever shall do the will of God, the same is my brother, and sister, and mother.

Chapter 4.

Mar 4:1 And again he began to teach by the sea side. And there is gathered unto him a very great multitude, so that he entered into a boat, and sat in the sea; and all the multitude were by the sea on the land.

Mar 4:2 And he taught them many things in parables, and said unto them in his teaching,

Mar 4:3 Hearken: Behold, the sower went forth to sow:

Mar 4:4 and it came to pass, as he sowed, some seed fell by the way side, and the birds came and devoured it.

Mar 4:5 And other fell on the rocky ground, where it had not much earth; and straightway it sprang up, because it had no deepness of earth:

Mar 4:6 and when the sun was risen, it was scorched; and because it had no root, it withered away.

Mar 4:7 And other fell among the thorns, and the thorns grew up, and choked it, and it yielded no fruit.

Mar 4:8 And others fell into the good ground, and yielded fruit, growing up and increasing; and brought forth, thirtyfold, and sixtyfold, and a hundredfold.

Mar 4:9 And he said, Who hath ears to hear, let him hear.

Mar 4:10 And when he was alone, they that were about him with the twelve asked of him the parables.

Mar 4:11 And he said unto them, Unto you is given the mystery of the kingdom of God: but unto them that are without, all things are done in parables:

Mar 4:12 that seeing they may see, and not perceive; and hearing they may hear, and not understand; lest haply they should turn again, and it should be forgiven them.

Mar 4:13 And he saith unto them, Know ye not this parable? and how shall ye know all the parables?

Mar 4:14 The sower soweth the word.

Mar 4:15 And these are they by the way side, where the word is sown; and when they have heard, straightway cometh Satan, and taketh away the word which hath been sown in them.

Mar 4:16 And these in like manner are they that are sown upon the rocky places, who, when they have heard the word, straightway receive it with joy;

Mar 4:17 and they have no root in themselves, but endure for a while; then, when tribulation or persecution ariseth because of the word, straightway they stumble.

Mar 4:18 And others are they that are sown among the thorns; these are they that have heard the word,

Mar 4:19 and the cares of the world, and the deceitfulness of riches, and the lusts of other things entering in, choke the word, and it becometh unfruitful.

Mar 4:20 And those are they that were sown upon the good ground; such as hear the word, and accept it, and bear fruit, thirtyfold, and sixtyfold, and a hundredfold.

Mar 4:21 And he said unto them, Is the lamp brought to be put under the bushel, or under the bed, and not to be put on the stand?

Mar 4:22 For there is nothing hid, save that it should be manifested; neither was anything made secret, but that it should come to light.

Mar 4:23 If any man hath ears to hear, let him hear.

Mar 4:24 And he said unto them, Take heed what ye hear: with what measure ye mete it shall be measured unto you; and more shall be given unto you.

Mar 4:25 For he that hath, to him shall be given: and he that hath not, from him shall be taken away even that which he hath.

Mar 4:26 And he said, So is the kingdom of God, as if a man should cast seed upon the earth;

Mar 4:27 and should sleep and rise night and day, and the seed should spring up and grow, he knoweth not how.

Mar 4:28 The earth beareth fruit of herself; first the blade, then the ear, then the full grain in the ear.

Mar 4:29 But when the fruit is ripe, straightway he putteth forth the sickle, because the harvest is come.

Mar 4:30 And he said, How shall we liken the kingdom of God? or in what parable shall we set it forth?

Mar 4:31 It is like a grain of mustard seed, which, when it is sown upon the earth, though it be less than all the seeds that are upon the earth,

Mar 4:32 yet when it is sown, groweth up, and becometh greater than all the herbs, and putteth out great branches; so that the birds of the heaven can lodge under the shadow thereof.

Mar 4:33 And with many such parables spake he the word unto them, as they were able to hear it;

Mar 4:34 and without a parable spake he not unto them: but privately to his own disciples he expounded all things.

Mar 4:35 And on that day, when even was come, he saith unto them, Let us go over unto the other side.

Mar 4:36 And leaving the multitude, they take him with them, even as he was, in the boat. And other boats were with him.

Mar 4:37 And there ariseth a great storm of wind, and the waves beat into the boat, insomuch that the boat was now filling.

Mar 4:38 And he himself was in the stern, asleep on the cushion: and they awake him, and say unto him, Teacher, carest thou not that we perish?

Mar 4:39 And he awoke, and rebuked the wind, and said unto the sea, Peace, be still. And the wind ceased, and there was a great calm.

Mar 4:40 And he said unto them, Why are ye fearful? have ye not yet faith?

Mar 4:41 And they feared exceedingly, and said one to another, Who then is this, that even the wind and the sea obey him?

Chapter 5.

Mar 5:1 And they came to the other side of the sea, into the country of the Gerasenes.

Mar 5:2 And when he was come out of the boat, straightway there met him out of the tombs a man with an unclean spirit,

Mar 5:3 who had his dwelling in the tombs: and no man could any more bind him, no, not with a chain;

Mar 5:4 because that he had been often bound with fetters and chains, and the chains had been rent asunder by him, and the fetters broken in pieces: and no man had strength to tame him.

Mar 5:5 And always, night and day, in the tombs and in the mountains, he was crying out, and cutting himself with stones.

Mar 5:6 And when he saw Jesus from afar, he ran and worshipped him;

Mar 5:7 and crying out with a loud voice, he saith, What have I to do with thee, Jesus, thou Son of the Most High God? I adjure thee by God, torment me not.

Mar 5:8 For he said unto him, Come forth, thou unclean spirit, out of the man.

Mar 5:9 And he asked him, What is thy name? And he saith unto him, My name is Legion; for we are many.

Mar 5:10 And he besought him much that he would not send them away out of the country.

Mar 5:11 Now there was there on the mountain side a great herd of swine feeding.

Mar 5:12 And they besought him, saying, Send us into the swine, that we may enter into them.

Mar 5:13 And he gave them leave. And the unclean spirits came out, and entered into the swine: and the herd rushed down the steep into the sea, in number about two thousand; and they were drowned in the sea.

Mar 5:14 And they that fed them fled, and told it in the city, and in the country. And they came to see what it was that had come to pass.

Mar 5:15 And they come to Jesus, and behold him that was possessed with demons sitting, clothed and in his right mind, even him that had the legion: and they were afraid.

Mar 5:16 And they that saw it declared unto them how it befell him that was possessed with demons, and concerning the swine.

Mar 5:17 And they began to beseech him to depart from their borders.

Mar 5:18 And as he was entering into the boat, he that had been possessed with demons besought him that he might be with him.

Mar 5:19 And he suffered him not, but saith unto him, Go to thy house unto thy friends, and tell them how great things the Lord hath done for thee, and how he had mercy on thee.

Mar 5:20 And he went his way, and began to publish in Decapolis how great things Jesus had done for him: and all men marvelled.

Mar 5:21 And when Jesus had crossed over again in the boat unto the other side, a great multitude was gathered unto him; and he was by the sea.

Mar 5:22 And there cometh one of the rulers of the synagogue, Jairus by name; and seeing him, he falleth at his feet,

Mar 5:23 and beseecheth him much, saying, My little daughter is at the point of death: I pray thee, that thou come and lay thy hands on her, that she may be made whole, and live.

Mar 5:24 And he went with him; and a great multitude followed him, and they thronged him.

Mar 5:25 And a woman, who had an issue of blood twelve years,

Mar 5:26 and had suffered many things of many physicians, and had spent all that she had, and was nothing bettered, but rather grew worse,

Mar 5:27 having heard the things concerning Jesus, came in the crowd behind, and touched his garment.

Mar 5:28 For she said, If I touch but his garments, I shall be made whole.

Mar 5:29 And straightway the fountain of her blood was dried up; and she felt in her body that she was healed of her plague.

Mar 5:30 And straightway Jesus, perceiving in himself that the power proceeding from him had gone forth, turned him about in the crowd, and said, Who touched my garments?

Mar 5:31 And his disciples said unto him, Thou seest the multitude thronging thee, and sayest thou, Who touched me?

Mar 5:32 And he looked round about to see her that had done this thing.

Mar 5:33 But the woman fearing and trembling, knowing what had been done to her, came and fell down before him, and told him all the truth.

Mar 5:34 And he said unto her, Daughter, thy faith hath made thee whole; go in peace, and be whole of thy plague.

Mar 5:35 While he yet spake, they come from the ruler of the synagogue's house saying, Thy daughter is dead: why troublest thou the Teacher any further?

Mar 5:36 But Jesus, not heeding the word spoken, saith unto the ruler of the synagogue, Fear not, only believe.

Mar 5:37 And he suffered no man to follow with him, save Peter, and James, and John the brother of James.

Mar 5:38 And they come to the house of the ruler of the synagogue; and he beholdeth a tumult, and many weeping and wailing greatly.

Mar 5:39 And when he was entered in, he saith unto them, Why make ye a tumult, and weep? the child is not dead, but sleepeth.

Mar 5:40 And they laughed him to scorn. But he, having put them all forth, taketh the father of the child and her mother and them that were with him, and goeth in where the child was.

Mar 5:41 And taking the child by the hand, he saith unto her, Talitha cumi; which is, being interpreted, Damsel, I say unto thee, Arise.

Mar 5:42 And straightway the damsel rose up, and walked; for she was twelve years old. And they were amazed straightway with a great amazement.

Mar 5:43 And he charged them much that no man should know this: and he commanded that something should be given her to eat.

Chapter 6.

Mar 6:1 And he went out from thence; and he cometh into his own country; and his disciples follow him.

Mar 6:2 And when the sabbath was come, he began to teach in the synagogue: and many hearing him were astonished, saying, Whence hath this man these things? and, What is the wisdom that is given unto this man, and what mean such mighty works wrought by his hands?

Mar 6:3 Is not this the carpenter, the son of Mary, and brother of James, and Joses, and Judas, and Simon? and are not his sisters here with us? And they were offended in him.

Mar 6:4 And Jesus said unto them, A prophet is not without honor, save in his own country, and among his own kin, and in his own house.

Mar 6:5 And he could there do no mighty work, save that he laid his hands upon a few sick folk, and healed them.

Mar 6:6 And he marvelled because of their unbelief. And he went round about the villages teaching.

Mar 6:7 And he calleth unto him the twelve, and began to send them forth by two and two; and he gave them authority over the unclean spirits;

Mar 6:8 and he charged them that they should take nothing for their journey, save a staff only; no bread, no wallet, no money in their purse;

Mar 6:9 but to go shod with sandals: and, said he, put not on two coats.

Mar 6:10 And he said unto them, Wheresoever ye enter into a house, there abide till ye depart thence.

Mar 6:11 And whatsoever place shall not receive you, and they hear you not, as ye go forth thence, shake off the dust that is under your feet for a testimony unto them.

Mar 6:12 And they went out, and preached that men should repent.

Mar 6:13 And they cast out many demons, and anointed with oil many that were sick, and healed them.

Mar 6:14 And king Herod heard thereof; for his name had become known: and he said, John the Baptizer is risen from the dead, and therefore do these powers work in him.

Mar 6:15 But others said, It is Elijah. And others said, It is a prophet, even as one of the prophets.

Mar 6:16 But Herod, when he heard thereof, said, John, whom I beheaded, he is risen.

Mar 6:17 For Herod himself had sent forth and laid hold upon John, and bound him in prison for the sake of Herodias, his brother Philip's wife; for he had married her.

Mar 6:18 For John said unto Herod, It is not lawful for thee to have thy brother's wife.

Mar 6:19 And Herodias set herself against him, and desired to kill him; and she could not;

Mar 6:20 for Herod feared John, knowing that he was a righteous and holy man, and kept him safe. And when he heard him, he was much perplexed; and he heard him gladly.

Mar 6:21 And when a convenient day was come, that Herod on his birthday made a supper to his lords, and the high captains, and the chief men of Galilee;

Mar 6:22 and when the daughter of Herodias herself came in and danced, she pleased Herod and them that sat at meat with him; and the king said unto the damsel, Ask of me whatsoever thou wilt, and I will give it thee.

Mar 6:23 And he sware unto her, Whatsoever thou shalt ask of me, I will give it thee, unto the half of my kingdom.

Mar 6:24 And she went out, and said unto her mother, What shall I ask? And she said, The head of John the Baptizer.

Mar 6:25 And she came in straightway with haste unto the king, and asked, saying, I will that thou forthwith give me on a platter the head of John the Baptist.

Mar 6:26 And the king was exceeding sorry; but for the sake of his oaths, and of them that sat at meat, he would not reject her.

Mar 6:27 And straightway the king sent forth a soldier of his guard, and commanded to bring his head: and he went and beheaded him in the prison,

Mar 6:28 and brought his head on a platter, and gave it to the damsel; and the damsel gave it to her mother.

Mar 6:29 And when his disciples heard thereof, they came and took up his corpse, and laid it in a tomb.

Mar 6:30 And the apostles gather themselves together unto Jesus; and they told him all things, whatsoever they had done, and whatsoever they had taught.

Mar 6:31 And he saith unto them, Come ye yourselves apart into a desert place, and rest a while. For there were many coming and going, and they had no leisure so much as to eat.

Mar 6:32 And they went away in the boat to a desert place apart.

Mar 6:33 And the people saw them going, and many knew them, and they ran together there on foot from all the cities, and outwent them.

Mar 6:34 And he came forth and saw a great multitude, and he had compassion on them, because they were as sheep not having a shepherd: and he began to teach them many things.

Mar 6:35 And when the day was now far spent, his disciples came unto him, and said, The place is desert, and the day is now far spent;

Mar 6:36 send them away, that they may go into the country and villages round about, and buy themselves somewhat to eat.

Mar 6:37 But he answered and said unto them, Give ye them to eat. And they say unto him, Shall we go and buy two hundred shillings' worth of bread, and give them to eat?

Mar 6:38 And he saith unto them, How many loaves have ye? go and see. And when they knew, they say, Five, and two fishes.

Mar 6:39 And he commanded them that all should sit down by companies upon the green grass.

Mar 6:40 And they sat down in ranks, by hundreds, and by fifties.

Mar 6:41 And he took the five loaves and the two fishes, and looking up to heaven, he blessed, and brake the loaves; and he gave to the disciples to set before them; and the two fishes divided he among them all.

Mar 6:42 And they all ate, and were filled.

Mar 6:43 And they took up broken pieces, twelve basketfuls, and also of the fishes.

Mar 6:44 And they that ate the loaves were five thousand men.

Mar 6:45 And straightway he constrained his disciples to enter into the boat, and to go before him unto the other side to Bethsaida, while he himself sendeth the multitude away.

Mar 6:46 And after he had taken leave of them, he departed into the mountain to pray.

Mar 6:47 And when even was come, the boat was in the midst of the sea, and he alone on the land.

Mar 6:48 And seeing them distressed in rowing, for the wind was contrary unto them, about the fourth watch of the night he cometh unto them, walking on the sea; and he would have passed by them:

Mar 6:49 but they, when they saw him walking on the sea, supposed that it was a ghost, and cried out;

Mar 6:50 for they all saw him, and were troubled. But he straightway spake with them, and saith unto them, Be of good cheer: it is I; be not afraid.

Mar 6:51 And he went up unto them into the boat; and the wind ceased: and they were sore amazed in themselves;

Mar 6:52 for they understood not concerning the loaves, but their heart was hardened.

Mar 6:53 And when they had crossed over, they came to the land unto Gennesaret, and moored to the shore.

Mar 6:54 And when they were come out of the boat, straightway the people knew him,

Mar 6:55 and ran round about that whole region, and began to carry about on their beds those that were sick, where they heard he was.

Mar 6:56 And wheresoever he entered, into villages, or into cities, or into the country, they laid the sick in the marketplaces, and besought him that they might touch if it were but the border of his garment: and as many as touched him were made whole.

Chapter 7.

Mar 7:1 And there are gathered together unto him the Pharisees, and certain of the scribes, who had come from Jerusalem,

Mar 7:2 and had seen that some of his disciples ate their bread with defiled, that is, unwashen, hands.

Mar 7:3 (For the Pharisees, and all the Jews, except they wash their hands diligently, eat not, holding the tradition of the elders;

Mar 7:4 and when they come from the market-place, except they bathe themselves, they eat not; and many other things there are, which they have received to hold, washings of cups, and pots, and brasen vessels.)

Mar 7:5 And the Pharisees and the scribes ask him, Why walk not thy disciples according to the tradition of the elders, but eat their bread with defiled hands?

Mar 7:6 And he said unto them, Well did Isaiah prophesy of you hypocrites, as it is written, This people honoreth me with their lips, But their heart is far from me.

Mar 7:7 But in vain do they worship me, Teaching as their doctrines the precepts of men.

Mar 7:8 Ye leave the commandment of God, and hold fast the tradition of men.

Mar 7:9 And he said unto them, Full well do ye reject the commandment of God, that ye may keep your tradition.

Mar 7:10 For Moses said, Honor thy father and thy mother; and, He that speaketh evil of father or mother, let him die the death:

Mar 7:11 but ye say, If a man shall say to his father or his mother, That wherewith thou mightest have been profited by me is Corban, that is to say, Given to God;

Mar 7:12 ye no longer suffer him to do aught for his father or his mother;

Mar 7:13 making void the word of God by your tradition, which ye have delivered: and many such like things ye do.

Mar 7:14 And he called to him the multitude again, and said unto them, Hear me all of you, and understand:

Mar 7:15 there is nothing from without the man, that going into him can defile him; but the things which proceed out of the man are those that defile the man.

Mar 7:16 If any man hath ears to hear, let him hear.

Mar 7:17 And when he was entered into the house from the multitude, his disciples asked of him the parable.

Mar 7:18 And he saith unto them, Are ye so without understanding also? Perceive ye not, that whatsoever from without goeth into the man, it cannot defile him;

Mar 7:19 because it goeth not into his heart, but into his belly, and goeth out into the draught? This he said, making all meats clean.

Mar 7:20 And he said, That which proceedeth out of the man, that defileth the man.

Mar 7:21 For from within, out of the heart of men, evil thoughts proceed, fornications, thefts, murders, adulteries,

Mar 7:22 covetings, wickednesses, deceit, lasciviousness, an evil eye, railing, pride, foolishness:

Mar 7:23 all these evil things proceed from within, and defile the man.

Mar 7:24 And from thence he arose, and went away into the borders of Tyre and Sidon. And he entered into a house, and would have no man know it; and he could not be hid.

Mar 7:25 But straightway a woman, whose little daughter had an unclean spirit, having heard of him, came and fell down at his feet.

Mar 7:26 Now the woman was a Greek, a Syrophoenician by race. And she besought him that he would cast forth the demon out of her daughter.

Mar 7:27 And he said unto her, Let the children first be filled: for it is not meet to take the children's bread and cast it to the dogs.

Mar 7:28 But she answered and saith unto him, Yea, Lord; even the dogs under the table eat of the children's crumbs.

Mar 7:29 And he said unto her, For this saying go thy way; the demon is gone out of thy daughter.

Mar 7:30 And she went away unto her house, and found the child laid upon the bed, and the demon gone out.

Mar 7:31 And again he went out from the borders of Tyre, and came through Sidon unto the sea of Galilee, through the midst of the borders of Decapolis.

Mar 7:32 And they bring unto him one that was deaf, and had an impediment in his speech; and they beseech him to lay his hand upon him.

Mar 7:33 And he took him aside from the multitude privately, and put his fingers into his ears, and he spat, and touched his tongue;

Mar 7:34 and looking up to heaven, he sighed, and saith unto him, Ephphatha, that is, Be opened.

Mar 7:35 And his ears were opened, and the bond of his tongue was loosed, and he spake plain.

Mar 7:36 And he charged them that they should tell no man: but the more he charged them, so much the more a great deal they published it.

Mar 7:37 And they were beyond measure astonished, saying, He hath done all things well; he maketh even the deaf to hear, and the dumb to speak.

Chapter 8.

Mar 8:1 In those days, when there was again a great multitude, and they had nothing to eat, he called unto him his disciples, and saith unto them,

Mar 8:2 I have compassion on the multitude, because they continue with me now three days, and have nothing to eat:

Mar 8:3 and if I send them away fasting to their home, they will faint on the way; and some of them are come from far.

Mar 8:4 And his disciples answered him, Whence shall one be able to fill these men with bread here in a desert place?

Mar 8:5 And he asked them, How many loaves have ye? And they said, Seven.

Mar 8:6 And he commandeth the multitude to sit down on the ground: and he took the seven loaves, and having given thanks, he brake, and gave to his disciples, to set before them; and they set them before the multitude.

Mar 8:7 And they had a few small fishes: and having blessed them, he commanded to set these also before them.

Mar 8:8 And they ate, and were filled: and they took up, of broken pieces that remained over, seven baskets.

Mar 8:9 And they were about four thousand: and he sent them away.

Mar 8:10 And straightway he entered into the boat with his disciples, and came into the parts of Dalmanutha.

Mar 8:11 And the Pharisees came forth, and began to question with him, seeking of him a sign from heaven, trying him.

Mar 8:12 And he sighed deeply in his spirit, and saith, Why doth this generation seek a sign? verily I say unto you, There shall no sign be given unto this generation.

Mar 8:13 And he left them, and again entering into the boat departed to the other side.

Mar 8:14 And they forgot to take bread; and they had not in the boat with them more than one loaf.

Mar 8:15 And he charged them, saying, Take heed, beware of the leaven of the Pharisees and the leaven of Herod.

Mar 8:16 And they reasoned one with another, saying, We have no bread.

Mar 8:17 And Jesus perceiving it saith unto them, Why reason ye, because ye have no bread? do ye not yet perceive, neither understand? have ye your heart hardened?

Mar 8:18 Having eyes, see ye not? and having ears, hear ye not? and do ye not remember?

Mar 8:19 When I brake the five loaves among the five thousand, how many baskets full of broken pieces took ye up? They say unto him, Twelve.

Mar 8:20 And when the seven among the four thousand, how many basketfuls of broken pieces took ye up? And they say unto him, Seven.

Mar 8:21 And he said unto them, Do ye not yet understand?

Mar 8:22 And they come unto Bethsaida. And they bring to him a blind man, and beseech him to touch him.

Mar 8:23 And he took hold of the blind man by the hand, and brought him out of the village; and when he had spit on his eyes, and laid his hands upon him, he asked him, Seest thou aught?

Mar 8:24 And he looked up, and said, I see men; for I behold them as trees, walking.

Mar 8:25 Then again he laid his hands upon his eyes; and he looked stedfastly, and was restored, and saw all things clearly.

Mar 8:26 And he sent him away to his home, saying, Do not even enter into the village.

Mar 8:27 And Jesus went forth, and his disciples, into the villages of Caesarea Philippi: and on the way he asked his disciples, saying unto them, Who do men say that I am?

Mar 8:28 And they told him, saying, John the Baptist; and others, Elijah; but others, One of the prophets.

Mar 8:29 And he asked them, But who say ye that I am? Peter answereth and saith unto him, Thou art the Christ.

Mar 8:30 And he charged them that they should tell no man of him.

Mar 8:31 And he began to teach them, that the Son of man must suffer many things, and be rejected by the elders, and the chief priests, and the scribes, and be killed, and after three days rise again.

Mar 8:32 And he spake the saying openly. And Peter took him, and began to rebuke him.

Mar 8:33 But he turning about, and seeing his disciples, rebuked Peter, and saith, Get thee behind me, Satan; for thou mindest not the things of God, but the things of men.

Mar 8:34 And he called unto him the multitude with his disciples, and said unto them, If any man would come after me, let him deny himself, and take up his cross, and follow me.

Mar 8:35 For whosoever would save his life shall lose it; and whosoever shall lose his life for my sake and the gospel's shall save it.

Mar 8:36 For what doth it profit a man, to gain the whole world, and forfeit his life?

Mar 8:37 For what should a man give in exchange for his life?

Mar 8:38 For whosoever shall be ashamed of me and of my words in this adulterous and sinful generation, the Son of man also shall be ashamed of him, when he cometh in the glory of his Father with the holy angels.

Chapter 9.

Mar 9:1 And he said unto them, Verily I say unto you, There are some here of them that stand by, who shall in no wise taste of death, till they see the kingdom of God come with power.

Mar 9:2 And after six days Jesus taketh with him Peter, and James, and John, and bringeth them up into a high mountain apart by themselves: and he was transfigured before them;

Mar 9:3 and his garments became glistering, exceeding white, so as no fuller on earth can whiten them.

Mar 9:4 And there appeared unto them Elijah with Moses: and they were talking with Jesus.

Mar 9:5 And Peter answereth and saith to Jesus, Rabbi, it is good for us to be here: and let us make three tabernacles; one for thee, and one for Moses, and one for Elijah.

Mar 9:6 For he knew not what to answer; for they became sore afraid.

Mar 9:7 And there came a cloud overshadowing them: and there came a voice out of the cloud, This is my beloved Son: hear ye him.

Mar 9:8 And suddenly looking round about, they saw no one any more, save Jesus only with themselves.

Mar 9:9 And as they were coming down from the mountain, he charged them that they should tell no man what things they had seen, save when the Son of man should have risen again from the dead.

Mar 9:10 And they kept the saying, questioning among themselves what the rising again from the dead should mean.

Mar 9:11 And they asked him, saying, How is it that the scribes say that Elijah must first come?

Mar 9:12 And he said unto them, Elijah indeed cometh first, and restoreth all things: and how is it written of the Son of man, that he should suffer many things and be set at nought?

Mar 9:13 But I say unto you, that Elijah is come, and they have also done unto him whatsoever they would, even as it is written of him.

Mar 9:14 And when they came to the disciples, they saw a great multitude about them, and scribes questioning with them.

Mar 9:15 And straightway all the multitude, when they saw him, were greatly amazed, and running to him saluted him.

Mar 9:16 And he asked them, What question ye with them?

Mar 9:17 And one of the multitude answered him, Teacher, I brought unto thee my son, who hath a dumb spirit;

Mar 9:18 and wheresoever it taketh him, it dasheth him down: and he foameth, and grindeth his teeth, and pineth away: and I spake to thy disciples that they should cast it out; and they were not able.

Mar 9:19 And he answereth them and saith, O faithless generation, how long shall I be with you? how long shall I bear with you? bring him unto me.

Mar 9:20 And they brought him unto him: and when he saw him, straightway the spirit tare him grievously; and he fell on the ground, and wallowed foaming.

Mar 9:21 And he asked his father, How long time is it since this hath come unto him? And he said, From a child.

Mar 9:22 And oft-times it hath cast him both into the fire and into the waters, to destroy him: but if thou canst do anything, have compassion on us, and help us.

Mar 9:23 And Jesus said unto him, If thou canst! All things are possible to him that believeth.

Mar 9:24 Straightway the father of the child cried out, and said, I believe; help thou mine unbelief.

Mar 9:25 And when Jesus saw that a multitude came running together, he rebuked the unclean spirit, saying unto him, Thou dumb and deaf spirit, I command thee, come out of him, and enter no more into him.

Mar 9:26 And having cried out, and torn him much, he came out: and the boy became as one dead; insomuch that the more part said, He is dead.

Mar 9:27 But Jesus took him by the hand, and raised him up; and he arose.

Mar 9:28 And when he was come into the house, his disciples asked him privately, How is it that we could not cast it out?

Mar 9:29 And he said unto them, This kind can come out by nothing, save by prayer.

Mar 9:30 And they went forth from thence, and passed through Galilee; and he would not that any man should know it.

Mar 9:31 For he taught his disciples, and said unto them, The Son of man is delivered up into the hands of men, and they shall kill him; and when he is killed, after three days he shall rise again.

Mar 9:32 But they understood not the saying, and were afraid to ask him.

Mar 9:33 And they came to Capernaum: and when he was in the house he asked them, What were ye reasoning on the way?

Mar 9:34 But they held their peace: for they had disputed one with another on the way, who was the greatest.

Mar 9:35 And he sat down, and called the twelve; and he saith unto them, If any man would be first, he shall be last of all, and servant of all.

Mar 9:36 And he took a little child, and set him in the midst of them: and taking him in his arms, he said unto them,

Mar 9:37 Whosoever shall receive one of such little children in my name, receiveth me: and whosoever receiveth me, receiveth not me, but him that sent me.

Mar 9:38 John said unto him, Teacher, we saw one casting out demons in thy name; and we forbade him, because he followed not us.

Mar 9:39 But Jesus said, Forbid him not: for there is no man who shall do a mighty work in my name, and be able quickly to speak evil of me.

Mar 9:40 For he that is not against us is for us.

Mar 9:41 For whosoever shall give you a cup of water to drink, because ye are Christ's, verily I say unto you, he shall in no wise lose his reward.

Mar 9:42 And whosoever shall cause one of these little ones that believe on me to stumble, it were better for him if a great millstone were hanged about his neck, and he were cast into the sea.

Mar 9:43 And if thy hand cause thee to stumble, cut it off: it is good for thee to enter into life maimed, rather than having thy two hands to go into hell, into the unquenchable fire;

Mar 9:44 where their worm dieth not, and the fire is not quenched.

Mar 9:45 And if thy foot cause thee to stumble, cut it off: it is good for thee to enter into life halt, rather than having thy two feet to be cast into hell;

Mar 9:46 where their worm dieth not, and the fire is not quenched.

Mar 9:47 And if thine eye cause thee to stumble, cast it out: it is good for thee to enter into the kingdom of God with one eye, rather than having two eyes to be cast into hell;

Mar 9:48 where their worm dieth not, and the fire is not quenched.

Mar 9:49 For every one shall be salted with fire.

Mar 9:50 Salt is good: but if the salt have lost its saltness, wherewith will ye season it? Have salt in yourselves, and be at peace one with another.

Chapter 10.

Mar 10:1 And he arose from thence and cometh into the borders of Judaea and beyond the Jordan: and multitudes come together unto him again; and, as he was wont, he taught them again.

Mar 10:2 And there came unto him Pharisees, and asked him, Is it lawful for a man to put away his wife? trying him.

Mar 10:3 And he answered and said unto them, What did Moses command you?

Mar 10:4 And they said, Moses suffered to write a bill of divorcement, and to put her away.

Mar 10:5 But Jesus said unto them, For your hardness of heart he wrote you this commandment.

Mar 10:6 But from the beginning of the creation, Male and female made he them.

Mar 10:7 For this cause shall a man leave his father and mother, and shall cleave to his wife;

Mar 10:8 and the two shall become one flesh: so that they are no more two, but one flesh.

Mar 10:9 What therefore God hath joined together, let not man put asunder.

Mar 10:10 And in the house the disciples asked him again of this matter.

Mar 10:11 And he saith unto them, Whosoever shall put away his wife, and marry another, committeth adultery against her:

Mar 10:12 and if she herself shall put away her husband, and marry another, she committeth adultery.

Mar 10:13 And they were bringing unto him little children, that he should touch them: and the disciples rebuked them.

Mar 10:14 But when Jesus saw it, he was moved with indignation, and said unto them, Suffer the little children to come unto me; forbid them not: for to such belongeth the kingdom of God.

Mar 10:15 Verily I say unto you, Whosoever shall not receive the kingdom of God as a little child, he shall in no wise enter therein.

Mar 10:16 And he took them in his arms, and blessed them, laying his hands upon them.

Mar 10:17 And as he was going forth into the way, there ran one to him, and kneeled to him, and asked him, Good Teacher, what shall I do that I may inherit eternal life?

Mar 10:18 And Jesus said unto him, Why callest thou me good? none is good save one, even God.

Mar 10:19 Thou knowest the commandments, Do not kill, Do not commit adultery, Do not steal, Do not bear false witness, Do not defraud, Honor thy father and mother.

Mar 10:20 And he said unto him, Teacher, all these things have I observed from my youth.

Mar 10:21 And Jesus looking upon him loved him, and said unto him, One thing thou lackest: go, sell whatsoever thou hast, and give to the poor, and thou shalt have treasure in heaven: and come, follow me.

Mar 10:22 But his countenance fell at the saying, and he went away sorrowful: for he was one that had great possessions.

Mar 10:23 And Jesus looked round about, and saith unto his disciples, How hardly shall they that have riches enter into the kingdom of God!

Mar 10:24 And the disciples were amazed at his words. But Jesus answereth again, and saith unto them, Children, how hard is it for them that trust in riches to enter into the kingdom of God!

Mar 10:25 It is easier for a camel to go through a needle's eye, than for a rich man to enter into the kingdom of God.

Mar 10:26 And they were astonished exceedingly, saying unto him, Then who can be saved?

Mar 10:27 Jesus looking upon them saith, With men it is impossible, but not with God: for all things are possible with God.

Mar 10:28 Peter began to say unto him, Lo, we have left all, and have followed thee.

Mar 10:29 Jesus said, Verily I say unto you, There is no man that hath left house, or brethren, or sisters, or mother, or father, or children, or lands, for my sake, and for the gospel's sake,

Mar 10:30 but he shall receive a hundredfold now in this time, houses, and brethren, and sisters, and mothers, and children, and lands, with persecutions; and in the world to come eternal life.

Mar 10:31 But many that are first shall be last; and the last first.

Mar 10:32 And they were on the way, going up to Jerusalem; and Jesus was going before them: and they were amazed; and they that followed were afraid. And he took again the twelve, and began to tell them the things that were to happen unto him,

Mar 10:33 saying, Behold, we go up to Jerusalem; and the Son of man shall be delivered unto the chief priests and the scribes; and they shall condemn him to death, and shall deliver him unto the Gentiles:

Mar 10:34 and they shall mock him, and shall spit upon him, and shall scourge him, and shall kill him; and after three days he shall rise again.

Mar 10:35 And there come near unto him James and John, the sons of Zebedee, saying unto him, Teacher, we would that thou shouldest do for us whatsoever we shall ask of thee.

Mar 10:36 And he said unto them, What would ye that I should do for you?

Mar 10:37 And they said unto him, Grant unto us that we may sit, one on thy right hand, and one on thy left hand, in thy glory.

Mar 10:38 But Jesus said unto them, Ye know not what ye ask. Are ye able to drink the cup that I drink? or to be baptized with the baptism that I am baptized with?

Mar 10:39 And they said unto him, We are able. And Jesus said unto them, The cup that I drink ye shall drink; and with the baptism that I am baptized withal shall ye be baptized:

Mar 10:40 but to sit on my right hand or on my left hand is not mine to give; but it is for them for whom it hath been prepared.

Mar 10:41 And when the ten heard it, they began to be moved with indignation concerning James and John.

Mar 10:42 And Jesus called them to him, and saith unto them, Ye know that they who are accounted to rule over the Gentiles lord it over them; and their great ones exercise authority over them.

Mar 10:43 But it is not so among you: but whosoever would become great among you, shall be your minister;

Mar 10:44 and whosoever would be first among you, shall be servant of all.

Mar 10:45 For the Son of man also came not to be ministered unto, but to minister, and to give his life a ransom for many.

Mar 10:46 And they come to Jericho: and as he went out from Jericho, with his disciples and a great multitude, the son of Timaeus, Bartimaeus, a blind beggar, was sitting by the way side.

Mar 10:47 And when he heard that it was Jesus the Nazarene, he began to cry out, and say, Jesus, thou son of David, have mercy on me.

Mar 10:48 And many rebuked him, that he should hold his peace: but he cried out the more a great deal, Thou son of David, have mercy on me.

Mar 10:49 And Jesus stood still, and said, Call ye him. And they call the blind man, saying unto him, Be of good cheer: rise, he calleth thee.

Mar 10:50 And he, casting away his garment, sprang up, and came to Jesus.

Mar 10:51 And Jesus answered him, and said, What wilt thou that I should do unto thee? And the blind man said unto him, Rabboni, that I may receive my sight.

Mar 10:52 And Jesus said unto him, Go thy way; thy faith hath made thee whole. And straightway he received his sight, and followed him in the way.

Chapter 11.

Mar 11:1 And when they draw nigh unto Jerusalem, unto Bethphage and Bethany, at the mount of Olives, he sendeth two of his disciples,

Mar 11:2 and saith unto them, Go your way into the village that is over against you: and straightway as ye enter into it, ye shall find a colt tied, whereon no man ever yet sat; loose him, and bring him.

Mar 11:3 And if any one say unto you, Why do ye this? say ye, The Lord hath need of him; and straightway he will send him back hither.

Mar 11:4 And they went away, and found a colt tied at the door without in the open street; and they loose him.

Mar 11:5 And certain of them that stood there said unto them, What do ye, loosing the colt?

Mar 11:6 And they said unto them even as Jesus had said: and they let them go.

Mar 11:7 And they bring the colt unto Jesus, and cast on him their garments; and he sat upon him.

Mar 11:8 And many spread their garments upon the way; and others branches, which they had cut from the fields.

Mar 11:9 And they that went before, and they that followed, cried, Hosanna; Blessed is he that cometh in the name of the Lord:

Mar 11:10 Blessed is the kingdom that cometh, the kingdom of our father David: Hosanna in the highest.

Mar 11:11 And he entered into Jerusalem, into the temple; and when he had looked round about upon all things, it being now eventide, he went out unto Bethany with the twelve.

Mar 11:12 And on the morrow, when they were come out from Bethany, he hungered.

Mar 11:13 And seeing a fig tree afar off having leaves, he came, if haply he might find anything thereon: and when he came to it, he found nothing but leaves; for it was not the season of figs.

Mar 11:14 And he answered and said unto it, No man eat fruit from thee henceforward for ever. And his disciples heard it.

Mar 11:15 And they come to Jerusalem: and he entered into the temple, and began to cast out them that sold and them that bought in the temple, and overthrew the tables of the money-changers, and the seats of them that sold the doves;

Mar 11:16 and he would not suffer that any man should carry a vessel through the temple.

Mar 11:17 And he taught, and said unto them, Is it not written, My house shall be called a house of prayer for all the nations? but ye have made it a den of robbers.

Mar 11:18 And the chief priests and the scribes heard it, and sought how they might destroy him: for they feared him, for all the multitude was astonished at his teaching.

Mar 11:19 And every evening he went forth out of the city.

Mar 11:20 And as they passed by in the morning, they saw the fig tree withered away from the roots.

Mar 11:21 And Peter calling to remembrance saith unto him, Rabbi, behold, the fig tree which thou cursedst is withered away.

Mar 11:22 And Jesus answering saith unto them, Have faith in God.

Mar 11:23 Verily I say unto you, Whosoever shall say unto this mountain, Be thou taken up and cast into the sea; and shall not doubt in his heart, but shall believe that what he saith cometh to pass; he shall have it.

Mar 11:24 Therefore I say unto you, All things whatsoever ye pray and ask for, believe that ye receive them, and ye shall have them.

Mar 11:25 And whensoever ye stand praying, forgive, if ye have aught against any one; that your Father also who is in heaven may forgive you your trespasses.

Mar 11:26 But if ye do not forgive, neither will your Father who is in heaven forgive your trespasses.

Mar 11:27 And they come again to Jerusalem: and as he was walking in the temple, there come to him the chief priests, and the scribes, and the elders;

Mar 11:28 and they said unto him, By what authority doest thou these things? or who gave thee this authority to do these things?

Mar 11:29 And Jesus said unto them, I will ask of you one question, and answer me, and I will tell you by what authority I do these things.

Mar 11:30 The baptism of John, was it from heaven, or from men? answer me.

Mar 11:31 And they reasoned with themselves, saying, If we shall say, From heaven; He will say, Why then did ye not believe him?

Mar 11:32 But should we say, From men - they feared the people: for all verily held John to be a prophet.

Mar 11:33 And they answered Jesus and say, We know not. And Jesus saith unto them, Neither tell I you by what authority I do these things.

Chapter 12.

Mar 12:1 And he began to speak unto them in parables. A man planted a vineyard, and set a hedge about it, and digged a pit for the winepress, and built a tower, and let it out to husbandmen, and went into another country.

Mar 12:2 And at the season he sent to the husbandmen a servant, that he might receive from the husbandmen of the fruits of the vineyard.

Mar 12:3 And they took him, and beat him, and sent him away empty.

Mar 12:4 And again he sent unto them another servant; and him they wounded in the head, and handled shamefully.

Mar 12:5 And he sent another; and him they killed: and many others; beating some, and killing some.

Mar 12:6 He had yet one, a beloved son: he sent him last unto them, saying, They will reverence my son.

Mar 12:7 But those husbandmen said among themselves, This is the heir; come, let us kill him, and the inheritance shall be ours.

Mar 12:8 And they took him, and killed him, and cast him forth out of the vineyard.

Mar 12:9 What therefore will the lord of the vineyard do? he will come and destroy the husbandmen, and will give the vineyard unto others.

Mar 12:10 Have ye not read even this scripture: The stone which the builders rejected, The same was made the head of the corner;

Mar 12:11 This was from the Lord, And it is marvellous in our eyes?

Mar 12:12 And they sought to lay hold on him; and they feared the multitude; for they perceived that he spake the parable against them: and they left him, and went away.

Mar 12:13 And they send unto him certain of the Pharisees and of the Herodians, that they might catch him in talk.

Mar 12:14 And when they were come, they say unto him, Teacher, we know that thou art true, and carest not for any one; for thou regardest not the person of men, but of a truth teachest the way of God: Is it lawful to give tribute unto Caesar, or not?

Mar 12:15 Shall we give, or shall we not give? But he, knowing their hypocrisy, said unto them, Why make ye trial of me? bring me a denarius, that I may see it.

Mar 12:16 And they brought it. And he saith unto them, Whose is this image and superscription? And they said unto him, Caesar's.

Mar 12:17 And Jesus said unto them, Render unto Caesar the things that are Caesar's, and unto God the things that are God's. And they marvelled greatly at him.

Mar 12:18 And there come unto him Sadducees, who say that there is no resurrection; and they asked him, saying,

Mar 12:19 Teacher, Moses wrote unto us, If a man's brother die, and leave a wife behind him, and leave no child, that his brother should take his wife, and raise up seed unto his brother.

Mar 12:20 There were seven brethren: and the first took a wife, and dying left no seed;

Mar 12:21 and the second took her, and died, leaving no seed behind him; and the third likewise:

Mar 12:22 and the seven left no seed. Last of all the woman also died.

Mar 12:23 In the resurrection whose wife shall she be of them? for the seven had her to wife.

Mar 12:24 Jesus said unto them, Is it not for this cause that ye err, that ye know not the scriptures, nor the power of God?

Mar 12:25 For when they shall rise from the dead, they neither marry, nor are given in marriage; but are as angels in heaven.

Mar 12:26 But as touching the dead, that they are raised; have ye not read in the book of Moses, in the place concerning the Bush, how God spake unto him, saying, I am the God of Abraham, and the God of Isaac, and the God of Jacob?

Mar 12:27 He is not the God of the dead, but of the living: ye do greatly err.

Mar 12:28 And one of the scribes came, and heard them questioning together, and knowing that he had answered them well, asked him, What commandment is the first of all?

Mar 12:29 Jesus answered, The first is, Hear, O Israel; The Lord our God, the Lord is one:

Mar 12:30 and thou shalt love the Lord thy God with all thy heart, and with all thy soul, and with all thy mind, and with all thy strength.

Mar 12:31 The second is this, Thou shalt love thy neighbor as thyself. There is none other commandment greater than these.

Mar 12:32 And the scribe said unto him, Of a truth, Teacher, thou hast well said that he is one; and there is none other but he:

Mar 12:33 and to love him with all the heart, and with all the understanding, and with all the strength, and to love his neighbor as himself, is much more than all whole burnt-offerings and sacrifices.

Mar 12:34 And when Jesus saw that he answered discreetly, he said unto him, Thou art not far from the kingdom of God. And no man after that durst ask him any question.

Mar 12:35 And Jesus answered and said, as he taught in the temple, How say the scribes that the Christ is the son of David?

Mar 12:36 David himself said in the Holy Spirit, The Lord said unto my Lord, Sit thou on my right hand, Till I make thine enemies the footstool of thy feet.

Mar 12:37 David himself calleth him Lord; and whence is he his son? And the common people heard him gladly.

Mar 12:38 And in his teaching he said, Beware of the scribes, who desire to walk in long robes, and to have salutations in the marketplaces,

Mar 12:39 and chief seats in the synagogues, and chief places at feasts:

Mar 12:40 they that devour widows' houses, and for a pretence make long prayers; these shall receive greater condemnation.

Mar 12:41 And he sat down over against the treasury, and beheld how the multitude cast money into the treasury: and many that were rich cast in much.

Mar 12:42 And there came a poor widow, and she cast in two mites, which make a farthing.

Mar 12:43 And he called unto him his disciples, and said unto them, Verily I say unto you, This poor widow cast in more than all they that are casting into the treasury:

Mar 12:44 for they all did cast in of their superfluity; but she of her want did cast in all that she had, even all her living.

Chapter 13.

Mar 13:1 And as he went forth out of the temple, one of his disciples saith unto him, Teacher, behold, what manner of stones and what manner of buildings!

Mar 13:2 And Jesus said unto him, Seest thou these great buildings? there shall not be left here one stone upon another, which shall not be thrown down.

Mar 13:3 And as he sat on the mount of Olives over against the temple, Peter and James and John and Andrew asked him privately,

Mar 13:4 Tell us, when shall these things be? and what shall be the sign when these things are all about to be accomplished?

Mar 13:5 And Jesus began to say unto them, Take heed that no man lead you astray.

Mar 13:6 Many shall come in my name, saying, I am he; and shall lead many astray.

Mar 13:7 And when ye shall hear of wars and rumors of wars, be not troubled: these things must needs come to pass; but the end is not yet.

Mar 13:8 For nation shall rise against nation, and kingdom against kingdom; there shall be earthquakes in divers places; there shall be famines: these things are the beginning of travail.

Mar 13:9 But take ye heed to yourselves: for they shall deliver you up to councils; and in synagogues shall ye be beaten; and before governors and kings shall ye stand for my sake, for a testimony unto them.

Mar 13:10 And the gospel must first be preached unto all the nations.

Mar 13:11 And when they lead you to judgment, and deliver you up, be not anxious beforehand what ye shall speak: but whatsoever shall be given you in that hour, that speak ye; for it is not ye that speak, but the Holy Spirit.

Mar 13:12 And brother shall deliver up brother to death, and the father his child; and children shall rise up against parents, and cause them to be put to death.

Mar 13:13 And ye shall be hated of all men for my name's sake: but he that endureth to the end, the same shall be saved.

Mar 13:14 But when ye see the abomination of desolation standing where he ought not (let him that readeth understand), then let them that are in Judaea flee unto the mountains:

Mar 13:15   and let him that is on the housetop not go down, nor enter in, to take anything out his house:

Mar 13:16 and let him that is in the field not return back to take his cloak.

Mar 13:17 But woe unto them that are with child and to them that give suck in those days!

Mar 13:18 And pray ye that it be not in the winter.

Mar 13:19 For those days shall be tribulation, such as there hath not been the like from the beginning of the creation which God created until now, and never shall be.

Mar 13:20 And except the Lord had shortened the days, no flesh would have been saved; but for the elect's sake, whom he chose, he shortened the days.

Mar 13:21 And then if any man shall say unto you, Lo, here is the Christ; or, Lo, there; believe it not:

Mar 13:22 for there shall arise false Christs and false prophets, and shall show signs and wonders, that they may lead astray, if possible, the elect.

Mar 13:23 But take ye heed: behold, I have told you all things beforehand.

Mar 13:24 But in those days, after that tribulation, the sun shall be darkened, and the moon shall not give her light,

Mar 13:25 and the stars shall be falling from heaven, and the powers that are in the heavens shall be shaken.

Mar 13:26 And then shall they see the Son of man coming in clouds with great power and glory.

Mar 13:27 And then shall he send forth the angels, and shall gather together his elect from the four winds, from the uttermost part of the earth to the uttermost part of heaven.

Mar 13:28 Now from the fig tree learn her parable: when her branch is now become tender, and putteth forth its leaves, ye know that the summer is nigh;

Mar 13:29 even so ye also, when ye see these things coming to pass, know ye that he is nigh, even at the doors.

Mar 13:30 Verily I say unto you, This generation shall not pass away, until all these things be accomplished.

Mar 13:31 Heaven and earth shall pass away: but my words shall not pass away.

Mar 13:32 But of that day or that hour knoweth no one, not even the angels in heaven, neither the Son, but the Father.

Mar 13:33 Take ye heed, watch and pray: for ye know not when the time is.

Mar 13:34 It is as when a man, sojourning in another country, having left his house, and given authority to his servants, to each one his work, commanded also the porter to watch.

Mar 13:35 Watch therefore: for ye know not when the lord of the house cometh, whether at even, or at midnight, or at cockcrowing, or in the morning;

Mar 13:36 lest coming suddenly he find you sleeping.

Mar 13:37 And what I say unto you I say unto all, Watch.

Chapter 14.

Mar 14:1 Now after two days was the feast of the passover and the unleavened bread: and the chief priests and the scribes sought how they might take him with subtlety, and kill him:

Mar 14:2 for they said, Not during the feast, lest haply there shall be a tumult of the people.

Mar 14:3 And while he was in Bethany in the house of Simon the leper, as he sat at meat, there came a woman having an alabaster cruse of ointment of pure nard very costly; and she brake the cruse, and poured it over his head.

Mar 14:4 But there were some that had indignation among themselves, saying, To what purpose hath this waste of the ointment been made?

Mar 14:5 For this ointment might have been sold for above three hundred shillings, and given to the poor. And they murmured against her.

Mar 14:6 But Jesus said, Let her alone; why trouble ye her? she hath wrought a good work on me.

Mar 14:7 For ye have the poor always with you, and whensoever ye will ye can do them good: but me ye have not always.

Mar 14:8 She hath done what she could; she hath anointed my body beforehand for the burying.

Mar 14:9 And verily I say unto you, Wheresoever the gospel shall be preached throughout the whole world, that also which this woman hath done shall be spoken of for a memorial of her.

Mar 14:10 And Judas Iscariot, he that was one of the twelve, went away unto the chief priests, that he might deliver him unto them.

Mar 14:11 And they, when they heard it, were glad, and promised to give him money. And he sought how he might conveniently deliver him unto them.

Mar 14:12 And on the first day of unleavened bread, when they sacrificed the passover, his disciples say unto him, Where wilt thou that we go and make ready that thou mayest eat the passover?

Mar 14:13 And he sendeth two of his disciples, and saith unto them, Go into the city, and there shall meet you a man bearing a pitcher of water: follow him;

Mar 14:14 and wheresoever he shall enter in, say to the master of the house, The Teacher saith, Where is my guest-chamber, where I shall eat the passover with my disciples?

Mar 14:15 And he will himself show you a large upper room furnished and ready: and there make ready for us.

Mar 14:16 And the disciples went forth, and came into the city, and found as he had said unto them: and they made ready the passover.

Mar 14:17 And when it was evening he cometh with the twelve.

Mar 14:18 And as they sat and were eating, Jesus said, Verily I say unto you, One of you shall betray me, even he that eateth with me.

Mar 14:19 They began to be sorrowful, and to say unto him one by one, Is it I?

Mar 14:20 And he said unto them, It is one of the twelve, he that dippeth with me in the dish.

Mar 14:21 For the Son of man goeth, even as it is written of him: but woe unto that man through whom the Son of man is betrayed! good were it for that man if he had not been born.

Mar 14:22 And as they were eating, he took bread, and when he had blessed, he brake it, and gave to them, and said, Take ye: this is my body.

Mar 14:23 And he took a cup, and when he had given thanks, he gave to them: and they all drank of it.

Mar 14:24 And he said unto them, This is my blood of the covenant, which is poured out for many.

Mar 14:25 Verily I say unto you, I shall no more drink of the fruit of the vine, until that day when I drink it new in the kingdom of God.

Mar 14:26 And when they had sung a hymn, they went out unto the mount of Olives.

Mar 14:27 And Jesus saith unto them, All ye shall be offended: for it is written, I will smite the shepherd, and the sheep shall be scattered abroad.

Mar 14:28 Howbeit, after I am raised up, I will go before you into Galilee.

Mar 14:29 But Peter said unto him, Although all shall be offended, yet will not I.

Mar 14:30 And Jesus saith unto him, Verily I say unto thee, that thou to-day, even this night, before the cock crow twice, shalt deny me thrice.

Mar 14:31 But he spake exceedingly vehemently, If I must die with thee, I will not deny thee. And in like manner also said they all.

Mar 14:32 And they come unto a place which was named Gethsemane: and he saith unto his disciples, Sit ye here, while I pray.

Mar 14:33 And he taketh with him Peter and James and John, and began to be greatly amazed, and sore troubled.

Mar 14:34 And he saith unto them, My soul is exceeding sorrowful even unto death: abide ye here, and watch.

Mar 14:35 And he went forward a little, and fell on the ground, and prayed that, if it were possible, the hour might pass away from him.

Mar 14:36 And he said, Abba, Father, all things are possible unto thee; remove this cup from me: howbeit not what I will, but what thou wilt.

Mar 14:37 And he cometh, and findeth them sleeping, and saith unto Peter, Simon, sleepest thou? couldest thou not watch one hour?

Mar 14:38 Watch and pray, that ye enter not into temptation: the spirit indeed is willing, but the flesh is weak.

Mar 14:39 And again he went away, and prayed, saying the same words.

Mar 14:40 And again he came, and found them sleeping, for their eyes were very heavy; and they knew not what to answer him.

Mar 14:41 And he cometh the third time, and saith unto them, Sleep on now, and take your rest: it is enough; the hour is come; behold, the Son of man is betrayed into the hands of sinners.

Mar 14:42 Arise, let us be going: behold, he that betrayeth me is at hand.

Mar 14:43 And straightway, while he yet spake, cometh Judas, one of the twelve, and with him a multitude with swords and staves, from the chief priests and the scribes and the elders.

Mar 14:44 Now he that betrayed him had given them a token, saying, Whomsoever I shall kiss, that is he; take him, and lead him away safely.

Mar 14:45 And when he was come, straightway he came to him, and saith, Rabbi; and kissed him.

Mar 14:46 And they laid hands on him, and took him.

Mar 14:47 But a certain one of them that stood by drew his sword, and smote the servant of the high priest, and struck off his ear.

Mar 14:48 And Jesus answered and said unto them, Are ye come out, as against a robber, with swords and staves to seize me?

Mar 14:49 I was daily with you in the temple teaching, and ye took me not: but this is done that the scriptures might be fulfilled.

Mar 14:50 And they all left him, and fled.

Mar 14:51 And a certain young man followed with him, having a linen cloth cast about him, over his naked body: and they lay hold on him;

Mar 14:52 but he left the linen cloth, and fled naked.

Mar 14:53 And they led Jesus away to the high priest: and there come together with him all the chief priests and the elders and the scribes.

Mar 14:54 And Peter had followed him afar off, even within, into the court of the high priest; and he was sitting with the officers, and warming himself in the light of the fire.

Mar 14:55 Now the chief priests and the whole council sought witness against Jesus to put him to death; and found it not.

Mar 14:56 For many bare false witness against him, and their witness agreed not together.

Mar 14:57 And there stood up certain, and bare false witness against him, saying,

Mar 14:58 We heard him say, I will destroy this temple that is made with hands, and in three days I will build another made without hands.

Mar 14:59 And not even so did their witness agree together.

Mar 14:60 And the high priest stood up in the midst, and asked Jesus, saying, Answerest thou nothing? what is it which these witness against thee?

Mar 14:61 But he held his peace, and answered nothing. Again the high priest asked him, and saith unto him, Art thou the Christ, the Son of the Blessed?

Mar 14:62 And Jesus said, I am: and ye shall see the Son of man sitting at the right hand of Power, and coming with the clouds of heaven.

Mar 14:63 And the high priest rent his clothes, and saith, What further need have we of witnesses?

Mar 14:64 Ye have heard the blasphemy: what think ye? And they all condemned him to be worthy of death.

Mar 14:65 And some began to spit on him, and to cover his face, and to buffet him, and to say unto him, Prophesy: and the officers received him with blows of their hands.

Mar 14:66 And as Peter was beneath in the court, there cometh one of the maids of the high priest;

Mar 14:67 and seeing Peter warming himself, she looked upon him, and saith, Thou also wast with the Nazarene, even Jesus.

Mar 14:68 But he denied, saying, I neither know, nor understand what thou sayest: and he went out into the porch; and the cock crew.

Mar 14:69 And the maid saw him, and began again to say to them that stood by, This is one of them.

Mar 14:70 But he again denied it. And after a little while again they that stood by said to Peter, of a truth thou art one of them; for thou art a Galilaean.

Mar 14:71 But he began to curse, and to swear, I know not this man of whom ye speak.

Mar 14:72 And straightway the second time the cock crew. And Peter called to mind the word, how that Jesus said unto him, Before the cock crow twice, thou shalt deny me thrice. And when he thought thereon, he wept.

Chapter 15.

Mar 15:1 And straightway in the morning the chief priests with the elders and scribes, and the whole council, held a consultation, and bound Jesus, and carried him away, and delivered him up to Pilate.

Mar 15:2 And Pilate asked him, Art thou the King of the Jews? And he answering saith unto him, Thou sayest.

Mar 15:3 And the chief priests accused him of many things.

Mar 15:4 And Pilate again asked him, saying, Answerest thou nothing? behold how many things they accuse thee of.

Mar 15:5 But Jesus no more answered anything; insomuch that Pilate marvelled.

Mar 15:6 Now at the feast he used to release unto them one prisoner, whom they asked of him.

Mar 15:7 And there was one called Barabbas, lying bound with them that had made insurrection, men who in the insurrection had committed murder.

Mar 15:8 And the multitude went up and began to ask him to do as he was wont to do unto them.

Mar 15:9 And Pilate answered them, saying, Will ye that I release unto you the King of the Jews?

Mar 15:10 For he perceived that for envy the chief priests had delivered him up.

Mar 15:11 But the chief priests stirred up the multitude, that he should rather release Barabbas unto them.

Mar 15:12 And Pilate again answered and said unto them, What then shall I do unto him whom ye call the King of the Jews?

Mar 15:13 And they cried out again, Crucify him.

Mar 15:14 And Pilate said unto them, Why, what evil hath he done? But they cried out exceedingly, Crucify him.

Mar 15:15 And Pilate, wishing to content the multitude, released unto them Barabbas, and delivered Jesus, when he had scourged him, to be crucified.

Mar 15:16 And the soldiers led him away within the court, which is the Praetorium; and they call together the whole band.

Mar 15:17 And they clothe him with purple, and platting a crown of thorns, they put it on him;

Mar 15:18 and they began to salute him, Hail, King of the Jews!

Mar 15:19 And they smote his head with a reed, and spat upon him, and bowing their knees worshipped him.

Mar 15:20 And when they had mocked him, they took off from him the purple, and put on him his garments. And they lead him out to crucify him.

Mar 15:21 And they compel one passing by, Simon of Cyrene, coming from the country, the father of Alexander and Rufus, to go with them, that he might bear his cross.

Mar 15:22 And they bring him unto the place Golgotha, which is, being interpreted, The place of a skull.

Mar 15:23 And they offered him wine mingled with myrrh: but he received it not.

Mar 15:24 And they crucify him, and part his garments among them, casting lots upon them, what each should take.

Mar 15:25 And it was the third hour, and they crucified him.

Mar 15:26 And the superscription of his accusation was written over, THE KING OF THE JEWS.

Mar 15:27 And with him they crucify two robbers; one on his right hand, and one on his left.

Mar 15:28 And the scripture was fulfilled, which saith, And he was reckoned with transgressors.

Mar 15:29 And they that passed by railed on him, wagging their heads, and saying, Ha! Thou that destroyest the temple, and buildest it in three days,

Mar 15:30 save thyself, and come down from the cross.

Mar 15:31 In like manner also the chief priests mocking him among themselves with the scribes said, He saved others; himself he cannot save.

Mar 15:32 Let the Christ, the King of Israel, now come down from the cross, that we may see and believe. And they that were crucified with him reproached him.

Mar 15:33 And when the sixth hour was come, there was darkness over the whole land until the ninth hour.

Mar 15:34 And at the ninth hour Jesus cried with a loud voice, Eloi, Eloi, lama sabachthani? which is, being interpreted, My God, my God, why hast thou forsaken me?

Mar 15:35 And some of them that stood by, when they heard it, said, Behold, he calleth Elijah.

Mar 15:36 And one ran, and filling a sponge full of vinegar, put it on a reed, and gave him to drink, saying, Let be; let us see whether Elijah cometh to take him down.

Mar 15:37 And Jesus uttered a loud voice, and gave up the ghost.

Mar 15:38 And the veil of the temple was rent in two from the top to the bottom.

Mar 15:39 And when the centurion, who stood by over against him, saw that he so gave up the ghost, he said, Truly this man was the Son of God.

Mar 15:40 And there were also women beholding from afar: among whom were both Mary Magdalene, and Mary the mother of James the less and of Joses, and Salome;

Mar 15:41 who, when he was in Galilee, followed him, and ministered unto him; and many other women that came up with him unto Jerusalem.

Mar 15:42 And when even was now come, because it was the Preparation, that is, the day before the sabbath,

Mar 15:43 there came Joseph of Arimathaea, a councillor of honorable estate, who also himself was looking for the kingdom of God; and he boldly went in unto Pilate, and asked for the body of Jesus.

Mar 15:44 And Pilate marvelled if he were already dead: and calling unto him the centurion, he asked him whether he had been any while dead.

Mar 15:45 And when he learned it of the centurion, he granted the corpse to Joseph.

Mar 15:46 And he bought a linen cloth, and taking him down, wound him in the linen cloth, and laid him in a tomb which had been hewn out of a rock; and he rolled a stone against the door of the tomb.

Mar 15:47 And Mary Magdalene and Mary the mother of Joses beheld where he was laid.

Chapter 16.

Mar 16:1 And when the sabbath was past, Mary Magdalene, and Mary the mother of James, and Salome, bought spices, that they might come and anoint him.

Mar 16:2 And very early on the first day of the week, they come to the tomb when the sun was risen.

Mar 16:3 And they were saying among themselves, Who shall roll us away the stone from the door of the tomb?

Mar 16:4 and looking up, they see that the stone is rolled back: for it was exceeding great.

Mar 16:5 And entering into the tomb, they saw a young man sitting on the right side, arrayed in a white robe; and they were amazed.

Mar 16:6 And he saith unto them, Be not amazed: ye seek Jesus, the Nazarene, who hath been crucified: he is risen; he is not here: behold, the place where they laid him!

Mar 16:7 But go, tell his disciples and Peter, He goeth before you into Galilee: there shall ye see him, as he said unto you.

Mar 16:8 And they went out, and fled from the tomb; for trembling and astonishment had come upon them: and they said nothing to any one; for they were afraid.

Mar 16:9 Now when he was risen early on the first day of the week, he appeared first to Mary Magdalene, from whom he had cast out seven demons.

Mar 16:10 She went and told them that had been with him, as they mourned and wept.

Mar 16:11 And they, when they heard that he was alive, and had been seen of her, disbelieved.

Mar 16:12 And after these things he was manifested in another form unto two of them, as they walked, on their way into the country.

Mar 16:13 And they went away and told it unto the rest: neither believed they them.

Mar 16:14 And afterward he was manifested unto the eleven themselves as they sat at meat; and he upbraided them with their unbelief and hardness of heart, because they believed not them that had seen him after he was risen.

Mar 16:15 And he said unto them, Go ye into all the world, and preach the gospel to the whole creation.

Mar 16:16 He that believeth and is baptized shall be saved; but he that disbelieveth shall be condemned.

Mar 16:17 And these signs shall accompany them that believe: in my name shall they cast out demons; they shall speak with new tongues;

Mar 16:18 they shall take up serpents, and if they drink any deadly thing, it shall in no wise hurt them; they shall lay hands on the sick, and they shall recover.

Mar 16:19 So then the Lord Jesus, after he had spoken unto them, was received up into heaven, and sat down at the right hand of God.

Mar 16:20 And they went forth, and preached everywhere, the Lord working with them, and confirming the word by the signs that followed. Amen.

4. Luke

Chapter 1.

Luk 1:1 Forasmuch as many have taken in hand to draw up a narrative concerning those matters which have been fulfilled among us,

Luk 1:2 even as they delivered them unto us, who from the beginning were eyewitnesses and ministers of the word,

Luk 1:3 it seemed good to me also, having traced the course of all things accurately from the first, to write unto thee in order, most excellent Theophilus;

Luk 1:4 that thou mightest know the certainty concerning the things wherein thou wast instructed.

Luk 1:5 There was in the days of Herod, king of Judaea, a certain priest named Zacharias, of the course of Abijah: and he had a wife of the daughters of Aaron, and her name was Elisabeth.

Luk 1:6 And they were both righteous before God, walking in all the commandments and ordinances of the Lord blameless.

Luk 1:7 And they had no child, because that Elisabeth was barren, and they both were now well stricken in years.

Luk 1:8 Now it came to pass, while he executed the priest's office before God in the order of his course,

Luk 1:9 according to the custom of the priest's office, his lot was to enter into the temple of the Lord and burn incense.

Luk 1:10 And the whole multitude of the people were praying without at the hour of incense.

Luk 1:11 And there appeared unto him an angel of the Lord standing on the right side of altar of incense.

Luk 1:12 And Zacharias was troubled when he saw him, and fear fell upon him.

Luk 1:13 But the angel said unto him, Fear not, Zacharias: because thy supplication is heard, and thy wife Elisabeth shall bear thee a son, and thou shalt call his name John.

Luk 1:14 And thou shalt have joy and gladness; and many shall rejoice at his birth.

Luk 1:15 For he shall be great in the sight of the Lord, and he shall drink no wine nor strong drink; and he shall be filled with the Holy Spirit, even from his mother's womb.

Luk 1:16 And many of the children of Israel shall be turn unto the Lord their God.

Luk 1:17 And he shall go before his face in the spirit and power of Elijah, to turn the hearts of the fathers to the children, and the disobedient to walk in the wisdom of the just; to make ready for the Lord a people prepared for him.

Luk 1:18 And Zacharias said unto the angel, Whereby shall I know this? for I am an old man, and my wife well stricken in years.

Luk 1:19 And the angel answering said unto him, I am Gabriel, that stand in the presence of God; and I was sent to speak unto thee, and to bring thee these good tidings.

Luk 1:20 And behold, thou shalt be silent and not able to speak, until the day that these things shall come to pass, because thou believedst not my words, which shall be fulfilled in their season.

Luk 1:21 And the people were waiting for Zacharias, and they marvelled while he tarried in the temple.

Luk 1:22 And when he came out, he could not speak unto them: and they perceived that he had seen a vision in the temple: and he continued making signs unto them, and remained dumb.

Luk 1:23 And it came to pass, when the days of his ministration were fulfilled, he departed unto his house.

Luk 1:24 And after these days Elisabeth his wife conceived; and she hid herself five months, saying,

Luk 1:25 Thus hath the Lord done unto me in the days wherein he looked upon me, to take away my reproach among men.

Luk 1:26 Now in the sixth month the angel Gabriel was sent from God unto a city of Galilee, named Nazareth,

Luk 1:27 to a virgin betrothed to a man whose name was Joseph, of the house of David; and the virgin's name was Mary.

Luk 1:28 And he came in unto her, and said, Hail, thou that art highly favored, the Lord is with thee.

Luk 1:29 But she was greatly troubled at the saying, and cast in her mind what manner of salutation this might be.

Luk 1:30 And the angel said unto her, Fear not, Mary: for thou hast found favor with God.

Luk 1:31 And behold, thou shalt conceive in thy womb, and bring forth a son, and shalt call his name JESUS.

Luk 1:32 He shall be great, and shall be called the Son of the Most High: and the Lord God shall give unto him the throne of his father David:

Luk 1:33 and he shall reign over the house of Jacob for ever; and of his kingdom there shall be no end.

Luk 1:34 And Mary said unto the angel, How shall this be, seeing I know not a man?

Luk 1:35 And the angel answered and said unto her, The Holy Spirit shall come upon thee, and the power of the Most High shall overshadow thee: wherefore also the holy thing which is begotten shall be called the Son of God.

Luk 1:36 And behold, Elisabeth thy kinswoman, she also hath conceived a son in her old age; and this is the sixth month with her that was called barren.

Luk 1:37 For no word from God shall be void of power.

Luk 1:38 And Mary said, Behold, the handmaid of the Lord; be it unto me according to thy word. And the angel departed from her.

Luk 1:39 And Mary arose in these days and went into the hill country with haste, into a city of Judah;

Luk 1:40 and entered into the house of Zacharias and saluted Elisabeth.

Luk 1:41 And it came to pass, when Elisabeth heard the salutation of Mary, the babe leaped in her womb; and Elisabeth was filled with the Holy Spirit;

Luk 1:42 and she lifted up her voice with a loud cry, and said, Blessed art thou among women, and blessed is the fruit of thy womb.

Luk 1:43 And whence is this to me, that the mother of my Lord should come unto me?

Luk 1:44 For behold, when the voice of thy salutation came into mine ears, the babe leaped in my womb for joy.

Luk 1:45 And blessed is she that believed; for there shall be a fulfilment of the things which have been spoken to her from the Lord.

Luk 1:46 And Mary said, My soul doth magnify the Lord,

Luk 1:47 And my spirit hath rejoiced in God my Saviour.

Luk 1:48 For he hath looked upon the low estate of his handmaid: For behold, from henceforth all generations shall call me blessed.

Luk 1:49 For he that is mighty hath done to me great things; And holy is his name.

Luk 1:50 And his mercy is unto generations and generations On them that fear him.

Luk 1:51 He hath showed strength with his arm; He hath scattered the proud in the imagination of their heart.

Luk 1:52 He hath put down princes from their thrones, And hath exalted them of low degree.

Luk 1:53 The hungry he hath filled with good things; And the rich he hath sent empty away.

Luk 1:54 He hath given help to Israel his servant, That he might remember mercy

Luk 1:55 (As he spake unto our fathers) Toward Abraham and his seed for ever.

Luk 1:56 And Mary abode with her about three months, and returned unto her house.

Luk 1:57 Now Elisabeth's time was fulfilled that she should be delivered; and she brought forth a son.

Luk 1:58 And her neighbors and her kinsfolk heard that the Lord had magnified his mercy towards her; and they rejoiced with her.

Luk 1:59 And it came to pass on the eighth day, that they came to circumcise the child; and they would have called him Zacharias, after the name of the father.

Luk 1:60 And his mother answered and said, Not so; but he shall be called John.

Luk 1:61 And they said unto her, There is none of thy kindred that is called by this name.

Luk 1:62 And they made signs to his father, what he would have him called.

Luk 1:63 And he asked for a writing tablet, and wrote, saying, His name is John. And they marvelled all.

Luk 1:64 And his mouth was opened immediately, and his tongue loosed, and he spake, blessing God.

Luk 1:65 And fear came on all that dwelt round about them: and all these sayings were noised abroad throughout all the hill country of Judaea.

Luk 1:66 And all that heard them laid them up in their heart, saying, What then shall this child be? For the hand of the Lord was with him.

Luk 1:67 And his father Zacharias was filled with the Holy Spirit, and prophesied, saying,

Luk 1:68 Blessed be the Lord, the God of Israel; For he hath visited and wrought redemption for his people,

Luk 1:69 And hath raised up a horn of salvation for us In the house of his servant David

Luk 1:70 (As he spake by the mouth of his holy prophets that have been from of old),

Luk 1:71 Salvation from our enemies, and from the hand of all that hate us;

Luk 1:72 To show mercy towards, our fathers, And to remember his holy covenant;

Luk 1:73 The oath which he spake unto Abraham our father,

Luk 1:74 To grant unto us that we being delivered out of the hand of our enemies Should serve him without fear,

Luk 1:75 In holiness and righteousness before him all our days.

Luk 1:76 Yea and thou, child, shalt be called the prophet of the Most High: For thou shalt go before the face of the Lord to make ready his ways;

Luk 1:77 To give knowledge of salvation unto his people In the remission of their sins,

Luk 1:78 Because of the tender mercy of our God, Whereby the dayspring from on high shall visit us,

Luk 1:79 To shine upon them that sit in darkness and the shadow of death; To guide our feet into the way of peace.

Luk 1:80 And the child grew, and waxed strong in spirit, and was in the deserts till the day of his showing unto Israel.

Chapter 2.

Luk 2:1 Now it came to pass in those days, there went out a decree from Caesar Augustus, that all the world should be enrolled.

Luk 2:2 This was the first enrolment made when Quirinius was governor of Syria.

Luk 2:3 And all went to enrol themselves, every one to his own city.

Luk 2:4 And Joseph also went up from Galilee, out of the city of Nazareth, into Judaea, to the city of David, which is called Bethlehem, because he was of the house and family of David;

Luk 2:5 to enrol himself with Mary, who was betrothed to him, being great with child.

Luk 2:6 And it came to pass, while they were there, the days were fulfilled that she should be delivered.

Luk 2:7 And she brought forth her firstborn son; and she wrapped him in swaddling clothes, and laid him in a manger, because there was no room for them in the inn.

Luk 2:8 And there were shepherds in the same country abiding in the field, and keeping watch by night over their flock.

Luk 2:9 And an angel of the Lord stood by them, and the glory of the Lord shone round about them: and they were sore afraid.

Luk 2:10 And the angel said unto them, Be not afraid; for behold, I bring you good tidings of great joy which shall be to all the people:

Luk 2:11 for there is born to you this day in the city of David a Saviour, who is Christ the Lord.

Luk 2:12 And this is the sign unto you: Ye shall find a babe wrapped in swaddling clothes, and lying in a manger.

Luk 2:13 And suddenly there was with the angel a multitude of the heavenly host praising God, and saying,

Luk 2:14 Glory to God in the highest, And on earth peace among men in whom he is well pleased.

Luk 2:15 And it came to pass, when the angels went away from them into heaven, the shepherds said one to another, Let us now go even unto Bethlehem, and see this thing that is come to pass, which the Lord hath made known unto us.

Luk 2:16 And they came with haste, and found both Mary and Joseph, and the babe lying in the manger.

Luk 2:17   And when they saw it, they made known concerning the saying which was spoken to them about this child.

Luk 2:18   And all that heard it wondered at the things which were spoken unto them by the shepherds.

Luk 2:19   But Mary kept all these sayings, pondering them in her heart.

Luk 2:20   And the shepherds returned, glorifying and praising God for all the things that they had heard and seen, even as it was spoken unto them.

Luk 2:21   And when eight days were fulfilled for circumcising him, his name was called JESUS, which was so called by the angel before he was conceived in the womb.

Luk 2:22   And when the days of their purification according to the law of Moses were fulfilled, they brought him up to Jerusalem, to present him to the Lord

Luk 2:23   (as it is written in the law of the Lord, Every male that openeth the womb shall be called holy to the Lord),

Luk 2:24   and to offer a sacrifice according to that which is said in the law of the Lord, A pair of turtledoves, or two young pigeons.

Luk 2:25   And behold, there was a man in Jerusalem, whose name was Simeon; and this man was righteous and devout, looking for the consolation of Israel: and the Holy Spirit was upon him.

Luk 2:26   And it had been revealed unto him by the Holy Spirit, that he should not see death, before he had seen the Lord's Christ.

Luk 2:27   And he came in the Spirit into the temple: and when the parents brought in the child Jesus, that they might do concerning him after the custom of the law,

Luk 2:28   then he received him into his arms, and blessed God, and said,

Luk 2:29   Now lettest thou thy servant depart, Lord, According to thy word, in peace;

Luk 2:30   For mine eyes have seen thy salvation,

Luk 2:31   Which thou hast prepared before the face of all peoples;

Luk 2:32   A light for revelation to the Gentiles, And the glory of thy people Israel.

Luk 2:33   And his father and his mother were marvelling at the things which were spoken concerning him;

Luk 2:34   and Simeon blessed them, and said unto Mary his mother, Behold, this child is set for the falling and the rising of many in Israel; and for a sign which is spoken against;

Luk 2:35   yea and a sword shall pierce through thine own soul; that thoughts out of many hearts may be revealed.

Luk 2:36   And there was one Anna, a prophetess, the daughter of Phanuel, of the tribe of Asher (she was of a great age, having lived with a husband seven years from her virginity,

Luk 2:37   and she had been a widow even unto fourscore and four years), who departed not from the temple, worshipping with fastings and supplications night and day.

Luk 2:38   And coming up at that very hour she gave thanks unto God, and spake of him to all them that were looking for the redemption of Jerusalem.

Luk 2:39   And when they had accomplished all things that were according to the law of the Lord, they returned into Galilee, to their own city Nazareth.

Luk 2:40   And the child grew, and waxed strong, filled with wisdom: and the grace of God was upon him.

Luk 2:41   And his parents went every year to Jerusalem at the feast of the passover.

Luk 2:42 And when he was twelve years old, they went up after the custom of the feast;

Luk 2:43 and when they had fulfilled the days, as they were returning, the boy Jesus tarried behind in Jerusalem: and his parents knew it not;

Luk 2:44 but supposing him to be in the company, they went a day's journey; and they sought for him among their kinsfolk and acquaintance:

Luk 2:45 and when they found him not, they returned to Jerusalem, seeking for him.

Luk 2:46 And it came to pass, after three days they found him in the temple, sitting in the midst of the teachers, both hearing them, and asking them questions:

Luk 2:47 and all that heard him were amazed at his understanding and his answers.

Luk 2:48 And when they saw him, they were astonished; and his mother said unto him, Son, why hast thou thus dealt with us? behold, thy father and I sought thee sorrowing.

Luk 2:49 And he said unto them, How is it that ye sought me? knew ye not that I must be in my Father's house?

Luk 2:50 And they understood not the saying which he spake unto them.

Luk 2:51 And he went down with them, and came to Nazareth; and he was subject unto them: and his mother kept all these sayings in her heart.

Luk 2:52 And Jesus advanced in wisdom and stature, and in favor with God and men.

Chapter 3.

Luk 3:1 Now in the fifteenth year of the reign of Tiberius Caesar, Pontius Pilate being governor of Judaea, and Herod being tetrarch of Galilee, and his brother Philip tetrarch of the region of Ituraea and Trachonitis, and Lysanias tetrarch of Abilene,

Luk 3:2 in the highpriesthood of Annas and Caiaphas, the word of God came unto John the son of Zacharias in the wilderness.

Luk 3:3 And he came into all the region round about the Jordan, preaching the baptism of repentance unto remission of sins;

Luk 3:4 as it is written in the book of the words of Isaiah the prophet, The voice of one crying in the wilderness, Make ye ready the way of the Lord, Make his paths straight.

Luk 3:5 Every valley shall be filled, And every mountain and hill shall be brought low; And the crooked shall become straight, And the rough ways smooth;

Luk 3:6 And all flesh shall see the salvation of God.

Luk 3:7 He said therefore to the multitudes that went out to be baptized of him, Ye offspring of vipers, who warned you to flee from the wrath to come?

Luk 3:8 Bring forth therefore fruits worthy of repentance, and begin not to say within yourselves, We have Abraham to our father: for I say unto you, that God is able of these stones to raise up children unto Abraham.

Luk 3:9 And even now the axe also lieth at the root of the trees: every tree therefore that bringeth not forth good fruit is hewn down, and cast into the fire.

Luk 3:10 And the multitudes asked him, saying, What then must we do?

Luk 3:11 And he answered and said unto them, He that hath two coats, let him impart to him that hath none; and he that hath food, let him do likewise.

Luk 3:12 And there came also publicans to be baptized, and they said unto him, Teacher, what must we do?

Luk 3:13 And he said unto them, Extort no more than that which is appointed you.

Luk 3:14 And soldiers also asked him, saying, And we, what must we do? And he said unto them, Extort from no man by violence, neither accuse any one wrongfully; and be content with your wages.

Luk 3:15 And as the people were in expectation, and all men reasoned in their hearts concerning John, whether haply he were the Christ;

Luk 3:16 John answered, saying unto them all, I indeed baptize you with water; but there cometh he that is mightier than I, the latchet of whose shoes I am not worthy to unloose: he shall baptize you in the Holy Spirit and in fire:

Luk 3:17 whose fan is in his hand, thoroughly to cleanse his threshing-floor, and to gather the wheat into his garner; but the chaff he will burn up with unquenchable fire.

Luk 3:18 With many other exhortations therefore preached he good tidings unto the people;

Luk 3:19 but Herod the tetrarch, being reproved by him for Herodias his brother's wife, and for all the evil things which Herod had done,

Luk 3:20 added this also to them all, that he shut up John in prison.

Luk 3:21 Now it came to pass, when all the people were baptized, that, Jesus also having been baptized, and praying, the heaven was opened,

Luk 3:22 and the Holy Spirit descended in a bodily form, as a dove, upon him, and a voice came out of heaven, Thou art my beloved Son; in thee I am well pleased.

Luk 3:23 And Jesus himself, when he began to teach, was about thirty years of age, being the son (as was supposed) of Joseph, the son of Heli,

Luk 3:24 the son of Matthat, the son of Levi, the son of Melchi, the son of Jannai, the son of Joseph,

Luk 3:25 the son of Mattathias, the son of Amos, the son of Nahum, the son of Esli, the son of Naggai,

Luk 3:26 the son of Maath, the son of Mattathias, the son of Semein, the son of Josech, the son of Joda,

Luk 3:27 the son of Joanan, the son of Rhesa, the son of Zerubbabel, the son of Shealtiel, the son of Neri,

Luk 3:28 the son of Melchi, the son of Addi, the son of Cosam, the son of Elmadam, the son of Er,

Luk 3:29 the son of Jesus, the son of Eliezer, the son of Jorim, the son of Matthat, the son of Levi,

Luk 3:30 the son of Symeon, the son of Judas, the son of Joseph, the son of Jonam, the son of Eliakim,

Luk 3:31 the son of Melea, the son of Menna, the son of Mattatha, the son of Nathan, the son of David,

Luk 3:32 the son of Jesse, the son of Obed, the son of Boaz, the son of Salmon, the son of Nahshon,

Luk 3:33 the son of Amminadab, the son of Arni, the son of Hezron, the son of Perez, the son of Judah,

Luk 3:34 the son of Jacob, the son of Isaac, the son of Abraham, the son of Terah, the son of Nahor,

Luk 3:35 the son of Serug, the son of Reu, the son of Peleg, the son of Eber, the son of Shelah,

Luk 3:36 the son of Cainan, the son of Arphaxad, the son of Shem, the son of Noah, the son of Lamech,

Luk 3:37   the son of Methuselah, the son of Enoch, the son of Jared, the son of
Mahalaleel, the son of Cainan,

Luk 3:38 the son of Enos, the son of Seth, the son of Adam, the son of God.

Chapter 4.

Luk 4:1 And Jesus, full of the Holy Spirit, returned from the Jordan, and was led in
the Spirit in the wilderness

Luk 4:2 during forty days, being tempted of the devil. And he did eat nothing in those
days: and when they were completed, he hungered.

Luk 4:3 And the devil said unto him, If thou art the Son of God, command this stone
that it become bread.

Luk 4:4 And Jesus answered unto him, It is written, Man shall not live by bread alone.

Luk 4:5 And he led him up, and showed him all the kingdoms of the world in a
moment of time.

Luk 4:6 And the devil said unto him, To thee will I give all this authority, and the
glory of them: for it hath been delivered unto me; and to whomsoever I will I give
it.

Luk 4:7 If thou therefore wilt worship before me, it shall all be thine.

Luk 4:8 And Jesus answered and said unto him, It is written, Thou shalt worship the
Lord thy God, and him only shalt thou serve.

Luk 4:9 And he led him to Jerusalem, and set him on the pinnacle of the temple, and
said unto him, If thou art the Son of God, cast thyself down from hence:

Luk 4:10 for it is written, He shall give his angels charge concerning thee, to guard
thee:

Luk 4:11 and, On their hands they shall bear thee up, Lest haply thou dash thy foot
against a stone.

Luk 4:12 And Jesus answering said unto him, It is said, Thou shalt not make trial of
the Lord thy God.

Luk 4:13 And when the devil had completed every temptation, he departed from him
for a season.

Luk 4:14 And Jesus returned in the power of the Spirit into Galilee: and a fame went
out concerning him through all the region round about.

Luk 4:15 And he taught in their synagogues, being glorified of all.

Luk 4:16 And he came to Nazareth, where he had been brought up: and he entered, as
his custom was, into the synagogue on the sabbath day, and stood up to read.

Luk 4:17 And there was delivered unto him the book of the prophet Isaiah. And he
opened the book, and found the place where it was written,

Luk 4:18 The Spirit of the Lord is upon me, Because he anointed me to preach good
tidings to the poor: He hath sent me to proclaim release to the captives, And
recovering of sight to the blind, To set at liberty them that are bruised,

Luk 4:19 To proclaim the acceptable year of the Lord.

Luk 4:20 And he closed the book, and gave it back to the attendant, and sat down: and
the eyes of all in the synagogue were fastened on him.

Luk 4:21 And he began to say unto them, To-day hath this scripture been fulfilled in
your ears.

Luk 4:22 And all bare him witness, and wondered at the words of grace which
proceeded out of his mouth: and they said, Is not this Joseph's son?

Luk 4:23   And he said unto them, Doubtless ye will say unto me this parable, Physician, heal thyself: whatsoever we have heard done at Capernaum, do also here in thine own country.

Luk 4:24   And he said, Verily I say unto you, No prophet is acceptable in his own country.

Luk 4:25   But of a truth I say unto you, There were many widows in Israel in the days of Elijah, when the heaven was shut up three years and six months, when there came a great famine over all the land;

Luk 4:26   and unto none of them was Elijah sent, but only to Zarephath, in the land of Sidon, unto a woman that was a widow.

Luk 4:27   And there were many lepers in Israel in the time of Elisha the prophet; and none of them was cleansed, but only Naaman the Syrian.

Luk 4:28   And they were all filled with wrath in the synagogue, as they heard these things;

Luk 4:29   and they rose up, and cast him forth out of the city, and led him unto the brow of the hill whereon their city was built, that they might throw him down headlong.

Luk 4:30   But he passing through the midst of them went his way.

Luk 4:31   And he came down to Capernaum, a city of Galilee. And he was teaching them on the sabbath day:

Luk 4:32   and they were astonished at his teaching; for his word was with authority.

Luk 4:33   And in the synagogue there was a man, that had a spirit of an unclean demon; and he cried out with a loud voice,

Luk 4:34   Ah! what have we to do with thee, Jesus thou Nazarene? art thou come to destroy us? I know thee who thou art, the Holy One of God.

Luk 4:35   And Jesus rebuked him, saying, Hold thy peace, and come out of him. And when the demon had thrown him down in the midst, he came out of him, having done him no hurt.

Luk 4:36   And amazement came upon all, and they spake together, one with another, saying, What is this word? for with authority and power he commandeth the unclean spirits, and they come out.

Luk 4:37   And there went forth a rumor concerning him into every place of the region round about.

Luk 4:38   And he rose up from the synagogue, and entered into the house of Simon. And Simon's wife's mother was holden with a great fever; and they besought him for her.

Luk 4:39   And he stood over her, and rebuked the fever; and it left her: and immediately she rose up and ministered unto them.

Luk 4:40   And when the sun was setting, all they that had any sick with divers diseases brought them unto him; and he laid his hands on every one of them, and healed them.

Luk 4:41   And demons also came out from many, crying out, and saying, Thou art the Son of God. And rebuking them, he suffered them not to speak, because they knew that he was the Christ.

Luk 4:42   And when it was day, he came out and went into a desert place: and the multitudes sought after him, and came unto him, and would have stayed him, that he should not go from them.

Luk 4:43 But he said unto them, I must preach the good tidings of the kingdom of God to the other cities also: for therefore was I sent.

Luk 4:44 And he was preaching in the synagogues of Galilee.

Chapter 5.

Luk 5:1 Now it came to pass, while the multitude pressed upon him and heard the word of God, that he was standing by the lake of Gennesaret;

Luk 5:2 and he saw two boats standing by the lake: but the fishermen had gone out of them, and were washing their nets.

Luk 5:3 And he entered into one of the boats, which was Simon's, and asked him to put out a little from the land. And he sat down and taught the multitudes out of the boat.

Luk 5:4 And when he had left speaking, he said unto Simon, Put out into the deep, and let down your nets for a draught.

Luk 5:5 And Simon answered and said, Master, we toiled all night, and took nothing: but at thy word I will let down the nets.

Luk 5:6 And when they had done this, they inclosed a great multitude of fishes; and their nets were breaking;

Luk 5:7 and they beckoned unto their partners in the other boat, that they should come and help them. And they came, and filled both the boats, so that they began to sink.

Luk 5:8 But Simon Peter, when he saw it, fell down at Jesus' knees, saying, Depart from me; for I am a sinful man, O Lord.

Luk 5:9 For he was amazed, and all that were with him, at the draught of the fishes which they had taken;

Luk 5:10 and so were also James and John, sons of Zebedee, who were partners with Simon. And Jesus said unto Simon, Fear not; from henceforth thou shalt catch men.

Luk 5:11 And when they had brought their boats to land, they left all, and followed him.

Luk 5:12 And it came to pass, while he was in one of the cities, behold, a man full of leprosy: and when he saw Jesus, he fell on his face, and besought him, saying, Lord, if thou wilt, thou canst make me clean.

Luk 5:13 And he stretched forth his hand, and touched him, saying, I will; be thou made clean. And straightway the leprosy departed from him.

Luk 5:14 And he charged him to tell no man: but go thy way, and show thyself to the priest, and offer for thy cleansing, according as Moses commanded, for a testimony unto them.

Luk 5:15 But so much the more went abroad the report concerning him: and great multitudes came together to hear, and to be healed of their infirmities.

Luk 5:16 But he withdrew himself in the deserts, and prayed.

Luk 5:17 And it came to pass on one of those days, that he was teaching; and there were Pharisees and doctors of the law sitting by, who were come out of every village of Galilee and Judaea and Jerusalem: and the power of the Lord was with him to heal.

Luk 5:18 And behold, men bring on a bed a man that was palsied: and they sought to bring him in, and to lay him before him.

Luk 5:19 And not finding by what way they might bring him in because of the multitude, they went up to the housetop, and let him down through the tiles with his couch into the midst before Jesus.

Luk 5:20 And seeing their faith, he said, Man, thy sins are forgiven thee.

Luk 5:21 And the scribes and the Pharisees began to reason, saying, Who is this that speaketh blasphemies? Who can forgive sins, but God alone?

Luk 5:22 But Jesus perceiving their reasonings, answered and said unto them, Why reason ye in your hearts?

Luk 5:23 Which is easier, to say, Thy sins are forgiven thee; or to say, Arise and walk?

Luk 5:24 But that ye may know that the Son of man hath authority on earth to forgive sins (he said unto him that was palsied), I say unto thee, Arise, and take up thy couch, and go unto thy house.

Luk 5:25 And immediately he rose up before them, and took up that whereon he lay, and departed to his house, glorifying God.

Luk 5:26 And amazement took hold on all, and they glorified God; and they were filled with fear, saying, We have seen strange things to-day.

Luk 5:27 And after these things he went forth, and beheld a publican, named Levi, sitting at the place of toll, and said unto him, Follow me.

Luk 5:28 And he forsook all, and rose up and followed him.

Luk 5:29 And Levi made him a great feast in his house: and there was a great multitude of publicans and of others that were sitting at meat with them.

Luk 5:30 And the Pharisees and their scribes murmured against his disciples, saying, Why do ye eat and drink with the publicans and sinners?

Luk 5:31 And Jesus answering said unto them, They that are in health have no need of a physician; but they that are sick.

Luk 5:32 I am not come to call the righteous but sinners to repentance.

Luk 5:33 And they said unto him, The disciples of John fast often, and make supplications; likewise also the disciples of the Pharisees; but thine eat and drink.

Luk 5:34 And Jesus said unto them, Can ye make the sons of the bride-chamber fast, while the bridegroom is with them?

Luk 5:35 But the days will come; and when the bridegroom shall be taken away from them, then will they fast in those days.

Luk 5:36 And he spake also a parable unto them: No man rendeth a piece from a new garment and putteth it upon an old garment; else he will rend the new, and also the piece from the new will not agree with the old.

Luk 5:37 And no man putteth new wine into old wine-skins; else the new wine will burst the skins, and itself will be spilled, and the skins will perish.

Luk 5:38 But new wine must be put into fresh wine-skins.

Luk 5:39 And no man having drunk old wine desireth new; for he saith, The old is good.

Chapter 6.

Luk 6:1 Now it came to pass on a sabbath, that he was going through the grainfields; and his disciples plucked the ears, and did eat, rubbing them in their hands.

Luk 6:2 But certain of the Pharisees said, Why do ye that which it is not lawful to do on the sabbath day?

Luk 6:3 And Jesus answering them said, Have ye not read even this, what David did, when he was hungry, he, and they that were with him;

Luk 6:4 how he entered into the house of God, and took and ate the showbread, and gave also to them that were with him; which it is not lawful to eat save for the priests alone?

Luk 6:5 And he said unto them, The Son of man is lord of the sabbath.

Luk 6:6 And it came to pass on another sabbath, that he entered into the synagogue and taught: and there was a man there, and his right hand was withered.

Luk 6:7 And the scribes and the Pharisees watched him, whether he would heal on the sabbath; that they might find how to accuse him.

Luk 6:8 But he knew their thoughts; and he said to the man that had his hand withered, Rise up, and stand forth in the midst. And he arose and stood forth.

Luk 6:9 And Jesus said unto them, I ask you, Is it lawful on the sabbath to do good, or to do harm? to save a life, or to destroy it?

Luk 6:10 And he looked round about on them all, and said unto him, Stretch forth thy hand. And he did so: and his hand was restored.

Luk 6:11 But they were filled with madness; and communed one with another what they might do to Jesus.

Luk 6:12 And it came to pass in these days, that he went out into the mountain to pray; and he continued all night in prayer to God.

Luk 6:13 And when it was day, he called his disciples; and he chose from them twelve, whom also he named apostles:

Luk 6:14 Simon, whom he also named Peter, and Andrew his brother, and James and John, and Philip and Bartholomew,

Luk 6:15 and Matthew and Thomas, and James the son of Alphaeus, and Simon who was called the Zealot,

Luk 6:16 and Judas the son of James, and Judas Iscariot, who became a traitor;

Luk 6:17 and he came down with them, and stood on a level place, and a great multitude of his disciples, and a great number of the people from all Judaea and Jerusalem, and the sea coast of Tyre and Sidon, who came to hear him, and to be healed of their diseases;

Luk 6:18 and they that were troubled with unclean spirits were healed.

Luk 6:19 And all the multitude sought to touch him; for power came forth from him, and healed them all.

Luk 6:20 And he lifted up his eyes on his disciples, and said, Blessed are ye poor: for yours is the kingdom of God.

Luk 6:21 Blessed are ye that hunger now: for ye shall be filled. Blessed are ye that weep now: for ye shall laugh.

Luk 6:22 Blessed are ye, when men shall hate you, and when they shall separate you from their company, and reproach you, and cast out your name as evil, for the Son of man's sake.

Luk 6:23 Rejoice in that day, and leap for joy for behold, your reward is great in heaven; for in the same manner did their fathers unto the prophets.

Luk 6:24 But woe unto you that are rich! for ye have received your consolation.

Luk 6:25 Woe unto you, ye that are full now! for ye shall hunger. Woe unto you, ye that laugh now! for ye shall mourn and weep.

Luk 6:26 Woe unto you, when all men shall speak well of you! for in the same manner did their fathers to the false prophets.

Luk 6:27 But I say unto you that hear, Love your enemies, do good to them that hate you,

Luk 6:28 bless them that curse you, pray for them that despitefully use you.

Luk 6:29 To him that smiteth thee on the one cheek offer also the other; and from him that taketh away thy cloak withhold not thy coat also.

Luk 6:30 Give to every one that asketh thee; and of him that taketh away thy goods ask them not again.

Luk 6:31 And as ye would that men should do to you, do ye also to them likewise.

Luk 6:32 And if ye love them that love you, what thank have ye? for even sinners love those that love them.

Luk 6:33 And if ye do good to them that do good to you, what thank have ye? for even sinners do the same.

Luk 6:34 And if ye lend to them of whom ye hope to receive, what thank have ye? even sinners lend to sinners, to receive again as much.

Luk 6:35 But love your enemies, and do them good, and lend, never despairing; and your reward shall be great, and ye shall be sons of the Most High: for he is kind toward the unthankful and evil.

Luk 6:36 Be ye merciful, even as your Father is merciful.

Luk 6:37 And judge not, and ye shall not be judged: and condemn not, and ye shall not be condemned: release, and ye shall be released:

Luk 6:38 give, and it shall be given unto you; good measure, pressed down, shaken together, running over, shall they give into your bosom. For with what measure ye mete it shall be measured to you again.

Luk 6:39 And he spake also a parable unto them, Can the blind guide the blind? shall they not both fall into a pit?

Luk 6:40 The disciple is not above his teacher: but every one when he is perfected shall be as his teacher.

Luk 6:41 And why beholdest thou the mote that is in thy brother's eye, but considerest not the beam that is in thine own eye?

Luk 6:42 Or how canst thou say to thy brother, Brother, let me cast out the mote that is in thine eye, when thou thyself beholdest not the beam that is in thine own eye? Thou hypocrite, cast out first the beam out of thine own eye, and then shalt thou see clearly to cast out the mote that is in thy brother's eye.

Luk 6:43 For there is no good tree that bringeth forth corrupt fruit; nor again a corrupt tree that bringeth forth good fruit.

Luk 6:44 For each tree is known by its own fruit. For of thorns men do not gather figs, nor of a bramble bush gather they grapes.

Luk 6:45 The good man out of the good treasure of his heart bringeth forth that which is good; and the evil man out of the evil treasure bringeth forth that which is evil: for out of the abundance of the heart his mouth speaketh.

Luk 6:46 And why call ye me, Lord, Lord, and do not the things which I say?

Luk 6:47 Every one that cometh unto me, and heareth my words, and doeth them, I will show you to whom he is like:

Luk 6:48 he is like a man building a house, who digged and went deep, and laid a foundation upon the rock: and when a flood arose, the stream brake against that house, and could not shake it: because it had been well builded.

Luk 6:49 But he that heareth, and doeth not, is like a man that built a house upon the earth without a foundation; against which the stream brake, and straightway it fell in; and the ruin of that house was great.

Chapter 7.

Luk 7:1 After he had ended all his sayings in the ears of the people, he entered into Capernaum.

Luk 7:2 And a certain centurion's servant, who was dear unto him, was sick and at the point of death.

Luk 7:3 And when he heard concerning Jesus, he sent unto him elders of the Jews, asking him that he would come and save his servant.

Luk 7:4 And they, when they came to Jesus, besought him earnestly, saying, He is worthy that thou shouldest do this for him;

Luk 7:5 for he loveth our nation, and himself built us our synagogue.

Luk 7:6 And Jesus went with them. And when he was now not far from the house, the centurion sent friends to him, saying unto him, Lord, trouble not thyself; for I am not worthy that thou shouldest come under my roof:

Luk 7:7 wherefore neither thought I myself worthy to come unto thee: but say the word, and my servant shall be healed.

Luk 7:8 For I also am a man set under authority, having under myself soldiers: and I say to this one, Go, and he goeth; and to another, Come, and he cometh; and to my servant, Do this, and he doeth it.

Luk 7:9 And when Jesus heard these things, he marvelled at him, and turned and said unto the multitude that followed him, I say unto you, I have not found so great faith, no, not in Israel.

Luk 7:10 And they that were sent, returning to the house, found the servant whole.

Luk 7:11 And it came to pass soon afterwards, that he went to a city called Nain; and his disciples went with him, and a great multitude.

Luk 7:12 Now when he drew near to the gate of the city, behold, there was carried out one that was dead, the only son of his mother, and she was a widow: and much people of the city was with her.

Luk 7:13 And when the Lord saw her, he had compassion on her, and said unto her, Weep not.

Luk 7:14 And he came nigh and touched the bier: and the bearers stood still. And he said, Young man, I say unto thee, Arise.

Luk 7:15 And he that was dead sat up, and began to speak. And he gave him to his mother.

Luk 7:16 And fear took hold on all: and they glorified God, saying, A great prophet is arisen among us: and, God hath visited his people.

Luk 7:17 And this report went forth concerning him in the whole of Judaea, and all the region round about.

Luk 7:18 And the disciples of John told him of all these things.

Luk 7:19 And John calling unto him two of his disciples sent them to the Lord, saying, Art thou he that cometh, or look we for another?

Luk 7:20 And when the men were come unto him, they said, John the Baptist hath sent us unto thee, saying, Art thou he that cometh, or look we for another?

Luk 7:21 In that hour he cured many of diseases and plagues and evil spirits; and on many that were blind he bestowed sight.

Luk 7:22 And he answered and said unto them, Go and tell John the things which ye have seen and heard; the blind receive their sight, the lame walk, the lepers are cleansed, and the deaf hear, the dead are raised up, the poor have good tidings preached to them.

Luk 7:23 And blessed is he, whosoever shall find no occasion of stumbling in me.

Luk 7:24 And when the messengers of John were departed, he began to say unto the multitudes concerning John, What went ye out into the wilderness to behold? a reed shaken with the wind?

Luk 7:25 But what went ye out to see? a man clothed in soft raiment? Behold, they that are gorgeously apparelled, and live delicately, are in kings' courts.

Luk 7:26 But what went ye out to see? a prophet? Yea, I say unto you, and much more than a prophet.

Luk 7:27 This is he of whom it is written, Behold, I send my messenger before thy face, Who shall prepare thy way before thee.

Luk 7:28 I say unto you, Among them that are born of women there is none greater than John: yet he that is but little in the kingdom of God is greater than he.

Luk 7:29 And all the people when they heard, and the publicans, justified God, being baptized with the baptism of John.

Luk 7:30 But the Pharisees and the lawyers rejected for themselves the counsel of God, being not baptized of him.

Luk 7:31 Whereunto then shall I liken the men of this generation, and to what are they like?

Luk 7:32 They are like unto children that sit in the marketplace, and call one to another; who say, We piped unto you, and ye did not dance; we wailed, and ye did not weep.

Luk 7:33 For John the Baptist is come eating no bread nor drinking wine; and ye say, He hath a demon.

Luk 7:34 The Son of man is come eating and drinking; and ye say, Behold, a gluttonous man, and a winebibber, a friend of publicans and sinners!

Luk 7:35 And wisdom is justified of all her children.

Luk 7:36 And one of the Pharisees desired him that he would eat with him. And he entered into the Pharisee's house, and sat down to meat.

Luk 7:37 And behold, a woman who was in the city, a sinner; and when she knew that he was sitting at meat in the Pharisee's house, she brought an alabaster cruse of ointment,

Luk 7:38 and standing behind at his feet, weeping, she began to wet his feet with her tears, and wiped them with the hair of her head, and kissed his feet, and anointed them with the ointment.

Luk 7:39 Now when the Pharisee that had bidden him saw it, he spake within himself, saying, This man, if he were a prophet, would have perceived who and what manner of woman this is that toucheth him, that she is a sinner.

Luk 7:40 And Jesus answering said unto him, Simon, I have somewhat to say unto thee. And he saith, Teacher, say on.

Luk 7:41 A certain lender had two debtors: the one owed five hundred shillings, and the other fifty.

Luk 7:42 When they had not wherewith to pay, he forgave them both. Which of them therefore will love him most?

Luk 7:43 Simon answered and said, He, I suppose, to whom he forgave the most. And he said unto him, Thou hast rightly judged.

Luk 7:44 And turning to the woman, he said unto Simon, Seest thou this woman? I entered into thy house, thou gavest me no water for my feet: but she hath wetted my feet with her tears, and wiped them with her hair.

Luk 7:45 Thou gavest me no kiss: but she, since the time I came in, hath not ceased to kiss my feet.

Luk 7:46 My head with oil thou didst not anoint: but she hath anointed my feet with ointment.

Luk 7:47 Wherefore I say unto thee, Her sins, which are many, are forgiven; for she loved much: but to whom little is forgiven, the same loveth little.

Luk 7:48 And he said unto her, Thy sins are forgiven.

Luk 7:49 And they that sat at meat with him began to say within themselves, Who is this that even forgiveth sins?

Luk 7:50 And he said unto the woman, Thy faith hath saved thee; go in peace.

Chapter 8.

Luk 8:1 And it came to pass soon afterwards, that he went about through cities and villages, preaching and bringing the good tidings of the kingdom of God, and with him the twelve,

Luk 8:2 and certain women who had been healed of evil spirits and infirmities: Mary that was called Magdalene, from whom seven demons had gone out,

Luk 8:3 and Joanna the wife of Chuzas Herod's steward, and Susanna, and many others, who ministered unto them of their substance.

Luk 8:4 And when a great multitude came together, and they of every city resorted unto him, he spake by a parable:

Luk 8:5 The sower went forth to sow his seed: and as he sowed, some fell by the way side; and it was trodden under foot, and the birds of the heaven devoured it.

Luk 8:6 And other fell on the rock; and as soon as it grew, it withered away, because it had no moisture.

Luk 8:7 And other fell amidst the thorns; and the thorns grew with it, and choked it.

Luk 8:8 And other fell into the good ground, and grew, and brought forth fruit a hundredfold. As he said these things, he cried, He that hath ears to hear, let him hear.

Luk 8:9 And his disciples asked him what this parable might be.

Luk 8:10 And he said, Unto you it is given to know the mysteries of the kingdom of God: but to the rest in parables; that seeing they may not see, and hearing they may not understand.

Luk 8:11 Now the parable is this: The seed is the word of God.

Luk 8:12 And those by the way side are they that have heard; then cometh the devil, and taketh away the word from their heart, that they may not believe and be saved.

Luk 8:13 And those on the rock are they who, when they have heard, receive the word with joy; and these have no root, who for a while believe, and in time of temptation fall away.

Luk 8:14 And that which fell among the thorns, these are they that have heard, and as they go on their way they are choked with cares and riches and pleasures of this life, and bring no fruit to perfection.

Luk 8:15 And that in the good ground, these are such as in an honest and good heart, having heard the word, hold it fast, and bring forth fruit with patience.

Luk 8:16 And no man, when he hath lighted a lamp, covereth it with a vessel, or putteth it under a bed; but putteth it on a stand, that they that enter in may see the light.

Luk 8:17 For nothing is hid, that shall not be made manifest; nor anything secret, that shall not be known and come to light.

Luk 8:18 Take heed therefore how ye hear: for whosoever hath, to him shall be given; and whosoever hath not, from him shall be taken away even that which he thinketh he hath.

Luk 8:19 And there came to him his mother and brethren, and they could not come at him for the crowd.

Luk 8:20 And it was told him, Thy mother and thy brethren stand without, desiring to see thee.

Luk 8:21 But he answered and said unto them, My mother and my brethren are these that hear the word of God, and do it.

Luk 8:22 Now it came to pass on one of those days, that he entered into a boat, himself and his disciples; and he said unto them, Let us go over unto the other side of the lake: and they launched forth.

Luk 8:23 But as they sailed he fell asleep: and there came down a storm of wind on the lake; and they were filling with water, and were in jeopardy.

Luk 8:24 And they came to him, and awoke him, saying, Master, master, we perish. And he awoke, and rebuked the wind and the raging of the water: and they ceased, and there was a calm.

Luk 8:25 And he said unto them, Where is your faith? And being afraid they marvelled, saying one to another, Who then is this, that he commandeth even the winds and the water, and they obey him?

Luk 8:26 And they arrived at the country of the Gerasenes, which is over against Galilee.

Luk 8:27 And when he was come forth upon the land, there met him a certain man out of the city, who had demons; and for a long time he had worn no clothes, and abode not in any house, but in the tombs.

Luk 8:28 And when he saw Jesus, he cried out, and fell down before him, and with a loud voice said, What have I to do with thee, Jesus, thou Son of the Most High God? I beseech thee, torment me not.

Luk 8:29 For he was commanding the unclean spirit to come out from the man. For oftentimes it had seized him: and he was kept under guard, and bound with chains and fetters; and breaking the bands asunder, he was driven of the demon into the deserts.

Luk 8:30 And Jesus asked him, What is thy name? And he said, Legion; for many demons were entered into him.

Luk 8:31 And they entreated him that he would not command them to depart into the abyss.

Luk 8:32 Now there was there a herd of many swine feeding on the mountain: and they entreated him that he would give them leave to enter into them. And he gave them leave.

Luk 8:33 And the demons came out from the man, and entered into the swine: and the herd rushed down the steep into the lake, and were drowned.

Luk 8:34 And when they that fed them saw what had come to pass, they fled, and told it in the city and in the country.

Luk 8:35 And they went out to see what had come to pass; and they came to Jesus, and found the man, from whom the demons were gone out, sitting, clothed and in his right mind, at the feet of Jesus: and they were afraid.

Luk 8:36 And they that saw it told them how he that was possessed with demons was made whole.

Luk 8:37 And all the people of the country of the Gerasenes round about asked him to depart from them; for they were holden with great fear: and he entered into a boat, and returned.

Luk 8:38 But the man from whom the demons were gone out prayed him that he might be with him: but he sent him away, saying,

Luk 8:39 Return to thy house, and declare how great things God hath done for thee. And he went his way, publishing throughout the whole city how great things Jesus had done for him.

Luk 8:40 And as Jesus returned, the multitude welcomed him; for they were all waiting for him.

Luk 8:41 And behold, there came a man named Jairus, and he was a ruler of the synagogue: and he fell down at Jesus' feet, and besought him to come into his house;

Luk 8:42 for he had an only daughter, about twelve years of age, and she was dying. But as he went the multitudes thronged him.

Luk 8:43 And a woman having an issue of blood twelve years, who had spent all her living upon physicians, and could not be healed of any,

Luk 8:44 came behind him, and touched the border of his garment: and immediately the issue of her blood stanched.

Luk 8:45 And Jesus said, Who is it that touched me? And when all denied, Peter said, and they that were with him, Master, the multitudes press thee and crush thee.

Luk 8:46 But Jesus said, Some one did touch me; for I perceived that power had gone forth from me.

Luk 8:47 And when the woman saw that she was not hid, she came trembling, and falling down before him declared in the presence of all the people for what cause she touched him, and how she was healed immediately.

Luk 8:48 And he said unto her, Daughter, thy faith hath made thee whole; go in peace.

Luk 8:49 While he yet spake, there cometh one from the ruler of the synagogue's house, saying, Thy daughter is dead; trouble not the Teacher.

Luk 8:50 But Jesus hearing it, answered him, Fear not: only believe, and she shall be made whole.

Luk 8:51 And when he came to the house, he suffered not any man to enter in with him, save Peter, and John, and James, and the father of the maiden and her mother.

Luk 8:52 And all were weeping, and bewailing her: but he said, Weep not; for she is not dead, but sleepeth.

Luk 8:53 And they laughed him to scorn, knowing that she was dead.

Luk 8:54 But he, taking her by the hand, called, saying, Maiden, arise.

Luk 8:55 And her spirit returned, and she rose up immediately: and he commanded that something be given her to eat.

Luk 8:56 And her parents were amazed: but he charged them to tell no man what had been done.

Chapter 9.

Luk 9:1 And he called the twelve together, and gave them power and authority over all demons, and to cure diseases.

Luk 9:2 And he sent them forth to preach the kingdom of God, and to heal the sick.

Luk 9:3 And he said unto them, Take nothing for your journey, neither staff, nor wallet, nor bread, nor money; neither have two coats.

Luk 9:4 And into whatsoever house ye enter, there abide, and thence depart.

Luk 9:5 And as many as receive you not, when ye depart from that city, shake off the dust from your feet for a testimony against them.

Luk 9:6 And they departed, and went throughout the villages, preaching the gospel, and healing everywhere.

Luk 9:7 Now Herod the tetrarch heard of all that was done: and he was much perplexed, because that it was said by some, that John was risen from the dead;

Luk 9:8 and by some, that Elijah had appeared; and by others, that one of the old prophets was risen again.

Luk 9:9 And Herod said, John I beheaded: but who is this, about whom I hear such things? And he sought to see him.

Luk 9:10 And the apostles, when they were returned, declared unto him what things they had done. And he took them, and withdrew apart to a city called Bethsaida.

Luk 9:11 But the multitudes perceiving it followed him: and he welcomed them, and spake to them of the kingdom of God, and them that had need of healing he cured.

Luk 9:12 And the day began to wear away; and the twelve came, and said unto him, Send the multitude away, that they may go into the villages and country round about, and lodge, and get provisions: for we are here in a desert place.

Luk 9:13 But he said unto them, Give ye them to eat. And they said, We have no more than five loaves and two fishes; except we should go and buy food for all this people.

Luk 9:14 For they were about five thousand men. And he said unto his disciples, Make them sit down in companies, about fifty each.

Luk 9:15 And they did so, and made them all sit down.

Luk 9:16 And he took the five loaves and the two fishes, and looking up to heaven, he blessed them, and brake; and gave to the disciples to set before the multitude.

Luk 9:17 And they ate, and were all filled: and there was taken up that which remained over to them of broken pieces, twelve baskets.

Luk 9:18 And it came to pass, as he was praying apart, the disciples were with him: and he asked them, saying, Who do the multitudes say that I am?

Luk 9:19 And they answering said, John the Baptist; but others say, Elijah; and others, that one of the old prophets is risen again.

Luk 9:20 And he said unto them, But who say ye that I am? And Peter answering said, The Christ of God.

Luk 9:21 But he charged them, and commanded them to tell this to no man;

Luk 9:22 saying, The Son of man must suffer many things, and be rejected of the elders and chief priests and scribes, and be killed, and the third day be raised up.

Luk 9:23 And he said unto all, If any man would come after me, let him deny himself, and take up his cross daily, and follow me.

Luk 9:24 For whosoever would save his life shall lose it; but whosoever shall lose his life for my sake, the same shall save it.

Luk 9:25 For what is a man profited, if he gain the whole world, and lose or forfeit his own self?

Luk 9:26 For whosoever shall be ashamed of me and of my words, of him shall the Son of man be ashamed, when he cometh in his own glory, and the glory of the Father, and of the holy angels.

Luk 9:27 But I tell you of a truth, There are some of them that stand here, who shall in no wise taste of death, till they see the kingdom of God.

Luk 9:28 And it came to pass about eight days after these sayings, that he took with him Peter and John and James, and went up into the mountain to pray.

Luk 9:29 And as he was praying, the fashion of his countenance was altered, and his raiment became white and dazzling.

Luk 9:30 And behold, there talked with him two men, who were Moses and Elijah;

Luk 9:31 who appeared in glory, and spake of his decease which he was about to accomplish at Jerusalem.

Luk 9:32 Now Peter and they that were with him were heavy with sleep: but when they were fully awake, they saw his glory, and the two men that stood with him.

Luk 9:33 And it came to pass, as they were parting from him, Peter said unto Jesus, Master, it is good for us to be here: and let us make three tabernacles; one for thee, and one for Moses, and one for Elijah: not knowing what he said.

Luk 9:34 And while he said these things, there came a cloud, and overshadowed them: and they feared as they entered into the cloud.

Luk 9:35 And a voice came out of the cloud, saying, This is my Son, my chosen: hear ye him.

Luk 9:36 And when the voice came, Jesus was found alone. And they held their peace, and told no man in those days any of the things which they had seen.

Luk 9:37 And it came to pass, on the next day, when they were come down from the mountain, a great multitude met him.

Luk 9:38 And behold, a man from the multitude cried, saying, Teacher, I beseech thee to look upon my son; for he is mine only child:

Luk 9:39 and behold, a spirit taketh him, and he suddenly crieth out; and it teareth him that he foameth, and it hardly departeth from him, bruising him sorely.

Luk 9:40 And I besought thy disciples to cast it out; and they could not.

Luk 9:41 And Jesus answered and said, O faithless and perverse generation, how long shall I be with you, and bear with you? bring hither thy son.

Luk 9:42 And as he was yet a coming, the demon dashed him down, and tare him grievously. But Jesus rebuked the unclean spirit, and healed the boy, and gave him back to his father.

Luk 9:43 And they were all astonished at the majesty of God. But while all were marvelling at all the things which he did, he said unto his disciples,

Luk 9:44 Let these words sink into your ears: for the Son of man shall be delivered up into the hands of men.

Luk 9:45 But they understood not this saying, and it was concealed from them, that they should not perceive it; and they were afraid to ask him about this saying.

Luk 9:46 And there arose a reasoning among them, which of them was the greatest.

Luk 9:47 But when Jesus saw the reasoning of their heart, he took a little child, and set him by his side,

Luk 9:48 and said unto them, Whosoever shall receive this little child in my name receiveth me: and whosoever shall receive me receiveth him that sent me: for he that is least among you all, the same is great.

Luk 9:49 And John answered and said, Master, we saw one casting out demons in thy name; and we forbade him, because he followeth not with us.

Luk 9:50 But Jesus said unto him, Forbid him not: for he that is not against you is for you.

Luk 9:51 And it came to pass, when the days were well-nigh come that he should be received up, he stedfastly set his face to go to Jerusalem,

Luk 9:52 and sent messengers before his face: and they went, and entered into a village of the Samaritans, to make ready for him.

Luk 9:53 And they did not receive him, because his face was as though he were going to Jerusalem.

Luk 9:54 And when his disciples James and John saw this, they said, Lord, wilt thou that we bid fire to come down from heaven, and consume them?

Luk 9:55 But he turned, and rebuked them.

Luk 9:56 And they went to another village.

Luk 9:57 And as they went on the way, a certain man said unto him, I will follow thee whithersoever thou goest.

Luk 9:58 And Jesus said unto him, The foxes have holes, and the birds of the heaven have nests; but the Son of man hath not where to lay his head.

Luk 9:59 And he said unto another, Follow me. But he said, Lord, suffer me first to go and bury my father.

Luk 9:60 But he said unto him, Leave the dead to bury their own dead; but go thou and publish abroad the kingdom of God.

Luk 9:61 And another also said, I will follow thee, Lord; but first suffer me to bid farewell to them that are at my house.

Luk 9:62 But Jesus said unto him, No man, having put his hand to the plow, and looking back, is fit for the kingdom of God.

Chapter 10.

Luk 10:1 Now after these things the Lord appointed seventy others, and sent them two and two before his face into every city and place, whither he himself was about to come.

Luk 10:2 And he said unto them, The harvest indeed is plenteous, but the laborers are few: pray ye therefore the Lord of the harvest, that he send forth laborers into his harvest.

Luk 10:3 Go your ways; behold, I send you forth as lambs in the midst of wolves.

Luk 10:4 Carry no purse, no wallet, no shoes; and salute no man on the way.

Luk 10:5 And into whatsoever house ye shall enter, first say, Peace be to this house.

Luk 10:6 And if a son of peace be there, your peace shall rest upon him: but if not, it shall turn to you again.

Luk 10:7 And in that same house remain, eating and drinking such things as they give: for the laborer is worthy of his hire. Go not from house to house.

Luk 10:8 And into whatsoever city ye enter, and they receive you, eat such things as are set before you:

Luk 10:9 and heal the sick that are therein, and say unto them, The kingdom of God is come nigh unto you.

Luk 10:10 But into whatsoever city ye shall enter, and they receive you not, go out into the streets thereof and say,

Luk 10:11 Even the dust from your city, that cleaveth to our feet, we wipe off against you: nevertheless know this, that the kingdom of God is come nigh.

Luk 10:12 I say unto you, it shall be more tolerable in that day for Sodom, than for that city.

Luk 10:13 Woe unto thee, Chorazin! woe unto thee, Bethsaida! for if the mighty works had been done in Tyre and Sidon, which were done in you, they would have repented long ago, sitting in sackcloth and ashes.

Luk 10:14 But it shall be more tolerable for Tyre and Sidon in the judgment, than for you.

Luk 10:15 And thou, Capernaum, shalt thou be exalted unto heaven? thou shalt be brought down unto Hades.

Luk 10:16 He that heareth you heareth me; and he that rejecteth you rejecteth me; and he that rejecteth me rejecteth him that sent me.

Luk 10:17 And the seventy returned with joy, saying, Lord, even the demons are subject unto us in thy name.

Luk 10:18 And he said unto them, I beheld Satan fallen as lightning from heaven.

Luk 10:19 Behold, I have given you authority to tread upon serpents and scorpions, and over all the power of the enemy: and nothing shall in any wise hurt you.

Luk 10:20 Nevertheless in this rejoice not, that the spirits are subject unto you; but rejoice that your names are written in heaven.

Luk 10:21 In that same hour he rejoiced in the Holy Spirit, and said, I thank thee, O Father, Lord of heaven and earth, that thou didst hide these things from the wise and understanding, and didst reveal them unto babes: yea, Father; for so it was well-pleasing in thy sight.

Luk 10:22 All things have been delivered unto me of my Father: and no one knoweth who the Son is, save the Father; and who the Father is, save the Son, and he to whomsoever the Son willeth to reveal him.

Luk 10:23 And turning to the disciples, he said privately, Blessed are the eyes which see the things that ye see:

Luk 10:24 for I say unto you, that many prophets and kings desired to see the things which ye see, and saw them not; and to hear the things which ye hear, and heard them not.

Luk 10:25 And behold, a certain lawyer stood up and made trial of him, saying, Teacher, what shall I do to inherit eternal life?

Luk 10:26 And he said unto him, What is written in the law? how readest thou?

Luk 10:27 And he answering said, Thou shalt love the Lord thy God with all thy heart, and with all thy soul, and with all thy strength, and with all thy mind; and thy neighbor as thyself.

Luk 10:28 And he said unto him, Thou hast answered right: this do, and thou shalt live.

Luk 10:29 But he, desiring to justify himself, said unto Jesus, And who is my neighbor?

Luk 10:30 Jesus made answer and said, A certain man was going down from Jerusalem to Jericho; and he fell among robbers, who both stripped him and beat him, and departed, leaving him half dead.

Luk 10:31 And by chance a certain priest was going down that way: and when he saw him, he passed by on the other side.

Luk 10:32 And in like manner a Levite also, when he came to the place, and saw him, passed by on the other side.

Luk 10:33 But a certain Samaritan, as he journeyed, came where he was: and when he saw him, he was moved with compassion,

Luk 10:34 and came to him, and bound up his wounds, pouring on them oil and wine; and he set him on his own beast, and brought him to an inn, and took care of him.

Luk 10:35 And on the morrow he took out two shillings, and gave them to the host, and said, Take care of him; and whatsoever thou spendest more, I, when I come back again, will repay thee.

Luk 10:36 Which of these three, thinkest thou, proved neighbor unto him that fell among the robbers?

Luk 10:37 And he said, He that showed mercy on him. And Jesus said unto him, Go, and do thou likewise.

Luk 10:38 Now as they went on their way, he entered into a certain village: and a certain woman named Martha received him into her house.

Luk 10:39 And she had a sister called Mary, who also sat at the Lord's feet, and heard his word.

Luk 10:40 But Martha was cumbered about much serving; and she came up to him, and said, Lord, dost thou not care that my sister did leave me to serve alone? bid her therefore that she help me.

Luk 10:41 But the Lord answered and said unto her, Martha, Martha, thou art anxious and troubled about many things:

Luk 10:42 but one thing is needful: for Mary hath chosen the good part, which shall not be taken away from her.

Chapter 11.

Luk 11:1 And it came to pass, as he was praying in a certain place, that when he ceased, one of his disciples said unto him, Lord, teach us to pray, even as John also taught his disciples.

Luk 11:2 And he said unto them, When ye pray, say, Father, Hallowed be thy name. Thy kingdom come.

Luk 11:3 Give us day by day our daily bread.

Luk 11:4 And forgive us our sins; for we ourselves also forgive every one that is indebted to us. And bring us not into temptation.

Luk 11:5 And he said unto them, Which of you shall have a friend, and shall go unto him at midnight, and say to him, Friend, lend me three loaves;

Luk 11:6 for a friend of mine is come to me from a journey, and I have nothing to set before him;

Luk 11:7 and he from within shall answer and say, Trouble me not: the door is now shut, and my children are with me in bed; I cannot rise and give thee?

Luk 11:8 I say unto you, Though he will not rise and give him because he is his friend, yet because of his importunity he will arise and give him as many as he needeth.

Luk 11:9 And I say unto you, Ask, and it shall be given you; seek, and ye shall find; knock, and it shall be opened unto you.

Luk 11:10 For every one that asketh receiveth; and he that seeketh findeth; and to him that knocketh it shall be opened.

Luk 11:11 And of which of you that is a father shall his son ask a loaf, and he give him a stone? or a fish, and he for a fish give him a serpent?

Luk 11:12 Or if he shall ask an egg, will he give him a scorpion?

Luk 11:13 If ye then, being evil, know how to give good gifts unto your children, how much more shall your heavenly Father give the Holy Spirit to them that ask him?

Luk 11:14 And he was casting out a demon that was dumb. And it came to pass, when the demon was gone out, the dumb man spake; and the multitudes marvelled.

Luk 11:15 But some of them said, By Beelzebub the prince of the demons casteth he out demons.

Luk 11:16 And others, trying him, sought of him a sign from heaven.

Luk 11:17 But he, knowing their thoughts, said unto them, Every kingdom divided against itself is brought to desolation; and a house divided against a house falleth.

Luk 11:18 And if Satan also is divided against himself, how shall his kingdom stand? because ye say that I cast out demons by Beelzebub.

Luk 11:19 And if I by Beelzebub cast out demons, by whom do your sons cast them out? therefore shall they be your judges.

Luk 11:20 But if I by the finger of God cast out demons, then is the kingdom of God come upon you.

Luk 11:21 When the strong man fully armed guardeth his own court, his goods are in peace:

Luk 11:22 but when a stronger than he shall come upon him, and overcome him, he taketh from him his whole armor wherein he trusted, and divideth his spoils.

Luk 11:23 He that is not with me is against me; and he that gathereth not with me scattereth.

Luk 11:24 The unclean spirit when he is gone out of the man, passeth through waterless places, seeking rest, and finding none, he saith, I will turn back unto my house whence I came out.

Luk 11:25 And when he is come, he findeth it swept and garnished.

Luk 11:26 Then goeth he, and taketh to him seven other spirits more evil than himself; and they enter in and dwell there: and the last state of that man becometh worse than the first.

Luk 11:27 And it came to pass, as he said these things, a certain woman out of the multitude lifted up her voice, and said unto him, Blessed is the womb that bare thee, and the breasts which thou didst suck.

Luk 11:28 But he said, Yea rather, blessed are they that hear the word of God, and keep it.

Luk 11:29 And when the multitudes were gathering together unto him, he began to say, This generation is an evil generation: it seeketh after a sign; and there shall no sign be given to it but the sign of Jonah.

Luk 11:30 For even as Jonah became a sign unto the Ninevites, so shall also the Son of man be to this generation.

Luk 11:31 The queen of the south shall rise up in the judgment with the men of this generation, and shall condemn them: for she came from the ends of the earth to hear the wisdom of Solomon; and behold, a greater than Solomon is here.

Luk 11:32 The men of Nineveh shall stand up in the judgment with this generation, and shall condemn it: for they repented at the preaching of Jonah; and behold, a greater than Jonah is here.

Luk 11:33 No man, when he hath lighted a lamp, putteth it in a cellar, neither under the bushel, but on the stand, that they which enter in may see the light.

Luk 11:34 The lamp of thy body is thine eye: when thine eye is single, thy whole body also is full of light; but when it is evil, thy body also is full of darkness.

Luk 11:35 Look therefore whether the light that is in thee be not darkness.

Luk 11:36 If therefore thy whole body be full of light, having no part dark, it shall be wholly full of light, as when the lamp with its bright shining doth give thee light.

Luk 11:37 Now as he spake, a Pharisee asketh him to dine with him: and he went in, and sat down to meat.

Luk 11:38 And when the Pharisee saw it, he marvelled that he had not first bathed himself before dinner.

Luk 11:39 And the Lord said unto him, Now ye the Pharisees cleanse the outside of the cup and of the platter; but your inward part is full of extortion and wickedness.

Luk 11:40 Ye foolish ones, did not he that made the outside make the inside also?

Luk 11:41 But give for alms those things which are within; and behold, all things are clean unto you.

Luk 11:42 But woe unto you Pharisees! for ye tithe mint and rue and every herb, and pass over justice and the love of God: but these ought ye to have done, and not to leave the other undone.

Luk 11:43 Woe unto you Pharisees! for ye love the chief seats in the synagogues, and the salutations in the marketplaces.

Luk 11:44 Woe unto you! for ye are as the tombs which appear not, and the men that walk over them know it not.

Luk 11:45 And one of the lawyers answering saith unto him, Teacher, in saying this thou reproachest us also.

Luk 11:46 And he said, Woe unto you lawyers also! for ye load men with burdens grievous to be borne, and ye yourselves touch not the burdens with one of your fingers.

Luk 11:47 Woe unto you! for ye build the tombs of the prophets, and your fathers killed them.

Luk 11:48 So ye are witnesses and consent unto the works of your fathers: for they killed them, and ye build their tombs.

Luk 11:49 Therefore also said the wisdom of God, I will send unto them prophets and apostles; and some of them they shall kill and persecute;

Luk 11:50 that the blood of all the prophets, which was shed from the foundation of the world, may be required of this generation;

Luk 11:51 from the blood of Abel unto the blood of Zachariah, who perished between the altar and the sanctuary: yea, I say unto you, it shall be required of this generation.

Luk 11:52 Woe unto you lawyers! for ye took away the key of knowledge: ye entered not in yourselves, and them that were entering in ye hindered.

Luk 11:53 And when he was come out from thence, the scribes and the Pharisees began to press upon him vehemently, and to provoke him to speak of many things;

Luk 11:54 laying wait for him, to catch something out of his mouth.

Chapter 12.

Luk 12:1 In the mean time, when the many thousands of the multitude were gathered together, insomuch that they trod one upon another, he began to say unto his disciples first of all, Beware ye of the leaven of the Pharisees, which is hypocrisy.

Luk 12:2 But there is nothing covered up, that shall not be revealed; and hid, that shall not be known.

Luk 12:3 Wherefore whatsoever ye have said in the darkness shall be heard in the light; and what ye have spoken in the ear in the inner chambers shall be proclaimed upon the housetops.

Luk 12:4 And I say unto you my friends, Be not afraid of them that kill the body, and after that have no more that they can do.

Luk 12:5 But I will warn you whom ye shall fear: Fear him, who after he hath killed hath power to cast into hell; yea, I say unto you, Fear him.

Luk 12:6 Are not five sparrows sold for two pence? and not one of them is forgotten in the sight of God.

Luk 12:7 But the very hairs of your head are all numbered. Fear not: ye are of more value than many sparrows.

Luk 12:8 And I say unto you, Every one who shall confess me before men, him shall the Son of man also confess before the angels of God:

Luk 12:9 but he that denieth me in the presence of men shall be denied in the presence of the angels of God.

Luk 12:10 And every one who shall speak a word against the Son of man, it shall be forgiven him: but unto him that blasphemeth against the Holy Spirit it shall not be forgiven.

Luk 12:11 And when they bring you before the synagogues, and the rulers, and the authorities, be not anxious how or what ye shall answer, or what ye shall say:

Luk 12:12 for the Holy Spirit shall teach you in that very hour what ye ought to say.

Luk 12:13 And one out of the multitude said unto him, Teacher, bid my brother divide the inheritance with me.

Luk 12:14 But he said unto him, Man, who made me a judge or a divider over you?

Luk 12:15 And he said unto them, Take heed, and keep yourselves from all covetousness: for a man's life consisteth not in the abundance of the things which he possesseth.

Luk 12:16 And he spake a parable unto them, saying, The ground of a certain rich man brought forth plentifully:

Luk 12:17 and he reasoned within himself, saying, What shall I do, because I have not where to bestow my fruits?

Luk 12:18 And he said, This will I do: I will pull down my barns, and build greater; and there will I bestow all my grain and my goods.

Luk 12:19 And I will say to my soul, Soul, thou hast much goods laid up for many years; take thine ease, eat, drink, be merry.

Luk 12:20 But God said unto him, Thou foolish one, this night is thy soul required of thee; and the things which thou hast prepared, whose shall they be?

Luk 12:21 So is he that layeth up treasure for himself, and is not rich toward God.

Luk 12:22 And he said unto his disciples, Therefore I say unto you, Be not anxious for your life, what ye shall eat; nor yet for your body, what ye shall put on.

Luk 12:23 For the life is more than the food, and the body than the raiment.

Luk 12:24 Consider the ravens, that they sow not, neither reap; which have no store-chamber nor barn; and God feedeth them: of how much more value are ye than the birds!

Luk 12:25 And which of you by being anxious can add a cubit unto the measure of his life?

Luk 12:26 If then ye are not able to do even that which is least, why are ye anxious concerning the rest?

Luk 12:27 Consider the lilies, how they grow: they toil not, neither do they spin; yet I say unto you, Even Solomon in all his glory was not arrayed like one of these.

Luk 12:28 But if God doth so clothe the grass in the field, which to-day is, and tomorrow is cast into the oven; how much more shall he clothe you, O ye of little faith?

Luk 12:29 And seek not ye what ye shall eat, and what ye shall drink, neither be ye of doubtful mind.

Luk 12:30 For all these things do the nations of the world seek after: but your Father knoweth that ye have need of these things.

Luk 12:31 Yet seek ye his kingdom, and these things shall be added unto you.

Luk 12:32 Fear not, little flock; for it is your Father's good pleasure to give you the kingdom.

Luk 12:33 Sell that which ye have, and give alms; make for yourselves purses which wax not old, a treasure in the heavens that faileth not, where no thief draweth near, neither moth destroyeth.

Luk 12:34 For where your treasure is, there will your heart be also.

Luk 12:35 Let your loins be girded about, and your lamps burning;

Luk 12:36 and be ye yourselves like unto men looking for their lord, when he shall return from the marriage feast; that, when he cometh and knocketh, they may straightway open unto him.

Luk 12:37 Blessed are those servants, whom the lord when he cometh shall find watching: verily I say unto you, that he shall gird himself, and make them sit down to meat, and shall come and serve them.

Luk 12:38 And if he shall come in the second watch, and if in the third, and find them so, blessed are those servants.

Luk 12:39 But know this, that if the master of the house had known in what hour the thief was coming, he would have watched, and not have left his house to be broken through.

Luk 12:40 Be ye also ready: for in an hour that ye think not the Son of man cometh.

Luk 12:41 And Peter said, Lord, speakest thou this parable unto us, or even unto all?

Luk 12:42 And the Lord said, Who then is the faithful and wise steward, whom his lord shall set over his household, to give them their portion of food in due season?

Luk 12:43 Blessed is that servant, whom his lord when he cometh shall find so doing.

Luk 12:44 Of a truth I say unto you, that he will set him over all that he hath.

Luk 12:45 But if that servant shall say in his heart, My lord delayeth his coming; and shall begin to beat the menservants and the maidservants, and to eat and drink, and to be drunken;

Luk 12:46 the lord of that servant shall come in a day when he expecteth not, and in an hour when he knoweth not, and shall cut him asunder, and appoint his portion with the unfaithful.

Luk 12:47 And that servant, who knew his lord's will, and made not ready, nor did according to his will, shall be beaten with many stripes;

Luk 12:48 but he that knew not, and did things worthy of stripes, shall be beaten with few stripes. And to whomsoever much is given, of him shall much be required: and to whom they commit much, of him will they ask the more.

Luk 12:49 I came to cast fire upon the earth; and what do I desire, if it is already kindled?

Luk 12:50 But I have a baptism to be baptized with; and how am I straitened till it be accomplished!

Luk 12:51 Think ye that I am come to give peace in the earth? I tell you, Nay; but rather division:

Luk 12:52 for there shall be from henceforth five in one house divided, three against two, and two against three.

Luk 12:53 They shall be divided, father against son, and son against father; mother against daughter, and daughter against her mother; mother in law against her daughter in law, and daughter in law against her mother in law.

Luk 12:54 And he said to the multitudes also, When ye see a cloud rising in the west, straightway ye say, There cometh a shower; and so it cometh to pass.

Luk 12:55 And when ye see a south wind blowing, ye say, There will be a scorching heat; and it cometh to pass.

Luk 12:56 Ye hypocrites, ye know how to interpret the face of the earth and the heaven; but how is it that ye know not how to interpret this time?

Luk 12:57 And why even of yourselves judge ye not what is right?

Luk 12:58 For as thou art going with thine adversary before the magistrate, on the way give diligence to be quit of him; lest haply he drag thee unto the judge, and the judge shall deliver thee to the officer, and the officer shall cast thee into prison.

Luk 12:59 I say unto thee, Thou shalt by no means come out thence, till thou have paid the very last mite.

Chapter 13.

Luk 13:1 Now there were some present at that very season who told him of the Galilaeans, whose blood Pilate had mingled with their sacrifices.

Luk 13:2 And he answered and said unto them, Think ye that these Galilaeans were sinners above all the Galilaeans, because they have suffered these things?

Luk 13:3 I tell you, Nay: but, except ye repent, ye shall all in like manner perish.

Luk 13:4 Or those eighteen, upon whom the tower in Siloam fell, and killed them, think ye that they were offenders above all the men that dwell in Jerusalem?

Luk 13:5 I tell you, Nay: but, except ye repent, ye shall all likewise perish.

Luk 13:6 And he spake this parable; A certain man had a fig tree planted in his vineyard; and he came seeking fruit thereon, and found none.

Luk 13:7 And he said unto the vinedresser, Behold, these three years I come seeking fruit on this fig tree, and find none: cut it down; why doth it also cumber the ground?

Luk 13:8 And he answering saith unto him, Lord, let it alone this year also, till I shall dig about it, and dung it:

Luk 13:9 and if it bear fruit thenceforth, well; but if not, thou shalt cut it down.

Luk 13:10 And he was teaching in one of the synagogues on the sabbath day.

Luk 13:11 And behold, a woman that had a spirit of infirmity eighteen years; and she was bowed together, and could in no wise lift herself up.

Luk 13:12 And when Jesus saw her, he called her, and said to her, Woman, thou art loosed from thine infirmity.

Luk 13:13 And he laid his hands upon her: and immediately she was made straight, and glorified God.

Luk 13:14 And the ruler of the synagogue, being moved with indignation because Jesus had healed on the sabbath, answered and said to the multitude, There are six days in which men ought to work: in them therefore come and be healed, and not on the day of the sabbath.

Luk 13:15 But the Lord answered him, and said, Ye hypocrites, doth not each one of you on the sabbath loose his ox or his ass from the stall, and lead him away to watering?

Luk 13:16 And ought not this woman, being a daughter of Abraham, whom Satan had bound, lo, these eighteen years, to have been loosed from this bond on the day of the sabbath?

Luk 13:17 And as he said these things, all his adversaries were put to shame: and all the multitude rejoiced for all the glorious things that were done by him.

Luk 13:18 He said therefore, Unto what is the kingdom of God like? and whereunto shall I liken it?

Luk 13:19 It is like unto a grain of mustard seed, which a man took, and cast into his own garden; and it grew, and became a tree; and the birds of the heaven lodged in the branches thereof.

Luk 13:20 And again he said, Whereunto shall I liken the kingdom of God?

Luk 13:21 It is like unto leaven, which a woman took and hid in three measures of meal, till it was all leavened.

Luk 13:22 And he went on his way through cities and villages, teaching, and journeying on unto Jerusalem.

Luk 13:23 And one said unto him, Lord, are they few that are saved? And he said unto them,

Luk 13:24 Strive to enter in by the narrow door: for many, I say unto you, shall seek to enter in, and shall not be able.

Luk 13:25 When once the master of the house is risen up, and hath shut to the door, and ye begin to stand without, and to knock at the door, saying, Lord, open to us; and he shall answer and say to you, I know you not whence ye are;

Luk 13:26 then shall ye begin to say, We did eat and drink in thy presence, and thou didst teach in our streets;

Luk 13:27 and he shall say, I tell you, I know not whence ye are; depart from me, all ye workers of iniquity.

Luk 13:28 There shall be the weeping and the gnashing of teeth, when ye shall see Abraham, and Isaac, and Jacob, and all the prophets, in the kingdom of God, and yourselves cast forth without.

Luk 13:29 And they shall come from the east and west, and from the north and south, and shall sit down in the kingdom of God.

Luk 13:30 And behold, there are last who shall be first, and there are first who shall be last.

Luk 13:31 In that very hour there came certain Pharisees, saying to him, Get thee out, and go hence: for Herod would fain kill thee.

Luk 13:32 And he said unto them, Go and say to that fox, Behold, I cast out demons and perform cures to-day and to-morrow, and the third day I am perfected.

Luk 13:33 Nevertheless I must go on my way to-day and to-morrow and the day following: for it cannot be that a prophet perish out of Jerusalem.

Luk 13:34 O Jerusalem, Jerusalem, that killeth the prophets, and stoneth them that are sent unto her! how often would I have gathered thy children together, even as a hen gathereth her own brood under her wings, and ye would not!

Luk 13:35 Behold, your house is left unto you desolate: and I say unto you, Ye shall not see me, until ye shall say, Blessed is he that cometh in the name of the Lord.

Chapter 14.

Luk 14:1 And it came to pass, when he went into the house of one of the rulers of the Pharisees on a sabbath to eat bread, that they were watching him.

Luk 14:2 And behold, there was before him a certain man that had the dropsy.

Luk 14:3 And Jesus answering spake unto the lawyers and Pharisees, saying, Is it lawful to heal on the sabbath, or not?

Luk 14:4 But they held their peace. And he took him, and healed him, and let him go.

Luk 14:5 And he said unto them, Which of you shall have an ass or an ox fallen into a well, and will not straightway draw him up on a sabbath day?

Luk 14:6 And they could not answer again unto these things.

Luk 14:7 And he spake a parable unto those that were bidden, when he marked how they chose out the chief seats; saying unto them,

Luk 14:8 When thou art bidden of any man to a marriage feast, sit not down in the chief seat; lest haply a more honorable man than thou be bidden of him,

Luk 14:9 and he that bade thee and him shall come and say to thee, Give this man place; and then thou shalt begin with shame to take the lowest place.

Luk 14:10 But when thou art bidden, go and sit down in the lowest place; that when he that hath bidden thee cometh, he may say to thee, Friend, go up higher: then shalt thou have glory in the presence of all that sit at meat with thee.

Luk 14:11 For every one that exalteth himself shall be humbled; and he that humbleth himself shall be exalted.

Luk 14:12 And he said to him also that had bidden him, When thou makest a dinner or a supper, call not thy friends, nor thy brethren, nor thy kinsmen, nor rich neighbors; lest haply they also bid thee again, and a recompense be made thee.

Luk 14:13 But when thou makest a feast, bid the poor, the maimed, the lame, the blind:

Luk 14:14 and thou shalt be blessed; because they have not wherewith to recompense thee: for thou shalt be recompensed in the resurrection of the just.

Luk 14:15 And when one of them that sat at meat with him heard these things, he said unto him, Blessed is he that shall eat bread in the kingdom of God.

Luk 14:16 But he said unto him, A certain man made a great supper; and he bade many:

Luk 14:17 and he sent forth his servant at supper time to say to them that were bidden, Come; for all things are now ready.

Luk 14:18 And they all with one consent began to make excuse. The first said unto him, I have bought a field, and I must needs go out and see it; I pray thee have me excused.

Luk 14:19 And another said, I have bought five yoke of oxen, and I go to prove them; I pray thee have me excused.

Luk 14:20 And another said, I have married a wife, and therefore I cannot come.

Luk 14:21 And the servant came, and told his lord these things. Then the master of the house being angry said to his servant, Go out quickly into the streets and lanes of the city, and bring in hither the poor and maimed and blind and lame.

Luk 14:22 And the servant said, Lord, what thou didst command is done, and yet there is room.

Luk 14:23 And the lord said unto the servant, Go out into the highways and hedges, and constrain them to come in, that my house may be filled.

Luk 14:24 For I say unto you, that none of those men that were bidden shall taste of my supper.

Luk 14:25 Now there went with him great multitudes: and he turned, and said unto them,

Luk 14:26 If any man cometh unto me, and hateth not his own father, and mother, and wife, and children, and brethren, and sisters, yea, and his own life also, he cannot be my disciple.

Luk 14:27 Whosoever doth not bear his own cross, and come after me, cannot be my disciple.

Luk 14:28 For which of you, desiring to build a tower, doth not first sit down and count the cost, whether he have wherewith to complete it?

Luk 14:29 Lest haply, when he hath laid a foundation, and is not able to finish, all that behold begin to mock him,

Luk 14:30 saying, This man began to build, and was not able to finish.

Luk 14:31 Or what king, as he goeth to encounter another king in war, will not sit down first and take counsel whether he is able with ten thousand to meet him that cometh against him with twenty thousand?

Luk 14:32 Or else, while the other is yet a great way off, he sendeth an ambassage, and asketh conditions of peace.

Luk 14:33 So therefore whosoever he be of you that renounceth not all that he hath, he cannot be my disciple.

Luk 14:34 Salt therefore is good: but if even the salt have lost its savor, wherewith shall it be seasoned?

Luk 14:35 It is fit neither for the land nor for the dunghill: men cast it out. He that hath ears to hear, let him hear.

Chapter 15.

Luk 15:1 Now all the publicans and sinners were drawing near unto him to hear him.

Luk 15:2 And both the Pharisees and the scribes murmured, saying, This man receiveth sinners, and eateth with them.

Luk 15:3 And he spake unto them this parable, saying,

Luk 15:4 What man of you, having a hundred sheep, and having lost one of them, doth not leave the ninety and nine in the wilderness, and go after that which is lost, until he find it?

Luk 15:5 And when he hath found it, he layeth it on his shoulders, rejoicing.

Luk 15:6 And when he cometh home, he calleth together his friends and his neighbors, saying unto them, Rejoice with me, for I have found my sheep which was lost.

Luk 15:7 I say unto you, that even so there shall be joy in heaven over one sinner that repenteth, more than over ninety and nine righteous persons, who need no repentance.

Luk 15:8 Or what woman having ten pieces of silver, if she lose one piece, doth not light a lamp, and sweep the house, and seek diligently until she find it?

Luk 15:9 And when she hath found it, she calleth together her friends and neighbors, saying, Rejoice with me, for I have found the piece which I had lost.

Luk 15:10 Even so, I say unto you, there is joy in the presence of the angels of God over one sinner that repenteth.

Luk 15:11 And he said, A certain man had two sons:

Luk 15:12 and the younger of them said to his father, Father, give me the portion of thy substance that falleth to me. And he divided unto them his living.

Luk 15:13 And not many days after, the younger son gathered all together and took his journey into a far country; and there he wasted his substance with riotous living.

Luk 15:14 And when he had spent all, there arose a mighty famine in that country; and he began to be in want.

Luk 15:15 And he went and joined himself to one of the citizens of that country; and he sent him into his fields to feed swine.

Luk 15:16 And he would fain have filled his belly with the husks that the swine did eat: and no man gave unto him.

Luk 15:17 But when he came to himself he said, How many hired servants of my father's have bread enough and to spare, and I perish here with hunger!

Luk 15:18 I will arise and go to my father, and will say unto him, Father, I have sinned against heaven, and in thy sight:

Luk 15:19 I am no more worthy to be called your son: make me as one of thy hired servants.

Luk 15:20 And he arose, and came to his father. But while he was yet afar off, his father saw him, and was moved with compassion, and ran, and fell on his neck, and kissed him.

Luk 15:21 And the son said unto him, Father, I have sinned against heaven, and in thy sight: I am no more worthy to be called thy son.

Luk 15:22 But the father said to his servants, Bring forth quickly the best robe, and put it on him; and put a ring on his hand, and shoes on his feet:

Luk 15:23 and bring the fatted calf, and kill it, and let us eat, and make merry:

Luk 15:24 for this my son was dead, and is alive again; he was lost, and is found. And they began to be merry.

Luk 15:25 Now his elder son was in the field: and as he came and drew nigh to the house, he heard music and dancing.

Luk 15:26 And he called to him one of the servants, and inquired what these things might be.

Luk 15:27 And he said unto him, Thy brother is come; and thy father hath killed the fatted calf, because he hath received him safe and sound.

Luk 15:28 But he was angry, and would not go in: and his father came out, and entreated him.

Luk 15:29 But he answered and said to his father, Lo, these many years do I serve thee, and I never transgressed a commandment of thine; and yet thou never gavest me a kid, that I might make merry with my friends:

Luk 15:30 but when this thy son came, who hath devoured thy living with harlots, thou killedst for him the fatted calf.

Luk 15:31 And he said unto him, Son, thou art ever with me, and all that is mine is thine.

Luk 15:32 But it was meet to make merry and be glad: for this thy brother was dead, and is alive again; and was lost, and is found.

Chapter 16.

Luk 16:1 And he said also unto the disciples, There was a certain rich man, who had a steward; and the same was accused unto him that he was wasting his goods.

Luk 16:2 And he called him, and said unto him, What is this that I hear of thee? render the account of thy stewardship; for thou canst be no longer steward.

Luk 16:3 And the steward said within himself, What shall I do, seeing that my lord taketh away the stewardship from me? I have not strength to dig; to beg I am ashamed.

Luk 16:4 I am resolved what to do, that, when I am put out of the stewardship, they may receive me into their houses.

Luk 16:5 And calling to him each one of his lord's debtors, he said to the first, How much owest thou unto my lord?

Luk 16:6 And he said, A hundred measures of oil. And he said unto him, Take thy bond, and sit down quickly and write fifty.

Luk 16:7 Then said he to another, And how much owest thou? And he said, A hundred measures of wheat. He saith unto him, Take thy bond, and write fourscore.

Luk 16:8 And his lord commended the unrighteous steward because he had done wisely: for the sons of this world are for their own generation wiser than the sons of the light.

Luk 16:9 And I say unto you, Make to yourselves friends by means of the mammon of unrighteousness; that, when it shall fail, they may receive you into the eternal tabernacles.

Luk 16:10 He that is faithful in a very little is faithful also in much: and he that is unrighteous in a very little is unrighteous also in much.

Luk 16:11 If therefore ye have not been faithful in the unrighteous mammon, who will commit to your trust the true riches?

Luk 16:12 And if ye have not been faithful in that which is another's, who will give you that which is your own?

Luk 16:13 No servant can serve two masters: for either he will hate the one, and love the other; or else he will hold to one, and despise the other. Ye cannot serve God and mammon.

Luk 16:14 And the Pharisees, who were lovers of money, heard all these things; and they scoffed at him.

Luk 16:15 And he said unto them, Ye are they that justify yourselves in the sight of men; but God knoweth your hearts: for that which is exalted among men is an abomination in the sight of God.

Luk 16:16 The law and the prophets were until John: from that time the gospel of the kingdom of God is preached, and every man entereth violently into it.

Luk 16:17 But it is easier for heaven and earth to pass away, than for one tittle of the law to fall.

Luk 16:18 Every one that putteth away his wife, and marrieth another, committeth adultery: and he that marrieth one that is put away from a husband committeth adultery.

Luk 16:19 Now there was a certain rich man, and he was clothed in purple and fine linen, faring sumptuously every day:

Luk 16:20 and a certain beggar named Lazarus was laid at his gate, full of sores,

Luk 16:21 and desiring to be fed with the crumbs that fell from the rich man's table; yea, even the dogs came and licked his sores.

Luk 16:22 And it came to pass, that the beggar died, and that he was carried away by the angels into Abraham's bosom: and the rich man also died, and was buried.

Luk 16:23 And in Hades he lifted up his eyes, being in torments, and seeth Abraham afar off, and Lazarus in his bosom.

Luk 16:24 And he cried and said, Father Abraham, have mercy on me, and send Lazarus, that he may dip the tip of his finger in water, and cool my tongue; for I am in anguish in this flame.

Luk 16:25 But Abraham said, Son, remember that thou in thy lifetime receivedst thy good things, and Lazarus in like manner evil things: but now here he is comforted, and thou art in anguish.

Luk 16:26 And besides all this, between us and you there is a great gulf fixed, that they that would pass from hence to you may not be able, and that none may cross over from thence to us.

Luk 16:27 And he said, I pray thee therefore, father, that thou wouldest send him to my father's house;

Luk 16:28 for I have five brethren; that he may testify unto them, lest they also come into this place of torment.

Luk 16:29 But Abraham saith, They have Moses and the prophets; let them hear them.

Luk 16:30 And he said, Nay, father Abraham: but if one go to them from the dead, they will repent.

Luk 16:31 And he said unto him, If they hear not Moses and the prophets, neither will they be persuaded, if one rise from the dead.

Chapter 17.

Luk 17:1 And he said unto his disciples, It is impossible but that occasions of stumbling should come; but woe unto him, through whom they come!

Luk 17:2 It were well for him if a millstone were hanged about his neck, and he were thrown into the sea, rather than that he should cause one of these little ones to stumble.

Luk 17:3 Take heed to yourselves: if thy brother sin, rebuke him; and if he repent, forgive him.

Luk 17:4 And if he sin against thee seven times in the day, and seven times turn again to thee, saying, I repent; thou shalt forgive him.

Luk 17:5 And the apostles said unto the Lord, Increase our faith.

Luk 17:6 And the Lord said, If ye had faith as a grain of mustard seed, ye would say unto this sycamine tree, Be thou rooted up, and be thou planted in the sea; and it would obey you.

Luk 17:7 But who is there of you, having a servant plowing or keeping sheep, that will say unto him, when he is come in from the field, Come straightway and sit down to meat;

Luk 17:8 and will not rather say unto him, Make ready wherewith I may sup, and gird thyself, and serve me, till I have eaten and drunken; and afterward thou shalt eat and drink?

Luk 17:9 Doth he thank the servant because he did the things that were commanded?

Luk 17:10 Even so ye also, when ye shall have done all the things that are commanded you, say, We are unprofitable servants; we have done that which it was our duty to do.

Luk 17:11 And it came to pass, as they were on the way to Jerusalem, that he was passing along the borders of Samaria and Galilee.

Luk 17:12 And as he entered into a certain village, there met him ten men that were lepers, who stood afar off:

Luk 17:13 and they lifted up their voices, saying, Jesus, Master, have mercy on us.

Luk 17:14 And when he saw them, he said unto them, Go and show yourselves unto the priests. And it came to pass, as they went, they were cleansed.

Luk 17:15 And one of them, when he saw that he was healed, turned back, with a loud voice glorifying God;

Luk 17:16 and he fell upon his face at his feet, giving him thanks: and he was a Samaritan.

Luk 17:17 And Jesus answering said, Were not the ten cleansed? but where are the nine?

Luk 17:18 Were there none found that returned to give glory to God, save this stranger?

Luk 17:19 And he said unto him, Arise, and go thy way: thy faith hath made thee whole.

Luk 17:20 And being asked by the Pharisees, when the kingdom of God cometh, he answered them and said, The kingdom of God cometh not with observation:

Luk 17:21 neither shall they say, Lo, here! or, There! for lo, the kingdom of God is within you.

Luk 17:22 And he said unto the disciples, The days will come, when ye shall desire to see one of the days of the Son of man, and ye shall not see it.

Luk 17:23 And they shall say to you, Lo, there! Lo, here! go not away, nor follow after them:

Luk 17:24 for as the lightning, when it lighteneth out of the one part under the heaven, shineth unto the other part under heaven; so shall the Son of man be in his day.

Luk 17:25 But first must he suffer many things and be rejected of this generation.

Luk 17:26 And as it came to pass in the days of Noah, even so shall it be also in the days of the Son of man.

Luk 17:27 They ate, they drank, they married, they were given in marriage, until the day that Noah entered into the ark, and the flood came, and destroyed them all.

Luk 17:28 Likewise even as it came to pass in the days of Lot; they ate, they drank, they bought, they sold, they planted, they builded;

Luk 17:29 but in the day that Lot went out from Sodom it rained fire and brimstone from heaven, and destroyed them all:

Luk 17:30 after the same manner shall it be in the day that the Son of man is revealed.

Luk 17:31 In that day, he that shall be on the housetop, and his goods in the house, let him not go down to take them away: and let him that is in the field likewise not return back.

Luk 17:32 Remember Lot's wife.

Luk 17:33 Whosoever shall seek to gain his life shall lose it: but whosoever shall lose his life shall preserve it.

Luk 17:34 I say unto you, In that night there shall be two men on one bed; the one shall be taken, and the other shall be left.

Luk 17:35 There shall be two women grinding together; the one shall be taken, and the other shall be left.

Luk 17:36 There shall be two men in the field; the one shall be taken, and the other shall be left.

Luk 17:37 And they answering say unto him, Where, Lord? And he said unto them, Where the body is, thither will the eagles also be gathered together.

Chapter 18.

Luk 18:1 And he spake a parable unto them to the end that they ought always to pray, and not to faint;

Luk 18:2 saying, There was in a city a judge, who feared not God, and regarded not man:

Luk 18:3 and there was a widow in that city; and she came oft unto him, saying, Avenge me of mine adversary.

Luk 18:4 And he would not for a while: but afterward he said within himself, Though I fear not God, nor regard man;

Luk 18:5 yet because this widow troubleth me, I will avenge her, lest she wear me out by her continual coming.

Luk 18:6 And the Lord said, Hear what the unrighteous judge saith.

Luk 18:7 And shall not God avenge his elect, that cry to him day and night, and yet he is longsuffering over them?

Luk 18:8 I say unto you, that he will avenge them speedily. Nevertheless, when the Son of man cometh, shall he find faith on the earth?

Luk 18:9 And he spake also this parable unto certain who trusted in themselves that they were righteous, and set all others at nought:

Luk 18:10 Two men went up into the temple to pray; the one a Pharisee, and the other a publican.

Luk 18:11 The Pharisee stood and prayed thus with himself, God, I thank thee, that I am not as the rest of men, extortioners, unjust, adulterers, or even as this publican.

Luk 18:12 I fast twice in the week; I give tithes of all that I get.

Luk 18:13 But the publican, standing afar off, would not lift up so much as his eyes unto heaven, but smote his breast, saying, God, be thou merciful to me a sinner.

Luk 18:14 I say unto you, This man went down to his house justified rather than the other: for every one that exalteth himself shall be humbled; but he that humbleth himself shall be exalted.

Luk 18:15 And they were bringing unto him also their babes, that he should touch them: but when the disciples saw it, they rebuked them.

Luk 18:16 But Jesus called them unto him, saying, Suffer the little children to come unto me, and forbid them not: for to such belongeth the kingdom of God.

Luk 18:17 Verily I say unto you, Whosoever shall not receive the kingdom of God as a little child, he shall in no wise enter therein.

Luk 18:18 And a certain ruler asked him, saying, Good Teacher, what shall I do to inherit eternal life?

Luk 18:19 And Jesus said unto him, Why callest thou me good? none is good, save one, even God.

Luk 18:20 Thou knowest the commandments, Do not commit adultery, Do not kill, Do not steal, Do not bear false witness, Honor thy father and mother.

Luk 18:21 And he said, All these things have I observed from my youth up.

Luk 18:22 And when Jesus heard it, he said unto him, One thing thou lackest yet: sell all that thou hast, and distribute unto the poor, and thou shalt have treasure in heaven: and come, follow me.

Luk 18:23 But when he heard these things, he became exceeding sorrowful; for he was very rich.

Luk 18:24 And Jesus seeing him said, How hardly shall they that have riches enter into the kingdom of God!

Luk 18:25 For it is easier for a camel to enter in through a needle's eye, than for a rich man to enter into the kingdom of God.

Luk 18:26 And they that heard it said, Then who can be saved?

Luk 18:27 But he said, The things which are impossible with men are possible with God.

Luk 18:28 And Peter said, Lo, we have left our own, and followed thee.

Luk 18:29 And he said unto them, Verily I say unto you, There is no man that hath left house, or wife, or brethren, or parents, or children, for the kingdom of God's sake,

Luk 18:30 who shall not receive manifold more in this time, and in the world to come eternal life.

Luk 18:31 And he took unto him the twelve, and said unto them, Behold, we go up to Jerusalem, and all the things that are written through the prophets shall be accomplished unto the Son of man.

Luk 18:32 For he shall be delivered up unto the Gentiles, and shall be mocked, and shamefully treated, and spit upon:

Luk 18:33 and they shall scourge and kill him: and the third day he shall rise again.

Luk 18:34 And they understood none of these things; and this saying was hid from them, and they perceived not the things that were said.

Luk 18:35 And it came to pass, as he drew nigh unto Jericho, a certain blind man sat by the way side begging:

Luk 18:36 and hearing a multitude going by, he inquired what this meant.

Luk 18:37 And they told him, that Jesus of Nazareth passeth by.

Luk 18:38 And he cried, saying, Jesus, thou son of David, have mercy on me.

Luk 18:39 And they that went before rebuked him, that he should hold his peace but he cried out the more a great deal, Thou son of David, have mercy on me.

Luk 18:40 And Jesus stood, and commanded him to be brought unto him: and when he was come near, he asked him,

Luk 18:41 What wilt thou that I should do unto thee? And he said, Lord, that I may receive my sight.

Luk 18:42 And Jesus said unto him, Receive thy sight: thy faith hath made thee whole.

Luk 18:43 And immediately he received his sight, and followed him, glorifying God: and all the people, when they saw it, gave praise unto God.

Chapter 19.

Luk 19:1 And he entered and was passing through Jericho.

Luk 19:2 And behold, a man called by name Zacchaeus; and he was a chief publican, and he was rich.

Luk 19:3 And he sought to see Jesus who he was; and could not for the crowd, because he was little of stature.

Luk 19:4 And he ran on before, and climbed up into a sycomore tree to see him: for he was to pass that way.

Luk 19:5 And when Jesus came to the place, he looked up, and said unto him, Zacchaeus, make haste, and come down; for to-day I must abide at thy house.

Luk 19:6 And he made haste, and came down, and received him joyfully.

Luk 19:7 And when they saw it, they all murmured, saying, He is gone in to lodge with a man that is a sinner.

Luk 19:8 And Zacchaeus stood, and said unto the Lord, Behold, Lord, the half of my goods I give to the poor, and if I have wrongfully exacted aught of any man, I restore fourfold.

Luk 19:9 And Jesus said unto him, To-day is salvation come to this house, forasmuch as he also is a son of Abraham.

Luk 19:10 For the Son of man came to seek and to save that which was lost.

Luk 19:11 And as they heard these things, he added and spake a parable, because he was nigh to Jerusalem, and because they supposed that the kingdom of God was immediately to appear.

Luk 19:12 He said therefore, A certain nobleman went into a far country, to receive for himself a kingdom, and to return.

Luk 19:13 And he called ten servants of his, and gave them ten pounds, and said unto them, Trade ye herewith till I come.

Luk 19:14 But his citizens hated him, and sent an ambassage after him, saying, We will not that this man reign over us.

Luk 19:15 And it came to pass, when he was come back again, having received the kingdom, that he commanded these servants, unto whom he had given the money, to be called to him, that he might know what they had gained by trading.

Luk 19:16 And the first came before him, saying, Lord, thy pound hath made ten pounds more.

Luk 19:17 And he said unto him, Well done, thou good servant: because thou wast found faithful in a very little, have thou authority over ten cities.

Luk 19:18 And the second came, saying, Thy pound, Lord, hath made five pounds.

Luk 19:19 And he said unto him also, Be thou also over five cities.

Luk 19:20 And another came, saying, Lord, behold, here is thy pound, which I kept laid up in a napkin:

Luk 19:21 for I feared thee, because thou art an austere man: thou takest up that which thou layedst not down, and reapest that which thou didst not sow.

Luk 19:22 He saith unto him, Out of thine own mouth will I judge thee, thou wicked servant. Thou knewest that I am an austere man, taking up that which I laid not down, and reaping that which I did not sow;

Luk 19:23 then wherefore gavest thou not my money into the bank, and I at my coming should have required it with interest?

Luk 19:24 And he said unto them that stood by, Take away from him the pound, and give it unto him that hath the ten pounds.

Luk 19:25 And they said unto him, Lord, he hath ten pounds.

Luk 19:26 I say unto you, that unto every one that hath shall be given; but from him that hath not, even that which he hath shall be taken away from him.

Luk 19:27 But these mine enemies, that would not that I should reign over them, bring hither, and slay them before me.

Luk 19:28 And when he had thus spoken, he went on before, going up to Jerusalem.

Luk 19:29 And it came to pass, when he drew nigh unto Bethphage and Bethany, at the mount that is called Olivet, he sent two of the disciples,

Luk 19:30 saying, Go your way into the village over against you; in which as ye enter ye shall find a colt tied, whereon no man ever yet sat: loose him, and bring him.

Luk 19:31 And if any one ask you, Why do ye loose him? thus shall ye say, The Lord hath need of him.

Luk 19:32 And they that were sent went away, and found even as he had said unto them.

Luk 19:33 And as they were loosing the colt, the owners thereof said unto them, Why loose ye the colt?

Luk 19:34 And they said, The Lord hath need of him.

Luk 19:35 And they brought him to Jesus: and they threw their garments upon the colt, and set Jesus thereon.

Luk 19:36 And as he went, they spread their garments in the way.

Luk 19:37 And as he was now drawing nigh, even at the descent of the mount of Olives, the whole multitude of the disciples began to rejoice and praise God with a loud voice for all the mighty works which they had seen;

Luk 19:38 saying, Blessed is the King that cometh in the name of the Lord: peace in heaven, and glory in the highest.

Luk 19:39 And some of the Pharisees from the multitude said unto him, Teacher, rebuke thy disciples.

Luk 19:40 And he answered and said, I tell you that, if these shall hold their peace, the stones will cry out.

Luk 19:41 And when he drew nigh, he saw the city and wept over it,

Luk 19:42 saying, If thou hadst known in this day, even thou, the things which belong unto peace! but now they are hid from thine eyes.

Luk 19:43 For the days shall come upon thee, when thine enemies shall cast up a bank about thee, and compass thee round, and keep thee in on every side,

Luk 19:44 and shall dash thee to the ground, and thy children within thee; and they shall not leave in thee one stone upon another; because thou knewest not the time of thy visitation.

Luk 19:45 And he entered into the temple, and began to cast out them that sold,

Luk 19:46 saying unto them, It is written, And my house shall be a house of prayer: but ye have made it a den of robbers.

Luk 19:47 And he was teaching daily in the temple. But the chief priests and the scribes and the principal men of the people sought to destroy him:

Luk 19:48 and they could not find what they might do; for the people all hung upon him, listening.

Chapter 20.

Luk 20:1 And it came to pass, on one of the days, as he was teaching the people in the temple, and preaching the gospel, there came upon him the chief priests and the scribes with the elders;

Luk 20:2 and they spake, saying unto him, Tell us: By what authority doest thou these things? or who is he that gave thee this authority?

Luk 20:3 And he answered and said unto them, I also will ask you a question; and tell me:

Luk 20:4 The baptism of John, was it from heaven, or from men?

Luk 20:5 And they reasoned with themselves, saying, If we shall say, From heaven; he will say, Why did ye not believe him?

Luk 20:6 But if we shall say, From men; all the people will stone us: for they are persuaded that John was a prophet.

Luk 20:7 And they answered, that they knew not whence it was.

Luk 20:8 And Jesus said unto them, neither tell I you by what authority I do these things.

Luk 20:9 And he began to speak unto the people this parable: A man planted a vineyard, and let it out to husbandmen, and went into another country for a long time.

Luk 20:10 And at the season he sent unto the husbandmen a servant, that they should give him of the fruit of the vineyard: but the husbandmen beat him, and sent him away empty.

Luk 20:11 And he sent yet another servant: and him also they beat, and handled him shamefully, and sent him away empty.

Luk 20:12 And he sent yet a third: and him also they wounded, and cast him forth.

Luk 20:13 And the lord of the vineyard said, What shall I do? I will send my beloved son; it may be they will reverence him.

Luk 20:14 But when the husbandmen saw him, they reasoned one with another, saying, This is the heir; let us kill him, that the inheritance may be ours.

Luk 20:15 And they cast him forth out of the vineyard, and killed him. What therefore will the lord of the vineyard do unto them?

Luk 20:16 He will come and destroy these husbandmen, and will give the vineyard unto others. And when they heard it, they said, God forbid.

Luk 20:17 But he looked upon them, and said, What then is this that is written, The stone which the builders rejected, The same was made the head of the corner?

Luk 20:18 Every one that falleth on that stone shall be broken to pieces; but on whomsoever it shall fall, it will scatter him as dust.

Luk 20:19 And the scribes and the chief priests sought to lay hands on him in that very hour; and they feared the people: for they perceived that he spake this parable against them.

Luk 20:20 And they watched him, and sent forth spies, who feigned themselves to be righteous, that they might take hold of his speech, so as to deliver him up to the rule and to the authority of the governor.

Luk 20:21   And they asked him, saying, Teacher, we know that thou sayest and teachest rightly, and acceptest not the person of any, but of a truth teachest the way of God:

Luk 20:22 Is it lawful for us to give tribute unto Caesar, or not?

Luk 20:23 But he perceived their craftiness, and said unto them,

Luk 20:24 Show me a denarius. Whose image and superscription hath it? And they said, Caesar's.

Luk 20:25   And he said unto them, Then render unto Caesar the things that are Caesar's, and unto God the things that are God's.

Luk 20:26 And they were not able to take hold of the saying before the people: and they marvelled at his answer, and held their peace.

Luk 20:27 And there came to him certain of the Sadducees, they that say that there is no resurrection;

Luk 20:28 and they asked him, saying, Teacher, Moses wrote unto us, that if a man's brother die, having a wife, and he be childless, his brother should take the wife, and raise up seed unto his brother.

Luk 20:29 There were therefore seven brethren: and the first took a wife, and died childless;

Luk 20:30 and the second:

Luk 20:31 and the third took her; and likewise the seven also left no children, and died.

Luk 20:32 Afterward the woman also died.

Luk 20:33 In the resurrection therefore whose wife of them shall she be? for the seven had her to wife.

Luk 20:34 And Jesus said unto them, The sons of this world marry, and are given in marriage:

Luk 20:35   but they that are accounted worthy to attain to that world, and the resurrection from the dead, neither marry, nor are given in marriage:

Luk 20:36 for neither can they die any more: for they are equal unto the angels; and are sons of God, being sons of the resurrection.

Luk 20:37 But that the dead are raised, even Moses showed, in the place concerning the Bush, when he calleth the Lord the God of Abraham, and the God of Isaac, and the God of Jacob.

Luk 20:38 Now he is not the God of the dead, but of the living: for all live unto him.

Luk 20:39 And certain of the scribes answering said, Teacher, thou hast well said.

Luk 20:40 For they durst not any more ask him any question.

Luk 20:41 And he said unto them, How say they that the Christ is David's son?

Luk 20:42 For David himself saith in the book of Psalms, The Lord said unto my Lord, Sit thou on my right hand,

Luk 20:43 Till I make thine enemies the footstool of thy feet.

Luk 20:44 David therefore calleth him Lord, and how is he his son?

Luk 20:45 And in the hearing of all the people he said unto his disciples,

Luk 20:46   Beware of the scribes, who desire to walk in long robes, and love salutations in the marketplaces, and chief seats in the synagogues, and chief places at feasts;

Luk 20:47 who devour widows' houses, and for a pretence make long prayers: these shall receive greater condemnation.

Chapter 21.

Luk 21:1 And he looked up, and saw the rich men that were casting their gifts into the treasury.

Luk 21:2 And he saw a certain poor widow casting in thither two mites.

Luk 21:3 And he said, Of a truth I say unto you, This poor widow cast in more than they all:

Luk 21:4 for all these did of their superfluity cast in unto the gifts; but she of her want did cast in all the living that she had.

Luk 21:5 And as some spake of the temple, how it was adorned with goodly stones and offerings, he said,

Luk 21:6 As for these things which ye behold, the days will come, in which there shall not be left here one stone upon another, that shall not be thrown down.

Luk 21:7 And they asked him, saying, Teacher, when therefore shall these things be? and what shall be the sign when these things are about to come to pass?

Luk 21:8 And he said, Take heed that ye be not led astray: for many shall come in my name, saying, I am he; and, The time is at hand: go ye not after them.

Luk 21:9 And when ye shall hear of wars and tumults, be not terrified: for these things must needs come to pass first; but the end is not immediately.

Luk 21:10 Then said he unto them, Nation shall rise against nation, and kingdom against kingdom;

Luk 21:11 and there shall be great earthquakes, and in divers places famines and pestilences; and there shall be terrors and great signs from heaven.

Luk 21:12 But before all these things, they shall lay their hands on you, and shall persecute you, delivering you up to the synagogues and prisons, bringing you before kings and governors for my name's sake.

Luk 21:13 It shall turn out unto you for a testimony.

Luk 21:14 Settle it therefore in your hearts, not to meditate beforehand how to answer:

Luk 21:15 for I will give you a mouth and wisdom, which all your adversaries shall not be able to withstand or to gainsay.

Luk 21:16 But ye shall be delivered up even by parents, and brethren, and kinsfolk, and friends; and some of you shall they cause to be put to death.

Luk 21:17 And ye shall be hated of all men for my name's sake.

Luk 21:18 And not a hair of your head shall perish.

Luk 21:19 In your patience ye shall win your souls.

Luk 21:20 But when ye see Jerusalem compassed with armies, then know that her desolation is at hand.

Luk 21:21 Then let them that are in Judaea flee unto the mountains; and let them that are in the midst of her depart out; and let not them that are in the country enter therein.

Luk 21:22 For these are days of vengeance, that all things which are written may be fulfilled.

Luk 21:23 Woe unto them that are with child and to them that give suck in those days! for there shall be great distress upon the land, and wrath unto this people.

Luk 21:24 And they shall fall by the edge of the sword, and shall be led captive into all the nations: and Jerusalem shall be trodden down of the Gentiles, until the times of the Gentiles be fulfilled.

Luk 21:25 And there shall be signs in sun and moon and stars; and upon the earth distress of nations, in perplexity for the roaring of the sea and the billows;

Luk 21:26 men fainting for fear, and for expectation of the things which are coming on the world: for the powers of the heavens shall be shaken.

Luk 21:27 And then shall they see the Son of man coming in a cloud with power and great glory.

Luk 21:28 But when these things begin to come to pass, look up, and lift up your heads; because your redemption draweth nigh.

Luk 21:29 And he spake to them a parable: Behold the fig tree, and all the trees:

Luk 21:30 when they now shoot forth, ye see it and know of your own selves that the summer is now nigh.

Luk 21:31 Even so ye also, when ye see these things coming to pass, know ye that the kingdom of God is nigh.

Luk 21:32 Verily I say unto you, This generation shall not pass away, till all things be accomplished.

Luk 21:33 Heaven and earth shall pass away: but my words shall not pass away.

Luk 21:34 But take heed to yourselves, lest haply your hearts be overcharged with surfeiting, and drunkenness, and cares of this life, and that day come on you suddenly as a snare:

Luk 21:35 for so shall it come upon all them that dwell on the face of all the earth.

Luk 21:36 But watch ye at every season, making supplication, that ye may prevail to escape all these things that shall come to pass, and to stand before the Son of man.

Luk 21:37 And every day he was teaching in the temple; and every night he went out, and lodged in the mount that is called Olivet.

Luk 21:38 And all the people came early in the morning to him in the temple, to hear him.

Chapter 22.

Luk 22:1 Now the feast of unleavened bread drew nigh, which is called the Passover.

Luk 22:2 And the chief priests and the scribes sought how they might put him to death; for they feared the people.

Luk 22:3 And Satan entered into Judas who was called Iscariot, being of the number of the twelve.

Luk 22:4 And he went away, and communed with the chief priests and captains, how he might deliver him unto them.

Luk 22:5 And they were glad, and covenanted to give him money.

Luk 22:6 And he consented, and sought opportunity to deliver him unto them in the absence of the multitude.

Luk 22:7 And the day of unleavened bread came on which the passover must be sacrificed.

Luk 22:8 And he sent Peter and John, saying, Go and make ready for us the passover, that we may eat.

Luk 22:9 And they said unto him, Where wilt thou that we make ready?

Luk 22:10 And he said unto them, Behold, when ye are entered into the city, there shall meet you a man bearing a pitcher of water; follow him into the house whereinto he goeth.

Luk 22:11 And ye shall say unto the master of the house, The Teacher saith unto thee, Where is the guestchamber, where I shall eat the passover with my disciples?

Luk 22:12 And he will show you a large upper room furnished: there make ready.

Luk 22:13 And they went, and found as he had said unto them: and they made ready the passover.

Luk 22:14 And when the hour was come, he sat down, and the apostles with him.

Luk 22:15 And he said unto them, With desire I have desired to eat this passover with you before I suffer:

Luk 22:16 for I say unto you, I shall not eat it, until it be fulfilled in the kingdom of God.

Luk 22:17 And he received a cup, and when he had given thanks, he said, Take this, and divide it among yourselves:

Luk 22:18 for I say unto you, I shall not drink from henceforth of the fruit of the vine, until the kingdom of God shall come.

Luk 22:19 And he took bread, and when he had given thanks, he brake it, and gave to them, saying, This is my body which is given for you: this do in remembrance of me.

Luk 22:20 And the cup in like manner after supper, saying, This cup is the new covenant in my blood, even that which is poured out for you.

Luk 22:21 But behold, the hand of him that betrayeth me is with me on the table.

Luk 22:22 For the Son of man indeed goeth, as it hath been determined: but woe unto that man through whom he is betrayed!

Luk 22:23 And they began to question among themselves, which of them it was that should do this thing.

Luk 22:24 And there arose also a contention among them, which of them was accounted to be greatest.

Luk 22:25 And he said unto them, The kings of the Gentiles have lordship over them; and they that have authority over them are called Benefactors.

Luk 22:26 But ye shall not be so: but he that is the greater among you, let him become as the younger; and he that is chief, as he that doth serve.

Luk 22:27 For which is greater, he that sitteth at meat, or he that serveth? is not he that sitteth at meat? but I am in the midst of you as he that serveth.

Luk 22:28 But ye are they that have continued with me in my temptations;

Luk 22:29 and I appoint unto you a kingdom, even as my Father appointed unto me,

Luk 22:30 that ye may eat and drink at my table in my kingdom; and ye shall sit on thrones judging the twelve tribes of Israel.

Luk 22:31 Simon, Simon, behold, Satan asked to have you, that he might sift you as wheat:

Luk 22:32 but I made supplication for thee, that thy faith fail not; and do thou, when once thou hast turned again, establish thy brethren.

Luk 22:33 And he said unto him, Lord, with thee I am ready to go both to prison and to death.

Luk 22:34 And he said, I tell thee, Peter, the cock shall not crow this day, until thou shalt thrice deny that thou knowest me.

Luk 22:35 And he said unto them, When I sent you forth without purse, and wallet, and shoes, lacked ye anything? And they said, Nothing.

Luk 22:36 And he said unto them, But now, he that hath a purse, let him take it, and likewise a wallet; and he that hath none, let him sell his cloak, and buy a sword.

Luk 22:37 For I say unto you, that this which is written must be fulfilled in me, And he was reckoned with transgressors: for that which concerneth me hath fulfilment.

Luk 22:38 And they said, Lord, behold, here are two swords. And he said unto them, It is enough.

Luk 22:39 And he came out, and went, as his custom was, unto the mount of Olives; and the disciples also followed him.

Luk 22:40 And when he was at the place, he said unto them, Pray that ye enter not into temptation.

Luk 22:41 And he was parted from them about a stone's cast; and he kneeled down and prayed,

Luk 22:42 saying, Father, if thou be willing, remove this cup from me: nevertheless not my will, but thine, be done.

Luk 22:43 And there appeared unto him an angel from heaven, strengthening him.

Luk 22:44 And being in an agony he prayed more earnestly; and his sweat became as it were great drops of blood falling down upon the ground.

Luk 22:45 And when he rose up from his prayer, he came unto the disciples, and found them sleeping for sorrow,

Luk 22:46 and said unto them, Why sleep ye? rise and pray, that ye enter not into temptation.

Luk 22:47 While he yet spake, behold, a multitude, and he that was called Judas, one of the twelve, went before them; and he drew near unto Jesus to kiss him.

Luk 22:48 But Jesus said unto him, Judas, betrayest thou the Son of man with a kiss?

Luk 22:49 And when they that were about him saw what would follow, they said, Lord, shall we smite with the sword?

Luk 22:50 And a certain one of them smote the servant of the high priest, and struck off his right ear.

Luk 22:51 But Jesus answered and said, Suffer ye them thus far. And he touched his ear, and healed him.

Luk 22:52 And Jesus said unto the chief priests, and captains of the temple, and elders, that were come against him, Are ye come out, as against a robber, with swords and staves?

Luk 22:53 When I was daily with you in the temple, ye stretched not forth your hands against me: but this is your hour, and the power of darkness.

Luk 22:54 And they seized him, and led him away, and brought him into the high priest's house. But Peter followed afar off.

Luk 22:55 And when they had kindled a fire in the midst of the court, and had sat down together, Peter sat in the midst of them.

Luk 22:56 And a certain maid seeing him as he sat in the light of the fire, and looking stedfastly upon him, said, This man also was with him.

Luk 22:57 But he denied, saying, Woman, I know him not.

Luk 22:58 And after a little while another saw him, and said, Thou also art one of them. But Peter said, Man, I am not.

Luk 22:59 And after the space of about one hour another confidently affirmed, saying, Of a truth this man also was with him; for he is a Galilaean.

Luk 22:60 But Peter said, Man, I know not what thou sayest. And immediately, while he yet spake, the cock crew.

Luk 22:61 And the Lord turned, and looked upon Peter. And Peter remembered the word of the Lord, how that he said unto him, Before the cock crow this day thou shalt deny me thrice.

Luk 22:62 And he went out, and wept bitterly.

Luk 22:63 And the men that held Jesus mocked him, and beat him.

Luk 22:64 And they blindfolded him, and asked him, saying, Prophesy: who is he that struck thee?

Luk 22:65 And many other things spake they against him, reviling him.

Luk 22:66 And as soon as it was day, the assembly of the elders of the people was gathered together, both chief priests and scribes; and they led him away into their council, saying,

Luk 22:67 If thou art the Christ, tell us. But he said unto them, If I tell you, ye will not believe:

Luk 22:68 and if I ask you, ye will not answer.

Luk 22:69 But from henceforth shall the Son of man be seated at the right hand of the power of God.

Luk 22:70 And they all said, Art thou then the Son of God? And he said unto them, Ye say that I am.

Luk 22:71 And they said, What further need have we of witness? for we ourselves have heard from his own mouth.

Chapter 23.

Luk 23:1 And the whole company of them rose up, and brought him before Pilate.

Luk 23:2 And they began to accuse him, saying, We found this man perverting our nation, and forbidding to give tribute to Caesar, and saying that he himself is Christ a king.

Luk 23:3 And Pilate asked him, saying, Art thou the King of the Jews? And he answered him and said, Thou sayest.

Luk 23:4 And Pilate said unto the chief priests and the multitudes, I find no fault in this man.

Luk 23:5 But they were the more urgent, saying, He stirreth up the people, teaching throughout all Judaea, and beginning from Galilee even unto this place.

Luk 23:6 But when Pilate heard it, he asked whether the man were a Galilaean.

Luk 23:7 And when he knew that he was of Herod's jurisdiction, he sent him unto Herod, who himself also was at Jerusalem in these days.

Luk 23:8 Now when Herod saw Jesus, he was exceeding glad: for he was of a long time desirous to see him, because he had heard concerning him; and he hoped to see some miracle done by him.

Luk 23:9 And he questioned him in many words; but he answered him nothing.

Luk 23:10 And the chief priests and the scribes stood, vehemently accusing him.

Luk 23:11 And Herod with his soldiers set him at nought, and mocked him, and arraying him in gorgeous apparel sent him back to Pilate.

Luk 23:12 And Herod and Pilate became friends with each other that very day: for before they were at enmity between themselves.

Luk 23:13 And Pilate called together the chief priests and the rulers and the people,

Luk 23:14 and said unto them, Ye brought unto me this man, as one that perverteth the people: and behold, I having examined him before you, found no fault in this man touching those things whereof ye accuse him:

Luk 23:15 no, nor yet Herod: for he sent him back unto us; and behold, nothing worthy of death hath been done by him.

Luk 23:16 I will therefore chastise him, and release him.

Luk 23:17 Now he must needs release unto them at the feast one prisoner.

Luk 23:18 But they cried out all together, saying, Away with this man, and release unto us Barabbas: -

Luk 23:19 one who for a certain insurrection made in the city, and for murder, was cast into prison.

Luk 23:20 And Pilate spake unto them again, desiring to release Jesus;

Luk 23:21 but they shouted, saying, Crucify, crucify him.

Luk 23:22 And he said unto them the third time, Why, what evil hath this man done? I have found no cause of death in him: I will therefore chastise him and release him.

Luk 23:23 But they were urgent with loud voices, asking that he might be crucified. And their voices prevailed.

Luk 23:24 And Pilate gave sentence that what they asked for should be done.

Luk 23:25 And he released him that for insurrection and murder had been cast into prison, whom they asked for; but Jesus he delivered up to their will.

Luk 23:26 And when they led him away, they laid hold upon one Simon of Cyrene, coming from the country, and laid on him the cross, to bear it after Jesus.

Luk 23:27 And there followed him a great multitude of the people, and of women who bewailed and lamented him.

Luk 23:28 But Jesus turning unto them said, Daughters of Jerusalem, weep not for me, but weep for yourselves, and for your children.

Luk 23:29 For behold, the days are coming, in which they shall say, Blessed are the barren, and the wombs that never bare, and the breasts that never gave suck.

Luk 23:30 Then shall they begin to say to the mountains, Fall on us; and to the hills, Cover us.

Luk 23:31 For if they do these things in the green tree, what shall be done in the dry?

Luk 23:32 And there were also two others, malefactors, led with him to be put to death.

Luk 23:33 And when they came unto the place which is called The skull, there they crucified him, and the malefactors, one on the right hand and the other on the left.

Luk 23:34 And Jesus said, Father, forgive them; for they know not what they do. And parting his garments among them, they cast lots.

Luk 23:35 And the people stood beholding. And the rulers also scoffed at him, saying, He saved others; let him save himself, if this is the Christ of God, his chosen.

Luk 23:36 And the soldiers also mocked him, coming to him, offering him vinegar,

Luk 23:37 and saying, If thou art the King of the Jews, save thyself.

Luk 23:38 And there was also a superscription over him, THIS IS THE KING OF THE JEWS.

Luk 23:39 And one of the malefactors that were hanged railed on him, saying, Art not thou the Christ? save thyself and us.

Luk 23:40 But the other answered, and rebuking him said, Dost thou not even fear God, seeing thou art in the same condemnation?

Luk 23:41 And we indeed justly; for we receive the due reward of our deeds: but this man hath done nothing amiss.

Luk 23:42 And he said, Jesus, remember me when thou comest in thy kingdom.

Luk 23:43 And he said unto him, Verily I say unto thee, Today shalt thou be with me in Paradise.

Luk 23:44 And it was now about the sixth hour, and a darkness came over the whole land until the ninth hour,

Luk 23:45 the sun's light failing: and the veil of the temple was rent in the midst.

Luk 23:46 And Jesus, crying with a loud voice, said, Father, into thy hands I commend my spirit: and having said this, he gave up the ghost.

Luk 23:47 And when the centurion saw what was done, he glorified God, saying, Certainly this was a righteous man.

Luk 23:48 And all the multitudes that came together to this sight, when they beheld the things that were done, returned smiting their breasts.

Luk 23:49 And all his acquaintance, and the women that followed with him from Galilee, stood afar off, seeing these things.

Luk 23:50 And behold, a man named Joseph, who was a councillor, a good and righteous man

Luk 23:51 (he had not consented to their counsel and deed), a man of Arimathaea, a city of the Jews, who was looking for the kingdom of God:

Luk 23:52 this man went to Pilate, and asked for the body of Jesus.

Luk 23:53 And he took it down, and wrapped it in a linen cloth, and laid him in a tomb that was hewn in stone, where never man had yet lain.

Luk 23:54 And it was the day of the Preparation, and the sabbath drew on.

Luk 23:55 And the women, who had come with him out of Galilee, followed after, and beheld the tomb, and how his body was laid.

Luk 23:56 And they returned, and prepared spices and ointments. And on the sabbath they rested according to the commandment.

Chapter 24.

Luk 24:1 But on the first day of the week, at early dawn, they came unto the tomb, bringing the spices which they had prepared.

Luk 24:2 And they found the stone rolled away from the tomb.

Luk 24:3 And they entered in, and found not the body of the Lord Jesus.

Luk 24:4 And it came to pass, while they were perplexed thereabout, behold, two men stood by them in dazzling apparel:

Luk 24:5 and as they were affrighted and bowed down their faces to the earth, they said unto them, Why seek ye the living among the dead?

Luk 24:6 He is not here, but is risen: remember how he spake unto you when he was yet in Galilee,

Luk 24:7 saying that the Son of man must be delivered up into the hands of sinful men, and be crucified, and the third day rise again.

Luk 24:8 And they remembered his words,

Luk 24:9 and returned from the tomb, and told all these things to the eleven, and to all the rest.

Luk 24:10 Now they were Mary Magdalene, and Joanna, and Mary the mother of James: and the other women with them told these things unto the apostles.

Luk 24:11 And these words appeared in their sight as idle talk; and they disbelieved them.

Luk 24:12 But Peter arose, and ran unto the tomb; and stooping and looking in, he seeth the linen cloths by themselves; and he departed to his home, wondering at that which was come to pass.

Luk 24:13 And behold, two of them were going that very day to a village named Emmaus, which was threescore furlongs from Jerusalem.

Luk 24:14 And they communed with each other of all these things which had happened.

Luk 24:15 And it came to pass, while they communed and questioned together, that Jesus himself drew near, and went with them.

Luk 24:16 But their eyes were holden that they should not know him.

Luk 24:17 And he said unto them, What communications are these that ye have one with another, as ye walk? And they stood still, looking sad.

Luk 24:18 And one of them, named Cleopas, answering said unto him, Dost thou alone sojourn in Jerusalem and not know the things which are come to pass there in these days?

Luk 24:19 And he said unto them, What things? And they said unto him, The things concerning Jesus the Nazarene, who was a prophet mighty in deed and word before God and all the people:

Luk 24:20 and how the chief priests and our rulers delivered him up to be condemned to death, and crucified him.

Luk 24:21 But we hoped that it was he who should redeem Israel. Yea and besides all this, it is now the third day since these things came to pass.

Luk 24:22 Moreover certain women of our company amazed us, having been early at the tomb;

Luk 24:23 and when they found not his body, they came, saying, that they had also seen a vision of angels, who said that he was alive.

Luk 24:24 And certain of them that were with us went to the tomb, and found it even so as the women had said: but him they saw not.

Luk 24:25 And he said unto them, O foolish men, and slow of heart to believe in all that the prophets have spoken!

Luk 24:26 Behooved it not the Christ to suffer these things, and to enter into his glory?

Luk 24:27 And beginning from Moses and from all the prophets, he interpreted to them in all the scriptures the things concerning himself.

Luk 24:28 And they drew nigh unto the village, whither they were going: and he made as though he would go further.

Luk 24:29 And they constrained him, saying, Abide with us; for it is toward evening, and the day is now far spent. And he went in to abide with them.

Luk 24:30 And it came to pass, when he had sat down with them to meat, he took the bread and blessed; and breaking it he gave to them.

Luk 24:31 And their eyes were opened, and they knew him; and he vanished out of their sight.

Luk 24:32 And they said one to another, Was not our heart burning within us, while he spake to us in the way, while he opened to us the scriptures?

Luk 24:33 And they rose up that very hour, and returned to Jerusalem, and found the eleven gathered together, and them that were with them,

Luk 24:34 saying, The Lord is risen indeed, and hath appeared to Simon.

Luk 24:35 And they rehearsed the things that happened in the way, and how he was known of them in the breaking of the bread.

Luk 24:36 And as they spake these things, he himself stood in the midst of them, and saith unto them, Peace be unto you.

Luk 24:37 But they were terrified and affrighted, and supposed that they beheld a spirit.

Luk 24:38 And he said unto them, Why are ye troubled? and wherefore do questionings arise in your heart?

Luk 24:39 See my hands and my feet, that it is I myself: handle me, and see; for a spirit hath not flesh and bones, as ye behold me having.

Luk 24:40 And when he had said this, he showed them his hands and his feet.

Luk 24:41 And while they still disbelieved for joy, and wondered, he said unto them, Have ye here anything to eat?

Luk 24:42 And they gave him a piece of a broiled fish.

Luk 24:43 And he took it, and ate before them.

Luk 24:44 And he said unto them, These are my words which I spake unto you, while I was yet with you, that all things must needs be fulfilled, which are written in the law of Moses, and the prophets, and the psalms, concerning me.

Luk 24:45 Then opened he their mind, that they might understand the scriptures;

Luk 24:46 and he said unto them, Thus it is written, that the Christ should suffer, and rise again from the dead the third day;

Luk 24:47 and that repentance and remission of sins should be preached in his name unto all the nations, beginning from Jerusalem.

Luk 24:48 Ye are witnesses of these things.

Luk 24:49 And behold, I send forth the promise of my Father upon you: but tarry ye in the city, until ye be clothed with power from on high.

Luk 24:50 And he led them out until they were over against Bethany: and he lifted up his hands, and blessed them.

Luk 24:51 And it came to pass, while he blessed them, he parted from them, and was carried up into heaven.

Luk 24:52 And they worshipped him, and returned to Jerusalem with great joy:

Luk 24:53 and were continually in the temple, blessing God.

5. John

Chapter 1.

Joh 1:1 In the beginning was the Word, and the Word was with God, and the Word was God.

Joh 1:2 The same was in the beginning with God.

Joh 1:3 All things were made through him; and without him was not anything made that hath been made.

Joh 1:4 In him was life; and the life was the light of men.

Joh 1:5 And the light shineth in the darkness; and the darkness apprehended it not.

Joh 1:6 There came a man, sent from God, whose name was John.

Joh 1:7 The same came for witness, that he might bear witness of the light, that all might believe through him.

Joh 1:8 He was not the light, but came that he might bear witness of the light.

Joh 1:9 There was the true light, even the light which lighteth every man, coming into the world.

Joh 1:10 He was in the world, and the world was made through him, and the world knew him not.

Joh 1:11 He came unto his own, and they that were his own received him not.

Joh 1:12 But as many as received him, to them gave he the right to become children of God, even to them that believe on his name:

Joh 1:13 who were born, not of blood, nor of the will of the flesh, nor of the will of man, but of God.

Joh 1:14 And the Word became flesh, and dwelt among us (and we beheld his glory, glory as of the only begotten from the Father), full of grace and truth.

Joh 1:15 John beareth witness of him, and crieth, saying, This was he of whom I said, He that cometh after me is become before me: for he was before me.

Joh 1:16 For of his fulness we all received, and grace for grace.

Joh 1:17 For the law was given through Moses; grace and truth came through Jesus Christ.

Joh 1:18 No man hath seen God at any time; the only begotten Son, who is in the bosom of the Father, he hath declared him.

Joh 1:19 And this is the witness of John, when the Jews sent unto him from Jerusalem priests and Levites to ask him, Who art thou?

Joh 1:20 And he confessed, and denied not; and he confessed, I am not the Christ.

Joh 1:21 And they asked him, What then? Art thou Elijah? And he saith, I am not. Art thou the prophet? And he answered, No.

Joh 1:22 They said therefore unto him, Who art thou? that we may give an answer to them that sent us. What sayest thou of thyself?

Joh 1:23 He said, I am the voice of one crying in the wilderness, Make straight the way of the Lord, as said Isaiah the prophet.

Joh 1:24 And they had been sent from the Pharisees.

Joh 1:25 And they asked him, and said unto him, Why then baptizest thou, if thou art not the Christ, neither Elijah, neither the prophet?

Joh 1:26 John answered them, saying, I baptize in water: in the midst of you standeth one whom ye know not,

Joh 1:27 even he that cometh after me, the latchet of whose shoe I am not worthy to unloose.

Joh 1:28 These things were done in Bethany beyond the Jordan, where John was baptizing.

Joh 1:29 On the morrow he seeth Jesus coming unto him, and saith, Behold, the Lamb of God, that taketh away the sin of the world!

Joh 1:30 This is he of whom I said, After me cometh a man who is become before me: for he was before me.

Joh 1:31 And I knew him not; but that he should be made manifest to Israel, for this cause came I baptizing in water.

Joh 1:32 And John bare witness, saying, I have beheld the Spirit descending as a dove out of heaven; and it abode upon him.

Joh 1:33 And I knew him not: but he that sent me to baptize in water, he said unto me, Upon whomsoever thou shalt see the Spirit descending, and abiding upon him, the same is he that baptizeth in the Holy Spirit.

Joh 1:34 And I have seen, and have borne witness that this is the Son of God.

Joh 1:35 Again on the morrow John was standing, and two of his disciples;

Joh 1:36 and he looked upon Jesus as he walked, and saith, Behold, the Lamb of God!

Joh 1:37 And the two disciples heard him speak, and they followed Jesus.

Joh 1:38 And Jesus turned, and beheld them following, and saith unto them, What seek ye? And they said unto him, Rabbi (which is to say, being interpreted, Teacher), where abidest thou?

Joh 1:39 He saith unto them, Come, and ye shall see. They came therefore and saw where he abode; and they abode with him that day: it was about the tenth hour.

Joh 1:40 One of the two that heard John speak, and followed him, was Andrew, Simon Peter's brother.

Joh 1:41 He findeth first his own brother Simon, and saith unto him, We have found the Messiah (which is, being interpreted, Christ).

Joh 1:42 He brought him unto Jesus. Jesus looked upon him, and said, Thou art Simon the son of John: thou shalt be called Cephas (which is by interpretation, Peter).

Joh 1:43 On the morrow he was minded to go forth into Galilee, and he findeth Philip: and Jesus saith unto him, Follow me.

Joh 1:44 Now Philip was from Bethsaida, of the city of Andrew and Peter.

Joh 1:45 Philip findeth Nathanael, and saith unto him, We have found him, of whom Moses in the law, and the prophets, wrote, Jesus of Nazareth, the son of Joseph.

Joh 1:46 And Nathanael said unto him, Can any good thing come out of Nazareth? Philip saith unto him, Come and see.

Joh 1:47 Jesus saw Nathanael coming to him, and saith of him, Behold, an Israelite indeed, in whom is no guile!

Joh 1:48 Nathanael saith unto him, Whence knowest thou me? Jesus answered and said unto him, Before Philip called thee, when thou wast under the fig tree, I saw thee.

Joh 1:49 Nathanael answered him, Rabbi, thou art the Son of God; thou art King of Israel.

Joh 1:50 Jesus answered and said unto him, Because I said unto thee, I saw thee underneath the fig tree, believest thou? thou shalt see greater things than these.

Joh 1:51 And he saith unto him, Verily, verily, I say unto you, Ye shall see the heaven opened, and the angels of God ascending and descending upon the Son of man.

Chapter 2.

Joh 2:1 And the third day there was a marriage in Cana of Galilee; and the mother of Jesus was there:

Joh 2:2 and Jesus also was bidden, and his disciples, to the marriage.

Joh 2:3 And when the wine failed, the mother of Jesus saith unto him, They have no wine.

Joh 2:4 And Jesus saith unto her, Woman, what have I to do with thee? mine hour is not yet come.

Joh 2:5 His mother saith unto the servants, Whatsoever he saith unto you, do it.

Joh 2:6 Now there were six waterpots of stone set there after the Jews' manner of purifying, containing two or three firkins apiece.

Joh 2:7 Jesus saith unto them, Fill the waterpots with water. And they filled them up to the brim.

Joh 2:8 And he saith unto them, Draw out now, and bear unto the ruler of the feast. And they bare it.

Joh 2:9 And when the ruler of the feast tasted the water now become wine, and knew not whence it was (but the servants that had drawn the water knew), the ruler of the feast calleth the bridegroom,

Joh 2:10 and saith unto him, Every man setteth on first the good wine; and when men have drunk freely, then that which is worse: thou hast kept the good wine until now.

Joh 2:11 This beginning of his signs did Jesus in Cana of Galilee, and manifested his glory; and his disciples believed on him.

Joh 2:12 After this he went down to Capernaum, he, and his mother, and his brethren, and his disciples; and there they abode not many days.

Joh 2:13 And the passover of the Jews was at hand, and Jesus went up to Jerusalem.

Joh 2:14 And he found in the temple those that sold oxen and sheep and doves, and the changers of money sitting:

Joh 2:15 and he made a scourge of cords, and cast all out of the temple, both the sheep and the oxen; and he poured out the changers' money, and overthrew their tables;

Joh 2:16 and to them that sold the doves he said, Take these things hence; make not my Father's house a house of merchandise.

Joh 2:17 His disciples remembered that it was written, Zeal for thy house shall eat me up.

Joh 2:18 The Jews therefore answered and said unto him, What sign showest thou unto us, seeing that thou doest these things?

Joh 2:19 Jesus answered and said unto them, Destroy this temple, and in three days I will raise it up.

Joh 2:20 The Jews therefore said, Forty and six years was this temple in building, and wilt thou raise it up in three days?

Joh 2:21 But he spake of the temple of his body.

Joh 2:22 When therefore he was raised from the dead, his disciples remembered that he spake this; and they believed the scripture, and the word which Jesus had said.

Joh 2:23 Now when he was in Jerusalem at the passover, during the feast, many believed on his name, beholding his signs which he did.

Joh 2:24 But Jesus did not trust himself unto them, for that he knew all men,

Joh 2:25 and because he needed not that any one should bear witness concerning man; for he himself knew what was in man.

Chapter 3.

Joh 3:1 Now there was a man of the Pharisees, named Nicodemus, a ruler of the Jews:

Joh 3:2 the same came unto him by night, and said to him, Rabbi, we know that thou art a teacher come from God; for no one can do these signs that thou doest, except God be with him.

Joh 3:3 Jesus answered and said unto him, Verily, verily, I say unto thee, Except one be born anew, he cannot see the kingdom of God.

Joh 3:4 Nicodemus saith unto him, How can a man be born when he is old? can he enter a second time into his mother's womb, and be born?

Joh 3:5 Jesus answered, Verily, verily, I say unto thee, Except one be born of water and the Spirit, he cannot enter into the kingdom of God!

Joh 3:6 That which is born of the flesh is flesh; and that which is born of the Spirit is spirit.

Joh 3:7 Marvel not that I said unto thee, Ye must be born anew.

Joh 3:8 The wind bloweth where it will, and thou hearest the voice thereof, but knowest not whence it cometh, and whither it goeth: so is every one that is born of the Spirit.

Joh 3:9 Nicodemus answered and said unto him, How can these things be?

Joh 3:10 Jesus answered and said unto him, Art thou the teacher of Israel, and understandest not these things?

Joh 3:11 Verily, verily, I say unto thee, We speak that which we know, and bear witness of that which we have seen; and ye receive not our witness.

Joh 3:12 If I told you earthly things and ye believe not, how shall ye believe if I tell you heavenly things?

Joh 3:13 And no one hath ascended into heaven, but he that descended out of heaven, even the Son of man, who is in heaven.

Joh 3:14 And as Moses lifted up the serpent in the wilderness, even so must the Son of man be lifted up;

Joh 3:15 that whosoever believeth may in him have eternal life.

Joh 3:16 For God so loved the world, that he gave his only begotten Son, that whosoever believeth on him should not perish, but have eternal life.

Joh 3:17 For God sent not the Son into the world to judge the world; but that the world should be saved through him.

Joh 3:18 He that believeth on him is not judged: he that believeth not hath been judged already, because he hath not believed on the name of the only begotten Son of God.

Joh 3:19 And this is the judgment, that the light is come into the world, and men loved the darkness rather than the light; for their works were evil.

Joh 3:20 For every one that doeth evil hateth the light, and cometh not to the light, lest his works should be reproved.

Joh 3:21 But he that doeth the truth cometh to the light, that his works may be made manifest, that they have been wrought in God.

Joh 3:22 After these things came Jesus and his disciples into the land of Judea; and there he tarried with them, and baptized.

Joh 3:23 And John also was baptizing in Enon near to Salim, because there was much water there: and they came, and were baptized.

Joh 3:24 For John was not yet cast into prison.

Joh 3:25 There arose therefore a questioning on the part of John's disciples with a Jew about purifying.

Joh 3:26 And they came unto John, and said to him, Rabbi, he that was with thee beyond the Jordan, to whom thou hast borne witness, behold, the same baptizeth, and all men come to him.

Joh 3:27 John answered and said, A man can receive nothing, except it have been given him from heaven.

Joh 3:28 Ye yourselves bear me witness, that I said, I am not the Christ, but, that I am sent before him.

Joh 3:29 He that hath the bride is the bridegroom: but the friend of the bridegroom, that standeth and heareth him, rejoiceth greatly because of the bridegroom's voice: this my joy therefore is made full.

Joh 3:30 He must increase, but I must decrease.

Joh 3:31 He that cometh from above is above all: he that is of the earth is of the earth, and of the earth he speaketh: he that cometh from heaven is above all.

Joh 3:32 What he hath seen and heard, of that he beareth witness; and no man receiveth his witness.

Joh 3:33 He that hath received his witness hath set his seal to this, that God is true.

Joh 3:34 For he whom God hath sent speaketh the words of God: for he giveth not the Spirit by measure.

Joh 3:35 The Father loveth the Son, and hath given all things into his hand.

Joh 3:36 He that believeth on the Son hath eternal life; but he that obeyeth not the Son shall not see life, but the wrath of God abideth on him.

Chapter 4.

Joh 4:1 When therefore the Lord knew that the Pharisees had heard that Jesus was making and baptizing more disciples than John

Joh 4:2 (although Jesus himself baptized not, but his disciples),

Joh 4:3 he left Judea, and departed again into Galilee.

Joh 4:4 And he must needs pass through Samaria.

Joh 4:5 so he cometh to a city of Samaria, called Sychar, near to the parcel of ground that Jacob gave to his son Joseph:

Joh 4:6 and Jacob's well was there. Jesus therefore, being wearied with his journey, sat thus by the well. It was about the sixth hour.

Joh 4:7 There cometh a woman of Samaria to draw water: Jesus saith unto her, Give me to drink.

Joh 4:8 For his disciples were gone away into the city to buy food.

Joh 4:9 The Samaritan woman therefore saith unto him, How is it that thou, being a Jew, askest drink of me, who am a Samaritan woman? (For Jews have no dealings with Samaritans.)

Joh 4:10 Jesus answered and said unto unto her, If thou knewest the gift of God, and who it is that saith to thee, Give me to drink; thou wouldest have asked of him, and he would have given thee living water.

Joh 4:11 The woman saith unto him, Sir, thou hast nothing to draw with, and the well is deep: whence then hast thou that living water?

Joh 4:12 Art thou greater than our father Jacob, who gave us the well, and drank thereof himself, and his sons, and his cattle?

Joh 4:13 Jesus answered and said unto her, Every one that drinketh of this water shall thirst again:

Joh 4:14 but whosoever drinketh of the water that I shall give him shall never thirst; but the water that I shall give him shall become in him a well of water springing up unto eternal life.

Joh 4:15 The woman saith unto him, Sir, give me this water, that I thirst not, neither come all the way hither to draw.

Joh 4:16 Jesus saith unto her, Go, call thy husband, and come hither.

Joh 4:17 The woman answered and said unto him, I have no husband. Jesus saith unto her, Thou saidst well, I have no husband:

Joh 4:18 for thou hast had five husbands; and he whom thou now hast is not thy husband: this hast thou said truly.

Joh 4:19 The woman saith unto him, Sir, I perceive that thou art a prophet.

Joh 4:20 Our fathers worshipped in this mountain; and ye say, that in Jerusalem is the place where men ought to worship.

Joh 4:21 Jesus saith unto her, Woman, believe me, the hour cometh, when neither in this mountain, nor in Jerusalem, shall ye worship the Father.

Joh 4:22 Ye worship that which ye know not: we worship that which we know; for salvation is from the Jews.

Joh 4:23 But the hour cometh, and now is, when the true worshippers shall worship the Father in spirit and truth: for such doth the Father seek to be his worshippers.

Joh 4:24 God is a Spirit: and they that worship him must worship in spirit and truth.

Joh 4:25 The woman saith unto him, I know that Messiah cometh (he that is called Christ): when he is come, he will declare unto us all things.

Joh 4:26 Jesus saith unto her, I that speak unto thee am he.

Joh 4:27 And upon this came his disciples; and they marvelled that he was speaking with a woman; yet no man said, What seekest thou? or, Why speakest thou with her?

Joh 4:28 So the woman left her waterpot, and went away into the city, and saith to the people,

Joh 4:29 Come, see a man, who told me all things that ever I did: can this be the Christ?

Joh 4:30 They went out of the city, and were coming to him.

Joh 4:31 In the mean while the disciples prayed him, saying, Rabbi, eat.

Joh 4:32 But he said unto them, I have meat to eat that ye know not.

Joh 4:33 The disciples therefore said one to another, Hath any man brought him aught to eat?

Joh 4:34 Jesus saith unto them, My meat is to do the will of him that sent me, and to accomplish his work.

Joh 4:35 say not ye, There are yet four months, and then cometh the harvest? behold, I say unto you, Lift up your eyes, and look on the fields, that they are white already unto harvest.

Joh 4:36 He that reapeth receiveth wages, and gathereth fruit unto life eternal; that he that soweth and he that reapeth may rejoice together.

Joh 4:37 For herein is the saying true, One soweth, and another reapeth.

Joh 4:38 I sent you to reap that whereon ye have not labored: others have labored, and ye are entered into their labor.

Joh 4:39 And from that city many of the Samaritans believed on him because of the word of the woman, who testified, He told me all things that ever I did.

Joh 4:40 So when the Samaritans came unto him, they besought him to abide with them: and he abode there two days.

Joh 4:41 And many more believed because of his word;

Joh 4:42 and they said to the woman, Now we believe, not because of thy speaking: for we have heard for ourselves, and know that this is indeed the Saviour of the world.

Joh 4:43 And after the two days he went forth from thence into Galilee.

Joh 4:44 For Jesus himself testified, that a prophet hath no honor in his own country.

Joh 4:45 So when he came into Galilee, the Galilaeans received him, having seen all the things that he did in Jerusalem at the feast: for they also went unto the feast.

Joh 4:46 He came therefore again unto Cana of Galilee, where he made the water wine. And there was a certain nobleman, whose son was sick at Capernaum.

Joh 4:47 When he heard that Jesus was come out of Judaea into Galilee, he went unto him, and besought him that he would come down, and heal his son; for he was at the point of death.

Joh 4:48 Jesus therefore said unto him, Except ye see signs and wonders, ye will in no wise believe.

Joh 4:49 The nobleman saith unto him, Sir, come down ere my child die.

Joh 4:50 Jesus saith unto him, Go thy way; thy son liveth. The man believed the word that Jesus spake unto him, and he went his way.

Joh 4:51 And as he was now going down, his servants met him, saying, that his son lived.

Joh 4:52 So he inquired of them the hour when he began to amend. They said therefore unto him, Yesterday at the seventh hour the fever left him.

Joh 4:53 So the father knew that it was at that hour in which Jesus said unto him, Thy son liveth: and himself believed, and his whole house.

Joh 4:54 This is again the second sign that Jesus did, having come out of Judaea into Galilee.

Chapter 5.

Joh 5:1 After these things there was a feast of the Jews; and Jesus went up to Jerusalem.

Joh 5:2 Now there is in Jerusalem by the sheep gate a pool, which is called in Hebrew Bethesda, having five porches.

Joh 5:3 In these lay a multitude of them that were sick, blind, halt, withered, waiting for the moving of the water,

Joh 5:4 for an angel of the Lord went down at certain seasons into the pool, and troubled the water: whosoever then first after the troubling of the waters stepped in was made whole, with whatsoever disease he was holden.

Joh 5:5 And a certain man was there, who had been thirty and eight years in his infirmity.

Joh 5:6 When Jesus saw him lying, and knew that he had been now a long time in that case, he saith unto him, Wouldest thou be made whole?

Joh 5:7 The sick man answered him, Sir, I have no man, when the water is troubled, to put me into the pool: but while I am coming, another steppeth down before me.

Joh 5:8 Jesus saith unto him, Arise, take up thy bed, and walk.

Joh 5:9 And straightway the man was made whole, and took up his bed and walked. Now it was the sabbath on that day.

Joh 5:10 So the Jews said unto him that was cured, It is the sabbath, and it is not lawful for thee to take up thy bed.

Joh 5:11 But he answered them, He that made me whole, the same said unto me, Take up thy bed, and walk.

Joh 5:12 They asked him, Who is the man that said unto thee, Take up thy bed, and walk?

Joh 5:13 But he that was healed knew not who it was; for Jesus had conveyed himself away, a multitude being in the place.

Joh 5:14 Afterward Jesus findeth him in the temple, and said unto him, Behold, thou art made whole: sin no more, lest a worse thing befall thee.

Joh 5:15 The man went away, and told the Jews that it was Jesus who had made him whole.

Joh 5:16 And for this cause the Jews persecuted Jesus, because he did these things on the sabbath.

Joh 5:17 But Jesus answered them, My Father worketh even until now, and I work.

Joh 5:18 For this cause therefore the Jews sought the more to kill him, because he not only brake the sabbath, but also called God his own Father, making himself equal with God.

Joh 5:19 Jesus therefore answered and said unto them, Verily, verily, I say unto you, The Son can do nothing of himself, but what he seeth the Father doing: for what things soever he doeth, these the Son also doeth in like manner.

Joh 5:20 For the Father loveth the Son, and showeth him all things that himself doeth: and greater works than these will he show him, that ye may marvel.

Joh 5:21 For as the Father raiseth the dead and giveth them life, even so the Son also giveth life to whom he will.

Joh 5:22 For neither doth the Father judge any man, but he hath given all judgment unto the Son;

Joh 5:23 that all may honor the Son, even as they honor the Father. He that honoreth not the Son honoreth not the Father that sent him.

Joh 5:24 Verily, verily, I say unto you, He that heareth my word, and believeth him that sent me, hath eternal life, and cometh not into judgment, but hath passed out of death into life.

Joh 5:25 Verily, verily, I say unto you, The hour cometh, and now is, when the dead shall hear the voice of the Son of God; and they that hear shall live.

Joh 5:26 For as the Father hath life in himself, even so gave he to the Son also to have life in himself:

Joh 5:27 and he gave him authority to execute judgment, because he is a son of man.

Joh 5:28 Marvel not at this: for the hour cometh, in which all that are in the tombs shall hear his voice,

Joh 5:29 and shall come forth; they that have done good, unto the resurrection of life; and they that have done evil, unto the resurrection of judgment.

Joh 5:30 I can of myself do nothing: as I hear, I judge: and my judgment is righteous; because I seek not mine own will, but the will of him that sent me.

Joh 5:31 If I bear witness of myself, my witness is not true.

Joh 5:32 It is another that beareth witness of me; and I know that the witness which he witnesseth of me is true.

Joh 5:33 Ye have sent unto John, and he hath borne witness unto the truth.

Joh 5:34 But the witness which I receive is not from man: howbeit I say these things, that ye may be saved.

Joh 5:35 He was the lamp that burneth and shineth; and ye were willing to rejoice for a season in his light.

Joh 5:36 But the witness which I have is greater than that of John; for the works which the Father hath given me to accomplish, the very works that I do, bear witness of me, that the Father hath sent me.

Joh 5:37 And the Father that sent me, he hath borne witness of me. Ye have neither heard his voice at any time, nor seen his form.

Joh 5:38 And ye have not his word abiding in you: for whom he sent, him ye believe not.

Joh 5:39 Ye search the scriptures, because ye think that in them ye have eternal life; and these are they which bear witness of me;

Joh 5:40 and ye will not come to me, that ye may have life.

Joh 5:41 I receive not glory from men.

Joh 5:42 But I know you, that ye have not the love of God in yourselves.

Joh 5:43 I am come in my Father's name, and ye receive me not: if another shall come in his own name, him ye will receive.

Joh 5:44 How can ye believe, who receive glory one of another, and the glory that cometh from the only God ye seek not?

Joh 5:45 Think not that I will accuse you to the Father: there is one that accuseth you, even Moses, on whom ye have set your hope.

Joh 5:46 For if ye believed Moses, ye would believe me; for he wrote of me.

Joh 5:47 But if ye believe not his writings, how shall ye believe my words?

Chapter 6.

Joh 6:1 After these things Jesus went away to the other side of the sea of Galilee, which is the sea of Tiberias.

Joh 6:2 And a great multitude followed him, because they beheld the signs which he did on them that were sick.

Joh 6:3 And Jesus went up into the mountain, and there he sat with his disciples.

Joh 6:4 Now the passover, the feast of the Jews, was at hand.

Joh 6:5 Jesus therefore lifting up his eyes, and seeing that a great multitude cometh unto him, saith unto Philip, Whence are we to buy bread, that these may eat?

Joh 6:6 And this he said to prove him: for he himself knew what he would do.

Joh 6:7 Philip answered him, Two hundred shillings' worth of bread is not sufficient for them, that every one may take a little.

Joh 6:8 One of his disciples, Andrew, Simon Peter's brother, saith unto him,

Joh 6:9 There is a lad here, who hath five barley loaves, and two fishes: but what are these among so many?

Joh 6:10 Jesus said, Make the people sit down. Now there was much grass in the place. So the men sat down, in number about five thousand.

Joh 6:11 Jesus therefore took the loaves; and having given thanks, he distributed to them that were set down; likewise also of the fishes as much as they would.

Joh 6:12 And when they were filled, he saith unto his disciples, Gather up the broken pieces which remain over, that nothing be lost.

Joh 6:13 So they gathered them up, and filled twelve baskets with broken pieces from the five barley loaves, which remained over unto them that had eaten.

Joh 6:14 When therefore the people saw the sign which he did, they said, This is of a truth the prophet that cometh into the world.

Joh 6:15 Jesus therefore perceiving that they were about to come and take him by force, to make him king, withdrew again into the mountain himself alone.

Joh 6:16 And when evening came, his disciples went down unto the sea;

Joh 6:17 and they entered into a boat, and were going over the sea unto Capernaum. And it was now dark, and Jesus had not yet come to them.

Joh 6:18 And the sea was rising by reason of a great wind that blew.

Joh 6:19 When therefore they had rowed about five and twenty or thirty furlongs, they behold Jesus walking on the sea, and drawing nigh unto the boat: and they were afraid.

Joh 6:20 But he saith unto them, It is I; be not afraid.

Joh 6:21 They were willing therefore to receive him into the boat: and straightway the boat was at the land whither they were going.

Joh 6:22 On the morrow the multitude that stood on the other side of the sea saw that there was no other boat there, save one, and that Jesus entered not with his disciples into the boat, but that his disciples went away alone

Joh 6:23 (howbeit there came boats from Tiberias nigh unto the place where they ate the bread after the Lord had given thanks):

Joh 6:24 when the multitude therefore saw that Jesus was not there, neither his disciples, they themselves got into the boats, and came to Capernaum, seeking Jesus.

Joh 6:25 And when they found him on the other side of the sea, they said unto him, Rabbi, when camest thou hither?

Joh 6:26 Jesus answered them and said, Verily, verily, I say unto you, Ye seek me, not because ye saw signs, but because ye ate of the loaves, and were filled.

Joh 6:27 Work not for the food which perisheth, but for the food which abideth unto eternal life, which the Son of man shall give unto you: for him the Father, even God, hath sealed.

Joh 6:28 They said therefore unto him, What must we do, that we may work the works of God?

Joh 6:29 Jesus answered and said unto them, This is the work of God, that ye believe on him whom he hath sent.

Joh 6:30 They said therefore unto him, What then doest thou for a sign, that we may see, and believe thee? what workest thou?

Joh 6:31 Our fathers ate the manna in the wilderness; as it is written, He gave them bread out of heaven to eat.

Joh 6:32 Jesus therefore said unto them, Verily, verily, I say unto you, It was not Moses that gave you the bread out of heaven; but my Father giveth you the true bread out of heaven.

Joh 6:33 For the bread of God is that which cometh down out of heaven, and giveth life unto the world.

Joh 6:34 They said therefore unto him, Lord, evermore give us this bread.

Joh 6:35 Jesus said unto them, I am the bread of life: he that cometh to me shall not hunger, and he that believeth on me shall never thirst.

Joh 6:36 But I said unto you, that ye have seen me, and yet believe not.

Joh 6:37 All that which the Father giveth me shall come unto me; and him that cometh to me I will in no wise cast out.

Joh 6:38 For I am come down from heaven, not to do mine own will, but the will of him that sent me.

Joh 6:39 And this is the will of him that sent me, that of all that which he hath given me I should lose nothing, but should raise it up at the last day.

Joh 6:40 For this is the will of my Father, that every one that beholdeth the Son, and believeth on him, should have eternal life; and I will raise him up at the last day.

Joh 6:41 The Jews therefore murmured concerning him, because he said, I am the bread which came down out of heaven.

Joh 6:42 And they said, Is not this Jesus, the son of Joseph, whose father and mother we know? how doth he now say, I am come down out of heaven?

Joh 6:43 Jesus answered and said unto them, Murmur not among yourselves.

Joh 6:44 No man can come to me, except the Father that sent me draw him: and I will raise him up in the last day.

Joh 6:45 It is written in the prophets, And they shall all be taught of God. Every one that hath heard from the Father, and hath learned, cometh unto me.

Joh 6:46 Not that any man hath seen the Father, save he that is from God, he hath seen the Father.

Joh 6:47 Verily, verily, I say unto you, He that believeth hath eternal life.

Joh 6:48 I am the bread of life.

Joh 6:49 Your fathers ate the manna in the wilderness, and they died.

Joh 6:50 This is the bread which cometh down out of heaven, that a man may eat thereof, and not die.

Joh 6:51 I am the living bread which came down out of heaven: if any man eat of this bread, he shall live for ever: yea and the bread which I will give is my flesh, for the life of the world.

Joh 6:52 The Jews therefore strove one with another, saying, How can this man give us his flesh to eat?

Joh 6:53 Jesus therefore said unto them, Verily, verily, I say unto you, Except ye eat the flesh of the Son of man and drink his blood, ye have not life in yourselves.

Joh 6:54 He that eateth my flesh and drinketh my blood hath eternal life: and I will raise him up at the last day.

Joh 6:55 For my flesh is meat indeed, and my blood is drink indeed.

Joh 6:56 He that eateth my flesh and drinketh my blood abideth in me, and I in him.

Joh 6:57 As the living Father sent me, and I live because of the Father; so he that eateth me, he also shall live because of me.

Joh 6:58 This is the bread which came down out of heaven: not as the fathers ate, and died; he that eateth this bread shall live for ever.

Joh 6:59 These things said he in the synagogue, as he taught in Capernaum.

Joh 6:60 Many therefore of his disciples, when the heard this, said, This is a hard saying; who can hear it?

Joh 6:61 But Jesus knowing in himself that his disciples murmured at this, said unto them, Doth this cause you to stumble?

Joh 6:62 What then if ye should behold the Son of man ascending where he was before?

Joh 6:63 It is the spirit that giveth life; the flesh profiteth nothing: the words that I have spoken unto you are spirit, are are life.

Joh 6:64 But there are some of you that believe not. For Jesus knew from the beginning who they were that believed not, and who it was that should betray him.

Joh 6:65 And he said, For this cause have I said unto you, that no man can come unto me, except it be given unto him of the Father.

Joh 6:66 Upon this many of his disciples went back, and walked no more with him.

Joh 6:67 Jesus said therefore unto the twelve, Would ye also go away?

Joh 6:68 Simon Peter answered him, Lord, to whom shall we go? thou hast the words of eternal life.

Joh 6:69 And we have believed and know that thou art the Holy One of God.

Joh 6:70 Jesus answered them, Did not I choose you the twelve, and one of you is a devil?

Joh 6:71 Now he spake of Judas the son of Simon Iscariot, for he it was that should betray him, being one of the twelve.

Chapter 7.

Joh 7:1 And after these things Jesus walked in Galilee: for he would not walk in Judaea, because the Jews sought to kill him.

Joh 7:2 Now the feast of the Jews, the feast of tabernacles, was at hand.

Joh 7:3 His brethren therefore said unto him, Depart hence, and go into Judaea, that thy disciples also may behold thy works which thou doest.

Joh 7:4 For no man doeth anything in secret, and himself seeketh to be known openly. If thou doest these things, manifest thyself to the world.

Joh 7:5 For even his brethren did not believe on him.

Joh 7:6 Jesus therefore saith unto them, My time is not yet come; but your time is always ready.

Joh 7:7 The world cannot hate you; but me it hateth, because I testify of it, that its works are evil.

Joh 7:8 Go ye up unto the feast: I go not up unto this feast; because my time is not yet fulfilled.

Joh 7:9 And having said these things unto them, he abode still in Galilee.

Joh 7:10 But when his brethren were gone up unto the feast, then went he also up, not publicly, but as it were in secret.

Joh 7:11 The Jews therefore sought him at the feast, and said, Where is he?

Joh 7:12 And there was much murmuring among the multitudes concerning him: some said, He is a good man; others said, Not so, but he leadeth the multitude astray.

Joh 7:13 Yet no man spake openly of him for fear of the Jews.

Joh 7:14 But when it was now the midst of the feast Jesus went up into the temple, and taught.

Joh 7:15 The Jews therefore marvelled, saying, How knoweth this man letters, having never learned?

Joh 7:16 Jesus therefore answered them and said, My teaching is not mine, but his that sent me.

Joh 7:17 If any man willeth to do his will, he shall know of the teaching, whether it is of God, or whether I speak from myself.

Joh 7:18 He that speaketh from himself seeketh his own glory: but he that seeketh the glory of him that sent him, the same is true, and no unrighteousness is in him.

Joh 7:19 Did not Moses give you the law, and yet none of you doeth the law? Why seek ye to kill me?

Joh 7:20 The multitude answered, Thou hast a demon: who seeketh to kill thee?

Joh 7:21 Jesus answered and said unto them, I did one work, and ye all marvel because thereof.

Joh 7:22 Moses hath given you circumcision (not that it is of Moses, but of the fathers); and on the sabbath ye circumcise a man.

Joh 7:23 If a man receiveth circumcision on the sabbath, that the law of Moses may not be broken; are ye wroth with me, because I made a man every whit whole on the sabbath?

Joh 7:24 Judge not according to appearance, but judge righteous judgment.

Joh 7:25 Some therefore of them of Jerusalem said, Is not this he whom they seek to kill?

Joh 7:26 And lo, he speaketh openly, and they say nothing unto him. Can it be that the rulers indeed know that this is the Christ?

Joh 7:27 Howbeit we know this man whence he is: but when the Christ cometh, no one knoweth whence he is.

Joh 7:28 Jesus therefore cried in the temple, teaching and saying, Ye both know me, and know whence I am; and I am not come of myself, but he that sent me is true, whom ye know not.

Joh 7:29 I know him; because I am from him, and he sent me.

Joh 7:30 They sought therefore to take him: and no man laid his hand on him, because his hour was not yet come.

Joh 7:31 But of the multitude many believed on him; and they said, When the Christ shall come, will he do more signs than those which this man hath done?

Joh 7:32 The Pharisees heard the multitude murmuring these things concerning him; and the chief priests and the Pharisees sent officers to take him.

Joh 7:33 Jesus therefore said, Yet a little while am I with you, and I go unto him that sent me.

Joh 7:34 Ye shall seek me, and shall not find me: and where I am, ye cannot come.

Joh 7:35 The Jews therefore said among themselves, Whither will this man go that we shall not find him? will he go unto the Dispersion among the Greeks, and teach the Greeks?

Joh 7:36 What is this word that he said, Ye shall seek me, and shall not find me; and where I am, ye cannot come?

Joh 7:37 Now on the last day, the great day of the feast, Jesus stood and cried, saying, If any man thirst, let him come unto me and drink.

Joh 7:38 He that believeth on me, as the scripture hath said, from within him shall flow rivers of living water.

Joh 7:39 But this spake he of the Spirit, which they that believed on him were to receive: for the Spirit was not yet given; because Jesus was not yet glorified.

Joh 7:40 Some of the multitude therefore, when they heard these words, said, This is of a truth the prophet.

Joh 7:41 Others said, This is the Christ. But some said, What, doth the Christ come out of Galilee?

Joh 7:42 Hath not the scripture said that the Christ cometh of the seed of David, and from Bethlehem, the village where David was?

Joh 7:43 So there arose a division in the multitude because of him.

Joh 7:44 And some of them would have taken him; but no man laid hands on him.

Joh 7:45 The officers therefore came to the chief priests and Pharisees; and they said unto them, Why did ye not bring him?

Joh 7:46 The officers answered, Never man so spake.

Joh 7:47 The Pharisees therefore answered them, Are ye also led astray?

Joh 7:48 Hath any of the rulers believed on him, or of the Pharisees?

Joh 7:49 But this multitude that knoweth not the law are accursed.

Joh 7:50 Nicodemus saith unto them (he that came to him before, being one of them),

Joh 7:51 Doth our law judge a man, except it first hear from himself and know what he doeth?

Joh 7:52 They answered and said unto him, Art thou also of Galilee? Search, and see that out of Galilee ariseth no prophet.

Joh 7:53 [And they went every man unto his own house:

Chapter 8.

Joh 8:1 but Jesus went unto the mount of Olives.

Joh 8:2 And early in the morning he came again into the temple, and all the people came unto him; and he sat down, and taught them.

Joh 8:3 And the scribes and the Pharisees bring a woman taken in adultery; and having set her in the midst,

Joh 8:4 they say unto him, Teacher, this woman hath been taken in adultery, in the very act.

Joh 8:5 Now in the law Moses commanded us to stone such: what then sayest thou of her?

Joh 8:6 And this they said, trying him, that they might have whereof to accuse him. But Jesus stooped down, and with his finger wrote on the ground.

Joh 8:7 But when they continued asking him, he lifted up himself, and said unto them, He that is without sin among you, let him first cast a stone at her.

Joh 8:8 And again he stooped down, and with his finger wrote on the ground.

Joh 8:9 And they, when they heard it, went out one by one, beginning from the eldest, even unto the last: and Jesus was left alone, and the woman, where she was, in the midst.

Joh 8:10 And Jesus lifted up himself, and said unto her, Woman, where are they? did no man condemn thee?

Joh 8:11 And she said, No man, Lord. And Jesus said, Neither do I condemn thee: go thy way; from henceforth sin no more.]

Joh 8:12 Again therefore Jesus spake unto them, saying, I am the light of the world: he that followeth me shall not walk in the darkness, but shall have the light of life.

Joh 8:13 The Pharisees therefore said unto him, Thou bearest witness of thyself; thy witness is not true.

Joh 8:14 Jesus answered and said unto them, Even if I bear witness of myself, my witness is true; for I know whence I came, and whither I go; but ye know not whence I come, or whither I go.

Joh 8:15 Ye judge after the flesh; I judge no man.

Joh 8:16 Yea and if I judge, my judgment is true; for I am not alone, but I and the Father that sent me.

Joh 8:17 Yea and in your law it is written, that the witness of two men is true.

Joh 8:18 I am he that beareth witness of myself, and the Father that sent me beareth witness of me.

Joh 8:19 They said therefore unto him, Where is thy Father? Jesus answered, Ye know neither me, nor my Father: if ye knew me, ye would know my Father also.

Joh 8:20 These words spake he in the treasury, as he taught in the temple: and no man took him; because his hour was not yet come.

Joh 8:21 He said therefore again unto them, I go away, and ye shall seek me, and shall die in your sin: whither I go, ye cannot come.

Joh 8:22 The Jews therefore said, Will he kill himself, that he saith, Whither I go, ye cannot come?

Joh 8:23 And he said unto them, Ye are from beneath; I am from above: ye are of this world; I am not of this world.

Joh 8:24 I said therefore unto you, that ye shall die in your sins: for except ye believe that I am he, ye shall die in your sins.

Joh 8:25 They said therefore unto him, Who art thou? Jesus said unto them, Even that which I have also spoken unto you from the beginning.

Joh 8:26 I have many things to speak and to judge concerning you: howbeit he that sent me is true; and the things which I heard from him, these speak I unto the world.

Joh 8:27 They perceived not that he spake to them of the Father.

Joh 8:28 Jesus therefore said, When ye have lifted up the Son of man, then shall ye know that I am he, and that I do nothing of myself, but as the Father taught me, I speak these things.

Joh 8:29 And he that sent me is with me; he hath not left me alone; for I do always the things that are pleasing to him.

Joh 8:30 As he spake these things, many believed on him.

Joh 8:31 Jesus therefore said to those Jews that had believed him, If ye abide in my word, then are ye truly my disciples;

Joh 8:32 and ye shall know the truth, and the truth shall make you free.

Joh 8:33 They answered unto him, We are Abraham's seed, and have never yet been in bondage to any man: how sayest thou, Ye shall be made free?

Joh 8:34 Jesus answered them, Verily, verily, I say unto you, Every one that committeth sin is the bondservant of sin.

Joh 8:35 And the bondservant abideth not in the house for ever: the son abideth for ever.

Joh 8:36 If therefore the Son shall make you free, ye shall be free indeed.

Joh 8:37 I know that ye are Abraham's seed: yet ye seek to kill me, because my word hath not free course in you.

Joh 8:38 I speak the things which I have seen with my Father: and ye also do the things which ye heard from your father.

Joh 8:39 They answered and said unto him, Our father is Abraham. Jesus saith unto them, If ye were Abraham's children, ye would do the works of Abraham.

Joh 8:40 But now ye seek to kill me, a man that hath told you the truth, which I heard from God: this did not Abraham.

Joh 8:41 Ye do the works of your father. They said unto him, We were not born of fornication; we have one Father, even God.

Joh 8:42 Jesus said unto them, If God were your Father, ye would love me: for I came forth and am come from God; for neither have I come of myself, but he sent me.

Joh 8:43 Why do ye not understand my speech? Even because ye cannot hear my word.

Joh 8:44 Ye are of your father the devil, and the lusts of your father it is your will to do. He was a murderer from the beginning, and standeth not in the truth, because there is no truth in him. When he speaketh a lie, he speaketh of his own: for he is a liar, and the father thereof.

Joh 8:45 But because I say the truth, ye believe me not.

Joh 8:46 Which of you convicteth me of sin? If I say truth, why do ye not believe me?

Joh 8:47 He that is of God heareth the words of God: for this cause ye hear them not, because ye are not of God.

Joh 8:48 The Jews answered and said unto him, Say we not well that thou art a Samaritan, and hast a demon?

Joh 8:49 Jesus answered, I have not a demon; but I honor my Father, and ye dishonor me.

Joh 8:50 But I seek not mine own glory: there is one that seeketh and judgeth.

Joh 8:51 Verily, verily, I say unto you, If a man keep my word, he shall never see death.

Joh 8:52 The Jews said unto him, Now we know that thou hast a demon. Abraham died, and the prophets; and thou sayest, If a man keep my word, he shall never taste of death.

Joh 8:53 Art thou greater than our father Abraham, who died? and the prophets died: whom makest thou thyself?

Joh 8:54 Jesus answered, If I glorify myself, my glory is nothing: it is my Father that glorifieth me; of whom ye say, that he is your God;

Joh 8:55 and ye have not known him: but I know him; and if I should say, I know him not, I shall be like unto you, a liar: but I know him, and keep his word.

Joh 8:56 Your father Abraham rejoiced to see my day; and he saw it, and was glad.

Joh 8:57 The Jews therefore said unto him, Thou art not yet fifty years old, and hast thou seen Abraham?

Joh 8:58 Jesus said unto them, Verily, verily, I say unto you, Before Abraham was born, I am.

Joh 8:59 They took up stones therefore to cast at him: but Jesus hid himself, and went out of the temple.

Chapter 9.

Joh 9:1 And as he passed by, he saw a man blind from his birth.

Joh 9:2 And his disciples asked him, saying, Rabbi, who sinned, this man, or his parents, that he should be born blind?

Joh 9:3 Jesus answered, Neither did this man sin, nor his parents: but that the works of God should be made manifest in him.

Joh 9:4 We must work the works of him that sent me, while it is day: the night cometh, when no man can work.

Joh 9:5 When I am in the world, I am the light of the world.

Joh 9:6 When he had thus spoken, he spat on the ground, and made clay of the spittle, and anointed his eyes with the clay,

Joh 9:7 and said unto him, Go, wash in the pool of Siloam (which is by interpretation, Sent). He went away therefore, and washed, and came seeing.

Joh 9:8 The neighbors therefore, and they that saw him aforetime, that he was a beggar, said, Is not this he that sat and begged?

Joh 9:9 Others said, It is he: others said, No, but he is like him. He said, I am he.

Joh 9:10 They said therefore unto him, How then were thine eyes opened?

Joh 9:11 He answered, The man that is called Jesus made clay, and anointed mine eyes, and said unto me, Go to Siloam, and wash: so I went away and washed, and I received sight.

Joh 9:12 And they said unto him, Where is he? He saith, I know not.

Joh 9:13 They bring to the Pharisees him that aforetime was blind.

Joh 9:14 Now it was the sabbath on the day when Jesus made the clay, and opened his eyes.

Joh 9:15 Again therefore the Pharisees also asked him how he received his sight. And he said unto them, He put clay upon mine eyes, and I washed, and I see.

Joh 9:16 Some therefore of the Pharisees said, This man is not from God, because he keepeth not the sabbath. But others said, How can a man that is a sinner do such signs? And there was division among them.

Joh 9:17 They say therefore unto the blind man again, What sayest thou of him, in that he opened thine eyes? And he said, He is a prophet.

Joh 9:18 The Jews therefore did not believe concerning him, that he had been blind, and had received his sight, until they called the parents of him that had received his sight,

Joh 9:19 and asked them, saying, Is this your son, who ye say was born blind? How then doth he now see?

Joh 9:20 His parents answered and said, We know that this is our son, and that he was born blind:

Joh 9:21 but how he now seeth, we know not; or who opened his eyes, we know not: ask him; he is of age; he shall speak for himself.

Joh 9:22 These things said his parents, because they feared the Jews: for the Jews had agreed already, that if any man should confess him to be Christ, he should be put out of the synagogue.

Joh 9:23 Therefore said his parents, He is of age; ask him.

Joh 9:24 So they called a second time the man that was blind, and said unto him, Give glory to God: we know that this man is a sinner.

Joh 9:25 He therefore answered, Whether he is a sinner, I know not: one thing I know, that, whereas I was blind, now I see.

Joh 9:26 They said therefore unto him, What did he to thee? How opened he thine eyes?

Joh 9:27 He answered them, I told you even now, and ye did not hear; wherefore would ye hear it again? would ye also become his disciples?

Joh 9:28 And they reviled him, and said, Thou art his disciple; but we are disciples of Moses.

Joh 9:29 We know that God hath spoken unto Moses: but as for this man, we know not whence he is.

Joh 9:30 The man answered and said unto them, Why, herein is the marvel, that ye know not whence he is, and yet he opened mine eyes.

Joh 9:31 We know that God heareth not sinners: but if any man be a worshipper of God, and do his will, him he heareth.

Joh 9:32 Since the world began it was never heard that any one opened the eyes of a man born blind.

Joh 9:33 If this man were not from God, he could do nothing.

Joh 9:34 They answered and said unto him, Thou wast altogether born in sins, and dost thou teach us? And they cast him out.

Joh 9:35 Jesus heard that they had cast him out; and finding him, he said, Dost thou believe on the Son of God?

Joh 9:36 He answered and said, And who is he, Lord, that I may believe on him?

Joh 9:37 Jesus said unto him, Thou hast both seen him, and he it is that speaketh with thee.

Joh 9:38 And he said, Lord, I believe. And he worshipped him.

Joh 9:39 And Jesus said, For judgment came I into this world, that they that see not may see; and that they that see may become blind.

Joh 9:40 Those of the Pharisees who were with him heard these things, and said unto him, Are we also blind?

Joh 9:41 Jesus said unto them, If ye were blind, ye would have no sin: but now ye say, We see: your sin remaineth.

Chapter 10.

Joh 10:1 Verily, verily, I say unto you, He that entereth not by the door into the fold of the sheep, but climbeth up some other way, the same is a thief and a robber.

Joh 10:2 But he that entereth in by the door is the shepherd of the sheep.

Joh 10:3 To him the porter openeth; and the sheep hear his voice: and he calleth his own sheep by name, and leadeth them out.

Joh 10:4 When he hath put forth all his own, he goeth before them, and the sheep follow him: for they know his voice.

Joh 10:5 And a stranger will they not follow, but will flee from him: for they know not the voice of strangers.

Joh 10:6 This parable spake Jesus unto them: but they understood not what things they were which he spake unto them.

Joh 10:7 Jesus therefore said unto them again, Verily, verily, I say unto you, I am the door of the sheep.

Joh 10:8 All that came before me are thieves and robbers: but the sheep did not hear them.

Joh 10:9 I am the door; by me if any man enter in, he shall be saved, and shall go in and go out, and shall find pasture.

Joh 10:10 The thief cometh not, but that he may steal, and kill, and destroy: I came that they may have life, and may have it abundantly.

Joh 10:11 I am the good shepherd: the good shepherd layeth down his life for the sheep.

Joh 10:12 He that is a hireling, and not a shepherd, whose own the sheep are not, beholdeth the wolf coming, and leaveth the sheep, and fleeth, and the wolf snatcheth them, and scattereth them:

Joh 10:13 he fleeth because he is a hireling, and careth not for the sheep.

Joh 10:14 I am the good shepherd; and I know mine own, and mine own know me,

Joh 10:15 even as the Father knoweth me, and I know the Father; and I lay down my life for the sheep.

Joh 10:16 And other sheep I have, which are not of this fold: them also I must bring, and they shall hear my voice: and they shall become one flock, one shepherd.

Joh 10:17 Therefore doth the Father love me, because I lay down my life, that I may take it again.

Joh 10:18 No one taketh it away from me, but I lay it down of myself. I have power to lay it down, and I have power to take it again. This commandment received I from my Father.

Joh 10:19 There arose a division again among the Jews because of these words.

Joh 10:20 And many of them said, He hath a demon, and is mad; why hear ye him?

Joh 10:21 Others said, These are not the sayings of one possessed with a demon. Can a demon open the eyes of the blind?

Joh 10:22 And it was the feast of the dedication at Jerusalem:

Joh 10:23 it was winter; and Jesus was walking in the temple in Solomon's porch.

Joh 10:24 The Jews therefore came round about him, and said unto him, How long dost thou hold us in suspense? If thou art the Christ, tell us plainly.

Joh 10:25 Jesus answered them, I told you, and ye believe not: the works that I do in my Father's name, these bear witness of me.

Joh 10:26 But ye believe not, because ye are not of my sheep.

Joh 10:27 My sheep hear my voice, and I know them, and they follow me:

Joh 10:28 and I give unto them eternal life; and they shall never perish, and no one shall snatch them out of my hand.

Joh 10:29 My Father, who hath given them unto me, is greater than all; and no one is able to snatch them out of the Father's hand.

Joh 10:30 I and the Father are one.

Joh 10:31 The Jews took up stones again to stone him.

Joh 10:32 Jesus answered them, Many good works have I showed you from the Father; for which of those works do ye stone me?

Joh 10:33 The Jews answered him, For a good work we stone thee not, but for blasphemy; and because that thou, being a man, makest thyself God.

Joh 10:34 Jesus answered them, Is it not written in your law, I said, ye are gods?

Joh 10:35 If he called them gods, unto whom the word of God came (and the scripture cannot be broken),

Joh 10:36 say ye of him, whom the Father sanctified and sent into the world, Thou blasphemest; because I said, I am the Son of God?

Joh 10:37 If I do not the works of my Father, believe me not.

Joh 10:38 But if I do them, though ye believe not me, believe the works: that ye may know and understand that the Father is in me, and I in the Father.

Joh 10:39 They sought again to take him: and he went forth out of their hand.

Joh 10:40 And he went away again beyond the Jordan into the place where John was at the first baptizing; and there be abode.

Joh 10:41 And many came unto him; and they said, John indeed did no sign: but all things whatsoever John spake of this man were true.

Joh 10:42 And many believed on him there.

Chapter 11.

Joh 11:1 Now a certain man was sick, Lazarus of Bethany, of the village of Mary and her sister Martha.

Joh 11:2 And it was that Mary who anointed the Lord with ointment, and wiped his feet with her hair, whose brother Lazarus was sick.

Joh 11:3 The sisters therefore sent unto him, saying, Lord, behold, he whom thou lovest is sick.

Joh 11:4 But when Jesus heard it, he said, This sickness is not unto death, but for the glory of God, that the Son of God may be glorified thereby.

Joh 11:5 Now Jesus loved Martha, and her sister, and Lazarus.

Joh 11:6 When therefore he heard that he was sick, he abode at that time two days in the place where he was.

Joh 11:7 Then after this he saith to the disciples, Let us go into Judaea again.

Joh 11:8 The disciples say unto him, Rabbi, the Jews were but now seeking to stone thee; and goest thou thither again?

Joh 11:9 Jesus answered, Are there not twelve hours in the day? If a man walk in the day, he stumbleth not, because he seeth the light of this world.

Joh 11:10 But if a man walk in the night, he stumbleth, because the light is not in him.

Joh 11:11 These things spake he: and after this he saith unto them, Our friend Lazarus is fallen asleep; but I go, that I may awake him out of sleep.

Joh 11:12 The disciples therefore said unto him, Lord, if he is fallen asleep, he will recover.

Joh 11:13 Now Jesus had spoken of his death: but they thought that he spake of taking rest in sleep.

Joh 11:14 Then Jesus therefore said unto them plainly, Lazarus is dead.

Joh 11:15 And I am glad for your sakes that I was not there, to the intent ye may believe; nevertheless let us go unto him.

Joh 11:16 Thomas therefore, who is called Didymus, said unto his fellow-disciples, Let us also go, that we may die with him.

Joh 11:17 So when Jesus came, he found that he had been in the tomb four days already.

Joh 11:18 Now Bethany was nigh unto Jerusalem, about fifteen furlongs off;

Joh 11:19 and many of the Jews had come to Martha and Mary, to console them concerning their brother.

Joh 11:20 Martha therefore, when she heard that Jesus was coming, went and met him: but Mary still sat in the house.

Joh 11:21 Martha therefore said unto Jesus, Lord, if thou hadst been here, my brother had not died.

Joh 11:22 And even now I know that, whatsoever thou shalt ask of God, God will give thee.

Joh 11:23 Jesus saith unto her, Thy brother shall rise again.

Joh 11:24 Martha saith unto him, I know that he shall rise again in the resurrection at the last day.

Joh 11:25 Jesus said unto her, I am the resurrection, and the life: he that believeth on me, though he die, yet shall he live;

Joh 11:26 and whosoever liveth and believeth on me shall never die. Believest thou this?

Joh 11:27 She saith unto him, Yea, Lord: I have believed that thou art the Christ, the Son of God, even he that cometh into the world.

Joh 11:28 And when she had said this, she went away, and called Mary her sister secretly, saying, The Teacher is her, and calleth thee.

Joh 11:29 And she, when she heard it, arose quickly, and went unto him.

Joh 11:30 (Now Jesus was not yet come into the village, but was still in the place where Martha met him.)

Joh 11:31 The Jews then who were with her in the house, and were consoling her, when they saw Mary, that she rose up quickly and went out, followed her, supposing that she was going unto the tomb to weep there.

Joh 11:32 Mary therefore, when she came where Jesus was, and saw him, fell down at his feet, saying unto him, Lord, if thou hadst been here, my brother had not died.

Joh 11:33 When Jesus therefore saw her weeping, and the Jews also weeping who came with her, he groaned in the spirit, and was troubled,

Joh 11:34 and said, Where have ye laid him? They say unto him, Lord, come and see.

Joh 11:35 Jesus wept.

Joh 11:36 The Jews therefore said, Behold how he loved him!

Joh 11:37 But some of them said, Could not this man, who opened the eyes of him that was blind, have caused that this man also should not die?

Joh 11:38 Jesus therefore again groaning in himself cometh to the tomb. Now it was a cave, and a stone lay against it.

Joh 11:39 Jesus saith, Take ye away the stone. Martha, the sister of him that was dead, saith unto him, Lord, by this time the body decayeth; for he hath been dead four days.

Joh 11:40   Jesus saith unto her, Said I not unto thee, that, if thou believedst, thou shouldest see the glory of God?

Joh 11:41 So they took away the stone. And Jesus lifted up his eyes, and said, Father, I thank thee that thou heardest me.

Joh 11:42 And I knew that thou hearest me always: but because of the multitude that standeth around I said it, that they may believe that thou didst send me.

Joh 11:43 And when he had thus spoken, he cried with a loud voice, Lazarus, come forth.

Joh 11:44 He that was dead came forth, bound hand and foot with grave-clothes; and his face was bound about with a napkin. Jesus saith unto them, Loose him, and let him go.

Joh 11:45 Many therefore of the Jews, who came to Mary and beheld that which he did, believed on him.

Joh 11:46 But some of them went away to the Pharisees, and told them the things which Jesus had done.

Joh 11:47 The chief priests therefore and the Pharisees gathered a council, and said, What do we? for this man doeth many signs.

Joh 11:48 If we let him thus alone, all men will believe on him: and the Romans will come and take away both our place and our nation.

Joh 11:49 But a certain one of them, Caiaphas, being high priest that year, said unto them, Ye know nothing at all,

Joh 11:50 nor do ye take account that it is expedient for you that one man should die for the people, and that the whole nation perish not.

Joh 11:51   Now this he said not of himself: but, being high priest that year, he prophesied that Jesus should die for the nation;

Joh 11:52 and not for the nation only, but that he might also gather together into one the children of God that are scattered abroad.

Joh 11:53 So from that day forth they took counsel that they might put him to death.

Joh 11:54   Jesus therefore walked no more openly among the Jews, but departed thence into the country near to the wilderness, into a city called Ephraim; and there he tarried with the disciples.

Joh 11:55 Now the passover of the Jews was at hand: and many went up to Jerusalem out of the country before the passover, to purify themselves.

Joh 11:56 They sought therefore for Jesus, and spake one with another, as they stood in the temple, What think ye? That he will not come to the feast?

Joh 11:57 Now the chief priests and the Pharisees had given commandment, that, if any man knew where he was, he should show it, that they might take him.

Chapter 12.

Joh 12:1 Jesus therefore six days before the passover came to Bethany, where Lazarus was, whom Jesus raised from the dead.

Joh 12:2 So they made him a supper there: and Martha served; but Lazarus was one of them that sat at meat with him.

Joh 12:3 Mary therefore took a pound of ointment of pure nard, very precious, and anointed the feet of Jesus, and wiped his feet with her hair: and the house was filled with the odor of the ointment.

Joh 12:4 But Judas Iscariot, one of his disciples, that should betray him, saith,

Joh 12:5 Why was not this ointment sold for three hundred shillings, and given to the poor?

Joh 12:6 Now this he said, not because he cared for the poor; but because he was a thief, and having the bag took away what was put therein.

Joh 12:7 Jesus therefore said, Suffer her to keep it against the day of my burying.

Joh 12:8 For the poor ye have always with you; but me ye have not always.

Joh 12:9 The common people therefore of the Jews learned that he was there: and they came, not for Jesus' sake only, but that they might see Lazarus also, whom he had raised from the dead.

Joh 12:10 But the chief priests took counsel that they might put Lazarus also to death;

Joh 12:11 because that by reason of him many of the Jews went away, and believed on Jesus.

Joh 12:12 On the morrow a great multitude that had come to the feast, when they heard that Jesus was coming to Jerusalem,

Joh 12:13 took the branches of the palm trees, and went forth to meet him, and cried out, Hosanna: Blessed is he that cometh in the name of the Lord, even the King of Israel.

Joh 12:14 And Jesus, having found a young ass, sat thereon; as it is written,

Joh 12:15 Fear not, daughter of Zion: behold, thy King cometh, sitting on an ass's colt.

Joh 12:16 These things understood not his disciples at the first: but when Jesus was glorified, then remembered they that these things were written of him, and that they had done these things unto him.

Joh 12:17 The multitude therefore that was with him when he called Lazarus out of the tomb, and raised him from the dead, bare witness.

Joh 12:18 For this cause also the multitude went and met him, for that they heard that he had done this sign.

Joh 12:19 The Pharisees therefore said among themselves, Behold how ye prevail nothing: lo, the world is gone after him.

Joh 12:20 Now there were certain Greeks among those that went up to worship at the feast:

Joh 12:21 these therefore came to Philip, who was of Bethsaida of Galilee, and asked him, saying, Sir, we would see Jesus.

Joh 12:22 Philip cometh and telleth Andrew: Andrew cometh, and Philip, and they tell Jesus.

Joh 12:23 And Jesus answereth them, saying, The hour is come, that the Son of man should be glorified.

Joh 12:24 Verily, verily, I say unto you, Except a grain of wheat fall into the earth and die, it abideth by itself alone; but if it die, it beareth much fruit.

Joh 12:25 He that loveth his life loseth it; and he that hateth his life in this world shall keep it unto life eternal.

Joh 12:26 If any man serve me, let him follow me; and where I am, there shall also my servant be: if any man serve me, him will the Father honor.

Joh 12:27 Now is my soul troubled; and what shall I say? Father, save me from this hour. But for this cause came I unto this hour.

Joh 12:28 Father, glorify thy name. There came therefore a voice out of heaven, saying, I have both glorified it, and will glorify it again.

Joh 12:29 The multitude therefore, that stood by, and heard it, said that it had thundered: others said, An angel hath spoken to him.

Joh 12:30 Jesus answered and said, This voice hath not come for my sake, but for your sakes.

Joh 12:31 Now is the judgment of this world: now shall the prince of this world be cast out.

Joh 12:32 And I, if I be lifted up from the earth, will draw all men unto myself.

Joh 12:33 But this he said, signifying by what manner of death he should die.

Joh 12:34 The multitude therefore answered him, We have heard out of the law that the Christ abideth for ever: and how sayest thou, The Son of man must be lifted up? who is this Son of man?

Joh 12:35 Jesus therefore said unto them, Yet a little while is the light among you. Walk while ye have the light, that darkness overtake you not: and he that walketh in the darkness knoweth not whither he goeth.

Joh 12:36 While ye have the light, believe on the light, that ye may become sons of light. These things spake Jesus, and he departed and hid himself from them.

Joh 12:37 But though he had done so many signs before them, yet they believed not on him:

Joh 12:38 that the word of Isaiah the prophet might be fulfilled, which he spake, Lord, who hath believed our report? And to whom hath the arm of the Lord been revealed?

Joh 12:39 For this cause they could not believe, for that Isaiah said again,

Joh 12:40 He hath blinded their eyes, and he hardened their heart; Lest they should see with their eyes, and perceive with their heart, And should turn, And I should heal them.

Joh 12:41 These things said Isaiah, because he saw his glory; and he spake of him.

Joh 12:42 Nevertheless even of the rulers many believed on him; but because of the Pharisees they did not confess it, lest they should be put out of the synagogue:

Joh 12:43 for they loved the glory that is of men more than the glory that is of God.

Joh 12:44 And Jesus cried and said, He that believeth on me, believeth not on me, but on him that sent me.

Joh 12:45 And he that beholdeth me beholdeth him that sent me.

Joh 12:46 I am come a light into the world, that whosoever believeth on me may not abide in the darkness.

Joh 12:47 And if any man hear my sayings, and keep them not, I judge him not: for I came not to judge the world, but to save the world.

Joh 12:48 He that rejecteth me, and receiveth not my sayings, hath one that judgeth him: the word that I spake, the same shall judge him in the last day.

Joh 12:49 For I spake not from myself; but the Father that sent me, he hath given me a commandment, what I should say, and what I should speak.

Joh 12:50 And I know that his commandment is life eternal: the things therefore which I speak, even as the Father hath said unto me, so I speak.

Chapter 13.

Joh 13:1 Now before the feast of the passover, Jesus knowing that his hour was come that he should depart out of this world unto his Father, having loved his own that were in the world, he loved them unto the end.

Joh 13:2 And during supper, the devil having already put into the heart of Judas Iscariot, Simon's son, to betray him,

Joh 13:3 Jesus, knowing that the Father had given all the things into his hands, and that he came forth from God, and goeth unto God,

Joh 13:4 riseth from supper, and layeth aside his garments; and he took a towel, and girded himself.

Joh 13:5 Then he poureth water into the basin, and began to wash the disciples' feet, and to wipe them with the towel wherewith he was girded.

Joh 13:6 So he cometh to Simon Peter. He saith unto him, Lord, dost thou wash my feet?

Joh 13:7 Jesus answered and said unto him, What I do thou knowest not now; but thou shalt understand hereafter.

Joh 13:8 Peter saith unto him, Thou shalt never wash my feet. Jesus answered him, If I wash thee not, thou hast no part with me.

Joh 13:9 Simon Peter saith unto him, Lord, not my feet only, but also my hands and my head.

Joh 13:10 Jesus saith to him, He that is bathed needeth not save to wash his feet, but is clean every whit: and ye are clean, but not all.

Joh 13:11 For he knew him that should betray him; therefore said he, Ye are not all clean.

Joh 13:12 So when he had washed their feet, and taken his garments, and sat down again, he said unto them, Know ye what I have done to you?

Joh 13:13 Ye call me, Teacher, and, Lord: and ye say well; for so I am.

Joh 13:14 If I then, the Lord and the Teacher, have washed your feet, ye also ought to wash one another's feet.

Joh 13:15 For I have given you an example, that ye also should do as I have done to you.

Joh 13:16 Verily, verily, I say unto you, a servant is not greater than his lord; neither one that is sent greater than he that sent him.

Joh 13:17 If ye know these things, blessed are ye if ye do them.

Joh 13:18 I speak not of you all: I know whom I have chosen: but that the scripture may be fulfilled: He that eateth my bread lifted up his heel against me.

Joh 13:19 From henceforth I tell you before it come to pass, that, when it is come to pass, ye may believe that I am he.

Joh 13:20 Verily, verily, I say unto you, he that receiveth whomsoever I send receiveth me; and he that receiveth me receiveth him that sent me.

Joh 13:21 When Jesus had thus said, he was troubled in the spirit, and testified, and said, Verily, verily, I say unto you, that one of you shall betray me.

Joh 13:22 The disciples looked one on another, doubting of whom he spake.

Joh 13:23 There was at the table reclining in Jesus' bosom one of his disciples, whom Jesus loved.

Joh 13:24 Simon Peter therefore beckoneth to him, and saith unto him, Tell us who it is of whom he speaketh.

Joh 13:25 He leaning back, as he was, on Jesus' breast saith unto him, Lord, who is it?

Joh 13:26 Jesus therefore answereth, He it is, for whom I shall dip the sop, and give it him. So when he had dipped the sop, he taketh and giveth it to Judas, the son of Simon Iscariot.

Joh 13:27 And after the sop, then entered Satan into him. Jesus therefore saith unto him, What thou doest, do quickly.

Joh 13:28 Now no man at the table knew for what intent he spake this unto him.

Joh 13:29 For some thought, because Judas had the bag, that Jesus said unto him, Buy what things we have need of for the feast; or, that he should give something to the poor.

Joh 13:30 He then having received the sop went out straightway: and it was night.

Joh 13:31 When therefore he was gone out, Jesus saith, Now is the Son of man glorified, and God is glorified in him;

Joh 13:32 and God shall glorify him in himself, and straightway shall he glorify him.

Joh 13:33 Little children, yet a little while I am with you. Ye shall seek me: and as I said unto the Jews, Whither I go, ye cannot come; so now I say unto you.

Joh 13:34 A new commandment I give unto you, that ye love one another; even as I have loved you, that ye also love one another.

Joh 13:35 By this shall all men know that ye are my disciples, if ye have love one to another.

Joh 13:36 Simon Peter saith unto him, Lord, whither goest thou? Jesus answered, Whither I go, thou canst not follow now; but thou shalt follow afterwards.

Joh 13:37 Peter saith unto him, Lord, why cannot I follow thee even now? I will lay down my life for thee.

Joh 13:38 Jesus answereth, Wilt thou lay down thy life for me? Verily, verily, I say unto thee, The cock shall not crow, till thou hast denied me thrice.

Chapter 14.

Joh 14:1 Let not your heart be troubled: believe in God, believe also in me.

Joh 14:2 In my Father's house are many mansions; if it were not so, I would have told you; for I go to prepare a place for you.

Joh 14:3 And if I go and prepare a place for you, I come again, and will receive you unto myself; that where I am, there ye may be also.

Joh 14:4 And whither I go, ye know the way.

Joh 14:5 Thomas saith unto him, Lord, we know not whither thou goest; how know we the way?

Joh 14:6 Jesus saith unto him, I am the way, and the truth, and the life: no one cometh unto the Father, but by me.

Joh 14:7 If ye had known me, ye would have known my Father also: from henceforth ye know him, and have seen him.

Joh 14:8 Philip saith unto him, Lord, show us the Father, and it sufficeth us.

Joh 14:9 Jesus saith unto him, Have I been so long time with you, and dost thou not know me, Philip? he that hath seen me hath seen the Father; how sayest thou, Show us the Father?

Joh 14:10 Believest thou not that I am in the Father, and the Father in me? the words that I say unto you I speak not from myself: but the Father abiding in me doeth his works.

Joh 14:11 Believe me that I am in the Father, and the Father in me: or else believe me for the very works' sake.

Joh 14:12 Verily, verily, I say unto you, he that believeth on me, the works that I do shall he do also; and greater works than these shall he do; because I go unto the Father.

Joh 14:13 And whatsoever ye shall ask in my name, that will I do, that the Father may be glorified in the Son.

Joh 14:14 If ye shall ask anything in my name, that will I do.

Joh 14:15 If ye love me, ye will keep my commandments.

Joh 14:16 And I will pray the Father, and he shall give you another Comforter, that he may be with you for ever,

Joh 14:17 even the Spirit of truth: whom the world cannot receive; for it beholdeth him not, neither knoweth him: ye know him; for he abideth with you, and shall be in you.

Joh 14:18 I will not leave you desolate: I come unto you.

Joh 14:19 Yet a little while, and the world beholdeth me no more; but ye behold me: because I live, ye shall live also.

Joh 14:20 In that day ye shall know that I am in my Father, and ye in me, and I in you.

Joh 14:21 He that hath my commandments, and keepeth them, he it is that loveth me: and he that loveth me shall be loved of my Father, and I will love him, and will manifest myself unto him.

Joh 14:22 Judas (not Iscariot) saith unto him, Lord, what is come to pass that thou wilt manifest thyself unto us, and not unto the world?

Joh 14:23 Jesus answered and said unto him, If a man love me, he will keep my word: and my Father will love him, and we will come unto him, and make our abode with him.

Joh 14:24 He that loveth me not keepeth not my words: and the word which ye hear is not mine, but the Father's who sent me.

Joh 14:25 These things have I spoken unto you, while yet abiding with you.

Joh 14:26 But the Comforter, even the Holy Spirit, whom the Father will send in my name, he shall teach you all things, and bring to your remembrance all that I said unto you.

Joh 14:27 Peace I leave with you; my peace I give unto you: not as the world giveth, give I unto you. Let not your heart be troubled, neither let it be fearful.

Joh 14:28 Ye heard how I said to you, I go away, and I come unto you. If ye loved me, ye would have rejoiced, because I go unto the Father: for the Father is greater than I.

Joh 14:29 And now I have told you before it come to pass, that, when it is come to pass, ye may believe.

Joh 14:30 I will no more speak much with you, for the prince of the world cometh: and he hath nothing in me;

Joh 14:31 but that the world may know that I love the Father, and as the Father gave me commandment, even so I do. Arise, let us go hence.

Chapter 15.

Joh 15:1 I am the true vine, and my Father is the husbandman.

Joh 15:2 Every branch in me that beareth not fruit, he taketh it away: and every branch that beareth fruit, he cleanseth it, that it may bear more fruit.

Joh 15:3 Already ye are clean because of the word which I have spoken unto you.

Joh 15:4 Abide in me, and I in you. As the branch cannot bear fruit of itself, except it abide in the vine; so neither can ye, except ye abide in me.

Joh 15:5 I am the vine, ye are the branches: He that abideth in me, and I in him, the same beareth much fruit: for apart from me ye can do nothing.

Joh 15:6 If a man abide not in me, he is cast forth as a branch, and is withered; and they gather them, and cast them into the fire, and they are burned.

Joh 15:7 If ye abide in me, and my words abide in you, ask whatsoever ye will, and it shall be done unto you.

Joh 15:8 Herein is my Father glorified, that ye bear much fruit; and so shall ye be my disciples.

Joh 15:9 Even as the Father hath loved me, I also have loved you: abide ye in my love.

Joh 15:10 If ye keep my commandments, ye shall abide in my love; even as I have kept my Father's commandments, and abide in his love.

Joh 15:11 These things have I spoken unto you, that my joy may be in you, and that your joy may be made full.

Joh 15:12 This is my commandment, that ye love one another, even as I have loved you.

Joh 15:13 Greater love hath no man than this, that a man lay down his life for his friends.

Joh 15:14 Ye are my friends, if ye do the things which I command you.

Joh 15:15 No longer do I call you servants; for the servant knoweth not what his lord doeth: but I have called you friends; for all things that I heard from my Father, I have made known unto you.

Joh 15:16 Ye did not choose me, but I chose you, and appointed you, that ye should go and bear fruit, and that your fruit should abide: that whatsoever ye shall ask of the Father in my name, he may give it you.

Joh 15:17 These things I command you, that ye may love one another.

Joh 15:18 If the world hateth you, ye know that it hath hated me before it hated you.

Joh 15:19 If ye were of the world, the world would love its own: but because ye are not of the world, but I chose you out of the world, therefore the world hateth you.

Joh 15:20 Remember the word that I said unto you, A servant is not greater than his lord. If they persecuted me, they will also persecute you; if they kept my word, they will keep yours also.

Joh 15:21 But all these things will they do unto you for my name's sake, because they know not him that sent me.

Joh 15:22 If I had not come and spoken unto them, they had not had sin: but now they have no excuse for their sin.

Joh 15:23 He that hateth me hateth my Father also.

Joh 15:24 If I had not done among them the works which none other did, they had not had sin: but now have they both seen and hated both me and my Father.

Joh 15:25 But this cometh to pass, that the word may be fulfilled that is written in their law, They hated me without a cause.

Joh 15:26 But when the Comforter is come, whom I will send unto you from the Father, even the Spirit of truth, which proceedeth from the Father, he shall bear witness of me:

Joh 15:27 and ye also bear witness, because ye have been with me from the beginning.

Chapter 16.

Joh 16:1 These things have I spoken unto you, that ye should not be caused to stumble.

Joh 16:2 They shall put you out of the synagogues: yea, the hour cometh, that whosoever killeth you shall think that he offereth service unto God.

Joh 16:3 And these things will they do, because they have not known the Father, nor me.

Joh 16:4 But these things have I spoken unto you, that when their hour is come, ye may remember them, how that I told you. And these things I said not unto you from the beginning, because I was with you.

Joh 16:5 But now I go unto him that sent me; and none of you asketh me, Whither goest thou?

Joh 16:6 But because I have spoken these things unto you, sorrow hath filled your heart.

Joh 16:7 Nevertheless I tell you the truth: It is expedient for you that I go away; for if I go not away, the Comforter will not come unto you; but if I go, I will send him unto you.

Joh 16:8 And he, when he is come, will convict the world in respect of sin, and of righteousness, and of judgment:

Joh 16:9 of sin, because they believe not on me;

Joh 16:10 of righteousness, because I go to the Father, and ye behold me no more;

Joh 16:11 of judgment, because the prince of this world hath been judged.

Joh 16:12 I have yet many things to say unto you, but ye cannot bear them now.

Joh 16:13 Howbeit when he, the Spirit of truth, is come, he shall guide you into all the truth: for he shall not speak from himself; but what things soever he shall hear, these shall he speak: and he shall declare unto you the things that are to come.

Joh 16:14 He shall glorify me: for he shall take of mine, and shall declare it unto you.

Joh 16:15 All things whatsoever the Father hath are mine: therefore said I, that he taketh of mine, and shall declare it unto you.

Joh 16:16 A little while, and ye behold me no more; and again a little while, and ye shall see me.

Joh 16:17 Some of his disciples therefore said one to another, What is this that he saith unto us, A little while, and ye behold me not; and again a little while, and ye shall see me: and, Because I go to the Father?

Joh 16:18 They said therefore, What is this that he saith, A little while? We know not what he saith.

Joh 16:19 Jesus perceived that they were desirous to ask him, and he said unto them, Do ye inquire among yourselves concerning this, that I said, A little while, and ye behold me not, and again a little while, and ye shall see me?

Joh 16:20 Verily, verily, I say unto you, that ye shall weep and lament, but the world shall rejoice: ye shall be sorrowful, but your sorrow shall be turned into joy.

Joh 16:21 A woman when she is in travail hath sorrow, because her hour is come: but when she is delivered of the child, she remembereth no more the anguish, for the joy that a man is born into the world.

Joh 16:22 And ye therefore now have sorrow: but I will see you again, and your heart shall rejoice, and your joy no one taketh away from you.

Joh 16:23 And in that day ye shall ask me no question. Verily, verily, I say unto you, if ye shall ask anything of the Father, he will give it you in my name.

Joh 16:24 Hitherto have ye asked nothing in my name: ask, and ye shall receive, that your joy may be made full.

Joh 16:25 These things have I spoken unto you in dark sayings: the hour cometh, when I shall no more speak unto you in dark sayings, but shall tell you plainly of the Father.

Joh 16:26 In that day ye shall ask in my name: and I say not unto you, that I will pray the Father for you;

Joh 16:27 for the Father himself loveth you, because ye have loved me, and have believed that I came forth from the Father.

Joh 16:28 I came out from the Father, and am come into the world: again, I leave the world, and go unto the Father.

Joh 16:29 His disciples say, Lo, now speakest thou plainly, and speakest no dark saying.

Joh 16:30 Now know we that thou knowest all things, and needest not that any man should ask thee: by this we believe that thou camest forth from God.

Joh 16:31 Jesus answered them, Do ye now believe?

Joh 16:32 Behold, the hour cometh, yea, is come, that ye shall be scattered, every man to his own, and shall leave me alone: and yet I am not alone, because the Father is with me.

Joh 16:33 These things have I spoken unto you, that in me ye may have peace. In the world ye have tribulation: but be of good cheer; I have overcome the world.

Chapter 17.

Joh 17:1 These things spake Jesus; and lifting up his eyes to heaven, he said, Father, the hour is come; glorify thy Son, that the son may glorify thee:

Joh 17:2 even as thou gavest him authority over all flesh, that to all whom thou hast given him, he should give eternal life.

Joh 17:3 And this is life eternal, that they should know thee the only true God, and him whom thou didst send, even Jesus Christ.

Joh 17:4 I glorified thee on the earth, having accomplished the work which thou hast given me to do.

Joh 17:5 And now, Father, glorify thou me with thine own self with the glory which I had with thee before the world was.

Joh 17:6 I manifested thy name unto the men whom thou gavest me out of the world: thine they were, and thou gavest them to me; and they have kept thy word.

Joh 17:7 Now they know that all things whatsoever thou hast given me are from thee:

Joh 17:8 for the words which thou gavest me I have given unto them; and they received them, and knew of a truth that I came forth from thee, and they believed that thou didst send me.

Joh 17:9 I pray for them: I pray not for the world, but for those whom thou hast given me; for they are thine:

Joh 17:10 and all things that are mine are thine, and thine are mine: and I am glorified in them.

Joh 17:11 And I am no more in the world, and these are in the world, and I come to thee. Holy Father, keep them in thy name which thou hast given me, that they may be one, even as we are.

Joh 17:12 While I was with them, I kept them in thy name which thou hast given me: and I guarded them, and not one of them perished, but the son of perdition; that the scripture might be fulfilled.

Joh 17:13 But now I come to thee; and these things I speak in the world, that they may have my joy made full in themselves.

Joh 17:14 I have given them thy word; and the world hated them, because they are not of the world, even as I am not of the world.

Joh 17:15 I pray not that thou shouldest take them from the world, but that thou shouldest keep them from the evil one.

Joh 17:16 They are not of the world even as I am not of the world.

Joh 17:17 Sanctify them in the truth: thy word is truth.

Joh 17:18 As thou didst send me into the world, even so sent I them into the world.

Joh 17:19 And for their sakes I sanctify myself, that they themselves also may be sanctified in truth.

Joh 17:20 Neither for these only do I pray, but for them also that believe on me through their word;

Joh 17:21 that they may all be one; even as thou, Father, art in me, and I in thee, that they also may be in us: that the world may believe that thou didst send me.

Joh 17:22 And the glory which thou hast given me I have given unto them; that they may be one, even as we are one;

Joh 17:23 I in them, and thou in me, that they may be perfected into one; that the world may know that thou didst send me, and lovedst them, even as thou lovedst me.

Joh 17:24 Father, I desire that they also whom thou hast given me be with me where I am, that they may behold my glory, which thou hast given me: for thou lovedst me before the foundation of the world.

Joh 17:25 O righteous Father, the world knew thee not, but I knew thee; and these knew that thou didst send me;

Joh 17:26 and I made known unto them thy name, and will make it known; that the love wherewith thou lovedst me may be in them, and I in them.

Chapter 18.

Joh 18:1 When Jesus had spoken these words, he went forth with his disciples over the brook Kidron, where was a garden, into which he entered, himself and his disciples.

Joh 18:2 Now Judas also, who betrayed him, knew the place: for Jesus oft-times resorted thither with his disciples.

Joh 18:3 Judas then, having received the band of soldiers, and officers from the chief priests and the Pharisees, cometh thither with lanterns and torches and weapons.

Joh 18:4 Jesus therefore, knowing all the things that were coming upon him, went forth, and saith unto them, Whom seek ye?

Joh 18:5 They answered him, Jesus of Nazareth. Jesus saith unto them, I am he. And Judas also, who betrayed him, was standing with them.

Joh 18:6 When therefore he said unto them, I am he, they went backward, and fell to the ground.

Joh 18:7 Again therefore he asked them, Whom seek ye? And they said, Jesus of Nazareth.

Joh 18:8 Jesus answered, I told you that I am he; if therefore ye seek me, let these go their way:

Joh 18:9 that the word might be fulfilled which he spake, Of those whom thou hast given me I lost not one.

Joh 18:10 Simon Peter therefore having a sword drew it, and struck the high priest's servant, and cut off his right ear. Now the servant's name was Malchus.

Joh 18:11 Jesus therefore said unto Peter, Put up the sword into the sheath: the cup which the Father hath given me, shall I not drink it?

Joh 18:12 So the band and the chief captain, and the officers of the Jews, seized Jesus and bound him,

Joh 18:13 and led him to Annas first; for he was father in law to Caiaphas, who was high priest that year.

Joh 18:14 Now Caiaphas was he that gave counsel to the Jews, that it was expedient that one man should die for the people.

Joh 18:15 And Simon Peter followed Jesus, and so did another disciple. Now that disciple was known unto the high priest, and entered in with Jesus into the court of the high priest;

Joh 18:16 but Peter was standing at the door without. So the other disciple, who was known unto the high priest, went out and spake unto her that kept the door, and brought in Peter.

Joh 18:17 The maid therefore that kept the door saith unto Peter, Art thou also one of this man's disciples? He saith, I am not.

Joh 18:18 Now the servants and the officers were standing there, having made a fire of coals; for it was cold; and they were warming themselves: and Peter also was with them, standing and warming himself.

Joh 18:19 The high priest therefore asked Jesus of his disciples, and of his teaching.

Joh 18:20 Jesus answered him, I have spoken openly to the world; I ever taught in synagogues, and in the temple, where all the Jews come together; and in secret spake I nothing.

Joh 18:21 Why askest thou me? Ask them that have heard me, what I spake unto them: behold, these know the things which I said.

Joh 18:22 And when he had said this, one of the officers standing by struck Jesus with his hand, saying, Answerest thou the high priest so?

Joh 18:23 Jesus answered him, If I have spoken evil, bear witness of the evil: but if well, why smitest thou me?

Joh 18:24 Annas therefore sent him bound unto Caiaphas the high priest.

Joh 18:25 Now Simon Peter was standing and warming himself. They said therefore unto him, Art thou also one of his disciples? He denied, and said, I am not.

Joh 18:26 One of the servants of the high priest, being a kinsman of him whose ear Peter cut off, saith, Did not I see thee in the garden with him?

Joh 18:27 Peter therefore denied again: and straightway the cock crew.

Joh 18:28 They lead Jesus therefore from Caiaphas into the Praetorium: and it was early; and they themselves entered not into the Praetorium, that they might not be defiled, but might eat the passover.

Joh 18:29 Pilate therefore went out unto them, and saith, What accusation bring ye against this man?

Joh 18:30 They answered and said unto him, If this man were not an evildoer, we should not have delivered him up unto thee.

Joh 18:31 Pilate therefore said unto them, Take him yourselves, and judge him according to your law. The Jews said unto him, It is not lawful for us to put any man to death:

Joh 18:32 that the word of Jesus might be fulfilled, which he spake, signifying by what manner of death he should die.

Joh 18:33 Pilate therefore entered again into the Praetorium, and called Jesus, and said unto him, Art thou the King of the Jews?

Joh 18:34 Jesus answered, Sayest thou this of thyself, or did others tell it thee concerning me?

Joh 18:35 Pilate answered, Am I a Jew? Thine own nation and the chief priests delivered thee unto me: what hast thou done?

Joh 18:36 Jesus answered, My kingdom is not of this world: if my kingdom were of this world, then would my servants fight, that I should not be delivered to the Jews: but now is my kingdom not from hence.

Joh 18:37 Pilate therefore said unto him, Art thou a king then? Jesus answered, Thou sayest that I am a king. To this end have I been born, and to this end am I come into the world, that I should bear witness unto the truth. Every one that is of the truth heareth my voice.

Joh 18:38 Pilate saith unto him, What is truth? And when he had said this, he went out again unto the Jews, and saith unto them, I find no crime in him.

Joh 18:39 But ye have a custom, that I should release unto you one at the passover: will ye therefore that I release unto you the King of the Jews?

Joh 18:40 They cried out therefore again, saying, Not this man, but Barabbas. Now Barabbas was a robber.

Chapter 19.

Joh 19:1 Then Pilate therefore took Jesus, and scourged him.

Joh 19:2 And the soldiers platted a crown of thorns, and put it on his head, and arrayed him in a purple garment;

Joh 19:3 and they came unto him, and said, Hail, King of the Jews! and they struck him with their hands.

Joh 19:4 And Pilate went out again, and saith unto them, Behold, I bring him out to you, that ye may know that I find no crime in him.

Joh 19:5 Jesus therefore came out, wearing the crown of thorns and the purple garment. And Pilate saith unto them, Behold, the man!

Joh 19:6 When therefore the chief priests and the officers saw him, they cried out, saying, Crucify him, crucify him! Pilate saith unto them, Take him yourselves, and crucify him: for I find no crime in him.

Joh 19:7 The Jews answered him, We have a law, and by that law he ought to die, because he made himself the Son of God.

Joh 19:8 When Pilate therefore heard this saying, he was the more afraid;

Joh 19:9 and he entered into the Praetorium again, and saith unto Jesus, Whence art thou? But Jesus gave him no answer.

Joh 19:10 Pilate therefore saith unto him, Speakest thou not unto me? Knowest thou not that I have power to release thee, and have power to crucify thee?

Joh 19:11 Jesus answered him, Thou wouldest have no power against me, except it were given thee from above: therefore he that delivered me unto thee hath greater sin.

Joh 19:12 Upon this Pilate sought to release him: but the Jews cried out, saying, If thou release this man, thou art not Caesar's friend: every one that maketh himself a king speaketh against Caesar.

Joh 19:13 When Pilate therefore heard these words, he brought Jesus out, and sat down on the judgment-seat at a place called The Pavement, but in Hebrew, Gabbatha.

Joh 19:14 Now it was the Preparation of the passover: it was about the sixth hour. And he saith unto the Jews, Behold, your King!

Joh 19:15 They therefore cried out, Away with him, away with him, crucify him! Pilate saith unto them, Shall I crucify your King? The chief priests answered, We have no king but Caesar.

Joh 19:16 Then therefore he delivered him unto them to be crucified.

Joh 19:17 They took Jesus therefore: and he went out, bearing the cross for himself, unto the place called The place of a skull, which is called in Hebrew, Golgotha:

Joh 19:18 where they crucified him, and with him two others, on either side one, and Jesus in the midst.

Joh 19:19 And Pilate wrote a title also, and put it on the cross. And there was written, JESUS OF NAZARETH, THE KING OF THE JEWS.

Joh 19:20 This title therefore read many of the Jews, for the place where Jesus was crucified was nigh to the city; and it was written in Hebrew, and in Latin, and in Greek.

Joh 19:21 The chief priests of the Jews therefore said to Pilate, Write not, The King of the Jews; but that he said, I am King of the Jews.

Joh 19:22 Pilate answered, What I have written I have written.

Joh 19:23 The soldiers therefore, when they had crucified Jesus, took his garments and made four parts, to every soldier a part; and also the coat: now the coat was without seam, woven from the top throughout.

Joh 19:24 They said therefore one to another, Let us not rend it, but cast lots for it, whose it shall be: that the scripture might be fulfilled, which saith, They parted my garments among them, And upon my vesture did they cast lots.

Joh 19:25 These things therefore the soldiers did. But there were standing by the cross of Jesus his mother, and his mother's sister, Mary the wife of Clopas, and Mary Magdalene.

Joh 19:26 When Jesus therefore saw his mother, and the disciple standing by whom he loved, he saith unto his mother, Woman, behold thy son!

Joh 19:27 Then saith he to the disciple, Behold, thy mother! And from that hour the disciple took her unto his own home.

Joh 19:28 After this Jesus, knowing that all things are now finished, that the scripture might be accomplished, saith, I thirst.

Joh 19:29 There was set there a vessel full of vinegar: so they put a sponge full of the vinegar upon hyssop, and brought it to his mouth.

Joh 19:30 When Jesus therefore had received the vinegar, he said, It is finished: and he bowed his head, and gave up his spirit.

Joh 19:31 The Jews therefore, because it was the Preparation, that the bodies should not remain on the cross upon the sabbath (for the day of that sabbath was a high day), asked of Pilate that their legs might be broken, and that they might be taken away.

Joh 19:32 The soldiers therefore came, and brake the legs of the first, and of the other that was crucified with him:

Joh 19:33 but when they came to Jesus, and saw that he was dead already, they brake not his legs:

Joh 19:34 howbeit one of the soldiers with a spear pierced his side, and straightway there came out blood and water.

Joh 19:35 And he that hath seen hath borne witness, and his witness is true: and he knoweth that he saith true, that ye also may believe.

Joh 19:36 For these things came to pass, that the scripture might be fulfilled, A bone of him shall not be broken.

Joh 19:37 And again another scripture saith, They shall look on him whom they pierced.

Joh 19:38 And after these things Joseph of Arimathaea, being a disciple of Jesus, but secretly for fear of the Jews, asked of Pilate that he might take away the body of Jesus: and Pilate gave him leave. He came therefore, and took away his body.

Joh 19:39 And there came also Nicodemus, he who at the first came to him by night, bringing a mixture of myrrh and aloes, about a hundred pounds.

Joh 19:40 So they took the body of Jesus, and bound it in linen cloths with the spices, as the custom of the Jews is to bury.

Joh 19:41 Now in the place where he was crucified there was a garden; and in the garden a new tomb wherein was never man yet laid.

Joh 19:42 There then because of the Jews' Preparation (for the tomb was nigh at hand) they laid Jesus.

Chapter 20.

Joh 20:1 Now on the first day of the week cometh Mary Magdalene early, while it was yet dark, unto the tomb, and seeth the stone taken away from the tomb.

Joh 20:2 She runneth therefore, and cometh to Simon Peter, and to the other disciple whom Jesus loved, and saith unto them, They have taken away the Lord out of the tomb, and we know not where they have laid him.

Joh 20:3 Peter therefore went forth, and the other disciple, and they went toward the tomb.

Joh 20:4 And they ran both together: and the other disciple outran Peter, and came first to the tomb;

Joh 20:5 and stooping and looking in, he seeth the linen cloths lying; yet entered he not in.

Joh 20:6 Simon Peter therefore also cometh, following him, and entered into the tomb; and he beholdeth the linen cloths lying,

Joh 20:7 and the napkin, that was upon his head, not lying with the linen cloths, but rolled up in a place by itself.

Joh 20:8 Then entered in therefore the other disciple also, who came first to the tomb, and he saw, and believed.

Joh 20:9 For as yet they knew not the scripture, that he must rise from the dead.

Joh 20:10 So the disciples went away again unto their own home.

Joh 20:11 But Mary was standing without at the tomb weeping: so, as she wept, she stooped and looked into the tomb;

Joh 20:12 and she beholdeth two angels in white sitting, one at the head, and one at the feet, where the body of Jesus had lain.

Joh 20:13 And they say unto her, Woman, why weepest thou? She saith unto them, Because they have taken away my Lord, and I know not where they have laid him.

Joh 20:14 When she had thus said, she turned herself back, and beholdeth Jesus standing, and knew not that it was Jesus.

Joh 20:15 Jesus saith unto her, Woman, why weepest thou? whom seekest thou? She, supposing him to be the gardener, saith unto him, Sir, if thou hast borne him hence, tell me where thou hast laid him, and I will take him away.

Joh 20:16 Jesus saith unto her, Mary. She turneth herself, and saith unto him in Hebrew, Rabboni; which is to say, Teacher.

Joh 20:17 Jesus saith to her, Touch me not; for I am not yet ascended unto the Father: but go unto my brethren, and say to them, I ascend unto my Father and your Father, and my God and your God.

Joh 20:18 Mary Magdalene cometh and telleth the disciples, I have seen the Lord; and that he had said these things unto her.

Joh 20:19 When therefore it was evening, on that day, the first day of the week, and when the doors were shut where the disciples were, for fear of the Jews, Jesus came and stood in the midst, and saith unto them, Peace be unto you.

Joh 20:20 And when he had said this, he showed unto them his hands and his side. The disciples therefore were glad, when they saw the Lord.

Joh 20:21 Jesus therefore said to them again, Peace be unto you: as the Father hath sent me, even so send I you.

Joh 20:22 And when he had said this, he breathed on them, and saith unto them, Receive ye the Holy Spirit:

Joh 20:23 whose soever sins ye forgive, they are forgiven unto them; whose soever sins ye retain, they are retained.

Joh 20:24 But Thomas, one of the twelve, called Didymus, was not with them when Jesus came.

Joh 20:25 The other disciples therefore said unto him, We have seen the Lord. But he said unto them, Except I shall see in his hands the print of the nails, and put my hand into his side, I will not believe.

Joh 20:26 And after eight days again his disciples were within, and Thomas with them. Jesus cometh, the doors being shut, and stood in the midst, and said, Peace be unto you.

Joh 20:27 Then saith he to Thomas, Reach hither thy finger, and see my hands; and reach hither thy hand, and put it into my side: and be not faithless, but believing.

Joh 20:28 Thomas answered and said unto him, My Lord and my God.

Joh 20:29 Jesus saith unto him, Because thou hast seen me, thou hast believed: blessed are they that have not seen, and yet have believed.

Joh 20:30 Many other signs therefore did Jesus in the presence of the disciples, which are not written in this book:

Joh 20:31 but these are written, that ye may believe that Jesus is the Christ, the Son of God; and that believing ye may have life in his name.

Chapter 21.

Joh 21:1 After these things Jesus manifested himself again to the disciples at the sea of Tiberias; and he manifested himself on this wise.

Joh 21:2   There was together Simon Peter, and Thomas called Didymus, and Nathanael of Cana in Galilee, and the sons of Zebedee, and two other of his disciples.

Joh 21:3   Simon Peter saith unto them, I go a fishing. They say unto him, We also come with thee. They went forth, and entered into the boat; and that night they took nothing.

Joh 21:4   But when day was now breaking, Jesus stood on the beach: yet the disciples knew not that it was Jesus.

Joh 21:5   Jesus therefore saith unto them, Children, have ye aught to eat? They answered him, No.

Joh 21:6   And he said unto them, Cast the net on the right side of the boat, and ye shall find. They cast therefore, and now they were not able to draw it for the multitude of fishes.

Joh 21:7   That disciple therefore whom Jesus loved saith unto Peter, It is the Lord. So when Simon Peter heard that it was the Lord, he girt his coat about him (for he was naked), and cast himself into the sea.

Joh 21:8   But the other disciples came in the little boat (for they were not far from the land, but about two hundred cubits off), dragging the net full of fishes.

Joh 21:9   So when they got out upon the land, they see a fire of coals there, and fish laid thereon, and bread.

Joh 21:10   Jesus saith unto them, Bring of the fish which ye have now taken.

Joh 21:11   Simon Peter therefore went up, and drew the net to land, full of great fishes, a hundred and fifty and three: and for all there were so many, the net was not rent.

Joh 21:12   Jesus saith unto them, Come and break your fast. And none of the disciples durst inquire of him, Who art thou? knowing that it was the Lord.

Joh 21:13   Jesus cometh, and taketh the bread, and giveth them, and the fish likewise.

Joh 21:14   This is now the third time that Jesus was manifested to the disciples, after that he was risen from the dead.

Joh 21:15   So when they had broken their fast, Jesus saith to Simon Peter, Simon, son of John, lovest thou me more than these? He saith unto him, Yea, Lord; thou knowest that I love thee. He saith unto him, Feed my lambs.

Joh 21:16   He saith to him again a second time, Simon, son of John, lovest thou me? He saith unto him, Yea, Lord; thou knowest that I love thee. He saith unto him, Tend my sheep.

Joh 21:17   He saith unto him the third time, Simon, son of John, lovest thou me? Peter was grieved because he said unto him the third time, Lovest thou me? And he said unto him, Lord, thou knowest all things; thou knowest that I love thee. Jesus saith unto him, Feed my sheep.

Joh 21:18   Verily, verily, I say unto thee, When thou wast young, thou girdedst thyself, and walkedst whither thou wouldest: but when thou shalt be old, thou shalt stretch forth thy hands, and another shall gird thee, and carry thee whither thou wouldest not.

Joh 21:19   Now this he spake, signifying by what manner of death he should glorify God. And when he had spoken this, he saith unto him, Follow me.

Joh 21:20   Peter, turning about, seeth the disciple whom Jesus loved following; who also leaned back on his breast at the supper, and said, Lord, who is he that betrayeth thee?

Joh 21:21   Peter therefore seeing him saith to Jesus, Lord, and what shall this man do?

Joh 21:22 Jesus saith unto him, If I will that he tarry till I come, what is that to thee? Follow thou me.

Joh 21:23 This saying therefore went forth among the brethren, that that disciple should not die: yet Jesus said not unto him, that he should not die; but, If I will that he tarry till I come, what is that to thee?

Joh 21:24 This is the disciple that beareth witness of these things, and wrote these things: and we know that his witness is true.

Joh 21:25 And there are also many other things which Jesus did, the which if they should be written every one, I suppose that even the world itself would not contain the books that should be written.

6. Acts

Chapter 1.

Act 1:1 The former treatise I made, O Theophilus, concerning all that Jesus began both to do and to teach,

Act 1:2 until the day in which he was received up, after that he had given commandment through the Holy Spirit unto the apostles whom he had chosen:

Act 1:3 to whom he also showed himself alive after his passion by many proofs, appearing unto them by the space of forty days, and speaking the things concerning the kingdom of God:

Act 1:4 and, being assembled together with them, he charged them not to depart from Jerusalem, but to wait for the promise of the Father, which, said he, ye heard from me:

Act 1:5 for John indeed baptized with water; but ye shall be baptized in the Holy Spirit not many days hence.

Act 1:6 They therefore, when they were come together, asked him, saying, Lord, dost thou at this time restore the kingdom to Israel?

Act 1:7 And he said unto them, It is not for you to know times or seasons, which the Father hath set within His own authority.

Act 1:8 But ye shall receive power, when the Holy Spirit is come upon you: and ye shall be my witnesses both in Jerusalem, and in all Judaea and Samaria, and unto the uttermost part of the earth.

Act 1:9 And when he had said these things, as they were looking, he was taken up; and a cloud received him out of their sight.

Act 1:10 And while they were looking stedfastly into heaven as he went, behold, two men stood by them in white apparel;

Act 1:11 who also said, Ye men of Galilee, why stand ye looking into heaven? this Jesus, who was received up from you into heaven shall so come in like manner as ye beheld him going into heaven.

Act 1:12 Then returned they unto Jerusalem from the mount called Olivet, which is nigh unto Jerusalem, a Sabbath day's journey off.

Act 1:13 And when they were come in, they went up into the upper chamber, where they were abiding; both Peter and John and James and Andrew, Philip and Thomas, Bartholomew and Matthew, James the son of Alphaeus, and Simon the Zealot, and Judas the son of James.

Act 1:14 These all with one accord continued stedfastly in prayer, with the women, and Mary the mother of Jesus, and with his brethren.

Act 1:15 And in these days Peter stood up in the midst of the brethren, and said (and there was a multitude of persons gathered together, about a hundred and twenty),

Act 1:16 Brethren, it was needful that the Scripture should be fulfilled, which the Holy Spirit spake before by the mouth of David concerning Judas, who was guide to them that took Jesus.

Act 1:17 For he was numbered among us, and received his portion in this ministry.

Act 1:18 (Now this man obtained a field with the reward of his iniquity; and falling headlong, he burst asunder in the midst, and all his bowels gushed out.

Act 1:19 And it became known to all the dwellers at Jerusalem; insomuch that in their language that field was called Akeldama, that is, The field of blood.)

Act 1:20 For it is written in the book of Psalms, Let his habitation be made desolate, And let no man dwell therein: and, His office let another take.

Act 1:21 Of the men therefore that have companied with us all the time that the Lord Jesus went in and went out among us,

Act 1:22 beginning from the baptism of John, unto the day that he was received up from us, of these must one become a witness with us of his resurrection.

Act 1:23 And they put forward two, Joseph called Barsabbas, who was surnamed Justus, and Matthias.

Act 1:24 And they prayed, and said, Thou, Lord, who knowest the hearts of all men, show of these two the one whom thou hast chosen,

Act 1:25 to take the place in this ministry and apostleship from which Judas fell away, that he might go to his own place.

Act 1:26 And they gave lots for them; and the lot fell upon Matthias; and he was numbered with the eleven apostles.

Chapter 2.

Act 2:1 And when the day of Pentecost was now come, they were all together in one place.

Act 2:2 And suddenly there came from heaven a sound as of the rushing of a mighty wind, and it filled all the house where they were sitting.

Act 2:3 And there appeared unto them tongues parting asunder, like as of fire; and it sat upon each one of them.

Act 2:4 And they were all filled with the Holy Spirit, and began to speak with other tongues, as the Spirit gave them utterance.

Act 2:5 Now there were dwelling at Jerusalem Jews, devout men, from every nation under heaven.

Act 2:6 And when this sound was heard, the multitude came together, and were confounded, because that every man heard them speaking in his own language.

Act 2:7 And they were all amazed and marvelled, saying, Behold, are not all these that speak Galilaeans?

Act 2:8 And how hear we, every man in our own language wherein we were born?

Act 2:9 Parthians and Medes and Elamites, and the dwellers in Mesopotamia, in Judaea and Cappadocia, in Pontus and Asia,

Act 2:10 in Phrygia and Pamphylia, in Egypt and the parts of Libya about Cyrene, and sojourners from Rome, both Jews and proselytes,

Act 2:11 Cretans and Arabians, we hear them speaking in our tongues the mighty works of God.

Act 2:12 And they were all amazed, and were perplexed, saying one to another, What meaneth this?

Act 2:13 But others mocking said, They are filled with new wine.

Act 2:14 But Peter, standing up with the eleven, lifted up his voice, and spake forth unto them, saying, Ye men of Judaea, and all ye that dwell at Jerusalem, be this known unto you, and give ear unto my words.

Act 2:15 For these are not drunken, as ye suppose; seeing it is but the third hour of the day;

Act 2:16 but this is that which hath been spoken through the prophet Joel:

Act 2:17 And it shall be in the last days, saith God, I will pour forth of My Spirit upon all flesh: And your sons and your daughters shall prophesy, And your young men shall see visions, And your old men shall dream dreams:

Act 2:18 Yea and on My servants and on My handmaidens in those days Will I pour forth of My Spirit; and they shall prophesy.

Act 2:19 And I will show wonders in the heaven above, And signs on the earth beneath; Blood, and fire, and vapor of smoke:

Act 2:20 The sun shall be turned into darkness, And the moon into blood, Before the day of the Lord come, That great and notable day.

Act 2:21 And it shall be, that whosoever shall call on the name of the Lord shall be saved.

Act 2:22 Ye men of Israel, hear these words: Jesus of Nazareth, a man approved of God unto you by mighty works and wonders and signs which God did by him in the midst of you, even as ye yourselves know;

Act 2:23 him, being delivered up by the determinate counsel and foreknowledge of God, ye by the hand of lawless men did crucify and slay:

Act 2:24 whom God raised up, having loosed the pangs of death: because it was not possible that he should be holden of it.

Act 2:25 For David saith concerning him, I beheld the Lord always before my face; For he is on my right hand, that I should not be moved:

Act 2:26 Therefore my heart was glad, and my tongue rejoiced; Moreover my flesh also shall dwell in hope:

Act 2:27 Because thou wilt not leave my soul unto Hades, Neither wilt thou give thy Holy One to see corruption.

Act 2:28 Thou madest known unto me the ways of life; Thou shalt make me full of gladness with thy countenance.

Act 2:29 Brethren, I may say unto you freely of the patriarch David, that he both died and was buried, and his tomb is with us unto this day.

Act 2:30 Being therefore a prophet, and knowing that God had sworn with an oath to him, that of the fruit of his loins he would set one upon his throne;

Act 2:31 he foreseeing this spake of the resurrection of the Christ, that neither was he left unto Hades, nor did his flesh see corruption.

Act 2:32 This Jesus did God raise up, whereof we all are witnesses.

Act 2:33 Being therefore by the right hand of God exalted, and having received of the Father the promise of the Holy Spirit, he hath poured forth this, which ye see and hear.

Act 2:34 For David ascended not into the heavens: but he saith himself, The Lord said unto my Lord, Sit thou on my right hand,

Act 2:35 Till I make thine enemies the footstool of thy feet.

Act 2:36 Let all the house of Israel therefore know assuredly, that God hath made him both Lord and Christ, this Jesus whom ye crucified.

Act 2:37 Now when they heard this, they were pricked in their heart, and said unto Peter and the rest of the apostles, Brethren, what shall we do?

Act 2:38 And Peter said unto them, Repent ye, and be baptized every one of you in the name of Jesus Christ unto the remission of your sins; and ye shall receive the gift of the Holy Spirit.

Act 2:39 For to you is the promise, and to your children, and to all that are afar off, even as many as the Lord our God shall call unto him.

Act 2:40 And with many other words he testified, and exhorted them, saying, Save yourselves from this crooked generation.

Act 2:41 They then that received his word were baptized: and there were added unto them in that day about three thousand souls.

Act 2:42 And they continued stedfastly in the apostles' teaching and fellowship, in the breaking of bread and the prayers.

Act 2:43 And fear came upon every soul: and many wonders and signs were done through the apostles.

Act 2:44 And all that believed were together, and had all things common;

Act 2:45 and they sold their possessions and goods, and parted them to all, according as any man had need.

Act 2:46 And day by day, continuing stedfastly with one accord in the temple, and breaking bread at home, they took their food with gladness and singleness of heart,

Act 2:47 praising God, and having favor with all the people. And the Lord added to them day by day those that were saved.

Chapter 3.

Act 3:1 Now Peter and John were going up into the temple at the hour of prayer, being the ninth hour.

Act 3:2 And a certain man that was lame from his mother's womb was carried, whom they laid daily at the door of the temple which is called Beautiful, to ask alms of them that entered into the temple;

Act 3:3 who seeing Peter and John about to go into the temple, asked to receive an alms.

Act 3:4 And Peter, fastening his eyes upon him, with John, said, Look on us.

Act 3:5 And he gave heed unto them, expecting to receive something from them.

Act 3:6 But Peter said, Silver and gold have I none; but what I have, that give I thee. In the name of Jesus Christ of Nazareth, walk.

Act 3:7 And he took him by the right hand, and raised him up: and immediately his feet and his ankle-bones received strength.

Act 3:8 And leaping up, he stood, and began to walk; and he entered with them into the temple, walking, and leaping, and praising God.

Act 3:9 And all the people saw him walking and praising God:

Act 3:10 and they took knowledge of him, that it was he that sat for alms at the Beautiful Gate of the temple; and they were filled with wonder and amazement at that which had happened unto him.

Act 3:11 And as he held Peter and John, all the people ran together unto them in the porch that is called Solomon's, greatly wondering.

Act 3:12 And when Peter saw it, he answered unto the people, Ye men of Israel, why marvel ye at this man? or why fasten ye your eyes on us, as though by our own power or godliness we had made him to walk?

Act 3:13 The God of Abraham, and of Isaac, and of Jacob, the God of our fathers, hath glorified his Servant Jesus; whom ye delivered up, and denied before the face of Pilate, when he had determined to release him.

Act 3:14 But ye denied the Holy and Righteous One, and asked for a murderer to be granted unto you,

Act 3:15 and killed the Prince of life; whom God raised from the dead; whereof we are witnesses.

Act 3:16 And by faith in his name hath his name made this man strong, whom ye behold and know: yea, the faith which is through him hath given him this perfect soundness in the presence of you all.

Act 3:17 And now, brethren, I know that in ignorance ye did it, as did also your rulers.

Act 3:18 But the things which God foreshowed by the mouth of all the prophets, that his Christ should suffer, he thus fulfilled.

Act 3:19 Repent ye therefore, and turn again, that your sins may be blotted out, that so there may come seasons of refreshing from the presence of the Lord;

Act 3:20 and that he may send the Christ who hath been appointed for you, even Jesus:

Act 3:21 whom the heaven must receive until the times of restoration of all things, whereof God spake by the mouth of His holy prophets that have been from of old.

Act 3:22 Moses indeed said, A prophet shall the Lord God raise up unto you from among your brethren, like unto me. To him shall ye hearken in all things whatsoever he shall speak unto you.

Act 3:23 And it shall be, that every soul that shall not hearken to that prophet, shall be utterly destroyed from among the people.

Act 3:24 Yea and all the prophets from Samuel and them that followed after, as many as have spoken, they also told of these days.

Act 3:25 Ye are the sons of the prophets, and of the covenant which God made with your fathers, saying unto Abraham, And in thy seed shall all the families of the earth be blessed.

Act 3:26 Unto you first God, having raised up his Servant, sent him to bless you, in turning away every one of you from your iniquities.

Chapter 4.

Act 4:1 And as they spake unto the people, the priests and the captain of the temple and the Sadducees came upon them,

Act 4:2 being sore troubled because they taught the people, and proclaimed in Jesus the resurrection from the dead.

Act 4:3 And they laid hands on them, and put them in ward unto the morrow: for it was now eventide.

Act 4:4 But many of them that heard the word believed; and the number of the men came to be about five thousand.

Act 4:5 And it came to pass on the morrow, that their rulers and elders and scribes were gathered together in Jerusalem;

Act 4:6 and Annas the high priest was there, and Caiaphas, and John, and Alexander, and as many as were of the kindred of the high priest.

Act 4:7 And when they had set them in the midst, they inquired, By what power, or in what name, have ye done this?

Act 4:8 Then Peter, filled with the Holy Spirit, said unto them, Ye rulers of the people, and elders,

Act 4:9 if we this day are examined concerning a good deed done to an impotent man, by what means this man is made whole;

Act 4:10 be it known unto you all, and to all the people of Israel, that in the name of Jesus Christ of Nazareth, whom ye crucified, whom God raised from the dead, even in him doth this man stand here before you whole.

Act 4:11 He is the stone which was set at nought of you the builders, which was made the head of the corner.

Act 4:12 And in none other is there salvation: for neither is there any other name under heaven, that is given among men, wherein we must be saved.

Act 4:13 Now when they beheld the boldness of Peter and John, and had perceived that they were unlearned and ignorant men, they marvelled; and they took knowledge of them, that they had been with Jesus.

Act 4:14 And seeing the man that was healed standing with them, they could say nothing against it.

Act 4:15 But when they had commanded them to go aside out of the council, they conferred among themselves,

Act 4:16 saying, What shall we do to these men? for that indeed a notable miracle hath been wrought through them, is manifest to all that dwell in Jerusalem; and we cannot deny it.

Act 4:17 But that it spread no further among the people, let us threaten them, that they speak henceforth to no man in this name.

Act 4:18 And they called them, and charged them not to speak at all nor teach in the name of Jesus.

Act 4:19 But Peter and John answered and said unto them, Whether it is right in the sight of God to hearken unto you rather than unto God, judge ye:

Act 4:20 for we cannot but speak the things which we saw and heard.

Act 4:21 And they, when they had further threatened them, let them go, finding nothing how they might punish them, because of the people; for all men glorified God for that which was done.

Act 4:22 For the man was more than forty years old, on whom this miracle of healing was wrought.

Act 4:23 And being let go, they came to their own company, and reported all that the chief priests and the elders had said unto them.

Act 4:24 And they, when they heard it, lifted up their voice to God with one accord, and said, O Lord, thou that didst make the heaven and the earth and the sea, and all that in them is:

Act 4:25 who by the Holy Spirit, by the mouth of our father David thy servant, didst say, Why did the Gentiles rage, And the peoples imagine vain things?

Act 4:26 The kings of the earth set themselves in array, And the rulers were gathered together, Against the Lord, and against his Anointed:

Act 4:27 for of a truth in this city against thy holy Servant Jesus, whom thou didst anoint, both Herod and Pontius Pilate, with the Gentiles and the peoples of Israel, were gathered together,

Act 4:28 to do whatsoever thy hand and thy council foreordained to come to pass.

Act 4:29 And now, Lord, look upon their threatenings: and grant unto thy servants to speak thy word with all boldness,

Act 4:30 while thy stretchest forth thy hand to heal; and that signs and wonders may be done through the name of thy holy Servant Jesus.

Act 4:31 And when they had prayed, the place was shaken wherein they were gathered together; and they were all filled with the Holy Spirit, and they spake the word of God with boldness.

Act 4:32 And the multitude of them that believed were of one heart and soul: and not one of them said that aught of the things which he possessed was his own; but they had all things common.

Act 4:33 And with great power gave the apostles their witness of the resurrection of the Lord Jesus: and great grace was upon them all.

Act 4:34 For neither was there among them any that lacked: for as many as were possessors of lands or houses sold them, and brought the prices of the things that were sold,

Act 4:35 and laid them at the apostles' feet: and distribution was made unto each, according as any one had need.

Act 4:36 And Joseph, who by the apostles was surnamed Barnabas (which is, being interpreted, Son of exhortation), a Levite, a man of Cyprus by race,

Act 4:37 having a field, sold it, and brought the money and laid it at the apostles' feet.

Chapter 5.

Act 5:1 But a certain man named Ananias, with Sapphira his wife, sold a possession,

Act 5:2 and kept back part of the price, his wife also being privy to it, and brought a certain part, and laid it at the apostles' feet.

Act 5:3 But Peter said, Ananias, why hath Satan filled thy heart to lie to the Holy Spirit, and to keep back part of the price of the land?

Act 5:4 While it remained, did it not remain thine own? and after it was sold, was it not in thy power? How is it that thou hast conceived this thing in thy heart? thou has not lied unto men, but unto God.

Act 5:5 And Ananias hearing these words fell down and gave up the ghost: and great fear came upon all that heard it.

Act 5:6 And the young men arose and wrapped him round, and they carried him out and buried him.

Act 5:7 And it was about the space of three hours after, when his wife, not knowing what was done, came in.

Act 5:8 And Peter answered unto her, Tell me whether ye sold the land for so much. And she said, Yea, for so much.

Act 5:9 But Peter said unto her, How is it that ye have agreed together to try the Spirit of the Lord? behold, the feet of them that have buried thy husband are at the door, and they shall carry thee out.

Act 5:10 And she fell down immediately at his feet, and gave up the ghost: and the young men came in and found her dead, and they carried her out and buried her by her husband.

Act 5:11 And great fear came upon the whole church, and upon all that heard these things.

Act 5:12 And by the hands of the apostles were many signs and wonders wrought among the people; and they were all with one accord in Solomon's porch.

Act 5:13 But of the rest durst no man join himself to them: howbeit the people magnified them;

Act 5:14 and believers were the more added to the Lord, multitudes both of them and women;

Act 5:15 insomuch that they even carried out the sick into the streets, and laid them on beds and couches, that, as Peter came by, at the least his shadow might overshadow some one of them.

Act 5:16 And there also came together the multitudes from the cities round about Jerusalem, bring sick folk, and them that were vexed with unclean spirits: and they were healed every one.

Act 5:17 But the high priest rose up, and all they that were with him (which is the sect of the Sadducees), and they were filled with jealousy,

Act 5:18 and laid hands on the apostles, and put them in public ward.

Act 5:19 But an angel of the Lord by night opened the prison doors, and brought them out, and said,

Act 5:20 Go ye, and stand and speak in the temple to the people all the words of this Life.

Act 5:21 And when they heard this, they entered into the temple about daybreak, and taught. But the high priest came, and they that were with him, and called the council together, and all the senate of the children of Israel, and sent to the prison-house to have them brought.

Act 5:22 But the officers that came found them not in the prison; and they returned, and told,

Act 5:23 saying, The prison-house we found shut in all safety, and the keepers standing at the doors: but when we had opened, we found no man within.

Act 5:24 Now when the captain of the temple and the chief priests heard these words, they were much perplexed concerning them whereunto this would grow.

Act 5:25 And there came one and told them, Behold, the men whom ye put in the prison are in the temple standing and teaching the people.

Act 5:26 Then went the captain with the officers, and brought them, but without violence; for they feared the people, lest they should be stoned.

Act 5:27 And when they had brought them, they set them before the council. And the high priest asked them,

Act 5:28 saying, We strictly charged you not to teach in this name: and behold, ye have filled Jerusalem with your teaching, and intend to bring this man's blood upon us.

Act 5:29 But Peter and the apostles answered and said, We must obey God rather than men.

Act 5:30 The God of our fathers raised up Jesus, whom ye slew, hanging him on a tree.

Act 5:31 Him did God exalt with his right hand to be a Prince and a Saviour, to give repentance to Israel, and remission of sins.

Act 5:32 And we are witnesses of these things; and so is the Holy Spirit, whom God hath given to them that obey him.

Act 5:33 But they, when they heard this, were cut to the heart, and minded to slay them.

Act 5:34 But there stood up one in the council, a Pharisee, named Gamaliel, a doctor of the law, had in honor of all the people, and commanded to put the men forth a little while.

Act 5:35 And he said unto them, Ye men of Israel, take heed to yourselves as touching these men, what ye are about to do.

Act 5:36 For before these days rose up Theudas, giving himself out to be somebody; to whom a number of men, about four hundred, joined themselves: who was slain; and all, as many as obeyed him, were dispersed, and came to nought.

Act 5:37 After this man rose up Judas of Galilee in the days of the enrolment, and drew away some of the people after him: he also perished; and all, as many as obeyed him, were scattered abroad.

Act 5:38 And now I say unto you, Refrain from these men, and let them alone: for if this counsel or this work be of men, it will be overthrown:

Act 5:39 but if it is of God, ye will not be able to overthrow them; lest haply ye be found even to be fighting against God.

Act 5:40 And to him they agreed: and when they had called the apostles unto them, they beat them and charged them not to speak in the name of Jesus, and let them go.

Act 5:41 They therefore departed from the presence of the council, rejoicing that they were counted worthy to suffer dishonor for the Name.

Act 5:42 And every day, in the temple and at home, they ceased not to teach and to preach Jesus as the Christ.

Chapter 6.

Act 6:1 Now in these days, when the number of the disciples was multiplying, there arose a murmuring of the Grecian Jews against the Hebrews, because their widows were neglected in the daily ministration.

Act 6:2 And the twelve called the multitude of the disciples unto them, and said, It is not fit that we should forsake the word of God, and serve tables.

Act 6:3 Look ye out therefore, brethren, from among you seven men of good report, full of the Spirit and of wisdom, whom we may appoint over this business.

Act 6:4 But we will continue stedfastly in prayer, and in the ministry of the word.

Act 6:5 And the saying pleased the whole multitude: and they chose Stephen, a man full of faith and of the Holy Spirit, and Philip, and Prochorus, and Nicanor, and Timon, and Parmenas, and Nicolaus a proselyte of Antioch;

Act 6:6 whom they set before the apostles: and when they had prayed, they laid their hands upon them.

Act 6:7 And the word of God increased; and the number of the disciples multiplied in Jerusalem exceedingly; and a great company of the priests were obedient to the faith.

Act 6:8 And Stephen, full of grace and power, wrought great wonders and signs among the people.

Act 6:9 But there arose certain of them that were of the synagogue called the synagogue of the Libertines, and of the Cyrenians, and of the Alexandrians, and of them of Cilicia and Asia, disputing with Stephen.

Act 6:10 And they were not able to withstand the wisdom and the Spirit by which he spake.

Act 6:11 Then they suborned men, who said, We have heard him speak blasphemous words against Moses, and against God.

Act 6:12 And they stirred up the people, and the elders, and the scribes, and came upon him, and seized him, and brought him into the council,

Act 6:13 and set up false witnesses, who said, This man ceaseth not to speak words against this holy place, and the law:

Act 6:14 for we have heard him say, that this Jesus of Nazareth shall destroy this place, and shall change the customs which Moses delivered unto us.

Act 6:15 And all that sat in the council, fastening their eyes on him, saw his face as it had been the face of an angel.

Chapter 7.

Act 7:1 And the high priest said, Are these things so?

Act 7:2 And he said, Brethren and fathers, hearken: The God of glory appeared unto our father Abraham, when he was in Mesopotamia, before he dwelt in Haran,

Act 7:3 and said unto him, Get thee out of thy land, and from thy kindred, and come into the land which I shall show thee.

Act 7:4 Then came he out of the land of the Chaldaeans, and dwelt in Haran: and from thence, when his father was dead, God removed him into this land, wherein ye now dwell:

Act 7:5 and he gave him none inheritance in it, no, not so much as to set his foot on: and he promised that he would give it to him in possession, and to his seed after him, when as yet he had no child.

Act 7:6 And God spake on this wise, that his seed should sojourn in a strange land, and that they should bring them into bondage, and treat them ill, four hundred years.

Act 7:7 And the nation to which they shall be in bondage will I judge, said God: and after that shall they come forth, and serve me in this place.

Act 7:8 And he gave him the covenant of circumcision: and so Abraham begat Isaac, and circumcised him the eighth day; and Isaac begat Jacob, and Jacob the twelve patriarchs.

Act 7:9 And the patriarchs, moved with jealousy against Joseph, sold him into Egypt: and God was with him,

Act 7:10 and delivered him out of all his afflictions, and gave him favor and wisdom before Pharaoh king of Egypt; and he made him governor over Egypt and all his house.

Act 7:11 Now there came a famine over all Egypt and Canaan, and great affliction: and our fathers found no sustenance.

Act 7:12 But when Jacob heard that there was grain in Egypt, he sent forth our fathers the first time.

Act 7:13 And at the second time Joseph was made known to his brethren; and Joseph's race became manifest unto Pharaoh.

Act 7:14 And Joseph sent, and called to him Jacob his father, and all his kindred, threescore and fifteen souls.

Act 7:15 And Jacob went down into Egypt; and he died, himself and our fathers;

Act 7:16 and they were carried over unto Shechem, and laid in the tomb that Abraham bought for a price in silver of the sons of Hamor in Shechem.

Act 7:17 But as the time of the promise drew nigh which God vouchsafed unto Abraham, the people grew and multiplied in Egypt,

Act 7:18 till there arose another king over Egypt, who knew not Joseph.

Act 7:19 The same dealt craftily with our race, and ill-treated our fathers, that they should cast out their babes to the end they might not live.

Act 7:20 At which season Moses was born, and was exceeding fair; and he was nourished three months in his father's house:

Act 7:21 and when he was cast out, Pharaoh's daughter took him up, and nourished him for her own son.

Act 7:22 And Moses was instructed in all the wisdom of the Egyptians; and he was mighty in his words and works.

Act 7:23 But when he was well-nigh forty years old, it came into his heart to visit his brethren the children of Israel.

Act 7:24 And seeing one of them suffer wrong, he defended him, and avenged him that was oppressed, smiting the Egyptian:

Act 7:25 and he supposed that his brethren understood that God by his hand was giving them deliverance; but they understood not.

Act 7:26 And the day following he appeared unto them as they strove, and would have set them at one again, saying, Sirs, ye are brethren; why do ye wrong one to another?

Act 7:27 But he that did his neighbor wrong thrust him away, saying, Who made thee a ruler and a judge over us?

Act 7:28 Wouldest thou kill me, as thou killedst the Egyptian yesterday?

Act 7:29 And Moses fled at this saying, and became a sojourner in the land of Midian, where he begat two sons.

Act 7:30 And when forty years were fulfilled, an angel appeared to him in the wilderness of Mount Sinai, in a flame of fire in a bush.

Act 7:31 And when Moses saw it, he wondered at the sight: and as he drew near to behold, there came a voice of the Lord,

Act 7:32 I am the God of thy fathers, the God of Abraham, and of Isaac, and of Jacob. And Moses trembled, and durst not behold.

Act 7:33 And the Lord said unto him, Loose the shoes from thy feet: for the place whereon thou standest is holy ground.

Act 7:34 I have surely seen the affliction of my people that is in Egypt, and have heard their groaning, and I am come down to deliver them: and now come, I will send thee into Egypt.

Act 7:35 This Moses whom they refused, saying, Who made thee a ruler and a judge? him hath God sent to be both a ruler and a deliverer with the hand of the angel that appeared to him in the bush.

Act 7:36 This man led them forth, having wrought wonders and signs in Egypt, and in the Red Sea, and in the wilderness forty years.

Act 7:37 This is that Moses, who said unto the children of Israel, A prophet shall God raise up unto you from among your brethren, like unto me.

Act 7:38 This is he that was in the church in the wilderness with the angel that spake to him in the Mount Sinai, and with our fathers: who received living oracles to give unto us:

Act 7:39 to whom our fathers would not be obedient, but thrust him from them, and turned back in their hearts unto Egypt,

Act 7:40 saying unto Aaron, Make us gods that shall go before us: for as for this Moses, who led us forth out of the land of Egypt, we know not what is become of him.

Act 7:41 And they made a calf in those days, and brought a sacrifice unto the idol, and rejoiced in the works of their hands.

Act 7:42 But God turned, and gave them up to serve the host of heaven; as it is written in the book of the prophets, Did ye offer unto me slain beasts and sacrifices Forty years in the wilderness, O house of Israel?

Act 7:43 And ye took up the tabernacle of Moloch, And the star of the god Rephan, The figures which ye made to worship them: And I will carry you away beyond Babylon.

Act 7:44 Our fathers had the tabernacle of the testimony in the wilderness, even as he appointed who spake unto Moses, that he should make it according to the figure that he had seen.

Act 7:45 Which also our fathers, in their turn, brought in with Joshua when they entered on the possession of the nations, that God thrust out before the face of our fathers, unto the days of David;

Act 7:46 who found favor in the sight of God, and asked to find a habitation for the God of Jacob.

Act 7:47 But Solomon built him a house.

Act 7:48 Howbeit the Most High dwelleth not in houses made with hands; as saith the prophet,

Act 7:49 The heaven is my throne, And the earth the footstool of my feet: What manner of house will ye build Me? saith the Lord: Or what is the place of My rest?

Act 7:50 Did not my hand make all these things?

Act 7:51 Ye stiffnecked and uncircumcised in heart and ears, ye do always resist the Holy Spirit: as your fathers did, so do ye.

Act 7:52 Which of the prophets did not your fathers persecute? and they killed them that showed before of the coming of the Righteous One; of whom ye have now become betrayers and murderers;

Act 7:53 ye who received the law as it was ordained by angels, and kept it not.

Act 7:54 Now when they heard these things, they were cut to the heart, and they gnashed on him with their teeth.

Act 7:55 But he, being full of the Holy Spirit, looked up stedfastly into heaven, and saw the glory of God, and Jesus standing on the right hand of God,

Act 7:56 and said, Behold, I see the heavens opened, and the Son of Man standing on the right hand of God.

Act 7:57 But they cried out with a loud voice, and stopped their ears, and rushed upon him with one accord;

Act 7:58 and they cast him out of the city, and stoned him: and the witnesses laid down their garments at the feet of a young man named Saul.

Act 7:59 And they stoned Stephen, calling upon the Lord, and saying, Lord Jesus, receive my spirit.

Act 7:60 And he kneeled down, and cried with a loud voice, Lord, lay not this sin to their charge. And when he had said this, he fell asleep.

Chapter 8.

Act 8:1 And Saul was consenting unto his death. And there arose on that day a great persecution against the church which was in Jerusalem; and they were all scattered abroad throughout the regions of Judaea and Samaria, except the apostles.

Act 8:2 And devout men buried Stephen, and made great lamentation over him.

Act 8:3 But Saul laid waste the church, entering into every house, and dragging men and women committed them to prison.

Act 8:4 They therefore that were scattered abroad, went about preaching the word.

Act 8:5 And Philip went down to the city of Samaria, and proclaimed unto them the Christ.

Act 8:6 And the multitudes gave heed with one accord unto the things that were spoken by Philip, when they heard, and saw the signs which he did.

Act 8:7 For from many of those that had unclean spirits, they came out, crying with a loud voice: and many that were palsied, and that were lame, were healed.

Act 8:8 And there was much joy in that city.

Act 8:9 But there was a certain man, Simon by name, who beforetime in the city used sorcery, and amazed the people of Samaria, giving out that himself was some great one:

Act 8:10 to whom they all gave heed, from the least to the greatest, saying, This man is that power of God which is called Great.

Act 8:11 And they gave heed to him, because that of long time he had amazed them with his sorceries.

Act 8:12 But when they believed Philip preaching good tidings concerning the kingdom of God and the name of Jesus Christ, they were baptized, both men and women.

Act 8:13 And Simon also himself believed: and being baptized, he continued with Philip; and beholding signs and great miracles wrought, he was amazed.

Act 8:14 Now when the apostles that were at Jerusalem heard that Samaria had received the word of God, they sent unto them Peter and John:

Act 8:15 who, when they were come down, prayed for them, that they might receive the Holy Spirit:

Act 8:16 for as yet it was fallen upon none of them: only they had been baptized into the name of the Lord Jesus.

Act 8:17 Then laid they their hands on them, and they received the Holy Spirit.

Act 8:18 Now when Simon saw that through the laying on of the apostles' hands the Holy Spirit was given, he offered them money,

Act 8:19 saying, Give me also this power, that on whomsoever I lay my hands, he may receive the Holy Spirit.

Act 8:20 But Peter said unto him, Thy silver perish with thee, because thou hast thought to obtain the gift of God with money.

Act 8:21 Thou hast neither part nor lot in this matter: for thy heart is not right before God.

Act 8:22 Repent therefore of this thy wickedness, and pray the Lord, if perhaps the thought of thy heart shall be forgiven thee.

Act 8:23 For I see that thou art in the gall of bitterness and in the bond of iniquity.

Act 8:24 And Simon answered and said, Pray ye for me to the Lord, that none of the things which ye have spoken come upon me.

Act 8:25 They therefore, when they had testified and spoken the word of the Lord, returned to Jerusalem, and preached the gospel to many villages of the Samaritans.

Act 8:26 But an angel of the Lord spake unto Philip, saying, Arise, and go toward the south unto the way that goeth down from Jerusalem unto Gaza: the same is desert.

Act 8:27 And he arose and went: and behold, a man of Ethiopia, a eunuch of great authority under Candace, queen of the Ethiopians, who was over all her treasure, who had come to Jerusalem to worship;

Act 8:28 and he was returning and sitting in his chariot, and was reading the prophet Isaiah.

Act 8:29 And the Spirit said unto Philip, Go near, and join thyself to this chariot.

Act 8:30 And Philip ran to him, and heard him reading Isaiah the prophet, and said, Understandest thou what thou readest?

Act 8:31 And he said, How can I, except some one shall guide me? And he besought Philip to come up and sit with him.

Act 8:32 Now the passage of the Scripture which he was reading was this, He was led as a sheep to the slaughter; And as a lamb before his shearer is dumb, So he openeth not his mouth:

Act 8:33 In his humiliation his judgment was taken away: His generation who shall declare? For his life is taken from the earth.

Act 8:34 And the eunuch answered Philip, and said, I pray thee, of whom speaketh the prophet this? of himself, or of some other?

Act 8:35 And Philip opened his mouth, and beginning from this Scripture, preached unto him Jesus.

Act 8:36 And as they went on the way, they came unto a certain water; and the eunuch saith, Behold, here is water; what doth hinder me to be baptized?

Act 8:37 And Philip said, If thou believest with all thy heart, thou mayest. And he answered and said, I believe that Jesus Christ is the Son of God.

Act 8:38 And he commanded the chariot to stand still: and they both went down into the water, both Philip and the eunuch, and he baptized him.

Act 8:39 And when they came up out of the water, the Spirit of the Lord caught away Philip; and the eunuch saw him no more, for he went on his way rejoicing.

Act 8:40 But Philip was found at Azotus: and passing through he preached the gospel to all the cities, till he came to Caesarea.

Chapter 9.

Act 9:1 But Saul, yet breathing threatening and slaughter against the disciples of the Lord, went unto the high priest,

Act 9:2 and asked of him letters to Damascus unto the synagogues, that if he found any that were of the Way, whether men or women, he might bring them bound to Jerusalem.

Act 9:3 And as he journeyed, it came to pass that he drew nigh unto Damascus: and suddenly there shone round about him a light out of heaven:

Act 9:4 and he fell upon the earth, and heard a voice saying unto him, Saul, Saul, why persecutest thou me?

Act 9:5 And he said, Who art thou, Lord? And he said, I am Jesus whom thou persecutest:

Act 9:6 but rise, and enter into the city, and it shall be told thee what thou must do.

Act 9:7 And the men that journeyed with him stood speechless, hearing the voice, but beholding no man.

Act 9:8 And Saul arose from the earth; and when his eyes were opened, he saw nothing; and they led him by the hand, and brought him into Damascus.

Act 9:9 And he was three days without sight, and did neither eat nor drink.

Act 9:10 Now there was a certain disciple at Damascus, named Ananias; and the Lord said unto him in a vision, Ananias. And he said, Behold, I am here, Lord.

Act 9:11 And the Lord said unto him, Arise, and go to the street which is called Straight, and inquire in the house of Judas for one named Saul, a man of Tarsus: for behold, he prayeth;

Act 9:12 and he hath seen a man named Ananias coming in, and laying his hands on him, that he might receive his sight.

Act 9:13 But Ananias answered, Lord, I have heard from many of this man, how much evil he did to thy saints at Jerusalem:

Act 9:14 and here he hath authority from the chief priests to bind all that call upon thy name.

Act 9:15 But the Lord said unto him, Go thy way: for he is a chosen vessel unto me, to bear my name before the Gentiles and kings, and the children of Israel:

Act 9:16 for I will show him how many things he must suffer for my name's sake.

Act 9:17 And Ananias departed, and entered into the house; and laying his hands on him said, Brother Saul, the Lord, even Jesus, who appeared unto thee in the way which thou camest, hath sent me, that thou mayest receive thy sight, and be filled with the Holy Spirit.

Act 9:18 And straightway there fell from his eyes as it were scales, and he received his sight; and he arose and was baptized;

Act 9:19 and he took food and was strengthened. And he was certain days with the disciples that were at Damascus.

Act 9:20 And straightway in the synagogues he proclaimed Jesus, that he is the Son of God.

Act 9:21 And all that heard him were amazed, and said, Is not this he that in Jerusalem made havoc of them that called on this name? and he had come hither for this intent, that he might bring them bound before the chief priests.

Act 9:22 But Saul increased the more in strength, and confounded the Jews that dwelt at Damascus, proving that this is the Christ.

Act 9:23 And when many days were fulfilled, the Jews took counsel together to kill him:

Act 9:24 but their plot became known to Saul. And they watched the gates also day and night that they might kill him:

Act 9:25 but his disciples took him by night, and let him down through the wall, lowering him in a basket.

Act 9:26 And when he was come to Jerusalem, he assayed to join himself to the disciples: and they were all afraid of him, not believing that he was a disciple.

Act 9:27 But Barnabas took him, and brought him to the apostles, and declared unto them how he had seen the Lord in the way, and that he had spoken to him, and how at Damascus he had preached boldly in the name of Jesus.

Act 9:28 And he was with them going in and going out at Jerusalem,

Act 9:29 preaching boldly in the name of the Lord: and he spake and disputed against the Grecian Jews; but they were seeking to kill him.

Act 9:30 And when the brethren knew it, they brought him down to Caesarea, and sent him forth to Tarsus.

Act 9:31 So the church throughout all Judaea and Galilee and Samaria had peace, being edified; and, walking in the fear of the Lord and in the comfort of the Holy Spirit, was multiplied.

Act 9:32 And it came to pass, as Peter went throughout all parts, he came down also to the saints that dwelt at Lydda.

Act 9:33 And there he found a certain man named Aeneas, who had kept his bed eight years; for he was palsied.

Act 9:34 And Peter said unto him, Aeneas, Jesus Christ healeth thee: arise and make thy bed. And straightway he arose.

Act 9:35 And all that dwelt at Lydda and in Sharon saw him, and they turned to the Lord.

Act 9:36 Now there was at Joppa a certain disciple named Tabitha, which by interpretation is called Dorcas: this woman was full of good works and almsdeeds which she did.

Act 9:37 And it came to pass in those days, that she fell sick, and died: and when they had washed her, they laid her in an upper chamber.

Act 9:38 And as Lydda was nigh unto Joppa, the disciples, hearing that Peter was there, sent two men unto him, entreating him, Delay not to come on unto us.

Act 9:39 And Peter arose and went with them. And when he was come, they brought him into the upper chamber: and all the widows stood by him weeping, and showing the coats and garments which Dorcas made, while she was with them.

Act 9:40 But Peter put them all forth, and kneeled down and prayed; and turning to the body, he said, Tabitha, arise. And she opened her eyes; and when she saw Peter, she sat up.

Act 9:41 And he gave her his hand, and raised her up; and calling the saints and widows, he presented her alive.

Act 9:42 And it became known throughout all Joppa: and many believed on the Lord.

Act 9:43 And it came to pass, that he abode many days in Joppa with one Simon a tanner.

Chapter 10.

Act 10:1 Now there was a certain man in Caesarea, Cornelius by name, a centurion of the band called the Italian band,

Act 10:2 a devout man, and one that feared God with all his house, who gave much alms to the people, and prayed to God always.

Act 10:3 He saw in a vision openly, as it were about the ninth hour of the day, an angel of God coming in unto him, and saying to him, Cornelius.

Act 10:4 And he, fastening his eyes upon him, and being affrighted, said, What is it, Lord? And he said unto him, Thy prayers and thine alms are gone up for a memorial before God.

Act 10:5 And now send men to Joppa, and fetch one Simon, who is surnamed Peter:

Act 10:6 he lodgeth with one Simon a tanner, whose house is by the sea side.

Act 10:7 And when the angel that spake unto him was departed, he called two of his household-servants, and a devout soldier of them that waited on him continually;

Act 10:8 and having rehearsed all things unto them, he sent them to Joppa.

Act 10:9 Now on the morrow, as they were on their journey, and drew nigh unto the city, Peter went up upon the housetop to pray, about the sixth hour:

Act 10:10 and he became hungry, and desired to eat: but while they made ready, he fell into a trance;

Act 10:11 and he beholdeth the heaven opened, and a certain vessel descending, as it were a great sheet, let down by four corners upon the earth:

Act 10:12 wherein were all manner of fourfooted beasts and creeping things of the earth and birds of the heaven.

Act 10:13 And there came a voice to him, Rise, Peter; kill and eat.

Act 10:14 But Peter said, Not so, Lord; for I have never eaten anything that is common and unclean.

Act 10:15 And a voice came unto him again the second time, What God hath cleansed, make not thou common.

Act 10:16 And this was done thrice: and straightway the vessel was received up into heaven.

Act 10:17 Now while Peter was much perplexed in himself what the vision which he had seen might mean, behold, the men that were sent by Cornelius, having made inquiry for Simon's house, stood before the gate,

Act 10:18 and called and asked whether Simon, who was surnamed Peter, were lodging there.

Act 10:19 And while Peter thought on the vision, the Spirit said unto him, Behold, three men seek thee.

Act 10:20 But arise, and get thee down, and go with them, nothing doubting: for I have sent them.

Act 10:21 And Peter went down to the men, and said, Behold, I am he whom ye seek: what is the cause wherefore ye are come?

Act 10:22 And they said, Cornelius a centurion, a righteous man and one that feareth God, and well reported of by all the nation of the Jews, was warned of God by a holy angel to send for thee into his house, and to hear words from thee.

Act 10:23 So he called them in and lodged them. And on the morrow he arose and went forth with them, and certain of the brethren from Joppa accompanied him.

Act 10:24 And on the morrow they entered into Caesarea. And Cornelius was waiting for them, having called together his kinsmen and his near friends.

Act 10:25 And when it came to pass that Peter entered, Cornelius met him, and fell down at his feet, and worshipped him.

Act 10:26 But Peter raised him up, saying, Stand up; I myself also am a man.

Act 10:27 And as he talked with him, he went in, and findeth many come together:

Act 10:28 and he said unto them, Ye yourselves know how it is an unlawful thing for a man that is a Jew to join himself or come unto one of another nation; and yet unto me hath God showed that I should not call any man common or unclean:

Act 10:29 wherefore also I came without gainsaying, when I was sent for. I ask therefore with what intent ye sent for me.

Act 10:30 And Cornelius said, Four days ago, until this hour, I was keeping the ninth hour of prayer in my house; and behold, a man stood before me in bright apparel,

Act 10:31 and saith, Cornelius, thy prayer is heard, and thine alms are had in remembrance in the sight of God.

Act 10:32 Send therefore to Joppa, and call unto thee Simon, who is surnamed Peter; he lodgeth in the house of Simon a tanner, by the sea side.

Act 10:33 Forthwith therefore I sent to thee; and thou hast well done that thou art come. Now therefore we are all here present in the sight of God, to hear all things that have been commanded thee of the Lord.

Act 10:34 And Peter opened his mouth and said, Of a truth I perceive that God is no respecter of persons:

Act 10:35 but in every nation he that feareth him, and worketh righteousness, is acceptable to him.

Act 10:36 The word which he sent unto the children of Israel, preaching good tidings of peace by Jesus Christ (He is Lord of all.) -

Act 10:37 that saying ye yourselves know, which was published throughout all Judaea, beginning from Galilee, after the baptism which John preached;

Act 10:38 even Jesus of Nazareth, how God anointed him with the Holy Spirit and with power: who went about doing good, and healing all that were oppressed of the devil; for God was with him.

Act 10:39 And we are witnesses of all things which he did both in the country of the Jews, and in Jerusalem; whom also they slew, hanging him on a tree.

Act 10:40 Him God raised up the third day, and gave him to be made manifest,

Act 10:41 not to all the people, but unto witnesses that were chosen before of God, even to us, who ate and drank with him after he rose from the dead.

Act 10:42 And he charged us to preach unto the people, and to testify that this is he who is ordained of God to be the Judge of the living and the dead.

Act 10:43 To him bear all the prophets witness, that through his name every one that believeth on him shall receive remission of sins.

Act 10:44 While Peter yet spake these words, the Holy Spirit fell on all them that heard the word.

Act 10:45 And they of the circumcision that believed were amazed, as many as came with Peter, because that on the Gentiles also was poured out the gift of the Holy Spirit.

Act 10:46 For they heard them speak with tongues, and magnify God. Then answered Peter,

Act 10:47 Can any man forbid the water, that these should not be baptized, who have received the Holy Spirit as well as we?

Act 10:48 And he commanded them to be baptized in the name of Jesus Christ. Then prayed they him to tarry certain days.

Chapter 11.

Act 11:1 Now the apostles and the brethren that were in Judaea heard that the Gentiles also had received the word of God.

Act 11:2 And when Peter was come up to Jerusalem, they that were of the circumcision contended with him,

Act 11:3 saying, Thou wentest in to men uncircumcised, and didst eat with them.

Act 11:4 But Peter began, and expounded the matter unto them in order, saying,

Act 11:5 I was in the city of Joppa praying: and in a trance I saw a vision, a certain vessel descending, as it were a great sheet let down from heaven by four corners; and it came even unto me:

Act 11:6 upon which when I had fastened mine eyes, I considered, and saw the fourfooted beasts of the earth and wild beasts and creeping things and birds of the heaven.

Act 11:7 And I heard also a voice saying unto me, Rise, Peter; kill and eat.

Act 11:8 But I said, Not so, Lord: for nothing common or unclean hath ever entered into my mouth.

Act 11:9 But a voice answered the second time out of heaven, What God hath cleansed, make not thou common.

Act 11:10 And this was done thrice: and all were drawn up again into heaven.

Act 11:11 And behold, forthwith three men stood before the house in which we were, having been sent from Caesarea unto me.

Act 11:12 And the Spirit bade me go with them, making no distinction. And these six brethren also accompanied me; and we entered into the man's house:

Act 11:13 and he told us how he had seen the angel standing in his house, and saying, Send to Joppa, and fetch Simon, whose surname is Peter;

Act 11:14 who shall speak unto thee words, whereby thou shalt be saved, thou and all thy house.

Act 11:15 And as I began to speak, the Holy Spirit fell on them, even as on us at the beginning.

Act 11:16 And I remembered the word of the Lord, how he said, John indeed baptized with water; but ye shall be baptized in the Holy Spirit.

Act 11:17 If then God gave unto them the like gift as he did also unto us, when we believed on the Lord Jesus Christ, who was I, that I could withstand God?

Act 11:18 And when they heard these things, they held their peace, and glorified God, saying, Then to the Gentiles also hath God granted repentance unto life.

Act 11:19 They therefore that were scattered abroad upon the tribulation that arose about Stephen travelled as far as Phoenicia, and Cyprus, and Antioch, speaking the word to none save only to Jews.

Act 11:20 But there were some of them, men of Cyprus and Cyrene, who, when they were come to Antioch, spake unto the Greeks also, preaching the Lord Jesus.

Act 11:21 And the hand of the Lord was with them: and a great number that believed turned unto the Lord.

Act 11:22 And the report concerning them came to the ears of the church which was in Jerusalem: and they sent forth Barnabas as far as Antioch:

Act 11:23 who, when he was come, and had seen the grace of God, was glad; and he exhorted them all, that with purpose of heart they would cleave unto the Lord:

Act 11:24 for he was a good man, and full of the Holy Spirit and of faith: and much people was added unto the Lord.

Act 11:25 And he went forth to Tarsus to seek for Saul;

Act 11:26 and when he had found him, he brought him unto Antioch. And it came to pass, that even for a whole year they were gathered together with the church, and taught much people, and that the disciples were called Christians first in Antioch.

Act 11:27 Now in these days there came down prophets from Jerusalem unto Antioch.

Act 11:28 And there stood up one of them named Agabus, and signified by the Spirit that there should be a great famine over all the world: which came to pass in the days of Claudius.

Act 11:29 And the disciples, every man according to his ability, determined to send relief unto the brethren that dwelt in Judea:

Act 11:30 which also they did, sending it to the elders by the hand of Barnabas and Saul.

Chapter 12.

Act 12:1 Now about that time Herod the king put forth his hands to afflict certain of the church.

Act 12:2 And he killed James the brother of John with the sword.

Act 12:3 And when he saw that it pleased the Jews, he proceeded to seize Peter also. And those were the days of unleavened bread.

Act 12:4 And when he had taken him, he put him in prison, and delivered him to four quaternions of soldiers to guard him; intending after the Passover to bring him forth to the people.

Act 12:5 Peter therefore was kept in the prison: but prayer was made earnestly of the church unto God for him.

Act 12:6 And when Herod was about to bring him forth, the same night Peter was sleeping between two soldiers, bound with two chains: and guards before the door kept the prison.

Act 12:7 And behold, an angel of the Lord stood by him, and a light shined in the cell: and he smote Peter on the side, and awoke him, saying, Rise up quickly. And his chains fell off from his hands.

Act 12:8 And the angel said unto him, Gird thyself, and bind on thy sandals. And he did so. And he saith unto him, Cast thy garment about thee, and follow me.

Act 12:9 And he went out, and followed; and he knew not that it was true which was done by the angel, but thought he saw a vision.

Act 12:10 And when they were past the first and the second guard, they came unto the iron gate that leadeth into the city; which opened to them of its own accord: and they went out, and passed on through one street; and straightway the angel departed from him.

Act 12:11 And when Peter was come to himself, he said, Now I know of a truth, that the Lord hath sent forth his angel and delivered me out of the hand of Herod, and from all the expectation of the people of the Jews.

Act 12:12 And when he had considered the thing, he came to the house of Mary the mother of John whose surname was Mark; where many were gathered together and were praying.

Act 12:13 And when he knocked at the door of the gate, a maid came to answer, named Rhoda.

Act 12:14 And when she knew Peter's voice, she opened not the gate for joy, but ran in, and told that Peter stood before the gate.

Act 12:15 And they said unto her, Thou art mad. But she confidently affirmed that it was even so. And they said, It is his angel.

Act 12:16 But Peter continued knocking: and when they had opened, they saw him, and were amazed.

Act 12:17 But he, beckoning unto them with the hand to hold their peace, declared unto them how the Lord had brought him forth out of the prison. And he said, Tell these things unto James, and to the brethren. And he departed, and went to another place.

Act 12:18 Now as soon as it was day, there was no small stir among the soldiers, what was become of Peter.

Act 12:19 And when Herod had sought for him, and found him not, he examined the guards, and commanded that they should be put to death. And he went down from Judaea to Caesarea, and tarried there.

Act 12:20 Now he was highly displeased with them of Tyre and Sidon: and they came with one accord to him, and, having made Blastus the king's chamberlain their friend, they asked for peace, because their country was fed from the king's country.

Act 12:21 And upon a set day Herod arrayed himself in royal apparel, and sat on the throne, and made an oration unto them.

Act 12:22 And the people shouted, saying, The voice of a god, and not of a man.

Act 12:23 And immediately an angel of the Lord smote him, because he gave not God the glory: and he was eaten of worms, and gave up the ghost.

Act 12:24 But the word of God grew and multiplied.

Act 12:25 And Barnabas and Saul returned from Jerusalem, when they had fulfilled their ministration, taking with them John whose surname was Mark.

Chapter 13.

Act 13:1 Now there were at Antioch, in the church that was there, prophets and teachers, Barnabas, and Symeon that was called Niger, and Lucius of Cyrene, and Manaen the foster-brother of Herod the tetrarch, and Saul.

Act 13:2 And as they ministered to the Lord, and fasted, the Holy Spirit said, Separate me Barnabas and Saul for the work whereunto I have called them.

Act 13:3 Then, when they had fasted and prayed and laid their hands on them, they sent them away.

Act 13:4 So they, being sent forth by the Holy Spirit, went down to Seleucia; and from thence they sailed to Cyprus.

Act 13:5 And when they were at Salamis, they proclaimed the word of God in the synagogues of the Jews: and they had also John as their attendant.

Act 13:6 And when they had gone through the whole island unto Paphos, they found a certain sorcerer, a false prophet, a Jew, whose name was Bar-Jesus;

Act 13:7 who was with the proconsul, Sergius Paulus, a man of understanding. The same called unto him Barnabas and Saul, and sought to hear the word of God.

Act 13:8 But Elymas the sorcerer (for so is his name by interpretation) withstood them, seeking to turn aside the proconsul from the faith.

Act 13:9 But Saul, who is also called Paul, filled with the Holy Spirit, fastened his eyes on him,

Act 13:10 and said, O full of all guile and all villany, thou son of the devil, thou enemy of all righteousness, wilt thou not cease to pervert the right ways of the Lord?

Act 13:11 And now, behold, the hand of the Lord is upon thee, and thou shalt be blind, not seeing the sun for a season. And immediately there fell on him a mist and a darkness; and he went about seeking some to lead him by the hand.

Act 13:12 Then the proconsul, when he saw what was done, believed, being astonished at the teaching of the Lord.

Act 13:13 Now Paul and his company set sail from Paphos, and came to Perga in Pamphylia: and John departed from them and returned to Jerusalem.

Act 13:14 But they, passing through from Perga, came to Antioch of Pisidia; and they went into the synagogue on the sabbath day, and sat down.

Act 13:15   And after the reading of the law and the prophets the rulers of the synagogue sent unto them, saying, Brethren, if ye have any word of exhortation for the people, say on.

Act 13:16   And Paul stood up, and beckoning with the hand said, Men of Israel, and ye that fear God, hearken:

Act 13:17   The God of this people Israel chose our fathers, and exalted the people when they sojourned in the land of Egypt, and with a high arm led he them forth out of it.

Act 13:18   And for about the time of forty years as a nursing-father bare he them in the wilderness.

Act 13:19   And when he had destroyed seven nations in the land of Canaan, he gave them their land for an inheritance, for about four hundred and fifty years:

Act 13:20   and after these things he gave them judges until Samuel the prophet.

Act 13:21   And afterward they asked for a king: and God gave unto them Saul the son of Kish, a man of the tribe of Benjamin, for the space of forty years.

Act 13:22   And when he had removed him, he raised up David to be their king; to whom also he bare witness and said, I have found David the son of Jesse, a man after My heart, who shall do all My will.

Act 13:23   Of this man's seed hath God according to promise brought unto Israel a Saviour, Jesus;

Act 13:24   when John had first preached before his coming the baptism of repentance to all the people of Israel.

Act 13:25   And as John was fulfilling his course, he said, What suppose ye that I am? I am not he. But behold, there cometh one after me the shoes of whose feet I am not worthy to unloose.

Act 13:26   Brethren, children of the stock of Abraham, and those among you that fear God, to us is the word of this salvation sent forth.

Act 13:27   For they that dwell in Jerusalem, and their rulers, because they knew him not, nor the voices of the prophets which are read every sabbath, fulfilled them by condemning him.

Act 13:28   And though they found no cause of death in him, yet asked they of Pilate that he should be slain.

Act 13:29   And when they had fulfilled all things that were written of him, they took him down from the tree, and laid him in a tomb.

Act 13:30   But God raised him from the dead:

Act 13:31   and he was seen for many days of them that came up with him from Galilee to Jerusalem, who are now his witnesses unto the people.

Act 13:32   And we bring you good tidings of the promise made unto the fathers,

Act 13:33   that God hath fulfilled the same unto our children, in that he raised up Jesus; as also it is written in the second psalm, Thou art my Son, this day have I begotten thee.

Act 13:34   And as concerning that he raised him up from the dead, now no more to return to corruption, he hath spoken on this wise, I will give you the holy and sure blessings of David.

Act 13:35   Because he saith also in another psalm, Thou wilt not give Thy Holy One to see corruption.

Act 13:36   For David, after he had in his own generation served the counsel of God, fell asleep, and was laid unto his fathers, and saw corruption:

Act 13:37 but he whom God raised up saw no corruption.

Act 13:38   Be it known unto you therefore, brethren, that through this man is proclaimed unto you remission of sins:

Act 13:39 and by him every one that believeth is justified from all things, from which ye could not be justified by the law of Moses.

Act 13:40 Beware therefore, lest that come upon you which is spoken in the prophets:

Act 13:41 Behold, ye despisers, and wonder, and perish; For I work a work in your days, A work which ye shall in no wise believe, if one declare it unto you.

Act 13:42 And as they went out, they besought that these words might be spoken to them the next sabbath.

Act 13:43 Now when the synagogue broke up, many of the Jews and of the devout proselytes followed Paul and Barnabas; who, speaking to them, urged them to continue in the grace of God.

Act 13:44 And the next sabbath almost the whole city was gathered together to hear the word of God.

Act 13:45 But when the Jews saw the multitudes, they were filled with jealousy, and contradicted the things which were spoken by Paul, and blasphemed.

Act 13:46 And Paul and Barnabas spake out boldly, and said, It was necessary that the word of God should first be spoken to you. Seeing ye thrust it from you, and judge yourselves unworthy of eternal life, lo, we turn to the Gentiles.

Act 13:47 For so hath the Lord commanded us, saying, I have set thee for a light of the Gentiles, That thou shouldest be for salvation unto the uttermost part of the earth.

Act 13:48 And as the Gentiles heard this, they were glad, and glorified the word of God: and as many as were ordained to eternal life believed.

Act 13:49 And the word of the Lord was spread abroad throughout all the region.

Act 13:50 But the Jews urged on the devout women of honorable estate, and the chief men of the city, and stirred up a persecution against Paul and Barnabas, and cast them out of their borders.

Act 13:51   But they shook off the dust of their feet against them, and came unto Iconium.

Act 13:52 And the disciples were filled with joy with the Holy Spirit.

Chapter 14.

Act 14:1 And it came to pass in Iconium that they entered together into the synagogue of the Jews, and so spake that a great multitude both of Jews and of Greeks believed.

Act 14:2 But the Jews that were disobedient stirred up the souls of the Gentiles, and made them evil affected against the brethren.

Act 14:3 Long time therefore they tarried there speaking boldly in the Lord, who bare witness unto the word of his grace, granting signs and wonders to be done by their hands.

Act 14:4 But the multitude of the city was divided; and part held with the Jews, and part with the apostles.

Act 14:5 And when there was made an onset both of the Gentiles and of the Jews with their rulers, to treat them shamefully and to stone them,

Act 14:6 they became aware of it, and fled unto the cities of Lycaonia, Lystra and Derbe, and the region round about:

Act 14:7 and there they preached the gospel.

Act 14:8 And at Lystra there sat a certain man, impotent in his feet, a cripple from his mother's womb, who never had walked.

Act 14:9 The same heard Paul speaking, who, fastening eyes upon him, and seeing that he had faith to be made whole,

Act 14:10 said with a loud voice, Stand upright on thy feet. And he leaped up and walked.

Act 14:11 And when the multitude saw what Paul had done, they lifted up their voice, saying in the speech of Lycaonia, The gods are come down to us in the likeness of men.

Act 14:12 And they called Barnabas, Jupiter; and Paul, Mercury, because he was the chief speaker.

Act 14:13 And the priest of Jupiter whose temple was before the city, brought oxen and garlands unto the gates, and would have done sacrifice with the multitudes.

Act 14:14 But when the apostles, Barnabas and Paul, heard of it, they rent their garments, and sprang forth among the multitude, crying out

Act 14:15 and saying, Sirs, why do ye these things? We also are men of like passions with you, and bring you good tidings, that ye should turn from these vain things unto a living God, who made the heaven and the earth and the sea, and all that in them is:

Act 14:16 who in the generations gone by suffered all the nations to walk in their own ways.

Act 14:17 And yet He left not himself without witness, in that he did good and gave you from heaven rains and fruitful seasons, filling your hearts with food and gladness.

Act 14:18 And with these sayings scarce restrained they the multitudes from doing sacrifice unto them.

Act 14:19 But there came Jews thither from Antioch and Iconium: and having persuaded the multitudes, they stoned Paul, and dragged him out of the city, supposing that he was dead.

Act 14:20 But as the disciples stood round about him, he rose up, and entered into the city: and on the morrow he went forth with Barnabas to Derbe.

Act 14:21 And when they had preached the gospel to that city, and had made many disciples, they returned to Lystra, and to Iconium, and to Antioch,

Act 14:22 confirming the souls of the disciples, exhorting them to continue in the faith, and that through many tribulations we must enter into the kingdom of God.

Act 14:23 And when they had appointed for them elders in every church, and had prayed with fasting, they commended them to the Lord, on whom they had believed.

Act 14:24 And they passed through Pisidia, and came to Pamphylia.

Act 14:25 And when they had spoken the word in Perga, they went down to Attalia;

Act 14:26 and thence they sailed to Antioch, from whence they had been committed to the grace of God for the work which they had fulfilled.

Act 14:27 And when they were come, and had gathered the church together, they rehearsed all things that God had done with them, and that he had opened a door of faith unto the Gentiles.

Act 14:28 And they tarried no little time with the disciples.

Chapter 15.

Act 15:1   And certain men came down from Judaea and taught the brethren, saying, Except ye be circumcised after the custom of Moses, ye cannot be saved.

Act 15:2   And when Paul and Barnabas had no small dissension and questioning with them, the brethren appointed that Paul and Barnabas, and certain other of them, should go up to Jerusalem unto the apostles and elders about this question.

Act 15:3   They therefore, being brought on their way by the church, passed through both Phoenicia and Samaria, declaring the conversion of the Gentiles: and they caused great joy unto all the brethren.

Act 15:4   And when they were come to Jerusalem, they were received of the church and the apostles and the elders, and they rehearsed all things that God had done with them.

Act 15:5   But there rose up certain of the sect of the Pharisees who believed, saying, It is needful to circumcise them, and to charge them to keep the law of Moses.

Act 15:6   And the apostles and the elders were gathered together to consider of this matter.

Act 15:7   And when there had been much questioning, Peter rose up, and said unto them, Brethren, ye know that a good while ago God made choice among you, that by my mouth the Gentiles should hear the word of the gospel, and believe.

Act 15:8   And God, who knoweth the heart, bare them witness, giving them the Holy Spirit, even as he did unto us;

Act 15:9   and he made no distinction between us and them, cleansing their hearts by faith.

Act 15:10   Now therefore why make ye trial of God, that ye should put a yoke upon the neck of the disciples which neither our fathers nor we were able to bear?

Act 15:11   But we believe that we shall be saved through the grace of the Lord Jesus, in like manner as they.

Act 15:12   And all the multitude kept silence; and they hearkened unto Barnabas and Paul rehearsing what signs and wonders God had wrought among the Gentiles through them.

Act 15:13   And after they had held their peace, James answered, saying, Brethren, hearken unto me:

Act 15:14   Symeon hath rehearsed how first God visited the Gentiles, to take out of them a people for his name.

Act 15:15   And to this agree the words of the prophets; as it is written,

Act 15:16   After these things I will return, And I will build again the tabernacle of David, which is fallen; And I will build again the ruins thereof, And I will set it up:

Act 15:17   That the residue of men may seek after the Lord, And all the Gentiles, upon whom my name is called,

Act 15:18   Saith the Lord, who maketh these things known from of old.

Act 15:19   Wherefore my judgment is, that we trouble not them that from among the Gentiles turn to God;

Act 15:20   but that we write unto them, that they abstain from the pollutions of idols, and from fornication, and from what is strangled, and from blood.

Act 15:21   For Moses from generations of old hath in every city them that preach him, being read in the synagogues every sabbath.

Act 15:22 Then it seemed good to the apostles and the elders, with the whole church, to choose men out of their company, and send them to Antioch with Paul and Barnabas; namely, Judas called Barsabbas, and Silas, chief men among the brethren:

Act 15:23 and they wrote thus by them, The apostles and the elders, brethren, unto the brethren who are of the Gentiles in Antioch and Syria and Cilicia, greeting:

Act 15:24 Forasmuch as we have heard that certain who went out from us have troubled you with words, subverting your souls; to whom we gave no commandment;

Act 15:25 it seemed good unto us, having come to one accord, to choose out men and send them unto you with our beloved Barnabas and Paul,

Act 15:26 men that have hazarded their lives for the name of our Lord Jesus Christ.

Act 15:27 We have sent therefore Judas and Silas, who themselves also shall tell you the same things by word of mouth.

Act 15:28 For it seemed good to the Holy Spirit, and to us, to lay upon you no greater burden than these necessary things:

Act 15:29 that ye abstain from things sacrificed to idols, and from blood, and from things strangled, and from fornication; from which if ye keep yourselves, it shall be well with you. Fare ye well.

Act 15:30 So they, when they were dismissed, came down to Antioch; and having gathered the multitude together, they delivered the epistle.

Act 15:31 And when they had read it, they rejoiced for the consolation.

Act 15:32 And Judas and Silas, being themselves also prophets, exhorted the brethren with many words, and confirmed them.

Act 15:33 And after they had spent some time there, they were dismissed in peace from the brethren unto those that had sent them forth.

Act 15:34 But it seemed good unto Silas to abide there.

Act 15:35 But Paul and Barnabas tarried in Antioch, teaching and preaching the word of the Lord, with many others also.

Act 15:36 And after some days Paul said unto Barnabas, Let us return now and visit the brethren in every city wherein we proclaimed the word of the Lord, and see how they fare.

Act 15:37 And Barnabas was minded to take with them John also, who was called Mark.

Act 15:38 But Paul thought not good to take with them him who withdrew from them from Pamphylia, and went not with them to the work.

Act 15:39 And there arose a sharp contention, so that they parted asunder one from the other, and Barnabas took Mark with him, and sailed away unto Cyprus;

Act 15:40 but Paul choose Silas, and went forth, being commended by the brethren to the grace of the Lord.

Act 15:41 And he went through Syria and Cilicia, confirming the churches.

Chapter 16.

Act 16:1 And he came also to Derbe and to Lystra: and behold, a certain disciple was there, named Timothy, the son of a Jewess that believed; but his father was a Greek.

Act 16:2 The same was well reported of by the brethren that were at Lystra and Iconium.

Act 16:3 Him would Paul have to go forth with him; and he took and circumcised him because of the Jews that were in those parts: for they all knew that his father was a Greek.

Act 16:4 And as they went on their way through the cities, they delivered them the decrees to keep which had been ordained of the apostles and elders that were at Jerusalem.

Act 16:5 So the churches were strengthened in the faith, and increased in number daily.

Act 16:6 And they went through the region of Phrygia and Galatia, having been forbidden of the Holy Spirit to speak the word in Asia;

Act 16:7 and when they were come over against Mysia, they assayed to go into Bithynia; and the Spirit of Jesus suffered them not;

Act 16:8 and passing by Mysia, they came down to Troas.

Act 16:9 And a vision appeared to Paul in the night: There was a man of Macedonia standing, beseeching him, and saying, Come over into Macedonia, and help us.

Act 16:10 And when he had seen the vision, straightway we sought to go forth into Macedonia, concluding that God had called us to preach the gospel to them.

Act 16:11 Setting sail therefore from Troas, we made a straight course to Samothrace, and the day following to Neapolis;

Act 16:12 and from thence to Philippi, which is a city of Macedonia, the first of the district, a Roman colony: and we were in this city tarrying certain days.

Act 16:13 And on the sabbath day we went forth without the gate by a river side, where we supposed there was a place of prayer; and we sat down, and spake unto the women that were come together.

Act 16:14 And a certain woman named Lydia, a seller of purple of the city of Thyatira, one that worshipped God, heard us: whose heart the Lord opened to give heed unto the things which were spoken by Paul.

Act 16:15 And when she was baptized, and her household, she besought us, saying, If ye have judged me to be faithful to the Lord, come into my house, and abide there. And she constrained us.

Act 16:16 And it came to pass, as we were going to the place of prayer, that a certain maid having a spirit of divination met us, who brought her masters much gain by soothsaying.

Act 16:17 The same following after Paul and us cried out, saying, These men are servants of the Most High God, who proclaim unto you the way of salvation.

Act 16:18 And this she did for many days. But Paul, being sore troubled, turned and said to the spirit, I charge thee in the name of Jesus Christ to come out of her. And it came out that very hour.

Act 16:19 But when her masters saw that the hope of their gain was gone, they laid hold on Paul and Silas, and dragged them into the marketplace before the rulers,

Act 16:20 and when they had brought them unto the magistrates, they said, These men, being Jews, do exceedingly trouble our city,

Act 16:21 and set forth customs which it is not lawful for us to receive, or to observe, being Romans.

Act 16:22 And the multitude rose up together against them: and the magistrates rent their garments off them, and commanded to beat them with rods.

Act 16:23 And when they had laid many stripes upon them, they cast them into prison, charging the jailor to keep them safely:

Act 16:24 who, having received such a charge, cast them into the inner prison, and made their feet fast in the stocks.

Act 16:25 But about midnight Paul and Silas were praying and singing hymns unto God, and the prisoners were listening to them;

Act 16:26 and suddenly there was a great earthquake, so that the foundations of the prison-house were shaken: and immediately all the doors were opened, and every one's bands were loosed.

Act 16:27 And the jailor, being roused out of sleep and seeing the prison doors open, drew his sword and was about to kill himself, supposing that the prisoners had escaped.

Act 16:28 But Paul cried with a loud voice, saying, Do thyself no harm: for we are all here.

Act 16:29 And he called for lights and sprang in, and, trembling for fear, fell down before Paul and Silas,

Act 16:30 and brought them out and said, Sirs, what must I do to be saved?

Act 16:31 And they said, Believe on the Lord Jesus, and thou shalt be saved, thou and thy house.

Act 16:32 And they spake the word of the Lord unto him, with all that were in his house.

Act 16:33 And he took them the same hour of the night, and washed their stripes; and was baptized, he and all his, immediately.

Act 16:34 And he brought them up into his house, and set food before them, and rejoiced greatly, with all his house, having believed in God.

Act 16:35 But when it was day, the magistrates sent the serjeants, saying, Let those men go.

Act 16:36 And the jailor reported the words to Paul, saying, The magistrates have sent to let you go: now therefore come forth, and go in peace.

Act 16:37 But Paul said unto them, They have beaten us publicly, uncondemned, men that are Romans, and have cast us into prison; and do they now cast us out privily? Nay verily; but let them come themselves and bring us out.

Act 16:38 And the serjeants reported these words unto the magistrates: and they feared when they heard that they were Romans;

Act 16:39 and they came and besought them; and when they had brought them out, they asked them to go away from the city.

Act 16:40 And they went out of the prison, and entered into the house of Lydia: and when they had seen the brethren, they comforted them, and departed.

Chapter 17.

Act 17:1 Now when they had passed through Amphipolis and Apollonia, they came to Thessalonica, where was a synagogue of the Jews:

Act 17:2 and Paul, as his custom was, went in unto them, and for three sabbath days reasoned with them from the Scriptures,

Act 17:3 opening and alleging that it behooved the Christ to suffer, and to rise again from the dead; and that this Jesus, whom, said he, I proclaim unto you, is the Christ.

Act 17:4 And some of them were persuaded, and consorted with Paul and Silas, and of the devout Greeks a great multitude, and of the chief women not a few.

Act 17:5 But the Jews, being moved with jealousy, took unto them certain vile fellows of the rabble, and gathering a crowd, set the city on an uproar; and assaulting the house of Jason, they sought to bring them forth to the people.

Act 17:6 And when they found them not, they dragged Jason and certain brethren before the rulers of the city, crying, These that have turned the world upside down are come hither also;

Act 17:7 whom Jason hath received: and these all act contrary to the decrees of Caesar, saying that there is another king, one Jesus.

Act 17:8 And they troubled the multitude and the rulers of the city, when they heard these things.

Act 17:9 And when they had taken security from Jason and the rest, they let them go.

Act 17:10 And the brethren immediately sent away Paul and Silas by night unto Beroea: who when they were come thither went into the synagogue of the Jews.

Act 17:11 Now these were more noble than those in Thessalonica, in that they received the word with all readiness of the mind, examining the Scriptures daily, whether these things were so.

Act 17:12 Many of them therefore believed; also of the Greek women of honorable estate, and of men, not a few.

Act 17:13 But when the Jews of Thessalonica had knowledge that the word of God was proclaimed of Paul at Beroea also, they came thither likewise, stirring up and troubling the multitudes.

Act 17:14 And then immediately the brethren sent forth Paul to go as far as to the sea: and Silas and Timothy abode there still.

Act 17:15 But they that conducted Paul brought him as far as Athens: and receiving a commandment unto Silas and Timothy that they should come to him with all speed, they departed.

Act 17:16 Now while Paul waited for them at Athens, his spirit was provoked within him as he beheld the city full of idols.

Act 17:17 So he reasoned in the synagogue with Jews and the devout persons, and in the marketplace every day with them that met him.

Act 17:18 And certain also of the Epicurean and Stoic philosophers encountered him. And some said, What would this babbler say? others, He seemeth to be a setter forth of strange gods: because he preached Jesus and the resurrection.

Act 17:19 And they took hold of him, and brought him unto the Areopagus, saying, May we know what this new teaching is, which is spoken by thee?

Act 17:20 For thou bringest certain strange things to our ears: we would know therefore what these things mean.

Act 17:21 (Now all the Athenians and the strangers sojourning there spent their time in nothing else, but either to tell or to hear some new thing.)

Act 17:22 And Paul stood in the midst of the Areopagus, and said, Ye men of Athens, in all things, I perceive that ye are very religious.

Act 17:23 For as I passed along, and observed the objects of your worship, I found also an altar with this inscription, TO AN UNKNOWN GOD. What therefore ye worship in ignorance, this I set forth unto you.

Act 17:24 The God that made the world and all things therein, he, being Lord of heaven and earth, dwelleth not in temples made with hands;

Act 17:25 neither is he served by men's hands, as though he needed anything, seeing he himself giveth to all life, and breath, and all things;

Act 17:26 and he made of one every nation of men to dwell on all the face of the earth, having determined their appointed seasons, and the bounds of their habitation;

Act 17:27 that they should seek God, if haply they might feel after him and find him, though he is not far from each one of us:

Act 17:28 for in him we live, and move, and have our being; as certain even of your own poets have said, For we are also his offspring.

Act 17:29 Being then the offspring of God, we ought not to think that the Godhead is like unto gold, or silver, or stone, graven by art and device of man.

Act 17:30 The times of ignorance therefore God overlooked; but now he commandeth men that they should all everywhere repent:

Act 17:31 inasmuch as he hath appointed a day in which he will judge the world in righteousness by the man whom he hath ordained; whereof he hath given assurance unto all men, in that he hath raised him from the dead.

Act 17:32 Now when they heard of the resurrection of the dead, some mocked; but others said, We will hear thee concerning this yet again.

Act 17:33 Thus Paul went out from among them.

Act 17:34 But certain men clave unto him, and believed: among whom also was Dionysius the Areopagite, and a woman named Damaris, and others with them.

Chapter 18.

Act 18:1 After these things he departed from Athens, and came to Corinth.

Act 18:2 And he found a certain Jew named Aquila, a man of Pontus by race, lately come from Italy, with his wife Priscilla, because Claudius had commanded all the Jews to depart from Rome: and he came unto them;

Act 18:3 and because he was of the same trade, he abode with them, and they wrought, for by their trade they were tentmakers.

Act 18:4 And he reasoned in the synagogue every sabbath, and persuaded Jews and Greeks.

Act 18:5 But when Silas and Timothy came down from Macedonia, Paul was constrained by the word, testifying to the Jews that Jesus was the Christ.

Act 18:6 And when they opposed themselves and blasphemed, he shook out his raiment and said unto them, Your blood be upon your own heads; I am clean: from henceforth I will go unto the Gentiles.

Act 18:7 And he departed thence, and went into the house of a certain man named Titus Justus, one that worshipped God, whose house joined hard to the synagogue.

Act 18:8 And Crispus, the ruler of the synagogue, believed in the Lord with all his house; and many of the Corinthians hearing believed, and were baptized.

Act 18:9 And the Lord said unto Paul in the night by a vision, Be not afraid, but speak and hold not thy peace:

Act 18:10 for I am with thee, and no man shall set on thee to harm thee: for I have much people in this city.

Act 18:11 And he dwelt there a year and six months, teaching the word of God among them.

Act 18:12 But when Gallio was proconsul of Achaia, the Jews with one accord rose up against Paul and brought him before the judgment-seat,

Act 18:13 saying, This man persuadeth men to worship God contrary to the law.

Act 18:14 But when Paul was about to open his mouth, Gallio said unto the Jews, If indeed it were a matter of wrong or of wicked villany, O ye Jews, reason would that I should bear with you:

Act 18:15 but if they are questions about words and names and your own law, look to it yourselves; I am not minded to be a judge of these matters.

Act 18:16 And he drove them from the judgment-seat.

Act 18:17 And they all laid hold on Sosthenes, the ruler of the synagogue, and beat him before the judgment-seat. And Gallio cared for none of these things.

Act 18:18 And Paul, having tarried after this yet many days, took his leave of the brethren, and sailed thence for Syria, and with him Priscilla and Aquila: having shorn his head in Cenchreae; for he had a vow.

Act 18:19 And they came to Ephesus, and he left them there: but he himself entered into the synagogue, and reasoned with the Jews.

Act 18:20 And when they asked him to abide a longer time, he consented not;

Act 18:21 but taking his leave of them, and saying, I will return again unto you if God will, he set sail from Ephesus.

Act 18:22 And when he had landed at Caesarea, he went up and saluted the church, and went down to Antioch.

Act 18:23 And having spent some time there, he departed, and went through the region of Galatia, and Phrygia, in order, establishing all the disciples.

Act 18:24 Now a certain Jew named Apollos, an Alexandrian by race, an eloquent man, came to Ephesus; and he was mighty in the scriptures.

Act 18:25 This man had been instructed in the way of the Lord; and being fervent in spirit, he spake and taught accurately the things concerning Jesus, knowing only the baptism of John:

Act 18:26 and he began to speak boldly in the synagogue. But when Priscilla and Aquila heard him, they took him unto them, and expounded unto him the way of God more accurately.

Act 18:27 And when he was minded to pass over into Achaia, the brethren encouraged him, and wrote to the disciples to receive him: and when he was come, he helped them much that had believed through grace;

Act 18:28 for he powerfully confuted the Jews, and that publicly, showing by the scriptures that Jesus was the Christ.

Chapter 19.

Act 19:1 And it came to pass, that, while Apollos was at Corinth, Paul having passed through the upper country came to Ephesus, and found certain disciples:

Act 19:2 and he said unto them, Did ye receive the Holy Spirit when ye believed? And they said unto him, Nay, we did not so much as hear whether the Holy Spirit was given.

Act 19:3 And he said, Into what then were ye baptized? And they said, Into John's baptism.

Act 19:4 And Paul said, John baptized with the baptism of repentance, saying unto the people that they should believe on him that should come after him, that is, on Jesus.

Act 19:5 And when they heard this, they were baptized into the name of the Lord Jesus.

Act 19:6 And when Paul had laid his hands upon them, the Holy Spirit came on them; and they spake with tongues, and prophesied.

Act 19:7 And they were in all about twelve men.

Act 19:8 And he entered into the synagogue, and spake boldly for the space of three months, reasoning and persuading as to the things concerning the kingdom of God.

Act 19:9 But when some were hardened and disobedient, speaking evil of the Way before the multitude, he departed from them, and separated the disciples, reasoning daily in the school of Tyrannus.

Act 19:10 And this continued for the space of two years; so that all they that dwelt in Asia heard the word of the Lord, both Jews and Greeks.

Act 19:11 And God wrought special miracles by the hands of Paul:

Act 19:12 insomuch that unto the sick were carried away from his body handkerchiefs or aprons, and the evil spirits went out.

Act 19:13 But certain also of the strolling Jews, exorcists, took upon them to name over them that had the evil spirits the name of the Lord Jesus, saying, I adjure you by Jesus whom Paul preacheth.

Act 19:14 And there were seven sons of one Sceva, a Jew, a chief priest, who did this.

Act 19:15 And the evil spirit answered and said unto them, Jesus I know, and Paul I know, but who are ye?

Act 19:16 And the man in whom the evil spirit was leaped on them, and mastered both of them, and prevailed against them, so that they fled out of that house naked and wounded.

Act 19:17 And this became known to all, both Jews and Greeks, that dwelt at Ephesus; and fear fell upon them all, and the name of the Lord Jesus was magnified.

Act 19:18 Many also of them that had believed came, confessing, and declaring their deeds.

Act 19:19 And not a few of them that practised magical arts brought their books together and burned them in the sight of all; and they counted the price of them, and found it fifty thousand pieces of silver.

Act 19:20 So mightily grew the word of the Lord and prevailed.

Act 19:21 Now after these things were ended, Paul purposed in the spirit, when he had passed through Macedonia and Achaia, to go to Jerusalem, saying, After I have been there, I must also see Rome.

Act 19:22 And having sent into Macedonia two of them that ministered unto him, Timothy and Erastus, he himself stayed in Asia for a while.

Act 19:23 And about that time there arose no small stir concerning the Way.

Act 19:24 For a certain man named Demetrius, a silversmith, who made silver shrines of Diana, brought no little business unto the craftsmen;

Act 19:25 whom he gathered together, with the workmen of like occupation, and said, Sirs, ye know that by this business we have our wealth.

Act 19:26 And ye see and hear, that not alone at Ephesus, but almost throughout all Asia, this Paul hath persuaded and turned away much people, saying that they are no gods, that are made with hands:

Act 19:27 and not only is there danger that this our trade come into disrepute; but also that the temple of the great goddess Diana be made of no account, and that she should even be deposed from her magnificence whom all Asia and the world worshippeth.

Act 19:28 And when they heard this they were filled with wrath, and cried out, saying, Great is Diana of the Ephesus.

Act 19:29 And the city was filled with the confusion: and they rushed with one accord into the theatre, having seized Gaius and Aristarchus, men of Macedonia, Paul's companions in travel.

Act 19:30 And when Paul was minded to enter in unto the people, the disciples suffered him not.

Act 19:31 And certain also of the Asiarchs, being his friends, sent unto him and besought him not to adventure himself into the theatre.

Act 19:32 Some therefore cried one thing, and some another: for the assembly was in confusion; and the more part knew not wherefore they were come together.

Act 19:33 And they brought Alexander out of the multitude, the Jews putting him forward. And Alexander beckoned with the hand, and would have made a defense unto the people.

Act 19:34 But when they perceived that he was a Jew, all with one voice about the space of two hours cried out, Great is Diana of the Ephesians.

Act 19:35 And when the townclerk had quieted the multitude, he saith, Ye men of Ephesus, what man is there who knoweth not that the city of the Ephesians is temple-keeper of the great Diana, and of the image which fell down from Jupiter?

Act 19:36 Seeing then that these things cannot be gainsaid, ye ought to be quiet, and to do nothing rash.

Act 19:37 For ye have brought hither these men, who are neither robbers of temples nor blasphemers of our goddess.

Act 19:38 If therefore Demetrius, and the craftsmen that are with him, have a matter against any man, the courts are open, and there are proconsuls: let them accuse one another.

Act 19:39 But if ye seek anything about other matters, it shall be settled in the regular assembly.

Act 19:40 For indeed we are in danger to be accused concerning this day's riot, there being no cause for it: and as touching it we shall not be able to give account of this concourse.

Act 19:41 And when he had thus spoken, he dismissed the assembly.

Chapter 20.

Act 20:1 And after the uproar ceased, Paul having sent for the disciples and exhorted them, took leave of them, and departed to go into Macedonia.

Act 20:2 And when he had gone through those parts, and had given them much exhortation, he came into Greece.

Act 20:3 And when he had spent three months there, and a plot was laid against him by Jews as he was about to set sail for Syria, he determined to return through Macedonia.

Act 20:4 And there accompanied him as far as Asia, Sopater of Beroea, the son of Pyrrhus; and of the Thessalonians, Aristarchus and Secundus; and Gaius of Derbe, and Timothy; and of Asia, Tychicus and Trophimus.

Act 20:5 But these had gone before, and were waiting for us at Troas.

Act 20:6 And we sailed away from Philippi after the days of unleavened bread, and came unto them to Troas in five days, where we tarried seven days.

Act 20:7 And upon the first day of the week, when we were gathered together to break bread, Paul discoursed with them, intending to depart on the morrow; and prolonged his speech until midnight.

Act 20:8 And there were many lights in the upper chamber where we were gathered together.

Act 20:9 And there sat in the window a certain young man named Eutychus, borne down with deep sleep; and as Paul discoursed yet longer, being borne down by his sleep he fell down from the third story, and was taken up dead.

Act 20:10 And Paul went down, and fell on him, and embracing him said, Make ye no ado; for his life is in him.

Act 20:11 And when he was gone up, and had broken the bread, and eaten, and had talked with them a long while, even till break of day, so he departed.

Act 20:12 And they brought the lad alive, and were not a little comforted.

Act 20:13 But we going before to the ship set sail for Assos, there intending to take in Paul: for so had he appointed, intending himself to go by land.

Act 20:14 And when he met us at Assos, we took him in, and came to Mitylene.

Act 20:15 And sailing from thence, we came the following day over against Chios; and the next day we touched at Samos; and the day after we came to Miletus.

Act 20:16 For Paul had determined to sail past Ephesus, that he might not have to spend time in Asia; for he was hastening, if it were possible for him, to be at Jerusalem the day of Pentecost.

Act 20:17 And from Miletus he sent to Ephesus, and called to him the elders of the church.

Act 20:18 And when they were come to him, he said unto them, Ye yourselves know, from the first day that I set foot in Asia, after what manner I was with you all the time,

Act 20:19 serving the Lord with all lowliness of mind, and with tears, and with trials which befell me by the plots of the Jews;

Act 20:20 how I shrank not from declaring unto you anything that was profitable, and teaching you publicly, and from house to house,

Act 20:21 testifying both to Jews and to Greeks repentance toward God, and faith toward our Lord Jesus Christ.

Act 20:22 And now, behold, I go bound in the spirit unto Jerusalem, not knowing the things that shall befall me there:

Act 20:23 save that the Holy Spirit testifieth unto me in every city, saying that bonds and afflictions abide me.

Act 20:24 But I hold not my life of any account as dear unto myself, so that I may accomplish my course, and the ministry which I received from the Lord Jesus, to testify the gospel of the grace of God.

Act 20:25 And now, behold, I know that ye all, among whom I went about preaching the kingdom, shall see my face no more.

Act 20:26 Wherefore I testify unto you this day, that I am pure from the blood of all men.

Act 20:27 For I shrank not from declaring unto you the whole counsel of God.

Act 20:28 Take heed unto yourselves, and to all the flock, in which the Holy Spirit hath made you bishops, to feed the church of the Lord which he purchased with his own blood.

Act 20:29 I know that after my departing grievous wolves shall enter in among you, not sparing the flock;

Act 20:30 and from among your own selves shall men arise, speaking perverse things, to draw away the disciples after them.

Act 20:31 Wherefore watch ye, remembering that by the space of three years I ceased not to admonish every one night and day with tears.

Act 20:32 And now I commend you to God, and to the word of his grace, which is able to build you up, and to give you the inheritance among all them that are sanctified.

Act 20:33 I coveted no man's silver, or gold, or apparel.

Act 20:34 Ye yourselves know that these hands ministered unto my necessities, and to them that were with me.

Act 20:35 In all things I gave you an example, that so laboring ye ought to help the weak, and to remember the words of the Lord Jesus, that he himself said, It is more blessed to give than to receive.

Act 20:36 And when he had thus spoken, he kneeled down and prayed with them all.

Act 20:37 And they all wept sore, and fell on Paul's neck and kissed him,

Act 20:38 sorrowing most of all for the word which he had spoken, that they should behold his face no more. And they brought him on his way unto the ship.

Chapter 21.

Act 21:1 And when it came to pass that were parted from them and had set sail, we came with a straight course unto Cos, and the next day unto Rhodes, and from thence unto Patara:

Act 21:2 and having found a ship crossing over unto Phoenicia, we went aboard, and set sail.

Act 21:3 And when we had come in sight of Cyprus, leaving it on the left hand, we sailed unto Syria, and landed at Tyre; for there the ship was to unlade her burden.

Act 21:4 And having found the disciples, we tarried there seven days: and these said to Paul through the Spirit, that he should not set foot in Jerusalem.

Act 21:5 And when it came to pass that we had accomplished the days, we departed and went on our journey; and they all, with wives and children, brought us on our way till we were out of the city: and kneeling down on the beach, we prayed, and bade each other farewell;

Act 21:6 and we went on board the ship, but they returned home again.

Act 21:7 And when we had finished the voyage from Tyre, we arrived at Ptolemais; and we saluted the brethren, and abode with them one day.

Act 21:8 And on the morrow we departed, and came unto Caesarea: and entering into the house of Philip the evangelist, who was one of the seven, we abode with him.

Act 21:9 Now this man had four virgin daughters, who prophesied.

Act 21:10 And as we tarried there some days, there came down from Judaea a certain prophet, named Agabus.

Act 21:11 And coming to us, and taking Paul's girdle, he bound his own feet and hands, and said, Thus saith the Holy Spirit, So shall the Jews at Jerusalem bind the man that owneth this girdle, and shall deliver him into the hands of the Gentiles.

Act 21:12 And when we heard these things, both we and they of that place besought him not to go up to Jerusalem.

Act 21:13 Then Paul answered, What do ye, weeping and breaking my heart? for I am ready not to be bound only, but also to die at Jerusalem for the name of the Lord Jesus.

Act 21:14 And when he would not be persuaded, we ceased, saying, The will of the Lord be done.

Act 21:15 And after these days we took up our baggage and went up to Jerusalem.

Act 21:16 And there went with us also certain of the disciples from Caesarea, bringing with them one Mnason of Cyprus, an early disciple, with whom we should lodge.

Act 21:17 And when we were come to Jerusalem, the brethren received us gladly.

Act 21:18 And the day following Paul went in with us unto James; and all the elders were present.

Act 21:19 And when he had saluted them, he rehearsed one by one the things which God had wrought among the Gentiles through his ministry.

Act 21:20 And they, when they heard it, glorified God; and they said unto him, Thou seest, brother, how many thousands there are among the Jews of them that have believed; and they are all zealous for the law:

Act 21:21 and they have been informed concerning thee, that thou teachest all the Jews who are among the Gentiles to forsake Moses, telling them not to circumcise their children neither to walk after the customs.

Act 21:22 What is it therefore? They will certainly hear that thou art come.

Act 21:23 Do therefore this that we say to thee: We have four men that have a vow on them;

Act 21:24 these take, and purify thyself with them, and be at charges for them, that they may shave their heads: and all shall know that there is no truth in the things whereof they have been informed concerning thee; but that thou thyself also walkest orderly, keeping the law.

Act 21:25 But as touching the Gentiles that have believed, we wrote, giving judgment that they should keep themselves from things sacrificed to idols, and from blood, and from what is strangled, and from fornication.

Act 21:26 Then Paul took the men, and the next day purifying himself with them went into the temple, declaring the fulfilment of the days of purification, until the offering was offered for every one of them.

Act 21:27 And when the seven days were almost completed, the Jews from Asia, when they saw him in the temple, stirred up all the multitude and laid hands on him,

Act 21:28 crying out, Men of Israel, help: This is the man that teacheth all men everywhere against the people, and the law, and this place; and moreover he brought Greeks also into the temple, and hath defiled this holy place.

Act 21:29 For they had before seen with him in the city Trophimus the Ephesian, whom they supposed that Paul had brought into the temple.

Act 21:30 And all the city was moved, and the people ran together; and they laid hold on Paul, and dragged him out of the temple: and straightway the doors were shut.

Act 21:31 And as they were seeking to kill him, tidings came up to the chief captain of the band, that all Jerusalem was in confusion.

Act 21:32 And forthwith he took soldiers and centurions, and ran down upon them: and they, when they saw the chief captain and the soldiers, left off beating Paul.

Act 21:33 Then the chief captain came near, and laid hold on him, and commanded him to be bound with two chains; and inquired who he was, and what he had done.

Act 21:34 And some shouted one thing, some another, among the crowd: and when he could not know the certainty for the uproar, he commanded him to be brought into the castle.

Act 21:35 And when he came upon the stairs, so it was that he was borne of the soldiers for the violence of the crowd;

Act 21:36 for the multitude of the people followed after, crying out, Away with him.

Act 21:37 And as Paul was about to be brought into the castle, he saith unto the chief captain, May I say something unto thee? And he said, Dost thou know Greek?

Act 21:38 Art thou not then the Egyptian, who before these days stirred up to sedition and led out into the wilderness the four thousand men of the Assassins?

Act 21:39 But Paul said, I am a Jew, of Tarsus in Cilicia, a citizen of no mean city: and I beseech thee, give me leave to speak unto the people.

Act 21:40 And when he had given him leave, Paul, standing on the stairs, beckoned with the hand unto the people; and when there was made a great silence, he spake unto them in the Hebrew language, saying,

Chapter 22.

Act 22:1 Brethren and fathers, hear ye the defence which I now make unto you.

Act 22:2 And when they heard that he spake unto them in the Hebrew language, they were the more quiet: and he saith,

Act 22:3 I am a Jew, born in Tarsus of Cilicia, but brought up in this city, at the feet of Gamaliel, instructed according to the strict manner of the law of our fathers, being zealous for God, even as ye all are this day:

Act 22:4 and I persecuted this Way unto the death, binding and delivering into prisons both men and women.

Act 22:5 As also the high priest doth bear me witness, and all the estate of the elders: from whom also I received letters unto the brethren, and journeyed to Damascus to bring them also that were there unto Jerusalem in bonds to be punished.

Act 22:6 And it came to pass, that, as I made my journey, and drew nigh unto Damascus, about noon, suddenly there shone from heaven a great light round about me.

Act 22:7 And I fell unto the ground, and heard a voice saying unto me, Saul, Saul, why persecutest thou me?

Act 22:8 And I answered, Who art thou, Lord? And he said unto me, I am Jesus of Nazareth, whom thou persecutest.

Act 22:9 And they that were with me beheld indeed the light, but they heard not the voice of him that spake to me.

Act 22:10 And I said, What shall I do, Lord? And the Lord said unto me, Arise, and go into Damascus; and there it shall be told thee of all things which are appointed for thee to do.

Act 22:11 And when I could not see for the glory of that light, being led by the hand of them that were with me I came into Damascus.

Act 22:12 And one Ananias, a devout man according to the law, well reported of by all the Jews that dwelt there,

Act 22:13 came unto me, and standing by me said unto me, Brother Saul, receive thy sight. And in that very hour I looked up on him.

Act 22:14 And he said, The God of our fathers hath appointed thee to know his will, and to see the Righteous One, and to hear a voice from his mouth.

Act 22:15 For thou shalt be a witness for him unto all men of what thou hast seen and heard.

Act 22:16 And now why tarriest thou? arise, and be baptized, and wash away thy sins, calling on his name.

Act 22:17 And it came to pass, that, when I had returned to Jerusalem, and while I prayed in the temple, I fell into a trance,

Act 22:18 and saw him saying unto me, Make haste, and get thee quickly out of Jerusalem; because they will not receive of thee testimony concerning me.

Act 22:19 And I said, Lord, they themselves know that I imprisoned and beat in every synagogue them that believed on thee:

Act 22:20 and when the blood of Stephen thy witness was shed, I also was standing by, and consenting, and keeping the garments of them that slew him.

Act 22:21 And he said unto me, Depart: for I will send thee forth far hence unto the Gentiles.

Act 22:22 And they gave him audience unto this word; and they lifted up their voice, and said, Away with such a fellow from the earth: for it is not fit that he should live.

Act 22:23 And as they cried out, and threw off their garments, and cast dust into the air,

Act 22:24 the chief captain commanded him be brought into the castle, bidding that he should be examined by scourging, that he might know for what cause they so shouted against him.

Act 22:25 And when they had tied him up with the thongs, Paul said unto the centurion that stood by, Is it lawful for you to scourge a man that is a Roman, and uncondemned?

Act 22:26 And when the centurion heard it, he went to the chief captain and told him, saying, What art thou about to do? for this man is a Roman.

Act 22:27 And the chief captain came and said unto him, Tell me, art thou a Roman? And he said, Yea.

Act 22:28 And the chief captain answered, With a great sum obtained I this citizenship. And Paul said, But I am a Roman born.

Act 22:29 They then that were about to examine him straightway departed from him: and the chief captain also was afraid when he knew that he was a Roman, and because he had bound him.

Act 22:30 But on the morrow, desiring to know the certainty wherefore he was accused of the Jews, he loosed him, and commanded the chief priests and all the council to come together, and brought Paul down and set him before them.

Chapter 23.

Act 23:1 And Paul, looking stedfastly on the council, said, Brethren, I have lived before God in all good conscience until this day.

Act 23:2 And the high priest Ananias commanded them that stood by him to smite him on the mouth.

Act 23:3 Then said Paul unto him, God shall smite thee, thou whited wall: and sittest thou to judge me according to the law, and commandest me to be smitten contrary to the law?

Act 23:4 And they that stood by said, Revilest thou God's high priest?

Act 23:5 And Paul said, I knew not, brethren, that he was high priest: for it is written, Thou shalt not speak evil of a ruler of thy people.

Act 23:6 But when Paul perceived that the one part were Sadducees and the other Pharisees, he cried out in the council, Brethren, I am a Pharisee, a son of Pharisees: touching the hope and resurrection of the dead I am called in question.

Act 23:7 And when he had so said, there arose a dissension between the Pharisees and Sadducees; and the assembly was divided.

Act 23:8 For the Sadducees say that there is no resurrection, neither angel, nor spirit; but the Pharisees confess both.

Act 23:9 And there arose a great clamor: and some of the scribes of the Pharisees part stood up, and strove, saying, We find no evil in this man: and what if a spirit hath spoken to him, or an angel?

Act 23:10 And when there arose a great dissension, the chief captain, fearing lest Paul should be torn in pieces by them, commanded the soldiers to go down and take him by force from among them, and bring him into the castle.

Act 23:11 And the night following the Lord stood by him, and said, Be of good cheer: for as thou hast testified concerning me at Jerusalem, so must thou bear witness also at Rome.

Act 23:12 And when it was day, the Jews banded together, and bound themselves under a curse, saying that they would neither eat nor drink till they had killed Paul.

Act 23:13 And they were more than forty that made this conspiracy.

Act 23:14 And they came to the chief priests and the elders, and said, We have bound ourselves under a great curse, to taste nothing until we have killed Paul.

Act 23:15 Now therefore do ye with the council signify to the chief captain that he bring him down unto you, as though ye would judge of his case more exactly: and we, before he comes near, are ready to slay him.

Act 23:16 But Paul's sister's son heard of their lying in wait, and he came and entered into the castle and told Paul.

Act 23:17 And Paul called unto him one of the centurions, and said, Bring this young man unto the chief captain; for he hath something to tell him.

Act 23:18 So he took him, and brought him to the chief captain, and saith, Paul the prisoner called me unto him, and asked me to bring this young man unto thee, who hath something to say to thee.

Act 23:19 And the chief captain took him by the hand, and going aside asked him privately, What is it that thou hast to tell me?

Act 23:20 And he said, The Jews have agreed to ask thee to bring down Paul tomorrow unto the council, as though thou wouldest inquire somewhat more exactly concerning him.

Act 23:21 Do not thou therefore yield unto them: for there lie in wait for him of them more than forty men, who have bound themselves under a curse, neither to eat nor to drink till they have slain him: and now are they ready, looking for the promise from thee.

Act 23:22 So the chief captain let the young man go, charging him, Tell no man that thou hast signified these things to me.

Act 23:23 And he called unto him two of the centurions, and said, Make ready two hundred soldiers to go as far as Caesarea, and horsemen threescore and ten, and spearmen two hundred, at the third hour of the night:

Act 23:24 and he bade them provide beasts, that they might set Paul thereon, and bring him safe unto Felix the governor.

Act 23:25 And he wrote a letter after this form:

Act 23:26 Claudius Lysias unto the most excellent governor Felix, greeting.

Act 23:27 This man was seized by the Jews, and was about to be slain of them, when I came upon them with the soldiers and rescued him, having learned that he was a Roman.

Act 23:28 And desiring to know the cause wherefore they accused him, I brought him down unto their council:

Act 23:29 whom I found to be accused about questions of their law, but to have nothing laid to his charge worthy of death or of bonds.

Act 23:30 And when it was shown to me that there would be a plot against the man, I sent him to thee forthwith, charging his accusers also to speak against him before thee.

Act 23:31 So the soldiers, as it was commanded them, took Paul and brought him by night to Antipatris.

Act 23:32 But on the morrow they left the horsemen to go with him, and returned to the castle:

Act 23:33 and they, when they came to Caesarea and delivered the letter to the governor, presented Paul also before him.

Act 23:34 And when he had read it, he asked of what province he was; and when he understood that he was of Cilicia,

Act 23:35 I will hear thee fully, said he, when thine accusers also are come: and he commanded him to be kept in Herod's palace.

Chapter 24.

Act 24:1 And after five days the high priest Ananias came down with certain elders, and with an orator, one Tertullus; and they informed the governor against Paul.

Act 24:2 And when he was called, Tertullus began to accuse him, saying, Seeing that by thee we enjoy much peace, and that by the providence evils are corrected for this nation,

Act 24:3 we accept it in all ways and in all places, most excellent Felix, with all thankfulness.

Act 24:4 But, that I be not further tedious unto thee, I entreat thee to hear us of thy clemency a few words.

Act 24:5 For we have found this man a pestilent fellow, and a mover of insurrections among all the Jews throughout the world, and a ringleader of the sect of the Nazarenes:

Act 24:6 who moreover assayed to profane the temple: on whom also we laid hold: and we would have judged him according to our law.

Act 24:7 But the chief captain Lysias came, and with great violence took him away out of our hands,

Act 24:8 commanding his accusers to come before thee. from whom thou wilt be able, by examining him thyself, to take knowledge of all these things whereof we accuse him.

Act 24:9 And the Jews also joined in the charge, affirming that these things were so.

Act 24:10 And when the governor had beckoned unto him to speak, Paul answered, Forasmuch as I know that thou hast been of many years a judge unto this nation, I cheerfully make my defense:

Act 24:11 seeing that thou canst take knowledge that it is not more than twelve days since I went up to worship at Jerusalem:

Act 24:12 and neither in the temple did they find me disputing with any man or stirring up a crowd, nor in the synagogues, nor in the city.

Act 24:13 Neither can they prove to thee the things whereof they now accuse me.

Act 24:14 But this I confess unto thee, that after the Way which they call a sect, so serve I the God of our fathers, believing all things which are according to the law, and which are written in the prophets;

Act 24:15 having hope toward God, which these also themselves look for, that there shall be a resurrection both of the just and unjust.

Act 24:16 Herein I also exercise myself to have a conscience void of offence toward God and men always.

Act 24:17 Now after some years I came to bring alms to my nation, and offerings:

Act 24:18 amidst which they found me purified in the temple, with no crowd, nor yet with tumult: but there were certain Jews from Asia -

Act 24:19 who ought to have been here before thee, and to make accusation, if they had aught against me.

Act 24:20 Or else let these men themselves say what wrong-doing they found when I stood before the council,

Act 24:21 except it be for this one voice, that I cried standing among them, Touching the resurrection of the dead I am called in question before you this day.

Act 24:22 But Felix, having more exact knowledge concerning the Way, deferred them, saying, When Lysias the chief captain shall come down, I will determine your matter.

Act 24:23 And he gave order to the centurion that he should be kept in charge, and should have indulgence; and not to forbid any of his friends to minister unto him.

Act 24:24 But after certain days, Felix came with Drusilla, his wife, who was a Jewess, and sent for Paul, and heard him concerning the faith in Christ Jesus.

Act 24:25 And as he reasoned of righteousness, and self-control, and the judgment to come, Felix was terrified, and answered, Go thy way for this time; and when I have a convenient season, I will call thee unto me.

Act 24:26 He hoped withal that money would be given him of Paul: wherefore also he sent for him the oftener, and communed with him.

Act 24:27 But when two years were fulfilled, Felix was succeeded by Porcius Festus; and desiring to gain favor with the Jews, Felix left Paul in bonds.

Chapter 25.

Act 25:1 Festus therefore, having come into the province, after three days went up to Jerusalem from Caesarea.

Act 25:2 And the chief priests and the principal men of the Jews informed him against Paul; and they besought him,

Act 25:3 asking a favor against him, that he would send for him to Jerusalem; laying a plot to kill him on the way.

Act 25:4 Howbeit Festus answered, that Paul was kept in charge at Caesarea, and that he himself was about to depart thither shortly.

Act 25:5 Let them therefore, saith he, that are of power among you go down with me, and if there is anything amiss in the man, let them accuse him.

Act 25:6 And when he had tarried among them not more than eight or ten days, he went down unto Caesarea; and on the morrow he sat on the judgment-seat, and commanded Paul to be brought.

Act 25:7 And when he was come, the Jews that had come down from Jerusalem stood round about him, bringing against him many and grievous charges which they could not prove;

Act 25:8 while Paul said in his defense, Neither against the law of the Jews, nor against the temple, nor against Caesar, have I sinned at all.

Act 25:9 But Festus, desiring to gain favor with the Jews, answered Paul and said, Wilt thou go up to Jerusalem, and there be judged of these things before me?

Act 25:10 But Paul said, I am standing before Caesar's judgment-seat, where I ought to be judged: to the Jews have I done no wrong, as thou also very well knowest.

Act 25:11 If then I am a wrong-doer, and have committed anything worthy of death, I refuse not to die; but if none of those things is true whereof these accuse me, no man can give me up unto them. I appeal unto Caesar.

Act 25:12 Then Festus, when he had conferred with the council, answered, Thou hast appealed unto Caesar: unto Caesar shalt thou go.

Act 25:13 Now when certain days were passed, Agrippa the King and Bernice arrived at Caesarea, and saluted Festus.

Act 25:14 And as they tarried there many days, Festus laid Paul's case before the King, saying, There is a certain man left a prisoner by Felix;

Act 25:15 about whom, when I was at Jerusalem, the chief priests and the elders of the Jews informed me, asking for sentence against him.

Act 25:16 To whom I answered, that it is not the custom of the Romans to give up any man, before that the accused have the accusers face to face, and have had opportunity to make his defense concerning the matter laid against him.

Act 25:17 When therefore they were come together here, I made no delay, but on the next day sat on the judgment-seat, and commanded the man to be brought.

Act 25:18 Concerning whom, when the accusers stood up, they brought no charge of such evil things as I supposed;

Act 25:19 but had certain questions against him of their own religion, and of one Jesus, who was dead, whom Paul affirmed to be alive.

Act 25:20 And I, being perplexed how to inquire concerning these things, asked whether he would go to Jerusalem and there be judged of these matters.

Act 25:21 But when Paul had appealed to be kept for the decision of the emperor, I commanded him to be kept till I should send him to Caesar.

Act 25:22 And Agrippa said unto Festus, I also could wish to hear the man myself. To-morrow, saith he, thou shalt hear him.

Act 25:23 So on the morrow, when Agrippa was come, and Bernice, with great pomp, and they were entered into the place of hearing with the chief captains and principal men of the city, at the command of Festus Paul was brought in.

Act 25:24 And Festus saith, King Agrippa, and all men who are here present with us, ye behold this man, about whom all the multitude of the Jews made suit to me, both at Jerusalem and here, crying that he ought not to live any longer.

Act 25:25 But I found that he had committed nothing worthy of death: and as he himself appealed to the emperor I determined to send him.

Act 25:26 Of whom I have no certain thing to write unto my lord. Wherefore I have brought him forth before you, and specially before thee, king Agrippa, that, after examination had, I may have somewhat to write.

Act 25:27 For it seemeth to me unreasonable, in sending a prisoner, not withal to signify the charges against him.

Chapter 26.

Act 26:1 And Agrippa said unto Paul, Thou art permitted to speak for thyself. Then Paul stretched forth his hand, and made his defence:

Act 26:2 I think myself happy, king Agrippa, that I am to make my defense before thee this day touching all the things whereof I am accused by the Jews:

Act 26:3 especially because thou art expert in all customs and questions which are among the Jews: wherefore I beseech thee to hear me patiently.

Act 26:4 My manner of life then from my youth up, which was from the beginning among mine own nation and at Jerusalem, know all the Jews;

Act 26:5 having knowledge of me from the first, if they be willing to testify, that after the straitest sect of our religion I lived a Pharisee.

Act 26:6 And now I stand here to be judged for the hope of the promise made of God unto our fathers;

Act 26:7 unto which promise our twelve tribes, earnestly serving God night and day, hope to attain. And concerning this hope I am accused by the Jews, O king!

Act 26:8 Why is it judged incredible with you, if God doth raise the dead?

Act 26:9 I verily thought with myself that I ought to do many things contrary to the name of Jesus of Nazareth.

Act 26:10 And this I also did in Jerusalem: and I both shut up many of the saints in prisons, having received authority from the chief priests, and when they were put to death I gave my vote against them.

Act 26:11 And punishing them oftentimes in all the synagogues, I strove to make them blaspheme; and being exceedingly mad against them, I persecuted them even unto foreign cities.

Act 26:12 Whereupon as I journeyed to Damascus with the authority and commission of the chief priests,

Act 26:13 at midday, O king, I saw on the way a light from heaven, above the brightness of the sun, shining round about me and them that journeyed with me.

Act 26:14 And when we were all fallen to the earth, I heard a voice saying unto me in the Hebrew language, Saul, Saul, why persecutest thou me? it is hard for thee to kick against the goad.

Act 26:15 And I said, Who art thou, Lord? And the Lord said, I am Jesus whom thou persecutest.

Act 26:16 But arise, and stand upon thy feet: for to this end have I appeared unto thee, to appoint thee a minister and a witness both of the things wherein thou hast seen me, and of the things wherein I will appear unto thee;

Act 26:17 delivering thee from the people, and from the Gentiles, unto whom I send thee,

Act 26:18 to open their eyes, that they may turn from darkness to light and from the power of Satan unto God, that they may receive remission of sins and an inheritance among them that are sanctified by faith in me.

Act 26:19 Wherefore, O king Agrippa, I was not disobedient unto the heavenly vision:

Act 26:20 but declared both to them of Damascus first and at Jerusalem, and throughout all the country of Judaea, and also to the Gentiles, that they should repent and turn to God, doing works worthy of repentance.

Act 26:21 For this cause the Jews seized me in the temple, and assayed to kill me.

Act 26:22 Having therefore obtained the help that is from God, I stand unto this day testifying both to small and great, saying nothing but what the prophets and Moses did say should come;

Act 26:23 how that the Christ must suffer, and how that he first by the resurrection of the dead should proclaim light both to the people and to the Gentiles.

Act 26:24 And as he thus made his defense, Festus saith with a loud voice, Paul, thou art mad; thy much learning is turning thee mad.

Act 26:25 But Paul saith, I am not mad, most excellent Festus; but speak forth words of truth and soberness.

Act 26:26 For the king knoweth of these things, unto whom also I speak freely: for I am persuaded that none of these things is hidden from him; for this hath not been done in a corner.

Act 26:27 King Agrippa, believest thou the prophets? I know that thou believest.

Act 26:28 And Agrippa said unto Paul, With but little persuasion thou wouldest fain make me a Christian.

Act 26:29 And Paul said, I would to God, that whether with little or with much, not thou only, but also all that hear me this day, might become such as I am, except these bonds.

Act 26:30 And the king rose up, and the governor, and Bernice, and they that sat with them:

Act 26:31 and when they had withdrawn, they spake one to another, saying, This man doeth nothing worthy of death or of bonds.

Act 26:32 And Agrippa said unto Festus, This man might have been set at liberty, if he had not appealed unto Caesar.

Chapter 27.

Act 27:1 And when it was determined that we should sail for Italy, they delivered Paul and certain other prisoners to a centurion named Julius, of the Augustan band.

Act 27:2 And embarking in a ship of Adramyttium, which was about to sail unto the places on the coast of Asia, we put to sea, Aristarchus, a Macedonian of Thessalonica, being with us.

Act 27:3 And the next day we touched at Sidon: and Julius treated Paul kindly, and gave him leave to go unto his friends and refresh himself.

Act 27:4 And putting to sea from thence, we sailed under the lee of Cyprus, because the winds were contrary.

Act 27:5 And when we had sailed across the sea which is off Cilicia and Pamphylia, we came to Myra, a city of Lycia.

Act 27:6 And there the centurion found a ship of Alexandria sailing for Italy; and he put us therein.

Act 27:7 And when we had sailed slowly many days, and were come with difficulty over against Cnidus, the wind not further suffering us, we sailed under the lee of Crete, over against Salmone;

Act 27:8 and with difficulty coasting along it we came unto a certain place called Fair Havens; nigh whereunto was the city of Lasea.

Act 27:9 And when much time was spent, and the voyage was now dangerous, because the Fast was now already gone by, Paul admonished them,

Act 27:10 and said unto them, Sirs, I perceive that the voyage will be with injury and much loss, not only of the lading and the ship, but also of our lives.

Act 27:11 But the centurion gave more heed to the master and to the owner of the ship, than to those things which were spoken by Paul.

Act 27:12 And because the haven was not commodious to winter in, the more part advised to put to sea from thence, if by any means they could reach Phoenix, and winter there; which is a haven of Crete, looking northeast and south-east.

Act 27:13 And when the south wind blew softly, supposing that they had obtained their purpose, they weighed anchor and sailed along Crete, close in shore.

Act 27:14 But after no long time there beat down from it a tempestuous wind, which is called Euraquilo:

Act 27:15 and when the ship was caught, and could not face the wind, we gave way to it, and were driven.

Act 27:16 And running under the lee of a small island called Cauda, we were able, with difficulty, to secure the boat:

Act 27:17 and when they had hoisted it up, they used helps, under-girding the ship; and, fearing lest they should be cast upon the Syrtis, they lowered the gear, and so were driven.

Act 27:18 And as we labored exceedingly with the storm, the next day they began to throw the the freight overboard;

Act 27:19 and the third day they cast out with their own hands the tackling of the ship.

Act 27:20 And when neither sun nor stars shone upon us for many days, and no small tempest lay on us, all hope that we should be saved was now taken away.

Act 27:21 And when they had been long without food, then Paul stood forth in the midst of them, and said, Sirs, ye should have hearkened unto me, and not have set sail from Crete, and have gotten this injury and loss.

Act 27:22 And now I exhort you to be of good cheer; for there shall be no loss of life among you, but only of the ship.

Act 27:23 For there stood by me this night an angel of the God whose I am, whom also I serve,

Act 27:24 saying, Fear not, Paul; thou must stand before Caesar: and lo, God hath granted thee all them that sail with thee.

Act 27:25 Wherefore, sirs, be of good cheer: for I believe God, that it shall be even so as it hath been spoken unto me.

Act 27:26 But we must be cast upon a certain island.

Act 27:27 But when the fourteenth night was come, as we were driven to and fro in the sea of Adria, about midnight the sailors surmised that they were drawing near to some country:

Act 27:28 and they sounded, and found twenty fathoms; and after a little space, they sounded again, and found fifteen fathoms.

Act 27:29 And fearing lest haply we should be cast ashore on rocky ground, they let go four anchors from the stern, and wished for the day.

Act 27:30 And as the sailors were seeking to flee out of the ship, and had lowered the boat into the sea, under color as though they would lay out anchors from the foreship,

Act 27:31 Paul said to the centurion and to the soldiers, Except these abide in the ship, ye cannot be saved.

Act 27:32 Then the soldiers cut away the ropes of the boat, and let her fall off.

Act 27:33 And while the day was coming on, Paul besought them all to take some food, saying, This day is the fourteenth day that ye wait and continue fasting, having taken nothing.

Act 27:34 Wherefore I beseech you to take some food: for this is for your safety: for there shall not a hair perish from the head of any of you.

Act 27:35 And when he had said this, and had taken bread, he gave thanks to God in the presence of all; and he brake it, and began to eat.

Act 27:36 Then were they all of good cheer, and themselves also took food.

Act 27:37 And we were in all in the ship two hundred threescore and sixteen souls.

Act 27:38 And when they had eaten enough, they lightened the ship, throwing out the wheat into the sea.

Act 27:39 And when it was day, they knew not the land: but they perceived a certain bay with a beach, and they took counsel whether they could drive the ship upon it.

Act 27:40 And casting off the anchors, they left them in the sea, at the same time loosing the bands of the rudders; and hoisting up the foresail to the wind, they made for the beach.

Act 27:41 But lighting upon a place where two seas met, they ran the vessel aground; and the foreship struck and remained unmoveable, but the stern began to break up by the violence of the waves.

Act 27:42 And the soldiers' counsel was to kill the prisoners, lest any of them should swim out, and escape.

Act 27:43 But the centurion, desiring to save Paul, stayed them from their purpose; and commanded that they who could swim should cast themselves overboard, and get first to the land;

Act 27:44 and the rest, some on planks, and some on other things from the ship. And so it came to pass, that they all escaped safe to the land.

Chapter 28.

Act 28:1 And when we were escaped, then we knew that the island was called Melita.

Act 28:2 And the barbarians showed us no common kindness; for they kindled a fire, and received us all, because of the present rain, and because of the cold.

Act 28:3 But when Paul had gathered a bundle of sticks and laid them on the fire, a viper came out by reason of the heat, and fastened on his hand.

Act 28:4 And when the barbarians saw the venomous creature hanging from his hand, they said one to another, No doubt this man is a murderer, whom, though he hath escaped from the sea, yet Justice hath not suffered to live.

Act 28:5 Howbeit he shook off the creature into the fire, and took no harm.

Act 28:6 But they expected that he would have swollen, or fallen down dead suddenly: but when they were long in expectation and beheld nothing amiss came to him, they changed their minds, and said that he was a god.

Act 28:7 Now in the neighborhood of that place were lands belonging to the chief man of the island, named Publius, who received us, and entertained us three days courteously.

Act 28:8 And it was so, that the father of Publius lay sick of fever and dysentery: unto whom Paul entered in, and prayed, and laying his hands on him healed him.

Act 28:9 And when this was done, the rest also that had diseases in the island came, and were cured:

Act 28:10 who also honored us with many honors; and when we sailed, they put on board such things as we needed.

Act 28:11 And after three months we set sail in a ship of Alexandria which had wintered in the island, whose sign was The Twin Brothers.

Act 28:12 And touching at Syracuse, we tarried there three days.

Act 28:13 And from thence we made a circuit, and arrived at Rhegium: and after one day a south wind sprang up, and on the second day we came to Puteoli;

Act 28:14 where we found brethren, and were entreated to tarry with them seven days: and so we came to Rome.

Act 28:15 And from thence the brethren, when they heard of us, came to meet us as far as The Market of Appius and The Three Taverns; whom when Paul saw, he thanked God, and took courage.

Act 28:16 And when we entered into Rome, Paul was suffered to abide by himself with the soldier that guarded him.

Act 28:17 And it came to pass, that after three days he called together those that were the chief of the Jews: and when they were come together, he said unto them, I, brethren, though I had done nothing against the people, or the customs of our fathers, yet was delivered prisoner from Jerusalem into the hands of the Romans:

Act 28:18 who, when they had examined me, desired to set me at liberty, because there was no cause of death in me.

Act 28:19 But when the Jews spake against it, I was constrained to appeal unto Caesar; not that I had aught whereof to accuse my nation.

Act 28:20 For this cause therefore did I entreat you to see and to speak with me: for because of the hope of Israel I am bound with this chain.

Act 28:21 And they said unto him, We neither received letters from Judaea concerning thee, nor did any of the brethren come hither and report or speak any harm of thee.

Act 28:22 But we desire to hear of thee what thou thinkest: for as concerning this sect, it is known to us that everywhere it is spoken against.

Act 28:23 And when they had appointed him a day, they came to him into his lodging in great number; to whom he expounded the matter, testifying the kingdom of God, and persuading them concerning Jesus, both from the law of Moses and from the prophets, from morning till evening.

Act 28:24 And some believed the things which were spoken, and some disbelieved.

Act 28:25 And when they agreed not among themselves, they departed after that Paul had spoken one word, Well spake the Holy Spirit through Isaiah the prophet unto your fathers,

Act 28:26 saying, Go thou unto this people, and say, By hearing ye shall hear, and shall in no wise understand; And seeing ye shall see, and shall in no wise perceive:

Act 28:27 For this people's heart is waxed gross, And their ears are dull of hearing, And their eyes they have closed; Lest, haply they should perceive with their eyes, And hear with their ears, And understand with their heart, And should turn again, And I should heal them.

Act 28:28 Be it known therefore unto you, that this salvation of God is sent unto the Gentiles: they will also hear.

Act 28:29 And when he had said these words, the Jews departed, having much disputing among themselves.

Act 28:30 And he abode two whole years in his own hired dwelling, and received all that went in unto him,

Act 28:31 preaching the kingdom of God, and teaching the things concerning the Lord Jesus Christ with all boldness, none forbidding him.

III. The Letters of the Apostle Paul

7. Romans

Chapter 1.

Rom 1:1 Paul, a servant of Jesus Christ, called to be an apostle, separated unto the gospel of God,

Rom 1:2 which he promised afore through his prophets in the holy scriptures,

Rom 1:3   concerning his Son, who was born of the seed of David according to the flesh,

Rom 1:4 who was declared to be the Son of God with power, according to the spirit of holiness, by the resurrection from the dead; even Jesus Christ our Lord,

Rom 1:5   through whom we received grace and apostleship, unto obedience of faith among all the nations, for his name's sake;

Rom 1:6 among whom are ye also called to be Jesus Christ's:

Rom 1:7 to all that are in Rome, beloved of God, called to be saints: Grace to you and peace from God our Father and the Lord Jesus Christ.

Rom 1:8   First, I thank my God through Jesus Christ for you all, that your faith is proclaimed throughout the whole world.

Rom 1:9 For God is my witness, whom I serve in my spirit in the gospel of his Son, how unceasingly I make mention of you, always in my prayers

Rom 1:10 making request, if by any means now at length I may be prospered by the will of God to come unto you.

Rom 1:11 For I long to see you, that I may impart unto you some spiritual gift, to the end ye may be established;

Rom 1:12 that is, that I with you may be comforted in you, each of us by the other's faith, both yours and mine.

Rom 1:13 And I would not have you ignorant, brethren, that oftentimes I purposed to come unto you (and was hindered hitherto), that I might have some fruit in you also, even as in the rest of the Gentiles.

Rom 1:14 I am debtor both to Greeks and to Barbarians, both to the wise and to the foolish.

Rom 1:15 So, as much as in me is, I am ready to preach the gospel to you also that are in Rome.

Rom 1:16 For I am not ashamed of the gospel: for it is the power of God unto salvation to every one that believeth; to the Jew first, and also to the Greek.

Rom 1:17 For therein is revealed a righteousness of God from faith unto faith: as it is written, But the righteous shall live by faith.

Rom 1:18 For the wrath of God is revealed from heaven against all ungodliness and unrighteousness of men, who hinder the truth in unrighteousness;

Rom 1:19   because that which is known of God is manifest in them; for God manifested it unto them.

Rom 1:20 For the invisible things of him since the creation of the world are clearly seen, being perceived through the things that are made, even his everlasting power and divinity; that they may be without excuse:

Rom 1:21 because that, knowing God, they glorified him not as God, neither gave thanks; but became vain in their reasonings, and their senseless heart was darkened.

Rom 1:22 Professing themselves to be wise, they became fools,

Rom 1:23 and changed the glory of the incorruptible God for the likeness of an image of corruptible man, and of birds, and four-footed beasts, and creeping things.

Rom 1:24 Wherefore God gave them up in the lusts of their hearts unto uncleanness, that their bodies should be dishonored among themselves:

Rom 1:25 for that they exchanged the truth of God for a lie, and worshipped and served the creature rather than the Creator, who is blessed for ever. Amen.

Rom 1:26 For this cause God gave them up unto vile passions: for their women changed the natural use into that which is against nature:

Rom 1:27 and likewise also the men, leaving the natural use of the woman, burned in their lust one toward another, men with men working unseemliness, and receiving in themselves that recompense of their error which was due.

Rom 1:28 And even as they refused to have God in their knowledge, God gave them up unto a reprobate mind, to do those things which are not fitting;

Rom 1:29   being filled with all unrighteousness, wickedness, covetousness, maliciousness; full of envy, murder, strife, deceit, malignity; whisperers,

Rom 1:30 backbiters, hateful to God, insolent, haughty, boastful, inventors of evil things, disobedient to parents,

Rom 1:31   without understanding, covenant-breakers, without natural affection, unmerciful:

Rom 1:32 who, knowing the ordinance of God, that they that practise such things are worthy of death, not only do the same, but also consent with them that practise them.

Chapter 2.

Rom 2:1 Wherefore thou art without excuse, O man, whosoever thou art that judgest: for wherein thou judges another, thou condemnest thyself; for thou that judgest dost practise the same things.

Rom 2:2 And we know that the judgment of God is according to truth against them that practise such things.

Rom 2:3 And reckonest thou this, O man, who judgest them that practise such things, and doest the same, that thou shalt escape the judgment of God?

Rom 2:4   Or despisest thou the riches of his goodness and forbearance and longsuffering, not knowing that the goodness of God leadeth thee to repentance?

Rom 2:5 but after thy hardness and impenitent heart treasurest up for thyself wrath in the day of wrath and revelation of the righteous judgment of God;

Rom 2:6 who will render to every man according to his works:

Rom 2:7   to them that by patience in well-doing seek for glory and honor and incorruption, eternal life:

Rom 2:8   but unto them that are factious, and obey not the truth, but obey unrighteousness, shall be wrath and indignation,

Rom 2:9 tribulation and anguish, upon every soul of man that worketh evil, of the Jew first, and also of the Greek;

Rom 2:10 but glory and honor and peace to every man that worketh good, to the Jew first, and also to the Greek:

Rom 2:11 for there is no respect of persons with God.

Rom 2:12 For as many as have sinned without law shall also perish without the law: and as many as have sinned under the law shall be judged by the law;

Rom 2:13 for not the hearers of the law are just before God, but the doers of the law shall be justified:

Rom 2:14 (for when Gentiles that have not the law do by nature the things of the law, these, not having the law, are the law unto themselves;

Rom 2:15 in that they show the work of the law written in their hearts, their conscience bearing witness therewith, and their thoughts one with another accusing or else excusing them);

Rom 2:16 in the day when God shall judge the secrets of men, according to my gospel, by Jesus Christ.

Rom 2:17 But if thou bearest the name of a Jew, and restest upon the law, and gloriest in God,

Rom 2:18 and knowest his will, and approvest the things that are excellent, being instructed out of the law,

Rom 2:19 and art confident that thou thyself art a guide of the blind, a light of them that are in darkness,

Rom 2:20 a corrector of the foolish, a teacher of babes, having in the law the form of knowledge and of the truth;

Rom 2:21 thou therefore that teachest another, teachest thou not thyself? thou that preachest a man should not steal, dost thou steal?

Rom 2:22 thou that sayest a man should not commit adultery, dost thou commit adultery? thou that abhorrest idols, dost thou rob temples?

Rom 2:23 thou who gloriest in the law, through thy transgression of the law dishonorest thou God?

Rom 2:24 For the name of God is blasphemed among the Gentiles because of you, even as it is written.

Rom 2:25 For circumcision indeed profiteth, if thou be a doer of the law: but if thou be a transgressor of the law, thy circumcision is become uncircumcision.

Rom 2:26 If therefore the uncircumcision keep the ordinances of the law, shall not his uncircumcision be reckoned for circumcision?

Rom 2:27 and shall not the uncircumcision which is by nature, if it fulfil the law, judge thee, who with the letter and circumcision art a transgressor of the law?

Rom 2:28 For he is not a Jew who is one outwardly; neither is that circumcision which is outward in the flesh:

Rom 2:29 but he is a Jew who is one inwardly; and circumcision is that of the heart, in the spirit not in the letter; whose praise is not of men, but of God.

Chapter 3.

Rom 3:1 What advantage then hath the Jew? or what is the profit of circumcision?

Rom 3:2 Much every way: first of all, that they were intrusted with the oracles of God.

Rom 3:3 For what if some were without faith? shall their want of faith make of none effect the faithfulness of God?

Rom 3:4 God forbid: yea, let God be found true, but every man a liar; as it is written, That thou mightest be justified in thy words, And mightest prevail when thou comest into judgment.

Rom 3:5 But if our righteousness commendeth the righteousness of God, what shall we say? Is God unrighteous who visiteth with wrath? (I speak after the manner of men.)

Rom 3:6 God forbid: for then how shall God judge the world?

Rom 3:7 But if the truth of God through my lie abounded unto his glory, why am I also still judged as a sinner?

Rom 3:8 and why not (as we are slanderously reported, and as some affirm that we say), Let us do evil, that good may come? whose condemnation is just.

Rom 3:9 What then? are we better than they? No, in no wise: for we before laid to the charge both of Jews and Greeks, that they are all under sin;

Rom 3:10 as it is written, There is none righteous, no, not one;

Rom 3:11 There is none that understandeth, There is none that seeketh after God;

Rom 3:12 They have all turned aside, they are together become unprofitable; There is none that doeth good, no, not, so much as one:

Rom 3:13 Their throat is an open sepulchre; With their tongues they have used deceit: The poison of asps is under their lips:

Rom 3:14 Whose mouth is full of cursing and bitterness:

Rom 3:15 Their feet are swift to shed blood;

Rom 3:16 Destruction and misery are in their ways;

Rom 3:17 And the way of peace have they not known:

Rom 3:18 There is no fear of God before their eyes.

Rom 3:19 Now we know that what things soever the law saith, it speaketh to them that are under the law; that every mouth may be stopped, and all the world may be brought under the judgment of God:

Rom 3:20 because by the works of the law shall no flesh be justified in his sight; for through the law cometh the knowledge of sin.

Rom 3:21 But now apart from the law a righteousness of God hath been manifested, being witnessed by the law and the prophets;

Rom 3:22 even the righteousness of God through faith in Jesus Christ unto all them that believe; for there is no distinction;

Rom 3:23 for all have sinned, and fall short of the glory of God;

Rom 3:24 being justified freely by his grace through the redemption that is in Christ Jesus:

Rom 3:25 whom God set forth to be a propitiation, through faith, in his blood, to show his righteousness because of the passing over of the sins done aforetime, in the forbearance of God;

Rom 3:26 for the showing, I say, of his righteousness at this present season: that he might himself be just, and the justifier of him that hath faith in Jesus.

Rom 3:27 Where then is the glorying? It is excluded. By what manner of law? of works? Nay: but by a law of faith.

Rom 3:28 We reckon therefore that a man is justified by faith apart from the works of the law.

Rom 3:29 Or is God the God of Jews only? is he not the God of Gentiles also? Yea, of Gentiles also:

Rom 3:30 if so be that God is one, and he shall justify the circumcision by faith, and the uncircumcision through faith.

Rom 3:31 Do we then make the law of none effect through faith? God forbid: nay, we establish the law.

Chapter 4.

Rom 4:1 What then shall we say that Abraham, our forefather, hath found according to the flesh?

Rom 4:2 For if Abraham was justified by works, he hath whereof to glory; but not toward God.

Rom 4:3 For what saith the scripture? And Abraham believed God, and it was reckoned unto him for righteousness.

Rom 4:4 Now to him that worketh, the reward is not reckoned as of grace, but as of debt.

Rom 4:5 But to him that worketh not, but believeth on him that justifieth the ungodly, his faith is reckoned for righteousness.

Rom 4:6 Even as David also pronounceth blessing upon the man, unto whom God reckoneth righteousness apart from works,

Rom 4:7 saying, Blessed are they whose iniquities are forgiven, And whose sins are covered.

Rom 4:8 Blessed is the man to whom, the Lord will not reckon sin.

Rom 4:9 Is this blessing then pronounced upon the circumcision, or upon the uncircumcision also? for we say, To Abraham his faith was reckoned for righteousness.

Rom 4:10 How then was it reckoned? when he was in circumcision, or in uncircumcision? Not in circumcision, but in uncircumcision:

Rom 4:11 and he received the sign of circumcision, a seal of the righteousness of the faith which he had while he was in uncircumcision; that he might be the father of all them that believe, though they be in uncircumcision, that righteousness might be reckoned unto them;

Rom 4:12 and the father of circumcision to them who not only are of the circumcision, but who also walk in the steps of that faith of our father Abraham which he had in uncircumcision.

Rom 4:13 For not through the law was the promise to Abraham or to his seed that he should be heir of the world, but through the righteousness of faith.

Rom 4:14 For if they that are of the law are heirs, faith is made void, and the promise is made of none effect:

Rom 4:15 for the law worketh wrath; but where there is no law, neither is there transgression.

Rom 4:16 For this cause it is of faith, that it may be according to grace; to the end that the promise may be sure to all the seed; not to that only which is of the law, but to that also which is of the faith of Abraham, who is the father of us all

Rom 4:17 (as it is written, A father of many nations have I made thee) before him whom he believed, even God, who giveth life to the dead, and calleth the things that are not, as though they were.

Rom 4:18 Who in hope believed against hope, to the end that he might become a father of many nations, according to that which had been spoken, So shall thy seed be.

Rom 4:19 And without being weakened in faith he considered his own body now as good as dead (he being about a hundred years old), and the deadness of Sarah's womb;

Rom 4:20 yet, looking unto the promise of God, he wavered not through unbelief, but waxed strong through faith, giving glory to God,

Rom 4:21   and being fully assured that what he had promised, he was able also to perform.

Rom 4:22   Wherefore also it was reckoned unto him for righteousness.

Rom 4:23   Now it was not written for his sake alone, that it was reckoned unto him;

Rom 4:24   but for our sake also, unto whom it shall be reckoned, who believe on him that raised Jesus our Lord from the dead,

Rom 4:25   who was delivered up for our trespasses, and was raised for our justification.

Chapter 5.

Rom 5:1   Being therefore justified by faith, we have peace with God through our Lord Jesus Christ;

Rom 5:2   through whom also we have had our access by faith into this grace wherein we stand; and we rejoice in hope of the glory of God.

Rom 5:3   And not only so, but we also rejoice in our tribulations: knowing that tribulation worketh stedfastness;

Rom 5:4   and stedfastness, approvedness; and approvedness, hope:

Rom 5:5   and hope putteth not to shame; because the love of God hath been shed abroad in our hearts through the Holy Spirit which was given unto us.

Rom 5:6   For while we were yet weak, in due season Christ died for the ungodly.

Rom 5:7   For scarcely for a righteous man will one die: for peradventure for the good man some one would even dare to die.

Rom 5:8   But God commendeth his own love toward us, in that, while we were yet sinners, Christ died for us.

Rom 5:9   Much more then, being now justified by his blood, shall we be saved from the wrath of God through him.

Rom 5:10   For if, while we were enemies, we were reconciled to God through the death of his Son, much more, being reconciled, shall we be saved by his life;

Rom 5:11   and not only so, but we also rejoice in God through our Lord Jesus Christ, through whom we have now received the reconciliation.

Rom 5:12   Therefore, as through one man sin entered into the world, and death through sin; and so death passed unto all men, for that all sinned: -

Rom 5:13   for until the law sin was in the world; but sin is not imputed when there is no law.

Rom 5:14   Nevertheless death reigned from Adam until Moses, even over them that had not sinned after the likeness of Adam's transgression, who is a figure of him that was to come.

Rom 5:15   But not as the trespass, so also is the free gift. For if by the trespass of the one the many died, much more did the grace of God, and the gift by the grace of the one man, Jesus Christ, abound unto the many.

Rom 5:16   And not as through one that sinned, so is the gift: for the judgment came of one unto condemnation, but the free gift came of many trespasses unto justification.

Rom 5:17   For if, by the trespass of the one, death reigned through the one; much more shall they that receive the abundance of grace and of the gift of righteousness reign in life through the one, even Jesus Christ.

Rom 5:18   So then as through one trespass the judgment came unto all men to condemnation; even so through one act of righteousness the free gift came unto all men to justification of life.

Rom 5:19   For as through the one man's disobedience the many were made sinners, even so through the obedience of the one shall the many be made righteous.

Rom 5:20   And the law came in besides, that the trespass might abound; but where sin abounded, grace did abound more exceedingly:

Rom 5:21   that, as sin reigned in death, even so might grace reign through righteousness unto eternal life through Jesus Christ our Lord.

Chapter 6.

Rom 6:1   What shall we say then? Shall we continue in sin, that grace may abound?

Rom 6:2   God forbid. We who died to sin, how shall we any longer live therein?

Rom 6:3   Or are ye ignorant that all we who were baptized into Christ Jesus were baptized into his death?

Rom 6:4   We were buried therefore with him through baptism unto death: that like as Christ was raised from the dead through the glory of the Father, so we also might walk in newness of life.

Rom 6:5   For if we have become united with him in the likeness of his death, we shall be also in the likeness of his resurrection;

Rom 6:6   knowing this, that our old man was crucified with him, that the body of sin might be done away, that so we should no longer be in bondage to sin;

Rom 6:7   for he that hath died is justified from sin.

Rom 6:8   But if we died with Christ, we believe that we shall also live with him;

Rom 6:9   knowing that Christ being raised from the dead dieth no more; death no more hath dominion over him.

Rom 6:10   For the death that he died, he died unto sin once: but the life that he liveth, he liveth unto God.

Rom 6:11   Even so reckon ye also yourselves to be dead unto sin, but alive unto God in Christ Jesus.

Rom 6:12   Let not sin therefore reign in your mortal body, that ye should obey the lusts thereof:

Rom 6:13   neither present your members unto sin as instruments of unrighteousness; but present yourselves unto God, as alive from the dead, and your members as instruments of righteousness unto God.

Rom 6:14   For sin shall not have dominion over you: for ye are not under law, but under grace.

Rom 6:15   What then? shall we sin, because we are not under law, but under grace? God forbid.

Rom 6:16   Know ye not, that to whom ye present yourselves as servants unto obedience, his servants ye are whom ye obey; whether of sin unto death, or of obedience unto righteousness?

Rom 6:17   But thanks be to God, that, whereas ye were servants of sin, ye became obedient from the heart to that form of teaching whereunto ye were delivered;

Rom 6:18   and being made free from sin, ye became servants of righteousness.

Rom 6:19   I speak after the manner of men because of the infirmity of your flesh: for as ye presented your members as servants to uncleanness and to iniquity unto iniquity, even so now present your members as servants to righteousness unto sanctification.

Rom 6:20 For when ye were servants of sin, ye were free in regard of righteousness.

Rom 6:21 What fruit then had ye at that time in the things whereof ye are now ashamed? for the end of those things is death.

Rom 6:22 But now being made free from sin and become servants to God, ye have your fruit unto sanctification, and the end eternal life.

Rom 6:23 For the wages of sin is death; but the free gift of God is eternal life in Christ Jesus our Lord.

Chapter 7.

Rom 7:1 Or are ye ignorant, brethren (for I speak to men who know the law), that the law hath dominion over a man for so long time as he liveth?

Rom 7:2 For the woman that hath a husband is bound by law to the husband while he liveth; but if the husband die, she is discharged from the law of the husband.

Rom 7:3 So then if, while the husband liveth, she be joined to another man, she shall be called an adulteress: but if the husband die, she is free from the law, so that she is no adulteress, though she be joined to another man.

Rom 7:4 Wherefore, my brethren, ye also were made dead to the law through the body of Christ; that ye should be joined to another, even to him who was raised from the dead, that we might bring forth fruit unto God.

Rom 7:5 For when we were in the flesh, the sinful passions, which were through the law, wrought in our members to bring forth fruit unto death.

Rom 7:6 But now we have been discharged from the law, having died to that wherein we were held; so that we serve in newness of the spirit, and not in oldness of the letter.

Rom 7:7 What shall we say then? Is the law sin? God forbid. Howbeit, I had not known sin, except through the law: for I had not known coveting, except the law had said, Thou shalt not covet:

Rom 7:8 but sin, finding occasion, wrought in me through the commandment all manner of coveting: for apart from the law sin is dead.

Rom 7:9 And I was alive apart from the law once: but when the commandment came, sin revived, and I died;

Rom 7:10 and the commandment, which was unto life, this I found to be unto death:

Rom 7:11 for sin, finding occasion, through the commandment beguiled me, and through it slew me.

Rom 7:12 So that the law is holy, and the commandment holy, and righteous, and good.

Rom 7:13 Did then that which is good become death unto me? God forbid. But sin, that it might be shown to be sin, by working death to me through that which is good; - that through the commandment sin might become exceeding sinful.

Rom 7:14 For we know that the law is spiritual: but I am carnal, sold under sin.

Rom 7:15 For that which I do I know not: for not what I would, that do I practise; but what I hate, that I do.

Rom 7:16 But if what I would not, that I do, I consent unto the law that it is good.

Rom 7:17 So now it is no more I that do it, but sin which dwelleth in me.

Rom 7:18 For I know that in me, that is, in my flesh, dwelleth no good thing: for to will is present with me, but to do that which is good is not.

Rom 7:19 For the good which I would I do not: but the evil which I would not, that I practise.

Rom 7:20 But if what I would not, that I do, it is no more I that do it, but sin which dwelleth in me.

Rom 7:21 I find then the law, that, to me who would do good, evil is present.

Rom 7:22 For I delight in the law of God after the inward man:

Rom 7:23 but I see a different law in my members, warring against the law of my mind, and bringing me into captivity under the law of sin which is in my members.

Rom 7:24 Wretched man that I am! who shall deliver me out of the body of this death?

Rom 7:25 I thank God through Jesus Christ our Lord. So then I of myself with the mind, indeed, serve the law of God; but with the flesh the law of sin.

Chapter 8.

Rom 8:1 There is therefore now no condemnation to them that are in Christ Jesus.

Rom 8:2 For the law of the Spirit of life in Christ Jesus made me free from the law of sin and of death.

Rom 8:3 For what the law could not do, in that it was weak through the flesh, God, sending his own Son in the likeness of sinful flesh and for sin, condemned sin in the flesh:

Rom 8:4 that the ordinance of the law might be fulfilled in us, who walk not after the flesh, but after the Spirit.

Rom 8:5 For they that are after the flesh mind the things of the flesh; but they that are after the Spirit the things of the Spirit.

Rom 8:6 For the mind of the flesh is death; but the mind of the Spirit is life and peace:

Rom 8:7 because the mind of the flesh is enmity against God; for it is not subject to the law of God, neither indeed can it be:

Rom 8:8 and they that are in the flesh cannot please God.

Rom 8:9 But ye are not in the flesh but in the Spirit, if so be that the Spirit of God dwelleth in you. But if any man hath not the Spirit of Christ, he is none of his.

Rom 8:10 And if Christ is in you, the body is dead because of sin; but the spirit is life because of righteousness.

Rom 8:11 But if the Spirit of him that raised up Jesus from the dead dwelleth in you, he that raised up Christ Jesus from the dead shall give life also to your mortal bodies through his Spirit that dwelleth in you.

Rom 8:12 So then, brethren, we are debtors, not to the flesh, to live after the flesh:

Rom 8:13 for if ye live after the flesh, ye must die; but if by the Spirit ye put to death the deeds of the body, ye shall live.

Rom 8:14 For as many as are led by the Spirit of God, these are sons of God.

Rom 8:15 For ye received not the spirit of bondage again unto fear; but ye received the spirit of adoption, whereby we cry, Abba, Father.

Rom 8:16 The Spirit himself beareth witness with our spirit, that we are children of God:

Rom 8:17 and if children, then heirs; heirs of God, and joint-heirs with Christ; if so be that we suffer with him, that we may be also glorified with him.

Rom 8:18 For I reckon that the sufferings of this present time are not worthy to be compared with the glory which shall be revealed to us-ward.

Rom 8:19 For the earnest expectation of the creation waiteth for the revealing of the sons of God.

Rom 8:20 For the creation was subjected to vanity, not of its own will, but by reason of him who subjected it, in hope

Rom 8:21 that the creation itself also shall be delivered from the bondage of corruption into the liberty of the glory of the children of God.

Rom 8:22 For we know that the whole creation groaneth and travaileth in pain together until now.

Rom 8:23 And not only so, but ourselves also, who have the first-fruits of the Spirit, even we ourselves groan within ourselves, waiting for our adoption, to wit, the redemption of our body.

Rom 8:24 For in hope were we saved: but hope that is seen is not hope: for who hopeth for that which he seeth?

Rom 8:25 But if we hope for that which we see not, then do we with patience wait for it.

Rom 8:26 And in like manner the Spirit also helpeth our infirmity: for we know not how to pray as we ought; but the Spirit himself maketh intercession for us with groanings which cannot be uttered;

Rom 8:27 and he that searcheth the hearts knoweth what is the mind of the Spirit, because he maketh intercession for the saints according to the will of God.

Rom 8:28 And we know that to them that love God all things work together for good, even to them that are called according to his purpose.

Rom 8:29 For whom he foreknew, he also foreordained to be conformed to the image of his Son, that he might be the firstborn among many brethren:

Rom 8:30 and whom he foreordained, them he also called: and whom he called, them he also justified: and whom he justified, them he also glorified.

Rom 8:31 What then shall we say to these things? If God is for us, who is against us?

Rom 8:32 He that spared not his own Son, but delivered him up for us all, how shall he not also with him freely give us all things?

Rom 8:33 Who shall lay anything to the charge of God's elect? It is God that justifieth;

Rom 8:34 who is he that condemneth? It is Christ Jesus that died, yea rather, that was raised from the dead, who is at the right hand of God, who also maketh intercession for us.

Rom 8:35 Who shall separate us from the love of Christ? shall tribulation, or anguish, or persecution, or famine, or nakedness, or peril, or sword?

Rom 8:36 Even as it is written, For thy sake we are killed all the day long; We were accounted as sheep for the slaughter.

Rom 8:37 Nay, in all these things we are more than conquerors through him that loved us.

Rom 8:38 For I am persuaded, that neither death, nor life, nor angels, nor principalities, nor things present, nor things to come, nor powers,

Rom 8:39 nor height, nor depth, nor any other creature, shall be able to separate us from the love of God, which is in Christ Jesus our Lord.

Chapter 9.

Rom 9:1 I say the truth in Christ, I lie not, my conscience bearing witness with me in the Holy Spirit,

Rom 9:2 that I have great sorrow and unceasing pain in my heart.

Rom 9:3 For I could wish that I myself were anathema from Christ for my brethren's sake, my kinsmen according to the flesh:

Rom 9:4 who are Israelites; whose is the adoption, and the glory, and the covenants, and the giving of the law, and the service of God, and the promises;

Rom 9:5 whose are the fathers, and of whom is Christ as concerning the flesh, who is over all, God blessed for ever. Amen.

Rom 9:6 But it is not as though the word of God hath come to nought. For they are not all Israel, that are of Israel:

Rom 9:7 neither, because they are Abraham's seed, are they all children: but, In Isaac shall thy seed be called.

Rom 9:8 That is, it is not the children of the flesh that are children of God; but the children of the promise are reckoned for a seed.

Rom 9:9 For this is a word of promise, According to this season will I come, and Sarah shall have a son.

Rom 9:10 And not only so; but Rebecca also having conceived by one, even by our father Isaac -

Rom 9:11 for the children being not yet born, neither having done anything good or bad, that the purpose of God according to election might stand, not of works, but of him that calleth,

Rom 9:12 it was said unto her, The elder shall serve the younger.

Rom 9:13 Even as it is written, Jacob I loved, but Esau I hated.

Rom 9:14 What shall we say then? Is there unrighteousness with God? God forbid.

Rom 9:15 For he saith to Moses, I will have mercy on whom I have mercy, and I will have compassion on whom I have compassion.

Rom 9:16 So then it is not of him that willeth, nor of him that runneth, but of God that hath mercy.

Rom 9:17 For the scripture saith unto Pharaoh, For this very purpose did I raise thee up, that I might show in thee my power, and that my name might be published abroad in all the earth.

Rom 9:18 So then he hath mercy on whom he will, and whom he will be hardeneth.

Rom 9:19 Thou wilt say then unto me, Why doth he still find fault? For who withstandeth his will?

Rom 9:20 Nay but, O man, who art thou that repliest against God? Shall the thing formed say to him that formed it, Why didst thou make me thus?

Rom 9:21 Or hath not the potter a right over the clay, from the same lump to make one part a vessel unto honor, and another unto dishonor?

Rom 9:22 What if God, willing to show his wrath, and to make his power known, endured with much longsuffering vessels of wrath fitted unto destruction:

Rom 9:23 and that he might make known the riches of his glory upon vessels of mercy, which he afore prepared unto glory,

Rom 9:24 even us, whom he also called, not from the Jews only, but also from the Gentiles?

Rom 9:25 As he saith also in Hosea, I will call that my people, which was not my people; And her beloved, that was not beloved.

Rom 9:26 And it shall be, that in the place where it was said unto them, Ye are not my people, There shall they be called sons of the living God.

Rom 9:27 And Isaiah crieth concerning Israel, If the number of the children of Israel be as the sand of the sea, it is the remnant that shall be saved:

Rom 9:28 for the Lord will execute his word upon the earth, finishing it and cutting it short.

Rom 9:29 And, as Isaiah hath said before, Except the Lord of Sabaoth had left us a seed, We had become as Sodom, and had been made like unto Gomorrah.

Rom 9:30 What shall we say then? That the Gentiles, who followed not after righteousness, attained to righteousness, even the righteousness which is of faith:

Rom 9:31 but Israel, following after a law of righteousness, did not arrive at that law.

Rom 9:32 Wherefore? Because they sought it not by faith, but as it were by works. They stumbled at the stone of stumbling;

Rom 9:33 even as it is written, Behold, I lay in Zion a stone of stumbling and a rock of offence: And he that believeth on him shall not be put to shame.

Chapter 10.

Rom 10:1 Brethren, my heart's desire and my supplication to God is for them, that they may be saved.

Rom 10:2 For I bear them witness that they have a zeal for God, but not according to knowledge.

Rom 10:3 For being ignorant of God's righteousness, and seeking to establish their own, they did not subject themselves to the righteousness of God.

Rom 10:4 For Christ is the end of the law unto righteousness to every one that believeth.

Rom 10:5 For Moses writeth that the man that doeth the righteousness which is of the law shall live thereby.

Rom 10:6 But the righteousness which is of faith saith thus, Say not in thy heart, Who shall ascend into heaven? (that is, to bring Christ down:)

Rom 10:7 or, Who shall descend into the abyss? (That is, to bring Christ up from the dead.)

Rom 10:8 But what saith it? The word is nigh thee, in thy mouth, and in thy heart: that is, the word of faith, which we preach:

Rom 10:9 because if thou shalt confess with thy mouth Jesus as Lord, and shalt believe in thy heart that God raised him from the dead, thou shalt be saved:

Rom 10:10 for with the heart man believeth unto righteousness; and with the mouth confession is made unto salvation.

Rom 10:11 For the scripture saith, Whosoever believeth on him shall not be put to shame.

Rom 10:12 For there is no distinction between Jew and Greek: for the same Lord is Lord of all, and is rich unto all that call upon him:

Rom 10:13 for, Whosoever shall call upon the name of the Lord shall be saved.

Rom 10:14 How then shall they call on him in whom they have not believed? and how shall they believe in him whom they have not heard? and how shall they hear without a preacher?

Rom 10:15 and how shall they preach, except they be sent? even as it is written, How beautiful are the feet of them that bring glad tidings of good things!

Rom 10:16 But they did not all hearken to the glad tidings. For Isaiah saith, Lord, who hath believed our report?

Rom 10:17 So belief cometh of hearing, and hearing by the word of Christ.

Rom 10:18 But I say, Did they not hear? Yea, verily, Their sound went out into all the earth, And their words unto the ends of the world.

Rom 10:19 But I say, Did Israel not know? First Moses saith, I will provoke you to jealousy with that which is no nation, With a nation void of understanding will I anger you.

Rom 10:20 And Isaiah is very bold, and saith, I was found of them that sought me not; I became manifest unto them that asked not of me.

Rom 10:21 But as to Israel he saith, All the day long did I spread out my hands unto a disobedient and gainsaying people.

Chapter 11.

Rom 11:1 I say then, Did God cast off his people? God forbid. For I also am an Israelite, of the seed of Abraham, of the tribe of Benjamin.

Rom 11:2 God did not cast off his people which he foreknew. Or know ye not what the scripture saith of Elijah? how he pleadeth with God against Israel:

Rom 11:3 Lord, they have killed thy prophets, they have digged down thine altars; and I am left alone, and they seek my life.

Rom 11:4 But what saith the answer of God unto him? I have left for myself seven thousand men, who have not bowed the knee to Baal.

Rom 11:5 Even so then at this present time also there is a remnant according to the election of grace.

Rom 11:6 But if it is by grace, it is no more of works: otherwise grace is no more grace.

Rom 11:7 What then? that which Israel seeketh for, that he obtained not; but the election obtained it, and the rest were hardened:

Rom 11:8 according as it is written, God gave them a spirit of stupor, eyes that they should not see, and ears that they should not hear, unto this very day.

Rom 11:9 And David saith, Let their table be made a snare, and a trap, And a stumblingblock, and a recompense unto them:

Rom 11:10 Let their eyes be darkened, that they may not see, And bow thou down their back always.

Rom 11:11 I say then, Did they stumble that they might fall? God forbid: but by their fall salvation is come unto the Gentiles, to provoke them to jealousy.

Rom 11:12 Now if their fall, is the riches of the world, and their loss the riches of the Gentiles; how much more their fulness?

Rom 11:13 But I speak to you that are Gentiles. Inasmuch then as I am an apostle of Gentiles, I glorify my ministry;

Rom 11:14 if by any means I may provoke to jealousy them that are my flesh, and may save some of them.

Rom 11:15 For if the casting away of them is the reconciling of the world, what shall the receiving of them be, but life from the dead?

Rom 11:16 And if the firstfruit is holy, so is the lump: and if the root is holy, so are the branches.

Rom 11:17 But if some of the branches were broken off, and thou, being a wild olive, wast grafted in among them, and didst become partaker with them of the root of the fatness of the olive tree;

Rom 11:18 glory not over the branches: but if thou gloriest, it is not thou that bearest the root, but the root thee.

Rom 11:19 Thou wilt say then, Branches were broken off, that I might be grafted in.

Rom 11:20 Well; by their unbelief they were broken off, and thou standest by thy faith. Be not highminded, but fear:

Rom 11:21 for if God spared not the natural branches, neither will he spare thee.

Rom 11:22 Behold then the goodness and severity of God: toward them that fell, severity; but toward thee, God's goodness, if thou continue in his goodness: otherwise thou also shalt be cut off.

Rom 11:23 And they also, if they continue not in their unbelief, shall be grafted in: for God is able to graft them in again.

Rom 11:24 For if thou wast cut out of that which is by nature a wild olive tree, and wast grafted contrary to nature into a good olive tree; how much more shall these, which are the natural branches, be grafted into their own olive tree?

Rom 11:25 For I would not, brethren, have you ignorant of this mystery, lest ye be wise in your own conceits, that a hardening in part hath befallen Israel, until the fulness of the Gentiles be come in;

Rom 11:26 and so all Israel shall be saved: even as it is written, There shall come out of Zion the Deliverer; He shall turn away ungodliness from Jacob:

Rom 11:27 And this is my covenant unto them, When I shall take away their sins.

Rom 11:28 As touching the gospel, they are enemies for your sake: but as touching the election, they are beloved for the fathers' sake.

Rom 11:29 For the gifts and the calling of God are not repented of.

Rom 11:30 For as ye in time past were disobedient to God, but now have obtained mercy by their disobedience,

Rom 11:31 even so have these also now been disobedient, that by the mercy shown to you they also may now obtain mercy.

Rom 11:32 For God hath shut up all unto disobedience, that he might have mercy upon all.

Rom 11:33 O the depth of the riches both of the wisdom and the knowledge of God! how unsearchable are his judgments, and his ways past tracing out!

Rom 11:34 For who hath known the mind of the Lord? or who hath been his counsellor?

Rom 11:35 or who hath first given to him, and it shall be recompensed unto him again?

Rom 11:36 For of him, and through him, and unto him, are all things. To him be the glory for ever. Amen.

Chapter 12.

Rom 12:1 I beseech you therefore, brethren, by the mercies of God, to present your bodies a living sacrifice, holy, acceptable to God, which is your spiritual service.

Rom 12:2 And be not fashioned according to this world: but be ye transformed by the renewing of your mind, and ye may prove what is the good and acceptable and perfect will of God.

Rom 12:3 For I say, through the grace that was given me, to every man that is among you, not to think of himself more highly than he ought to think; but to think as to think soberly, according as God hath dealt to each man a measure of faith.

Rom 12:4 For even as we have many members in one body, and all the members have not the same office:

Rom 12:5 so we, who are many, are one body in Christ, and severally members one of another.

Rom 12:6 And having gifts differing according to the grace that was given to us, whether prophecy, let us prophesy according to the proportion of our faith;

Rom 12:7 or ministry, let us give ourselves to our ministry; or he that teacheth, to his teaching;

Rom 12:8 or he that exhorteth, to his exhorting: he that giveth, let him do it with liberality; he that ruleth, with diligence; he that showeth mercy, with cheerfulness.

Rom 12:9 Let love be without hypocrisy. Abhor that which is evil; cleave to that which is good.

Rom 12:10 In love of the brethren be tenderly affectioned one to another; in honor preferring one another;

Rom 12:11 in diligence not slothful; fervent in spirit; serving the Lord;

Rom 12:12 rejoicing in hope; patient in tribulation; continuing stedfastly in prayer;

Rom 12:13 communicating to the necessities of the saints; given to hospitality.

Rom 12:14 Bless them that persecute you; bless, and curse not.

Rom 12:15 Rejoice with them that rejoice; weep with them that weep.

Rom 12:16 Be of the same mind one toward another. Set not your mind on high things, but condescend to things that are lowly. Be not wise in your own conceits.

Rom 12:17 Render to no man evil for evil. Take thought for things honorable in the sight of all men.

Rom 12:18 If it be possible, as much as in you lieth, be at peace with all men.

Rom 12:19 Avenge not yourselves, beloved, but give place unto the wrath of God: for it is written, Vengeance belongeth unto me; I will recompense, saith the Lord.

Rom 12:20 But if thine enemy hunger, feed him; if he thirst, give him to drink: for in so doing thou shalt heap coals of fire upon his head.

Rom 12:21 Be not overcome of evil, but overcome evil with good.

Chapter 13.

Rom 13:1 Let every soul be in subjection to the higher powers: for there is no power but of God; and the powers that be are ordained of God.

Rom 13:2 Therefore he that resisteth the power, withstandeth the ordinance of God: and they that withstand shall receive to themselves judgment.

Rom 13:3 For rulers are not a terror to the good work, but to the evil. And wouldest thou have no fear of the power? do that which is good, and thou shalt have praise from the same:

Rom 13:4 for he is a minister of God to thee for good. But if thou do that which is evil, be afraid; for he beareth not the sword in vain: for he is a minister of God, an avenger for wrath to him that doeth evil.

Rom 13:5 Wherefore ye must needs be in subjection, not only because of the wrath, but also for conscience' sake.

Rom 13:6 For this cause ye pay tribute also; for they are ministers of God's service, attending continually upon this very thing.

Rom 13:7 Render to all their dues: tribute to whom tribute is due; custom to whom custom; fear to whom fear; honor to whom honor.

Rom 13:8 Owe no man anything, save to love one another: for he that loveth his neighbor hath fulfilled the law.

Rom 13:9 For this, Thou shalt not commit adultery, Thou shalt not kill, Thou shalt not steal, Thou shalt not covet, and if there be any other commandment, it is summed up in this word, namely, Thou shalt love thy neighbor as thyself.

Rom 13:10 Love worketh no ill to his neighbor: love therefore is the fulfilment of the law.

Rom 13:11 And this, knowing the season, that already it is time for you to awake out of sleep: for now is salvation nearer to us than when we first believed.

Rom 13:12 The night is far spent, and the day is at hand: let us therefore cast off the works of darkness, and let us put on the armor of light.

Rom 13:13 Let us walk becomingly, as in the day; not in revelling and drunkenness, not in chambering and wantonness, not in strife and jealousy.

Rom 13:14 But put ye on the Lord Jesus Christ, and make not provision for the flesh, to fulfil the lusts thereof.

Chapter 14.

Rom 14:1 But him that is weak in faith receive ye, yet not for decision of scruples.

Rom 14:2 One man hath faith to eat all things: but he that is weak eateth herbs.

Rom 14:3 Let not him that eateth set at nought him that eateth not; and let not him that eateth not judge him that eateth: for God hath received him.

Rom 14:4 Who art thou that judgest the servant of another? to his own lord he standeth or falleth. Yea, he shall be made to stand; for the Lord hath power to make him stand.

Rom 14:5 One man esteemeth one day above another: another esteemeth every day alike. Let each man be fully assured in his own mind.

Rom 14:6 He that regardeth the day, regardeth it unto the Lord: and he that eateth, eateth unto the Lord, for he giveth God thanks; and he that eateth not, unto the Lord he eateth not, and giveth God thanks.

Rom 14:7 For none of us liveth to himself, and none dieth to himself.

Rom 14:8 For whether we live, we live unto the Lord; or whether we die, we die unto the Lord: whether we live therefore, or die, we are the Lord's.

Rom 14:9 For to this end Christ died and lived again, that he might be Lord of both the dead and the living.

Rom 14:10 But thou, why dost thou judge thy brother? or thou again, why dost thou set at nought thy brother? for we shall all stand before the judgment-seat of God.

Rom 14:11 For it is written, As I live, saith the Lord, to me every knee shall bow, And every tongue shall confess to God.

Rom 14:12 So then each one of us shall give account of himself to God.

Rom 14:13 Let us not therefore judge one another any more: but judge ye this rather, that no man put a stumblingblock in his brother's way, or an occasion of falling.

Rom 14:14 I know, and am persuaded in the Lord Jesus, that nothing is unclean of itself: save that to him who accounteth anything to be unclean, to him it is unclean.

Rom 14:15 For if because of meat thy brother is grieved, thou walkest no longer in love. Destroy not with thy meat him for whom Christ died.

Rom 14:16 Let not then your good be evil spoken of:

Rom 14:17 for the kingdom of God is not eating and drinking, but righteousness and peace and joy in the Holy Spirit.

Rom 14:18 For he that herein serveth Christ is well-pleasing to God, and approved of men.

Rom 14:19 So then let us follow after things which make for peace, and things whereby we may edify one another.

Rom 14:20 Overthrow not for meat's sake the work of God. All things indeed are clean; howbeit it is evil for that man who eateth with offence.

Rom 14:21 It is good not to eat flesh, nor to drink wine, nor to do anything whereby thy brother stumbleth.

Rom 14:22 The faith which thou hast, have thou to thyself before God. Happy is he that judgeth not himself in that which he approveth.

Rom 14:23 But he that doubteth is condemned if he eat, because he eateth not of faith; and whatsoever is not of faith is sin.

Chapter 15.

Rom 15:1 Now we that are strong ought to bear the infirmities of the weak, and not to please ourselves.

Rom 15:2 Let each one of us please his neighbor for that which is good, unto edifying.

Rom 15:3 For Christ also pleased not himself; but, as it is written, The reproaches of them that reproached thee fell upon me.

Rom 15:4 For whatsoever things were written aforetime were written for our learning, that through patience and through comfort of the scriptures we might have hope.

Rom 15:5 Now the God of patience and of comfort grant you to be of the same mind one with another according to Christ Jesus:

Rom 15:6 that with one accord ye may with one mouth glorify the God and Father of our Lord Jesus Christ.

Rom 15:7 Wherefore receive ye one another, even as Christ also received you, to the glory of God.

Rom 15:8 For I say that Christ hath been made a minister of the circumcision for the truth of God, that he might confirm the promises given unto the fathers,

Rom 15:9 and that the Gentiles might glorify God for his mercy; as it is written, Therefore will I give praise unto thee among the Gentiles, And sing unto thy name.

Rom 15:10 And again he saith, Rejoice, ye Gentiles, with his people.

Rom 15:11 And again, Praise the Lord, all ye Gentiles; And let all the peoples praise him.

Rom 15:12 And again, Isaiah saith, There shall be the root of Jesse, And he that ariseth to rule over the Gentiles; On him shall the Gentiles hope.

Rom 15:13 Now the God of hope fill you with all joy and peace in believing, that ye may abound in hope, in the power of the Holy Spirit.

Rom 15:14 And I myself also am persuaded of you, my brethren, that ye yourselves are full of goodness, filled with all knowledge, able also to admonish one another.

Rom 15:15 But I write the more boldly unto you in some measure, as putting you again in remembrance, because of the grace that was given me of God,

Rom 15:16 that I should be a minister of Christ Jesus unto the Gentiles, ministering the gospel of God, that the offering up of the Gentiles might be made acceptable, being sanctified by the Holy Spirit.

Rom 15:17 I have therefore my glorifying in Christ Jesus in things pertaining to God.

Rom 15:18 For I will not dare to speak of any things save those which Christ wrought through me, for the obedience of the Gentiles, by word and deed,

Rom 15:19 in the power of signs and wonders, in the power of the Holy Spirit; so that from Jerusalem, and round about even unto Illyricum, I have fully preached the gospel of Christ;

Rom 15:20 yea, making it my aim so to preach the gospel, not where Christ was already named, that I might not build upon another man's foundation;

Rom 15:21 but, as it is written, They shall see, to whom no tidings of him came, And they who have not heard shall understand.

Rom 15:22 Wherefore also I was hindered these many times from coming to you:

Rom 15:23 but now, having no more any place in these regions, and having these many years a longing to come unto you,

Rom 15:24 whensoever I go unto Spain (for I hope to see you in my journey, and to be brought on my way thitherward by you, if first in some measure I shall have been satisfied with your company) -

Rom 15:25 but now, I say, I go unto Jerusalem, ministering unto the saints.

Rom 15:26 For it hath been the good pleasure of Macedonia and Achaia to make a certain contribution for the poor among the saints that are at Jerusalem.

Rom 15:27 Yea, it hath been their good pleasure; and their debtors they are. For if the Gentiles have been made partakers of their spiritual things, they owe it to them also to minister unto them in carnal things.

Rom 15:28 When therefore I have accomplished this, and have sealed to them this fruit, I will go on by you unto Spain.

Rom 15:29 And I know that, when I come unto you, I shall come in the fulness of the blessing of Christ.

Rom 15:30 Now I beseech you, brethren, by our Lord Jesus Christ, and by the love of the Spirit, that ye strive together with me in your prayers to God for me;

Rom 15:31 that I may be delivered from them that are disobedient in Judaea, and that my ministration which I have for Jerusalem may be acceptable to the saints;

Rom 15:32 that I may come unto you in joy through the will of God, and together with you find rest.

Rom 15:33 Now the God of peace be with you all. Amen.

Chapter 16.

Rom 16:1 I commend unto you Phoebe our sister, who is a servant of the church that is at Cenchreae:

Rom 16:2 that ye receive her in the Lord, worthily of the saints, and that ye assist her in whatsoever matter she may have need of you: for she herself also hath been a helper of many, and of mine own self.

Rom 16:3 Salute Prisca and Aquila my fellow-workers in Christ Jesus,

Rom 16:4 who for my life laid down their own necks; unto whom not only I give thanks, but also all the churches of the Gentiles:

Rom 16:5 and salute the church that is in their house. Salute Epaenetus my beloved, who is the first-fruits of Asia unto Christ.

Rom 16:6 Salute Mary, who bestowed much labor on you.

Rom 16:7 Salute Andronicus and Junias, my kinsmen, and my fellow-prisoners, who are of note among the apostles, who also have been in Christ before me.

Rom 16:8 Salute Ampliatus my beloved in the Lord.

Rom 16:9 Salute Urbanus our fellow-worker in Christ, and Stachys my beloved.

Rom 16:10 Salute Apelles the approved in Christ. Salute them that are of the household of Aristobulus.

Rom 16:11 Salute Herodion my kinsman. Salute them of the household of Narcissus, that are in the Lord.

Rom 16:12 Salute Tryphaena and Tryphosa, who labor in the Lord. Salute Persis the beloved, who labored much in the Lord.

Rom 16:13 Salute Rufus the chosen in the Lord, and his mother and mine.

Rom 16:14 Salute Asyncritus, Phlegon, Hermes, Patrobas, Hermas, and the brethren that are with them.

Rom 16:15 Salute Philologus and Julia, Nereus and his sister, and Olympas, and all the saints that are with them.

Rom 16:16 Salute one another with a holy kiss. All the churches of Christ salute you.

Rom 16:17 Now I beseech you, brethren, mark them that are causing the divisions and occasions of stumbling, contrary to the doctrine which ye learned: and turn away from them.

Rom 16:18 For they that are such serve not our Lord Christ, but their own belly; and by their smooth and fair speech they beguile the hearts of the innocent.

Rom 16:19 For your obedience is come abroad unto all men. I rejoice therefore over you: but I would have you wise unto that which is good, and simple unto that which is evil.

Rom 16:20 And the God of peace shall bruise Satan under your feet shortly. The grace of our Lord Jesus Christ be with you.

Rom 16:21 Timothy my fellow-worker saluteth you; and Lucius and Jason and Sosipater, my kinsmen.

Rom 16:22 I Tertius, who write the epistle, salute you in the Lord.

Rom 16:23 Gaius my host, and of the whole church, saluteth you. Erastus the treasurer of the city saluteth you, and Quartus the brother.

Rom 16:24 The grace of our Lord Jesus Christ be with you all. Amen.

Rom 16:25 Now to him that is able to establish you according to my gospel and the preaching of Jesus Christ, according to the revelation of the mystery which hath been kept in silence through times eternal,

Rom 16:26 but now is manifested, and by the scriptures of the prophets, according to the commandment of the eternal God, is made known unto all the nations unto obedience of faith:

Rom 16:27 to the only wise God, through Jesus Christ, to whom be the glory for ever. Amen.

8. 1 Corinthians

Chapter 1.

1Co 1:1 Paul, called to be an apostle of Jesus Christ through the will of God, and Sosthenes our brother,

1Co 1:2 unto the church of God which is at Corinth, even them that are sanctified in Christ Jesus, called to be saints, with all that call upon the name of our Lord Jesus Christ in every place, their Lord and ours:

1Co 1:3 Grace to you and peace from God our Father and the Lord Jesus Christ.

1Co 1:4 I thank my God always concerning you, for the grace of God which was given you in Christ Jesus;

1Co 1:5 that in everything ye were enriched in him, in all utterance and all knowledge;

1Co 1:6 even as the testimony of Christ was confirmed in you:

1Co 1:7 so that ye come behind in no gift; waiting for the revelation of our Lord Jesus Christ;

1Co 1:8 who shall also confirm you unto the end, that ye be unreproveable in the day of our Lord Jesus Christ.

1Co 1:9 God is faithful, through whom ye were called into the fellowship of his Son Jesus Christ our Lord.

1Co 1:10 Now I beseech you, brethren, through the name of our Lord Jesus Christ, that ye all speak the same thing and that there be no divisions among you; but that ye be perfected together in the same mind and in the same judgment.

1Co 1:11 For it hath been signified unto me concerning you, my brethren, by them that are of the household of Chloe, that there are contentions among you.

1Co 1:12 Now this I mean, that each one of you saith, I am of Paul; and I of Apollos: and I of Cephas; and I of Christ.

1Co 1:13 Is Christ divided? was Paul crucified for you? or were ye baptized into the name of Paul?

1Co 1:14 I thank God that I baptized none of you, save Crispus and Gaius;

1Co 1:15 lest any man should say that ye were baptized into my name.

1Co 1:16 And I baptized also the household of Stephanas: besides, I know not whether I baptized any other.

1Co 1:17 For Christ sent me not to baptize, but to preach the gospel: not in wisdom of words, lest the cross of Christ should be made void.

1Co 1:18 For the word of the cross is to them that perish foolishness; but unto us who are saved it is the power of God.

1Co 1:19 For it is written, I will destroy the wisdom of the wise, And the discernment of the discerning will I bring to nought.

1Co 1:20 Where is the wise? where is the scribe? where is the disputer of this world? hath not God made foolish the wisdom of the world?

1Co 1:21 For seeing that in the wisdom of God the world through its wisdom knew not God, it was God's good pleasure through the foolishness of the preaching to save them that believe.

1Co 1:22 Seeing that Jews ask for signs, and Greeks seek after wisdom:

1Co 1:23 but we preach Christ crucified, unto Jews a stumblingblock, and unto Gentiles foolishness;

1Co 1:24 but unto them that are called, both Jews and Greeks, Christ the power of God, and the wisdom of God.

1Co 1:25 Because the foolishness of God is wiser than men; and the weakness of God is stronger than men.

1Co 1:26 For behold your calling, brethren, that not many wise after the flesh, not many mighty, not many noble, are called:

1Co 1:27 but God chose the foolish things of the world, that he might put to shame them that are wise; and God chose the weak things of the world, that he might put to shame the things that are strong;

1Co 1:28 and the base things of the world, and the things that are despised, did God choose, yea and the things that are not, that he might bring to nought the things that are:

1Co 1:29 that no flesh should glory before God.

1Co 1:30 But of him are ye in Christ Jesus, who was made unto us wisdom from God, and righteousness and sanctification, and redemption:

1Co 1:31 that, according as it is written, He that glorieth, let him glory in the Lord.

Chapter 2.

1Co 2:1 And I, brethren, when I came unto you, came not with excellency of speech or of wisdom, proclaiming to you the testimony of God.

1Co 2:2 For I determined not to know anything among you, save Jesus Christ, and him crucified.

1Co 2:3 And I was with you in weakness, and in fear, and in much trembling.

1Co 2:4 And my speech and my preaching were not in persuasive words of wisdom, but in demonstration of the Spirit and of power:

1Co 2:5 that your faith should not stand in the wisdom of men, but in the power of God.

1Co 2:6 We speak wisdom, however, among them that are fullgrown: yet a wisdom not of this world, nor of the rulers of this world, who are coming to nought:

1Co 2:7 but we speak God's wisdom in a mystery, even the wisdom that hath been hidden, which God foreordained before the worlds unto our glory:

1Co 2:8 which none of the rulers of this world hath known: for had they known it, they would not have crucified the Lord of glory:

1Co 2:9 but as it is written, Things which eye saw not, and ear heard not, And which entered not into the heart of man, Whatsoever things God prepared for them that love him.

1Co 2:10 But unto us God revealed them through the Spirit: for the Spirit searcheth all things, yea, the deep things of God.

1Co 2:11 For who among men knoweth the things of a man, save the spirit of the man, which is in him? even so the things of God none knoweth, save the Spirit of God.

1Co 2:12 But we received, not the spirit of the world, but the spirit which is from God; that we might know the things that were freely given to us of God.

1Co 2:13 Which things also we speak, not in words which man's wisdom teacheth, but which the Spirit teacheth; combining spiritual things with spiritual words.

1Co 2:14 Now the natural man receiveth not the things of the Spirit of God: for they are foolishness unto him; and he cannot know them, because they are spiritually judged.

1Co 2:15 But he that is spiritual judgeth all things, and he himself is judged of no man.

1Co 2:16 For who hath known the mind of the Lord, that he should instruct him? But we have the mind of Christ.

Chapter 3.

1Co 3:1 And I, brethren, could not speak unto you as unto spiritual, but as unto carnal, as unto babes in Christ.

1Co 3:2 I fed you with milk, not with meat; for ye were not yet able to bear it: nay, not even now are ye able;

1Co 3:3 for ye are yet carnal: for whereas there is among you jealousy and strife, are ye not carnal, and do ye not walk after the manner of men?

1Co 3:4 For when one saith, I am of Paul; and another, I am of Apollos; are ye not men?

1Co 3:5 What then is Apollos? and what is Paul? Ministers through whom ye believed; and each as the Lord gave to him.

1Co 3:6 I planted, Apollos watered; but God gave the increase.

1Co 3:7 So then neither is he that planteth anything, neither he that watereth; but God that giveth the increase.

1Co 3:8 Now he that planteth and he that watereth are one: but each shall receive his own reward according to his own labor.

1Co 3:9 For we are God's fellow-workers: ye are God's husbandry, God's building.

1Co 3:10 According to the grace of God which was given unto me, as a wise masterbuilder I laid a foundation; and another buildeth thereon. But let each man take heed how he buildeth thereon.

1Co 3:11 For other foundation can no man lay than that which is laid, which is Jesus Christ.

1Co 3:12 But if any man buildeth on the foundation gold, silver, costly stones, wood, hay, stubble;

1Co 3:13 each man's work shall be made manifest: for the day shall declare it, because it is revealed in fire; and the fire itself shall prove each man's work of what sort it is.

1Co 3:14 If any man's work shall abide which he built thereon, he shall receive a reward.

1Co 3:15 If any man's work shall be burned, he shall suffer loss: but he himself shall be saved; yet so as through fire.

1Co 3:16 Know ye not that ye are a temple of God, and that the Spirit of God dwelleth in you?

1Co 3:17 If any man destroyeth the temple of God, him shall God destroy; for the temple of God is holy, and such are ye.

1Co 3:18 Let no man deceive himself. If any man thinketh that he is wise among you in this world, let him become a fool, that he may become wise.

1Co 3:19 For the wisdom of this world is foolishness with God. For it is written, He that taketh the wise in their craftiness:

1Co 3:20 and again, The Lord knoweth the reasonings of the wise that they are vain.

1Co 3:21 Wherefore let no one glory in men. For all things are yours;

1Co 3:22 whether Paul, or Apollos, or Cephas, or the world, or life, or death, or things present, or things to come; all are yours;

1Co 3:23 and ye are Christ's; and Christ is God's.

Chapter 4.

1Co 4:1 Let a man so account of us, as of ministers of Christ, and stewards of the mysteries of God.

1Co 4:2 Here, moreover, it is required in stewards, that a man be found faithful.

1Co 4:3 But with me it is a very small thing that I should be judged of you, or of man's judgment: yea, I judge not mine own self.

1Co 4:4 For I know nothing against myself; yet am I not hereby justified: but he that judgeth me is the Lord.

1Co 4:5 Wherefore judge nothing before the time, until the Lord come, who will both bring to light the hidden things of darkness, and make manifest the counsels of the hearts; and then shall each man have his praise from God.

1Co 4:6 Now these things, brethren, I have in a figure transferred to myself and Apollos for your sakes; that in us ye might learn not to go beyond the things which are written; that no one of you be puffed up for the one against the other.

1Co 4:7 For who maketh thee to differ? and what hast thou that thou didst not receive? but if thou didst receive it, why dost thou glory as if thou hadst not received it?

1Co 4:8 Already are ye filled, already ye are become rich, ye have come to reign without us: yea and I would that ye did reign, that we also might reign with you.

1Co 4:9 For, I think, God hath set forth us the apostles last of all, as men doomed to death: for we are made a spectacle unto the world, both to angels and men.

1Co 4:10 We are fools for Christ's sake, but ye are wise in Christ; we are weak, but ye are strong; ye have glory, but we have dishonor.

1Co 4:11 Even unto this present hour we both hunger, and thirst, and are naked, and are buffeted, and have no certain dwelling-place;

1Co 4:12 and we toil, working with our own hands: being reviled, we bless; being persecuted, we endure;

1Co 4:13 being defamed, we entreat: we are made as the filth of the world, the offscouring of all things, even until now.

1Co 4:14 I write not these things to shame you, but to admonish you as my beloved children.

1Co 4:15 For though ye have ten thousand tutors in Christ, yet have ye not many fathers; for in Christ Jesus I begat you through the gospel.

1Co 4:16 I beseech you therefore, be ye imitators of me.

1Co 4:17 For this cause have I sent unto you Timothy, who is my beloved and faithful child in the Lord, who shall put you in remembrance of my ways which are in Christ, even as I teach everywhere in every church.

1Co 4:18 Now some are puffed up, as though I were not coming to you.

1Co 4:19 But I will come to you shortly, if the Lord will; and I will know, not the word of them that are puffed up, but the power.

1Co 4:20 For the kingdom of God is not in word, but in power.

1Co 4:21 What will ye? shall I come unto you with a rod, or in love and a spirit of gentleness?

Chapter 5.

1Co 5:1   It is actually reported that there is fornication among you, and such fornication as is not even among the Gentiles, that one of you hath his father's wife.

1Co 5:2   And ye are puffed up, and did not rather mourn, that he that had done this deed might be taken away from among you.

1Co 5:3   For I verily, being absent in body but present in spirit, have already as though I were present judged him that hath so wrought this thing,

1Co 5:4   in the name of our Lord Jesus, ye being gathered together, and my spirit, with the power of our Lord Jesus,

1Co 5:5   to deliver such a one unto Satan for the destruction of the flesh, that the spirit may be saved in the day of the Lord Jesus.

1Co 5:6   Your glorying is not good. Know ye not that a little leaven leaveneth the whole lump?

1Co 5:7   Purge out the old leaven, that ye may be a new lump, even as ye are unleavened. For our passover also hath been sacrificed, even Christ:

1Co 5:8   wherefore let us keep the feast, not with old leaven, neither with the leaven of malice and wickedness, but with the unleavened bread of sincerity and truth.

1Co 5:9   I wrote unto you in my epistle to have no company with fornicators;

1Co 5:10   not at all meaning with the fornicators of this world, or with the covetous and extortioners, or with idolaters; for then must ye needs go out of the world:

1Co 5:11   but as it is, I wrote unto you not to keep company, if any man that is named a brother be a fornicator, or covetous, or an idolater, or a reviler, or a drunkard, or an extortioner; with such a one no, not to eat.

1Co 5:12   For what have I to do with judging them that are without? Do not ye judge them that are within?

1Co 5:13   But them that are without God judgeth. Put away the wicked man from among yourselves.

Chapter 6.

1Co 6:1   Dare any of you, having a matter against his neighbor, go to law before the unrighteous, and not before the saints?

1Co 6:2   Or know ye not that the saints shall judge the world? and if the world is judged by you, are ye unworthy to judge the smallest matters?

1Co 6:3   Know ye not that we shall judge angels? how much more, things that pertain to this life?

1Co 6:4   If then ye have to judge things pertaining to this life, do ye set them to judge who are of no account in the church?

1Co 6:5   I say this to move you to shame. What, cannot there be found among you one wise man who shall be able to decide between his brethren,

1Co 6:6   but brother goeth to law with brother, and that before unbelievers?

1Co 6:7   Nay, already it is altogether a defect in you, that ye have lawsuits one with another. Why not rather take wrong? why not rather be defrauded?

1Co 6:8   Nay, but ye yourselves do wrong, and defraud, and that your brethren.

1Co 6:9   Or know ye not that the unrighteous shall not inherit the kingdom of God? Be not deceived: neither fornicators, nor idolaters, nor adulterers, nor effeminate, nor abusers of themselves with men,

1Co 6:10 nor thieves, nor covetous, nor drunkards, nor revilers, nor extortioners, shall inherit the kingdom of God.

1Co 6:11 And such were some of you: but ye were washed, but ye were sanctified, but ye were justified in the name of the Lord Jesus Christ, and in the Spirit of our God.

1Co 6:12 All things are lawful for me; but not all things are expedient. All things are lawful for me; but I will not be brought under the power of any.

1Co 6:13 Meats for the belly, and the belly for meats: but God shall bring to nought both it and them. But the body is not for fornication, but for the Lord; and the Lord for the body:

1Co 6:14 and God both raised the Lord, and will raise up as through his power.

1Co 6:15 Know ye not that your bodies are members of Christ? shall I then take away the members of Christ, and make them members of a harlot? God forbid.

1Co 6:16 Or know ye not that he that is joined to a harlot is one body? for, The twain, saith he, shall become one flesh.

1Co 6:17 But he that is joined unto the Lord is one spirit.

1Co 6:18 Flee fornication. Every sin that a man doeth is without the body; but he that committeth fornication sinneth against his own body.

1Co 6:19 Or know ye not that your body is a temple of the Holy Spirit which is in you, which ye have from God? and ye are not your own;

1Co 6:20 for ye were bought with a price: glorify God therefore in your body.

Chapter 7.

1Co 7:1 Now concerning the things whereof ye wrote: It is good for a man not to touch a woman.

1Co 7:2 But, because of fornications, let each man have his own wife, and let each woman have her own husband.

1Co 7:3 Let the husband render unto the wife her due: and likewise also the wife unto the husband.

1Co 7:4 The wife hath not power over her own body, but the husband: and likewise also the husband hath not power over his own body, but the wife.

1Co 7:5 Defraud ye not one the other, except it be by consent for a season, that ye may give yourselves unto prayer, and may be together again, that Satan tempt you not because of your incontinency.

1Co 7:6 But this I say by way of concession, not of commandment.

1Co 7:7 Yet I would that all men were even as I myself. Howbeit each man hath his own gift from God, one after this manner, and another after that.

1Co 7:8 But I say to the unmarried and to widows, It is good for them if they abide even as I.

1Co 7:9 But if they have not continency, let them marry: for it is better to marry than to burn.

1Co 7:10 But unto the married I give charge, yea not I, but the Lord, That the wife depart not from her husband

1Co 7:11 (but should she depart, let her remain unmarried, or else be reconciled to her husband); and that the husband leave not his wife.

1Co 7:12 But to the rest say I, not the Lord: If any brother hath an unbelieving wife, and she is content to dwell with him, let him not leave her.

1Co 7:13 And the woman that hath an unbelieving husband, and he is content to dwell with her, let her not leave her husband.

1Co 7:14 For the unbelieving husband is sanctified in the wife, and the unbelieving wife is sanctified in the brother: else were your children unclean; but now are they holy.

1Co 7:15 Yet if the unbelieving departeth, let him depart: the brother or the sister is not under bondage in such cases: but God hath called us in peace.

1Co 7:16 For how knowest thou, O wife, whether thou shalt save thy husband? Or how knowest thou, O husband, whether thou shalt save thy wife?

1Co 7:17 Only, as the Lord hath distributed to each man, as God hath called each, so let him walk. And so ordain I in all the churches.

1Co 7:18 Was any man called being circumcised? Let him not become uncircumcised. Hath any been called in uncircumcision? Let him not be circumcised.

1Co 7:19 Circumcision is nothing, and uncircumcision is nothing; but the keeping of the commandments of God.

1Co 7:20 Let each man abide in that calling wherein he was called.

1Co 7:21 Wast thou called being a bondservant? Care not for it: nay, even if thou canst become free, use it rather.

1Co 7:22 For he that was called in the Lord being a bondservant, is the Lord's freedman: likewise he that was called being free, is Christ's bondservant.

1Co 7:23 Ye were bought with a price; become not bondservants of men.

1Co 7:24 Brethren, let each man, wherein he was called, therein abide with God.

1Co 7:25 Now concerning virgins I have no commandment of the Lord: but I give my judgment, as one that hath obtained mercy of the Lord to be trustworthy.

1Co 7:26 I think therefore that this is good by reason of the distress that is upon us, namely, that it is good for a man to be as he is.

1Co 7:27 Art thou bound unto a wife? Seek not to be loosed. Art thou loosed from a wife? Seek not a wife.

1Co 7:28 But shouldest thou marry, thou hast not sinned; and if a virgin marry, she hath not sinned. Yet such shall have tribulation in the flesh: and I would spare you.

1Co 7:29 But this I say, brethren, the time is shortened, that henceforth both those that have wives may be as though they had none;

1Co 7:30 and those that weep, as though they wept not; and those that rejoice, as though they rejoiced not; and those that buy, as though they possessed not;

1Co 7:31 and those that use the world, as not using it to the full: for the fashion of this world passeth away.

1Co 7:32 But I would have you to be free from cares. He that is unmarried is careful for the things of the Lord, how he may please the Lord:

1Co 7:33 but he that is married is careful for the things of the world, how he may please his wife,

1Co 7:34 and is divided. So also the woman that is unmarried and the virgin is careful for the things of the Lord, that she may be holy both in body and in spirit: but she that is married is careful for the things of the world, how she may please her husband.

1Co 7:35 And this I say for your own profit; not that I may cast a snare upon you, but for that which is seemly, and that ye may attend upon the Lord without distraction.

1Co 7:36 But if any man thinketh that he behaveth himself unseemly toward his virgin daughter, if she be past the flower of her age, and if need so requireth, let him do what he will; he sinneth not; let them marry.

1Co 7:37 But he that standeth stedfast in his heart, having no necessity, but hath power as touching in his own heart, to keep his own virgin daughter, shall do well.

1Co 7:38 So then both he that giveth his own virgin daughter in marriage doeth well; and he that giveth her not in marriage shall do better.

1Co 7:39 A wife is bound for so long time as her husband liveth; but if the husband be dead, she is free to be married to whom she will; only in the Lord.

1Co 7:40 But she is happier if she abide as she is, after my judgment: and I think that I also have the Spirit of God.

Chapter 8.

1Co 8:1 Now concerning things sacrificed to idols: We know that we all have knowledge. Knowledge puffeth up, but love edifieth.

1Co 8:2 If any man thinketh that he knoweth anything, he knoweth not yet as he ought to know;

1Co 8:3 but if any man loveth God, the same is known by him.

1Co 8:4 Concerning therefore the eating of things sacrificed to idols, we know that no idol is anything in the world, and that there is no God but one.

1Co 8:5 For though there be that are called gods, whether in heaven or on earth; as there are gods many, and lords many;

1Co 8:6 yet to us there is one God, the Father, of whom are all things, and we unto him; and one Lord, Jesus Christ, through whom are all things, and we through him.

1Co 8:7 Howbeit there is not in all men that knowledge: but some, being used until now to the idol, eat as of a thing sacrificed to an idol; and their conscience being weak is defiled.

1Co 8:8 But food will not commend us to God: neither, if we eat not, are we the worse; nor, if we eat, are we the better.

1Co 8:9 But take heed lest by any means this liberty of yours become a stumblingblock to the weak.

1Co 8:10 For if a man see thee who hast knowledge sitting at meat in an idol's temple, will not his conscience, if he is weak, be emboldened to eat things sacrificed to idols?

1Co 8:11 For through thy knowledge he that is weak perisheth, the brother for whose sake Christ died.

1Co 8:12 And thus, sinning against the brethren, and wounding their conscience when it is weak, ye sin against Christ.

1Co 8:13 Wherefore, if meat causeth my brother to stumble, I will eat no flesh for evermore, that I cause not my brother to stumble.

Chapter 9.

1Co 9:1 Am I not free? Am I not an apostle? Have I not seen Jesus our Lord? Are not ye my work in the Lord?

1Co 9:2 If to others I am not an apostle, yet at least I am to you; for the seal of mine apostleship are ye in the Lord.

1Co 9:3 My defence to them that examine me is this.

1Co 9:4 Have we no right to eat and to drink?

1Co 9:5 Have we no right to lead about a wife that is a believer, even as the rest of the apostles, and the brethren of the Lord, and Cephas?

1Co 9:6 Or I only and Barnabas, have we not a right to forbear working?

1Co 9:7 What soldier ever serveth at his own charges? who planteth a vineyard, and eateth not the fruit thereof? Or who feedeth a flock, and eateth not of the milk of the flock?

1Co 9:8 Do I speak these things after the manner of men? or saith not the law also the same?

1Co 9:9 For it is written in the law of Moses, Thou shalt not muzzle the ox when he treadeth out the corn. Is it for the oxen that God careth,

1Co 9:10 or saith he it assuredly for our sake? Yea, for our sake it was written: because he that ploweth ought to plow in hope, and he that thresheth, to thresh in hope of partaking.

1Co 9:11 If we sowed unto you spiritual things, is it a great matter if we shall reap your carnal things?

1Co 9:12 If others partake of this right over you, do not we yet more? Nevertheless we did not use this right; but we bear all things, that we may cause no hindrance to the gospel of Christ.

1Co 9:13 Know ye not that they that minister about sacred things eat of the things of the temple, and they that wait upon the altar have their portion with the altar?

1Co 9:14 Even so did the Lord ordain that they that proclaim the gospel should live of the gospel.

1Co 9:15 But I have used none of these things: and I write not these things that it may be so done in my case; for it were good for me rather to die, than that any man should make my glorifying void.

1Co 9:16 For if I preach the gospel, I have nothing to glory of; for necessity is laid upon me; for woe is unto me, if I preach not the gospel.

1Co 9:17 For if I do this of mine own will, I have a reward: but if not of mine own will, I have a stewardship intrusted to me.

1Co 9:18 What then is my reward? That, when I preach the gospel, I may make the gospel without charge, so as not to use to the full my right in the gospel.

1Co 9:19 For though I was free from all men, I brought myself under bondage to all, that I might gain the more.

1Co 9:20 And to the Jews I became as a Jew, that I might gain Jews; to them that are under the law, as under the law, not being myself under the law, that I might gain them that are under the law;

1Co 9:21 to them that are without law, as without law, not being without law to God, but under law to Christ, that I might gain them that are without law.

1Co 9:22 To the weak I became weak, that I might gain the weak: I am become all things to all men, that I may by all means save some.

1Co 9:23 And I do all things for the gospel's sake, that I may be a joint partaker thereof.

1Co 9:24 Know ye not that they that run in a race run all, but one receiveth the prize? Even so run; that ye may attain.

1Co 9:25 And every man that striveth in the games exerciseth self-control in all things. Now they do it to receive a corruptible crown; but we an incorruptible.

1Co 9:26 I therefore so run, as not uncertainly; so fight I, as not beating the air:

1Co 9:27 but I buffet my body, and bring it into bondage: lest by any means, after that I have preached to others, I myself should be rejected.

Chapter 10.

1Co 10:1 For I would not, brethren, have you ignorant, that our fathers were all under the cloud, and all passed through the sea;

1Co 10:2 and were all baptized unto Moses in the cloud and in the sea;

1Co 10:3 and did all eat the same spiritual food;

1Co 10:4 and did all drink the same spiritual drink: for they drank of a spiritual rock that followed them: and the rock was Christ.

1Co 10:5 Howbeit with most of them God was not well pleased: for they were overthrown in the wilderness.

1Co 10:6 Now these things were our examples, to the intent we should not lust after evil things, as they also lusted.

1Co 10:7 Neither be ye idolaters, as were some of them; as it is written, The people sat down to eat and drink, and rose up to play.

1Co 10:8 Neither let us commit fornication, as some of them committed, and fell in one day three and twenty thousand.

1Co 10:9 Neither let us make trial of the Lord, as some of them made trial, and perished by the serpents.

1Co 10:10 Neither murmur ye, as some of them murmured, and perished by the destroyer.

1Co 10:11 Now these things happened unto them by way of example; and they were written for our admonition, upon whom the ends of the ages are come.

1Co 10:12 Wherefore let him that thinketh he standeth take heed lest he fall.

1Co 10:13 There hath no temptation taken you but such as man can bear: but God is faithful, who will not suffer you to be tempted above that ye are able; but will with the temptation make also the way of escape, that ye may be able to endure it.

1Co 10:14 Wherefore, my beloved, flee from idolatry.

1Co 10:15 I speak as to wise men; judge ye what I say.

1Co 10:16 The cup of blessing which we bless, is it not a communion of the blood of Christ? The bread which we break, is it not a communion of the body of Christ?

1Co 10:17 seeing that we, who are many, are one bread, one body: for we are all partake of the one bread.

1Co 10:18 Behold Israel after the flesh: have not they that eat the sacrifices communion with the altar?

1Co 10:19 What say I then? that a thing sacrificed to idols is anything, or that an idol is anything?

1Co 10:20 But I say, that the things which the Gentiles sacrifice, they sacrifice to demons, and not to God: and I would not that ye should have communion with demons.

1Co 10:21 Ye cannot drink the cup of the Lord, and the cup of demons: ye cannot partake of the table of the Lord, and of the table of demons.

1Co 10:22 Or do we provoke the Lord to jealousy? are we stronger than he?

1Co 10:23 All things are lawful; but not all things are expedient. All things are lawful; but not all things edify.

1Co 10:24 Let no man seek his own, but each his neighbor's good.

1Co 10:25 Whatsoever is sold in the shambles, eat, asking no question for conscience' sake,

1Co 10:26 for the earth is the Lord's, and the fulness thereof.

1Co 10:27 If one of them that believe not biddeth you to a feast, and ye are disposed to go; whatsoever is set before you, eat, asking no question for conscience' sake.

1Co 10:28 But if any man say unto you, This hath been offered in sacrifice, eat not, for his sake that showed it, and for conscience sake:

1Co 10:29 conscience, I say, not thine own, but the other's; for why is my liberty judged by another conscience?

1Co 10:30 If I partake with thankfulness, why am I evil spoken of for that for which I give thanks?

1Co 10:31 Whether therefore ye eat, or drink, or whatsoever ye do, do all to the glory of God.

1Co 10:32 Give no occasions of stumbling, either to Jews, or to Greeks, or to the church of God:

1Co 10:33 even as I also please all men in all things, not seeking mine own profit, but the profit of the many, that they may be saved.

Chapter 11.

1Co 11:1 Be ye imitators of me, even as I also am of Christ.

1Co 11:2 Now I praise you that ye remember me in all things, and hold fast the traditions, even as I delivered them to you.

1Co 11:3 But I would have you know, that the head of every man is Christ; and the head of the woman is the man; and the head of Christ is God.

1Co 11:4 Every man praying or prophesying, having his head covered, dishonoreth his head.

1Co 11:5 But every woman praying or prophesying with her head unveiled dishonoreth her head; for it is one and the same thing as if she were shaven.

1Co 11:6 For if a woman is not veiled, let her also be shorn: but if it is a shame to a woman to be shorn or shaven, let her be veiled.

1Co 11:7 For a man indeed ought not to have his head veiled, forasmuch as he is the image and glory of God: but the woman is the glory of the man.

1Co 11:8 For the man is not of the woman; but the woman of the man:

1Co 11:9 for neither was the man created for the woman; but the woman for the man:

1Co 11:10 for this cause ought the woman to have a sign of authority on her head, because of the angels.

1Co 11:11 Nevertheless, neither is the woman without the man, nor the man without the woman, in the Lord.

1Co 11:12 For as the woman is of the man, so is the man also by the woman; but all things are of God.

1Co 11:13 Judge ye in yourselves: is it seemly that a woman pray unto God unveiled?

1Co 11:14 Doth not even nature itself teach you, that, if a man have long hair, it is a dishonor to him?

1Co 11:15 But if a woman have long hair, it is a glory to her: for her hair is given her for a covering.

1Co 11:16 But if any man seemeth to be contentious, we have no such custom, neither the churches of God.

1Co 11:17 But in giving you this charge, I praise you not, that ye come together not for the better but for the worse.

1Co 11:18 For first of all, when ye come together in the church, I hear that divisions exist among you; and I partly believe it.

1Co 11:19 For there must be also factions among you, that they that are approved may be made manifest among you.

1Co 11:20 When therefore ye assemble yourselves together, it is not possible to eat the Lord's supper:

1Co 11:21 for in your eating each one taketh before other his own supper; and one is hungry, and another is drunken.

1Co 11:22 What, have ye not houses to eat and to drink in? or despise ye the church of God, and put them to shame that have not? What shall I say to you? shall I praise you? In this I praise you not.

1Co 11:23 For I received of the Lord that which also I delivered unto you, that the Lord Jesus in the night in which he was betrayed took bread;

1Co 11:24 and when he had given thanks, he brake it, and said, This is my body, which is for you: this do in remembrance of me.

1Co 11:25 In like manner also the cup, after supper, saying, This cup is the new covenant in my blood: this do, as often as ye drink it, in remembrance of me.

1Co 11:26 For as often as ye eat this bread, and drink the cup, ye proclaim the Lord's death till he come.

1Co 11:27 Wherefore whosoever shall eat the bread or drink the cup of the Lord in an unworthy manner, shall be guilty of the body and the blood of the Lord.

1Co 11:28 But let a man prove himself, and so let him eat of the bread, and drink of the cup.

1Co 11:29 For he that eateth and drinketh, eateth and drinketh judgment unto himself, if he discern not the body.

1Co 11:30 For this cause many among you are weak and sickly, and not a few sleep.

1Co 11:31 But if we discerned ourselves, we should not be judged.

1Co 11:32 But when we are judged, we are chastened of the Lord, that we may not be condemned with the world.

1Co 11:33 Wherefore, my brethren, when ye come together to eat, wait one for another.

1Co 11:34 If any man is hungry, let him eat at home; that your coming together be not unto judgment. And the rest will I set in order whensoever I come.

Chapter 12.

1Co 12:1 Now concerning spiritual gifts, brethren, I would not have you ignorant.

1Co 12:2 Ye know that when ye were Gentiles ye were led away unto those dumb idols, howsoever ye might led.

1Co 12:3 Wherefore I make known unto you, that no man speaking in the Spirit of God saith, Jesus is anathema; and no man can say, Jesus is Lord, but in the Holy Spirit.

1Co 12:4 Now there are diversities of gifts, but the same Spirit.

1Co 12:5 And there are diversities of ministrations, and the same Lord.

1Co 12:6 And there are diversities of workings, but the same God, who worketh all things in all.

1Co 12:7 But to each one is given the manifestation of the Spirit to profit withal.

1Co 12:8 For to one is given through the Spirit the word of wisdom; and to another the word of knowledge, according to the same Spirit:

1Co 12:9 to another faith, in the same Spirit; and to another gifts of healings, in the one Spirit;

1Co 12:10 and to another workings of miracles; and to another prophecy; and to another discernings of spirits; to another divers kinds of tongues; and to another the interpretation of tongues:

1Co 12:11 but all these worketh the one and the same Spirit, dividing to each one severally even as he will.

1Co 12:12 For as the body is one, and hath many members, and all the members of the body, being many, are one body; so also is Christ.

1Co 12:13 For in one Spirit were we all baptized into one body, whether Jews or Greeks, whether bond or free; and were all made to drink of one Spirit.

1Co 12:14 For the body is not one member, but many.

1Co 12:15 If the foot shall say, Because I am not the hand, I am not of the body; it is not therefore not of the body.

1Co 12:16 And if the ear shall say, Because I am not the eye, I am not of the body; it is not therefore not of the body.

1Co 12:17 If the whole body were an eye, where were the hearing? If the whole were hearing, where were the smelling?

1Co 12:18 But now hath God set the members each one of them in the body, even as it pleased him.

1Co 12:19 And if they were all one member, where were the body?

1Co 12:20 But now they are many members, but one body.

1Co 12:21 And the eye cannot say to the hand, I have no need of thee: or again the head to the feet, I have no need of you.

1Co 12:22 Nay, much rather, those members of the body which seem to be more feeble are necessary:

1Co 12:23 and those parts of the body, which we think to be less honorable, upon these we bestow more abundant honor; and our uncomely parts have more abundant comeliness;

1Co 12:24 whereas our comely parts have no need: but God tempered the body together, giving more abundant honor to that part which lacked;

1Co 12:25 that there should be no schism in the body; but that the members should have the same care one for another.

1Co 12:26 And whether one member suffereth, all the members suffer with it; or one member is honored, all the members rejoice with it.

1Co 12:27 Now ye are the body of Christ, and severally members thereof.

1Co 12:28 And God hath set some in the church, first apostles, secondly prophets, thirdly teachers, then miracles, then gifts of healings, helps, governments, divers kinds of tongues.

1Co 12:29 Are all apostles? are all prophets? are all teachers? are all workers of miracles?

1Co 12:30 have all gifts of healings? do all speak with tongues? do all interpret?

1Co 12:31 But desire earnestly the greater gifts. And moreover a most excellent way show I unto you.

Chapter 13.

1Co 13:1 If I speak with the tongues of men and of angels, but have not love, I am become sounding brass, or a clanging cymbal.

1Co 13:2   And if I have the gift of prophecy, and know all mysteries and all knowledge; and if I have all faith, so as to remove mountains, but have not love, I am nothing.

1Co 13:3 And if I bestow all my goods to feed the poor, and if I give my body to be burned, but have not love, it profiteth me nothing.

1Co 13:4 Love suffereth long, and is kind; love envieth not; love vaunteth not itself, is not puffed up,

1Co 13:5 doth not behave itself unseemly, seeketh not its own, is not provoked, taketh not account of evil;

1Co 13:6 rejoiceth not in unrighteousness, but rejoiceth with the truth;

1Co 13:7 beareth all things, believeth all things, hopeth all things, endureth all things.

1Co 13:8   Love never faileth: but whether there be prophecies, they shall be done away; whether there be tongues, they shall cease; whether there be knowledge, it shall be done away.

1Co 13:9 For we know in part, and we prophesy in part;

1Co 13:10 but when that which is perfect is come, that which is in part shall be done away.

1Co 13:11 When I was a child, I spake as a child, I felt as a child, I thought as a child: now that I am become a man, I have put away childish things.

1Co 13:12 For now we see in a mirror, darkly; but then face to face: now I know in part; but then shall I know fully even as also I was fully known.

1Co 13:13 But now abideth faith, hope, love, these three; and the greatest of these is love.

Chapter 14.

1Co 14:1 Follow after love; yet desire earnestly spiritual gifts, but rather that ye may prophesy.

1Co 14:2 For he that speaketh in a tongue speaketh not unto men, but unto God; for no man understandeth; but in the spirit he speaketh mysteries.

1Co 14:3 But he that prophesieth speaketh unto men edification, and exhortation, and consolation.

1Co 14:4   He that speaketh in a tongue edifieth himself; but he that prophesieth edifieth the church.

1Co 14:5 Now I would have you all speak with tongues, but rather that ye should prophesy: and greater is he that prophesieth than he that speaketh with tongues, except he interpret, that the church may receive edifying.

1Co 14:6 But now, brethren, if I come unto you speaking with tongues, what shall I profit you, unless I speak to you either by way of revelation, or of knowledge, or of prophesying, or of teaching?

1Co 14:7 Even things without life, giving a voice, whether pipe or harp, if they give not a distinction in the sounds, how shall it be known what is piped or harped?

1Co 14:8 For if the trumpet give an uncertain voice, who shall prepare himself for war?

1Co 14:9 So also ye, unless ye utter by the tongue speech easy to understood, how shall it be known what is spoken? for ye will be speaking into the air.

1Co 14:10 There are, it may be, so many kinds of voices in the world, and no kind is without signification.

1Co 14:11 If then I know not the meaning of the voice, I shall be to him that speaketh a barbarian, and he that speaketh will be a barbarian unto me.

1Co 14:12 So also ye, since ye are zealous of spiritual gifts, seek that ye may abound unto the edifying of the church.

1Co 14:13 Wherefore let him that speaketh in a tongue pray that he may interpret.

1Co 14:14 For if I pray in a tongue, my spirit prayeth, but my understanding is unfruitful.

1Co 14:15 What is it then? I will pray with the spirit, and I will pray with the understanding also: I will sing with the spirit, and I will sing with the understanding also.

1Co 14:16 Else if thou bless with the spirit, how shall he that filleth the place of the unlearned say the Amen at thy giving of thanks, seeing he knoweth not what thou sayest?

1Co 14:17 For thou verily givest thanks well, but the other is not edified.

1Co 14:18 I thank God, I speak with tongues more than you all:

1Co 14:19 howbeit in the church I had rather speak five words with my understanding, that I might instruct others also, than ten thousand words in a tongue.

1Co 14:20 Brethren, be not children in mind: yet in malice be ye babes, but in mind be men.

1Co 14:21 In the law it is written, By men of strange tongues and by the lips of strangers will I speak unto this people; and not even thus will they hear me, saith the Lord.

1Co 14:22 Wherefore tongues are for a sign, not to them that believe, but to the unbelieving: but prophesying is for a sign, not to the unbelieving, but to them that believe.

1Co 14:23 If therefore the whole church be assembled together and all speak with tongues, and there come in men unlearned or unbelieving, will they not say that ye are mad?

1Co 14:24 But if all prophesy, and there come in one unbelieving or unlearned, he is reproved by all, he is judged by all;

1Co 14:25 the secrets of his heart are made manifest; and so he will fall down on his face and worship God, declaring that God is among you indeed.

1Co 14:26 What is it then, brethren? When ye come together, each one hath a psalm, hath a teaching, hath a revelation, hath a tongue, hath an interpretation. Let all things be done unto edifying.

1Co 14:27 If any man speaketh in a tongue, let it be by two, or at the most three, and that in turn; and let one interpret:

1Co 14:28 but if there be no interpreter, let him keep silence in the church; and let him speak to himself, and to God.

1Co 14:29 And let the prophets speak by two or three, and let the others discern.

1Co 14:30 But if a revelation be made to another sitting by, let the first keep silence.

1Co 14:31 For ye all can prophesy one by one, that all may learn, and all may be exhorted;

1Co 14:32 and the spirits of the prophets are subject to the prophets;

1Co 14:33 for God is not a God of confusion, but of peace. As in all the churches of the saints,

1Co 14:34 let the women keep silence in the churches: for it is not permitted unto them to speak; but let them be in subjection, as also saith the law.

1Co 14:35 And if they would learn anything, let them ask their own husbands at home: for it is shameful for a woman to speak in the church.

1Co 14:36 What? was it from you that the word of God went forth? or came it unto you alone?

1Co 14:37 If any man thinketh himself to be a prophet, or spiritual, let him take knowledge of the things which I write unto you, that they are the commandment of the Lord.

1Co 14:38 But if any man is ignorant, let him be ignorant.

1Co 14:39 Wherefore, my brethren, desire earnestly to prophesy, and forbid not to speak with tongues.

1Co 14:40 But let all things be done decently and in order.

Chapter 15.

1Co 15:1 Now I make known unto you brethren, the gospel which I preached unto you, which also ye received, wherein also ye stand,

1Co 15:2 by which also ye are saved, if ye hold fast the word which I preached unto you, except ye believed in vain.

1Co 15:3 For I delivered unto you first of all that which also I received: that Christ died for our sins according to the scriptures;

1Co 15:4 and that he was buried; and that he hath been raised on the third day according to the scriptures;

1Co 15:5 and that he appeared to Cephas; then to the twelve;

1Co 15:6 then he appeared to above five hundred brethren at once, of whom the greater part remain until now, but some are fallen asleep;

1Co 15:7 then he appeared to James; then to all the apostles;

1Co 15:8 and last of all, as to the child untimely born, he appeared to me also.

1Co 15:9 For I am the least of the apostles, that am not meet to be called an apostle, because I persecuted the church of God.

1Co 15:10 But by the grace of God I am what I am: and his grace which was bestowed upon me was not found vain; but I labored more abundantly than they all: yet not I, but the grace of God which was with me.

1Co 15:11 Whether then it be I or they, so we preach, and so ye believed.

1Co 15:12 Now if Christ is preached that he hath been raised from the dead, how say some among you that there is no resurrection of the dead?

1Co 15:13 But if there is no resurrection of the dead, neither hath Christ been raised:

1Co 15:14 and if Christ hath not been raised, then is our preaching vain, your faith also is vain.

1Co 15:15 Yea, we are found false witnesses of God; because we witnessed of God that he raised up Christ: whom he raised not up, if so be that the dead are not raised.

1Co 15:16 For if the dead are not raised, neither hath Christ been raised:

1Co 15:17 and if Christ hath not been raised, your faith is vain; ye are yet in your sins.

1Co 15:18 Then they also that are fallen asleep in Christ have perished.

1Co 15:19 If we have only hoped in Christ in this life, we are of all men most pitiable.

1Co 15:20 But now hath Christ been raised from the dead, the firstfruits of them that are asleep.

1Co 15:21 For since by man came death, by man came also the resurrection of the dead.

1Co 15:22 For as in Adam all die, so also in Christ shall all be made alive.

1Co 15:23 But each in his own order: Christ the firstfruits; then they that are Christ's, at his coming.

1Co 15:24 Then cometh the end, when he shall deliver up the kingdom to God, even the Father; when he shall have abolished all rule and all authority and power.

1Co 15:25 For he must reign, till he hath put all his enemies under his feet.

1Co 15:26 The last enemy that shall be abolished is death.

1Co 15:27 For, He put all things in subjection under his feet. But when he saith, All things are put in subjection, it is evident that he is excepted who did subject all things unto him.

1Co 15:28 And when all things have been subjected unto him, then shall the Son also himself be subjected to him that did subject all things unto him, that God may be all in all.

1Co 15:29 Else what shall they do that are baptized for the dead? If the dead are not raised at all, why then are they baptized for them?

1Co 15:30 Why do we also stand in jeopardy every hour?

1Co 15:31 I protest by that glorifying in you, brethren, which I have in Christ Jesus our Lord, I die daily.

1Co 15:32 If after the manner of men I fought with beasts at Ephesus, what doth it profit me? If the dead are not raised, let us eat and drink, for to-morrow we die.

1Co 15:33 Be not deceived: Evil companionships corrupt good morals.

1Co 15:34 Awake to soberness righteously, and sin not; for some have no knowledge of God: I speak this to move you to shame.

1Co 15:35 But some one will say, How are the dead raised? and with what manner of body do they come?

1Co 15:36 Thou foolish one, that which thou thyself sowest is not quickened except it die:

1Co 15:37 and that which thou sowest, thou sowest not the body that shall be, but a bare grain, it may chance of wheat, or of some other kind;

1Co 15:38 but God giveth it a body even as it pleased him, and to each seed a body of its own.

1Co 15:39 All flesh is not the same flesh: but there is one flesh of men, and another flesh of beasts, and another flesh of birds, and another of fishes.

1Co 15:40 There are also celestial bodies, and bodies terrestrial: but the glory of the celestial is one, and the glory of the terrestrial is another.

1Co 15:41 There is one glory of the sun, and another glory of the moon, and another glory of the stars; for one star differeth from another star in glory.

1Co 15:42 So also is the resurrection of the dead. It is sown in corruption; it is raised in incorruption:

1Co 15:43 it is sown in dishonor; it is raised in glory: it is sown in weakness; it is raised in power:

1Co 15:44 it is sown a natural body; it is raised a spiritual body. If there is a natural body, there is also a spiritual body.

1Co 15:45 So also it is written, The first man Adam became a living soul. The last Adam became a life-giving spirit.

1Co 15:46 Howbeit that is not first which is spiritual, but that which is natural; then that which is spiritual.

1Co 15:47 The first man is of the earth, earthy: the second man is of heaven.

1Co 15:48 As is the earthy, such are they also that are earthy: and as is the heavenly, such are they also that are heavenly.

1Co 15:49 And as we have borne the image of the earthy, we shall also bear the image of the heavenly.

1Co 15:50 Now this I say, brethren, that flesh and blood cannot inherit the kingdom of God; neither doth corruption inherit incorruption.

1Co 15:51 Behold, I tell you a mystery: We all shall not sleep, but we shall all be changed,

1Co 15:52 in a moment, in the twinkling of an eye, at the last trump: for the trumpet shall sound, and the dead shall be raised incorruptible, and we shall be changed.

1Co 15:53 For this corruptible must put on incorruption, and this mortal must put on immortality.

1Co 15:54 But when this corruptible shall have put on incorruption, and this mortal shall have put on immortality, then shall come to pass the saying that is written, Death is swallowed up in victory.

1Co 15:55 O death, where is thy victory? O death, where is thy sting?

1Co 15:56 The sting of death is sin; and the power of sin is the law:

1Co 15:57 but thanks be to God, who giveth us the victory through our Lord Jesus Christ.

1Co 15:58 Wherefore, my beloved brethren, be ye stedfast, unmoveable, always abounding in the work of the Lord, forasmuch as ye know that your labor is not vain in the Lord.

Chapter 16.

1Co 16:1 Now concerning the collection for the saints, as I gave order to the churches of Galatia, so also do ye.

1Co 16:2 Upon the first day of the week let each one of you lay by him in store, as he may prosper, that no collections be made when I come.

1Co 16:3 And when I arrive, whomsoever ye shall approve, them will I send with letters to carry your bounty unto Jerusalem:

1Co 16:4 and if it be meet for me to go also, they shall go with me.

1Co 16:5 But I will come unto you, when I shall have passed through Macedonia; for I pass through Macedonia;

1Co 16:6 but with you it may be that I shall abide, or even winter, that ye may set me forward on my journey whithersoever I go.

1Co 16:7 For I do not wish to see you now by the way; for I hope to tarry a while with you, if the Lord permit.

1Co 16:8 But I will tarry at Ephesus until Pentecost;

1Co 16:9 for a great door and effectual is opened unto me, and there are many adversaries.

1Co 16:10 Now if Timothy come, see that he be with you without fear; for he worketh the work of the Lord, as I also do:

1Co 16:11 let no man therefore despise him. But set him forward on his journey in peace, that he may come unto me: for I expect him with the brethren.

1Co 16:12 But as touching Apollos the brother, I besought him much to come unto you with the brethren: and it was not all his will to come now; but he will come when he shall have opportunity.

1Co 16:13 Watch ye, stand fast in the faith, quit you like men, be strong.

1Co 16:14 Let all that ye do be done in love.

1Co 16:15 Now I beseech you, brethren (ye know the house of Stephanas, that it is the firstfruits of Achaia, and that they have set themselves to minister unto the saints),

1Co 16:16 that ye also be in subjection unto such, and to every one that helpeth in the work and laboreth.

1Co 16:17 And I rejoice at the coming of Stephanas and Fortunatus and Achaicus: for that which was lacking on your part they supplied.

1Co 16:18 For they refreshed my spirit and yours: acknowledge ye therefore them that are such.

1Co 16:19 The churches of Asia salute you. Aquila and Prisca salute you much in the Lord, with the church that is in their house.

1Co 16:20 All the brethren salute you. Salute one another with a holy kiss.

1Co 16:21 The salutation of me Paul with mine own hand.

1Co 16:22 If any man loveth not the Lord, let him be anathema. Maranatha.

1Co 16:23 The grace of the Lord Jesus Christ be with you.

1Co 16:24 My love be with you all in Christ Jesus. Amen.

9. 2 Corinthians

Chapter 1.

2Co 1:1 Paul, an apostle of Christ Jesus through the will of God, and Timothy our brother, unto the church of God which is at Corinth, with all the saints that are in the whole of Achaia:

2Co 1:2 Grace to you and peace from God our Father and the Lord Jesus Christ.

2Co 1:3 Blessed be the God and Father of our Lord Jesus Christ, the Father of mercies and God of all comfort;

2Co 1:4 who comforteth us in all our affliction, that we may be able to comfort them that are in any affliction, through the comfort wherewith we ourselves are comforted of God.

2Co 1:5 For as the sufferings of Christ abound unto us, even so our comfort also aboundeth through Christ.

2Co 1:6 But whether we are afflicted, it is for your comfort and salvation; or whether we are comforted, it is for your comfort, which worketh in the patient enduring of the same sufferings which we also suffer:

2Co 1:7 and our hope for you is stedfast; knowing that, as ye are partakers of the sufferings, so also are ye of the comfort.

2Co 1:8 For we would not have you ignorant, brethren, concerning our affliction which befell us in Asia, that we were weighed down exceedingly, beyond our power, insomuch that we despaired even of life:

2Co 1:9 yea, we ourselves have had the sentence of death within ourselves, that we should not trust in ourselves, but in God who raiseth the dead:

2Co 1:10 who delivered us out of so great a death, and will deliver: on whom we have set our hope that he will also still deliver us;

2Co 1:11 ye also helping together on our behalf by your supplication; that, for the gift bestowed upon us by means of many, thanks may be given by many persons on our behalf.

2Co 1:12 For our glorifying is this, the testimony of our conscience, that in holiness and sincerity of God, not in fleshly wisdom but in the grace of God, we behaved ourselves in the world, and more abundantly to you-ward.

2Co 1:13 For we write no other things unto you, than what ye read or even acknowledge, and I hope ye will acknowledge unto the end:

2Co 1:14 as also ye did acknowledge us in part, that we are your glorying, even as ye also are ours, in the day of our Lord Jesus.

2Co 1:15 And in this confidence I was minded to come first unto you, that ye might have a second benefit;

2Co 1:16 and by you to pass into Macedonia, and again from Macedonia to come unto you, and of you to be set forward on my journey unto Judaea.

2Co 1:17 When I therefore was thus minded, did I show fickleness? or the things that I purpose, do I purpose according to the flesh, that with me there should be the yea yea and the nay nay?

2Co 1:18 But as God is faithful, our word toward you is not yea and nay.

2Co 1:19 For the Son of God, Jesus Christ, who was preached among you by us, even by me and Silvanus and Timothy, was not yea and nay, but in him is yea.

2Co 1:20 For how many soever be the promises of God, in him is the yea: wherefore also through him is the Amen, unto the glory of God through us.

2Co 1:21 Now he that establisheth us with you in Christ, and anointed us, is God;

2Co 1:22 who also sealed us, and gave us the earnest of the Spirit in our hearts.

2Co 1:23 But I call God for a witness upon my soul, that to spare you I forbare to come unto Corinth.

2Co 1:24 Not that we have lordship over your faith, but are helpers of your joy: for in faith ye stand fast.

Chapter 2.

2Co 2:1 But I determined this for myself, that I would not come again to you with sorrow.

2Co 2:2 For if I make you sorry, who then is he that maketh me glad but he that is made sorry by me?

2Co 2:3 And I wrote this very thing, lest, when I came, I should have sorrow from them of whom I ought to rejoice; having confidence in you all, that my joy is the joy of you all.

2Co 2:4 For out of much affliction and anguish of heart I wrote unto you with many tears; not that ye should be made sorry, but that ye might know the love that I have more abundantly unto you.

2Co 2:5 But if any hath caused sorrow, he hath caused sorrow, not to me, but in part (that I press not too heavily) to you all.

2Co 2:6 Sufficient to such a one is this punishment which was inflicted by the many;

2Co 2:7 so that contrariwise ye should rather forgive him and comfort him, lest by any means such a one should be swallowed up with his overmuch sorrow.

2Co 2:8 Wherefore I beseech you to confirm your love toward him.

2Co 2:9 For to this end also did I write, that I might know the proof of you, whether ye are obedient in all things.

2Co 2:10 But to whom ye forgive anything, I forgive also: for what I also have forgiven, if I have forgiven anything, for your sakes have I forgiven it in the presence of Christ;

2Co 2:11 that no advantage may be gained over us by Satan: for we are not ignorant of his devices.

2Co 2:12 Now when I came to Troas for the gospel of Christ, and when a door was opened unto me in the Lord,

2Co 2:13 I had no relief for my spirit, because I found not Titus my brother: but taking my leave of them, I went forth into Macedonia.

2Co 2:14 But thanks be unto God, who always leadeth us in triumph in Christ, and maketh manifest through us the savor of his knowledge in every place.

2Co 2:15 For we are a sweet savor of Christ unto God, in them that are saved, and in them that perish;

2Co 2:16 to the one a savor from death unto death; to the other a savor from life unto life. And who is sufficient for these things?

2Co 2:17 For we are not as the many, corrupting the word of God: but as of sincerity, but as of God, in the sight of God, speak we in Christ.

Chapter 3.

2Co 3:1 Are we beginning again to commend ourselves? or need we, as do some, epistles of commendation to you or from you?

2Co 3:2 Ye are our epistle, written in our hearts, known and read of all men;

2Co 3:3 being made manifest that ye are an epistle of Christ, ministered by us, written not with ink, but with the Spirit of the living God; not in tables of stone, but in tables that are hearts of flesh.

2Co 3:4 And such confidence have we through Christ to God-ward:

2Co 3:5 not that we are sufficient of ourselves, to account anything as from ourselves; but our sufficiency is from God;

2Co 3:6 who also made us sufficient as ministers of a new covenant; not of the letter, but of the spirit: for the letter killeth, but the spirit giveth life.

2Co 3:7 But if the ministration of death, written, and engraven on stones, came with glory, so that the children of Israel could not look stedfastly upon the face of Moses for the glory of his face; which glory was passing away:

2Co 3:8 how shall not rather the ministration of the spirit be with glory?

2Co 3:9 For if the ministration of condemnation hath glory, much rather doth the ministration of righteousness exceed in glory.

2Co 3:10 For verily that which hath been made glorious hath not been made glorious in this respect, by reason of the glory that surpasseth.

2Co 3:11 For if that which passeth away was with glory, much more that which remaineth is in glory.

2Co 3:12 Having therefore such a hope, we use great boldness of speech,

2Co 3:13 and are not as Moses, who put a veil upon his face, that the children of Israel should not look stedfastly on the end of that which was passing away:

2Co 3:14 but their minds were hardened: for until this very day at the reading of the old covenant the same veil remaineth, it not being revealed to them that it is done away in Christ.

2Co 3:15 But unto this day, whensoever Moses is read, a veil lieth upon their heart.

2Co 3:16 But whensoever it shall turn to the Lord, the veil is taken away.

2Co 3:17 Now the Lord is the Spirit: and where the Spirit of the Lord is, there is liberty.

2Co 3:18 But we all, with unveiled face beholding as in a mirror the glory of the Lord, are transformed into the same image from glory to glory, even as from the Lord the Spirit.

Chapter 4.

2Co 4:1 Therefore seeing we have this ministry, even as we obtained mercy, we faint not:

2Co 4:2 but we have renounced the hidden things of shame, not walking in craftiness, nor handling the word of God deceitfully; but by the manifestation of the truth commending ourselves to every man's conscience in the sight of God.

2Co 4:3 And even if our gospel is veiled, it is veiled in them that perish:

2Co 4:4 in whom the god of this world hath blinded the minds of the unbelieving, that the light of the gospel of the glory of Christ, who is the image of God, should not dawn upon them.

2Co 4:5 For we preach not ourselves, but Christ Jesus as Lord, and ourselves as your servants for Jesus' sake.

2Co 4:6 Seeing it is God, that said, Light shall shine out of darkness, who shined in our hearts, to give the light of the knowledge of the glory of God in the face of Jesus Christ.

2Co 4:7 But we have this treasure in earthen vessels, that the exceeding greatness of the power may be of God, and not from ourselves;

2Co 4:8 we are pressed on every side, yet not straitened; perplexed, yet not unto despair;

2Co 4:9 pursued, yet not forsaken; smitten down, yet not destroyed;

2Co 4:10 always bearing about in the body the dying of Jesus, that the life also of Jesus may be manifested in our body.

2Co 4:11 For we who live are always delivered unto death for Jesus' sake, that the life also of Jesus may be manifested in our mortal flesh.

2Co 4:12 So then death worketh in us, but life in you.

2Co 4:13 But having the same spirit of faith, according to that which is written, I believed, and therefore did I speak; we also believe, and therefore also we speak;

2Co 4:14 knowing that he that raised up the Lord Jesus shall raise up us also with Jesus, and shall present us with you.

2Co 4:15 For all things are for your sakes, that the grace, being multiplied through the many, may cause the thanksgiving to abound unto the glory of God.

2Co 4:16 Wherefore we faint not; but though our outward man is decaying, yet our inward man is renewed day by day.

2Co 4:17 For our light affliction, which is for the moment, worketh for us more and more exceedingly an eternal weight of glory;

2Co 4:18 while we look not at the things which are seen, but at the things which are not seen: for the things which are seen are temporal; but the things which are not seen are eternal.

Chapter 5.

2Co 5:1 For we know that if the earthly house of our tabernacle be dissolved, we have a building from God, a house not made with hands, eternal, in the heavens.

2Co 5:2 For verily in this we groan, longing to be clothed upon with our habitation which is from heaven:

2Co 5:3 if so be that being clothed we shall not be found naked.

2Co 5:4 For indeed we that are in this tabernacle do groan, being burdened; not for that we would be unclothed, but that we would be clothed upon, that what is mortal may be swallowed up of life.

2Co 5:5 Now he that wrought us for this very thing is God, who gave unto us the earnest of the Spirit.

2Co 5:6 Being therefore always of good courage, and knowing that, whilst we are at home in the body, we are absent from the Lord

2Co 5:7 (for we walk by faith, not by sight);

2Co 5:8 we are of good courage, I say, and are willing rather to be absent from the body, and to be at home with the Lord.

2Co 5:9 Wherefore also we make it our aim, whether at home or absent, to be well-pleasing unto him.

2Co 5:10 For we must all be made manifest before the judgment-seat of Christ; that each one may receive the things done in the body, according to what he hath done, whether it be good or bad.

2Co 5:11 Knowing therefore the fear of the Lord, we persuade men, but we are made manifest unto God; and I hope that we are made manifest also in your consciences.

2Co 5:12 We are not again commending ourselves unto you, but speak as giving you occasion of glorying on our behalf, that ye may have wherewith to answer them that glory in appearance, and not in heart.

2Co 5:13 For whether we are beside ourselves, it is unto God; or whether we are of sober mind, it is unto you.

2Co 5:14 For the love of Christ constraineth us; because we thus judge, that one died for all, therefore all died;

2Co 5:15 and he died for all, that they that live should no longer live unto themselves, but unto him who for their sakes died and rose again.

2Co 5:16 Wherefore we henceforth know no man after the flesh: even though we have known Christ after the flesh, yet now we know him so no more.

2Co 5:17 Wherefore if any man is in Christ, he is a new creature: the old things are passed away; behold, they are become new.

2Co 5:18 But all things are of God, who reconciled us to himself through Christ, and gave unto us the ministry of reconciliation;

2Co 5:19 to wit, that God was in Christ reconciling the world unto himself, not reckoning unto them their trespasses, and having committed unto us the word of reconciliation.

2Co 5:20 We are ambassadors therefore on behalf of Christ, as though God were entreating by us: we beseech you on behalf of Christ, be ye reconciled to God.

2Co 5:21 Him who knew no sin he made to be sin on our behalf; that we might become the righteousness of God in him.

Chapter 6.

2Co 6:1 And working together with him we entreat also that ye receive not the grace of God in vain

2Co 6:2 (for he saith, At an acceptable time I hearkened unto thee, And in a day of salvation did I succor thee: behold, now is the acceptable time; behold, now is the day of salvation):

2Co 6:3 giving no occasion of stumbling in anything, that our ministration be not blamed;

2Co 6:4 but in everything commending ourselves, as ministers of God, in much patience, in afflictions, in necessities, in distresses,

2Co 6:5 in stripes, in imprisonments, in tumults, in labors, in watchings, in fastings;

2Co 6:6 in pureness, in knowledge, in long suffering, in kindness, in the Holy Spirit, in love unfeigned,

2Co 6:7 in the word of truth, in the power of God; by the armor of righteousness on the right hand and on the left,

2Co 6:8 by glory and dishonor, by evil report and good report; as deceivers, and yet true;

2Co 6:9 as unknown, and yet well known; as dying, and behold, we live; as chastened, and not killed;

2Co 6:10 as sorrowful, yet always rejoicing; as poor, yet making many rich; as having nothing, and yet possessing all things.

2Co 6:11 Our mouth is open unto you, O Corinthians, our heart is enlarged.

2Co 6:12 Ye are not straitened in us, but ye are straitened in your own affections.

2Co 6:13 Now for a recompense in like kind (I speak as unto my children), be ye also enlarged.

2Co 6:14 Be not unequally yoked with unbelievers: for what fellowship have righteousness and iniquity? or what communion hath light with darkness?

2Co 6:15 And what concord hath Christ with Belial? or what portion hath a believer with an unbeliever?

2Co 6:16 And what agreement hath a temple of God with idols? for we are a temple of the living God; even as God said, I will dwell in them, and walk in them; and I will be their God, and they shall be my people.

2Co 6:17 Wherefore Come ye out from among them, and be ye separate, saith the Lord, And touch no unclean thing; And I will receive you,

2Co 6:18 And will be to you a Father, And ye shall be to me sons and daughters, saith the Lord Almighty.

Chapter 7.

2Co 7:1 Having therefore these promises, beloved, let us cleanse ourselves from all defilement of flesh and spirit, perfecting holiness in the fear of God.

2Co 7:2 Open your hearts to us: we wronged no man, we corrupted no man, we took advantage of no man.

2Co 7:3 I say it not to condemn you: for I have said before, that ye are in our hearts to die together and live together.

2Co 7:4 Great is my boldness of speech toward you, great is my glorying on your behalf: I am filled with comfort, I overflow with joy in all our affliction.

2Co 7:5 For even when we were come into Macedonia our flesh had no relief, but we were afflicted on every side; without were fightings, within were fears.

2Co 7:6 Nevertheless he that comforteth the lowly, even God, comforted us by the coming of Titus;

2Co 7:7 and not by his coming only, but also by the comfort wherewith he was comforted in you, while he told us your longing, your mourning, your zeal for me; so that I rejoiced yet more.

2Co 7:8 For though I made you sorry with my epistle, I do not regret it: though I did regret it (for I see that that epistle made you sorry, though but for a season),

2Co 7:9 I now rejoice, not that ye were made sorry, but that ye were made sorry unto repentance; for ye were made sorry after a godly sort, that ye might suffer loss by us in nothing.

2Co 7:10 For godly sorrow worketh repentance unto salvation, a repentance which bringeth no regret: but the sorrow of the world worketh death.

2Co 7:11 For behold, this selfsame thing, that ye were made sorry after a godly sort, what earnest care it wrought in you, yea what clearing of yourselves, yea what indignation, yea what fear, yea what longing, yea what zeal, yea what avenging! In everything ye approved yourselves to be pure in the matter.

2Co 7:12 So although I wrote unto you, I wrote not for his cause that did the wrong, nor for his cause that suffered the wrong, but that your earnest care for us might be made manifest unto you in the sight of God.

2Co 7:13 Therefore we have been comforted: And in our comfort we joyed the more exceedingly for the joy of Titus, because his spirit hath been refreshed by you all.

2Co 7:14 For if in anything I have gloried to him on your behalf, I was not put to shame; but as we spake all things to you in truth, so our glorying also which I made before Titus was found to be truth.

2Co 7:15 And his affection is more abundantly toward you, while he remembereth the obedience of you all, how with fear and trembling ye received him.

2Co 7:16 I rejoice that in everything I am of good courage concerning you.

Chapter 8.

2Co 8:1 Moreover, brethren, we make known to you the grace of God which hath been given in the churches of Macedonia;

2Co 8:2 how that in much proof of affliction the abundance of their joy and their deep poverty abounded unto the riches of their liberality.

2Co 8:3 For according to their power, I bear witness, yea and beyond their power, they gave of their own accord,

2Co 8:4 beseeching us with much entreaty in regard of this grace and the fellowship in the ministering to the saints:

2Co 8:5 and this, not as we had hoped, but first they gave their own selves to the Lord, and to us through the will of God.

2Co 8:6 Insomuch that we exhorted Titus, that as he made a beginning before, so he would also complete in you this grace also.

2Co 8:7 But as ye abound in everything, in faith, and utterance, and knowledge, and in all earnestness, and in your love to us, see that ye abound in this grace also.

2Co 8:8 I speak not by way of commandment, but as proving through the earnestness of others the sincerity also of your love.

2Co 8:9 For ye know the grace of our Lord Jesus Christ, that, though he was rich, yet for your sakes he became poor, that ye through his poverty might become rich.

2Co 8:10 And herein I give my judgment: for this is expedient for you, who were the first to make a beginning a year ago, not only to do, but also to will.

2Co 8:11 But now complete the doing also; that as there was the readiness to will, so there may be the completion also out of your ability.

2Co 8:12 For if the readiness is there, it is acceptable according as a man hath, not according as he hath not.

2Co 8:13 For I say not this that others may be eased and ye distressed;

2Co 8:14 but by equality: your abundance being a supply at this present time for their want, that their abundance also may become a supply for your want; that there may be equality:

2Co 8:15 as it is written, He that gathered much had nothing over; and he that gathered little had no lack.

2Co 8:16 But thanks be to God, who putteth the same earnest care for you into the heart of Titus.

2Co 8:17 For he accepted indeed our exhortation; but being himself very earnest, he went forth unto you of his own accord.

2Co 8:18 And we have sent together with him the brother whose praise in the gospel is spread through all the churches;

2Co 8:19 and not only so, but who was also appointed by the churches to travel with us in the matter of this grace, which is ministered by us to the glory of the Lord, and to show our readiness:

2Co 8:20 avoiding this, that any man should blame us in the matter of this bounty which is ministered by us:

2Co 8:21 for we take thought for things honorable, not only in the sight of the Lord, but also in the sight of men.

2Co 8:22 And we have sent with them our brother, whom we have many times proved earnest in many things, but now much more earnest, by reason of the great confidence which he hath in you.

2Co 8:23 Whether any inquire about Titus, he is my partner and my fellow-worker to you-ward, or our brethren, they are the messengers of the churches, they are the glory of Christ.

2Co 8:24 Show ye therefore unto them in the face of the churches the proof of your love, and of our glorying on your behalf.

Chapter 9.

2Co 9:1 For as touching the ministering to the saints, it is superfluous for me to write to you:

2Co 9:2 for I know your readiness, of which I glory on your behalf to them of Macedonia, that Achaia hath been prepared for a year past; and your zeal hath stirred up very many of them.

2Co 9:3 But I have sent the brethren, that our glorying on your behalf may not be made void in this respect; that, even as I said, ye may be prepared:

2Co 9:4 lest by any means, if there come with me any of Macedonia and find you unprepared, we (that we say not, ye) should be put to shame in this confidence.

2Co 9:5 I thought it necessary therefore to entreat the brethren, that they would go before unto you, and make up beforehand your aforepromised bounty, that the same might be ready as a matter of bounty, and not of extortion.

2Co 9:6 But this I say, He that soweth sparingly shall reap also sparingly; and he that soweth bountifully shall reap also bountifully.

2Co 9:7 Let each man do according as he hath purposed in his heart: not grudgingly, or of necessity: for God loveth a cheerful giver.

2Co 9:8 And God is able to make all grace abound unto you; that ye, having always all sufficiency in everything, may abound unto every good work:

2Co 9:9 as it is written, He hath scattered abroad, he hath given to the poor; His righteousness abideth for ever.

2Co 9:10 And he that supplieth seed to the sower and bread for food, shall supply and multiply your seed for sowing, and increase the fruits of your righteousness:

2Co 9:11 ye being enriched in everything unto all liberality, which worketh through us thanksgiving to God.

2Co 9:12 For the ministration of this service not only filleth up the measure of the wants of the saints, but aboundeth also through many thanksgivings unto God;

2Co 9:13 seeing that through the proving of you by this ministration they glorify God for the obedience of your confession unto the gospel of Christ, and for the liberality of your contribution unto them and unto all;

2Co 9:14 while they themselves also, with supplication on your behalf, long after you by reason of the exceeding grace of God in you.

2Co 9:15 Thanks be to God for his unspeakable gift.

Chapter 10.

2Co 10:1 Now I Paul myself entreat you by the meekness and gentleness of Christ, I who in your presence am lowly among you, but being absent am of good courage toward you:

2Co 10:2 yea, I beseech you, that I may not when present show courage with the confidence wherewith I count to be bold against some, who count of us as if we walked according to the flesh.

2Co 10:3 For though we walk in the flesh, we do not war according to the flesh

2Co 10:4 (for the weapons of our warfare are not of the flesh, but mighty before God to the casting down of strongholds),

2Co 10:5 casting down imaginations, and every high thing that is exalted against the knowledge of God, and bringing every thought into captivity to the obedience of Christ;

2Co 10:6 and being in readiness to avenge all disobedience, when your obedience shall be made full.

2Co 10:7 Ye look at the things that are before your face. If any man trusteth in himself that he is Christ's, let him consider this again with himself, that, even as he is Christ's, so also are we.

2Co 10:8 For though I should glory somewhat abundantly concerning our authority (which the Lord gave for building you up, and not for casting you down), I shall not be put to shame:

2Co 10:9 that I may not seem as if I would terrify you by my letters.

2Co 10:10 For, His letters, they say, are weighty and strong; but his bodily presence is weak, and his speech of no account.

2Co 10:11 Let such a one reckon this, that, what we are in word by letters when we are absent, such are we also in deed when we are present.

2Co 10:12 For we are not bold to number or compare ourselves with certain of them that commend themselves: but they themselves, measuring themselves by themselves, and comparing themselves with themselves, are without understanding.

2Co 10:13 But we will not glory beyond our measure, but according to the measure of the province which God apportioned to us as a measure, to reach even unto you.

2Co 10:14 For we stretch not ourselves overmuch, as though we reached not unto you: for we came even as far as unto you in the gospel of Christ:

2Co 10:15 not glorying beyond our measure, that is, in other men's labors; but having hope that, as your faith groweth, we shall be magnified in you according to our province unto further abundance,

2Co 10:16 so as to preach the gospel even unto the parts beyond you, and not to glory in another's province in regard of things ready to our hand.

2Co 10:17 But he that glorieth, let him glory in the Lord.

2Co 10:18 For not he that commendeth himself is approved, but whom the Lord commendeth.

Chapter 11.

2Co 11:1 Would that ye could bear with me in a little foolishness: but indeed ye do bear with me.

2Co 11:2 For I am jealous over you with a godly jealousy: for I espoused you to one husband, that I might present you as a pure virgin to Christ.

2Co 11:3 But I fear, lest by any means, as the serpent beguiled Eve in his craftiness, your minds should be corrupted from the simplicity and the purity that is toward Christ.

2Co 11:4 For if he that cometh preacheth another Jesus, whom we did not preach, or if ye receive a different spirit, which ye did not receive, or a different gospel, which ye did not accept, ye do well to bear with him.

2Co 11:5 For I reckon that I am not a whit behind the very chiefest apostles.

2Co 11:6 But though I be rude in speech, yet am I not in knowledge; nay, in every way have we made this manifest unto you in all things.

2Co 11:7 Or did I commit a sin in abasing myself that ye might be exalted, because I preached to you the gospel of God for nought?

2Co 11:8 I robbed other churches, taking wages of them that I might minister unto you;

2Co 11:9 and when I was present with you and was in want, I was not a burden on any man; for the brethren, when they came from Macedonia, supplied the measure of my want; and in everything I kept myself from being burdensome unto you, and so will I keep myself.

2Co 11:10 As the truth of Christ is in me, no man shall stop me of this glorying in the regions of Achaia.

2Co 11:11 Wherefore? because I love you not? God knoweth.

2Co 11:12 But what I do, that I will do, that I may cut off occasion from them that desire an occasion; that wherein they glory, they may be found even as we.

2Co 11:13 For such men are false apostles, deceitful workers, fashioning themselves into apostles of Christ.

2Co 11:14 And no marvel; for even Satan fashioneth himself into an angel of light.

2Co 11:15 It is no great thing therefore if his ministers also fashion themselves as ministers of righteousness, whose end shall be according to their works.

2Co 11:16 I say again, let no man think me foolish; but if ye do, yet as foolish receive me, that I also may glory a little.

2Co 11:17 That which I speak, I speak not after the Lord, but as in foolishness, in this confidence of glorying.

2Co 11:18 Seeing that many glory after the flesh, I will glory also.

2Co 11:19 For ye bear with the foolish gladly, being wise yourselves.

2Co 11:20 For ye bear with a man, if he bringeth you into bondage, if he devoureth you, if he taketh you captive, if he exalteth himself, if he smiteth you on the face.

2Co 11:21 I speak by way of disparagement, as though we had been weak. Yet whereinsoever any is bold (I speak in foolishness), I am bold also.

2Co 11:22 Are they Hebrews? so am I. Are they Israelites? so am I. Are they the seed of Abraham? so am I.

2Co 11:23 Are they ministers of Christ? (I speak as one beside himself) I more; in labors more abundantly, in prisons more abundantly, in stripes above measure, in deaths oft.

2Co 11:24 Of the Jews five times received I forty stripes save one.

2Co 11:25 Thrice was I beaten with rods, once was I stoned, thrice I suffered shipwreck, a night and a day have I been in the deep;

2Co 11:26 in journeyings often, in perils of rivers, in perils of robbers, in perils from my countrymen, in perils from the Gentiles, in perils in the city, in perils in the wilderness, in perils in the sea, in perils among false brethren;

2Co 11:27 in labor and travail, in watchings often, in hunger and thirst, in fastings often, in cold and nakedness.

2Co 11:28 Besides those things that are without, there is that which presseth upon me daily, anxiety for all the churches.

2Co 11:29 Who is weak, and I am not weak? who is caused to stumble, and I burn not?

2Co 11:30 If I must needs glory, I will glory of the things that concern my weakness.

2Co 11:31 The God and Father of the Lord Jesus, he who is blessed for evermore knoweth that I lie not.

2Co 11:32 In Damascus the governor under Aretas the king guarded the city of the Damascenes in order to take me:

2Co 11:33 and through a window was I let down in a basket by the wall, and escaped his hands.

Chapter 12.

2Co 12:1 I must needs glory, though it is not expedient; but I will come to visions and revelations of the Lord.

2Co 12:2 I know a man in Christ, fourteen years ago (whether in the body, I know not; or whether out of the body, I know not; God knoweth), such a one caught up even to the third heaven.

2Co 12:3 And I know such a man (whether in the body, or apart from the body, I know not; God knoweth),

2Co 12:4 how that he was caught up into Paradise, and heard unspeakable words, which it is not lawful for a man to utter.

2Co 12:5 On behalf of such a one will I glory: but on mine own behalf I will not glory, save in my weaknesses.

2Co 12:6 For if I should desire to glory, I shall not be foolish; for I shall speak the truth: but I forbear, lest any man should account of me above that which he seeth me to be, or heareth from me.

2Co 12:7 And by reason of the exceeding greatness of the revelations, that I should not be exalted overmuch, there was given to me a thorn in the flesh, a messenger of Satan to buffet me, that I should not be exalted overmuch.

2Co 12:8 Concerning this thing I besought the Lord thrice, that it might depart from me.

2Co 12:9 And he hath said unto me, My grace is sufficient for thee: for my power is made perfect in weakness. Most gladly therefore will I rather glory in my weaknesses, that the power of Christ may rest upon me.

2Co 12:10 Wherefore I take pleasure in weaknesses, in injuries, in necessities, in persecutions, in distresses, for Christ's sake: for when I am weak, then am I strong.

2Co 12:11 I am become foolish: ye compelled me; for I ought to have been commended of you: for in nothing was I behind the very chiefest apostles, though I am nothing.

2Co 12:12 Truly the signs of an apostle were wrought among you in all patience, by signs and wonders and mighty works.

2Co 12:13 For what is there wherein ye were made inferior to the rest of the churches, except it be that I myself was not a burden to you? forgive me this wrong.

2Co 12:14 Behold, this is the third time I am ready to come to you; and I will not be a burden to you: for I seek not yours, but you: for the children ought not to lay up for the parents, but the parents for the children.

2Co 12:15 And I will most gladly spend and be spent for your souls. If I love you more abundantly, am I loved the less?

2Co 12:16 But be it so, I did not myself burden you; but, being crafty, I caught you with guile.

2Co 12:17 Did I take advantage of you by any one of them whom I have sent unto you?

2Co 12:18 I exhorted Titus, and I sent the brother with him. Did Titus take any advantage of you? walked we not in the same spirit? walked we not in the same steps?

2Co 12:19 Ye think all this time that we are excusing ourselves unto you. In the sight of God speak we in Christ. But all things, beloved, are for your edifying.

2Co 12:20 For I fear, lest by any means, when I come, I should find you not such as I would, and should myself be found of you such as ye would not; lest by any means there should be strife, jealousy, wraths, factions, backbitings, whisperings, swellings, tumults;

2Co 12:21 lest again when I come my God should humble me before you, and I should mourn for many of them that have sinned heretofore, and repented not of the uncleanness and fornication and lasciviousness which they committed.

Chapter 13.

2Co 13:1 This is the third time I am coming to you. At the mouth of two witnesses or three shall every word be established.

2Co 13:2 I have said beforehand, and I do say beforehand, as when I was present the second time, so now, being absent, to them that have sinned heretofore, and to all the rest, that, if I come again, I will not spare;

2Co 13:3 seeing that ye seek a proof of Christ that speaketh in me; who to you-ward is not weak, but is powerful in you:

2Co 13:4 for he was crucified through weakness, yet he liveth through the power of God. For we also are weak in him, but we shall live with him through the power of God toward you.

2Co 13:5 Try your own selves, whether ye are in the faith; prove your own selves. Or know ye not as to your own selves, that Jesus Christ is in you? unless indeed ye be reprobate.

2Co 13:6 But I hope that ye shall know that we are not reprobate.

2Co 13:7 Now we pray to God that ye do no evil; not that we may appear approved, but that ye may do that which is honorable, though we be as reprobate.

2Co 13:8 For we can do nothing against the truth, but for the truth.

2Co 13:9 For we rejoice, when we are weak, and ye are strong: this we also pray for, even your perfecting.

2Co 13:10 For this cause I write these things while absent, that I may not when present deal sharply, according to the authority which the Lord gave me for building up, and not for casting down.

2Co 13:11 Finally, brethren, farewell. Be perfected; be comforted; be of the same mind; live in peace: and the God of love and peace shall be with you.

2Co 13:12 Salute one another with a holy kiss.

2Co 13:13 All the saints salute you.

2Co 13:14 The grace of the Lord Jesus Christ, and the love of God, and the communion of the Holy Spirit, be with you all.

10. Galatians

Chapter 1.

Gal 1:1 Paul, an apostle (not from men, neither through man, but through Jesus Christ, and God the Father, who raised him from the dead),

Gal 1:2 and all the brethren that are with me, unto the churches of Galatia:

Gal 1:3 Grace to you and peace from God the Father, and our Lord Jesus Christ,

Gal 1:4 who gave himself for our sins, that he might deliver us out of this present evil world, according to the will of our God and Father:

Gal 1:5 to whom be the glory for ever and ever. Amen.

Gal 1:6 I marvel that ye are so quickly removing from him that called you in the grace of Christ unto a different gospel;

Gal 1:7 which is not another gospel only there are some that trouble you, and would pervert the gospel of Christ.

Gal 1:8 But though we, or an angel from heaven, should preach unto you any gospel other than that which we preached unto you, let him be anathema.

Gal 1:9 As we have said before, so say I now again, if any man preacheth unto you any gospel other than that which ye received, let him be anathema.

Gal 1:10 For am I now seeking the favor of men, or of God? or am I striving to please men? if I were still pleasing men, I should not be a servant of Christ.

Gal 1:11 For I make known to you, brethren, as touching the gospel which was preached by me, that it is not after man.

Gal 1:12 For neither did I receive it from man, nor was I taught it, but it came to me through revelation of Jesus Christ.

Gal 1:13 For ye have heard of my manner of life in time past in the Jews' religion, how that beyond measure I persecuted the church of God, and made havoc of it:

Gal 1:14 and I advanced in the Jews' religion beyond many of mine own age among my countrymen, being more exceedingly zealous for the traditions of my fathers.

Gal 1:15 But when it was the good pleasure of God, who separated me, even from my mother's womb, and called me through his grace,

Gal 1:16 to reveal his Son in me, that I might preach him among the Gentiles; straightway I conferred not with flesh and blood:

Gal 1:17 neither went I up to Jerusalem to them that were apostles before me: but I went away into Arabia; and again I returned unto Damascus.

Gal 1:18 Then after three years I went up to Jerusalem to visit Cephas, and tarried with him fifteen days.

Gal 1:19 But other of the apostles saw I none, save James the Lord's brother.

Gal 1:20 Now touching the things which I write unto you, behold, before God, I lie not.

Gal 1:21 Then I came unto the regions of Syria and Cilicia.

Gal 1:22 And I was still unknown by face unto the churches of Judaea which were in Christ:

Gal 1:23 but they only heard say, He that once persecuted us now preacheth the faith of which he once made havoc;

Gal 1:24 and they glorified God in me.

Chapter 2.

Gal 2:1 Then after the space of fourteen years I went up again to Jerusalem with Barnabas, taking Titus also with me.

Gal 2:2 And I went up by revelation; and I laid before them the gospel which I preach among the Gentiles but privately before them who were of repute, lest by any means I should be running, or had run, in vain.

Gal 2:3 But not even Titus who was with me, being a Greek, was compelled to be circumcised:

Gal 2:4 and that because of the false brethren privily brought in, who came in privily to spy out our liberty which we have in Christ Jesus, that they might bring us into bondage:

Gal 2:5 to whom we gave place in the way of subjection, no, not for an hour; that the truth of the gospel might continue with you.

Gal 2:6 But from those who were reputed to be somewhat (whatsoever they were, it maketh no matter to me: God accepteth not man's person) - they, I say, who were of repute imparted nothing to me:

Gal 2:7 but contrariwise, when they saw that I had been intrusted with the gospel of the uncircumcision, even as Peter with the gospel of the circumcision

Gal 2:8 (for he that wrought for Peter unto the apostleship of the circumcision wrought for me also unto the Gentiles);

Gal 2:9 and when they perceived the grace that was given unto me, James and Cephas and John, they who were reputed to be pillars, gave to me and Barnabas the right hands of fellowship, that we should go unto the Gentiles, and they unto the circumcision;

Gal 2:10 only they would that we should remember the poor; which very thing I was also zealous to do.

Gal 2:11 But when Cephas came to Antioch, I resisted him to the face, because he stood condemned.

Gal 2:12 For before that certain came from James, he ate with the Gentiles; but when they came, he drew back and separated himself, fearing them that were of the circumcision.

Gal 2:13 And the rest of the Jews dissembled likewise with him; insomuch that even Barnabas was carried away with their dissimulation.

Gal 2:14 But when I saw that they walked not uprightly according to the truth of the gospel, I said unto Cephas before them all, If thou, being a Jew, livest as do the Gentiles, and not as do the Jews, how compellest thou the Gentiles to live as do the Jews?

Gal 2:15 We being Jews by nature, and not sinners of the Gentiles,

Gal 2:16 yet knowing that a man is not justified by the works of the law but through faith in Jesus Christ, even we believed on Christ Jesus, that we might be justified by faith in Christ, and not by the works of the law: because by the works of the law shall no flesh be justified.

Gal 2:17 But if, while we sought to be justified in Christ, we ourselves also were found sinners, is Christ a minister of sin? God forbid.

Gal 2:18 For if I build up again those things which I destroyed, I prove myself a transgressor.

Gal 2:19 For I through the law died unto the law, that I might live unto God.

Gal 2:20 I have been crucified with Christ; and it is no longer I that live, but Christ living in me: and that life which I now live in the flesh I live in faith, the faith which is in the Son of God, who loved me, and gave himself up for me.

Gal 2:21 I do not make void the grace of God: for if righteousness is through the law, then Christ died for nought.

Chapter 3.

Gal 3:1 O foolish Galatians, who did bewitch you, before whose eyes Jesus Christ was openly set forth crucified?

Gal 3:2 This only would I learn from you. Received ye the Spirit by the works of the law, or by the hearing of faith?

Gal 3:3 Are ye so foolish? having begun in the Spirit, are ye now perfected in the flesh?

Gal 3:4 Did ye suffer so many things in vain? if it be indeed in vain.

Gal 3:5 He therefore that supplieth to you the Spirit, and worketh miracles among you, doeth he it by the works of the law, or by the hearing of faith?

Gal 3:6 Even as Abraham believed God, and it was reckoned unto him for righteousness.

Gal 3:7 Know therefore that they that are of faith, the same are sons of Abraham.

Gal 3:8 And the scripture, foreseeing that God would justify the Gentiles by faith, preached the gospel beforehand unto Abraham, saying, In thee shall all the nations be blessed.

Gal 3:9 So then they that are of faith are blessed with the faithful Abraham.

Gal 3:10 For as many as are of the works of the law are under a curse: for it is written, Cursed is every one who continueth not in all things that are written in the book of the law, to do them.

Gal 3:11 Now that no man is justified by the law before God, is evident: for, The righteous shall live by faith;

Gal 3:12 and the law is not of faith; but, He that doeth them shall live in them.

Gal 3:13 Christ redeemed us from the curse of the law, having become a curse for us; for it is written, Cursed is every one that hangeth on a tree:

Gal 3:14 that upon the Gentiles might come the blessing of Abraham in Christ Jesus; that we might receive the promise of the Spirit through faith.

Gal 3:15 Brethren, I speak after the manner of men: Though it be but a man's covenant, yet when it hath been confirmed, no one maketh it void, or addeth thereto.

Gal 3:16 Now to Abraham were the promises spoken, and to his seed. He saith not, And to seeds, as of many; but as of one, And to thy seed, which is Christ.

Gal 3:17 Now this I say: A covenant confirmed beforehand by God, the law, which came four hundred and thirty years after, doth not disannul, so as to make the promise of none effect.

Gal 3:18 For if the inheritance is of the law, it is no more of promise: but God hath granted it to Abraham by promise.

Gal 3:19 What then is the law? It was added because of transgressions, till the seed should come to whom the promise hath been made; and it was ordained through angels by the hand of a mediator.

Gal 3:20 Now a mediator is not a mediator of one; but God is one.

Gal 3:21 Is the law then against the promises of God? God forbid: for if there had been a law given which could make alive, verily righteousness would have been of the law.

Gal 3:22 But the scriptures shut up all things under sin, that the promise by faith in Jesus Christ might be given to them that believe.

Gal 3:23 But before faith came, we were kept in ward under the law, shut up unto the faith which should afterwards be revealed.

Gal 3:24 So that the law is become our tutor to bring us unto Christ, that we might be justified by faith.

Gal 3:25 But now that faith is come, we are no longer under a tutor.

Gal 3:26 For ye are all sons of God, through faith, in Christ Jesus.

Gal 3:27 For as many of you as were baptized into Christ did put on Christ.

Gal 3:28 There can be neither Jew nor Greek, there can be neither bond nor free, there can be no male and female; for ye all are one man in Christ Jesus.

Gal 3:29 And if ye are Christ's, then are ye Abraham's seed, heirs according to promise.

Chapter 4.

Gal 4:1 But I say that so long as the heir is a child, he differeth nothing from a bondservant though he is lord of all;

Gal 4:2 but is under guardians and stewards until the day appointed of the father.

Gal 4:3 So we also, when we were children, were held in bondage under the rudiments of the world:

Gal 4:4 but when the fulness of the time came, God sent forth his Son, born of a woman, born under the law,

Gal 4:5 that he might redeem them that were under the law, that we might receive the adoption of sons.

Gal 4:6 And because ye are sons, God sent forth the Spirit of his Son into our hearts, crying, Abba, Father.

Gal 4:7 So that thou art no longer a bondservant, but a son; and if a son, then an heir through God.

Gal 4:8 Howbeit at that time, not knowing God, ye were in bondage to them that by nature are no gods:

Gal 4:9 but now that ye have come to know God, or rather to be known by God, how turn ye back again to the weak and beggarly rudiments, whereunto ye desire to be in bondage over again?

Gal 4:10 Ye observe days, and months, and seasons, and years.

Gal 4:11 I am afraid of you, lest by any means I have bestowed labor upon you in vain.

Gal 4:12 I beseech you, brethren, become as I am, for I also am become as ye are. Ye did me no wrong:

Gal 4:13 but ye know that because of an infirmity of the flesh I preached the gospel unto you the first time:

Gal 4:14 and that which was a temptation to you in my flesh ye despised not, nor rejected; but ye received me as an angel of God, even as Christ Jesus.

Gal 4:15 Where then is that gratulation of yourselves? for I bear you witness, that, if possible, ye would have plucked out your eyes and given them to me.

Gal 4:16 So then am I become your enemy, by telling you the truth?

Gal 4:17 They zealously seek you in no good way; nay, they desire to shut you out, that ye may seek them.

Gal 4:18 But it is good to be zealously sought in a good matter at all times, and not only when I am present with you.

Gal 4:19 My little children, of whom I am again in travail until Christ be formed in you -

Gal 4:20 but I could wish to be present with you now, and to change my tone; for I am perplexed about you.

Gal 4:21 Tell me, ye that desire to be under the law, do ye not hear the law?

Gal 4:22 For it is written, that Abraham had two sons, one by the handmaid, and one by the freewoman.

Gal 4:23 Howbeit the son by the handmaid is born after the flesh; but the son by the freewoman is born through promise.

Gal 4:24 Which things contain an allegory: for these women are two covenants; one from mount Sinai, bearing children unto bondage, which is Hagar.

Gal 4:25 Now this Hagar is mount Sinai in Arabia and answereth to the Jerusalem that now is: for she is in bondage with her children.

Gal 4:26 But the Jerusalem that is above is free, which is our mother.

Gal 4:27 For it is written, Rejoice, thou barren that bearest not; Break forth and cry, thou that travailest not: For more are the children of the desolate than of her that hath the husband.

Gal 4:28 Now we, brethren, as Isaac was, are children of promise.

Gal 4:29 But as then he that was born after the flesh persecuted him that was born after the Spirit, so also it is now.

Gal 4:30 Howbeit what saith the scripture? Cast out the handmaid and her son: for the son of the handmaid shall not inherit with the son of the freewoman.

Gal 4:31 Wherefore, brethren, we are not children of a handmaid, but of the freewoman.

Chapter 5.

Gal 5:1 For freedom did Christ set us free: stand fast therefore, and be not entangled again in a yoke of bondage.

Gal 5:2 Behold, I Paul say unto you, that, if ye receive circumcision, Christ will profit you nothing.

Gal 5:3 Yea, I testify again to every man that receiveth circumcision, that he is a debtor to do the whole law.

Gal 5:4 Ye are severed from Christ, ye who would be justified by the law; ye are fallen away from grace.

Gal 5:5 For we through the Spirit by faith wait for the hope of righteousness.

Gal 5:6 For in Christ Jesus neither circumcision availeth anything, nor uncircumcision; but faith working through love.

Gal 5:7 Ye were running well; who hindered you that ye should not obey the truth?

Gal 5:8 This persuasion came not of him that calleth you.

Gal 5:9 A little leaven leaveneth the whole lump.

Gal 5:10 I have confidence to you-ward in the Lord, that ye will be none otherwise minded: but he that troubleth you shall bear his judgment, whosoever he be.

Gal 5:11 But I, brethren, if I still preach circumcision, why am I still persecuted? then hath the stumbling-block of the cross been done away.

Gal 5:12 I would that they that unsettle you would even go beyond circumcision.

Gal 5:13 For ye, brethren, were called for freedom; only use not your freedom for an occasion to the flesh, but through love be servants one to another.

Gal 5:14 For the whole law is fulfilled in one word, even in this: Thou shalt love thy neighbor as thyself.

Gal 5:15 But if ye bite and devour one another, take heed that ye be not consumed one of another.

Gal 5:16 But I say, walk by the Spirit, and ye shall not fulfil the lust of the flesh.

Gal 5:17 For the flesh lusteth against the Spirit, and the Spirit against the flesh; for these are contrary the one to the other; that ye may not do the things that ye would.

Gal 5:18 But if ye are led by the Spirit, ye are not under the law.

Gal 5:19 Now the works of the flesh are manifest, which are these: fornication, uncleanness, lasciviousness,

Gal 5:20 idolatry, sorcery, enmities, strife, jealousies, wraths, factions, divisions, parties,

Gal 5:21 envyings, drunkenness, revellings, and such like; of which I forewarn you, even as I did forewarn you, that they who practise such things shall not inherit the kingdom of God.

Gal 5:22 But the fruit of the Spirit is love, joy, peace, longsuffering, kindness, goodness, faithfulness,

Gal 5:23 meekness, self-control; against such there is no law.

Gal 5:24 And they that are of Christ Jesus have crucified the flesh with the passions and the lusts thereof.

Gal 5:25 If we live by the Spirit, by the Spirit let us also walk.

Gal 5:26 Let us not become vainglorious, provoking one another, envying one another.

Chapter 6.

Gal 6:1 Brethren, even if a man be overtaken in any trespass, ye who are spiritual, restore such a one in a spirit of gentleness; looking to thyself, lest thou also be tempted.

Gal 6:2 Bear ye one another's burdens, and so fulfil the law of Christ.

Gal 6:3 For if a man thinketh himself to be something when he is nothing, he deceiveth himself.

Gal 6:4 But let each man prove his own work, and then shall he have his glorying in regard of himself alone, and not of his neighbor.

Gal 6:5 For each man shall bear his own burden.

Gal 6:6 But let him that is taught in the word communicate unto him that teacheth in all good things.

Gal 6:7 Be not deceived; God is not mocked: for whatsoever a man soweth, that shall he also reap.

Gal 6:8 For he that soweth unto his own flesh shall of the flesh reap corruption; but he that soweth unto the Spirit shall of the Spirit reap eternal life.

Gal 6:9 And let us not be weary in well-doing: for in due season we shall reap, if we faint not.

Gal 6:10 So then, as we have opportunity, let us work that which is good toward all men, and especially toward them that are of the household of the faith.

Gal 6:11 See with how large letters I write unto you with mine own hand.

Gal 6:12 As many as desire to make a fair show in the flesh, they compel you to be circumcised; only that they may not be persecuted for the cross of Christ.

Gal 6:13 For not even they who receive circumcision do themselves keep the law; but they desire to have you circumcised, that they may glory in your flesh.

Gal 6:14 But far be it from me to glory, save in the cross of our Lord Jesus Christ, through which the world hath been crucified unto me, and I unto the world.

Gal 6:15 For neither is circumcision anything, nor uncircumcision, but a new creature.

Gal 6:16 And as many as shall walk by this rule, peace be upon them, and mercy, and upon the Israel of God.

Gal 6:17 Henceforth, let no man trouble me; for I bear branded on my body the marks of Jesus.

Gal 6:18 The grace of our Lord Jesus Christ be with your spirit, brethren. Amen.

11. Ephesians

Chapter 1.

Eph 1:1 Paul, an apostle of Christ Jesus through the will of God, to the saints that are at Ephesus, and the faithful in Christ Jesus:

Eph 1:2 Grace to you and peace from God our Father and the Lord Jesus Christ.

Eph 1:3 Blessed be the God and Father of our Lord Jesus Christ, who hath blessed us with every spiritual blessing in the heavenly places in Christ:

Eph 1:4 even as he chose us in him before the foundation of the world, that we should be holy and without blemish before him in love:

Eph 1:5 having foreordained us unto adoption as sons through Jesus Christ unto himself, according to the good pleasure of his will,

Eph 1:6 to the praise of the glory of his grace, which he freely bestowed on us in the Beloved:

Eph 1:7 in whom we have our redemption through his blood, the forgiveness of our trespasses, according to the riches of his grace,

Eph 1:8 which he made to abound toward us in all wisdom and prudence,

Eph 1:9 making known unto us the mystery of his will, according to his good pleasure which he purposed in him

Eph 1:10 unto a dispensation of the fulness of the times, to sum up all things in Christ, the things in the heavens, and the things upon the earth; in him, I say,

Eph 1:11 in whom also we were made a heritage, having been foreordained according to the purpose of him who worketh all things after the counsel of his will;

Eph 1:12 to the end that we should be unto the praise of his glory, we who had before hoped in Christ:

Eph 1:13 in whom ye also, having heard the word of the truth, the gospel of your salvation, - in whom, having also believed, ye were sealed with the Holy Spirit of promise,

Eph 1:14 which is an earnest of our inheritance, unto the redemption of God's own possession, unto the praise of his glory.

Eph 1:15 For this cause I also, having heard of the faith in the Lord Jesus which is among you, and the love which ye show toward all the saints,

Eph 1:16 cease not to give thanks for you, making mention of you in my prayers;

Eph 1:17 that the God of our Lord Jesus Christ, the Father of glory, may give unto you a spirit of wisdom and revelation in the knowledge of him;

Eph 1:18 having the eyes of your heart enlightened, that ye may know what is the hope of his calling, what the riches of the glory of his inheritance in the saints,

Eph 1:19 and what the exceeding greatness of his power to us-ward who believe, according to that working of the strength of his might

Eph 1:20 which he wrought in Christ, when he raised him from the dead, and made him to sit at his right hand in the heavenly places,

Eph 1:21 far above all rule, and authority, and power, and dominion, and every name that is named, not only in this world, but also in that which is to come:

Eph 1:22 and he put all things in subjection under his feet, and gave him to be head over all things to the church,

Eph 1:23 which is his body, the fulness of him that filleth all in all.

Chapter 2.

Eph 2:1 And you did he make alive, when ye were dead through your trespasses and sins,

Eph 2:2 wherein ye once walked according to the course of this world, according to the prince of the powers of the air, of the spirit that now worketh in the sons of disobedience;

Eph 2:3 among whom we also all once lived in the lust of our flesh, doing the desires of the flesh and of the mind, and were by nature children of wrath, even as the rest: -

Eph 2:4 but God, being rich in mercy, for his great love wherewith he loved us,

Eph 2:5 even when we were dead through our trespasses, made us alive together with Christ (by grace have ye been saved),

Eph 2:6 and raised us up with him, and made us to sit with him in the heavenly places, in Christ Jesus:

Eph 2:7 that in the ages to come he might show the exceeding riches of his grace in kindness toward us in Christ Jesus:

Eph 2:8 for by grace have ye been saved through faith; and that not of yourselves, it is the gift of God;

Eph 2:9 not of works, that no man should glory.

Eph 2:10 For we are his workmanship, created in Christ Jesus for good works, which God afore prepared that we should walk in them.

Eph 2:11 Wherefore remember, that once ye, the Gentiles in the flesh, who are called Uncircumcision by that which is called Circumcision, in the flesh, made by hands;

Eph 2:12 that ye were at that time separate from Christ, alienated from the commonwealth of Israel, and strangers from the covenants of the promise, having no hope and without God in the world.

Eph 2:13 But now in Christ Jesus ye that once were far off are made nigh in the blood of Christ.

Eph 2:14 For he is our peace, who made both one, and brake down the middle wall of partition,

Eph 2:15 having abolished in the flesh the enmity, even the law of commandments contained in ordinances; that he might create in himself of the two one new man, so making peace;

Eph 2:16 and might reconcile them both in one body unto God through the cross, having slain the enmity thereby:

Eph 2:17 and he came and preached peace to you that were far off, and peace to them that were nigh:

Eph 2:18 for through him we both have our access in one Spirit unto the Father.

Eph 2:19 So then ye are no more strangers and sojourners, but ye are fellow-citizens with the saints, and of the household of God,

Eph 2:20 being built upon the foundation of the apostles and prophets, Christ Jesus himself being the chief corner stone;

Eph 2:21 in whom each several building, fitly framed together, groweth into a holy temple in the Lord;

Eph 2:22 in whom ye also are builded together for a habitation of God in the Spirit.

Chapter 3.

Eph 3:1 For this cause I Paul, the prisoner of Christ Jesus in behalf of you Gentiles, -

Eph 3:2 if so be that ye have heard of the dispensation of that grace of God which was given me to you-ward;

Eph 3:3 how that by revelation was made known unto me the mystery, as I wrote before in few words,

Eph 3:4 whereby, when ye read, ye can perceive my understanding in the mystery of Christ;

Eph 3:5 which in other generations was not made known unto the sons of men, as it hath now been revealed unto his holy apostles and prophets in the Spirit;

Eph 3:6 to wit, that the Gentiles are fellow-heirs, and fellow-members of the body, and fellow-partakers of the promise in Christ Jesus through the gospel,

Eph 3:7 whereof I was made a minister, according to the gift of that grace of God which was given me according to the working of his power.

Eph 3:8 Unto me, who am less than the least of all saints, was this grace given, to preach unto the Gentiles the unsearchable riches of Christ;

Eph 3:9 and to make all men see what is the dispensation of the mystery which for ages hath been hid in God who created all things;

Eph 3:10 to the intent that now unto the principalities and the powers in the heavenly places might be made known through the church the manifold wisdom of God,

Eph 3:11 according to the eternal purpose which he purposed in Christ Jesus our Lord:

Eph 3:12 in whom we have boldness and access in confidence through our faith in him.

Eph 3:13 Wherefore I ask that ye may not faint at my tribulations for you, which are your glory.

Eph 3:14 For this cause I bow my knees unto the Father,

Eph 3:15 from whom every family in heaven and on earth is named,

Eph 3:16 that he would grant you, according to the riches of his glory, that ye may be strengthened with power through his Spirit in the inward man;

Eph 3:17 that Christ may dwell in your hearts through faith; to the end that ye, being rooted and grounded in love,

Eph 3:18 may be strong to apprehend with all the saints what is the breadth and length and height and depth,

Eph 3:19 and to know the love of Christ which passeth knowledge, that ye may be filled unto all the fulness of God.

Eph 3:20 Now unto him that is able to do exceeding abundantly above all that we ask or think, according to the power that worketh in us,

Eph 3:21 unto him be the glory in the church and in Christ Jesus unto all generations for ever and ever. Amen.

Chapter 4.

Eph 4:1 I therefore, the prisoner in the Lord, beseech you to walk worthily of the calling wherewith ye were called,

Eph 4:2 with all lowliness and meekness, with longsuffering, forbearing one another in love;

Eph 4:3 giving diligence to keep the unity of the Spirit in the bond of peace.

Eph 4:4 There is one body, and one Spirit, even as also ye were called in one hope of your calling;

Eph 4:5 one Lord, one faith, one baptism,

Eph 4:6 one God and Father of all, who is over all, and through all, and in all.

Eph 4:7 But unto each one of us was the grace given according to the measure of the gift of Christ.

Eph 4:8 Wherefore he saith, When he ascended on high, he led captivity captive, And gave gifts unto men.

Eph 4:9 (Now this, He ascended, what is it but that he also descended into the lower parts of the earth?

Eph 4:10 He that descended is the same also that ascended far above all the heavens, that he might fill all things.)

Eph 4:11   And he gave some to be apostles; and some, prophets; and some, evangelists; and some, pastors and teachers;

Eph 4:12 for the perfecting of the saints, unto the work of ministering, unto the building up of the body of Christ:

Eph 4:13 till we all attain unto the unity of the faith, and of the knowledge of the Son of God, unto a fullgrown man, unto the measure of the stature of the fulness of Christ:

Eph 4:14 that we may be no longer children, tossed to and fro and carried about with every wind of doctrine, by the sleight of men, in craftiness, after the wiles of error;

Eph 4:15 but speaking truth in love, we may grow up in all things into him, who is the head, even Christ;

Eph 4:16 from whom all the body fitly framed and knit together through that which every joint supplieth, according to the working in due measure of each several part, maketh the increase of the body unto the building up of itself in love.

Eph 4:17 This I say therefore, and testify in the Lord, that ye no longer walk as the Gentiles also walk, in the vanity of their mind,

Eph 4:18   being darkened in their understanding, alienated from the life of God, because of the ignorance that is in them, because of the hardening of their heart;

Eph 4:19 who being past feeling gave themselves up to lasciviousness, to work all uncleanness with greediness.

Eph 4:20 But ye did not so learn Christ;

Eph 4:21 if so be that ye heard him, and were taught in him, even as truth is in Jesus:

Eph 4:22 that ye put away, as concerning your former manner of life, the old man, that waxeth corrupt after the lusts of deceit;

Eph 4:23 and that ye be renewed in the spirit of your mind,

Eph 4:24 and put on the new man, that after God hath been created in righteousness and holiness of truth.

Eph 4:25   Wherefore, putting away falsehood, speak ye truth each one with his neighbor: for we are members one of another.

Eph 4:26 Be ye angry, and sin not: let not the sun go down upon your wrath:

Eph 4:27 neither give place to the devil.

Eph 4:28 Let him that stole steal no more: but rather let him labor, working with his hands the thing that is good, that he may have whereof to give to him that hath need.

Eph 4:29 Let no corrupt speech proceed out of your mouth, but such as is good for edifying as the need may be, that it may give grace to them that hear.

Eph 4:30 And grieve not the Holy Spirit of God, in whom ye were sealed unto the day of redemption.

Eph 4:31 Let all bitterness, and wrath, and anger, and clamor, and railing, be put away from you, with all malice:

Eph 4:32 and be ye kind one to another, tenderhearted, forgiving each other, even as God also in Christ forgave you.

Chapter 5.

Eph 5:1 Be ye therefore imitators of God, as beloved children;

Eph 5:2 and walk in love, even as Christ also loved you, and gave himself up for us, an offering and a sacrifice to God for an odor of a sweet smell.

Eph 5:3 But fornication, and all uncleanness, or covetousness, let it not even be named among you, as becometh saints;

Eph 5:4 nor filthiness, nor foolish talking, or jesting, which are not befitting: but rather giving of thanks.

Eph 5:5 For this ye know of a surety, that no fornicator, nor unclean person, nor covetous man, who is an idolater, hath any inheritance in the kingdom of Christ and God.

Eph 5:6 Let no man deceive you with empty words: for because of these things cometh the wrath of God upon the sons of disobedience.

Eph 5:7 Be not ye therefore partakers with them;

Eph 5:8 For ye were once darkness, but are now light in the Lord: walk as children of light

Eph 5:9 (for the fruit of the light is in all goodness and righteousness and truth),

Eph 5:10 proving what is well-pleasing unto the Lord;

Eph 5:11 and have no fellowship with the unfruitful works of darkness, but rather even reprove them;

Eph 5:12 for the things which are done by them in secret it is a shame even to speak of.

Eph 5:13 But all things when they are reproved are made manifest by the light: for everything that is made manifest is light.

Eph 5:14 Wherefore he saith, Awake, thou that sleepest, and arise from the dead, and Christ shall shine upon thee.

Eph 5:15 Look therefore carefully how ye walk, not as unwise, but as wise;

Eph 5:16 redeeming the time, because the days are evil.

Eph 5:17 Wherefore be ye not foolish, but understand what the will of the Lord is.

Eph 5:18 And be not drunken with wine, wherein is riot, but be filled with the Spirit;

Eph 5:19 speaking one to another in psalms and hymns and spiritual songs, singing and making melody with your heart to the Lord;

Eph 5:20 giving thanks always for all things in the name of our Lord Jesus Christ to God, even the Father;

Eph 5:21 subjecting yourselves one to another in the fear of Christ.

Eph 5:22 Wives, be in subjection unto your own husbands, as unto the Lord.

Eph 5:23 For the husband is the head of the wife, as Christ also is the head of the church, being himself the saviour of the body.

Eph 5:24 But as the church is subject to Christ, so let the wives also be to their husbands in everything.

Eph 5:25 Husbands, love your wives, even as Christ also loved the church, and gave himself up for it;

Eph 5:26 that he might sanctify it, having cleansed it by the washing of water with the word,

Eph 5:27 that he might present the church to himself a glorious church, not having spot or wrinkle or any such thing; but that it should be holy and without blemish.

Eph 5:28 Even so ought husbands also to love their own wives as their own bodies. He that loveth his own wife loveth himself:

Eph 5:29 for no man ever hated his own flesh; but nourisheth and cherisheth it, even as Christ also the church;

Eph 5:30 because we are members of his body.

Eph 5:31 For this cause shall a man leave his father and mother, and shall cleave to his wife; and the two shall become one flesh.

Eph 5:32 This mystery is great: but I speak in regard of Christ and of the church.

Eph 5:33 Nevertheless do ye also severally love each one his own wife even as himself; and let the wife see that she fear her husband.

Chapter 6.

Eph 6:1 Children, obey your parents in the Lord: for this is right.

Eph 6:2 Honor thy father and mother (which is the first commandment with promise),

Eph 6:3 that it may be well with thee, and thou mayest live long on the earth.

Eph 6:4 And, ye fathers, provoke not your children to wrath: but nurture them in the chastening and admonition of the Lord.

Eph 6:5 Servants, be obedient unto them that according to the flesh are your masters, with fear and trembling, in singleness of your heart, as unto Christ;

Eph 6:6 not in the way of eyeservice, as men-pleasers; but as servants of Christ, doing the will of God from the heart;

Eph 6:7 with good will doing service, as unto the Lord, and not unto men:

Eph 6:8 knowing that whatsoever good thing each one doeth, the same shall he receive again from the Lord, whether he be bond or free.

Eph 6:9 And, ye masters, do the same things unto them, and forbear threatening: knowing that he who is both their Master and yours is in heaven, and there is no respect of persons with him.

Eph 6:10 Finally, be strong in the Lord, and in the strength of his might.

Eph 6:11 Put on the whole armor of God, that ye may be able to stand against the wiles of the devil.

Eph 6:12 For our wrestling is not against flesh and blood, but against the principalities, against the powers, against the world-rulers of this darkness, against the spiritual hosts of wickedness in the heavenly places.

Eph 6:13 Wherefore take up the whole armor of God, that ye may be able to withstand in the evil day, and, having done all, to stand.

Eph 6:14 Stand therefore, having girded your loins with truth, and having put on the breastplate of righteousness,

Eph 6:15 and having shod your feet with the preparation of the gospel of peace;

Eph 6:16 withal taking up the shield of faith, wherewith ye shall be able to quench all the fiery darts of the evil one.

Eph 6:17 And take the helmet of salvation, and the sword of the Spirit, which is the word of God:

Eph 6:18 with all prayer and supplication praying at all seasons in the Spirit, and watching thereunto in all perseverance and supplication for all the saints,

Eph 6:19 and on my behalf, that utterance may be given unto me in opening my mouth, to make known with boldness the mystery of the gospel,

Eph 6:20 for which I am an ambassador in chains; that in it I may speak boldly, as I ought to speak.

Eph 6:21 But that ye also may know my affairs, how I do, Tychicus, the beloved brother and faithful minister in the Lord, shall make known to you all things:

Eph 6:22 whom I have sent unto you for this very purpose, that ye may know our state, and that he may comfort your hearts.

Eph 6:23 Peace be to the brethren, and love with faith, from God the Father and the Lord Jesus Christ.

Eph 6:24 Grace be with all them that love our Lord Jesus Christ with a love incorruptible.

12. Philippians

Chapter 1.

Php 1:1 Paul and Timothy, servants of Christ Jesus, to all the saints in Christ Jesus that are at Philippi, with the bishops and deacons:

Php 1:2 Grace to you and peace from God our Father and the Lord Jesus Christ.

Php 1:3 I thank my God upon all my remembrance of you,

Php 1:4 always in every supplication of mine on behalf of you all making my supplication with joy,

Php 1:5 for your fellowship in furtherance of the gospel from the first day until now;

Php 1:6 being confident of this very thing, that he who began a good work in you will perfect it until the day of Jesus Christ:

Php 1:7 even as it is right for me to be thus minded on behalf of you all, because I have you in my heart, inasmuch as, both in my bonds and in the defence and confirmation of the gospel, ye all are partakers with me of grace.

Php 1:8 For God is my witness, how I long after you all in the tender mercies of Christ Jesus.

Php 1:9 And this I pray, that your love may abound yet more and more in knowledge and all discernment;

Php 1:10 so that ye may approve the things that are excellent; that ye may be sincere and void of offence unto the day of Christ;

Php 1:11 being filled with the fruits of righteousness, which are through Jesus Christ, unto the glory and praise of God.

Php 1:12 Now I would have you know, brethren, that the things which happened unto me have fallen out rather unto the progress of the gospel;

Php 1:13 so that my bonds became manifest in Christ throughout the whole praetorian guard, and to all the rest;

Php 1:14 and that most of the brethren in the Lord, being confident through my bonds, are more abundantly bold to speak the word of God without fear.

Php 1:15 Some indeed preach Christ even of envy and strife; and some also of good will:

Php 1:16 the one do it of love, knowing that I am set for the defence of the gospel;

Php 1:17 but the other proclaim Christ of faction, not sincerely, thinking to raise up affliction for me in my bonds.

Php 1:18 What then? only that in every way, whether in pretence or in truth, Christ is proclaimed; and therein I rejoice, yea, and will rejoice.

Php 1:19 For I know that this shall turn out to my salvation, through your supplication and the supply of the Spirit of Jesus Christ,

Php 1:20 according to my earnest expectation and hope, that in nothing shall I be put to shame, but that with all boldness, as always, so now also Christ shall be magnified in my body, whether by life, or by death.

Php 1:21 For to me to live is Christ, and to die is gain.

Php 1:22 But if to live in the flesh, - if this shall bring fruit from my work, then what I shall choose I know not.

Php 1:23 But I am in a strait betwixt the two, having the desire to depart and be with Christ; for it is very far better:

Php 1:24 yet to abide in the flesh is more needful for your sake.

Php 1:25 And having this confidence, I know that I shall abide, yea, and abide with you all, for your progress and joy in the faith;

Php 1:26 that your glorying may abound in Christ Jesus in me through my presence with you again.

Php 1:27 Only let your manner of life be worthy of the gospel of Christ: that, whether I come and see you or be absent, I may hear of your state, that ye stand fast in one spirit, with one soul striving for the faith of the gospel;

Php 1:28 and in nothing affrighted by the adversaries: which is for them an evident token of perdition, but of your salvation, and that from God;

Php 1:29 because to you it hath been granted in the behalf of Christ, not only to believe on him, but also to suffer in his behalf:

Php 1:30 having the same conflict which ye saw in me, and now hear to be in me.

Chapter 2.

Php 2:1 If there is therefore any exhortation in Christ, if any consolation of love, if any fellowship of the Spirit, if any tender mercies and compassions,

Php 2:2 make full my joy, that ye be of the same mind, having the same love, being of one accord, of one mind;

Php 2:3 doing nothing through faction or through vainglory, but in lowliness of mind each counting other better than himself;

Php 2:4 not looking each of you to his own things, but each of you also to the things of others.

Php 2:5 Have this mind in you, which was also in Christ Jesus:

Php 2:6 who, existing in the form of God, counted not the being on an equality with God a thing to be grasped,

Php 2:7 but emptied himself, taking the form of a servant, being made in the likeness of men;

Php 2:8 and being found in fashion as a man, he humbled himself, becoming obedient even unto death, yea, the death of the cross.

Php 2:9 Wherefore also God highly exalted him, and gave unto him the name which is above every name;

Php 2:10 that in the name of Jesus every knee should bow, of things in heaven and things on earth and things under the earth,

Php 2:11 and that every tongue should confess that Jesus Christ is Lord, to the glory of God the Father.

Php 2:12 So then, my beloved, even as ye have always obeyed, not as in my presence only, but now much more in my absence, work out your own salvation with fear and trembling;

Php 2:13 for it is God who worketh in you both to will and to work, for his good pleasure.

Php 2:14 Do all things without murmurings and questionings:

Php 2:15 that ye may become blameless and harmless, children of God without blemish in the midst of a crooked and perverse generation, among whom ye are seen as lights in the world,

Php 2:16 holding forth the word of life; that I may have whereof to glory in the day of Christ, that I did not run in vain neither labor in vain.

Php 2:17 Yea, and if I am offered upon the sacrifice and service of your faith, I joy, and rejoice with you all:

Php 2:18 and in the same manner do ye also joy, and rejoice with me.

Php 2:19 But I hope in the Lord Jesus to send Timothy shortly unto you, that I also may be of good comfort, when I know your state.

Php 2:20 For I have no man likeminded, who will care truly for your state.

Php 2:21 For they all seek their own, not the things of Jesus Christ.

Php 2:22 But ye know the proof of him, that, as a child serveth a father, so he served with me in furtherance of the gospel.

Php 2:23 Him therefore I hope to send forthwith, so soon as I shall see how it will go with me:

Php 2:24 but I trust in the Lord that I myself also shall come shortly.

Php 2:25 But I counted it necessary to send to you Epaphroditus, my brother and fellow-worker and fellow-soldier, and your messenger and minister to my need;

Php 2:26 since he longed after you all, and was sore troubled, because ye had heard that he was sick:

Php 2:27 for indeed he was sick nigh unto death: but God had mercy on him; and not on him only, but on me also, that I might not have sorrow upon sorrow.

Php 2:28 I have sent him therefore the more diligently, that, when ye see him again, ye may rejoice, and that I may be the less sorrowful.

Php 2:29 Receive him therefore in the Lord with all joy; and hold such in honor:

Php 2:30 because for the work of Christ he came nigh unto death, hazarding his life to supply that which was lacking in your service toward me.

Chapter 3.

Php 3:1 Finally, my brethren, rejoice in the Lord. To write the same things to you, to me indeed is not irksome, but for you it is safe.

Php 3:2 Beware of the dogs, beware of the evil workers, beware of the concision:

Php 3:3 for we are the circumcision, who worship by the Spirit of God, and glory in Christ Jesus, and have no confidence in the flesh:

Php 3:4 though I myself might have confidence even in the flesh: if any other man thinketh to have confidence in the flesh, I yet more:

Php 3:5 circumcised the eighth day, of the stock of Israel, of the tribe of Benjamin, a Hebrew of Hebrews; as touching the law, a Pharisee;

Php 3:6 as touching zeal, persecuting the church; as touching the righteousness which is in the law, found blameless.

Php 3:7 Howbeit what things were gain to me, these have I counted loss for Christ.

Php 3:8 Yea verily, and I count all things to be loss for the excellency of the knowledge of Christ Jesus my Lord: for whom I suffered the loss of all things, and do count them but refuse, that I may gain Christ,

Php 3:9 and be found in him, not having a righteousness of mine own, even that which is of the law, but that which is through faith in Christ, the righteousness which is from God by faith:

Php 3:10 that I may know him, and the power of his resurrection, and the fellowship of his sufferings, becoming conformed unto his death;

Php 3:11 if by any means I may attain unto the resurrection from the dead.

Php 3:12 Not that I have already obtained, or am already made perfect: but I press on, if so be that I may lay hold on that for which also I was laid hold on by Christ Jesus.

Php 3:13 Brethren, I count not myself yet to have laid hold: but one thing I do, forgetting the things which are behind, and stretching forward to the things which are before,

Php 3:14 I press on toward the goal unto the prize of the high calling of God in Christ Jesus.

Php 3:15 Let us therefore, as many as are perfect, be thus minded: and if in anything ye are otherwise minded, this also shall God reveal unto you:

Php 3:16 only, whereunto we have attained, by that same rule let us walk.

Php 3:17 Brethren, be ye imitators together of me, and mark them that so walk even as ye have us for an ensample.

Php 3:18 For many walk, of whom I told you often, and now tell you even weeping, that they are the enemies of the cross of Christ:

Php 3:19 whose end is perdition, whose god is the belly, and whose glory is in their shame, who mind earthly things.

Php 3:20 For our citizenship is in heaven; whence also we wait for a Saviour, the Lord Jesus Christ:

Php 3:21 who shall fashion anew the body of our humiliation, that it may be conformed to the body of his glory, according to the working whereby he is able even to subject all things unto himself.

Chapter 4.

Php 4:1 Wherefore, my brethren beloved and longed for, my joy and crown, so stand fast in the Lord, my beloved.

Php 4:2 I exhort Euodia, and I exhort Syntyche, to be of the same mind in the Lord.

Php 4:3 Yea, I beseech thee also, true yokefellow, help these women, for they labored with me in the gospel, with Clement also, and the rest of my fellow-workers, whose names are in the book of life.

Php 4:4 Rejoice in the Lord always: again I will say, Rejoice.

Php 4:5 Let your forbearance be known unto all men. The Lord is at hand.

Php 4:6 In nothing be anxious; but in everything by prayer and supplication with thanksgiving let your requests be made known unto God.

Php 4:7 And the peace of God, which passeth all understanding, shall guard your hearts and your thoughts in Christ Jesus.

Php 4:8 Finally, brethren, whatsoever things are true, whatsoever things are honorable, whatsoever things are just, whatsoever things are pure, whatsoever things are lovely, whatsoever things are of good report; if there be any virtue, and if there be any praise, think on these things.

Php 4:9 The things which ye both learned and received and heard and saw in me, these things do: and the God of peace shall be with you.

Php 4:10 But I rejoice in the Lord greatly, that now at length ye have revived your thought for me; wherein ye did indeed take thought, but ye lacked opportunity.

Php 4:11 Not that I speak in respect of want: for I have learned, in whatsoever state I am, therein to be content.

Php 4:12 I know how to be abased, and I know also how to abound: in everything and in all things have I learned the secret both to be filled and to be hungry, both to abound and to be in want.

Php 4:13 I can do all things in him that strengtheneth me.

Php 4:14 Howbeit ye did well that ye had fellowship with my affliction.

Php 4:15 And ye yourselves also know, ye Philippians, that in the beginning of the gospel, when I departed from Macedonia, no church had fellowship with me in the matter of giving and receiving but ye only;

Php 4:16 for even in Thessalonica ye sent once and again unto my need.

Php 4:17 Not that I seek for the gift; but I seek for the fruit that increaseth to your account.

Php 4:18 But I have all things, and abound: I am filled, having received from Epaphroditus the things that came from you, an odor of a sweet smell, a sacrifice acceptable, well-pleasing to God.

Php 4:19 And my God shall supply every need of yours according to his riches in glory in Christ Jesus.

Php 4:20 Now unto our God and Father be the glory for ever and ever. Amen.

Php 4:21 Salute every saint in Christ Jesus. The brethren that are with me salute you.

Php 4:22 All the saints salute you, especially they that are of Caesar's household.

Php 4:23 The grace of the Lord Jesus Christ be with your spirit.

13. Colossians

Chapter 1.

Col 1:1 Paul, an apostle of Christ Jesus through the will of God, and Timothy our brother,

Col 1:2 To the saints and faithful brethren in Christ that are at Colossae: Grace to you and peace from God our Father.

Col 1:3 We give thanks to God the Father of our Lord Jesus Christ, praying always for you,

Col 1:4 having heard of your faith in Christ Jesus, and of the love which ye have toward all the saints,

Col 1:5 because of the hope which is laid up for you in the heavens, whereof ye heard before in the word of the truth of the gospel,

Col 1:6 which is come unto you; even as it is also in all the world bearing fruit and increasing, as it doth in you also, since the day ye heard and knew the grace of God in truth;

Col 1:7 even as ye learned of Epaphras our beloved fellow-servant, who is a faithful minister of Christ on our behalf,

Col 1:8 who also declared unto us your love in the Spirit.

Col 1:9 For this cause we also, since the day we heard it, do not cease to pray and make request for you, that ye may be filled with the knowledge of his will in all spiritual wisdom and understanding,

Col 1:10 to walk worthily of the Lord unto all pleasing, bearing fruit in every good work, and increasing in the knowledge of God;

Col 1:11 strengthened with all power, according to the might of his glory, unto all patience and longsuffering with joy;

Col 1:12 giving thanks unto the Father, who made us meet to be partakers of the inheritance of the saints in light;

Col 1:13 who delivered us out of the power of darkness, and translated us into the kingdom of the Son of his love;

Col 1:14 in whom we have our redemption, the forgiveness of our sins:

Col 1:15 who is the image of the invisible God, the firstborn of all creation;

Col 1:16 for in him were all things created, in the heavens and upon the earth, things visible and things invisible, whether thrones or dominions or principalities or powers; all things have been created through him, and unto him;

Col 1:17 and he is before all things, and in him all things consist.

Col 1:18 And he is the head of the body, the church: who is the beginning, the firstborn from the dead; that in all things he might have the preeminence.

Col 1:19 For it was the good pleasure of the Father that in him should all the fulness dwell;

Col 1:20 and through him to reconcile all things unto himself, having made peace through the blood of his cross; through him, I say, whether things upon the earth, or things in the heavens.

Col 1:21 And you, being in time past alienated and enemies in your mind in your evil works,

Col 1:22 yet now hath he reconciled in the body of his flesh through death, to present you holy and without blemish and unreproveable before him:

Col 1:23 if so be that ye continue in the faith, grounded and stedfast, and not moved away from the hope of the gospel which ye heard, which was preached in all creation under heaven; whereof I Paul was made a minister.

Col 1:24 Now I rejoice in my sufferings for your sake, and fill up on my part that which is lacking of the afflictions of Christ in my flesh for his body's sake, which is the church;

Col 1:25 whereof I was made a minister, according to the dispensation of God which was given me to you-ward, to fulfil the word of God,

Col 1:26 even the mystery which hath been hid for ages and generations: but now hath it been manifested to his saints,

Col 1:27 to whom God was pleased to make known what is the riches of the glory of this mystery among the Gentiles, which is Christ in you, the hope of glory:

Col 1:28 whom we proclaim, admonishing every man and teaching every man in all wisdom, that we may present every man perfect in Christ;

Col 1:29 whereunto I labor also, striving according to his working, which worketh in me mightily.

Chapter 2.

Col 2:1 For I would have you know how greatly I strive for you, and for them at Laodicea, and for as many as have not seen my face in the flesh;

Col 2:2 that their hearts may be comforted, they being knit together in love, and unto all riches of the full assurance of understanding, that they may know the mystery of God, even Christ,

Col 2:3 in whom are all the treasures of wisdom and knowledge hidden.

Col 2:4 This I say, that no one may delude you with persuasiveness of speech.

Col 2:5 For though I am absent in the flesh, yet am I with you in the spirit, joying and beholding your order, and the stedfastness of your faith in Christ.

Col 2:6 As therefore ye received Christ Jesus the Lord, so walk in him,

Col 2:7 rooted and builded up in him, and established in your faith, even as ye were taught, abounding in thanksgiving.

Col 2:8 Take heed lest there shall be any one that maketh spoil of you through his philosophy and vain deceit, after the tradition of men, after the rudiments of the world, and not after Christ:

Col 2:9 for in him dwelleth all the fulness of the Godhead bodily,

Col 2:10 and in him ye are made full, who is the head of all principality and power:

Col 2:11 in whom ye were also circumcised with a circumcision not made with hands, in the putting off of the body of the flesh, in the circumcision of Christ;

Col 2:12 having been buried with him in baptism, wherein ye were also raised with him through faith in the working of God, who raised him from the dead.

Col 2:13 And you, being dead through your trespasses and the uncircumcision of your flesh, you, I say, did he make alive together with him, having forgiven us all our trespasses;

Col 2:14 having blotted out the bond written in ordinances that was against us, which was contrary to us: and he hath taken it out that way, nailing it to the cross;

Col 2:15 having despoiled the principalities and the powers, he made a show of them openly, triumphing over them in it.

Col 2:16 Let no man therefore judge you in meat, or in drink, or in respect of a feast day or a new moon or a sabbath day:

Col 2:17 which are a shadow of the things to come; but the body is Christ's.

Col 2:18 Let no man rob you of your prize by a voluntary humility and worshipping of the angels, dwelling in the things which he hath seen, vainly puffed up by his fleshly mind,

Col 2:19 and not holding fast the Head, from whom all the body, being supplied and knit together through the joints and bands, increasing with the increase of God.

Col 2:20 If ye died with Christ from the rudiments of the world, why, as though living in the world, do ye subject yourselves to ordinances,

Col 2:21 Handle not, nor taste, nor touch

Col 2:22 (all which things are to perish with the using), after the precepts and doctrines of men?

Col 2:23 Which things have indeed a show of wisdom in will-worship, and humility, and severity to the body; but are not of any value against the indulgence of the flesh.

Chapter 3.

Col 3:1 If then ye were raised together with Christ, seek the things that are above, where Christ is, seated on the right hand of God.

Col 3:2 Set your mind on the things that are above, not on the things that are upon the earth.

Col 3:3 For ye died, and your life is hid with Christ in God.

Col 3:4 When Christ, who is our life, shall be manifested, then shall ye also with him be manifested in glory.

Col 3:5 Put to death therefore your members which are upon the earth: fornication, uncleanness, passion, evil desire, and covetousness, which is idolatry;

Col 3:6   for which things' sake cometh the wrath of God upon the sons of disobedience:

Col 3:7 wherein ye also once walked, when ye lived in these things;

Col 3:8 but now do ye also put them all away: anger, wrath, malice, railing, shameful speaking out of your mouth:

Col 3:9 lie not one to another; seeing that ye have put off the old man with his doings,

Col 3:10 and have put on the new man, that is being renewed unto knowledge after the image of him that created him:

Col 3:11 where there cannot be Greek and Jew, circumcision and uncircumcision, barbarian, Scythian, bondman, freeman; but Christ is all, and in all.

Col 3:12 Put on therefore, as God's elect, holy and beloved, a heart of compassion, kindness, lowliness, meekness, longsuffering;

Col 3:13 forbearing one another, and forgiving each other, if any man have a complaint against any; even as the Lord forgave you, so also do ye:

Col 3:14 and above all these things put on love, which is the bond of perfectness.

Col 3:15 And let the peace of Christ rule in your hearts, to the which also ye were called in one body; and be ye thankful.

Col 3:16 Let the word of Christ dwell in you richly; in all wisdom teaching and admonishing one another with psalms and hymns and spiritual songs, singing with grace in your hearts unto God.

Col 3:17 And whatsoever ye do, in word or in deed, do all in the name of the Lord Jesus, giving thanks to God the Father through him.

Col 3:18 Wives, be in subjection to your husbands, as is fitting in the Lord.

Col 3:19 Husbands, love your wives, and be not bitter against them.

Col 3:20 Children, obey your parents in all things, for this is well-pleasing in the Lord.

Col 3:21 Fathers, provoke not your children, that they be not discouraged.

Col 3:22 Servants, obey in all things them that are your masters according to the flesh; not with eye-service, as men-pleasers, but in singleness of heart, fearing the Lord:

Col 3:23 whatsoever ye do, work heartily, as unto the Lord, and not unto men;

Col 3:24 knowing that from the Lord ye shall receive the recompense of the inheritance: ye serve the Lord Christ.

Col 3:25 For he that doeth wrong shall receive again for the wrong that he hath done: and there is no respect of persons.

Chapter 4.

Col 4:1 Masters, render unto your servants that which is just and equal; knowing that ye also have a Master in heaven.

Col 4:2 Continue stedfastly in prayer, watching therein with thanksgiving;

Col 4:3 withal praying for us also, that God may open unto us a door for the word, to speak the mystery of Christ, for which I am also in bonds;

Col 4:4 that I may make it manifest, as I ought to speak.

Col 4:5 Walk in wisdom toward them that are without, redeeming the time.

Col 4:6 Let your speech be always with grace, seasoned with salt, that ye may know how ye ought to answer each one.

Col 4:7 All my affairs shall Tychicus make known unto you, the beloved brother and faithful minister and fellow-servant in the Lord:

Col 4:8 whom I have sent you for this very purpose, that ye may know our state, and that he may comfort your hearts;

Col 4:9 together with Onesimus, the faithful and beloved brother, who is one of you. They shall make known unto you all things that are done here.

Col 4:10 Aristarchus my fellow-prisoner saluteth you, and Mark, the cousin of Barnabas (touching whom ye received commandments; if he come unto you, receive him),

Col 4:11 and Jesus that is called Justus, who are of the circumcision: these only are my fellow-workers unto the kingdom of God, men that have been a comfort unto me.

Col 4:12 Epaphras, who is one of you, a servant of Christ Jesus, saluteth you, always striving for you in his prayers, that ye may stand perfect and fully assured in all the will of God.

Col 4:13 For I bear him witness, that he hath much labor for you, and for them in Laodicea, and for them in Hierapolis.

Col 4:14 Luke, the beloved physician, and Demas salute you.

Col 4:15 Salute the brethren that are in Laodicea, and Nymphas, and the church that is in their house.

Col 4:16 And when this epistle hath been read among you, cause that it be read also in the church of the Laodiceans; and that ye also read the epistle from Laodicea.

Col 4:17 And say to Archippus, Take heed to the ministry which thou hast received in the Lord, that thou fulfil it.

Col 4:18 The salutation of me Paul with mine own hand. Remember my bonds. Grace be with you.

14. 1 Thessalonians

Chapter 1.

1Th 1:1 Paul, and Silvanus, and Timothy, unto the church of the Thessalonians in God the Father and the Lord Jesus Christ: Grace to you and peace.

1Th 1:2 We give thanks to God always for you all, making mention of you in our prayers;

1Th 1:3 remembering without ceasing your work of faith and labor of love and patience of hope in our Lord Jesus Christ, before our God and Father;

1Th 1:4 knowing, brethren beloved of God, your election,

1Th 1:5 how that our gospel came not unto you in word only, but also in power, and in the Holy Spirit, and in much assurance; even as ye know what manner of men we showed ourselves toward you for your sake.

1Th 1:6 And ye became imitators of us, and of the Lord, having received the word in much affliction, with joy of the Holy Spirit;

1Th 1:7 so that ye became an ensample to all that believe in Macedonia and in Achaia.

1Th 1:8 For from you hath sounded forth the word of the Lord, not only in Macedonia and Achaia, but in every place your faith to God-ward is gone forth; so that we need not to speak anything.

1Th 1:9 For they themselves report concerning us what manner of entering in we had unto you; and how ye turned unto God from idols, to serve a living and true God,

1Th 1:10 and to wait for his Son from heaven, whom he raised from the dead, even Jesus, who delivereth us from the wrath to come.

Chapter 2.

1Th 2:1 For yourselves, brethren, know our entering in unto you, that it hath not been found vain:

1Th 2:2 but having suffered before and been shamefully treated, as ye know, at Philippi, we waxed bold in our God to speak unto you the gospel of God in much conflict.

1Th 2:3 For our exhortation is not of error, nor of uncleanness, nor in guile:

1Th 2:4 but even as we have been approved of God to be intrusted with the gospel, so we speak; not as pleasing men, but God who proveth our hearts.

1Th 2:5 For neither at any time were we found using words of flattery, as ye know, nor a cloak of covetousness, God is witness;

1Th 2:6 nor seeking glory of men, neither from you nor from others, when we might have claimed authority as apostles of Christ.

1Th 2:7 But we were gentle in the midst of you, as when a nurse cherisheth her own children:

1Th 2:8 even so, being affectionately desirous of you, we were well pleased to impart unto you, not the gospel of God only, but also our own souls, because ye were become very dear to us.

1Th 2:9 For ye remember, brethren, our labor and travail: working night and day, that we might not burden any of you, we preached unto you the gospel of God.

1Th 2:10 Ye are witnesses, and God also, how holily and righteously and unblameably we behaved ourselves toward you that believe:

1Th 2:11 as ye know how we dealt with each one of you, as a father with his own children, exhorting you, and encouraging you, and testifying,

1Th 2:12 to the end that ye should walk worthily of God, who calleth you into his own kingdom and glory.

1Th 2:13 And for this cause we also thank God without ceasing, that, when ye received from us the word of the message, even the word of God, ye accepted it not as the word of men, but, as it is in truth, the word of God, which also worketh in you that believe.

1Th 2:14 For ye, brethren, became imitators of the churches of God which are in Judaea in Christ Jesus: for ye also suffered the same things of your own countrymen, even as they did of the Jews;

1Th 2:15 who both killed the Lord Jesus and the prophets, and drove out us, and pleased not God, and are contrary to all men;

1Th 2:16 forbidding us to speak to the Gentiles that they may be saved; to fill up their sins always: but the wrath is come upon them to the uttermost.

1Th 2:17 But we, brethren, being bereaved of you for a short season, in presence not in heart, endeavored the more exceedingly to see your face with great desire:

1Th 2:18 because we would fain have come unto you, I Paul once and again; and Satan hindered us.

1Th 2:19 For what is our hope, or joy, or crown of glorying? Are not even ye, before our Lord Jesus at his coming?

1Th 2:20 For ye are our glory and our joy.

Chapter 3.

1Th 3:1 Wherefore when we could no longer forbear, we thought it good to be left behind at Athens alone;

1Th 3:2 and sent Timothy, our brother and God's minister in the gospel of Christ, to establish you, and to comfort you concerning your faith;

1Th 3:3 that no man be moved by these afflictions; for yourselves know that hereunto we are appointed.

1Th 3:4 For verily, when we were with you, we told you beforehand that we are to suffer affliction; even as it came to pass, and ye know.

1Th 3:5 For this cause I also, when I could no longer forbear, sent that I might know your faith, lest by any means the tempter had tempted you, and our labor should be in vain.

1Th 3:6 But when Timothy came even now unto us from you, and brought us glad tidings of your faith and love, and that ye have good remembrance of us always, longing to see us, even as we also to see you;

1Th 3:7 for this cause, brethren, we were comforted over you in all our distress and affliction through your faith:

1Th 3:8 for now we live, if ye stand fast in the Lord.

1Th 3:9 For what thanksgiving can we render again unto God for you, for all the joy wherewith we joy for your sakes before our God;

1Th 3:10 night and day praying exceedingly that we may see your face, and may perfect that which is lacking in your faith?

1Th 3:11 Now may our God and Father himself, and our Lord Jesus, direct our way unto you:

1Th 3:12 and the Lord make you to increase and abound in love one toward another, and toward all men, even as we also do toward you;

1Th 3:13 to the end he may establish your hearts unblameable in holiness before our God and Father, at the coming of our Lord Jesus with all his saints.

Chapter 4.

1Th 4:1 Finally then, brethren, we beseech and exhort you in the Lord Jesus, that, as ye received of us how ye ought to walk and to please God, even as ye do walk, - that ye abound more and more.

1Th 4:2 For ye know what charge we gave you through the Lord Jesus.

1Th 4:3 For this is the will of God, even your sanctification, that ye abstain from fornication;

1Th 4:4 that each one of you know how to possess himself of his own vessel in sanctification and honor,

1Th 4:5 not in the passion of lust, even as the Gentiles who know not God;

1Th 4:6 that no man transgress, and wrong his brother in the matter: because the Lord is an avenger in all these things, as also we forewarned you and testified.

1Th 4:7 For God called us not for uncleanness, but in sanctification.

1Th 4:8 Therefore he that rejecteth, rejecteth not man, but God, who giveth his Holy Spirit unto you.

1Th 4:9 But concerning love of the brethren ye have no need that one write unto you: for ye yourselves are taught of God to love one another;

1Th 4:10 for indeed ye do it toward all the brethren that are in all Macedonia. But we exhort you, brethren, that ye abound more and more;

1Th 4:11 and that ye study to be quiet, and to do your own business, and to work with your hands, even as we charged you;

1Th 4:12 that ye may walk becomingly toward them that are without, and may have need of nothing.

1Th 4:13 But we would not have you ignorant, brethren, concerning them that fall asleep; that ye sorrow not, even as the rest, who have no hope.

1Th 4:14 For if we believe that Jesus died and rose again, even so them also that are fallen asleep in Jesus will God bring with him.

1Th 4:15 For this we say unto you by the word of the Lord, that we that are alive, that are left unto the coming of the Lord, shall in no wise precede them that are fallen asleep.

1Th 4:16 For the Lord himself shall descend from heaven, with a shout, with the voice of the archangel, and with the trump of God: and the dead in Christ shall rise first;

1Th 4:17 then we that are alive, that are left, shall together with them be caught up in the clouds, to meet the Lord in the air: and so shall we ever be with the Lord.

1Th 4:18 Wherefore comfort one another with these words.

Chapter 5.

1Th 5:1 But concerning the times and the seasons, brethren, ye have no need that aught be written unto you.

1Th 5:2 For yourselves know perfectly that the day of the Lord so cometh as a thief in the night.

1Th 5:3 When they are saying, Peace and safety, then sudden destruction cometh upon them, as travail upon a woman with child; and they shall in no wise escape.

1Th 5:4 But ye, brethren, are not in darkness, that that day should overtake you as a thief:

1Th 5:5 for ye are all sons of light, and sons of the day: we are not of the night, nor of darkness;

1Th 5:6 so then let us not sleep, as do the rest, but let us watch and be sober.

1Th 5:7 For they that sleep sleep in the night: and they that are drunken are drunken in the night.

1Th 5:8 But let us, since we are of the day, be sober, putting on the breastplate of faith and love; and for a helmet, the hope of salvation.

1Th 5:9 For God appointed us not into wrath, but unto the obtaining of salvation through our Lord Jesus Christ,

1Th 5:10 who died for us, that, whether we wake or sleep, we should live together with him.

1Th 5:11 Wherefore exhort one another, and build each other up, even as also ye do.

1Th 5:12 But we beseech you, brethren, to know them that labor among you, and are over you in the Lord, and admonish you;

1Th 5:13 and to esteem them exceeding highly in love for their work's sake. Be at peace among yourselves.

1Th 5:14 And we exhort you, brethren, admonish the disorderly, encourage the fainthearted, support the weak, be longsuffering toward all.

1Th 5:15 See that none render unto any one evil for evil; but always follow after that which is good, one toward another, and toward all.

1Th 5:16 Rejoice always;

1Th 5:17 pray without ceasing;

1Th 5:18 in everything give thanks: for this is the will of God in Christ Jesus to you-ward.

1Th 5:19 Quench not the Spirit;

1Th 5:20 despise not prophesyings;

1Th 5:21 prove all things; hold fast that which is good;

1Th 5:22 abstain from every form of evil.

1Th 5:23 And the God of peace himself sanctify you wholly; and may your spirit and soul and body be preserved entire, without blame at the coming of our Lord Jesus Christ.

1Th 5:24 Faithful is he that calleth you, who will also do it.

1Th 5:25 Brethren, pray for us.

1Th 5:26 Salute all the brethren with a holy kiss.

1Th 5:27 I adjure you by the Lord that this epistle be read unto all the brethren.

1Th 5:28 The grace of our Lord Jesus Christ be with you.

15. 2 Thessalonians

Chapter 1.

2Th 1:1 Paul, and Silvanus, and Timothy, unto the church of the Thessalonians in God our Father and the Lord Jesus Christ;

2Th 1:2 Grace to you and peace from God the Father and the Lord Jesus Christ.

2Th 1:3 We are bound to give thanks to God always to you, brethren, even as it is meet, for that your faith growth exceedingly, and the love of each one of you all toward one another aboundeth;

2Th 1:4 so that we ourselves glory in you in the churches of God for your patience and faith in all your persecutions and in the afflictions which ye endure;

2Th 1:5 which is a manifest token of the righteous judgment of God; to the end that ye may be counted worthy of the kingdom of God, for which ye also suffer:

2Th 1:6 if so be that it is righteous thing with God to recompense affliction to them that afflict you,

2Th 1:7 and to you that are afflicted rest with us, at the revelation of the Lord Jesus from heaven with the angels of his power in flaming fire,

2Th 1:8 rendering vengeance to them that know not God, and to them that obey not the gospel of our Lord Jesus:

2Th 1:9 who shall suffer punishment, even eternal destruction from the face of the Lord and from the glory of his might,

2Th 1:10 when he shall come to be glorified in his saints, and to be marvelled at in all them that believed (because our testimony unto you was believed) in that day.

2Th 1:11 To which end we also pray always for you, that our God may count you worthy of your calling, and fulfil every desire of goodness and every work of faith, with power;

2Th 1:12 that the name of our Lord Jesus may be glorified in you, and ye in him, according to the grace of our God and the Lord Jesus Christ.

Chapter 2.

2Th 2:1 Now we beseech you, brethren, touching the coming of our Lord Jesus Christ, and our gathering together unto him;

2Th 2:2 to the end that ye be not quickly shaken from your mind, nor yet be troubled, either by spirit, or by word, or by epistle as from us, as that the day of the Lord is just at hand;

2Th 2:3 let no man beguile you in any wise: for it will not be, except the falling away come first, and the man of sin be revealed, the son of perdition,

2Th 2:4 he that opposeth and exalteth himself against all that is called God or that is worshipped; so that he sitteth in the temple of God, setting himself forth as God.

2Th 2:5 Remember ye not, that, when I was yet with you, I told you these things?

2Th 2:6 And now ye know that which restraineth, to the end that he may be revealed in his own season.

2Th 2:7 For the mystery of lawlessness doth already work: only there is one that restraineth now, until he be taken out of the way.

2Th 2:8 And then shall be revealed the lawless one, whom the Lord Jesus shall slay with the breath of his mouth, and bring to nought by the manifestation of his coming;

2Th 2:9 even he, whose coming is according to the working of Satan with all power and signs and lying wonders,

2Th 2:10 and with all deceit of unrighteousness for them that perish; because they received not the love of the truth, that they might be saved.

2Th 2:11 And for this cause God sendeth them a working of error, that they should believe a lie:

2Th 2:12 that they all might be judged who believed not the truth, but had pleasure in unrighteousness.

2Th 2:13 But we are bound to give thanks to God always for you, brethren beloved of the Lord, for that God chose you from the beginning unto salvation in sanctification of the Spirit and belief of the truth:

2Th 2:14 whereunto he called you through our gospel, to the obtaining of the glory of our Lord Jesus Christ.

2Th 2:15 So then, brethren, stand fast, and hold the traditions which ye were taught, whether by word, or by epistle of ours.

2Th 2:16 Now our Lord Jesus Christ himself, and God our Father who loved us and gave us eternal comfort and good hope through grace,

2Th 2:17 comfort your hearts and establish them in every good work and word.

Chapter 3.

2Th 3:1 Finally, brethren, pray for us, that the word of the Lord may run and be glorified, even as also it is with you;

2Th 3:2 and that we may be delivered from unreasonable and evil men; for all have not faith.

2Th 3:3 But the Lord is faithful, who shall establish you, and guard you from the evil one.

2Th 3:4 And we have confidence in the Lord touching you, that ye both do and will do the things which we command.

2Th 3:5 And the Lord direct your hearts into the love of God, and into the patience of Christ.

2Th 3:6 Now we command you, brethren, in the name of our Lord Jesus Christ, that ye withdraw yourselves from every brother that walketh disorderly, and not after the tradition which they received of us.

2Th 3:7 For yourselves know how ye ought to imitate us: for we behaved not ourselves disorderly among you;

2Th 3:8 neither did we eat bread for nought at any man's hand, but in labor and travail, working night and day, that we might not burden any of you:

2Th 3:9 not because we have not the right, but to make ourselves an ensample unto you, that ye should imitate us.

2Th 3:10 For even when we were with you, this we commanded you, If any will not work, neither let him eat.

2Th 3:11 For we hear of some that walk among you disorderly, that work not at all, but are busybodies.

2Th 3:12 Now them that are such we command and exhort in the Lord Jesus Christ, that with quietness they work, and eat their own bread.

2Th 3:13 But ye, brethren, be not weary in well-doing.

2Th 3:14 And if any man obeyeth not our word by this epistle, note that man, that ye have no company with him, to the end that he may be ashamed.

2Th 3:15 And yet count him not as an enemy, but admonish him as a brother.

2Th 3:16 Now the Lord of peace himself give you peace at all times in all ways. The Lord be with you all.

2Th 3:17 The salutation of me Paul with mine own hand, which is the token in every epistle: so I write.

2Th 3:18 The grace of our Lord Jesus Christ be with you all.

16. 1 Timothy

Chapter 1.

1Ti 1:1 Paul, an apostle of Christ Jesus according to the commandment of God our Saviour, and Christ Jesus our hope;

1Ti 1:2 unto Timothy, my true child in faith: Grace, mercy, peace, from God the Father and Christ Jesus our Lord.

1Ti 1:3 As I exhorted thee to tarry at Ephesus, when I was going into Macedonia, that thou mightest charge certain men not to teach a different doctrine,

1Ti 1:4 neither to give heed to fables and endless genealogies, which minister questionings, rather than a dispensation of God which is in faith; so do I now.

1Ti 1:5 But the end of the charge is love out of a pure heart and a good conscience and faith unfeigned:

1Ti 1:6 from which things some having swerved have turned aside unto vain talking;

1Ti 1:7 desiring to be teachers of the law, though they understand neither what they say, nor whereof they confidently affirm.

1Ti 1:8 But we know that the law is good, if a man use it lawfully,

1Ti 1:9 as knowing this, that law is not made for a righteous man, but for the lawless and unruly, for the ungodly and sinners, for the unholy and profane, for murderers of fathers and murderers of mothers, for manslayers,

1Ti 1:10 for fornicators, for abusers of themselves with men, for menstealers, for liars, for false swearers, and if there be any other thing contrary to the sound doctrine;

1Ti 1:11   according to the gospel of the glory of the blessed God, which was committed to my trust.

1Ti 1:12 I thank him that enabled me, even Christ Jesus our Lord, for that he counted me faithful, appointing me to his service;

1Ti 1:13 though I was before a blasphemer, and a persecutor, and injurious: howbeit I obtained mercy, because I did it ignorantly in unbelief;

1Ti 1:14 and the grace of our Lord abounded exceedingly with faith and love which is in Christ Jesus.

1Ti 1:15 Faithful is the saying, and worthy of all acceptation, that Christ Jesus came into the world to save sinners; of whom I am chief:

1Ti 1:16 howbeit for this cause I obtained mercy, that in me as chief might Jesus Christ show forth all his longsuffering, for an ensample of them that should thereafter believe on him unto eternal life.

1Ti 1:17 Now unto the King eternal, immortal, invisible, the only God, be honor and glory forever and ever. Amen.

1Ti 1:18   This charge I commit unto thee, my child Timothy, according to the prophecies which led the way to thee, that by them thou mayest war the good warfare;

1Ti 1:19 holding faith and a good conscience; which some having thrust from them made shipwreck concerning the faith:

1Ti 1:20 of whom is Hymenaeus and Alexander; whom I delivered unto Satan, that they might be taught not to blaspheme.

Chapter 2.

1Ti 2:1   I exhort therefore, first of all, that supplications, prayers, intercessions, thanksgivings, be made for all men;

1Ti 2:2 for kings and all that are in high place; that we may lead a tranquil and quiet life in all godliness and gravity.

1Ti 2:3 This is good and acceptable in the sight of God our Saviour;

1Ti 2:4 who would have all men to be saved, and come to the knowledge of the truth.

1Ti 2:5 For there is one God, one mediator also between God and men, himself man, Christ Jesus,

1Ti 2:6 who gave himself a ransom for all; the testimony to be borne in its own times;

1Ti 2:7 whereunto I was appointed a preacher and an apostle (I speak the truth, I lie not), a teacher of the Gentiles in faith and truth.

1Ti 2:8 I desire therefore that the men pray in every place, lifting up holy hands, without wrath and disputing.

1Ti 2:9   In like manner, that women adorn themselves in modest apparel, with shamefastness and sobriety; not with braided hair, and gold or pearls or costly raiment;

1Ti 2:10 but (which becometh women professing godliness) through good works.

1Ti 2:11 Let a woman learn in quietness with all subjection.

1Ti 2:12 But I permit not a woman to teach, nor to have dominion over a man, but to be in quietness.

1Ti 2:13 For Adam was first formed, then Eve;

1Ti 2:14 and Adam was not beguiled, but the woman being beguiled hath fallen into transgression:

1Ti 2:15 but she shall be saved through her child-bearing, if they continue in faith and love and sanctification with sobriety.

Chapter 3.

1Ti 3:1 Faithful is the saying, If a man seeketh the office of a bishop, he desireth a good work.

1Ti 3:2 The bishop therefore must be without reproach, the husband of one wife, temperate, sober-minded, orderly, given to hospitality, apt to teach;

1Ti 3:3 no brawler, no striker; but gentle, not contentious, no lover of money;

1Ti 3:4 one that ruleth well his own house, having his children in subjection with all gravity;

1Ti 3:5 (but if a man knoweth not how to rule his own house, how shall he take care of the church of God?)

1Ti 3:6 not a novice, lest being puffed up he fall into the condemnation of the devil.

1Ti 3:7 Moreover he must have good testimony from them that are without; lest he fall into reproach and the snare of the devil.

1Ti 3:8 Deacons in like manner must be grave, not double-tongued, not given to much wine, not greedy of filthy lucre;

1Ti 3:9 holding the mystery of the faith in a pure conscience.

1Ti 3:10 And let these also first be proved; then let them serve as deacons, if they be blameless.

1Ti 3:11 Women in like manner must be grave, not slanderers, temperate, faithful in all things.

1Ti 3:12 Let deacons be husbands of one wife, ruling their children and their own houses well.

1Ti 3:13 For they that have served well as deacons gain to themselves a good standing, and great boldness in the faith which is in Christ Jesus.

1Ti 3:14 These things write I unto thee, hoping to come unto thee shortly;

1Ti 3:15 but if I tarry long, that thou mayest know how men ought to behave themselves in the house of God, which is the church of the living God, the pillar and ground of the truth.

1Ti 3:16 And without controversy great is the mystery of godliness; He who was manifested in the flesh, Justified in the spirit, Seen of angels, Preached among the nations, Believed on in the world, Received up in glory.

Chapter 4.

1Ti 4:1 But the Spirit saith expressly, that in later times some shall fall away from the faith, giving heed to seducing spirits and doctrines of demons,

1Ti 4:2 through the hypocrisy of men that speak lies, branded in their own conscience as with a hot iron;

1Ti 4:3 forbidding to marry, and commanding to abstain from meats, which God created to be received with thanksgiving by them that believe and know the truth.

1Ti 4:4 For every creature of God is good, and nothing is to be rejected, if it be received with thanksgiving:

1Ti 4:5 for it is sanctified through the word of God and prayer.

1Ti 4:6 If thou put the brethren in mind of these things, thou shalt be a good minister of Christ Jesus, nourished in the words of the faith, and of the good doctrine which thou hast followed until now:

1Ti 4:7 but refuse profane and old wives' fables. And exercise thyself unto godliness:

1Ti 4:8 for bodily exercise is profitable for a little; but godliness is profitable for all things, having promise of the life which now is, and of that which is to come.

1Ti 4:9 Faithful is the saying, and worthy of all acceptation.

1Ti 4:10 For to this end we labor and strive, because we have our hope set on the living God, who is the Saviour of all men, specially of them that believe.

1Ti 4:11 These things command and teach.

1Ti 4:12 Let no man despise thy youth; but be thou an ensample to them that believe, in word, in manner of life, in love, in faith, in purity.

1Ti 4:13 Till I come, give heed to reading, to exhortation, to teaching.

1Ti 4:14 Neglect not the gift that is in thee, which was given thee by prophecy, with the laying on of the hands of the presbytery.

1Ti 4:15 Be diligent in these things; give thyself wholly to them; that thy progress may be manifest unto all.

1Ti 4:16 Take heed to thyself, and to thy teaching. Continue in these things; for in doing this thou shalt save both thyself and them that hear thee.

Chapter 5.

1Ti 5:1 Rebuke not an elder, but exhort him as a father; the younger men as brethren:

1Ti 5:2 the elder women as mothers; the younger as sisters, in all purity.

1Ti 5:3 Honor widows that are widows indeed.

1Ti 5:4 But if any widow hath children or grandchildren, let them learn first to show piety towards their own family, and to requite their parents: for this is acceptable in the sight of God.

1Ti 5:5 Now she that is a widow indeed, and desolate, hath her hope set on God, and continueth in supplications and prayers night and day.

1Ti 5:6 But she that giveth herself to pleasure is dead while she liveth.

1Ti 5:7 These things also command, that they may be without reproach.

1Ti 5:8 But if any provideth not for his own, and specially his own household, he hath denied the faith, and is worse than an unbeliever.

1Ti 5:9 Let none be enrolled as a widow under threescore years old, having been the wife of one man,

1Ti 5:10 well reported of for good works; if she hath brought up children, if she hath used hospitality to strangers, if she hath washed the saints' feet, if she hath relieved the afflicted, if she hath diligently followed every good work.

1Ti 5:11 But younger widows refuse: for when they have waxed wanton against Christ, they desire to marry;

1Ti 5:12 having condemnation, because they have rejected their first pledge.

1Ti 5:13 And withal they learn also to be idle, going about from house to house; and not only idle, but tattlers also and busybodies, speaking things which they ought not.

1Ti 5:14 I desire therefore that the younger widows marry, bear children, rule the household, give no occasion to the adversary for reviling:

1Ti 5:15 for already some are turned aside after Satan.

1Ti 5:16 If any woman that believeth hath widows, let her relieve them, and let not the church be burdened; that it may relieve them that are widows indeed.

1Ti 5:17 Let the elders that rule well be counted worthy of double honor, especially those who labor in the word and in teaching.

1Ti 5:18 For the scripture saith, Thou shalt not muzzle the ox when he treadeth out the corn. And, The laborer is worthy of his hire.

1Ti 5:19 Against an elder receive not an accusation, except at the mouth of two or three witnesses.

1Ti 5:20 Them that sin reprove in the sight of all, that the rest also may be in fear.

1Ti 5:21 I charge thee in the sight of God, and Christ Jesus, and the elect angels, that thou observe these things without prejudice, doing nothing by partiality.

1Ti 5:22 Lay hands hastily on no man, neither be partaker of other men's sins: keep thyself pure.

1Ti 5:23 Be no longer a drinker of water, but use a little wine for thy stomach's sake and thine often infirmities.

1Ti 5:24 Some men's sins are evident, going before unto judgment; and some men also they follow after.

1Ti 5:25 In like manner also there are good works that are evident; and such as are otherwise cannot be hid.

Chapter 6.

1Ti 6:1 Let as many as are servants under the yoke count their own masters worthy of all honor, that the name of God and the doctrine be not blasphemed.

1Ti 6:2 And they that have believing masters, let them not despise them, because they are brethren; but let them serve them the rather, because they that partake of the benefit are believing and beloved. These things teach and exhort.

1Ti 6:3 If any man teacheth a different doctrine, and consenteth not to sound words, even the words of our Lord Jesus Christ, and to the doctrine which is according to godliness;

1Ti 6:4 he is puffed up, knowing nothing, but doting about questionings and disputes of words, whereof cometh envy, strife, railings, evil surmisings,

1Ti 6:5 wranglings of men corrupted in mind and bereft of the truth, supposing that godliness is a way of gain.

1Ti 6:6 But godliness with contentment is great gain:

1Ti 6:7 for we brought nothing into the world, for neither can we carry anything out;

1Ti 6:8 but having food and covering we shall be therewith content.

1Ti 6:9 But they that are minded to be rich fall into a temptation and a snare and many foolish and hurtful lusts, such as drown men in destruction and perdition.

1Ti 6:10 For the love of money is a root of all kinds of evil: which some reaching after have been led astray from the faith, and have pierced themselves through with many sorrows.

1Ti 6:11 But thou, O man of God, flee these things; and follow after righteousness, godliness, faith, love, patience, meekness.

1Ti 6:12 Fight the good fight of the faith, lay hold on the life eternal, whereunto thou wast called, and didst confess the good confession in the sight of many witnesses.

1Ti 6:13 I charge thee in the sight of God, who giveth life to all things, and of Christ Jesus, who before Pontius Pilate witnessed the good confession;

1Ti 6:14 that thou keep the commandment, without spot, without reproach, until the appearing of our Lord Jesus Christ:

1Ti 6:15 which in its own times he shall show, who is the blessed and only Potentate, the King of kings, and Lord of lords;

1Ti 6:16 who only hath immortality, dwelling in light unapproachable; whom no man hath seen, nor can see: to whom be honor and power eternal. Amen.

1Ti 6:17 Charge them that are rich in this present world, that they be not highminded, nor have their hope set on the uncertainty of riches, but on God, who giveth us richly all things to enjoy;

1Ti 6:18 that they do good, that they be rich in good works, that they be ready to distribute, willing to communicate;

1Ti 6:19 laying up in store for themselves a good foundation against the time to come, that they may lay hold on the life which is life indeed.

1Ti 6:20 O Timothy, guard that which is committed unto thee, turning away from the profane babblings and oppositions of the knowledge which is falsely so called;

1Ti 6:21 which some professing have erred concerning the faith. Grace be with you.

17. 2 Timothy

Chapter 1.

2Ti 1:1 Paul, an apostle of Christ Jesus through the will of God, according to the promise of the life which is in Christ Jesus,

2Ti 1:2 to Timothy, my beloved child: Grace, mercy, peace, from God the Father and Christ Jesus our Lord.

2Ti 1:3 I thank God, whom I serve from my forefathers in a pure conscience, how unceasing is my remembrance of thee in my supplications, night and day

2Ti 1:4 longing to see thee, remembering thy tears, that I may be filled with joy;

2Ti 1:5 having been reminded of the unfeigned faith that is in thee; which dwelt first in thy grandmother Lois, and thy mother Eunice; and, I am persuaded, in thee also.

2Ti 1:6 For which cause I put thee in remembrance that thou stir up the gift of God, which is in thee through the laying on of my hands.

2Ti 1:7 For God gave us not a spirit of fearfulness; but of power and love and discipline.

2Ti 1:8 Be not ashamed therefore of the testimony of our Lord, nor of me his prisoner: but suffer hardship with the gospel according to the power of God;

2Ti 1:9 who saved us, and called us with a holy calling, not according to our works, but according to his own purpose and grace, which was given us in Christ Jesus before times eternal,

2Ti 1:10 but hath now been manifested by the appearing of our Saviour Christ Jesus, who abolished death, and brought life and immortality to light through the gospel,

2Ti 1:11 whereunto I was appointed a preacher, and an apostle, and a teacher.

2Ti 1:12 For which cause I suffer also these things: yet I am not ashamed; for I know him whom I have believed, and I am persuaded that he is able to guard that which I have committed unto him against that day.

2Ti 1:13 Hold the pattern of sound words which thou hast heard from me, in faith and love which is in Christ Jesus.

2Ti 1:14 That good thing which was committed unto thee guard through the Holy Spirit which dwelleth in us.

2Ti 1:15 This thou knowest, that all that are in Asia turned away from me; of whom are Phygelus and Hermogenes.

2Ti 1:16 The Lord grant mercy unto the house of Onesiphorus: for he oft refreshed me, and was not ashamed of my chain;

2Ti 1:17 but, when he was in Rome, he sought me diligently, and found me

2Ti 1:18 (the Lord grant unto him to find mercy of the Lord in that day); and in how many things he ministered at Ephesus, thou knowest very well.

Chapter 2.

2Ti 2:1 Thou therefore, my child, be strengthened in the grace that is in Christ Jesus.

2Ti 2:2 And the things which thou hast heard from me among many witnesses, the same commit thou to faithful men, who shall be able to teach others also.

2Ti 2:3 Suffer hardship with me, as a good soldier of Christ Jesus.

2Ti 2:4 No soldier on service entangleth himself in the affairs of this life; that he may please him who enrolled him as a soldier.

2Ti 2:5 And if also a man contend in the games, he is not crowned, except he have contended lawfully.

2Ti 2:6 The husbandmen that laboreth must be the first to partake of the fruits.

2Ti 2:7 Consider what I say; for the Lord shall give thee understanding in all things.

2Ti 2:8 Remember Jesus Christ, risen from the dead, of the seed of David, according to my gospel:

2Ti 2:9 wherein I suffer hardship unto bonds, as a malefactor; but the word of God is not bound.

2Ti 2:10 Therefore I endure all things for the elect's sake, that they also may obtain the salvation which is in Christ Jesus with eternal glory.

2Ti 2:11 Faithful is the saying: For if we died with him, we shall also live with him:

2Ti 2:12 if we endure, we shall also reign with him: if we shall deny him, he also will deny us:

2Ti 2:13 if we are faithless, he abideth faithful; for he cannot deny himself.

2Ti 2:14 Of these things put them in remembrance, charging them in the sight of the Lord, that they strive not about words, to no profit, to the subverting of them that hear.

2Ti 2:15 Give diligence to present thyself approved unto God, a workman that needeth not to be ashamed, handling aright the word of truth.

2Ti 2:16 But shun profane babblings: for they will proceed further in ungodliness,

2Ti 2:17 and their word will eat as doth a gangrene: or whom is Hymenaeus an Philetus;

2Ti 2:18 men who concerning the truth have erred, saying that the resurrection is past already, and overthrow the faith of some.

2Ti 2:19 Howbeit the firm foundation of God standeth, having this seal, The Lord knoweth them that are his: and, Let every one that nameth the name of the Lord depart from unrighteousness.

2Ti 2:20 Now in a great house there are not only vessels of gold and of silver, but also of wood and of earth; and some unto honor, and some unto dishonor.

2Ti 2:21 If a man therefore purge himself from these, he shall be a vessel unto honor, sanctified, meet for the master's use, prepared unto every good work.

2Ti 2:22 But flee youthful lusts, and follow after righteousness, faith, love, peace, with them that call on the Lord out of a pure heart.

2Ti 2:23 But foolish and ignorant questionings refuse, knowing that they gender strifes.

2Ti 2:24 And the Lord's servant must not strive, but be gentle towards all, apt to teach, forbearing,

2Ti 2:25 in meekness correcting them that oppose themselves; if peradventure God may give them repentance unto the knowledge of the truth,

2Ti 2:26 and they may recover themselves out of the snare of the devil, having been taken captive by him unto his will.

Chapter 3.

2Ti 3:1 But know this, that in the last days grievous times shall come.

2Ti 3:2 For men shall be lovers of self, lovers of money, boastful, haughty, railers, disobedient to parents, unthankful, unholy,

2Ti 3:3 without natural affection, implacable, slanderers, without self-control, fierce, no lovers of good,

2Ti 3:4 traitors, headstrong, puffed up, lovers of pleasure rather than lovers of God;

2Ti 3:5 holding a form of godliness, but having denied the power thereof: from these also turn away.

2Ti 3:6 For of these are they that creep into houses, and take captive silly women laden with sins, led away by divers lusts,

2Ti 3:7 ever learning, and never able to come to the knowledge of the truth.

2Ti 3:8 And even as Jannes and Jambres withstood Moses, so do these also withstand the truth. Men corrupted in mind, reprobate concerning the faith.

2Ti 3:9 But they shall proceed no further. For their folly shall be evident unto all men, as theirs also came to be.

2Ti 3:10 But thou didst follow my teaching, conduct, purpose, faith, longsuffering, love, patience,

2Ti 3:11 persecutions, sufferings. What things befell me at Antioch, at Iconium, at Lystra; what persecutions I endured. And out of them all the Lord delivered me.

2Ti 3:12 Yea, and all that would live godly in Christ Jesus shall suffer persecution.

2Ti 3:13 But evil men and impostors shall wax worse and worse, deceiving and being deceived.

2Ti 3:14 But abide thou in the things which thou hast learned and hast been assured of, knowing of whom thou hast learned them.

2Ti 3:15 And that from a babe thou hast known the sacred writings which are able to make thee wise unto salvation through faith which is in Christ Jesus.

2Ti 3:16 Every scripture inspired of God is also profitable for teaching, for reproof, for correction, for instruction which is in righteousness.

2Ti 3:17 That the man of God may be complete, furnished completely unto every good work.

Chapter 4.

2Ti 4:1 I charge thee in the sight of God, and of Christ Jesus, who shall judge the living and the dead, and by his appearing and his kingdom:

2Ti 4:2 preach the word; be urgent in season, out of season; reprove, rebuke, exhort, with all longsuffering and teaching.

2Ti 4:3 For the time will come when they will not endure the sound doctrine; but, having itching ears, will heap to themselves teachers after their own lusts;

2Ti 4:4 and will turn away their ears from the truth, and turn aside unto fables.

2Ti 4:5 But be thou sober in all things, suffer hardship, do the work of an evangelist, fulfil thy ministry.

2Ti 4:6 For I am already being offered, and the time of my departure is come.

2Ti 4:7 I have fought the good fight, I have finished the course, I have kept the faith:

2Ti 4:8 henceforth there is laid up for me the crown of righteousness, which the Lord, the righteous judge, shall give to me at that day; and not to me only, but also to all them that have loved his appearing.

2Ti 4:9 Give diligence to come shortly unto me:

2Ti 4:10 for Demas forsook me, having loved this present world, and went to Thessalonica; Crescens to Galatia, Titus to Dalmatia.

2Ti 4:11 Only Luke is with me. Take Mark, and bring him with thee; for he is useful to me for ministering.

2Ti 4:12 But Tychicus I sent to Ephesus.

2Ti 4:13 The cloak that I left at Troas with Carpus, bring when thou comest, and the books, especially the parchments.

2Ti 4:14 Alexander the coppersmith did me much evil: the Lord will render to him according to his works:

2Ti 4:15 of whom do thou also beware; for he greatly withstood our words.

2Ti 4:16 At my first defence no one took my part, but all forsook me: may it not be laid to their account.

2Ti 4:17 But the Lord stood by me, and strengthened me; that through me the message might me fully proclaimed, and that all the Gentiles might hear: and I was delivered out of the mouth of the lion.

2Ti 4:18 The Lord will deliver me from every evil work, and will save me unto his heavenly kingdom: to whom be the glory forever and ever. Amen.

2Ti 4:19 Salute Prisca and Aquila, and the house of Onesiphorus.

2Ti 4:20 Erastus remained at Corinth: but Trophimus I left at Miletus sick.

2Ti 4:21 Give diligence to come before winter. Eubulus saluteth thee, and Pudens, and Linus, and Claudia, and all the brethren.

2Ti 4:22 The Lord be with thy spirit. Grace be with you.

18. Titus

Chapter 1.

Tit 1:1 Paul, a servant of God, and an apostle of Jesus Christ, according to the faith of God's elect, and the knowledge of the truth which is according to godliness,

Tit 1:2 in hope of eternal life, which God, who cannot lie, promised before times eternal;

Tit 1:3 but in his own seasons manifested his word in the message, wherewith I was intrusted according to the commandment of God our Saviour;

Tit 1:4 to Titus, my true child after a common faith: Grace and peace from God the Father and Christ Jesus our Saviour.

Tit 1:5 For this cause left I thee in Crete, that thou shouldest set in order the things that were wanting, and appoint elders in every city, as I gave thee charge;

Tit 1:6 if any man is blameless, the husband of one wife, having children that believe, who are not accused of riot or unruly.

Tit 1:7 For the bishop must be blameless, as God's steward; not self-willed, not soon angry, no brawler, no striker, not greedy of filthy lucre;

Tit 1:8 but given to hospitality, a lover of good, sober-minded, just, holy, self-controlled;

Tit 1:9 holding to the faithful word which is according to the teaching, that he may be able to exhort in the sound doctrine, and to convict the gainsayers.

Tit 1:10 For there are many unruly men, vain talkers and deceivers, specially they of the circumcision,

Tit 1:11 whose mouths must be stopped; men who overthrow whole houses, teaching things which they ought not, for filthy lucre's sake.

Tit 1:12 One of themselves, a prophet of their own, said, Cretans are always liars, evil beasts, idle gluttons.

Tit 1:13 This testimony is true. For which cause reprove them sharply, that they may be sound in the faith,

Tit 1:14 not giving heed to Jewish fables, and commandments of men who turn away from the truth.

Tit 1:15 To the pure all things are pure: but to them that are defiled and unbelieving nothing is pure; but both their mind and their conscience are defiled.

Tit 1:16 They profess that they know God; but by their works they deny him, being abominable, and disobedient, and unto every good work reprobate.

Chapter 2.

Tit 2:1 But speak thou the things which befit the sound doctrine:

Tit 2:2 that aged men be temperate, grave, sober-minded, sound in faith, in love, in patience:

Tit 2:3 that aged women likewise be reverent in demeanor, not slanderers nor enslaved to much wine, teachers of that which is good;

Tit 2:4 that they may train the young women to love their husbands, to love their children,

Tit 2:5 to be sober-minded, chaste, workers at home, kind, being in subjection to their own husbands, that the word of God be not blasphemed:

Tit 2:6 the younger men likewise exhort to be sober-minded:

Tit 2:7 in all things showing thyself an ensample of good works; in thy doctrine showing uncorruptness, gravity,

Tit 2:8 sound speech, that cannot be condemned; that he that is of the contrary part may be ashamed, having no evil thing to say of us.

Tit 2:9 Exhort servants to be in subjection to their own masters, and to be well-pleasing to them in all things; not gainsaying;

Tit 2:10 not purloining, but showing all good fidelity; that they may adorn the doctrine of God our Saviour in all things.

Tit 2:11 For the grace of God hath appeared, bringing salvation to all men,

Tit 2:12 instructing us, to the intent that, denying ungodliness and worldly lusts, we should live soberly and righteously and godly in this present world;

Tit 2:13 looking for the blessed hope and appearing of the glory of the great God and our Saviour Jesus Christ;

Tit 2:14 who gave himself for us, that he might redeem us from all iniquity, and purify unto himself a people for his own possession, zealous of good works.

Tit 2:15 These things speak and exhort and reprove with all authority. Let no man despise thee.

Chapter 3.

Tit 3:1 Put them in mind to be in subjection to rulers, to authorities, to be obedient, to be ready unto every good work,

Tit 3:2 to speak evil of no man, not to be contentious, to be gentle, showing all meekness toward all men.

Tit 3:3 For we also once were foolish, disobedient, deceived, serving divers lusts and pleasures, living in malice and envy, hateful, hating one another.

Tit 3:4 But when the kindness of God our Saviour, and his love toward man, appeared,

Tit 3:5 not by works done in righteousness, which we did ourselves, but according to his mercy he saved us, through the washing of regeneration and renewing of the Holy Spirit,

Tit 3:6 which he poured out upon us richly, through Jesus Christ our Saviour;

Tit 3:7 that, being justified by his grace, we might be made heirs according to the hope of eternal life.

Tit 3:8 Faithful is the saying, and concerning these things I desire that thou affirm confidently, to the end that they who have believed God may be careful to maintain good works. These things are good and profitable unto men:

Tit 3:9 but shun foolish questionings, and genealogies, and strifes, and fightings about law; for they are unprofitable and vain.

Tit 3:10 A factious man after a first and second admonition refuse;

Tit 3:11 knowing that such a one is perverted, and sinneth, being self-condemned.

Tit 3:12 When I shall send Artemas unto thee, or Tychicus, give diligence to come unto me to Nicopolis: for there I have determined to winter.

Tit 3:13 Set forward Zenas the lawyer and Apollos on their journey diligently, that nothing be wanting unto them.

Tit 3:14 And let our people also learn to maintain good works for necessary uses, that they be not unfruitful.

Tit 3:15 All that are with me salute thee. Salute them that love us in faith. Grace be with you all.

19. Philemon

Chapter 1.

Phm 1:1 Paul, a prisoner of Christ Jesus, and Timothy our brother, to Philemon our beloved and fellow-worker,

Phm 1:2 and to Apphia our sister, and to Archippus our fellow-soldier, and to the church in thy house:

Phm 1:3 Grace to you and peace from God our Father and the Lord Jesus Christ.

Phm 1:4 I thank my God always, making mention of thee in my prayers,

Phm 1:5 hearing of thy love, and of the faith which thou hast toward the Lord Jesus, and toward all the saints;

Phm 1:6 that the fellowship of thy faith may become effectual, in the knowledge of every good thing which is in you, unto Christ.

Phm 1:7 For I had much joy and comfort in thy love, because the hearts of the saints have been refreshed through thee, brother.

Phm 1:8 Wherefore, though I have all boldness in Christ to enjoin thee that which is befitting,

Phm 1:9 yet for love's sake I rather beseech, being such a one as Paul the aged, and now a prisoner also of Christ Jesus:

Phm 1:10 I beseech thee for my child, whom I have begotten in my bonds, Onesimus,

Phm 1:11 who once was unprofitable to thee, but now is profitable to thee and to me:

Phm 1:12 whom I have sent back to thee in his own person, that is, my very heart:

Phm 1:13 whom I would fain have kept with me, that in thy behalf he might minister unto me in the bonds of the gospel:

Phm 1:14 but without thy mind I would do nothing; that thy goodness should not be as of necessity, but of free will.

Phm 1:15 For perhaps he was therefore parted from thee for a season, that thou shouldest have him for ever;

Phm 1:16 no longer as a servant, but more than a servant, a brother beloved, specially to me, but how much rather to thee, both in the flesh and in the Lord.

Phm 1:17 If then thou countest me a partner, receive him as myself.

Phm 1:18 But if he hath wronged thee at all, or oweth thee aught, put that to mine account;

Phm 1:19 I Paul write it with mine own hand, I will repay it: that I say not unto thee that thou owest to me even thine own self besides.

Phm 1:20 Yea, brother, let me have joy of thee in the Lord: refresh my heart in Christ.

Phm 1:21 Having confidence in thine obedience I write unto thee, knowing that thou wilt do even beyond what I say.

Phm 1:22 But withal prepare me also a lodging: for I hope that through your prayers I shall be granted unto you.

Phm 1:23 Epaphras, my fellow-prisoner in Christ Jesus, saluteth thee;

Phm 1:24 and so do Mark, Aristarchus, Demas, Luke, my fellow-workers.

Phm 1:25 The grace of our Lord Jesus Christ be with your spirit. Amen.

IV. Letters of Other Apostles and Prophets

20. Hebrews

Chapter 1.

Heb 1:1 God, having of old time spoken unto the fathers in the prophets by divers portions and in divers manners,

Heb 1:2 hath at the end of these days spoken unto us in his Son, whom he appointed heir of all things, through whom also he made the worlds;

Heb 1:3 who being the effulgence of his glory, and the very image of his substance, and upholding all things by the word of his power, when he had made purification of sins, sat down on the right hand of the Majesty on high;

Heb 1:4 having become by so much better than the angels, as he hath inherited a more excellent name than they.

Heb 1:5 For unto which of the angels said he at any time, Thou art my Son, This day have I begotten thee? and again, I will be to him a Father, And he shall be to me a Son?

Heb 1:6 And when he again bringeth in the firstborn into the world he saith, And let all the angels of God worship him.

Heb 1:7 And of the angels he saith, Who maketh his angels winds, And his ministers a flame a fire:

Heb 1:8 but of the Son he saith, Thy throne, O God, is for ever and ever; And the sceptre of uprightness is the sceptre of thy kingdom.

Heb 1:9 Thou hast loved righteousness, and hated iniquity; Therefore God, thy God, hath anointed thee With the oil of gladness above thy fellows.

Heb 1:10 And, Thou, Lord, in the beginning didst lay the foundation of the earth, And the heavens are the works of thy hands:

Heb 1:11 They shall perish; but thou continuest: And they all shall wax old as doth a garment;

Heb 1:12 And as a mantle shalt thou roll them up, As a garment, and they shall be changed: But thou art the same, And thy years shall not fail.

Heb 1:13 But of which of the angels hath he said at any time, Sit thou on my right hand, Till I make thine enemies the footstool of thy feet?

Heb 1:14 Are they not all ministering spirits, sent forth to do service for the sake of them that shall inherit salvation?

Chapter 2.

Heb 2:1 Therefore we ought to give the more earnest heed to the things that were heard, lest haply we drift away from them.

Heb 2:2   For if the word spoken through angels proved stedfast, and every transgression and disobedience received a just recompense of reward;

Heb 2:3 how shall we escape, if we neglect so great a salvation? which having at the first been spoken through the Lord, was confirmed unto us by them that heard;

Heb 2:4   God also bearing witness with them, both by signs and wonders, and by manifold powers, and by gifts of the Holy Spirit, according to his own will.

Heb 2:5 For not unto angels did he subject the world to come, whereof we speak.

Heb 2:6 But one hath somewhere testified, saying, What is man, that thou art mindful of him? Or the son of man, that thou visitest him?

Heb 2:7 Thou madest him a little lower than the angels; Thou crownedst him with glory and honor, And didst set him over the works of thy hands:

Heb 2:8 Thou didst put all things in subjection under his feet. For in that he subjected all things unto him, he left nothing that is not subject to him. But now we see not yet all things subjected to him.

Heb 2:9 But we behold him who hath been made a little lower than the angels, even Jesus, because of the suffering of death crowned with glory and honor, that by the grace of God he should taste of death for every man.

Heb 2:10 For it became him, for whom are all things, and through whom are all things, in bringing many sons unto glory, to make the author of their salvation perfect through sufferings.

Heb 2:11 For both he that sanctifieth and they that are sanctified are all of one: for which cause he is not ashamed to call them brethren,

Heb 2:12 saying, I will declare thy name unto my brethren, In the midst of the congregation will I sing thy praise.

Heb 2:13 And again, I will put my trust in him. And again, Behold, I and the children whom God hath given me.

Heb 2:14 Since then the children are sharers in flesh and blood, he also himself in like manner partook of the same; that through death he might bring to nought him that had the power of death, that is, the devil;

Heb 2:15 and might deliver all them who through fear of death were all their lifetime subject to bondage.

Heb 2:16 For verily not to angels doth he give help, but he giveth help to the seed of Abraham.

Heb 2:17 Wherefore it behooved him in all things to be made like unto his brethren, that he might become a merciful and faithful high priest in things pertaining to God, to make propitiation for the sins of the people.

Heb 2:18 For in that he himself hath suffered being tempted, he is able to succor them that are tempted.

Chapter 3.

Heb 3:1 Wherefore, holy brethren, partakers of a heavenly calling, consider the Apostle and High Priest of our confession, even Jesus;

Heb 3:2 who was faithful to him that appointed him, as also was Moses in all his house.

Heb 3:3 For he hath been counted worthy of more glory than Moses, by so much as he that built the house hath more honor than the house.

Heb 3:4 For every house is builded by some one; but he that built all things is God.

Heb 3:5 And Moses indeed was faithful in all his house as a servant, for a testimony of those things which were afterward to be spoken;

Heb 3:6 but Christ as a son, over his house; whose house are we, if we hold fast our boldness and the glorying of our hope firm unto the end.

Heb 3:7 Wherefore, even as the Holy Spirit saith, To-day if ye shall hear his voice,

Heb 3:8 Harden not your hearts, as in the provocation, Like as in the day of the trial in the wilderness,

Heb 3:9 Where your fathers tried me by proving me, And saw my works forty years.

Heb 3:10 Wherefore I was displeased with this generation, And said, They do always err in their heart: But they did not know my ways;

Heb 3:11 As I sware in my wrath, They shall not enter into my rest.

Heb 3:12 Take heed, brethren, lest haply there shall be in any one of you an evil heart of unbelief, in falling away from the living God:

Heb 3:13 but exhort one another day by day, so long as it is called To-day; lest any one of you be hardened by the deceitfulness of sin:

Heb 3:14 for we are become partakers of Christ, if we hold fast the beginning of our confidence firm unto the end:

Heb 3:15 while it is said, To-day if ye shall hear his voice, Harden not your hearts, as in the provocation.

Heb 3:16 For who, when they heard, did provoke? nay, did not all they that came out of Egypt by Moses?

Heb 3:17 And with whom was he displeased forty years? was it not with them that sinned, whose bodies fell in the wilderness?

Heb 3:18 And to whom sware he that they should not enter into his rest, but to them that were disobedient?

Heb 3:19 And we see that they were not able to enter in because of unbelief.

Chapter 4.

Heb 4:1 Let us fear therefore, lest haply, a promise being left of entering into his rest, any one of you should seem to have come short of it.

Heb 4:2 For indeed we have had good tidings preached unto us, even as also they: but the word of hearing did not profit them, because it was not united by faith with them that heard.

Heb 4:3 For we who have believed do enter into that rest; even as he hath said, As I sware in my wrath, They shall not enter into my rest: although the works were finished from the foundation of the world.

Heb 4:4 For he hath said somewhere of the seventh day on this wise, And God rested on the seventh day from all his works;

Heb 4:5 and in this place again, They shall not enter into my rest.

Heb 4:6 Seeing therefore it remaineth that some should enter thereinto, and they to whom the good tidings were before preached failed to enter in because of disobedience,

Heb 4:7 he again defineth a certain day, To-day, saying in David so long a time afterward (even as hath been said before), To-day if ye shall hear his voice, Harden not your hearts.

Heb 4:8 For if Joshua had given them rest, he would not have spoken afterward of another day.

Heb 4:9 There remaineth therefore a sabbath rest for the people of God.

Heb 4:10 For he that is entered into his rest hath himself also rested from his works, as God did from his.

Heb 4:11 Let us therefore give diligence to enter into that rest, that no man fall after the same example of disobedience.

Heb 4:12 For the word of God is living, and active, and sharper than any two-edged sword, and piercing even to the dividing of soul and spirit, of both joints and marrow, and quick to discern the thoughts and intents of the heart.

Heb 4:13 And there is no creature that is not manifest in his sight: but all things are naked and laid open before the eyes of him with whom we have to do.

Heb 4:14 Having then a great high priest, who hath passed through the heavens, Jesus the Son of God, let us hold fast our confession.

Heb 4:15 For we have not a high priest that cannot be touched with the feeling of our infirmities; but one that hath been in all points tempted like as we are, yet without sin.

Heb 4:16 Let us therefore draw near with boldness unto the throne of grace, that we may receive mercy, and may find grace to help us in time of need.

Chapter 5.

Heb 5:1 For every high priest, being taken from among men, is appointed for men in things pertaining to God, that he may offer both gifts and sacrifices for sins:

Heb 5:2 who can bear gently with the ignorant and erring, for that he himself also is compassed with infirmity;

Heb 5:3 and by reason thereof is bound, as for the people, so also for himself, to offer for sins.

Heb 5:4 And no man taketh the honor unto himself, but when he is called of God, even as was Aaron.

Heb 5:5 So Christ also glorified not himself to be made a high priest, but he that spake unto him, Thou art my Son, This day have I begotten thee:

Heb 5:6 as he saith also in another place, Thou art a priest for ever After the order of Melchizedek.

Heb 5:7 Who in the days of his flesh, having offered up prayers and supplications with strong crying and tears unto him that was able to save him from death, and having been heard for his godly fear,

Heb 5:8 though he was a Son, yet learned obedience by the things which he suffered;

Heb 5:9 and having been made perfect, he became unto all them that obey him the author of eternal salvation;

Heb 5:10 named of God a high priest after the order of Melchizedek.

Heb 5:11 Of whom we have many things to say, and hard of interpretation, seeing ye are become dull of hearing.

Heb 5:12 For when by reason of the time ye ought to be teachers, ye have need again that some one teach you the rudiments of the first principles of the oracles of God; and are become such as have need of milk, and not of solid food.

Heb 5:13 For every one that partaketh of milk is without experience of the word of righteousness; for he is a babe.

Heb 5:14 But solid food is for fullgrown men, even those who by reason of use have their senses exercised to discern good and evil.

Chapter 6.

Heb 6:1 Wherefore leaving the doctrine of the first principles of Christ, let us press on unto perfection; not laying again a foundation of repentance from dead works, and of faith toward God,

Heb 6:2 of the teaching of baptisms, and of laying on of hands, and of resurrection of the dead, and of eternal judgment.

Heb 6:3 And this will we do, if God permit.

Heb 6:4 For as touching those who were once enlightened and tasted of the heavenly gift, and were made partakers of the Holy Spirit,

Heb 6:5 and tasted the good word of God, and the powers of the age to come,

Heb 6:6 and then fell away, it is impossible to renew them again unto repentance; seeing they crucify to themselves the Son of God afresh, and put him to an open shame.

Heb 6:7 For the land which hath drunk the rain that cometh oft upon it, and bringeth forth herbs meet for them for whose sake it is also tilled, receiveth blessing from God:

Heb 6:8 but if it beareth thorns and thistles, it is rejected and nigh unto a curse; whose end is to be burned.

Heb 6:9 But, beloved, we are persuaded better things of you, and things that accompany salvation, though we thus speak:

Heb 6:10 for God is not unrighteous to forget your work and the love which ye showed toward his name, in that ye ministered unto the saints, and still do minister.

Heb 6:11 And we desire that each one of you may show the same diligence unto the fulness of hope even to the end:

Heb 6:12 that ye be not sluggish, but imitators of them who through faith and patience inherit the promises.

Heb 6:13 For when God made promise to Abraham, since he could swear by none greater, he sware by himself,

Heb 6:14 saying, Surely blessing I will bless thee, and multiplying I will multiply thee.

Heb 6:15 And thus, having patiently endured, he obtained the promise.

Heb 6:16 For men swear by the greater: and in every dispute of theirs the oath is final for confirmation.

Heb 6:17 Wherein God, being minded to show more abundantly unto the heirs of the promise the immutability of his counsel, interposed with an oath;

Heb 6:18 that by two immutable things, in which it is impossible for God to lie, we may have a strong encouragement, who have fled for refuge to lay hold of the hope set before us:

Heb 6:19 which we have as an anchor of the soul, a hope both sure and stedfast and entering into that which is within the veil;

Heb 6:20 whither as a forerunner Jesus entered for us, having become a high priest for ever after the order of Melchizedek.

Chapter 7.

Heb 7:1 For this Melchizedek, king of Salem, priest of God Most High, who met Abraham returning from the slaughter of the kings and blessed him,

Heb 7:2 to whom also Abraham divided a tenth part of all (being first, by interpretation, King of righteousness, and then also King of Salem, which is King of peace;

Heb 7:3 without father, without mother, without genealogy, having neither beginning of days nor end of life, but made like unto the Son of God), abideth a priest continually.

Heb 7:4 Now consider how great this man was, unto whom Abraham, the patriarch, gave a tenth out of the chief spoils.

Heb 7:5   And they indeed of the sons of Levi that receive the priest's office have commandment to take tithes of the people according to the law, that is, of their brethren, though these have come out of the loins of Abraham:

Heb 7:6   but he whose genealogy is not counted from them hath taken tithes of Abraham, and hath blessed him that hath the promises.

Heb 7:7   But without any dispute the less is blessed of the better.

Heb 7:8   And here men that die receive tithes; but there one, of whom it is witnessed that he liveth.

Heb 7:9   And, so to say, through Abraham even Levi, who receiveth tithes, hath paid tithes;

Heb 7:10   for he was yet in the loins of his father, when Melchizedek met him.

Heb 7:11   Now if there was perfection through the Levitical priesthood (for under it hath the people received the law), what further need was there that another priest should arise after the order of Melchizedek, and not be reckoned after the order of Aaron?

Heb 7:12   For the priesthood being changed, there is made of necessity a change also of the law.

Heb 7:13   For he of whom these things are said belongeth to another tribe, from which no man hath given attendance at the altar.

Heb 7:14   For it is evident that our Lord hath sprung out of Judah; as to which tribe Moses spake nothing concerning priests.

Heb 7:15   And what we say is yet more abundantly evident, if after the likeness of Melchizedek there ariseth another priest,

Heb 7:16   who hath been made, not after the law of a carnal commandment, but after the power of an endless life:

Heb 7:17   for it is witnessed of him, Thou art a priest for ever After the order of Melchizedek.

Heb 7:18   For there is a disannulling of a foregoing commandment because of its weakness and unprofitableness

Heb 7:19   (for the law made nothing perfect), and a bringing in thereupon of a better hope, through which we draw nigh unto God.

Heb 7:20   And inasmuch as it is not without the taking of an oath

Heb 7:21   (for they indeed have been made priests without an oath; but he with an oath by him that saith of him, The Lord sware and will not repent himself, Thou art a priest for ever);

Heb 7:22   by so much also hath Jesus become the surety of a better covenant.

Heb 7:23   And they indeed have been made priests many in number, because that by death they are hindered from continuing:

Heb 7:24   but he, because he abideth for ever, hath his priesthood unchangeable.

Heb 7:25   Wherefore also he is able to save to the uttermost them that draw near unto God through him, seeing he ever liveth to make intercession for them.

Heb 7:26   For such a high priest became us, holy, guileless, undefiled, separated from sinners, and made higher than the heavens;

Heb 7:27   who needeth not daily, like those high priests, to offer up sacrifices, first for his own sins, and then for the sins of the people: for this he did once for all, when he offered up himself.

Heb 7:28   For the law appointeth men high priests, having infirmity; but the word of the oath, which was after the law, appointeth a Son, perfected for evermore.

Chapter 8.

Heb 8:1 Now in the things which we are saying the chief point is this: We have such a high priest, who sat down on the right hand of the throne of the Majesty in the heavens,

Heb 8:2 a minister of the sanctuary, and of the true tabernacle, which the Lord pitched, not man.

Heb 8:3 For every high priest is appointed to offer both gifts and sacrifices: wherefore it is necessary that this high priest also have somewhat to offer.

Heb 8:4 Now if he were on earth, he would not be a priest at all, seeing there are those who offer the gifts according to the law;

Heb 8:5 who serve that which is a copy and shadow of the heavenly things, even as Moses is warned of God when he is about to make the tabernacle: for, See, saith he, that thou make all things according to the pattern that was showed thee in the mount.

Heb 8:6 But now hath he obtained a ministry the more excellent, by so much as he is also the mediator of a better covenant, which hath been enacted upon better promises.

Heb 8:7 For if that first covenant had been faultless, then would no place have been sought for a second.

Heb 8:8 For finding fault with them, he saith, Behold, the days come, saith the Lord, That I will make a new covenant with the house of Israel and with the house of Judah;

Heb 8:9 Not according to the covenant that I made with their fathers In the day that I took them by the hand to lead them forth out of the land of Egypt; For they continued not in my covenant, And I regarded them not, saith the Lord.

Heb 8:10 For this is the covenant that I will make with the house of Israel After those days, saith the Lord; I will put my laws into their mind, And on their heart also will I write them: And I will be to them a God, And they shall be to me a people:

Heb 8:11 And they shall not teach every man his fellow-citizen, And every man his brother, saying, Know the Lord: For all shall know me, From the least to the greatest of them.

Heb 8:12 For I will be merciful to their iniquities, And their sins will I remember no more.

Heb 8:13 In that he saith, A new covenant he hath made the first old. But that which is becoming old and waxeth aged is nigh unto vanishing away.

Chapter 9.

Heb 9:1 Now even a first covenant had ordinances of divine service, and its sanctuary, a sanctuary of this world.

Heb 9:2 For there was a tabernacle prepared, the first, wherein were the candlestick, and the table, and the showbread; which is called the Holy place.

Heb 9:3 And after the second veil, the tabernacle which is called the Holy of holies;

Heb 9:4 having a golden altar of incense, and the ark of the covenant overlaid round about with gold, wherein was a golden pot holding the manna, and Aaron's rod that budded, and the tables of the covenant;

Heb 9:5 and above it cherubim of glory overshadowing the mercy-seat; of which things we cannot now speak severally.

Heb 9:6 Now these things having been thus prepared, the priests go in continually into the first tabernacle, accomplishing the services;

Heb 9:7 but into the second the high priest alone, once in the year, not without blood, which he offereth for himself, and for the errors of the people:

Heb 9:8 the Holy Spirit this signifying, that the way into the holy place hath not yet been made manifest, while the first tabernacle is yet standing;

Heb 9:9 which is a figure for the time present; according to which are offered both gifts and sacrifices that cannot, as touching the conscience, make the worshipper perfect,

Heb 9:10 being only (with meats and drinks and divers washings) carnal ordinances, imposed until a time of reformation.

Heb 9:11 But Christ having come a high priest of the good things to come, through the greater and more perfect tabernacle, not made with hands, that is to say, not of this creation,

Heb 9:12 nor yet through the blood of goats and calves, but through his own blood, entered in once for all into the holy place, having obtained eternal redemption.

Heb 9:13 For if the blood of goats and bulls, and the ashes of a heifer sprinkling them that have been defiled, sanctify unto the cleanness of the flesh:

Heb 9:14 how much more shall the blood of Christ, who through the eternal Spirit offered himself without blemish unto God, cleanse your conscience from dead works to serve the living God?

Heb 9:15 And for this cause he is the mediator of a new covenant, that a death having taken place for the redemption of the transgressions that were under the first covenant, they that have been called may receive the promise of the eternal inheritance.

Heb 9:16 For where a testament is, there must of necessity be the death of him that made it.

Heb 9:17 For a testament is of force where there hath been death: for it doth never avail while he that made it liveth.

Heb 9:18 Wherefore even the first covenant hath not been dedicated without blood.

Heb 9:19 For when every commandment had been spoken by Moses unto all the people according to the law, he took the blood of the calves and the goats, with water and scarlet wool and hyssop, and sprinkled both the book itself and all the people,

Heb 9:20 saying, This is the blood of the covenant which God commanded to you-ward.

Heb 9:21 Moreover the tabernacle and all the vessels of the ministry he sprinkled in like manner with the blood.

Heb 9:22 And according to the law, I may almost say, all things are cleansed with blood, and apart from shedding of blood there is no remission.

Heb 9:23 It was necessary therefore that the copies of the things in the heavens should be cleansed with these; but the heavenly things themselves with better sacrifices than these.

Heb 9:24 For Christ entered not into a holy place made with hands, like in pattern to the true; but into heaven itself, now to appear before the face of God for us:

Heb 9:25 nor yet that he should offer himself often, as the high priest entereth into the holy place year by year with blood not his own;

Heb 9:26 else must he often have suffered since the foundation of the world: but now once at the end of the ages hath he been manifested to put away sin by the sacrifice of himself.

Heb 9:27 And inasmuch as it is appointed unto men once to die, and after this cometh judgment;

Heb 9:28 so Christ also, having been once offered to bear the sins of many, shall appear a second time, apart from sin, to them that wait for him, unto salvation.

Chapter 10.

Heb 10:1 For the law having a shadow of the good things to come, not the very image of the things, can never with the same sacrifices year by year, which they offer continually, make perfect them that draw nigh.

Heb 10:2 Else would they not have ceased to be offered? because the worshippers, having been once cleansed, would have had no more consciousness of sins.

Heb 10:3 But in those sacrifices there is a remembrance made of sins year by year.

Heb 10:4 For it is impossible that the blood of bulls and goats should take away sins.

Heb 10:5 Wherefore when he cometh into the world, he saith, Sacrifice and offering thou wouldest not, But a body didst thou prepare for me;

Heb 10:6 In whole burnt offerings and sacrifices for sin thou hadst no pleasure:

Heb 10:7 Then said I, Lo, I am come (In the roll of the book it is written of me) To do thy will, O God.

Heb 10:8 Saying above, Sacrifices and offerings and whole burnt offerings and sacrifices for sin thou wouldest not, neither hadst pleasure therein (the which are offered according to the law),

Heb 10:9 then hath he said, Lo, I am come to do thy will. He taketh away the first, that he may establish the second.

Heb 10:10 By which will we have been sanctified through the offering of the body of Jesus Christ once for all.

Heb 10:11 And every priest indeed standeth day by day ministering and offering oftentimes the same sacrifices, the which can never take away sins:

Heb 10:12 but he, when he had offered one sacrifice for sins for ever, sat down on the right hand of God;

Heb 10:13 henceforth expecting till his enemies be made the footstool of his feet.

Heb 10:14 For by one offering he hath perfected for ever them that are sanctified.

Heb 10:15 And the Holy Spirit also beareth witness to us; for after he hath said,

Heb 10:16 This is the covenant that I will make with them After those days, saith the Lord: I will put my laws on their heart, And upon their mind also will I write them; then saith he,

Heb 10:17 And their sins and their iniquities will I remember no more.

Heb 10:18 Now where remission of these is, there is no more offering for sin.

Heb 10:19 Having therefore, brethren, boldness to enter into the holy place by the blood of Jesus,

Heb 10:20 by the way which he dedicated for us, a new and living way, through the veil, that is to say, his flesh;

Heb 10:21 and having a great priest over the house of God;

Heb 10:22 let us draw near with a true heart in fulness of faith, having our hearts sprinkled from an evil conscience: and having our body washed with pure water,

Heb 10:23 let us hold fast the confession of our hope that it waver not; for he is faithful that promised:

Heb 10:24 and let us consider one another to provoke unto love and good works;

Heb 10:25 not forsaking our own assembling together, as the custom of some is, but exhorting one another; and so much the more, as ye see the day drawing nigh.

Heb 10:26 For if we sin wilfully after that we have received the knowledge of the truth, there remaineth no more a sacrifice for sins,

Heb 10:27 but a certain fearful expectation of judgment, and a fierceness of fire which shall devour the adversaries.

Heb 10:28 A man that hath set at nought Moses law dieth without compassion on the word of two or three witnesses:

Heb 10:29 of how much sorer punishment, think ye, shall he be judged worthy, who hath trodden under foot the Son of God, and hath counted the blood of the covenant wherewith he was sanctified an unholy thing, and hath done despite unto the Spirit of grace?

Heb 10:30 For we know him that said, Vengeance belongeth unto me, I will recompense. And again, The Lord shall judge his people.

Heb 10:31 It is a fearful thing to fall into the hands of the living God.

Heb 10:32 But call to remembrance the former days, in which, after ye were enlightened, ye endured a great conflict of sufferings;

Heb 10:33 partly, being made a gazingstock both by reproaches and afflictions; and partly, becoming partakers with them that were so used.

Heb 10:34 For ye both had compassion on them that were in bonds, and took joyfully the spoiling of you possessions, knowing that ye have for yourselves a better possession and an abiding one.

Heb 10:35 Cast not away therefore your boldness, which hath great recompense of reward.

Heb 10:36 For ye have need of patience, that, having done the will of God, ye may receive the promise.

Heb 10:37 For yet a very little while, He that cometh shall come, and shall not tarry.

Heb 10:38 But my righteous one shall live by faith: And if he shrink back, my soul hath no pleasure in him.

Heb 10:39 But we are not of them that shrink back unto perdition; but of them that have faith unto the saving of the soul.

Chapter 11.

Heb 11:1 Now faith is assurance of things hoped for, a conviction of things not seen.

Heb 11:2 For therein the elders had witness borne to them.

Heb 11:3 By faith we understand that the worlds have been framed by the word of God, so that what is seen hath not been made out of things which appear.

Heb 11:4 By faith Abel offered unto God a more excellent sacrifice than Cain, through which he had witness borne to him that he was righteous, God bearing witness in respect of his gifts: and through it he being dead yet speaketh.

Heb 11:5 By faith Enoch was translated that he should not see death; and he was not found, because God translated him: for he hath had witness borne to him that before his translation he had been well-pleasing unto God:

Heb 11:6 and without faith it is impossible to be well-pleasing unto him; for he that cometh to God must believe that he is, and that he is a rewarder of them that seek after him.

Heb 11:7 By faith Noah, being warned of God concerning things not seen as yet, moved with godly fear, prepared an ark to the saving of his house; through which he condemned the world, and became heir of the righteousness which is according to faith.

Heb 11:8 By faith Abraham, when he was called, obeyed to go out unto a place which he was to receive for an inheritance; and he went out, not knowing whither he went.

Heb 11:9 By faith he became a sojourner in the land of promise, as in a land not his own, dwelling in tents, with Isaac and Jacob, the heirs with him of the same promise:

Heb 11:10 for he looked for the city which hath the foundations, whose builder and maker is God.

Heb 11:11 By faith even Sarah herself received power to conceive seed when she was past age, since she counted him faithful who had promised:

Heb 11:12 wherefore also there sprang of one, and him as good as dead, so many as the stars of heaven in multitude, and as the sand, which is by the sea-shore, innumerable.

Heb 11:13 These all died in faith, not having received the promises, but having seen them and greeted them from afar, and having confessed that they were strangers and pilgrims on the earth.

Heb 11:14 For they that say such things make it manifest that they are seeking after a country of their own.

Heb 11:15 And if indeed they had been mindful of that country from which they went out, they would have had opportunity to return.

Heb 11:16 But now they desire a better country, that is, a heavenly: wherefore God is not ashamed of them, to be called their God; for he hath prepared for them a city.

Heb 11:17 By faith Abraham, being tried, offered up Isaac: yea, he that had gladly received the promises was offering up his only begotten son;

Heb 11:18 even he to whom it was said, In Isaac shall thy seed be called:

Heb 11:19 accounting that God is able to raise up, even from the dead; from whence he did also in a figure receive him back.

Heb 11:20 By faith Isaac blessed Jacob and Esau, even concerning things to come.

Heb 11:21 By faith Jacob, when he was dying, blessed each of the sons of Joseph; and worshipped, leaning upon the top of his staff.

Heb 11:22 By faith Joseph, when his end was nigh, made mention of the departure of the children of Israel; and gave commandment concerning his bones.

Heb 11:23 By faith Moses, when he was born, was hid three months by his parents, because they saw he was a goodly child; and they were not afraid of the king's commandment.

Heb 11:24 By faith Moses, when he was grown up, refused to be called the son of Pharaoh's daughter;

Heb 11:25 choosing rather to share ill treatment with the people of God, than to enjoy the pleasures of sin for a season;

Heb 11:26 accounting the reproach of Christ greater riches than the treasures of Egypt: for he looked unto the recompense of reward.

Heb 11:27 By faith he forsook Egypt, not fearing the wrath of the king: for he endured, as seeing him who is invisible.

Heb 11:28 By faith he kept the passover, and the sprinkling of the blood, that the destroyer of the firstborn should not touch them.

Heb 11:29 By faith they passed through the Red sea as by dry land: which the Egyptians assaying to do were swallowed up.

Heb 11:30 By faith the walls of Jericho fell down, after they had been compassed about for seven days.

Heb 11:31 By faith Rahab the harlot perished not with them that were disobedient, having received the spies with peace.

Heb 11:32 And what shall I more say? for the time will fail me if I tell of Gideon, Barak, Samson, Jephthah; of David and Samuel and the prophets:

Heb 11:33 who through faith subdued kingdoms, wrought righteousness, obtained promises, stopped the mouths of lions,

Heb 11:34 quenched the power of fire, escaped the edge of the sword, from weakness were made strong, waxed mighty in war, turned to flight armies of aliens.

Heb 11:35 Women received their dead by a resurrection: and others were tortured, not accepting their deliverance; that they might obtain a better resurrection:

Heb 11:36 and others had trial of mockings and scourgings, yea, moreover of bonds and imprisonment:

Heb 11:37 they were stoned, they were sawn asunder, they were tempted, they were slain with the sword: they went about in sheepskins, in goatskins; being destitute, afflicted, ill-treated

Heb 11:38 (of whom the world was not worthy), wandering in deserts and mountains and caves, and the holes of the earth.

Heb 11:39 And these all, having had witness borne to them through their faith, received not the promise,

Heb 11:40 God having provided some better thing concerning us, that apart from us they should not be made perfect.

Chapter 12.

Heb 12:1 Therefore let us also, seeing we are compassed about with so great a cloud of witnesses, lay aside every weight, and the sin which doth so easily beset us, and let us run with patience the race that is set before us,

Heb 12:2 looking unto Jesus the author and perfecter of our faith, who for the joy that was set before him endured the cross, despising shame, and hath sat down at the right hand of the throne of God.

Heb 12:3 For consider him that hath endured such gainsaying of sinners against himself, that ye wax not weary, fainting in your souls.

Heb 12:4 Ye have not yet resisted unto blood, striving against sin:

Heb 12:5 and ye have forgotten the exhortation which reasoneth with you as with sons, My son, regard not lightly the chastening of the Lord, Nor faint when thou art reproved of him;

Heb 12:6 For whom the Lord loveth he chasteneth, And scourgeth every son whom he receiveth.

Heb 12:7 It is for chastening that ye endure; God dealeth with you as with sons; for what son is there whom his father chasteneth not?

Heb 12:8 But if ye are without chastening, whereof all have been made partakers, then are ye bastards, and not sons.

Heb 12:9 Furthermore, we had the fathers of our flesh to chasten us, and we gave them reverence: shall we not much rather be in subjection unto the Father of spirits, and live?

Heb 12:10 For they indeed for a few days chastened us as seemed good to them; but he for our profit, that we may be partakers of his holiness.

Heb 12:11 All chastening seemeth for the present to be not joyous but grievous; yet afterward it yieldeth peaceable fruit unto them that have been exercised thereby, even the fruit of righteousness.

Heb 12:12 Wherefore lift up the hands that hang down, and the palsied knees;

Heb 12:13 and make straight paths for your feet, that that which is lame be not turned out of the way, but rather be healed.

Heb 12:14 Follow after peace with all men, and the sanctification without which no man shall see the Lord:

Heb 12:15 looking carefully lest there be any man that falleth short of the grace of God; lest any root of bitterness springing up trouble you, and thereby the many be defiled;

Heb 12:16 lest there be any fornicator, or profane person, as Esau, who for one mess of meat sold his own birthright.

Heb 12:17 For ye know that even when he afterward desired to inherit the blessing, he was rejected; for he found no place for a change of mind in his father, though he sought is diligently with tears.

Heb 12:18 For ye are not come unto a mount that might be touched, and that burned with fire, and unto blackness, and darkness, and tempest,

Heb 12:19 and the sound of a trumpet, and the voice of words; which voice they that heard entreated that no word more should be spoken unto them;

Heb 12:20 for they could not endure that which was enjoined, If even a beast touch the mountain, it shall be stoned;

Heb 12:21 and so fearful was the appearance, that Moses said, I exceedingly fear and quake:

Heb 12:22 but ye are come unto mount Zion, and unto the city of the living God, the heavenly Jerusalem, and to innumerable hosts of angels,

Heb 12:23 to the general assembly and church of the firstborn who are enrolled in heaven, and to God the Judge of all, and to the spirits of just men made perfect,

Heb 12:24 and to Jesus the mediator of a new covenant, and to the blood of sprinkling that speaketh better than that of Abel.

Heb 12:25 See that ye refuse not him that speaketh. For if they escaped not when they refused him that warned them on earth, much more shall not we escape who turn away from him that warneth from heaven:

Heb 12:26 whose voice then shook the earth: but now he hath promised, saying, Yet once more will I make to tremble not the earth only, but also the heaven.

Heb 12:27 And this word, Yet once more, signifieth the removing of those things that are shaken, as of things that have been made, that those things which are not shaken may remain.

Heb 12:28 Wherefore, receiving a kingdom that cannot be shaken, let us have grace, whereby we may offer service well-pleasing to God with reverence and awe:

Heb 12:29 for our God is a consuming fire.

Chapter 13.

Heb 13:1 Let love of the brethren continue.

Heb 13:2 Forget not to show love unto strangers: for thereby some have entertained angels unawares.

Heb 13:3 Remember them that are in bonds, as bound with them; them that are illtreated, as being yourselves also in the body.

Heb 13:4 Let marriage be had in honor among all, and let the bed be undefiled: for fornicators and adulterers God will judge.

Heb 13:5 Be ye free from the love of money; content with such things as ye have: for himself hath said, I will in no wise fail thee, neither will I in any wise forsake thee.

Heb 13:6 So that with good courage we say, The Lord is my helper; I will not fear: What shall man do unto me?

Heb 13:7 Remember them that had the rule over you, men that spake unto you the word of God; and considering the issue of their life, imitate their faith.

Heb 13:8 Jesus Christ is the same yesterday and to-day, yea and for ever.

Heb 13:9 Be not carried away by divers and strange teachings: for it is good that the heart be established by grace; not by meats, wherein they that occupied themselves were not profited.

Heb 13:10 We have an altar, whereof they have no right to eat that serve the tabernacle.

Heb 13:11 For the bodies of those beasts whose blood is brought into the holy place by the high priest as an offering for sin, are burned without the camp.

Heb 13:12 Wherefore Jesus also, that he might sanctify the people through his own blood, suffered without the gate.

Heb 13:13 Let us therefore go forth unto him without the camp, bearing his reproach.

Heb 13:14 For we have not here an abiding city, but we seek after the city which is to come.

Heb 13:15 Through him then let us offer up a sacrifice of praise to God continually, that is, the fruit of lips which make confession to his name.

Heb 13:16 But to do good and to communicate forget not: for with such sacrifices God is well pleased.

Heb 13:17 Obey them that have the rule over you, and submit to them: for they watch in behalf of your souls, as they that shall give account; that they may do this with joy, and not with grief: for this were unprofitable for you.

Heb 13:18 Pray for us: for we are persuaded that we have a good conscience, desiring to live honorably in all things.

Heb 13:19 And I exhort you the more exceedingly to do this, that I may be restored to you the sooner.

Heb 13:20 Now the God of peace, who brought again from the dead the great shepherd of the sheep with the blood of an eternal covenant, even our Lord Jesus,

Heb 13:21 make you perfect in every good thing to do his will, working in us that which is well-pleasing in his sight, through Jesus Christ; to whom be the glory for ever and ever. Amen.

Heb 13:22 But I exhort you, brethren, bear with the word of exhortation, for I have written unto you in few words.

Heb 13:23 Know ye that our brother Timothy hath been set at liberty; with whom, if he come shortly, I will see you.

Heb 13:24 Salute all them that have the rule over you, and all the saints. They of Italy salute you.

Heb 13:25 Grace be with you all. Amen.

21. James

Chapter 1.

Jas 1:1 James, a servant of God and of the Lord Jesus Christ, to the twelve tribes which are of the Dispersion, greeting.

Jas 1:2 Count it all joy, my brethren, when ye fall into manifold temptations;

Jas 1:3 Knowing that the proving of your faith worketh patience.

Jas 1:4 And let patience have its perfect work, that ye may be perfect and entire, lacking in nothing.

Jas 1:5 But if any of you lacketh wisdom, let him ask of God, who giveth to all liberally and upbraideth not; and it shall be given him.

Jas 1:6 But let him ask in faith, nothing doubting: for he that doubteth is like the surge of the sea driven by the wind and tossed.

Jas 1:7 For let not that man think that he shall receive anything of the Lord;

Jas 1:8 a doubleminded man, unstable in all his ways.

Jas 1:9 But let the brother of low degree glory in his high estate:

Jas 1:10 and the rich, in that he is made low: because as the flower of the grass he shall pass away.

Jas 1:11 For the sun ariseth with the scorching wind, and withereth the grass: and the flower thereof falleth, and the grace of the fashion of it perisheth: so also shall the rich man fade away in his goings.

Jas 1:12 Blessed is the man that endureth temptation; for when he hath been approved, he shall receive the crown of life, which the Lord promised to them that love him.

Jas 1:13 Let no man say when he is tempted, I am tempted of God; for God cannot be tempted with evil, and he himself tempteth no man:

Jas 1:14 but each man is tempted, when he is drawn away by his own lust, and enticed.

Jas 1:15 Then the lust, when it hath conceived, beareth sin: and the sin, when it is fullgrown, bringeth forth death.

Jas 1:16 Be not deceived, my beloved brethren.

Jas 1:17 Every good gift and every perfect gift is from above, coming down from the Father of lights, with whom can be no variation, neither shadow that is cast by turning.

Jas 1:18 Of his own will he brought us forth by the word of truth, that we should be a kind of firstfruits of his creatures.

Jas 1:19 Ye know this, my beloved brethren. But let every man be swift to hear, slow to speak, slow to wrath:

Jas 1:20 for the wrath of man worketh not the righteousness of God.

Jas 1:21 Wherefore putting away all filthiness and overflowing of wickedness, receive with meekness the implanted word, which is able to save your souls.

Jas 1:22 But be ye doers of the word, and not hearers only, deluding your own selves.

Jas 1:23 For if any one is a hearer of the word and not a doer, he is like unto a man beholding his natural face in a mirror:

Jas 1:24 for he beholdeth himself, and goeth away, and straightway forgetteth what manner of man he was.

Jas 1:25 But he that looketh into the perfect law, the law of liberty, and so continueth, being not a hearer that forgetteth but a doer that worketh, this man shall be blessed in his doing.

Jas 1:26 If any man thinketh himself to be religious, while he bridleth not his tongue but deceiveth his heart, this man's religion is vain.

Jas 1:27 Pure religion and undefiled before our God and Father is this, to visit the fatherless and widows in their affliction, and to keep oneself unspotted from the world.

Chapter 2.

Jas 2:1 My brethren, hold not the faith of our Lord Jesus Christ, the Lord of glory, with respect of persons.

Jas 2:2 For if there come into your synagogue a man with a gold ring, in fine clothing, and there come in also a poor man in vile clothing;

Jas 2:3 and ye have regard to him that weareth the fine clothing, and say, Sit thou here in a good place; and ye say to the poor man, Stand thou there, or sit under my footstool;

Jas 2:4 Do ye not make distinctions among yourselves, and become judges with evil thoughts?

Jas 2:5 Hearken, my beloved brethren; did not God choose them that are poor as to the world to be rich in faith, and heirs of the kingdom which he promised to them that love him?

Jas 2:6 But ye have dishonored the poor man. Do not the rich oppress you, and themselves drag you before the judgment-seats?

Jas 2:7 Do not they blaspheme the honorable name by which ye are called?

Jas 2:8 Howbeit if ye fulfil the royal law, according to the scripture, Thou shalt love thy neighbor as thyself, ye do well:

Jas 2:9 but if ye have respect of persons, ye commit sin, being convicted by the law as transgressors.

Jas 2:10 For whosoever shall keep the whole law, and yet stumble in one point, he is become guilty of all.

Jas 2:11 For he that said, Do not commit adultery, said also, Do not kill. Now if thou dost not commit adultery, but killest, thou art become a transgressor of the law.

Jas 2:12 So speak ye, and so do, as men that are to be judged by a law of liberty.

Jas 2:13 For judgment is without mercy to him that hath showed no mercy: mercy glorieth against judgment.

Jas 2:14 What doth it profit, my brethren, if a man say he hath faith, but have not works? can that faith save him?

Jas 2:15 If a brother or sister be naked and in lack of daily food,

Jas 2:16 and one of you say unto them, Go in peace, be ye warmed and filled; and yet ye give them not the things needful to the body; what doth it profit?

Jas 2:17 Even so faith, if it have not works, is dead in itself.

Jas 2:18 Yea, a man will say, Thou hast faith, and I have works: show me thy faith apart from thy works, and I by my works will show thee my faith.

Jas 2:19 Thou believest that God is one; thou doest well: the demons also believe, and shudder.

Jas 2:20 But wilt thou know, O vain man, that faith apart from works is barren?

Jas 2:21 Was not Abraham our father justified by works, in that he offered up Isaac his son upon the altar?

Jas 2:22 Thou seest that faith wrought with his works, and by works was faith made perfect;

Jas 2:23 and the scripture was fulfilled which saith, And Abraham believed God, and it was reckoned unto him for righteousness; and he was called the friend of God.

Jas 2:24 Ye see that by works a man is justified, and not only by faith.

Jas 2:25 And in like manner was not also Rahab the harlot justified by works, in that she received the messengers, and sent them out another way?

Jas 2:26 For as the body apart from the spirit is dead, even so faith apart from works is dead.

Chapter 3.

Jas 3:1 Be not many of you teachers, my brethren, knowing that we shall receive heavier judgment.

Jas 3:2 For in many things we all stumble. If any stumbleth not in word, the same is a perfect man, able to bridle the whole body also.

Jas 3:3 Now if we put the horses' bridles into their mouths that they may obey us, we turn about their whole body also.

Jas 3:4 Behold, the ships also, though they are so great and are driven by rough winds, are yet turned about by a very small rudder, whither the impulse of the steersman willeth.

Jas 3:5 So the tongue also is a little member, and boasteth great things. Behold, how much wood is kindled by how small a fire!

Jas 3:6 And the tongue is a fire: the world of iniquity among our members is the tongue, which defileth the whole body, and setteth on fire the wheel of nature, and is set on fire by hell.

Jas 3:7 For every kind of beasts and birds, of creeping things and things in the sea, is tamed, and hath been tamed by mankind.

Jas 3:8 But the tongue can no man tame; it is a restless evil, it is full of deadly poison.

Jas 3:9 Therewith bless we the Lord and Father; and therewith curse we men, who are made after the likeness of God:

Jas 3:10 out of the same mouth cometh forth blessing and cursing. My brethren, these things ought not so to be.

Jas 3:11 Doth the fountain send forth from the same opening sweet water and bitter?

Jas 3:12 Can a fig tree, my brethren, yield olives, or a vine figs? Neither can salt water yield sweet.

Jas 3:13 Who is wise and understanding among you? let him show by his good life his works in meekness of wisdom.

Jas 3:14 But if ye have bitter jealousy and faction in your heart, glory not and lie not against the truth.

Jas 3:15 This wisdom is not a wisdom that cometh down from above, but is earthly, sensual, devilish.

Jas 3:16 For where jealousy and faction are, there is confusion and every vile deed.

Jas 3:17 But the wisdom that is from above is first pure, then peaceable, gentle, easy
to be entreated, full of mercy and good fruits, without variance, without hypocrisy.

Jas 3:18 And the fruit of righteousness is sown in peace for them that make peace.

Chapter 4.

Jas 4:1 Whence come wars and whence come fightings among you? come they not
hence, even of your pleasures that war in your members?

Jas 4:2 Ye lust, and have not: ye kill, and covet, and cannot obtain: ye fight and war;
ye have not, because ye ask not.

Jas 4:3 Ye ask, and receive not, because ye ask amiss, that ye may spend it in your
pleasures.

Jas 4:4 Ye adulteresses, know ye not that the friendship of the world is enmity with
God? Whosoever therefore would be a friend of the world maketh himself an
enemy of God.

Jas 4:5 Or think ye that the scripture speaketh in vain? Doth the spirit which he made
to dwell in us long unto envying?

Jas 4:6 But he giveth more grace. Wherefore the scripture saith, God resisteth the
proud, but giveth grace to the humble.

Jas 4:7 Be subject therefore unto God; but resist the devil, and he will flee from you.

Jas 4:8 Draw nigh to God, and he will draw nigh to you. Cleanse your hands, ye
sinners; and purify your hearts, ye doubleminded.

Jas 4:9 Be afflicted, and mourn, and weep: let your laughter be turned to mourning,
and your joy to heaviness.

Jas 4:10 Humble yourselves in the sight of the Lord, and he shall exalt you.

Jas 4:11 Speak not one against another, brethren. He that speaketh against a brother,
or judgeth his brother, speaketh against the law, and judgeth the law: but if thou
judgest the law, thou art not a doer of the law, but a judge.

Jas 4:12 One only is the lawgiver and judge, even he who is able to save and to
destroy: but who art thou that judgest thy neighbor?

Jas 4:13 Come now, ye that say, To-day or to-morrow we will go into this city, and
spend a year there, and trade, and get gain:

Jas 4:14 whereas ye know not what shall be on the morrow. What is your life? For ye
are a vapor, that appeareth for a little time, and then vanisheth away.

Jas 4:15 For that ye ought to say, If the Lord will, we shall both live, and do this or
that.

Jas 4:16 But now ye glory in your vauntings: all such glorying is evil.

Jas 4:17 To him therefore that knoweth to do good, and doeth it not, to him it is sin.

Chapter 5.

Jas 5:1 Come now, ye rich, weep and howl for your miseries that are coming upon
you.

Jas 5:2 Your riches are corrupted, and your garments are moth-eaten.

Jas 5:3 Your gold and your silver are rusted; and their rust shall be for a testimony
against you, and shall eat your flesh as fire. Ye have laid up your treasure in the
last days.

Jas 5:4 Behold, the hire of the laborers who mowed your fields, which is of you kept back by fraud, crieth out: and the cries of them that reaped have entered into the ears of the Lord of Sabaoth.

Jas 5:5 Ye have lived delicately on the earth, and taken your pleasure; ye have nourished your hearts in a day of slaughter.

Jas 5:6 Ye have condemned, ye have killed the righteous one; he doth not resist you.

Jas 5:7 Be patient therefore, brethren, until the coming of the Lord. Behold, the husbandman waiteth for the precious fruit of the earth, being patient over it, until it receive the early and latter rain.

Jas 5:8 Be ye also patient; establish your hearts: for the coming of the Lord is at hand.

Jas 5:9 Murmur not, brethren, one against another, that ye be not judged: behold, the judge standeth before the doors.

Jas 5:10 Take, brethren, for an example of suffering and of patience, the prophets who spake in the name of the Lord.

Jas 5:11 Behold, we call them blessed that endured: ye have heard of the patience of Job, and have seen the end of the Lord, how that the Lord is full of pity, and merciful.

Jas 5:12 But above all things, my brethren, swear not, neither by the heaven, nor by the earth, nor by any other oath: but let your yea be yea, and your nay, nay; that ye fall not under judgment.

Jas 5:13 Is any among you suffering? Let him pray. Is any cheerful? Let him sing praise.

Jas 5:14 Is any among you sick? Let him call for the elders of the church; and let them pray over him, anointing him with oil in the name of the Lord:

Jas 5:15 and the prayer of faith shall save him that is sick, and the Lord shall raise him up; and if he have committed sins, it shall be forgiven him.

Jas 5:16 Confess therefore your sins one to another, and pray one for another, that ye may be healed. The supplication of a righteous man availeth much in its working.

Jas 5:17 Elijah was a man of like passions with us, and he prayed fervently that it might not rain; and it rained not on the earth for three years and six months.

Jas 5:18 And he prayed again; and the heaven gave rain, and the earth brought forth her fruit.

Jas 5:19 My brethren, if any among you err from the truth, and one convert him;

Jas 5:20 let him know, that he who converteth a sinner from the error of his way shall save a soul from death, and shall cover a multitude of sins.

22. 1 Peter

Chapter 1.

1Pe 1:1 Peter, an apostle of Jesus Christ, to the elect who are sojourners of the Dispersion in Pontus, Galatia, Cappadocia, Asia, and Bithynia,

1Pe 1:2 according to the foreknowledge of God the Father, in sanctification of the Spirit, unto obedience and sprinkling of the blood of Jesus Christ: Grace to you and peace be multiplied.

1Pe 1:3 Blessed be the God and Father of our Lord Jesus Christ, who according to his great mercy begat us again unto a living hope by the resurrection of Jesus Christ from the dead,

1Pe 1:4 unto an inheritance incorruptible, and undefiled, and that fadeth not away, reserved in heaven for you,

1Pe 1:5 who by the power of God are guarded through faith unto a salvation ready to be revealed in the last time.

1Pe 1:6 Wherein ye greatly rejoice, though now for a little while, if need be, ye have been put to grief in manifold trials,

1Pe 1:7 that the proof of your faith, being more precious than gold that perisheth though it is proved by fire, may be found unto praise and glory and honor at the revelation of Jesus Christ:

1Pe 1:8 whom not having seen ye love; on whom, though now ye see him not, yet believing, ye rejoice greatly with joy unspeakable and full of glory:

1Pe 1:9 receiving the end of your faith, even the salvation of your souls.

1Pe 1:10 Concerning which salvation the prophets sought and searched diligently, who prophesied of the grace that should come unto you:

1Pe 1:11 searching what time or what manner of time the Spirit of Christ which was in them did point unto, when it testified beforehand the sufferings of Christ, and the glories that should follow them.

1Pe 1:12 To whom it was revealed, that not unto themselves, but unto you, did they minister these things, which now have been announced unto you through them that preached the gospel unto you by the Holy Spirit sent forth from heaven; which things angel desire to look into.

1Pe 1:13 Wherefore girding up the loins of your mind, be sober and set your hope perfectly on the grace that is to be brought unto you at the revelation of Jesus Christ;

1Pe 1:14 as children of obedience, not fashioning yourselves according to your former lusts in the time of your ignorance:

1Pe 1:15 but like as he who called you is holy, be ye yourselves also holy in all manner of living;

1Pe 1:16 because it is written, Ye shall be holy; for I am holy.

1Pe 1:17 And if ye call on him as Father, who without respect of persons judgeth according to each man's work, pass the time of your sojourning in fear:

1Pe 1:18 knowing that ye were redeemed, not with corruptible things, with silver or gold, from your vain manner of life handed down from your fathers;

1Pe 1:19 but with precious blood, as of a lamb without spot, even the blood of Christ:

1Pe 1:20 who was foreknown indeed before the foundation of the world, but was manifested at the end of times for your sake,

1Pe 1:21 who through him are believers in God, that raised him from the dead, and gave him glory; so that your faith and hope might be in God.

1Pe 1:22 Seeing ye have purified your souls in your obedience to the truth unto unfeigned love of the brethren, love one another from the heart fervently:

1Pe 1:23 having been begotten again, not of corruptible seed, but of incorruptible, through the word of God, which liveth and abideth.

1Pe 1:24 For, All flesh is as grass, And all the glory thereof as the flower of grass. The grass withereth, and the flower falleth:

1Pe 1:25 But the word of the Lord abideth for ever. And this is the word of good tidings which was preached unto you.

Chapter 2.

1Pe 2:1 Putting away therefore all wickedness, and all guile, and hypocrisies, and envies, and all evil speakings,

1Pe 2:2 as newborn babes, long for the spiritual milk which is without guile, that ye may grow thereby unto salvation;

1Pe 2:3 if ye have tasted that the Lord is gracious:

1Pe 2:4 unto whom coming, a living stone, rejected indeed of men, but with God elect, precious,

1Pe 2:5 ye also, as living stones, are built up a spiritual house, to be a holy priesthood, to offer up spiritual sacrifices, acceptable to God through Jesus Christ.

1Pe 2:6 Because it is contained in scripture, Behold, I lay in Zion a chief corner stone, elect, precious: And he that believeth on him shall not be put to shame.

1Pe 2:7 For you therefore that believe is the preciousness: but for such as disbelieve, The stone which the builders rejected, The same was made the head of the corner;

1Pe 2:8 and, A stone of stumbling, and a rock of offence; for they stumble at the word, being disobedient: whereunto also they were appointed.

1Pe 2:9 But ye are an elect race, a royal priesthood, a holy nation, a people for God's own possession, that ye may show forth the excellencies of him who called you out of darkness into his marvellous light:

1Pe 2:10 who in time past were no people, but now are the people of God: who had not obtained mercy, but now have obtained mercy.

1Pe 2:11 Beloved, I beseech you as sojourners and pilgrims, to abstain from fleshly lusts, which war against the soul;

1Pe 2:12 having your behavior seemly among the Gentiles; that, wherein they speak against you as evil-doers, they may by your good works, which they behold, glorify God in the day of visitation.

1Pe 2:13 Be subject to every ordinance of man for the Lord's sake: whether to the king, as supreme;

1Pe 2:14 or unto governors, as sent by him for vengeance on evil-doers and for praise to them that do well.

1Pe 2:15 For so is the will of God, that by well-doing ye should put to silence the ignorance of foolish men:

1Pe 2:16 as free, and not using your freedom for a cloak of wickedness, but as bondservants of God.

1Pe 2:17 Honor all men. Love the brotherhood. Fear God. Honor the king.

1Pe 2:18 Servants, be in subjection to your masters with all fear; not only to the good and gentle, but also to the froward.

1Pe 2:19 For this is acceptable, if for conscience toward God a man endureth griefs, suffering wrongfully.

1Pe 2:20 For what glory is it, if, when ye sin, and are buffeted for it, ye shall take it patiently? but if, when ye do well, and suffer for it, ye shall take it patiently, this is acceptable with God.

1Pe 2:21 For hereunto were ye called: because Christ also suffered for you, leaving you an example, that ye should follow his steps:

1Pe 2:22 who did no sin, neither was guile found in his mouth:

1Pe 2:23 who, when he was reviled, reviled not again; when he suffered threatened not; but committed himself to him that judgeth righteously:

1Pe 2:24 who his own self bare our sins in his body upon the tree, that we, having died unto sins, might live unto righteousness; by whose stripes ye were healed.

1Pe 2:25 For ye were going astray like sheep; but are now returned unto the Shepherd and Bishop of your souls.

Chapter 3.

1Pe 3:1 In like manner, ye wives, be in subjection to your own husbands; that, even if any obey not the word, they may without the word be gained by the behavior of their wives;

1Pe 3:2 beholding your chaste behavior coupled with fear.

1Pe 3:3 Whose adorning let it not be the outward adorning of braiding the hair, and of wearing jewels of gold, or of putting on apparel;

1Pe 3:4 but let it be the hidden man of the heart, in the incorruptible apparel of a meek and quiet spirit, which is in the sight of God of great price.

1Pe 3:5 For after this manner aforetime the holy women also, who hoped in God, adorned themselves, being in subjection to their own husbands:

1Pe 3:6 as Sarah obeyed Abraham, calling him lord: whose children ye now are, if ye do well, and are not put in fear by any terror.

1Pe 3:7 Ye husbands, in like manner, dwell with your wives according to knowledge, giving honor unto the woman, as unto the weaker vessel, as being also joint-heirs of the grace of life; to the end that your prayers be not hindered.

1Pe 3:8 Finally, be ye all likeminded, compassionate, loving as brethren, tenderhearted, humbleminded:

1Pe 3:9 not rendering evil for evil, or reviling for reviling; but contrariwise blessing; for hereunto were ye called, that ye should inherit a blessing.

1Pe 3:10 For, He that would love life, And see good days, Let him refrain his tongue from evil, And his lips that they speak no guile:

1Pe 3:11 And let him turn away from evil, and do good; Let him seek peace, and pursue it.

1Pe 3:12 For the eyes of the Lord are upon the righteous, And his ears unto their supplication: But the face of the Lord is upon them that do evil.

1Pe 3:13 And who is he that will harm you, if ye be zealous of that which is good?

1Pe 3:14 But even if ye should suffer for righteousness' sake, blessed are ye: and fear not their fear, neither be troubled;

1Pe 3:15 but sanctify in your hearts Christ as Lord: being ready always to give answer to every man that asketh you a reason concerning the hope that is in you, yet with meekness and fear:

1Pe 3:16 having a good conscience; that, wherein ye are spoken against, they may be put to shame who revile your good manner of life in Christ.

1Pe 3:17 For it is better, if the will of God should so will, that ye suffer for well-doing than for evil-doing.

1Pe 3:18 Because Christ also suffered for sins once, the righteous for the unrighteous, that he might bring us to God; being put to death in the flesh, but made alive in the spirit;

1Pe 3:19 in which also he went and preached unto the spirits in prison,

1Pe 3:20 that aforetime were disobedient, when the longsuffering of God waited in the days of Noah, while the ark was a preparing, wherein few, that is, eight souls, were saved through water:

1Pe 3:21 which also after a true likeness doth now save you, even baptism, not the putting away of the filth of the flesh, but the interrogation of a good conscience toward God, through the resurrection of Jesus Christ;

1Pe 3:22 who is on the right hand of God, having gone into heaven; angels and authorities and powers being made subject unto him.

Chapter 4.

1Pe 4:1 Forasmuch then as Christ suffered in the flesh, arm ye yourselves also with the same mind; for he that hath suffered in the flesh hath ceased from sin;

1Pe 4:2 that ye no longer should live the rest of your time in flesh to the lusts of men, but to the will of God.

1Pe 4:3 For the time past may suffice to have wrought the desire of the Gentiles, and to have walked in lasciviousness, lusts, winebibbings, revellings, carousings, and abominable idolatries:

1Pe 4:4 wherein they think strange that ye run not with them into the same excess of riot, speaking evil of you:

1Pe 4:5 who shall give account to him that is ready to judge the living and the dead.

1Pe 4:6 For unto this end was the gospel preached even to the dead, that they might be judged indeed according to men in the flesh, but live according to God in the spirit.

1Pe 4:7 But the end of all things is at hand: be ye therefore of sound mind, and be sober unto prayer:

1Pe 4:8 above all things being fervent in your love among yourselves; for love covereth a multitude of sins:

1Pe 4:9 using hospitality one to another without murmuring:

1Pe 4:10 according as each hath received a gift, ministering it among yourselves, as good stewards of the manifold grace of God;

1Pe 4:11 if any man speaketh, speaking as it were oracles of God; if any man ministereth, ministering as of the strength which God supplieth: that in all things God may be glorified through Jesus Christ, whose is the glory and the dominion for ever and ever. Amen.

1Pe 4:12 Beloved, think it not strange concerning the fiery trial among you, which cometh upon you to prove you, as though a strange thing happened unto you:

1Pe 4:13 but insomuch as ye are partakers of Christ's sufferings, rejoice; that at the revelation of his glory also ye may rejoice with exceeding joy.

1Pe 4:14 If ye are reproached for the name of Christ, blessed are ye; because the Spirit of glory and the Spirit of God resteth upon you.

1Pe 4:15 For let none of you suffer as a murderer, or a thief, or an evil-doer, or as a meddler in other men's matters:

1Pe 4:16 but if a man suffer as a Christian, let him not be ashamed; but let him glorify God in this name.

1Pe 4:17 For the time is come for judgment to begin at the house of God: and if it begin first at us, what shall be the end of them that obey not the gospel of God?

1Pe 4:18 And if the righteous is scarcely saved, where shall the ungodly and sinner appear?

1Pe 4:19 Wherefore let them also that suffer according to the will of God commit their souls in well-doing unto a faithful Creator.

Chapter 5.

1Pe 5:1 The elders among you I exhort, who am a fellow-elder, and a witness of the sufferings of Christ, who am also a partaker of the glory that shall be revealed:

1Pe 5:2 Tend the flock of God which is among you, exercising the oversight, not of constraint, but willingly, according to the will of God; nor yet for filthy lucre, but of a ready mind;

1Pe 5:3 neither as lording it over the charge allotted to you, but making yourselves ensamples to the flock.

1Pe 5:4 And when the chief Shepherd shall be manifested, ye shall receive the crown of glory that fadeth not away.

1Pe 5:5 Likewise, ye younger, be subject unto the elder. Yea, all of you gird yourselves with humility, to serve one another: for God resisteth the proud, but giveth grace to the humble.

1Pe 5:6 Humble yourselves therefore under the mighty hand of God, that he may exalt you in due time;

1Pe 5:7 casting all your anxiety upon him, because he careth for you.

1Pe 5:8 Be sober, be watchful: your adversary the devil, as a roaring lion, walketh about, seeking whom he may devour,

1Pe 5:9 whom withstand stedfast in your faith, knowing that the same sufferings are accomplished in your brethren who are in the world.

1Pe 5:10 And the God of all grace, who called you unto his eternal glory in Christ, after that ye have suffered a little while, shall himself perfect, establish, strengthen you.

1Pe 5:11 To him be the dominion for ever and ever. Amen.

1Pe 5:12 By Silvanus, our faithful brother, as I account him, I have written unto you briefly, exhorting, and testifying that this is the true grace of God. Stand ye fast therein.

1Pe 5:13 She that is in Babylon, elect together with you, saluteth you; and so doth Mark my son.

1Pe 5:14 Salute one another with a kiss of love. Peace be unto you all that are in Christ.

23. 2 Peter

Chapter 1.

2Pe 1:1 Simon Peter, a servant and apostle of Jesus Christ, to them that have obtained a like precious faith with us in the righteousness of our God and the Saviour Jesus Christ:

2Pe 1:2 Grace to you and peace be multiplied in the knowledge of God and of Jesus our Lord;

2Pe 1:3 seeing that his divine power hath granted unto us all things that pertain unto life and godliness, through the knowledge of him that called us by his own glory and virtue;

2Pe 1:4 whereby he hath granted unto us his precious and exceeding great promises; that through these ye may become partakers of the divine nature, having escaped from the corruption that is in that world by lust.

2Pe 1:5 Yea, and for this very cause adding on your part all diligence, in your faith supply virtue; and in your virtue knowledge;

2Pe 1:6 and in your knowledge self-control; and in your self-control patience; and in your patience godliness;

2Pe 1:7 and in your godliness brotherly kindness; and in your brotherly kindness love.

2Pe 1:8 For if these things are yours and abound, they make you to be not idle nor unfruitful unto the knowledge of our Lord Jesus Christ.

2Pe 1:9 For he that lacketh these things is blind, seeing only what is near, having forgotten the cleansing from his old sins.

2Pe 1:10 Wherefore, brethren, give the more diligence to make your calling and election sure: for if ye do these things, ye shall never stumble:

2Pe 1:11 for thus shall be richly supplied unto you the entrance into the eternal kingdom of our Lord and Saviour Jesus Christ.

2Pe 1:12 Wherefore I shall be ready always to put you in remembrance of these things, though ye know them, and are established in the truth which is with you.

2Pe 1:13 And I think it right, as long as I am in this tabernacle, to stir you up by putting you in remembrance;

2Pe 1:14 knowing that the putting off of my tabernacle cometh swiftly, even as our Lord Jesus Christ signified unto me.

2Pe 1:15 Yea, I will give diligence that at every time ye may be able after my decease to call these things to remembrance.

2Pe 1:16 For we did not follow cunningly devised fables, when we made known unto you the power and coming of our Lord Jesus Christ, but we were eyewitnesses of his majesty.

2Pe 1:17 For he received from God the Father honor and glory, when there was borne such a voice to him by the Majestic Glory, This is my beloved Son, in whom I am well pleased:

2Pe 1:18 and this voice we ourselves heard borne out of heaven, when we were with him in the holy mount.

2Pe 1:19 And we have the word of prophecy made more sure; whereunto ye do well that ye take heed, as unto a lamp shining in a dark place, until the day dawn, and the day-star arise in your hearts:

2Pe 1:20 knowing this first, that no prophecy of scripture is of private interpretation.

2Pe 1:21 For no prophecy ever came by the will of man: but men spake from God, being moved by the Holy Spirit.

Chapter 2.

2Pe 2:1 But there arose false prophets also among the people, as among you also there shall be false teachers, who shall privily bring in destructive heresies, denying even the Master that bought them, bringing upon themselves swift destruction.

2Pe 2:2 And many shall follow their lascivious doings; by reason of whom the way of the truth shall be evil spoken of.

2Pe 2:3 And in covetousness shall they with feigned words make merchandise of you: whose sentence now from of old lingereth not, and their destruction slumbereth not.

2Pe 2:4 For if God spared not angels when they sinned, but cast them down to hell, and committed them to pits of darkness, to be reserved unto judgment;

2Pe 2:5 and spared not the ancient world, but preserved Noah with seven others, a preacher of righteousness, when he brought a flood upon the world of the ungodly;

2Pe 2:6 and turning the cities of Sodom and Gomorrah into ashes condemned them with an overthrow, having made them an example unto those that should live ungodly;

2Pe 2:7 and delivered righteous Lot, sore distressed by the lascivious life of the wicked

2Pe 2:8 (for that righteous man dwelling among them, in seeing and hearing, vexed his righteous soul from day to day with their lawless deeds):

2Pe 2:9 the Lord knoweth how to deliver the godly out of temptation, and to keep the unrighteous under punishment unto the day of judgment;

2Pe 2:10 but chiefly them that walk after the flesh in the lust of defilement, and despise dominion. Daring, self-willed, they tremble not to rail at dignities:

2Pe 2:11 whereas angels, though greater in might and power, bring not a railing judgment against them before the Lord.

2Pe 2:12 But these, as creatures without reason, born mere animals to be taken and destroyed, railing in matters whereof they are ignorant, shall in their destroying surely be destroyed,

2Pe 2:13 suffering wrong as the hire of wrong-doing; men that count it pleasure to revel in the day-time, spots and blemishes, revelling in their deceivings while they feast with you;

2Pe 2:14 having eyes full of adultery, and that cannot cease from sin; enticing unstedfast souls; having a heart exercised in covetousness; children of cursing;

2Pe 2:15 forsaking the right way, they went astray, having followed the way of Balaam the son of Beor, who loved the hire of wrong-doing;

2Pe 2:16 but he was rebuked for his own transgression: a dumb ass spake with man's voice and stayed the madness of the prophet.

2Pe 2:17 These are springs without water, and mists driven by a storm; for whom the blackness of darkness hath been reserved.

2Pe 2:18 For, uttering great swelling words of vanity, they entice in the lusts of the flesh, by lasciviousness, those who are just escaping from them that live in error;

2Pe 2:19 promising them liberty, while they themselves are bondservants of corruption; for of whom a man is overcome, of the same is he also brought into bondage.

2Pe 2:20 For if, after they have escaped the defilements of the world through the knowledge of the Lord and Saviour Jesus Christ, they are again entangled therein and overcome, the last state is become worse with them than the first.

2Pe 2:21 For it were better for them not to have known the way of righteousness, than, after knowing it, to turn back from the holy commandment delivered unto them.

2Pe 2:22 It has happened unto them according to the true proverb, The dog turning to his own vomit again, and the sow that had washed to wallowing in the mire.

Chapter 3.

2Pe 3:1 This is now, beloved, the second epistle that I write unto you; and in both of them I stir up your sincere mind by putting you in remembrance;

2Pe 3:2 that ye should remember the words which were spoken before by the holy prophets, and the commandments of the Lord and Saviour through your apostles:

2Pe 3:3 knowing this first, that in the last days mockers shall come with mockery, walking after their own lusts,

2Pe 3:4 and saying, Where is the promise of his coming? for, from the day that the fathers fell asleep, all things continue as they were from the beginning of the creation.

2Pe 3:5 For this they willfully forget, that there were heavens from of old, and an earth compacted out of water and amidst water, by the word of God;

2Pe 3:6 by which means the world that then was, being overflowed with water, perished:

2Pe 3:7 but the heavens that now are, and the earth, by the same word have been stored up for fire, being reserved against the day of judgment and destruction of ungodly men.

2Pe 3:8 But forget not this one thing, beloved, that one day is with the Lord as a thousand years, and a thousand years as one day.

2Pe 3:9 The Lord is not slack concerning his promise, as some count slackness; but is longsuffering to you-ward, not wishing that any should perish, but that all should come to repentance.

2Pe 3:10 But the day of the Lord will come as a thief; in the which the heavens shall pass away with a great noise, and the elements shall be dissolved with fervent heat, and the earth and the works that are therein shall be burned up.

2Pe 3:11 Seeing that these things are thus all to be dissolved, what manner of persons ought ye to be in all holy living and godliness,

2Pe 3:12 looking for and earnestly desiring the coming of the day of God, by reason of which the heavens being on fire shall be dissolved, and the elements shall melt with fervent heat?

2Pe 3:13 But, according to his promise, we look for new heavens and a new earth, wherein dwelleth righteousness.

2Pe 3:14 Wherefore, beloved, seeing that ye look for these things, give diligence that ye may be found in peace, without spot and blameless in his sight.

2Pe 3:15 And account that the longsuffering of our Lord is salvation; even as our beloved brother Paul also, according to the wisdom given to him, wrote unto you;

2Pe 3:16 as also in all his epistles, speaking in them of these things; wherein are some things hard to be understood, which the ignorant and unstedfast wrest, as they do also the other scriptures, unto their own destruction.

2Pe 3:17 Ye therefore, beloved, knowing these things beforehand, beware lest, being carried away with the error of the wicked, ye fall from your own stedfastness.

2Pe 3:18 But grow in the grace and knowledge of our Lord and Saviour Jesus Christ. To him be the glory both now and for ever. Amen.

24. 1 John

Chapter 1.

1Jn 1:1 That which was from the beginning, that which we have heard, that which we have seen with our eyes, that which we beheld, and our hands handled, concerning the Word of life

1Jn 1:2 (and the life was manifested, and we have seen, and bear witness, and declare unto you the life, the eternal life, which was with the Father, and was manifested unto us);

1Jn 1:3 that which we have seen and heard declare we unto you also, that ye also may have fellowship with us: yea, and our fellowship is with the Father, and with his Son Jesus Christ:

1Jn 1:4 and these things we write, that our joy may be made full.

1Jn 1:5 And this is the message which we have heard from him and announce unto you, that God is light, and in him is no darkness at all.

1Jn 1:6 If we say that we have fellowship with him and walk in the darkness, we lie, and do not the truth:

1Jn 1:7 but if we walk in the light, as he is in the light, we have fellowship one with another, and the blood of Jesus his Son cleanseth us from all sin.

1Jn 1:8 If we say that we have no sin, we deceive ourselves, and the truth is not in us.

1Jn 1:9 If we confess our sins, he is faithful and righteous to forgive us our sins, and to cleanse us from all unrighteousness.

1Jn 1:10 If we say that we have not sinned, we make him a liar, and his word is not in us.

Chapter 2.

1Jn 2:1 My little children, these things write I unto you that ye may not sin. And if any man sin, we have an Advocate with the Father, Jesus Christ the righteous:

1Jn 2:2 and he is the propitiation for our sins; and not for ours only, but also for the whole world.

1Jn 2:3 And hereby we know that we know him, if we keep his commandments.

1Jn 2:4 He that saith, I know him, and keepeth not his commandments, is a liar, and the truth is not in him;

1Jn 2:5 but whoso keepeth his word, in him verily hath the love of God been perfected. Hereby we know that we are in him:

1Jn 2:6 he that saith he abideth in him ought himself also to walk even as he walked.

1Jn 2:7 Beloved, no new commandment write I unto you, but an old commandment which ye had from the beginning: the old commandment is the word which ye heard.

1Jn 2:8 Again, a new commandment write I unto you, which thing is true in him and in you; because the darkness is passing away, and the true light already shineth.

1Jn 2:9 He that saith he is in the light and hateth his brother, is in the darkness even until now.

1Jn 2:10 He that loveth his brother abideth in the light, and there is no occasion of stumbling in him.

1Jn 2:11 But he that hateth his brother is in the darkness, and walketh in the darkness, and knoweth not whither he goeth, because the darkness hath blinded his eyes.

1Jn 2:12 I write unto you, my little children, because your sins are forgiven you for his name's sake.

1Jn 2:13 I write unto you, fathers, because ye know him who is from the beginning. I write unto you, young men, because ye have overcome the evil one. I have written unto you, little children, because ye know the Father.

1Jn 2:14 I have written unto you, fathers, because ye know him who is from the beginning. I have written unto you, young men, because ye are strong, and the word of God abideth in you, and ye have overcome the evil one.

1Jn 2:15 Love not the world, neither the things that are in the world. If any man love the world, the love of the Father is not in him.

1Jn 2:16 For all that is in the world, the lust of the flesh and the lust of the eyes and the vain glory of life, is not of the Father, but is of the world.

1Jn 2:17 And the world passeth away, and the lust thereof: but he that doeth the will of God abideth for ever.

1Jn 2:18 Little children, it is the last hour: and as ye heard that antichrist cometh, even now have there arisen many antichrists; whereby we know that it is the last hour.

1Jn 2:19 They went out from us, but they were not of us; for if they had been of us, they would have continued with us: but they went out, that they might be made manifest that they all are not of us.

1Jn 2:20 And ye have an anointing from the Holy One, and ye know all the things.

1Jn 2:21 I have not written unto you because ye know not the truth, but because ye know it, and because no lie is of the truth.

1Jn 2:22 Who is the liar but he that denieth that Jesus is the Christ? This is the antichrist, even he that denieth the Father and the Son.

1Jn 2:23 Whosoever denieth the Son, the same hath not the Father: he that confesseth the Son hath the Father also.

1Jn 2:24 As for you, let that abide in you which ye heard from the beginning. If that which ye heard from the beginning abide in you, ye also shall abide in the Son, and in the Father.

1Jn 2:25 And this is the promise which he promised us, even the life eternal.

1Jn 2:26 These things have I written unto you concerning them that would lead you astray.

1Jn 2:27 And as for you, the anointing which ye received of him abideth in you, and ye need not that any one teach you; but as his anointing teacheth you; concerning all things, and is true, and is no lie, and even as it taught you, ye abide in him.

1Jn 2:28 And now, my little children, abide in him; that, if he shall be manifested, we may have boldness, and not be ashamed before him at his coming.

1Jn 2:29 If ye know that he is righteous, ye know that every one also that doeth righteousness is begotten of him.

Chapter 3.

1Jn 3:1 Behold what manner of love the Father hath bestowed upon us, that we should be called children of God; and such we are. For this cause the world knoweth us not, because it knew him not.

1Jn 3:2 Beloved, now are we children of God, and it is not yet made manifest what we shall be. We know that, if he shall be manifested, we shall be like him; for we shall see him even as he is.

1Jn 3:3 And every one that hath this hope set on him purifieth himself, even as he is pure.

1Jn 3:4 Every one that doeth sin doeth also lawlessness; and sin is lawlessness.

1Jn 3:5 And ye know that he was manifested to take away sins; and in him is no sin.

1Jn 3:6 Whosoever abideth in him sinneth not: whosoever sinneth hath not seen him, neither knoweth him.

1Jn 3:7 My little children, let no man lead you astray: he that doeth righteousness is righteous, even as he is righteous:

1Jn 3:8 he that doeth sin is of the devil; for the devil sinneth from the beginning. To this end was the Son of God manifested, that he might destroy the works of the devil.

1Jn 3:9 Whosoever is begotten of God doeth no sin, because his seed abideth in him: and he cannot sin, because he is begotten of God.

1Jn 3:10 In this the children of God are manifest, and the children of the devil: whosoever doeth not righteousness is not of God, neither he that loveth not his brother.

1Jn 3:11 For this is the message which ye heard from the beginning, that we should love one another:

1Jn 3:12 not as Cain was of the evil one, and slew his brother. And wherefore slew he him? Because his works were evil, and his brother's righteous.

1Jn 3:13 Marvel not, brethren, if the world hateth you.

1Jn 3:14 We know that we have passed out of death into life, because we love the brethren. He that loveth not abideth in death.

1Jn 3:15 Whosoever hateth his brother is a murderer: and ye know that no murderer hath eternal life abiding in him.

1Jn 3:16 Hereby know we love, because he laid down his life for us: and we ought to lay down our lives for the brethren.

1Jn 3:17 But whoso hath the world's goods, and beholdeth his brother in need, and shutteth up his compassion from him, how doth the love of God abide in him?

1Jn 3:18 My Little children, let us not love in word, neither with the tongue; but in deed and truth.

1Jn 3:19 Hereby shall we know that we are of the truth, and shall assure our heart before him:

1Jn 3:20 because if our heart condemn us, God is greater than our heart, and knoweth all things.

1Jn 3:21 Beloved, if our heart condemn us not, we have boldness toward God;

1Jn 3:22 and whatsoever we ask we receive of him, because we keep his commandments and do the things that are pleasing in his sight.

1Jn 3:23 And this is his commandment, that we should believe in the name of his Son Jesus Christ, and love one another, even as he gave us commandment.

1Jn 3:24 And he that keepeth his commandments abideth in him, and he in him. And hereby we know that he abideth in us, by the Spirit which he gave us.

Chapter 4.

1Jn 4:1 Beloved, believe not every spirit, but prove the spirits, whether they are of God; because many false prophets are gone out into the world.

1Jn 4:2 Hereby know ye the Spirit of God: every spirit that confesseth that Jesus Christ is come in the flesh is of God:

1Jn 4:3 and every spirit that confesseth not Jesus is not of God: and this is the spirit of the antichrist, whereof ye have heard that it cometh; and now it is in the world already.

1Jn 4:4 Ye are of God, my little children, and have overcome them: because greater is he that is in you than he that is in the world.

1Jn 4:5 They are of the world: therefore speak they as of the world, and the world heareth them.

1Jn 4:6 We are of God: he that knoweth God heareth us; he who is not of God heareth us not. By this we know the spirit of truth, and the spirit of error.

1Jn 4:7 Beloved, let us love one another: for love is of God; and every one that loveth is begotten of God, and knoweth God.

1Jn 4:8 He that loveth not knoweth not God; for God is love.

1Jn 4:9 Herein was the love of God manifested in us, that God hath sent his only begotten Son into the world that we might live through him.

1Jn 4:10 Herein is love, not that we loved God, but that he loved us, and sent his Son to be the propitiation for our sins.

1Jn 4:11 Beloved, if God so loved us, we also ought to love one another.

1Jn 4:12 No man hath beheld God at any time: if we love one another, God abideth in us, and his love is perfected in us:

1Jn 4:13 hereby we know that we abide in him and he in us, because he hath given us of his Spirit.

1Jn 4:14 And we have beheld and bear witness that the Father hath sent the Son to be the Saviour of the world.

1Jn 4:15 Whosoever shall confess that Jesus is the Son of God, God abideth in him, and he in God.

1Jn 4:16 And we know and have believed the love which God hath in us. God is love; and he that abideth in love abideth in God, and God abideth in him.

1Jn 4:17 Herein is love made perfect with us, that we may have boldness in the day of judgment; because as he is, even so are we in this world.

1Jn 4:18 There is no fear in love: but perfect love casteth out fear, because fear hath punishment; and he that feareth is not made perfect in love.

1Jn 4:19 We love, because he first loved us.

1Jn 4:20 If a man say, I love God, and hateth his brother, he is a liar: for he that loveth not his brother whom he hath seen, cannot love God whom he hath not seen.

1Jn 4:21 And this commandment have we from him, that he who loveth God love his brother also.

Chapter 5.

1Jn 5:1 Whosoever believeth that Jesus is the Christ is begotten of God: and whosoever loveth him that begat loveth him also that is begotten of him.

1Jn 5:2 Hereby we know that we love the children of God, when we love God and do his commandments.

1Jn 5:3 For this is the love of God, that we keep his commandments: and his commandments are not grievous.

1Jn 5:4 For whatsoever is begotten of God overcometh the world: and this is the victory that hath overcome the world, even our faith.

1Jn 5:5 And who is he that overcometh the world, but he that believeth that Jesus is the Son of God?

1Jn 5:6 This is he that came by water and blood, even Jesus Christ; not with the water only, but with the water and with the blood.

1Jn 5:7 And it is the Spirit that beareth witness, because the Spirit is the truth.

1Jn 5:8 For there are three who bear witness, the Spirit, and the water, and the blood: and the three agree in one.

1Jn 5:9 If we receive the witness of men, the witness of God is greater: for the witness of God is this, that he hath borne witness concerning his Son.

1Jn 5:10 He that believeth on the Son of God hath the witness in him: he that believeth not God hath made him a liar; because he hath not believed in the witness that God hath borne concerning his Son.

1Jn 5:11 And the witness is this, that God gave unto us eternal life, and this life is in his Son.

1Jn 5:12 He that hath the Son hath the life; he that hath not the Son of God hath not the life.

1Jn 5:13 These things have I written unto you, that ye may know that ye have eternal life, even unto you that believe on the name of the Son of God.

1Jn 5:14 And this is the boldness which we have toward him, that, if we ask anything according to his will, he heareth us:

1Jn 5:15 and if we know that he heareth us whatsoever we ask, we know that we have the petitions which we have asked of him.

1Jn 5:16 If any man see his brother sinning a sin not unto death, he shall ask, and God will give him life for them that sin not unto death. There is a sin unto death: not concerning this do I say that he should make request.

1Jn 5:17 All unrighteousness is sin: and there is a sin not unto death.

1Jn 5:18 We know that whosoever is begotten of God sinneth not; but he that was begotten of God keepeth himself, and the evil one toucheth him not.

1Jn 5:19 We know that we are of God, and the whole world lieth in the evil one.

1Jn 5:20 And we know that the Son of God is come, and hath given us an understanding, that we know him that is true, and we are in him that is true, even in his Son Jesus Christ. This is the true God, and eternal life.

1Jn 5:21 My little children, guard yourselves from idols.

25. 2 John

Chapter 1.

2Jn 1:1 The elder unto the elect lady and her children, whom I love in truth; and not I only, but also all they that know the truth;

2Jn 1:2 for the truth's sake which abideth in us, and it shall be with us for ever:

2Jn 1:3 Grace, mercy, peace shall be with us, from God the Father, and from Jesus Christ, the Son of the Father, in truth and love.

2Jn 1:4 I rejoice greatly that I have found certain of thy children walking in truth, even as we received commandment from the Father.

2Jn 1:5 And now I beseech thee, lady, not as though I wrote to thee a new commandment, but that which we had from the beginning, that we love one another.

2Jn 1:6 And this is love, that we should walk after his commandments. This is the commandment, even as ye heard from the beginning, that ye should walk in it.

2Jn 1:7 For many deceivers are gone forth into the world, even they that confess not that Jesus Christ cometh in the flesh. This is the deceiver and the antichrist.

2Jn 1:8 Look to yourselves, that ye lose not the things which we have wrought, but that ye receive a full reward.

2Jn 1:9 Whosoever goeth onward and abideth not in the teaching of Christ, hath not God: he that abideth in the teaching, the same hath both the Father and the Son.

2Jn 1:10 If any one cometh unto you, and bringeth not this teaching, receive him not into your house, and give him no greeting:

2Jn 1:11 for he that giveth him greeting partaketh in his evil works.

2Jn 1:12 Having many things to write unto you, I would not write them with paper and ink: but I hope to come unto you, and to speak face to face, that your joy may be made full.

2Jn 1:13 The children of thine elect sister salute thee.

26. 3 John

Chapter 1.

3Jn 1:1 The elder unto Gaius the beloved, whom I love in truth.

3Jn 1:2 Beloved, I pray that in all things thou mayest prosper and be in health, even as thy soul prospereth.

3Jn 1:3 For I rejoiced greatly, when brethren came and bare witness unto thy truth, even as thou walkest in truth.

3Jn 1:4 Greater joy have I none than this, to hear of my children walking in the truth.

3Jn 1:5 Beloved, thou doest a faithful work in whatsoever thou doest toward them that are brethren and strangers withal;

3Jn 1:6 who bare witness to thy love before the church: whom thou wilt do well to set forward on their journey worthily of God:

3Jn 1:7 because that for the sake of the Name they went forth, taking nothing of the Gentiles.

3Jn 1:8 We therefore ought to welcome such, that we may be fellow-workers for the truth.

3Jn 1:9 I wrote somewhat unto the church: but Diotrephes, who loveth to have the preeminence among them, receiveth us not.

3Jn 1:10 Therefore, if I come, I will bring to remembrance his works which he doeth, prating against us with wicked words: and not content therewith, neither doth he himself receive the brethren, and them that would he forbiddeth and casteth them out of the church.

3Jn 1:11 Beloved, imitate not that which is evil, but that which is good. He that doeth good is of God: he that doeth evil hath not seen God.

3Jn 1:12 Demetrius hath the witness of all men, and of the truth itself: yea, we also bear witness: and thou knowest that our witness is true.

3Jn 1:13 I had many things to write unto thee, but I am unwilling to write them to thee with ink and pen:

3Jn 1:14 but I hope shortly to see thee, and we shall speak face to face. Peace be unto thee. The friends salute thee. Salute the friends by name.

27. Jude

Chapter 1.

Jud 1:1 Jude, a servant of Jesus Christ, and brother of James, to them that are called, beloved in God the Father, and kept for Jesus Christ:

Jud 1:2 Mercy unto you and peace and love be multiplied.

Jud 1:3 Beloved, while I was giving all diligence to write unto you of our common salvation, I was constrained to write unto you exhorting you to contend earnestly for the faith which was once for all delivered unto the saints.

Jud 1:4 For there are certain men crept in privily, even they who were of old written of beforehand unto this condemnation, ungodly men, turning the grace of our God into lasciviousness, and denying our only Master and Lord, Jesus Christ.

Jud 1:5 Now I desire to put you in remembrance, though ye know all things once for all, that the Lord, having saved a people out of the land of Egypt, afterward destroyed them that believed not.

Jud 1:6 And angels that kept not their own principality, but left their proper habitation, he hath kept in everlasting bonds under darkness unto the judgment of the great day.

Jud 1:7 Even as Sodom and Gomorrah, and the cities about them, having in like manner with these given themselves over to fornication and gone after strange flesh, are set forth as an example, suffering the punishment of eternal fire.

Jud 1:8 Yet in like manner these also in their dreamings defile the flesh, and set at nought dominion, and rail at dignities.

Jud 1:9 But Michael the archangel, when contending with the devil he disputed about the body of Moses, durst not bring against him a railing judgment, but said, The Lord rebuke thee.

Jud 1:10 But these rail at whatsoever things they know not: and what they understand naturally, like the creatures without reason, in these things are they destroyed.

Jud 1:11 Woe unto them! For they went in the way of Cain, and ran riotously in the error of Balaam for hire, and perished in the gainsaying of Korah.

Jud 1:12 These are they who are hidden rocks in your love-feasts when they feast with you, shepherds that without fear feed themselves; clouds without water, carried along by winds; autumn leaves without fruit, twice dead, plucked up by the roots;

Jud 1:13 Wild waves of the sea, foaming out their own shame; wandering stars, for whom the blackness of darkness hath been reserved forever.

Jud 1:14 And to these also Enoch, the seventh from Adam, prophesied, saying, Behold, the Lord came with ten thousands of his holy ones,

Jud 1:15 to execute judgment upon all, and to convict all the ungodly of all their works of ungodliness which they have ungodly wrought, and of all the hard things which ungodly sinners have spoken against him.

Jud 1:16 These are murmurers, complainers, walking after their lusts (and their mouth speaketh great swelling words), showing respect of persons for the sake of advantage.

Jud 1:17 But ye, beloved, remember ye the words which have been spoken before by the apostles of our Lord Jesus Christ;

Jud 1:18 That they said to you, In the last time there shall be mockers, walking after their own ungodly lusts.

Jud 1:19 These are they who make separations, sensual, having not the Spirit.

Jud 1:20 But ye, beloved, building up yourselves on your most holy faith, praying in the Holy Spirit,

Jud 1:21 keep yourselves in the love of God, looking for the mercy of our Lord Jesus Christ unto eternal life.

Jud 1:22 And on some have mercy, who are in doubt;

Jud 1:23 and some save, snatching them out of the fire; and on some have mercy with fear; hating even the garment spotted by the flesh.

Jud 1:24 Now unto him that is able to guard you from stumbling, and to set you before the presence of his glory without blemish in exceeding joy,

Jud 1:25   to the only God our Saviour, through Jesus Christ our Lord, be glory, majesty, dominion and power, before all time, and now, and for evermore. Amen.

V. Revelation

28. Revelation of Jesus Christ

Chapter 1.

Rev 1:1 The Revelation of Jesus Christ, which God gave him to show unto his servants, even the things which must shortly come to pass: and he sent and signified it by his angel unto his servant John;

Rev 1:2 who bare witness of the word of God, and of the testimony of Jesus Christ, even of all things that he saw.

Rev 1:3 Blessed is he that readeth, and they that hear the words of the prophecy, and keep the things that are written therein: for the time is at hand.

Rev 1:4 John to the seven churches that are in Asia: Grace to you and peace, from him who is and who was and who is to come; and from the seven Spirits that are before his throne;

Rev 1:5 and from Jesus Christ, who is the faithful witness, the firstborn of the dead, and the ruler of the kings of the earth. Unto him that loveth us, and loosed us from our sins by his blood;

Rev 1:6 and he made us to be a kingdom, to be priests unto his God and Father; to him be the glory and the dominion for ever and ever. Amen.

Rev 1:7 Behold, he cometh with the clouds; and every eye shall see him, and they that pierced him; and all the tribes of the earth shall mourn over him. Even so, Amen.

Rev 1:8 I am the Alpha and the Omega, saith the Lord God, who is and who was and who is to come, the Almighty.

Rev 1:9 I John, your brother and partaker with you in tribulation and kingdom and patience which are in Jesus, was in the isle that is called Patmos, for the word of God and the testimony of Jesus.

Rev 1:10 I was in the Spirit on the Lord's day, and I heard behind me a great voice, as of a trumpet

Rev 1:11 saying, What thou seest, write in a book and send it to the seven churches: unto Ephesus, and unto Smyrna, and unto Pergamum, and unto Thyatira, and unto Sardis, and unto Philadelphia, and unto Laodicea.

Rev 1:12 And I turned to see the voice that spake with me. And having turned I saw seven golden candlesticks;

Rev 1:13 and in the midst of the candlesticks one like unto a son of man, clothed with a garment down to the foot, and girt about at the breasts with a golden girdle.

Rev 1:14 And his head and his hair were white as white wool, white as snow; and his eyes were as a flame of fire;

Rev 1:15 and his feet like unto burnished brass, as if it had been refined in a furnace; and his voice as the voice of many waters.

Rev 1:16 And he had in his right hand seven stars: and out of his mouth proceeded a sharp two-edged sword: and his countenance was as the sun shineth in his strength.

Rev 1:17 And when I saw him, I fell at his feet as one dead. And he laid his right hand upon me, saying, Fear not; I am the first and the last,

Rev 1:18 and the Living one; and I was dead, and behold, I am alive for evermore, and I have the keys of death and of Hades.

Rev 1:19 Write therefore the things which thou sawest, and the things which are, and the things which shall come to pass hereafter;

Rev 1:20 the mystery of the seven stars which thou sawest in my right hand, and the seven golden candlesticks. The seven stars are the angels of the seven churches: and the seven candlesticks are seven churches.

Chapter 2.

Rev 2:1 To the angel of the church in Ephesus write: These things saith he that holdeth the seven stars in his right hand, he that walketh in the midst of the seven golden candlesticks:

Rev 2:2 I know thy works, and thy toil and patience, and that thou canst not bear evil men, and didst try them that call themselves apostles, and they are not, and didst find them false;

Rev 2:3 and thou hast patience and didst bear for my name's sake, and hast not grown weary.

Rev 2:4 But I have this against thee, that thou didst leave thy first love.

Rev 2:5 Remember therefore whence thou art fallen, and repent and do the first works; or else I come to thee, and will move thy candlestick out of its place, except thou repent.

Rev 2:6 But this thou hast, that thou hatest the works of the Nicolaitans, which I also hate.

Rev 2:7 He that hath an ear, let him hear what the Spirit saith to the churches. To him that overcometh, to him will I give to eat of the tree of life, which is in the Paradise of God.

Rev 2:8 And to the angel of the church in Smyrna write: These things saith the first and the last, who was dead, and lived again:

Rev 2:9 I know thy tribulation, and thy poverty (but thou art rich), and the blasphemy of them that say they are Jews, and they art not, but are a synagogue of Satan.

Rev 2:10 Fear not the things which thou art about to suffer: behold, the devil is about to cast some of you into prison, that ye may be tried; and ye shall have tribulation ten days. Be thou faithful unto death, and I will give thee the crown of life.

Rev 2:11 He that hath an ear, let him hear what the Spirit saith to the churches. He that overcometh shall not be hurt of the second death.

Rev 2:12 And to the angel of the church in Pergamum write: These things saith he that hath the sharp two-edged sword:

Rev 2:13 I know where thou dwellest, even where Satan's throne is; and thou holdest fast my name, and didst not deny my faith, even in the days of Antipas my witness, my faithful one, who was killed among you, where Satan dwelleth.

Rev 2:14 But I have a few things against thee, because thou hast there some that hold the teaching of Balaam, who taught Balak to cast a stumblingblock before the children of Israel, to eat things sacrificed to idols, and to commit fornication.

Rev 2:15 So hast thou also some that hold the teaching of the Nicolaitans in like manner.

Rev 2:16 Repent therefore; or else I come to thee quickly, and I will make war against them with the sword of my mouth.

Rev 2:17 He that hath an ear, let him hear what the Spirit saith to the churches. To him that overcometh, to him will I give of the hidden manna, and I will give him a white stone, and upon the stone a new name written, which no one knoweth but he that receiveth it.

Rev 2:18 And to the angel of the church in Thyatira write: These things saith the Son of God, who hath his eyes like a flame of fire, and his feet are like unto burnished brass:

Rev 2:19 I know thy works, and thy love and faith and ministry and patience, and that thy last works are more than the first.

Rev 2:20 But I have this against thee, that thou sufferest the woman Jezebel, who calleth herself a prophetess; and she teacheth and seduceth my servants to commit fornication, and to eat things sacrificed to idols.

Rev 2:21 And I gave her time that she should repent; and she willeth not to repent of her fornication.

Rev 2:22 Behold, I cast her into a bed, and them that commit adultery with her into great tribulation, except they repent of her works.

Rev 2:23 And I will kill her children with death; and all the churches shall know that I am he that searcheth the reins and hearts: and I will give unto each one of you according to your works.

Rev 2:24 But to you I say, to the rest that are in Thyatira, as many as have not this teaching, who know not the deep things of Satan, as they are wont to say; I cast upon you none other burden.

Rev 2:25 Nevertheless that which ye have, hold fast till I come.

Rev 2:26 And he that overcometh, and he that keepeth my works unto the end, to him will I give authority over the nations:

Rev 2:27 and he shall rule them with a rod of iron, as the vessels of the potter are broken to shivers; as I also have received of my Father:

Rev 2:28 and I will give him the morning star.

Rev 2:29 He that hath an ear, let him hear what the Spirit saith to the churches.

Chapter 3.

Rev 3:1 And to the angel of the church in Sardis write: These things saith he that hath the seven Spirits of God, and the seven stars: I know thy works, that thou hast a name that thou livest, and thou art dead.

Rev 3:2 Be thou watchful, and establish the things that remain, which were ready to die: for I have found no works of thine perfected before my God.

Rev 3:3 Remember therefore how thou hast received and didst hear; and keep it, and repent. If therefore thou shalt not watch, I will come as a thief, and thou shalt not know what hour I will come upon thee.

Rev 3:4 But thou hast a few names in Sardis that did not defile their garments: and they shall walk with me in white; for they are worthy.

Rev 3:5 He that overcometh shall thus be arrayed in white garments; and I will in no wise blot his name out of the book of life, and I will confess his name before my Father, and before his angels.

Rev 3:6 He that hath an ear, let him hear what the Spirit saith to the churches.

Rev 3:7 And to the angel of the church in Philadelphia write: These things saith he that is holy, he that is true, he that hath the key of David, he that openeth and none shall shut, and that shutteth and none openeth:

Rev 3:8 I know thy works (behold, I have set before thee a door opened, which none can shut), that thou hast a little power, and didst keep my word, and didst not deny my name.

Rev 3:9 Behold, I give of the synagogue of Satan, of them that say they are Jews, and they are not, but do lie; behold, I will make them to come and worship before thy feet, and to know that I have loved thee.

Rev 3:10 Because thou didst keep the word of my patience, I also will keep thee from the hour of trial, that hour which is to come upon the whole world, to try them that dwell upon the earth.

Rev 3:11 I come quickly: hold fast that which thou hast, that no one take thy crown.

Rev 3:12 He that overcometh, I will make him a pillar in the temple of my God, and he shall go out thence no more: and I will write upon him the name of my God, and the name of the city of my God, the new Jerusalem, which cometh down out of heaven from my God, and mine own new name.

Rev 3:13 He that hath an ear, let him hear what the Spirit saith to the churches.

Rev 3:14 And to the angel of the church in Laodicea write: These things saith the Amen, the faithful and true witness, the beginning of the creation of God:

Rev 3:15 I know thy works, that thou art neither cold nor hot: I would thou wert cold or hot.

Rev 3:16 So because thou art lukewarm, and neither hot nor cold, I will spew thee out of my mouth.

Rev 3:17 Because thou sayest, I am rich, and have gotten riches, and have need of nothing; and knowest not that thou art the wretched one and miserable and poor and blind and naked:

Rev 3:18 I counsel thee to buy of me gold refined by fire, that thou mayest become rich; and white garments, that thou mayest clothe thyself, and that the shame of thy nakedness be not made manifest; and eyesalve to anoint thine eyes, that thou mayest see.

Rev 3:19 As many as I love, I reprove and chasten: be zealous therefore, and repent.

Rev 3:20 Behold, I stand at the door and knock: if any man hear my voice and open the door, I will come in to him, and will sup with him, and he with me.

Rev 3:21 He that overcometh, I will give to him to sit down with me in my throne, as I also overcame, and sat down with my Father in his throne.

Rev 3:22 He that hath an ear, let him hear what the Spirit saith to the churches.

Chapter 4.

Rev 4:1 After these things I saw, and behold, a door opened in heaven, and the first voice that I heard, a voice as of a trumpet speaking with me, one saying, Come up hither, and I will show thee the things which must come to pass hereafter.

Rev 4:2 Straightway I was in the Spirit: and behold, there was a throne set in heaven, and one sitting upon the throne;

Rev 4:3 and he that sat was to look upon like a jasper stone and a sardius: and there was a rainbow round about the throne, like an emerald to look upon.

Rev 4:4 And round about the throne were four and twenty thrones: and upon the thrones I saw four and twenty elders sitting, arrayed in white garments; and on their heads crowns of gold.

Rev 4:5 And out of the throne proceed lightnings and voices and thunders. And there were seven lamps of fire burning before the throne, which are the seven Spirits of God;

Rev 4:6 and before the throne, as it were a sea of glass like a crystal; and in the midst of the throne, and round about the throne, four living creatures full of eyes before and behind.

Rev 4:7 And the first creature was like a lion, and the second creature like a calf, and the third creature had a face as of a man, and the fourth creature was like a flying eagle.

Rev 4:8 And the four living creatures, having each one of them six wings, are full of eyes round about and within: and they have no rest day and night, saying, Holy, holy, holy, is the Lord God, the Almighty, who was and who is and who is to come.

Rev 4:9 And when the living creatures shall give glory and honor and thanks to him that sitteth on the throne, to him that liveth for ever and ever,

Rev 4:10 the four and twenty elders shall fall down before him that sitteth on the throne, and shall worship him that liveth for ever and ever, and shall cast their crowns before the throne, saying,

Rev 4:11 Worthy art thou, our Lord and our God, to receive the glory and the honor and the power: for thou didst create all things, and because of thy will they were, and were created.

Chapter 5.

Rev 5:1 And I saw in the right hand of him that sat on the throne a book written within and on the back, close sealed with seven seals.

Rev 5:2 And I saw a strong angel proclaiming with a great voice, Who is worthy to open the book, and to loose the seals thereof?

Rev 5:3 And no one in the heaven, or on the earth, or under the earth, was able to open the book, or to look thereon.

Rev 5:4 And I wept much, because no one was found worthy to open the book, or to look thereon:

Rev 5:5 and one of the elders saith unto me, Weep not; behold, the Lion that is of the tribe of Judah, the Root of David, hath overcome to open the book and the seven seals thereof.

Rev 5:6 And I saw in the midst of the throne and of the four living creatures, and in the midst of the elders, a Lamb standing, as though it had been slain, having seven horns, and seven eyes, which are the seven Spirits of God, sent forth into all the earth.

Rev 5:7 And he came, and he taketh it out of the right hand of him that sat on the throne.

Rev 5:8 And when he had taken the book, the four living creatures and the four and twenty elders fell down before the Lamb, having each one a harp, and golden bowls full of incense, which are the prayers of the saints.

Rev 5:9 And they sing a new song, saying, Worthy art thou to take the book, and to open the seals thereof: for thou was slain, and didst purchase unto God with thy blood men of every tribe, and tongue, and people, and nation,

Rev 5:10 and madest them to be unto our God a kingdom and priests; and they reign upon earth.

Rev 5:11 And I saw, and I heard a voice of many angels round about the throne and the living creatures and the elders; and the number of them was ten thousand times ten thousand, and thousands of thousands;

Rev 5:12 saying with a great voice, Worthy is the Lamb that hath been slain to receive the power, and riches, and wisdom, and might and honor, and glory, and blessing.

Rev 5:13 And every created thing which is in the heaven, and on the earth, and under the earth, and on the sea, and all things are in them, heard I saying, Unto him that sitteth on the throne, and unto the Lamb, be the blessing, and the honor, and the glory, and the dominion, for ever and ever.

Rev 5:14 And the four living creatures said, Amen. And the elders fell down and worshipped.

Chapter 6.

Rev 6:1 And I saw when the Lamb opened one of the seven seals, and I heard one of the four living creatures saying as with a voice of thunder, Come.

Rev 6:2 And I saw, and behold, a white horse, and he that sat thereon had a bow; and there was given unto him a crown: and he came forth conquering, and to conquer.

Rev 6:3 And when he opened the second seal, I heard the second living creature saying, Come.

Rev 6:4 And another horse came forth, a red horse: and to him that sat thereon it was given to take peace from the earth, and that they should slay one another: and there was given unto him a great sword.

Rev 6:5 And when he opened the third seal, I heard the third living creature saying, Come. And I saw, and behold, a black horse; and he that sat thereon had a balance in his hand.

Rev 6:6 And I heard as it were a voice in the midst of the four living creatures saying, A measure of wheat for a shilling, and three measures of barley for a shilling; and the oil and the wine hurt thou not.

Rev 6:7 And when he opened the fourth seal, I heard the voice of the fourth living creature saying, Come.

Rev 6:8 And I saw, and behold, a pale horse: and he that sat upon him, his name was Death; and Hades followed with him. And there was given unto them authority over the fourth part of the earth, to kill with sword, and with famine, and with death, and by the wild beasts of the earth.

Rev 6:9 And when he opened the fifth seal, I saw underneath the altar the souls of them that had been slain for the word of God, and for the testimony which they held:

Rev 6:10 and they cried with a great voice, saying, How long, O Master, the holy and true, dost thou not judge and avenge our blood on them that dwell on the earth?

Rev 6:11 And there was given them to each one a white robe; and it was said unto them, that they should rest yet for a little time, until their fellow-servants also and their brethren, who should be killed even as they were, should have fulfilled their course.

Rev 6:12 And I saw when he opened the sixth seal, and there was a great earthquake; and the sun became black as sackcloth of hair, and the whole moon became as blood;

Rev 6:13 and the stars of the heaven fell unto the earth, as a fig tree casteth her unripe figs when she is shaken of a great wind.

Rev 6:14 And the heaven was removed as a scroll when it is rolled up; and every mountain and island were moved out of their places.

Rev 6:15 And the kings of the earth, and the princes, and the chief captains, and the rich, and the strong, and every bondman and freeman, hid themselves in the caves and in the rocks of the mountains;

Rev 6:16 and they say to the mountains and to the rocks, Fall on us, and hide us from the face of him that sitteth on the throne, and from the wrath of the Lamb:

Rev 6:17 for the great day of their wrath is come; and who is able to stand?

Chapter 7.

Rev 7:1 After his I saw four angels standing at the four corners of the earth, holding the four winds of the earth, that no wind should blow on the earth, or on the sea, or upon any tree.

Rev 7:2 And I saw another angel ascend from the sunrising, having the seal of the living God: and he cried with a great voice to the four angels to whom it was given to hurt the earth and the sea,

Rev 7:3 saying, Hurt not the earth, neither the sea, nor the trees, till we shall have sealed the servants of our God on their foreheads.

Rev 7:4 And I heard the number of them that were sealed, a hundred and forty and four thousand, sealed out of every tribe of the children of Israel:

Rev 7:5 Of the tribe of Judah were sealed twelve thousand: Of the tribe of Reuben twelve thousand; Of the tribe of Gad twelve thousand;

Rev 7:6 Of the tribe of Asher twelve thousand; Of the tribe of Naphtali twelve thousand; Of the tribe of Manasseh twelve thousand;

Rev 7:7 Of the tribe of Simeon twelve thousand; Of the tribe of Levi twelve thousand; Of the tribe of Issachar twelve thousand;

Rev 7:8 Of the tribe of Zebulun twelve thousand; Of the tribe of Joseph twelve thousand; Of the tribe of Benjamin were sealed twelve thousand.

Rev 7:9 After these things I saw, and behold, a great multitude, which no man could number, out of every nation and of all tribes and peoples and tongues, standing before the throne and before the Lamb, arrayed in white robes, and palms in their hands;

Rev 7:10 and they cry with a great voice, saying, Salvation unto our God who sitteth on the throne, and unto the Lamb.

Rev 7:11 And all the angels were standing round about the throne, and about the elders and the four living creatures; and they fell before the throne on their faces, and worshipped God,

Rev 7:12 saying, Amen: Blessing, and glory, and wisdom, and thanksgiving, and honor, and power, and might, be unto our God for ever and ever. Amen.

Rev 7:13 And one of the elders answered, saying unto me, These that are arrayed in white robes, who are they, and whence came they?

Rev 7:14 And I say unto him, My lord, thou knowest. And he said to me, These are they that come of the great tribulation, and they washed their robes, and made them white in the blood of the Lamb.

Rev 7:15 Therefore are they before the throne of God; and they serve him day and night in his temple: and he that sitteth on the throne shall spread his tabernacle over them.

Rev 7:16 They shall hunger no more, neither thirst any more; neither shall the sun strike upon them, nor any heat:

Rev 7:17 for the Lamb that is in the midst of the throne shall be their shepherd, and shall guide them unto fountains of waters of life: and God shall wipe away every tear from their eyes.

Chapter 8.

Rev 8:1 And when he opened the seventh seal, there followed a silence in heaven about the space of half an hour.

Rev 8:2 And I saw the seven angels that stand before God; and there were given unto them seven trumpets.

Rev 8:3 And another angel came and stood over the altar, having a golden censer; and there was given unto him much incense, that he should add it unto the prayers of all the saints upon the golden altar which was before the throne.

Rev 8:4 And the smoke of the incense, with the prayers of the saints, went up before God out of the angel's hand.

Rev 8:5 And the angel taketh the censer; and he filled it with the fire of the altar, and cast it upon the earth: and there followed thunders, and voices, and lightnings, and an earthquake.

Rev 8:6 And the seven angels that had the seven trumpets prepared themselves to sound.

Rev 8:7 And the first sounded, and there followed hail and fire, mingled with blood, and they were cast upon the earth: and the third part of the earth was burnt up, and the third part of the trees was burnt up, and all green grass was burnt up.

Rev 8:8 And the second angel sounded, and as it were a great mountain burning with fire was cast into the sea: and the third part of the sea became blood;

Rev 8:9 and there died the third part of the creatures which were in the sea, even they that had life; and the third part of the ships was destroyed.

Rev 8:10 And the third angel sounded, and there fell from heaven a great star, burning as a torch, and it fell upon the third part of the rivers, and upon the fountains of the waters;

Rev 8:11 and the name of the star is called Wormwood: and the third part of the waters became wormwood; and many men died of the waters, because they were made bitter.

Rev 8:12 And the fourth angel sounded, and the third part of the sun was smitten, and the third part of the moon, and the third part of the stars; that the third part of them should be darkened, and the day should not shine for the third part of it, and the night in like manner.

Rev 8:13 And I saw, and I heard an eagle, flying in mid heaven, saying with a great voice, Woe, woe, woe, for them that dwell on the earth, by reason of the other voices of the trumpet of the three angels, who are yet to sound.

Chapter 9.

Rev 9:1 And the fifth angel sounded, and I saw a star from heaven fallen unto the earth: and there was given to him the key of the pit of the abyss.

Rev 9:2 And he opened the pit of the abyss; and there went up a smoke out of the pit, as the smoke of a great furnace; and the sun and the air were darkened by reason of the smoke of the pit.

Rev 9:3 And out of the smoke came forth locusts upon the earth; and power was given them, as the scorpions of the earth have power.

Rev 9:4 And it was said unto them that they should not hurt the grass of the earth, neither any green thing, neither any tree, but only such men as have not the seal of God on their foreheads.

Rev 9:5 And it was given them that they should not kill them, but that they should be tormented five months: and their torment was as the torment of a scorpion, when it striketh a man.

Rev 9:6 And in those days men shall seek death, and shall in no wise find it; and they shall desire to die, and death fleeth from them.

Rev 9:7 And the shapes of the locusts were like unto horses prepared for war; and upon their heads as it were crowns like unto gold, and their faces were as men's faces.

Rev 9:8 And they had hair as the hair of women, and their teeth were as the teeth of lions.

Rev 9:9 And they had breastplates, as it were breastplates of iron; and the sound of their wings was as the sound of chariots, of many horses rushing to war.

Rev 9:10 And they have tails like unto scorpions, and stings; and in their tails is their power to hurt men five months.

Rev 9:11 They have over them as king the angel of the abyss: his name in Hebrew is Abaddon, and in the Greek tongue he hath the name Apollyon.

Rev 9:12 The first Woe is past: behold, there come yet two Woes hereafter.

Rev 9:13 And the sixth angel sounded, and I heard a voice from the horns of the golden altar which is before God,

Rev 9:14 one saying to the sixth angel that had one trumpet, Loose the four angels that are bound at the great river Euphrates.

Rev 9:15 And the four angels were loosed, that had been prepared for the hour and day and month and year, that they should kill the third part of men.

Rev 9:16 And the number of the armies of the horsemen was twice ten thousand times ten thousand: I heard the number of them.

Rev 9:17 And thus I saw the horses in the vision, and them that sat on them, having breastplates as of fire and of hyacinth and of brimstone: and the heads of lions; and out of their mouths proceedeth fire and smoke and brimstone.

Rev 9:18 By these three plagues was the third part of men killed, by the fire and the smoke and the brimstone, which proceeded out of their mouths.

Rev 9:19 For the power of the horses is in their mouth, and in their tails: for their tails are like unto serpents, and have heads; and with them they hurt.

Rev 9:20 And the rest of mankind, who were not killed with these plagues, repented not of the works of their hands, that they should not worship demons, and the idols of gold, and of silver, and of brass, and of stone, and of wood; which can neither see, nor hear, nor walk:

Rev 9:21 and they repented not of their murders, nor of their sorceries, nor of their fornication, nor of their thefts.

Chapter 10.

Rev 10:1 And I saw another strong angel coming down out of heaven, arrayed with a cloud; and the rainbow was upon his head, and his face was as the sun, and his feet as pillars of fire;

Rev 10:2 and he had in his hand a little book open: and he set his right foot upon the sea, and his left upon the earth;

Rev 10:3 and he cried with a great voice, as a lion roareth: and when he cried, the seven thunders uttered their voices.

Rev 10:4 And when the seven thunders uttered their voices, I was about to write: and I heard a voice from heaven saying, Seal up the things which the seven thunders uttered, and write them not.

Rev 10:5 And the angel that I saw standing upon the sea and upon the earth lifted up his right hand to heaven,

Rev 10:6 and sware by him that liveth for ever and ever, who created the heaven and the things that are therein, and the earth and the things that are therein, and the sea and the things that are therein, that there shall be delay no longer:

Rev 10:7 but in the days of the voice of the seventh angel, when he is about to sound, then is finished the mystery of God, according to the good tidings which he declared to his servants the prophets.

Rev 10:8 And the voice which I heard from heaven, I heard it again speaking with me, and saying, Go, take the book which is open in the hand of the angel that standeth upon the sea and upon the earth.

Rev 10:9 And I went unto the angel, saying unto him that he should give me the little book. And he saith unto me, Take it, and eat it up; and it shall make thy belly bitter, but in thy mouth it shall be sweet as honey.

Rev 10:10 And I took the little book out of the angel's hand, and ate it up; and it was in my mouth sweet as honey: and when I had eaten it, my belly was made bitter.

Rev 10:11 And they say unto me, Thou must prophesy again over many peoples and nations and tongues and kings.

Chapter 11.

Rev 11:1 And there was given me a reed like unto a rod: and one said, Rise, and measure the temple of God, and the altar, and them that worship therein.

Rev 11:2 And the court which is without the temple leave without, and measure it not; for it hath been given unto the nations: and the holy city shall they tread under foot forty and two months.

Rev 11:3 And I will give unto my two witnesses, and they shall prophesy a thousand two hundred and threescore days, clothed in sackcloth.

Rev 11:4 These are the two olive trees and the two candlesticks, standing before the Lord of the earth.

Rev 11:5 And if any man desireth to hurt them, fire proceedeth out of their mouth and devoureth their enemies; and if any man shall desire to hurt them, in this manner must he be killed.

Rev 11:6 These have the power to shut the heaven, that it rain not during the days of their prophecy: and they have power over the waters to turn them into blood, and to smite the earth with every plague, as often as they shall desire.

Rev 11:7 And when they shall have finished their testimony, the beast that cometh up out of the abyss shall make war with them, and overcome them, and kill them.

Rev 11:8 And their dead bodies lie in the street of the great city, which spiritually is called Sodom and Egypt, where also their Lord was crucified.

Rev 11:9 And from among the peoples and tribes and tongues and nations do men look upon their dead bodies three days and a half, and suffer not their dead bodies to be laid in a tomb.

Rev 11:10 And they that dwell on the earth rejoice over them, and make merry; and they shall send gifts one to another; because these two prophets tormented them that dwell on the earth.

Rev 11:11 And after the three days and a half the breath of life from God entered into them, and they stood upon their feet; and great fear fell upon them that beheld them.

Rev 11:12 And they heard a great voice from heaven saying unto them, Come up hither. And they went up into heaven in the cloud; and their enemies beheld them.

Rev 11:13 And in that hour there was a great earthquake, and the tenth part of the city fell; and there were killed in the earthquake seven thousand persons: and the rest were affrighted, and gave glory to the God of heaven.

Rev 11:14 The second Woe is past: behold, the third Woe cometh quickly.

Rev 11:15 And the seventh angel sounded; and there followed great voices in heaven, and they said, The kingdom of the world is become the kingdom of our Lord, and of his Christ: and he shall reign for ever and ever.

Rev 11:16 And the four and twenty elders, who sit before God on their thrones, fell upon their faces and worshipped God,

Rev 11:17 saying, We give thee thanks, O Lord God, the Almighty, who art and who wast; because thou hast taken thy great power, and didst reign.

Rev 11:18 And the nations were wroth, and thy wrath came, and the time of the dead to be judged, and the time to give their reward to thy servants the prophets, and to the saints, and to them that fear thy name, the small and the great; and to destroy them that destroy the earth.

Rev 11:19 And there was opened the temple of God that is in heaven; and there was seen in his temple the ark of his covenant; and there followed lightnings, and voices, and thunders, and an earthquake, and great hail.

Chapter 12.

Rev 12:1 And a great sign was seen in heaven: a woman arrayed with the sun, and the moon under her feet, and upon her head a crown of twelve stars;

Rev 12:2 and she was with child; and she crieth out, travailing in birth, and in pain to be delivered.

Rev 12:3 And there was seen another sign in heaven: and behold, a great red dragon, having seven heads and ten horns, and upon his heads seven diadems.

Rev 12:4 And his tail draweth the third part of the stars of heaven, and did cast them to the earth: and the dragon standeth before the woman that is about to be delivered, that when she is delivered he may devour her child.

Rev 12:5 And she was delivered of a son, a man child, who is to rule all the nations with a rod of iron: and her child was caught up unto God, and unto his throne.

Rev 12:6 And the woman fled into the wilderness, where she hath a place prepared of God, that there they may nourish her a thousand two hundred and threescore days.

Rev 12:7 And there was war in heaven: Michael and his angels going forth to war with the dragon; and the dragon warred and his angels;

Rev 12:8 And they prevailed not, neither was their place found any more in heaven.

Rev 12:9 And the great dragon was cast down, the old serpent, he that is called the Devil and Satan, the deceiver of the whole world; he was cast down to the earth, and his angels were cast down with him.

Rev 12:10 And I heard a great voice in heaven, saying, Now is come the salvation, and the power, and the kingdom of our God, and the authority of his Christ: for the accuser of our brethren is cast down, who accuseth them before our God day and night.

Rev 12:11 And they overcame him because of the blood of the Lamb, and because of the word of their testimony; and they loved not their life even unto death.

Rev 12:12 Therefore rejoice, O heavens, and ye that dwell in them. Woe for the earth and for the sea: because the devil is gone down unto you, having great wrath, knowing that he hath but a short time.

Rev 12:13 And when the dragon saw that he was cast down to the earth, he persecuted the woman that brought forth the man child.

Rev 12:14 And there were given to the woman the two wings of the great eagle, that she might fly into the wilderness unto her place, where she is nourished for a time, and times, and half a time, from the face of the serpent.

Rev 12:15 And the serpent cast out of his mouth after the woman water as a river, that he might cause her to be carried away by the stream.

Rev 12:16 And the earth helped the woman, and the earth opened her mouth and swallowed up the river which the dragon cast out of his mouth.

Rev 12:17 And the dragon waxed wroth with the woman, and went away to make war with the rest of her seed, that keep the commandments of God, and hold the testimony of Jesus:

Chapter 13.

Rev 13:1 And he stood upon the sand of the sea. And I saw a beast coming up out of the sea, having ten horns, and seven heads, and on his horns ten diadems, and upon his heads names of blasphemy.

Rev 13:2 And the beast which I saw was like unto a leopard, and his feet were as the feet of a bear, and his mouth as the mouth of a lion: and the dragon gave him his power, and his throne, and great authority.

Rev 13:3 And I saw one of his heads as though it had been smitten unto death; and his death-stroke was healed: and the whole earth wondered after the beast;

Rev 13:4 and they worshipped the dragon, because he gave his authority unto the beast; and they worshipped the beast, saying, Who is like unto the beast? And who is able to war with him?

Rev 13:5 and there was given to him a mouth speaking great things and blasphemies; and there was given to him authority to continue forty and two months.

Rev 13:6 And he opened his mouth for blasphemies against God, to blaspheme his name, and his tabernacle, even them that dwell in the heaven.

Rev 13:7 And it was given unto him to make war with the saints, and to overcome them: and there was given to him authority over every tribe and people and tongue and nation.

Rev 13:8 And all that dwell on the earth shall worship him, every one whose name hath not been written from the foundation of the world in the book of life of the Lamb that hath been slain.

Rev 13:9 If any man hath an ear, let him hear.

Rev 13:10 If any man is for captivity, into captivity he goeth: if any man shall kill with the sword, with the sword must he be killed. Here is the patience and the faith of the saints.

Rev 13:11 And I saw another beast coming up out of the earth; and he had two horns like unto a lamb, and he spake as a dragon.

Rev 13:12 And he exerciseth all the authority of the first beast in his sight. And he maketh the earth and them dwell therein to worship the first beast, whose death-stroke was healed.

Rev 13:13 And he doeth great signs, that he should even make fire to come down out of heaven upon the earth in the sight of men.

Rev 13:14 And he deceiveth them that dwell on the earth by reason of the signs which it was given him to do in the sight of the beast; saying to them that dwell on the earth, that they should make an image to the beast who hath the stroke of the sword and lived.

Rev 13:15 And it was given unto him to give breath to it, even to the image to the beast, that the image of the beast should both speak, and cause that as many as should not worship the image of the beast should be killed.

Rev 13:16 And he causeth all, the small and the great, and the rich and the poor, and the free and the bond, that there be given them a mark on their right hand, or upon their forehead;

Rev 13:17 and that no man should be able to buy or to sell, save he that hath the mark, even the name of the beast or the number of his name.

Rev 13:18 Here is wisdom. He that hath understanding, let him count the number of the beast; for it is the number of a man: and his number is Six hundred and sixty and six.

Chapter 14.

Rev 14:1 And I saw, and behold, the Lamb standing on the mount Zion, and with him a hundred and forty and four thousand, having his name, and the name of his Father, written on their foreheads.

Rev 14:2 And I heard a voice from heaven, as the voice of many waters, and as the voice of a great thunder: and the voice which I heard was as the voice of harpers harping with their harps:

Rev 14:3 and they sing as it were a new song before the throne, and before the four living creatures and the elders: and no man could learn the song save the hundred and forty and four thousand, even they that had been purchased out of the earth.

Rev 14:4 These are they that were not defiled with women; for they are virgins. These are they that follow the Lamb whithersoever he goeth. These were purchased from among men, to be the firstfruits unto God and unto the Lamb.

Rev 14:5 And in their mouth was found no lie: they are without blemish.

Rev 14:6 And I saw another angel flying in mid heaven, having eternal good tidings to proclaim unto them that dwell on the earth, and unto every nation and tribe and tongue and people;

Rev 14:7 and he saith with a great voice, Fear God, and give him glory; for the hour of his judgment is come: and worship him that made the heaven and the earth and sea and fountains of waters.

Rev 14:8 And another, a second angel, followed, saying, Fallen, fallen is Babylon the great, that hath made all the nations to drink of the wine of the wrath of her fornication.

Rev 14:9 And another angel, a third, followed them, saying with a great voice, If any man worshippeth the beast and his image, and receiveth a mark on his forehead, or upon his hand,

Rev 14:10 he also shall drink of the wine of the wrath of God, which is prepared unmixed in the cup of his anger; and he shall be tormented with fire and brimstone in the presence of the holy angels, and in the presence of the Lamb:

Rev 14:11 and the smoke of their torment goeth up for ever and ever; and they have no rest day and night, they that worship the beast and his image, and whoso receiveth the mark of his name.

Rev 14:12 Here is the patience of the saints, they that keep the commandments of God, and the faith of Jesus.

Rev 14:13 And I heard the voice from heaven saying, Write, Blessed are the dead who die in the Lord from henceforth: yea, saith the Spirit, that they may rest from their labors; for their works follow with them.

Rev 14:14 And I saw, and behold, a white cloud; and on the cloud I saw one sitting like unto a son of man, having on his head a golden crown, and in his hand sharp sickle.

Rev 14:15 And another angel came out from the temple, crying with a great voice to him that sat on the cloud, Send forth thy sickle, and reap: for the hour to reap is come; for the harvest of the earth is ripe.

Rev 14:16 And he that sat on the cloud cast his sickle upon the earth; and the earth was reaped.

Rev 14:17 Another angel came out from the temple which is in heaven, he also having a sharp sickle.

Rev 14:18 And another angel came out from the altar, he that hath power over fire; and he called with a great voice to him that had the sharp sickle, saying, Send forth thy sharp sickle, and gather the clusters of the vine of the earth; for her grapes are fully ripe.

Rev 14:19 And the angel cast his sickle into the earth, and gathered the vintage of the earth, and cast it into the winepress, the great winepress, of the wrath of God.

Rev 14:20 And the winepress was trodden without the city, and there came out blood from the winepress, even unto the bridles of the horses, as far as a thousand and six hundred furlongs.

Chapter 15.

Rev 15:1 And I saw another sign in heaven, great and marvellous, seven angels having seven plagues, which are the last, for in them is finished the wrath of God.

Rev 15:2 And I saw as it were a sea of glass mingled with fire; and them that come off victorious from the beast, and from his image, and from the number of his name, standing by the sea of glass, having harps of God.

Rev 15:3 And they sing the song of Moses the servant of God, and the song of the Lamb, saying, Great and marvellous are thy works, O Lord God, the Almighty; righteous and true are thy ways, thou King of the ages.

Rev 15:4 Who shall not fear, O Lord, and glorify thy name? for thou only art holy; for all the nations shall come and worship before thee; for thy righteous acts have been made manifest.

Rev 15:5 And after these things I saw, and the temple of the tabernacle of the testimony in heaven was opened:

Rev 15:6 and there came out from the temple the seven angels that had the seven plagues, arrayed with precious stone, pure and bright, and girt about their breasts with golden girdles.

Rev 15:7 And one of the four living creatures gave unto the seven angels seven golden bowls full of the wrath of God, who liveth for ever and ever.

Rev 15:8 And the temple was filled with smoke from the glory of God, and from his power; and none was able to enter into the temple, till the seven plagues of the seven angels should be finished.

Chapter 16.

Rev 16:1 And I heard a great voice out of the temple, saying to the seven angels, Go ye, and pour out the seven bowls of the wrath of God into the earth.

Rev 16:2 And the first went, and poured out his bowl into the earth; and it became a noisome and grievous sore upon the men that had the mark of the beast, and that worshipped his image.

Rev 16:3 And the second poured out his bowl into the sea; and it became blood as of a dead man; and every living soul died, even the things that were in the sea.

Rev 16:4 And the third poured out his bowl into the rivers and the fountains of the waters; and it became blood.

Rev 16:5 And I heard the angel of the waters saying, Righteous art thou, who art and who wast, thou Holy One, because thou didst thus judge:

Rev 16:6 for they poured out the blood of the saints and the prophets, and blood hast thou given them to drink: they are worthy.

Rev 16:7 And I heard the altar saying, Yea, O Lord God, the Almighty, true and righteous are thy judgments.

Rev 16:8 And the fourth poured out his bowl upon the sun; and it was given unto it to scorch men with fire.

Rev 16:9 And men were scorched with great heat: and they blasphemed the name of God who hath the power over these plagues; and they repented not to give him glory.

Rev 16:10 And the fifth poured out his bowl upon the throne of the beast; and his kingdom was darkened; and they gnawed their tongues for pain,

Rev 16:11 and they blasphemed the God of heaven because of their pains and their sores; and they repented not of their works.

Rev 16:12 And the sixth poured out his bowl upon the great river, the river Euphrates; and the water thereof was dried up, that the way might by made ready for the kings that come from the sunrising.

Rev 16:13 And I saw coming out of the mouth of the dragon, and out of the mouth of the beast, and out of the mouth of the false prophet, three unclean spirits, as it were frogs:

Rev 16:14 for they are spirits of demons, working signs; which go forth unto the kings of the whole world, to gather them together unto the war of the great day of God, the Almighty.

Rev 16:15 (Behold, I come as a thief. Blessed is he that watcheth, and keepeth his garments, lest he walk naked, and they see his shame.)

Rev 16:16 And they gathered them together into the place which is called in Hebrew Har-Magedon.

Rev 16:17 And the seventh poured out his bowl upon the air; and there came forth a great voice out of the temple, from the throne, saying, It is done:

Rev 16:18 and there were lightnings, and voices, and thunders; and there was a great earthquake, such as was not since there were men upon the earth, so great an earthquake, so mighty.

Rev 16:19 And the great city was divided into three parts, and the cities of the nations fell: and Babylon the great was remembered in the sight of God, to give unto her the cup of the wine of the fierceness of his wrath.

Rev 16:20 And every island fled away, and the mountains were not found.

Rev 16:21 And great hail, every stone about the weight of a talent, cometh down out of heaven upon men: and men blasphemed God because of the plague of the hail; for the plague thereof is exceeding great.

Chapter 17.

Rev 17:1 And there came one of the seven angels that had the seven bowls, and spake with me, saying, Come hither, I will show thee the judgment of the great harlot that sitteth upon many waters;

Rev 17:2 with whom the kings of the earth committed fornication, and they that dwell in the earth were made drunken with the wine of her fornication.

Rev 17:3 And he carried me away in the Spirit into a wilderness: and I saw a woman sitting upon a scarlet-colored beast, full of names of blasphemy, having seven heads and ten horns.

Rev 17:4 And the woman was arrayed in purple and scarlet, and decked with gold and precious stone and pearls, having in her hand a golden cup full of abominations, even the unclean things of her fornication,

Rev 17:5 and upon her forehead a name written, MYSTERY, BABYLON THE GREAT, THE MOTHER OF THE HARLOTS AND OF THE ABOMINATIONS OF THE EARTH.

Rev 17:6 And I saw the woman drunken with the blood of the saints, and with the blood of the martyrs of Jesus. And when I saw her, I wondered with a great wonder.

Rev 17:7 And the angel said unto me, Wherefore didst thou wonder? I will tell thee the mystery of the woman, and of the beast that carrieth her, which hath the seven heads and the ten horns.

Rev 17:8 The beast that thou sawest was, and is not; and is about to come up out of the abyss, and to go into perdition. And they that dwell on the earth shall wonder, they whose name hath not been written in the book of life from the foundation of the world, when they behold the beast, how that he was, and is not, and shall come.

Rev 17:9 Here is the mind that hath wisdom. The seven heads are seven mountains, on which the woman sitteth:

Rev 17:10 and they are seven kings; the five are fallen, the one is, the other is not yet come; and when he cometh, he must continue a little while.

Rev 17:11 And the beast that was, and is not, is himself also an eighth, and is of the seven; and he goeth into perdition.

Rev 17:12 And the ten horns that thou sawest are ten kings, who have received no kingdom as yet; but they receive authority as kings, with the beast, for one hour.

Rev 17:13 These have one mind, and they give their power and authority unto the beast.

Rev 17:14 These shall war against the Lamb, and the Lamb shall overcome them, for he is Lord of lords, and King of kings; and they also shall overcome that are with him, called and chosen and faithful.

Rev 17:15 And he saith unto me, The waters which thou sawest, where the harlot sitteth, are peoples, and multitudes, and nations, and tongues.

Rev 17:16 And the ten horns which thou sawest, and the beast, these shall hate the harlot, and shall make her desolate and naked, and shall eat her flesh, and shall burn her utterly with fire.

Rev 17:17 For God did put in their hearts to do his mind, and to come to one mind, and to give their kingdom unto the beast, until the words of God should be accomplished.

Rev 17:18 And the woman whom thou sawest is the great city, which reigneth over the kings of the earth.

Chapter 18.

Rev 18:1 After these things I saw another angel coming down out of heaven, having great authority; and the earth was lightened with his glory.

Rev 18:2 And he cried with a mighty voice, saying, Fallen, fallen is Babylon the great, and is become a habitation of demons, and a hold of every unclean spirit, and a hold of every unclean and hateful bird.

Rev 18:3 For by the wine of the wrath of her fornication all the nations are fallen; and the kings of the earth committed fornication with her, and the merchants of the earth waxed rich by the power of her wantonness.

Rev 18:4 And I heard another voice from heaven, saying, Come forth, my people, out of her, that ye have no fellowship with her sins, and that ye receive not of her plagues:

Rev 18:5 for her sins have reached even unto heaven, and God hath remembered her iniquities.

Rev 18:6 Render unto her even as she rendered, and double unto her the double according to her works: in the cup which she mingled, mingle unto her double.

Rev 18:7 How much soever she glorified herself, and waxed wanton, so much give her of torment and mourning: for she saith in her heart, I sit a queen, and am no widow, and shall in no wise see mourning.

Rev 18:8 Therefore in one day shall her plagues come, death, and mourning, and famine; and she shall be utterly burned with fire; for strong is the Lord God who judged her.

Rev 18:9 And the kings of the earth, who committed fornication and lived wantonly with her, shall weep and wail over her, when they look upon the smoke of her burning,

Rev 18:10 standing afar off for the fear of her torment, saying, Woe, woe, the great city, Babylon, the strong city! for in one hour is thy judgment come.

Rev 18:11   And the merchants of the earth weep and mourn over her, for no man buyeth their merchandise any more;

Rev 18:12   merchandise of gold, and silver, and precious stone, and pearls, and fine linen, and purple, and silk, and scarlet; and all thyine wood, and every vessel of ivory, and every vessel made of most precious wood, and of brass, and iron, and marble;

Rev 18:13   and cinnamon, and spice, and incense, and ointment, and frankincense, and wine, and oil, and fine flour, and wheat, and cattle, and sheep; and merchandise of horses and chariots and slaves; and souls of men.

Rev 18:14   And the fruits which thy soul lusted after are gone from thee, and all things that were dainty and sumptuous are perished from thee, and men shall find them no more at all.

Rev 18:15   The merchants of these things, who were made rich by her, shall stand afar off for the fear of her torment, weeping and mourning;

Rev 18:16   saying, Woe, woe, the great city, she that was arrayed in fine linen and purple and scarlet, and decked with gold and precious stone and pearl!

Rev 18:17   for in an hour so great riches is made desolate. And every shipmaster, and every one that saileth any wither, and mariners, and as many as gain their living by sea, stood afar off,

Rev 18:18   and cried out as they looked upon the smoke of her burning, saying, What city is like the great city?

Rev 18:19   And they cast dust on their heads, and cried, weeping and mourning, saying, Woe, woe, the great city, wherein all that had their ships in the sea were made rich by reason of her costliness! for in one hour is she made desolate.

Rev 18:20   Rejoice over her, thou heaven, and ye saints, and ye apostles, and ye prophets; for God hath judged your judgment on her.

Rev 18:21   And a strong angel took up a stone as it were a great millstone and cast it into the sea, saying, Thus with a mighty fall shall Babylon, the great city, be cast down, and shall be found no more at all.

Rev 18:22   And the voice of harpers and minstrels and flute-players and trumpeters shall be heard no more at all in thee; and no craftsman, of whatsoever craft, shall be found any more at all in thee; and the voice of a mill shall be heard no more at all in thee;

Rev 18:23   and the light of a lamp shall shine no more at all in thee; and the voice of the bridegroom and of the bride shall be heard no more at all in thee: for thy merchants were the princes of the earth; for with thy sorcery were all the nations deceived.

Rev 18:24   And in her was found the blood of prophets and of saints, and of all that have been slain upon the earth.

Chapter 19.

Rev 19:1   After these things I heard as it were a great voice of a great multitude in heaven, saying, Hallelujah; Salvation, and glory, and power, belong to our God:

Rev 19:2   for true and righteous are his judgments; for he hath judged the great harlot, her that corrupted the earth with her fornication, and he hath avenged the blood of his servants at her hand.

Rev 19:3 And a second time they say, Hallelujah. And her smoke goeth up for ever and ever.

Rev 19:4 And the four and twenty elders and the four living creatures fell down and worshipped God that sitteth on the throne, saying, Amen; Hallelujah.

Rev 19:5 And a voice came forth from the throne, saying, Give praise to our God, all ye his servants, ye that fear him, the small and the great.

Rev 19:6 And I heard as it were the voice of a great multitude, and as the voice of many waters, and as the voice of mighty thunders, saying, Hallelujah: for the Lord our God, the Almighty, reigneth.

Rev 19:7 Let us rejoice and be exceeding glad, and let us give the glory unto him: for the marriage of the Lamb is come, and his wife hath made herself ready.

Rev 19:8 And it was given unto her that she should array herself in fine linen, bright and pure: for the fine linen is the righteous acts of the saints.

Rev 19:9 And he saith unto me, Write, Blessed are they that are bidden to the marriage supper of the Lamb. And he saith unto me, These are true words of God.

Rev 19:10 And I fell down before his feet to worship him. And he saith unto me, See thou do it not: I am a fellow-servant with thee and with thy brethren that hold the testimony of Jesus: worship God; for the testimony of Jesus is the spirit of prophecy.

Rev 19:11 And I saw the heaven opened; and behold, a white horse, and he that sat thereon called Faithful and True; and in righteousness he doth judge and make war.

Rev 19:12 And his eyes are a flame of fire, and upon his head are many diadems; and he hath a name written which no one knoweth but he himself.

Rev 19:13 And he is arrayed in a garment sprinkled with blood: and his name is called The Word of God.

Rev 19:14 And the armies which are in heaven followed him upon white horses, clothed in fine linen, white and pure.

Rev 19:15 And out of his mouth proceedeth a sharp sword, that with it he should smite the nations: and he shall rule them with a rod of iron: and he treadeth the winepress of the fierceness of the wrath of God, the Almighty.

Rev 19:16 And he hath on his garment and on his thigh a name written, KINGS OF KINGS, AND LORD OF LORDS.

Rev 19:17 And I saw an angel standing in the sun; and he cried with a loud voice, saying to all the birds that fly in mid heaven, Come and be gathered together unto the great supper of God;

Rev 19:18 that ye may eat the flesh of kings, and the flesh of captains, and the flesh of mighty men, and the flesh of horses and of them that sit thereon, and the flesh of all men, both free and bond, and small and great.

Rev 19:19 And I saw the beast, and the kings of the earth, and their armies, gathered together to make war against him that sat upon the horse, and against his army.

Rev 19:20 And the beast was taken, and with him the false prophet that wrought the signs in his sight, wherewith he deceived them that had received the mark of the beast and them that worshipped his image: they two were cast alive into the lake of fire that burneth with brimstone:

Rev 19:21 and the rest were killed with the sword of him that sat upon the horse, even the sword which came forth out of his mouth: and all the birds were filled with their flesh.

Chapter 20.

Rev 20:1 And I saw an angel coming down out of heaven, having the key of the abyss and a great chain in his hand.

Rev 20:2 And he laid hold on the dragon, the old serpent, which is the Devil and Satan, and bound him for a thousand years,

Rev 20:3 and cast him into the abyss, and shut it, and sealed it over him, that he should deceive the nations no more, until the thousand years should be finished: after this he must be loosed for a little time.

Rev 20:4 And I saw thrones, and they sat upon them, and judgment was given unto them: and I saw the souls of them that had been beheaded for the testimony of Jesus, and for the word of God, and such as worshipped not the beast, neither his image, and received not the mark upon their forehead and upon their hand; and they lived, and reigned with Christ a thousand years.

Rev 20:5 The rest of the dead lived not until the thousand years should be finished. This is the first resurrection.

Rev 20:6 Blessed and holy is he that hath part in the first resurrection: over these the second death hath no power; but they shall be priests of God and of Christ, and shall reign with him a thousand years.

Rev 20:7 And when the thousand years are finished, Satan shall be loosed out of his prison,

Rev 20:8 and shall come forth to deceive the nations which are in the four corners of the earth, Gog and Magog, to gather them together to the war: the number of whom is as the sand of the sea.

Rev 20:9 And they went up over the breadth of the earth, and compassed the camp of the saints about, and the beloved city: and fire came down out of heaven, and devoured them.

Rev 20:10 And the devil that deceived them was cast into the lake of fire and brimstone, where are also the beast and the false prophet; and they shall be tormented day and night for ever and ever.

Rev 20:11 And I saw a great white throne, and him that sat upon it, from whose face the earth and the heaven fled away; and there was found no place for them.

Rev 20:12 And I saw the dead, the great and the small, standing before the throne; and books were opened: and another book was opened, which is the book of life: and the dead were judged out of the things which were written in the books, according to their works.

Rev 20:13 And the sea gave up the dead that were in it; and death and Hades gave up the dead that were in them: and they were judged every man according to their works.

Rev 20:14 And death and Hades were cast into the lake of fire. This is the second death, even the lake of fire.

Rev 20:15 And if any was not found written in the book of life, he was cast into the lake of fire.

Chapter 21.

Rev 21:1 And I saw a new heaven and a new earth: for the first heaven and the first earth are passed away; and the sea is no more.

Rev 21:2 And I saw the holy city, new Jerusalem, coming down out of heaven from God, made ready as a bride adorned for her husband.

Rev 21:3 And I heard a great voice out of the throne saying, Behold, the tabernacle of God is with men, and he shall dwell with them, and they shall be his peoples, and God himself shall be with them, and be their God:

Rev 21:4 and he shall wipe away every tear from their eyes; and death shall be no more; neither shall there be mourning, nor crying, nor pain, any more: the first things are passed away.

Rev 21:5 And he that sitteth on the throne said, Behold, I make all things new. And he saith, Write: for these words are faithful and true.

Rev 21:6 And he said unto me, They are come to pass. I am the Alpha and the Omega, the beginning and the end. I will give unto him that is athirst of the fountain of the water of life freely.

Rev 21:7 He that overcometh shall inherit these things; and I will be his God, and he shall be my son.

Rev 21:8 But for the fearful, and unbelieving, and abominable, and murderers, and fornicators, and sorcerers, and idolaters, and all liars, their part shall be in the lake that burneth with fire and brimstone; which is the second death.

Rev 21:9 And there came one of the seven angels who had the seven bowls, who were laden with the seven last plagues; and he spake with me, saying, Come hither, I will show thee the bride, the wife of the Lamb.

Rev 21:10 And he carried me away in the Spirit to a mountain great and high, and showed me the holy city Jerusalem, coming down out of heaven from God,

Rev 21:11 having the glory of God: her light was like unto a stone most precious, as it were a jasper stone, clear as crystal:

Rev 21:12 having a wall great and high; having twelve gates, and at the gates twelve angels; and names written thereon, which are the names of the twelve tribes of the children of Israel:

Rev 21:13 on the east were three gates; and on the north three gates; and on the south three gates; and on the west three gates.

Rev 21:14 And the wall of the city had twelve foundations, and on them twelve names of the twelve apostles of the Lamb.

Rev 21:15 And he that spake with me had for a measure a golden reed to measure the city, and the gates thereof, and the wall thereof.

Rev 21:16 And the city lieth foursquare, and the length thereof is as great as the breadth: and he measured the city with the reed, twelve thousand furlongs: the length and the breadth and the height thereof are equal.

Rev 21:17 And he measured the wall thereof, a hundred and forty and four cubits, according to the measure of a man, that is, of an angel.

Rev 21:18 And the building of the wall thereof was jasper: and the city was pure gold, like unto pure glass.

Rev 21:19 The foundations of the wall of the city were adorned with all manner of precious stones. The first foundation was jasper; the second, sapphire; the third, chalcedony; the fourth, emerald;

Rev 21:20 the fifth, sardonyx; the sixth, sardius; the seventh, chrysolite; the eighth, beryl; the ninth, topaz; the tenth, chrysoprase; the eleventh, jacinth; the twelfth, amethyst.

Rev 21:21 And the twelve gates were twelve pearls; each one of the several gates was of one pearl: and the street of the city was pure gold, as it were transparent glass.

Rev 21:22 And I saw no temple therein: for the Lord God the Almighty, and the Lamb, are the temple thereof.

Rev 21:23 And the city hath no need of the sun, neither of the moon, to shine upon it: for the glory of God did lighten it, and the lamp thereof is the Lamb.

Rev 21:24 And the nations shall walk amidst the light thereof: and the kings of the earth bring their glory into it.

Rev 21:25 And the gates thereof shall in no wise be shut by day (for there shall be no night there):

Rev 21:26 and they shall bring the glory and the honor of the nations into it:

Rev 21:27 and there shall in no wise enter into it anything unclean, or he that maketh an abomination and a lie: but only they that are written in the Lamb's book of life.

Chapter 22.

Rev 22:1 And he showed me a river of water of life, bright as crystal, proceeding out of the throne of God and of the Lamb,

Rev 22:2 in the midst of the street thereof. And on this side of the river and on that was the tree of life, bearing twelve manner of fruits, yielding its fruit every month: and the leaves of the tree were for the healing of the nations.

Rev 22:3 And there shall be no curse any more: and the throne of God and of the Lamb shall be therein: and his servants shall serve him;

Rev 22:4 and they shall see his face; and his name shall be on their foreheads.

Rev 22:5 And there shall be night no more; and they need no light of lamp, neither light of sun; for the Lord God shall give them light: and they shall reign for ever and ever.

Rev 22:6 And he said unto me, These words are faithful and true: and the Lord, the God of the spirits of the prophets, sent his angels to show unto his servants the things which must shortly come to pass.

Rev 22:7 And behold, I come quickly. Blessed is he that keepeth the words of the prophecy of this book.

Rev 22:8 And I John am he that heard and saw these things. And when I heard and saw, I fell down to worship before the feet of the angel that showed me these things.

Rev 22:9 And he saith unto me, See thou do it not: I am a fellow-servant with thee and with thy brethren the prophets, and with them that keep the words of this book: worship God.

Rev 22:10 And he saith unto me, Seal not up the words of the prophecy of this book; for the time is at hand.

Rev 22:11 He that is unrighteous, let him do unrighteousness still: and he that is filthy, let him be made filthy still: and he that is righteous, let him do righteousness still: and he that is holy, let him be made holy still.

Rev 22:12 Behold, I come quickly; and my reward is with me, to render to each man according as his work is.

Rev 22:13 I am the Alpha and the Omega, the first and the last, the beginning and the end.

Rev 22:14 Blessed are they that wash their robes, that they may have the right to come to the tree of life, and may enter in by the gates into the city.

Rev 22:15 Without are the dogs, and the sorcerers, and the fornicators, and the murderers, and the idolaters, and every one that loveth and maketh a lie.

Rev 22:16 I Jesus have sent mine angel to testify unto you these things for the churches. I am the root and the offspring of David, the bright, the morning star.

Rev 22:17 And the Spirit and the bride say, Come. And he that heareth, let him say, Come. And he that is athirst, let him come: he that will, let him take the water of life freely.

Rev 22:18 I testify unto every man that heareth the words of the prophecy of this book, if any man shall add unto them, God shall add unto him the plagues which are written in this book:

Rev 22:19 and if any man shall take away from the words of the book of this prophecy, God shall take away his part from the tree of life, and out of the holy city, which are written in this book.

Rev 22:20 He who testifieth these things saith, Yea: I come quickly. Amen: come, Lord Jesus.

Rev 22:21 The grace of the Lord Jesus be with the saints. Amen.